Inflation Rate

(GDP Deflator)

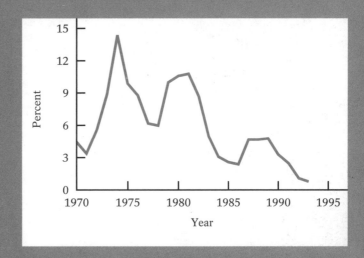

Nominal Interest Rate

(Three-Month Treasury Bills)

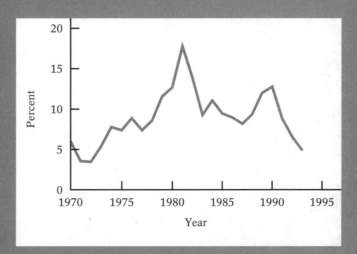

Macroeconomics

Macroeconomics
Canadian Edition

N. Gregory Mankiw

Harvard University

William Scarth

McMaster University

Worth Publishers

Macroeconomics, Canadian Edition

Copyright © 1995 by Worth Publishers

All rights reserved

Manufactured in the United States of America

Library of Congress Catalog Card Number: 94–061334

ISBN: 1–57259–001–7

Printing: 2 3 4 5–99

Development editors: Paul Shensa and Elisa Adams

Design: Malcolm Grear Designers

Art director: George Touloumes

Production editor: Laura Rubin

Production supervisor: Patricia Lawson

Line art: Academy Artworks

Layout: Matthew Dvorozniak

Composition: TSI Graphics

Printing and binding: R.R. Donnelley & Sons

Worth Publishers
41 Madison Avenue
New York, NY 10010

to
Deborah
and
Kathy

About the Authors

N. Gregory Mankiw is Professor of Economics at Harvard University. He began his study of economics at Princeton University, where in 1980 he received an A.B. *summa cum laude*. After earning a Ph.D. in economics from MIT, he began teaching at Harvard in 1985 and was promoted to full professor in 1987, at the age of 29. Today, he regularly teaches both undergraduate and graduate courses in macroeconomics.

Professor Mankiw is a prolific writer and a regular contributor to scholarly journals. His research ranges across many fields within economics and includes work on price adjustment, consumer behaviour, financial markets, housing, monetary and fiscal policy, and economic growth. In addition to his duties at Harvard, he is Director of the Monetary Economics Program of the National Bureau of Economic Research, a nonprofit think tank in Cambridge, Massachusetts.

Professor Mankiw lives in Wellesley, Massachusetts, with his wife Deborah and their children Catherine and Nicholas. In his free time, he plays with his border terrier, Keynes.

William M. Scarth is Professor of Economics at McMaster University. His introduction to the subject came at Queen's University, where he obtained the Gold Medal in economics upon graduating with his B.A. After receiving M.A. and Ph.D. degrees at the universities of Essex and Toronto, he began teaching at McMaster. He has held a number of visiting positions at other universities in Canada, Australia, and England.

Professor Scarth has published many articles in academic journals, often writing on such topics as the stabilization policy problems faced by small open economies and the challenges posed by ever-increasing government debt. He is also the author of other textbooks—one that introduces graduate students to advanced methods in macroeconomics, and two introductory books (one accompanies the TVOntario series, which he wrote). In addition to research and teaching at McMaster, he is an Adjunct Scholar at the C. D. Howe Institute, Canada's leading nonprofit policy institute.

Professor Scarth lives in Ancaster, Ontario, with his wife Kathy and their two sons Brian and David. Professor Scarth enjoys frequent hikes with his family and their dog, Samantha.

Those branches of politics, or of the laws of social life, in which there exists a collection of facts sufficiently sifted and methodized to form the beginning of a science should be taught *ex professo*. Among the chief of these is Political Economy, the sources and conditions of wealth and material prosperity for aggregate bodies of human beings. . . .

The same persons who cry down Logic will generally warn you against Political Economy. It is unfeeling, they will tell you. It recognises unpleasant facts. For my part, the most unfeeling thing I know of is the law of gravitation: it breaks the neck of the best and most amiable person without scruple, if he forgets for a single moment to give heed to it. The winds and waves too are very unfeeling. Would you advise those who go to sea to deny the winds and waves—or to make use of them, and find the means of guarding against their dangers? My advice to you is to study the great writers on Political Economy, and hold firmly by whatever in them you find true; and depend upon it that if you are not selfish or hard-hearted already, Political Economy will not make you so.

John Stuart Mill
1867

Brief Table of Contents

Table of Contents

Part Three

The Economy in the Short Run   231

CHAPTER ◆ 8

Introduction to Economic Fluctuations   233

List of Case Studies

Preface

Although poets may get pleasure from the sheer act of writing poetry, textbook authors are pleased only if their work is read, understood, and enjoyed by students. I was, therefore, gratified by the response to the first U.S. edition of this book and delighted when William Scarth offered to adapt the second edition for the Canadian market. Professors at more than 350 schools in 27 countries chose to use the first edition in their courses. Student reaction, as reported in course evaluations and letters from students, was as enthusiastic as I could have hoped. This strong response has resulted in the translation of the book into six other languages, and it has prompted the publication of both the second U.S. edition and the book that you now hold—one that has been fully adapted for use in Canada.

As was the case with the U.S. editions, we maintain a commitment to reorient the teaching of macroeconomics in this book. It differs markedly from those we used as students in four ways.

First, we attempt to achieve a balance between short-run and long-run macroeconomics. Courses in macroeconomics will always present the theory of short-run economic fluctuations, for it provides the basis for understanding most discussions of monetary and fiscal policy. Yet if students are to understand fully the implications of public policies, courses must give ample attention to long-run topics as well, including economic growth, the natural rate of unemployment, persistent inflation, and government debt. As if we needed reminding, recent years have highlighted the importance of understanding the effects of policies at all time horizons: any intelligent discussion of continuing budget deficits requires balancing short-run and long-run concerns.

Second, we integrate the insights of both Keynesian and classical economics. The prominent role of the Keynesian approach to economic fluctuations in this and most other textbooks is a testament to the influence and importance of Keynes's *General Theory*. Yet, in the aftermath of the Keynesian revolution, too many economists forgot that classical economics provides the right answers to many fundamental questions. In this book we incorporate many of the contributions of the classical economists before Keynes and the new classical economists of the past two decades. Substantial coverage is given, for example, to the loanable-funds theory of the interest rate, the quantity theory of money, and the problem of time inconsistency. At the same time, however, we recognize that many of the ideas of Keynes and the new Keynesians are necessary for understanding economic fluctuations. Substantial coverage is given also to the *IS-LM* model of aggregate demand, the short-run tradeoff between inflation and unemployment, and modern theories of wage and price rigidity.

Third, we present macroeconomics using a variety of simple models. Instead of pretending that there is one model that is complete enough to explain all facets of the economy, we encourage students to learn how to use and compare a set of prominent models. This approach has the pedagogical value that each model can be kept relatively simple and can be presented within one or two chapters. More important, this approach asks students to think like economists, who always keep various models in mind when analyzing economic events or public policies.

Fourth, we emphasize that macroeconomics is an empirical discipline, motivated and guided by a wide array of experience. This book contains 78 case studies that use macroeconomic theory to shed light on real-world data or events. To highlight the broad applicability of the basic theory, we have drawn the case studies both from current issues facing the world's economies and from dramatic historical episodes. The case studies analyze the policies of Paul Martin and Gordon Thiessen, many former Canadian politicians and central bankers, government initiatives in other countries, and even the policies of Henry Ford. They teach the reader how to apply economic principles to issues from fourteenth-century Europe, the island of Yap, the land of Oz, and today's newspaper.

The Canadian Perspective

Traditional education stressed the "three Rs—reading, writing and 'rithmetic." We think three different Rs are fundamental in the teaching of macroeconomics—*readability, rigour,* and *relevance.*

Concerning readability, we have always kept in mind the benefits of brevity. From our own experience as students, we know that long books are less likely to be read. Our goal in this book is to offer the clearest, most up-to-date, most accessible course in macroeconomics in the fewest words possible.

The central goal for many students taking macroeconomics is to achieve a level of understanding that permits participation in policy debates with the confidence that can only follow from solid knowledge. Students know when propositions are simply being asserted rather than being derived, and they are dissatisfied when their pursuit of understanding is thereby frustrated. We have met this challenge directly by rigorously explaining all the theory that students need to understand the issues in Canadian macroeconomic policy. But we have not let the pursuit of rigour contaminate the user-friendly nature of this book. One strategy we have adopted for keeping this objective squarely within our sights is that we have not numbered any equations. The formal material is truly worked in with the flow of the prose, so that students do not need to flip through pages to follow an argument.

Of course readability without loss of rigour would not amount to much if the book lacked relevance. And relevance is not achieved if the applications are relegated to separate sections of the book. Given the case study format of this text, it may appear that our discussions of policy may be separated in this way. But this is not the case. The book truly integrates theory and policy—both because the case studies are an integral part of the flow of each chapter and because there is focus on actual macroeconomic phenomena in many other places. Discussions of the productivity growth slowdown that started in the 1970s (Chapter 4), the detailed changes in Canadian unemployment that have taken place over the same period (Chapter 5), the interaction of inflation and the nonindexed tax system (Chapter 6), and the details of the Canadian monetary policy process (Chapter 18) are just several of countless policy discussions that are not highlighted as case studies.

But the case studies have proven to be an organizing device that is particularly appreciated by students, and many of these studies address the most pressing macroeconomic concerns of Canadians. Here is a sample:

Fiscal Policy

Concerning short-run issues, some case studies (9-1 and 10-1) explain why the estimates of the Canadian expenditure multiplier have shrunk over the years. Others (13-1 and 13-4) emphasize the importance of exchange-rate policy for determining the power of fiscal changes overall and the contribution of provincial fiscal efforts to regional tensions within the country. Still other case studies (15-4 and 17-2) evaluate particular taxes as instruments of short-run fiscal policy. Canadian experiences with personal-income, sales, and corporate tax rate changes are considered. Concerning long-run issues, there are case studies (4-5, 4-6, and 7-2) that focus on Canadian attempts to stimulate economic growth and the challenge posed by the aging of the Canadian populace. Case Study 7-4 evaluates the analytical underpinnings of the entire neoclassical conservative agenda, which considers together the long-run implications of tax reform, deficit reduction, disinflation, and free trade.

Monetary/Exchange-Rate Policy

As this heading suggests, we treat monetary and exchange-rate policy as one and the same—the only treatment that is appropriate for a small open economy like Canada's. Case studies discuss the importance of Bank of Canada credibility (6-7), the recent recession (8-3 and 10-2), how Canada's experience in the 1980s can be used to calculate the sacrifice ratio involved in disinflation (11-4), the implications of the Bank of Canada's low-inflation target for the "built-in stability" features of the Canadian economy (12-5), experience with devaluations (13-3), and the relative merits of fixed and floating exchange rates (13-5).

Deficit Reduction

There is little doubt that the deficit reduction challenge will remain a primary focus of Canadian macroeconomic policy consideration for the next several years. As a result, we have highlighted this question, and it is a particularly good issue for illustrating the payoff that follows from our determination to give long-run and short-run analysis equal emphasis. Deficit reduction involves short-term pain for an anticipated long-term gain. As a result, a thorough investigation requires that we give significant attention to establishing a realistic value for Canada's short-run expenditure multiplier (which we do, as noted previously) *and* that we give at least as much attention to estimating the potential for long-term gain. This is why we devote much space to evaluating the Ricardian equivalence controversy, and we have case studies that evaluate the federal government's deficit reduction targets (16-3) and the benefits to the Canadian economy that can be expected to follow from lower interest rates (17-1). The appendix to Chapter 16 estimates the long-run benefits of deficit reduction that follow from the standard model of a small open economy, even when it is assumed that the Canadian initiative will bring no reduction in interest rates.

The Arrangement of Topics

We first examine the long run when prices are flexible and then the short run when prices are sticky. Thus, the book begins with classical models of the economy and explains fully the long-run equilibrium before discussing deviations from that equilibrium. This strategy has several advantages:

- Because the classical dichotomy permits the separation of real and monetary issues, the long-run material is easier for students to understand.

- When students begin studying short-run fluctuations, they understand fully the long-run equilibrium around which the economy is fluctuating.

- Beginning with market-clearing models makes clearer the link between macroeconomics and microeconomics.

- Students learn first the material that is less controversial among macroeconomists.

When this organizational strategy was proposed in the first U.S. edition, some instructors were skeptical about making such a major change in their courses. With time and experience, however, the skepticism has faded, and we are pleased to see that today this organization is becoming standard.

Here is a whirlwind tour of the book:

Part One: Introduction

We have kept the introductory material as brief as possible in order to get to the core topics quickly. Chapter 1 discusses the broad questions that macroeconomists address and the economist's approach of building models to explain the world. Chapter 2 introduces the key data of macroeconomics, emphasizing gross domestic product, the consumer price index, and the unemployment rate.

Part Two: The Economy in the Long Run

Part Two examines the long run over which prices are flexible. Chapter 3 presents the basic classical model of national income. In this model, the factors of production and the production technology determine the level of income, and the marginal products of the factors determine its distribution to households. In addition, the model shows how fiscal policy influences the allocation of the economy's resources among consumption, investment, and government purchases, and it highlights how the real interest rate equilibrates the supply and demand for goods and services.

Chapter 4 makes the classical analysis of the economy dynamic. It uses the Solow growth model to examine the evolution of the economy over time. The Solow model provides the basis for discussing why the standard of living varies so widely across countries and how public policies influence the level and growth of the standard of living.

Chapter 5 relaxes the assumption of full employment by discussing the dynamics of the labour market and the natural rate of unemployment. It examines various causes of unemployment, including job search, minimum-wage laws, union power, and efficiency wages. It also presents many important facts about patterns of unemployment.

Money and the price level are introduced in Chapter 6. Because prices are assumed to be fully flexible, the chapter presents the prominent ideas of classical monetary theory: the quantity theory of money, the inflation tax, the Fisher effect, the causes of hyperinflation, the social costs of inflation, and the importance of central bank credibility.

The study of open-economy macroeconomics begins in Chapter 7. Maintaining the assumption of full employment, this chapter presents models to explain the trade balance and the exchange rate. Various policy issues are addressed: the relationship between the budget deficit and the trade deficit, the macroeconomic impact of protectionist trade policies, the effect of monetary policy on the value of a currency in the market for foreign exchange, and the effects of deficit reduction and tax reform on standards of living.

Part Three: The Economy in the Short Run

Part Three examines the short run when prices are sticky. It begins in Chapter 8 by introducing the model of aggregate supply and aggregate demand as well as the role of stabilization policy. Subsequent chapters refine the ideas introduced here.

Chapters 9 and 10 look more closely at aggregate demand. Chapter 9 presents the Keynesian cross and the theory of liquidity preference and uses these models as building blocks for developing the *IS-LM* model. Chapter 10 uses the *IS-LM* model to explain economic fluctuations and the aggregate demand curve. It concludes with an extended case study of the Great Depression.

Chapter 11 looks more closely at aggregate supply. It examines various approaches to explaining the short-run aggregate supply curve and discusses the short-run tradeoff between inflation and unemployment. It also covers some recent developments in the theory of aggregate supply.

After the model of aggregate supply and aggregate demand has been fully developed, Chapter 12 turns to the debate over how this model should be applied to economic policy. It emphasizes two broad questions. Should monetary and fiscal policy be active or passive? Should policy be conducted by rule or by discretion? The chapter presents arguments on both sides of these questions.

The study of open-economy macroeconomics continues in Chapter 13, which focuses on short-run fluctuations in an open economy. This chapter presents the Mundell-Fleming model and shows how monetary and fiscal policies and foreign developments affect the economy under floating and fixed exchange-rate systems. It also discusses the debate over whether exchange rates should be floating or fixed.

Finally, Chapter 14 presents the theory of real business cycles as an alternative way to view economic fluctuations. It discusses the basic elements of this new classical approach and the arguments advanced by its advocates and its critics.

Part Four: More on the Microeconomics Behind Macroeconomics

After developing the long-run and short-run models, the book discusses several topics that refine our understanding of the economy by analyzing more fully the microeconomics behind macroeconomics. Chapter 15 presents the various theories of consumer behaviour, including the Keynesian consumption function, Fisher's model of intertemporal choice, Modigliani's life-cycle hypothesis, and Friedman's permanent-income hypothesis. Chapter 16 focuses on the various debates over government debt, including the debate over Ricardian equivalence; it emphasizes that these debates arise largely because economists have different views of consumer behaviour. Chapter 17 examines the theory behind the investment function. Chapter 18 provides additional material on the money market, including the role of the banking system in determining the money supply and the Baumol-Tobin model of money demand.

Epilogue

The book ends with a brief epilogue that reviews the broad lessons on which most macroeconomists would agree and some of the most important unresolved questions. Here and throughout the book, we emphasize that despite the disagreements among macroeconomists, there is much that we know about how the economy works.

Alternative Syllabus

Instructors differ in the emphasis they place on various topics and in the sequence of topics they prefer. Also, some universities offer intermediate-level macroeconomics as a sequence of two courses. We have, therefore, tried to make this book as flexible as possible. Many of the chapters are self-contained. Instructors can change the emphases of their courses by rearranging chapters or by omitting some chapters entirely.

One possible alternative syllabus is presented here as an example. This syllabus maintains the strategy of first examining output and prices in the long run when prices are flexible, but it introduces sticky prices and short-run fluctuations earlier in the course. It defers the study of economic growth and the natural rate of unemployment until the end of the course or until the second of a two-course sequence. Instructors can interchange the sequence of parts C and D in the following syllabus. For instructors in a two-course sequence, this would depend on whether they were more comfortable leaving open economy considerations for the second course or leaving the debates concerning active or passive policy, rules versus discretion, and alternative approaches to business cycle theory until the second course.

A. Introduction

1. The Science of Macroeconomics
2. The Data of Macroeconomics

B. Income and Prices

3. National Income: Its Production, Distribution, and Allocation
6. Money and Inflation (pp. 162–186 can be left until later)
8. Introduction to Economic Fluctuations
9. Aggregate Demand I
10. Aggregate Demand II
11. Aggregate Supply

C. Open-Economy Macroeconomics

7. The Open Economy (pp. 94–99 and 205–220 can be left until later)
13. The Open Economy in the Short Run

D. Stabilization Policy Controversies

12. The Macroeconomic Policy Debate
14. The Theory of Real Business Cycles

E. More on the Microeconomics Behind Macroeconomics

15. Consumption
16. The Debates Over Government Debt
17. Investment
18. Money Supply and Money Demand (plus part of Chapter 6 if deferred earlier)
5. Unemployment
4. Economic Growth (plus part of Chapter 7 if deferred earlier)

Learning Tools

We have tried to make this book as user-friendly as possible.

Case Studies

Economics comes to life when it is applied to understanding actual events. Therefore, the 78 case studies are an important learning tool. The frequency with which these case studies occur ensures that a student does not have to grapple with an overdose of theory before seeing the theory applied. Students using earlier editions have reported that the case studies are their favourite part of the book.

FYI Boxes

These boxes present ancillary material "for your information." We use these boxes to clarify difficult concepts, to provide additional information about the tools of economics, and to show how economics relates to our daily lives.

Mathematical Notes

We use occasional mathematical footnotes to keep more difficult material out of the body of the text. These notes make an argument more rigorous or present a proof of a mathematical result. They can easily be skipped by those students who have not been introduced to the necessary mathematical tools.

Chapter Summaries

Every chapter ends with a brief, nontechnical summary of its major lessons. Students can use the summaries to place the material in perspective and to review for exams.

Key Concepts

Learning the language of a field is a major part of any course. Within the chapter, each key concept is in **boldface** when it is introduced. At the end of the chapter, the key concepts are listed for review.

Questions for Review

After studying a chapter, students can immediately test their understanding of its basic lessons by answering the "Questions for Review."

Problems and Applications

The "Problems and Applications" at the end of each chapter are designed for homework assignments. Some of these are numerical applications of the theory in the chapter. Others encourage the student to go beyond the material in the chapter by addressing new issues that are closely related to the chapter topics.

Chapter Appendixes

Eight chapters include appendixes that offer additional material, sometimes at a higher level of mathematical sophistication. These are designed so that professors can cover certain topics in greater depth if they wish. The appendixes can be skipped altogether without loss of continuity.

Glossary

To help students become familiar with the language of macroeconomics, a glossary of more than 250 terms is provided at the back of the book.

Supplements for Students

There are two supplements for students that instructors can order to use in their courses. Like the ancillaries that are available for instructors, these have not been specially adapted for Canada. They are useful, however, because they are designed to help students understand the *analytical* issues.

Student Guide and Workbook

This guide, by Roger Kaufman, offers various ways for students to learn the material in the text and assess their understanding.

- *Fill-In Questions* give students the opportunity to review and check their knowledge of the key terms and concepts in the chapter.
- *Multiple-Choice Questions* allow students to test themselves on the chapter material.

- *Exercises* guide students step by step through the various models using graphs and numerical examples.

- *Problems* ask students to apply the models on their own.

- *Questions to Think About* require critical thinking as well as economic analysis.

MacroBytes

David Weil has written an innovative software package for students. *MacroBytes* provides a range of activities to aid and motivate the student throughout the course.

- *Self-Tests.* Students can test their knowledge of the material in the book by taking multiple-choice tests on any chapter or combination of chapters. After the student responds, the program explains the answer and directs the student to specific sections in the book for additional study.

- *Macro Models.* These modules provide simulations of the models presented in the book. Students can change the exogenous variables and see the outcomes in terms of shifting curves and recalculated numerical values of the endogenous variables. Each module contains exercises that instructors can assign as homework.

- *2001: A Game for Macroeconomists.* The game allows students to become President of the United States in the year 2001 and to make macroeconomic policy decisions based on news events, economic statistics, and approval ratings. It gives students a sense of the complex interconnections that influence the economy. It is also fun to play.

MacroBytes is available for the IBM PC.

Supplements for Instructors

Additional supplements are available from Worth Publishers to help instructors enhance their courses.

Instructor's Resources

Andrew John has constructed an impressive resource manual for instructors. For each chapter of this book, the manual contains notes to the instructor, a detailed lecture outline, additional case studies, and coverage of advanced topics. Instructors can use the manual to prepare their lectures, and they can reproduce whatever pages they choose as handouts for students.

Solutions Manual

John Fernald and Paula DeMasi have written a solutions manual for all of the "Questions for Review" and "Problems and Applications." The manual also contains the answers to selected questions from the *Student Guide and Workbook* and the answers to the software exercises.

Test Bank

The Test Bank, by Charles Bischoff, includes over 900 multiple-choice questions to accompany the text. Several short numerical problems are also provided for each chapter. The multiple-choice questions that appear in *Macrobytes* are also included in the Test Bank. The Test Bank is available both as a printed book and on disks. The disks include a test-generation program and are available for the IBM PC and Apple Macintosh.

Transparency Masters

Instructors can obtain enlarged master copies of most of the figures in the text to prepare overhead transparencies for use in lectures.

Acknowledgments

We benefited from the input of many reviewers, colleagues, and government agencies. Four Canadian economists were particularly helpful. Norm Cameron (University of Manitoba), Bryan Campbell (Concordia University), Ron Kneebone (University of Calgary), and Tony Myatt (University of New Brunswick) all read extensive portions of the book at the manuscript stage and made many useful suggestions. In addition, we wish to acknowledge the discussions we have had with colleagues at our own universities and the input given by a number of economists teaching in the United States (whose helpful comments found their way into this Canadian edition). This latter group is thanked in the second U.S. edition of the book.

Much of the Canadian data was provided by Statistics Canada. Readers wishing additional information on data provided through the cooperation of Statistics Canada may obtain copies of related publications by writing to Publications Sales, Statistics Canada, Ottawa, Ontario K1A 0T6, or by calling (613) 951-7277 or 800-267-6677. Readers may also facsimile their orders by dialing (613) 951-1584.

The people at Worth Publishers have been congenial, dedicated, and efficient. We are grateful to Elisa Adams, Patricia Lawson, Paul Shensa, Laura Rubin, George Touloumes, and Demetrios Zangos.

Finally, we would like to thank our families for being so understanding, supportive, and inspirational.

N. Gregory Mankiw   *William Scarth*

Cambridge, Massachusetts
December 1994

Hamilton, Ontario
December 1994

Macroeconomics

Introduction

Part One introduces you to the study of macroeconomics. Chapter 1 discusses why macroeconomics is an exciting and important subject; it explains the tools that economists use to analyze the economy; and it outlines the plan of this book. Chapter 2 discusses the types of data that economists and policymakers use to monitor the economy.

The Science of Macroeconomics

The whole of science is nothing more than the refinement of everyday thinking.

Albert Einstein

1•1 Why Study Macroeconomics?

Why are incomes higher today than they were in 1960, and why were they higher in 1960 than in 1925? Why do some countries have high rates of inflation while others maintain stable prices? What causes recessions and depressions—the recurrent periods of falling incomes and rising unemployment—and how can public policy be used to reduce their frequency and severity? **Macroeconomics**, the study of the economy as a whole, attempts to answer these and many related questions.

To appreciate the importance of macroeconomics, you need only read the newspaper or listen to the news. The media report macroeconomic developments daily. Headlines such as GDP RISES 4 PERCENT, THE BANK OF CANADA MOVES TO COMBAT INFLATION, THE NATIONAL DEBT EXCEEDS $500 BILLION, or STOCKS FALL AMID FEARS OF RECESSION are routine.

Macroeconomic events touch all of our lives. Business executives forecasting the demand for their products must guess how fast consumers' incomes will grow. Senior citizens living on fixed incomes wonder how fast prices will rise. Unemployed workers looking for jobs hope that the economy will boom and that firms will be hiring. All are affected by the state of the economy.

It is no surprise that macroeconomic issues play a central role in political debate. In the 1970s, Prime Minister Elliott Trudeau wrestled unsuccessfully with a rising rate of inflation. In the 1980s, both the Liberal and Conservative parties presided over large federal budget deficits. In 1993, Prime Minister Jean Chrétien moved into 24 Sussex Drive committed to reducing the deficit and increasing economic growth. Historically, the popularity of incumbent prime ministers rises during booms and falls during recessions. Voters are keenly aware of macroeconomic events, and politicians are equally aware of the importance of macroeconomic policy.

The influence of economic events on politics is most apparent during political election campaigns. Economic policy is a prime topic of debate for the candidates, and the state of the economy has a powerful influence on the out-

3

come of the election. During the election of 1993, Liberal strategists wanted to keep the campaign focused on the key issue. Every speech included the refrain "jobs, jobs, jobs."

Macroeconomic issues also play a pivotal role in international relations. In the 1950s and 1960s, most major industrial countries maintained constant rates of exchange between their currencies and those of other countries. In the early 1970s, this system of fixed exchange rates broke down, and a new era of flexible and highly volatile exchange rates began. In the 1980s and early 1990s, Canada's foreign debt grew dramatically, and international bond rating agencies downgraded Canadian government bonds to lower levels of reliability. Also in the early 1990s, important world events, such as German reunification, forced up Canadian interest rates and delayed the country's economic recovery. International economic developments like these events and the signing of the Free Trade Agreements with the United States in 1989 and Mexico in 1994 are often a source of heated debate and tension.

Macroeconomists are the scientists who try to explain the working of the economy as a whole. They collect data on incomes, prices, unemployment, and many other economic variables from different periods of time and from different countries. They then attempt to formulate general theories that help to explain these data.

Like astronomers studying the evolution of stars or biologists studying the evolution of species, macroeconomists cannot conduct controlled experiments—experimenting with the economy would be too costly. Instead, they rely on natural experiments. Macroeconomists observe that economies differ from one another and that they change over time. These observations provide both the motivation for developing macroeconomic theories and the data for testing them.

To be sure, macroeconomics is a young and an imperfect science. The macroeconomist's ability to predict the future course of economic events is no better than the meteorologist's ability to predict next month's weather. But, as you will see, we do know quite a lot about how the economy works.

Our goal in studying macroeconomics, however, is not just to explain economic events but also to improve economic policy. The monetary and fiscal tools of government can influence the economy in powerful ways—both for good and for ill—and macroeconomics helps policymakers evaluate alternative policies. Macroeconomists are asked to explain the economic world as it is and to consider what it could be.

CASE STUDY

1•1

The Historical Performance of the Canadian Economy

Economists use many types of data to measure the performance of an economy. Three macroeconomic variables are particularly important: real gross domestic product (GDP), the inflation rate, and the unemployment rate. **Real GDP** measures the total output of the economy, and so it represents the total income that is available to everyone in the economy. ("Real" means that this measure of total income has been adjusted for any changes in the level of prices.) The **inflation rate** measures how quickly prices are rising. And the **unemployment rate** measures the fraction of the labour force that is out of work. Macroeconomists study how these variables are determined, why they change over time, and how they interact with one another.

Figure 1-1 shows real GDP per person for the Canadian economy. Two aspects of this figure are noteworthy. First, real GDP grows over time. Real GDP per person today is about seven and one half times its level in 1900. Second, the growth in real GDP is not steady. There are repeated periods during which real GDP is falling, a dramatic example being the 1930s. Such periods are called **recessions** if they are mild and **depressions** if they are more severe.

Figure 1-1

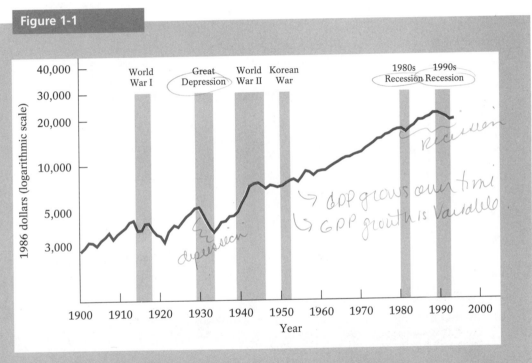

Real GDP per Person in the Canadian Economy Real GDP measures the total output of the economy. Real GDP per person measures the income of the typical person in the economy.

Note: Real GDP is plotted here on a logarithmic scale. On such a scale, equal distances on the vertical axis represent equal *percentage* changes. Thus, the distance between $5,000 and $10,000 is the same as the distance between $10,000 and $20,000.

Source: Reproduced and adapted by authority of the Minister of Industry, 1994, "Statistics Canada," *Canadian Economic Observer, Catalogue 11-210,* Series D20463, D4 (Historical Statistical Supplement 1991/92): 7, 98 and *Catalogue 11-010* (Statistical Summary, March 1994): 4, 12; Morris Altman, "Revised Real GNP Estimates and Canadian Economic Growth, 1870-1926," *Review of Income and Wealth,* Series 38, No. 4 (December 1992): 458-59; and *Canada 1930: A Handbook of Present Conditions and Recent Progress in the Dominion Bureau of Statistics* (Ottawa: Dominion Bureau of Statistics): 40.

Figure 1-2 shows the Canadian inflation rate. You can see that inflation varies substantially. Before 1945, the inflation rate averaged about zero. Periods of falling prices, called **deflation**, were almost as common as periods of rising prices. In more recent history, inflation has been the norm. The inflation problem became most severe during the mid-1970s, when prices rose persistently at a rate of almost 10 percent per year.

Figure 1-2

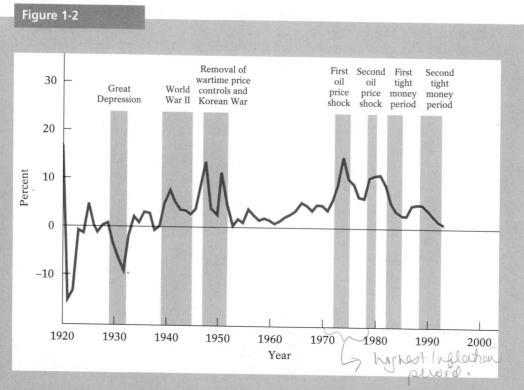

The Inflation Rate in the Canadian Economy
The inflation rate measures the percentage change in the average level of prices from the year before. A negative inflation rate indicates that prices are falling.

Note: The inflation rate is measured here using the GDP deflator.

Source: Reproduced and adapted by authority of the Minister of Industry, 1994, "Statistics Canada," *Canadian Economic Observer*, Series D20556 (Historical Statistical Supplement, 1991/92): 27 and (Statistical Summary, March 1994): 22; Morris Altman, "Revised Real GNP Estimates and Canadian Economic Growth, 1870-1926," *Review of Income and Wealth*, Series 38, No. 4.

Figure 1-3 shows the Canadian unemployment rate since 1921, the first year for which data exist. This figure shows that there is always some unemployment and that the amount varies from year to year. Recessions and depressions are associated with unusually high unemployment. The highest rates of unemployment were reached during the Great Depression of the 1930s. As the figure shows, since World War II, there is a gradual upward trend in unemployment. We will discuss the likely causes of this troubling fact in Chapter 5.

Figure 1-3

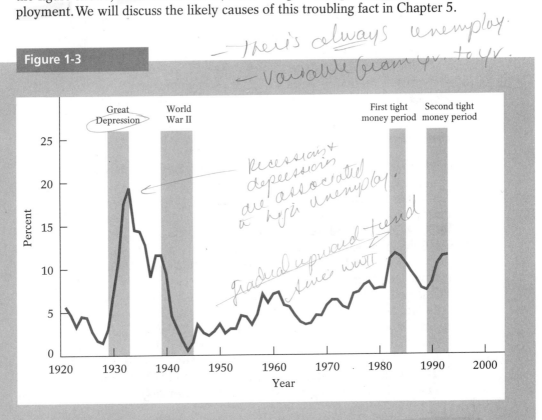

The Unemployment Rate in the Canadian Economy The unemployment rate measures the fraction of the labour force that does not have a job.

Source: Reproduced and adapted by authority of the Minister of Industry, 1994, "Statistics Canada," *Canadian Economic Observer*, Series D767863 (Historical Statistical Supplement 1991/92): 38 and (Statistical Summary, March 1994): 16; Frank Leacy (Ed.), "Statistics Canada," *Historical Statistics of Canada*, 2e, *Catalogue 11-516*, Series D223, D132 (1983).

These three figures offer a glimpse at the history of the Canadian economy. They show that unemployment falls and inflation rises when total spending is high (such as during World War II and the early 1960s), and that unemployment rises when inflation is reduced by government policy that decreases total spending (such as during the early 1980s and 1990s).

In the chapters that follow, we first discuss how these variables are measured and then explain how they behave—both in the long run and in the short run. We are then in a position to evaluate the government's fiscal policy (its changes in government spending and taxing) and its monetary policy (changes in the growth of the nation's money supply).

1·2 How Economists Think

Economists try to address the issues they study—even those that are politically charged—with a scientist's objectivity. Like any science, economics has its own set of tools: terminology, data, and a way of thinking. These tools can seem foreign and arcane to the uninitiated. The best way to become familiar with them is to practice using them. This book will afford you ample opportunity to do so. To make these tools less forbidding, however, let's discuss a few of them here.

Economic Models

Economists try to understand the economy by using models. **Models** are theories that summarize, often in mathematical terms, the relationships among economic variables. Models are useful because they help us to dispense with irrelevant details and to focus on important economic connections more clearly.

Models have two kinds of variables: exogenous variables and endogenous variables. **Exogenous variables** come from outside the model—they are the inputs into the model. **Endogenous variables** come from inside the model—they are the model's output. In other words, exogenous variables are fixed at the moment they enter the model, whereas endogenous variables are determined within the model. As Figure 1-4 illustrates, the purpose of a model is to show how the exogenous variables affect the endogenous variables.

For example, consider how an economist might develop a model of the market for bread. The economist supposes that the quantity of bread demanded by consumers, Q^d, depends on the price of bread, P_b, and on aggregate income, Y. This relationship is expressed in the equation

$$Q^d = D(P_b, Y),$$

where $D(\ )$ denotes the demand function and the letters within the brackets

Figure 1-4

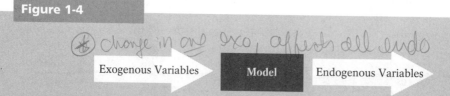

Exogenous Variables → Model → Endogenous Variables

How Models Work Models are simplified theories that show the key relationships among economic variables. The exogenous variables are those that come from outside the model. The endogenous variables are those that the model explains. The model shows how a change in one of the exogenous variables affects all the endogenous variables.

indicate the arguments of that function. (The FYI box on page 13 discusses this notation.). Similarly, the economist supposes that the quantity of bread supplied by bakers, Q^s, depends on the price of bread, P_b, and on the price of flour, P_f, since flour is used to make bread. This relationship is expressed as

$$Q^s = S(P_b, P_f),$$

where $S(\ )$ denotes the supply function. Finally, the economist assumes that the price of bread adjusts to equilibrate supply and demand:

$$Q^s = Q^d.$$

These three equations compose a model of the market for bread.

The economist illustrates the model with the supply-and-demand diagram, as in Figure 1-5. The demand curve shows the relationship between the quantity of bread demanded and the price of bread, while holding aggregate income constant. The demand curve slopes downward because the higher the

Figure 1-5

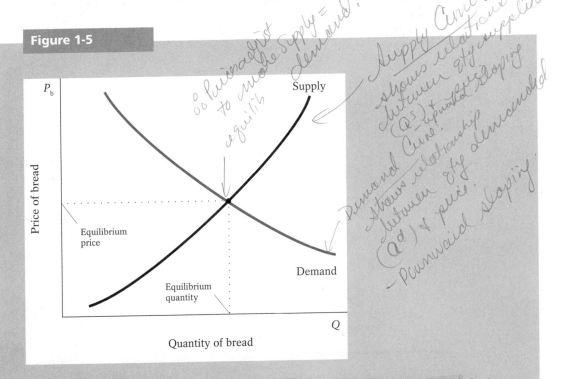

Supply and Demand Curves The most famous economic model is that of supply and demand for a good or service—in this case, bread. The demand curve is a downward-sloping curve relating the price of bread to the quantity of bread that consumers demand. The supply curve is an upward-sloping curve relating the price of bread to the quantity of bread that bakeries supply. The price of bread adjusts until the quantity supplied equals the quantity demanded. The point where the two curves cross is the market equilibrium, which shows the equilibrium price of bread and the equilibrium quantity of bread.

price of bread, the more consumers switch to other foods and the less bread they buy. The supply curve shows the relationship between the quantity of bread supplied and the price of bread, while holding the price of flour constant. The supply curve slopes upward because the higher the price of bread, the more bread bakers produce. The equilibrium for the market is the price and quantity at which the supply and demand curves intersect. At the equilibrium price, consumers choose to buy exactly the amount of bread that bakeries choose to produce.

This model of the bread market has two exogenous variables and two endogenous variables. The exogenous variables are aggregate income and the price of flour. The model does not attempt to explain them but takes them as already determined (perhaps to be explained by another model). The endogenous variables are the price of bread and the quantity of bread exchanged. These are the variables that the model attempts to explain.

The model shows how a change in one of the exogenous variables affects both endogenous variables. For example, if aggregate income increases, then the demand for bread increases, as illustrated in Figure 1-6. The model shows that both the equilibrium price and the equilibrium quantity of bread rise.

Figure 1-6

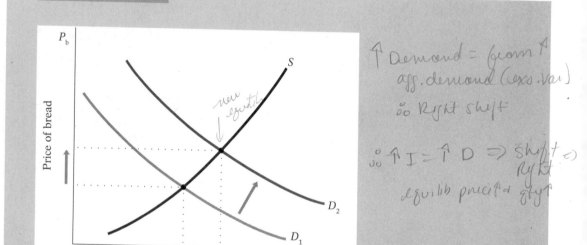

An Increase in Demand If aggregate income rises, so does the demand for bread: at any given price, consumers now want to buy more bread. This is represented by an outward shift in the demand curve. The market moves to the new intersection of supply and demand. The equilibrium price and the equilibrium quantity of bread rise.

Similarly, if the price of flour increases, then the supply of bread decreases, as illustrated in Figure 1-7. The model shows that in this case the equilibrium price of bread rises and the equilibrium quantity of bread falls. Thus, the model shows how changes in aggregate income or in the price of flour affect the market for bread.

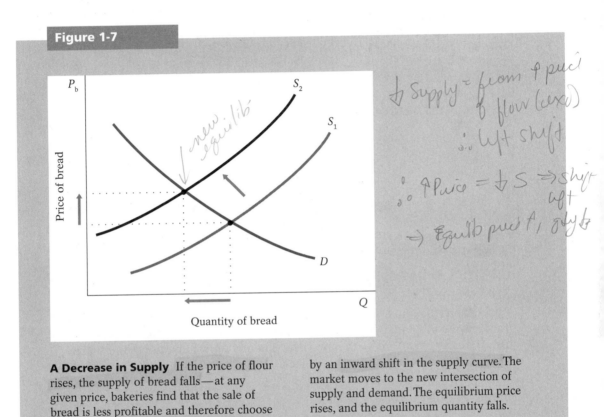

Figure 1-7

A Decrease in Supply If the price of flour rises, the supply of bread falls—at any given price, bakeries find that the sale of bread is less profitable and therefore choose to produce less bread. This is represented by an inward shift in the supply curve. The market moves to the new intersection of supply and demand. The equilibrium price rises, and the equilibrium quantity falls.

Like all models, this model of the bread market makes many simplifying assumptions. The model does not take into account, for example, that every bakery is in a different location. For each customer, one bakery is more convenient than the others, and thus bakeries have some ability to set their own prices. Although the model assumes that there is a single price for bread, in fact there could be a different price at every bakery.

How should we react to the model's lack of realism? Should we discard the simple model of bread supply and bread demand? Should we attempt to build a more complex model that allows for diverse bread prices? The answers to these questions depend on our purpose. On the one hand, if our goal is to explain how the price of flour affects the average price of bread and the amount of bread sold, then the diversity of bread prices is probably not important. The simple model of the bread market does a good job of answering that question. On the other hand, if our goal is to explain why towns with three bakeries have lower bread prices than towns with one bakery, the simple model is less useful.

The art in economics is in judging when an assumption is clarifying and when it is misleading. Any model constructed to be completely realistic would be too complicated for anyone to understand. Simplification is a necessary part of building a useful model. Yet models lead to incorrect conclusions when they ignore crucial features of the economy. Economic modeling therefore requires the use of care and common sense.

Eclectic Macroeconomics

Macroeconomists address many different questions. For example, they examine the influence of fiscal policy on national saving, the impact of unemployment insurance on the unemployment rate, and the role of monetary policy in maintaining stable prices. Macroeconomics is as diverse as the economy.

Because no single model can answer all questions, macroeconomists use many different models. One of the most important and difficult tasks for the student of macroeconomics is to keep in mind that there is no single "correct" model. Instead, there are many models—each of which is useful for a different purpose.

This book therefore presents many different models that address different questions and that make different assumptions. Remember that a model is only as good as its assumptions and that an assumption that is useful for some purposes may be misleading for others. When using a model to address a question, the economist must keep in mind the underlying assumptions and judge whether these assumptions are reasonable for the matter at hand.

Prices: Flexible versus Sticky

One crucial assumption of macroeconomic models concerns the adjustment of wages and prices. Economists normally presume that the price of a good or a service adjusts to equilibrate supply and demand. In other words, they assume that, at the going price, demanders have bought all they want and suppliers have sold all they want. This assumption is called **market clearing** and is central to the model of the bread market discussed earlier. For answering most questions, economists use market-clearing models.

But the assumption of *continuous* market clearing is not entirely realistic. For markets to clear continuously, prices must adjust instantly to changes in supply and demand. In fact, however, many wages and prices adjust slowly. Labour contracts often set wages for up to three years. Many firms leave their product prices unchanged for long periods of time—for example, magazine publishers change their newsstand prices only every three or four years. Although market-clearing models assume that all wages and prices are **flexible**, in the real world some wages and prices are **sticky**.

Using Functions to Express Relationships Among Variables

All economic models express relationships among economic variables. Often, these relationships are expressed as functions. A *function* is a mathematical concept that shows how one variable depends on a set of other variables. For example, in the model of the bread market, we said that the quantity of bread demanded depends on the price of bread and on aggregate income. To express this, we use functional notation to write

$$Q^d = D(P_b, Y).$$

This equation says that the quantity of bread demanded Q^d is a function of the price of bread P_b and aggregate income Y. In functional notation, the variable preceding the parentheses denotes the function. In this case, $D(\ )$ is the function expressing how the variables in parentheses determine the quantity of bread demanded.

If we knew more about the bread market, we could give a numerical formula for the quantity of bread demanded. We might be able to write

$$Q^d = 60 - 10P_b + 2Y.$$

In this case, the demand function is

$$D(P_b, Y) = 60 - 10P_b + 2Y.$$

For any price of bread and aggregate income, this function gives the corresponding quantity of bread demanded. For example, if aggregate income is 10 and the price of bread is 2, then the quantity of bread demanded is 60; if the price of bread rises to 3, the quantity of bread demanded falls to 50.

Functional notation allows us to express a relationship among variables even when the precise numerical relationship among the variables is unknown. For example, we might know that the quantity of bread demanded falls when the price rises from 2 to 3, but we might not know by how much it falls. In this case, functional notation is useful: as long as we know that a relationship among the variables exists, we can express it using functional notation.

The apparent stickiness of prices does not necessarily make market-clearing models useless. After all, prices are not stuck forever; eventually, they do adjust to changes in supply and demand. Market-clearing models might not describe the economy at every instant, but they do describe the equilibrium toward which the economy slowly gravitates. Therefore, most macroeconomists believe that price flexibility is a good assumption for studying long-run issues, such as the economic growth we observe from decade to decade.

Yet, for studying short-run issues, such as year-to-year economic fluctuations, the assumption of price flexibility is less plausible. Over short periods,
many prices are fixed at predetermined levels. Therefore, most macroeconomists believe that price stickiness is a better assumption for studying the behaviour of the economy in the short run.

The Role of Microeconomics in Macroeconomics

Microeconomics, the study of the economy in the small, examines the activities
of individual units in the economy. Microeconomists study how households
and firms make decisions and how these decisionmakers interact in the marketplace. The central principle of microeconomics is that households and firms
"optimize"—they do the best they can, given their objectives and the constraints they face. In microeconomic models, households choose their purchases to maximize their level of satisfaction, which economists call *utility*, and
firms make production decisions to maximize profit.

Because the economy-wide events studied by macroeconomists arise
from the interaction of many households and many firms, macroeconomics
and microeconomics are inextricably linked. When we study the economy as a
whole, we must consider the decisions of individual economic actors. For example, to understand what determines total consumer spending, we must think
about a family deciding how much to spend today and how much to save for
the future. To understand what determines total investment spending, we must
think about a firm deciding whether to build a new factory. Because aggregate
variables are simply the sum of the variables describing many individual decisions, macroeconomics is inevitably founded in microeconomics.

Although microeconomic decisions always underlie economic models, in
many models the optimizing behaviour of households and firms is implicit
rather than explicit. The model of the bread market we discussed earlier is an
example. Households' decisions about how much bread to buy underlie the demand for bread, and bakeries' decisions about how much bread to produce underlie the supply of bread. Presumably, households make their decisions to
maximize utility, and bakeries make their decisions to maximize profit. Yet the
model did not focus on these microeconomic decisions; it left them in the background. Similarly, in much of macroeconomics, the optimizing behaviour of
households and firms is left implicit.

1•3 How This Book Proceeds

This book has four parts. This chapter and the next one form the "Introduction." Chapter 2 discusses how economists measure economic variables,
such as aggregate income, the inflation rate, and the unemployment rate.

Part Two, "The Economy in the Long Run," presents the classical model
of the economy. The key feature of the classical model is that, with only a few

exceptions, it assumes that prices adjust to equilibrate markets; that is, it assumes market clearing. For the reasons we have discussed, this assumption is best viewed as describing the economy in the long run.

Part Three, "The Economy in the Short Run," examines the behaviour of the economy when prices are sticky. It describes a non-market-clearing model of the economy and shows how the conclusions of the classical model need to be modified when the stickiness of prices is taken into account. This model with sticky prices is designed to analyze short-run issues, such as the reasons for economic fluctuations and the role of monetary and fiscal policy in stabilizing the economy.

The last chapter of Part Three presents an alternative view of economic fluctuations. It examines a "new classical" theory that attempts to explain the economy in the short run without invoking the assumption that prices are sticky. This approach stands in stark contrast to the one advocated by most economists, which posits that the failure of prices to equilibrate supply and demand is crucial for explaining short-run economic fluctuations.

Part Four, "More on the Microeconomics Behind Macroeconomics," examines some of the microeconomic models that are useful for analyzing macroeconomic issues. For example, it examines the household's decisions regarding how much to consume and how much money to hold and the firm's decisions regarding how much to invest. These individual decisions together form the larger macroeconomic picture. The goal of studying these microeconomic decisions in detail is to refine our understanding of the aggregate economy.

Summary

1. Macroeconomics is the study of the economy as a whole—including growth in incomes, changes in prices, and the rate of unemployment. Macroeconomists attempt both to explain economic events and to devise policies to improve economic performance.

2. To understand the economy, economists use models—theories that simplify reality in order to reveal how exogenous variables influence endogenous variables. The art in economics is in judging whether a model usefully captures the important economic relationships. Because no single model can answer all questions, macroeconomists use different models for different purposes.

3. Whether prices are flexible or sticky is a crucial assumption for a macroeconomic model. Most macroeconomists believe that market-clearing models describe the economy in the long run, but that prices are sticky in the short run.

4. Microeconomics is the study of how firms and individuals make decisions and how these decisionmakers interact. Since macroeconomic events arise from many microeconomic interactions, macroeconomists use many of the tools of microeconomics.

KEY CONCEPTS

Macroeconomics

Real GDP

Inflation rate

Unemployment rate

Recessions

Depressions

Deflation

Models

Exogenous and endogenous variables

Market clearing

Flexible and sticky prices

Microeconomics

QUESTIONS FOR REVIEW

1. Explain the difference between macroeconomics and microeconomics. How are these two fields related?

2. Why do economists build models?

3. What is a market-clearing model? When is the assumption of market clearing appropriate?

PROBLEMS AND APPLICATIONS

1. What macroeconomic issues have been in the news lately?

2. What do you think are the defining characteristics of a science? Does the study of the economy have these characteristics? Do you think macroeconomics should be called a science? Why or why not?

3. How often does the price you pay for a haircut change? What does your answer imply about the usefulness of market-clearing models for analyzing the market for haircuts?

The Data of Macroeconomics

It is a capital mistake to theorize before one has data. Insensibly one begins to twist facts to suit theories, instead of theories to fit facts.

Sherlock Holmes

Like all scientists, economists rely on both theory and observation. Since our goal is to understand how the economy works, observing the economy provides the basis for our theories. Once we have developed these theories, we turn again to observation to test them. This chapter discusses the types of observations that macroeconomists use to create and test their theories.

Casual observation provides one source of economic information. When shopping, you see how fast prices are rising. When looking for a job, you learn whether firms are hiring. Because we are all participants in the economy, we all gain some sense of economic conditions as we go about our lives.

Economic statistics provide a more systematic and an objective source of information. The government regularly surveys households and firms to learn about their economic activity—how much they are earning, what they are buying, what prices they are charging, and so on. From these surveys, various statistics are computed that summarize the state of the economy. These statistics are the data that economists use to study the economy. They also help policymakers to monitor economic developments and formulate appropriate policies.

This chapter focuses on the three economic statistics that economists and policymakers use most often. **Gross domestic product**, or **GDP**, tells us the nation's total income and the total expenditure on its output of goods and services. The **consumer price index (CPI)** measures the level of prices. The **unemployment rate** tells us the fraction of workers who are unemployed. We see below how these statistics are computed and what they tell us about the economy.

2•1 Measuring the Value of Economic Activity: Gross Domestic Product

Gross domestic product is often considered the best measure of how well the economy is performing. This measure, which Statistics Canada computes every three months, attempts to summarize in a single number the dollar value of

economic activity. More precisely, GDP equals the total value of all final goods
and services produced within Canada during a particular year or quarter. *If* it
were the case that (1) no Canadian worker had a job in another country, (2) no
foreigner had a job in Canada, and (3) all machines and factories used both
here and elsewhere were owned by domestic residents, then this total value of
goods produced would also measure the total value of Canadians' incomes.
But, since some income *is* received from individuals owning capital equipment
in other countries, GDP is not a perfect measure of total Canadian income.
Thus, statisticians also compute **gross national product (GNP)**.

GDP versus GNP

Here is the distinction between GDP and GNP:

- *GDP* is total income earned *domestically*. It includes income earned domestically by foreigners, but it does not include income earned by domestic residents on foreign ground.

- *GNP* is total income earned by *nationals* (that is, by residents of a nation). It includes the income that nationals earn abroad, but it does not include the income earned within a country by foreigners.

As noted, these two measures of income differ because a person can earn income and reside in different countries.

   To further understand the difference between GDP and GNP, consider
several examples. Suppose a resident of Hong Kong comes temporarily to Vancouver to work. The income he earns in Canada is part of Canadian GDP because it is earned domestically. But the income is not part of Canadian GNP
because the worker is not a Canadian national.

   As another example, suppose a Japanese resident owns a factory in Ontario. The profit she earns is part of Canadian GDP because this income is
earned domestically. But the profit is not part of Canadian GNP, because the
Japanese owner is not a Canadian.

   For the purpose of stabilizing employment, we are interested in a broad
measure of job-creating activity within Canada. GDP is that measure. For evaluating trends in the standard of living of Canadians, GNP is more appropriate.
In 1993, GNP was almost 4 percent less than GDP, primarily because (1) foreigners owned some capital equipment operating within Canada and (2) Canadians were in debt to foreigners. This gap meant that only 96 percent of the
economic activity taking place within Canada actually generated income for
Canadians. Despite this gap, we simplify by ignoring the difference between
GDP and GNP (and focus only on GDP) for many discussions within this book.
This is partly because it is GDP that is reported in the media, and partly because the cyclical swings in GDP and GNP are almost identical, so this simplification does not limit the applicability of our analysis.

   Thus, throughout much of this book, we abstract from the phenomenon
of foreign-owned factors of production, and we assume that GDP simultane-
ously measures all three of the following concepts:

CHAPTER 2 The Data of Macroeconomics   19

(handwritten margin notes: "GDP measures 3 things", "national income accounting system is used to measure these 3 things (GDP)")

- • The total output of goods and services
- • The total income of all individuals
- • The total expenditure of all individuals

To see how GDP can measure all these things at once, we must discuss **national income accounting**, the accounting system used to measure GDP and many related statistics.

Income, Expenditure, and the Circular Flow

Imagine an economy that produces a single good, bread, from a single input, domestic labour. Figure 2-1 illustrates all the economic transactions that occur between households and firms in this economy.

The inner loop in Figure 2-1 represents the flows of bread and labour. The households sell their labour to the firms. The firms use the labour of their workers to produce bread, which the firms in turn sell to the households.

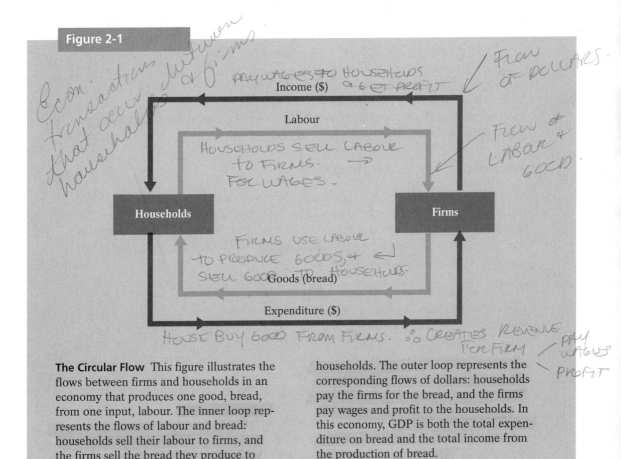

Figure 2-1

(handwritten notes on figure: "Econ. transactions that occur between households & firms", "Pay wages to households & get profit", "Flow of dollars", "Households sell labour to firms for wages", "Flow of labour & good", "Firms use labour to produce goods, & sell good to households", "House buy good from firms ∴ creates revenue for firm / pay wages / profit")

Income ($)

Labour

Households

Firms

Goods (bread)

Expenditure ($)

The Circular Flow This figure illustrates the flows between firms and households in an economy that produces one good, bread, from one input, labour. The inner loop represents the flows of labour and bread: households sell their labour to firms, and the firms sell the bread they produce to households. The outer loop represents the corresponding flows of dollars: households pay the firms for the bread, and the firms pay wages and profit to the households. In this economy, GDP is both the total expenditure on bread and the total income from the production of bread.

Hence, labour flows from households to firms, and bread flows from firms to households.

The outer loop in Figure 2-1 represents the corresponding flow of dollars. The households buy bread from the firms. The firms use some of the revenue from these sales to pay the wages of their workers, and the remainder is the profit belonging to the owners of the firms (who themselves are part of the household sector). Hence, expenditure on bread flows from households to firms, and income in the form of wages and profit flows from firms to households.

GDP measures the flow of dollars in this economy. We can compute it in two ways. GDP is the total income from the production of bread, which equals the sum of wages and profit—the top half of the circular flow of dollars. GDP is also the total expenditure on purchases of bread—the bottom half of the circular flow of dollars. Thus, we can look at the flow of dollars from firms to households or at the flow of dollars from households to firms.

The economy's total expenditure and its total income must be equal because every transaction has two sides—a buyer and a seller. The expenditure of buyers on purchases of products is, by the rules of accounting, income to the sellers of the products. Therefore, every transaction that affects expenditure must affect income, and every transaction that affects income must affect expenditure. For example, suppose that a firm produces and sells one more loaf of bread to a household. Clearly this transaction raises total expenditure on bread, but it also has an equal effect on total income. If the firm produces the extra loaf without hiring any more labour (such as by making the production process more efficient), then profit increases. If the firm produces the extra loaf by hiring more labour, then wages increase. In both cases, output, expenditure, and income all increase by the same amount.

Some Rules for Computing GDP

In the hypothetical economy that produces only bread, we can compute GDP simply by adding up the total expenditure on bread. By contrast, because a nation's economy is so large and complex, adding up the expenditure on all goods and services is less straightforward. To interpret GDP correctly, we must understand some of the rules that govern its construction.

The Treatment of Inventories Suppose that a firm in our one-good economy hires workers to produce more bread, pays their wages, and then fails to sell the additional bread. How does this transaction affect GDP?

The answer depends on what happens to the unsold bread. If the bread spoils, then profit is reduced by the amount that wages are increased—the firm has paid the workers more wages but has not received any benefit from doing so. Because the transaction affects neither expenditure nor income, it leaves GDP unaltered (although more is distributed as wages and less as profit). By contrast, if the bread is put into inventory to be sold later, the transaction is treated differently. In this case, profit is not reduced, and the owners of the firm are assumed to have "purchased" the bread for the firm's inventory. Because the higher wages raise total income, and greater inventory accumulation raises total expenditure, GDP rises.

Stocks and Flows

Many of the variables that economists study involve a quantity of something—a quantity of money, a quantity of goods, and so on. Economists distinguish between two types of quantity variables: stocks and flows. A **stock** is a quantity measured at a given point in time, whereas a **flow** is a quantity measured per unit of time.

The bathtub, shown in Figure 2-2, is the classic example used to illustrate stocks and flows. The amount of water in the tub is a stock: it is the quantity of water in the tub at a given point in time. The amount of water coming out of the faucet is a flow: it is the quantity of water being added to the tub per unit of time. Note that the units with which we measure stocks and flows differ. We say that the bathtub contains 200 *litres* of water, but that water is coming out of the faucet at 20 *litres per minute*.

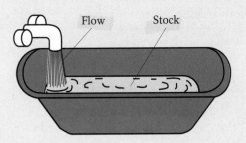

Flow   Stock

Figure 2-2

Stocks and Flows The amount of water in a bathtub is a stock; it is a quantity measured at a given moment in time. The amount of water coming out of the faucet is a flow: it is a quantity measured per unit of time.

Stocks and flows are often related. In the bathtub example, these relationships are clear. The stock of water in the tub represents the accumulation of the flow out of the faucet, and the flow of water represents the change in the stock. When building theories to explain economic variables, it is essential to think about whether the variables are stocks or flows and whether any relationships link them.

Here are some examples of related stocks and flows that we study in future chapters:

- The amount of capital equipment in the economy is a stock; the amount of investment on new plant and equipment is a flow.

- A consumer's wealth is a stock; his or her income and expenditure are flows.

- The number of unemployed people is a stock; the number of people losing their jobs is a flow.

- The government debt is a stock; the government budget deficit is a flow.

The general rule is that when a firm increases its inventory of goods, this investment in inventory is counted both as part of expenditure and as part of income. Thus, production for inventory increases GDP just as production for final sales does.

Adding Apples and Oranges   We have been discussing GDP as if bread were the only item produced. Our economy, however, produces many different goods and services—bread, beef, cars, haircuts, and so on. GDP combines the value of these goods and services into one summary measure. The diversity of products in the economy complicates the calculation of GDP because different products have different values.

Suppose, for example, that the economy produces four apples and three oranges. How do we compute GDP? We could simply add apples and oranges and conclude that GDP equals seven pieces of fruit. But this makes sense only if apples and oranges have equal value, which is generally not true. (This would be even clearer if the economy had produced four watermelons and three grapes.)

To compute the total value of different goods and services, we use the market price as the measure of value. The market price is used because it reflects how much people are willing to pay for a good or service. Thus, if apples cost $0.50 each and oranges cost $1.00 each, GDP would be

$$
\begin{aligned}
\text{GDP} &= (\text{Price of Apples} \times \text{Quantity of Apples}) \\
&\quad + (\text{Price of Oranges} \times \text{Quantity of Oranges}) \\
&= (\$0.50 \times 4) + (\$1.00 \times 3) \\
&= \$5.00.
\end{aligned}
$$

GDP equals $5.00—the value of all the apples, $2.00, plus the value of all the oranges, $3.00.

Intermediate Goods and Value-Added   Many goods are produced in stages: raw materials are processed into intermediate goods by one firm and then sold to another firm for final processing. How should we treat such products when computing GDP? For example, suppose a cattle rancher sells one-quarter pound of meat to McDonald's for $0.50, and then McDonald's sells you a hamburger for $1.50. Should GDP include both the meat and the hamburger (a total of $2.00), or just the hamburger ($1.50)?

The answer is that GDP includes only the value of final goods. Thus, the hamburger is included in GDP but the meat is not: GDP increases by $1.50, not by $2.00. The reason is that the value of intermediate goods is already included as part of the price of the final goods. To add the intermediate goods to the final goods would be double-counting—that is, the meat would be counted twice. Hence, GDP is the total value of final goods and services produced.

One way to compute the value of all final goods and services is to sum the value-added at each stage of production. The **value-added** of a firm equals the value of the firm's output less the value of the intermediate goods that the firm purchases. In the case of the hamburger, the value-added of the rancher is

$0.50 (assuming the rancher bought no intermediate goods), and the value-added of McDonald's is $1.50 − $0.50, or $1.00. Total value-added is $0.50 + $1.00, which equals $1.50. For the economy as a whole, the sum of all value-added must equal the value of all final goods and services. Hence, GDP is also the total value-added of all firms in the economy.

Housing Services and Other Imputations Although most goods and services are valued at their market prices when computing GDP, some are not sold in the marketplace and therefore do not have market prices. If GDP is to include the value of these goods and services, we must use an estimate of their value, an estimate that is called an **imputed value**.

One area in which imputations are important is housing. A person who rents a house is buying housing services and is providing income for the landlord; the rent is part of GDP, both as expenditure by the renter and as income of the landlord. Many people, however, live in their own homes. Although they do not pay rent to a landlord, they are enjoying housing services similar to those of renters. To take account of the housing services enjoyed by homeowners, GDP includes the "rent" that these homeowners "pay" to themselves. Of course, homeowners do not in fact pay themselves this rent. Statistics Canada estimates what the market rent for a house would be if it were rented and includes that imputed rent as part of GDP. This imputed rent is included both in the homeowner's expenditure and in the homeowner's income.

Another area in which imputations arise is in valuing the services provided by the government. For example, police officers, fire fighters, and legislators provide services to the public. Measuring the value of these services is difficult because they are not sold in a marketplace and therefore do not have a market price. GDP includes these services by valuing them at their cost. Thus, the wages of these public servants are used as a measure of the value of their output.

In many circumstances, an imputation is called for in principle but, to keeps things simple, is not made in practice. Since GDP includes the imputed rent on owner-occupied houses, one might expect it also to include the imputed rent on cars, lawnmowers, jewelry, and other durable goods owned by households. Yet the value of these services is left out of GDP. In addition, some of the output of the economy is produced and consumed at home and never enters the marketplace. For example, meals cooked at home are similar to meals cooked at a restaurant, yet the value-added in meals at home is left out of GDP. Statistics Canada does not try to estimate the value of "household production" like this on any regular basis. Just to give some idea of the magnitude involved, however, the agency published an estimate for 1991. According to this study, household production in Canada is equal to about one third of the measured GDP.

Finally, no imputation is made for the value of goods and services sold in the *underground economy*. The underground economy is that part of the economy that people hide from the government either because they wish to evade taxation or because the activity is illegal. Home construction, repairs, and cleaning services paid "under the table" are examples of the underground economy. The illegal drug trade is another.

Since the imputations necessary for computing GDP are only approximate, and since the value of many goods and services is left out altogether, GDP is an imperfect measure of economic activity. These imperfections are most problematic when comparing standards of living across countries. The size of the underground economy, for instance, varies from country to country. Yet as long as the magnitude of these imperfections remains fairly constant over time, GDP is useful for comparing economic activity from year to year.

Real GDP versus Nominal GDP

Now that we have examined some of the rules used in constructing GDP, let us return to the question of whether GDP is a good measure of economic well-being. Consider once again the economy that produces only apples and oranges. In this economy GDP is the sum of the value of all the apples produced and the value of all the oranges produced. That is,

$$\text{GDP} = (\text{Price of Apples} \times \text{Quantity of Apples})$$
$$+ (\text{Price of Oranges} \times \text{Quantity of Oranges}).$$

GDP can increase either because prices rise or because quantities rise.

GDP computed this way is not a good measure of economic well-being. That is, it does not accurately reflect how well the economy can satisfy the demands of households, firms, and the government. If all prices doubled without any change in quantities, GDP would double. Yet it would be misleading to say that the economy's ability to satisfy demands has doubled, because the quantity of every good produced remains the same. Economists call the value of goods and services measured at current prices **nominal GDP**.

A better measure of economic well-being would tally the economy's output of goods and services and would not be influenced by changes in prices. For this purpose, economists use **real GDP**, which is the value of goods and services measured at constant prices. To compute real GDP, a base year is chosen—say, 1986. Goods and services are then added up using 1986 prices to value the different goods. In our apple-and-orange economy, real GDP for 1994 would be

$$\text{Real GDP} = (1986 \text{ Price of Apples} \times 1994 \text{ Quantity of Apples})$$
$$+ (1986 \text{ Price of Oranges} \times 1994 \text{ Quantity of Oranges}).$$

Similarly, real GDP in 1995 would be

$$\text{Real GDP} = (1986 \text{ Price of Apples} \times 1995 \text{ Quantity of Apples})$$
$$+ (1986 \text{ Price of Oranges} \times 1995 \text{ Quantity of Oranges}).$$

Because the prices are held constant, real GDP varies from year to year only if the quantities vary. Thus, real GDP summarizes the output of the economy measured in base-year (in this case, 1986) dollars. Because a society's ability to provide economic satisfaction for its members ultimately depends on the quantities of goods and services produced, real GDP provides a better measure of economic well-being than nominal GDP.

The GDP Deflator

From nominal GDP and real GDP we can compute a third statistic: the GDP deflator. The **GDP deflator**, also called the implicit price deflator for GDP, is defined as

$$\text{GDP Deflator} = \frac{\text{Nominal GDP}}{\text{Real GDP}}.$$

The GDP deflator is the ratio of nominal GDP to real GDP.

To better understand nominal GDP, real GDP, and the GDP deflator, consider again an economy with only one good, bread. In any year, nominal GDP is the total number of dollars spent on bread in that year. Real GDP is the number of loaves of bread produced in that year times the price of bread in some base year. The GDP deflator is the price of bread in that year relative to the price of bread in the base year.

Actual economies, however, produce many goods. Nominal GDP, real GDP, and the GDP deflator aggregate the many different prices and quantities. Consider an economy with apples and oranges. Letting P denote the price of a good, Q the quantity, and a superscript "86" the base year 1986, the GDP deflator would be

$$\text{GDP Deflator} = \frac{(P_{\text{apples}} \times Q_{\text{apples}}) + (P_{\text{oranges}} \times Q_{\text{oranges}})}{(P^{86}_{\text{apples}} \times Q_{\text{apples}}) + (P^{86}_{\text{oranges}} \times Q_{\text{oranges}})}.$$

The numerator of this expression is nominal GDP, and the denominator is real GDP. Both nominal GDP and real GDP can be viewed as the price of a basket of goods; in this case, the basket consists of the quantities of apples and oranges currently produced. The GDP deflator compares the current price of this basket to the price of the same basket in the base year.

The definition of the GDP deflator allows us to separate nominal GDP into two parts: one part measures quantities and the other measures prices. That is,

$$\text{Nominal GDP} = \text{Real GDP} \times \text{GDP Deflator}.$$

Nominal GDP measures the dollar value of the output of the economy. Real GDP measures the amount of output—that is, output valued at constant (base-year) prices. The GDP deflator measures the price of the typical unit of output relative to its price in the base year.

The Components of Expenditure

Economists and policymakers care not only about the economy's total output of goods and services but also about the allocation of this output among alternative uses. National income accounts allocate GDP among four broad categories:

- Consumption (*C*)
- Investment (*I*)
- Government purchases (*G*)
- Net exports (*NX*)

Thus, letting *Y* stand for GDP,

$$Y = C + I + G + NX.$$

GDP is the sum of consumption, investment, government purchases, and net exports. Each dollar of GDP is placed in one of these categories. This equation is an *identity*—an equation that must hold because of the way the variables are defined. It is called the **national income accounts identity**.

Consumption consists of the goods and services bought by households. It is divided into three subcategories: durable goods, nondurable goods, and services. Durable goods are goods that last a long time, such as cars and TVs. Nondurable goods are goods that last only a short time, such as food and clothing. Services include the work done for consumers by individuals and firms, such as haircuts and doctor visits.

Investment consists of goods bought for future use. Investment is also divided into three subcategories: business fixed investment, residential construction, and inventory investment. Business fixed investment is the purchase of new plants and equipment by firms. Residential construction is the purchase of new housing by households and landlords. Inventory investment is the increase in firms' inventory of goods (if the inventory is falling, inventory investment is negative).

Government purchases are the goods and services bought by federal, provincial, and municipal governments. This category includes military equipment, highways, and the services that government workers provide. It does not include transfer payments to individuals, such as the Canada Pension, unemployment insurance benefits, and welfare. Because these payments are merely reallocating existing income, and are not made in exchange for goods and services, they are not part of GDP.

The last category, **net exports**, takes into account trade with other countries. Net exports are the value of goods and services exported to other countries minus the value of goods and services that foreigners provide us. It represents the net expenditure from abroad for our goods and services, which provides income for domestic producers.

What Is Investment?

The term "investment" sometimes creates confusion for newcomers to macro-economics. The confusion arises because what looks like investment for an individual may not be investment for the economy as a whole.

Suppose we observe these two events:

- Smith buys for himself a 100-year-old Victorian house.

- Jones builds for herself a brand-new contemporary house.

What is total investment here? One house, two houses, or none?

A macroeconomist seeing these two transactions counts only the Jones house as investment. Smith's transaction has not created new housing for the economy; it has merely reallocated existing housing. Smith's purchase is investment for Smith, but it is disinvestment for the person selling the house. By contrast, Jones has added new housing to the economy; her new house is counted as investment.

Similarly, consider these two events:

- Clarke buys $5 million in Air Canada stock from White on the Toronto Stock Exchange.

- General Motors sells $10 million in stock to the public and uses the proceeds to build a new car factory.

Here, investment is $10 million. In the first transaction, Clarke is investing in Air Canada stock, and White is disinvesting; there is no investment for the economy. By contrast, General Motors is using some of the economy's output of goods and services to add to its stock of capital; hence, its new factory is counted as investment.

The general rule is that purchases that reallocate existing assets among different individuals are not investment for the economy. Investment, as macroeconomists use the term, entails the creation of new capital.

CASE STUDY

2·1 GDP and Its Components

In 1993 the GDP of Canada totaled almost $710.7 billion. This number is so large that it is almost impossible to comprehend. We can make it easier to understand by dividing it by the 1993 Canadian population of 28.753 million. In this way, we obtain GDP per person—the amount of expenditure for the average Canadian—which equaled $24,717 in 1993.

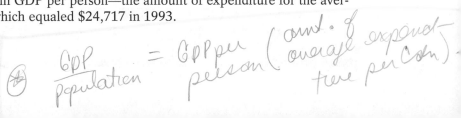

How did we use this GDP? Table 2-1 shows that about 60 percent of it, or
$15,025 per person, was spent on consumption. Investment was $3,920 per
person, and government purchases were $5,801 per person.

Table 2-1

GDP and the Components of Expenditure: 1993

	Total (billions of dollars)	Per Person (dollars)
Gross Domestic Product	$710.7	$24,717
Consumption	432.0	15,025
Durables and semi-durables	94.7	3,294
Nondurables and services	337.3	11,731
Investment	112.7	3,920
Business fixed investment (factories, machinery)	68.8	2,393
Residential construction	43.1	1,499
Inventory investment	0.8	28
Government Purchases	166.8	5,801
Current goods and services	150.3	5,227
Capital goods	16.5	574
Net Exports	− 0.8	− 28
Exports	208.3	7,244
Imports	209.1	7,272

Source: Reproduced and adapted by authority of the Minister of Industry, 1994, "Statistics Canada," *National Income and Expenditure Accounts, Catalogue 13-001* (Quarterly Estimates, 1993): 5.

The average person bought $7,272 of goods imported from abroad and
produced $7,244 of goods that were exported to other countries. Thus, net ex-
ports were negative. Since we earned less from selling to foreigners than we
spent on foreign goods, we must have financed the difference by taking out
loans from foreigners (or, equivalently, by selling them some of our assets).
Thus, the average Canadian borrowed $28 from abroad in 1993.

It is interesting to compare how Canadians use their GDP to the spending
patterns in other countries. Even when compared to Americans, there are significant differences. While Canadians spend almost 30 percent of per-capita
GDP on imports, Americans limit spending on imports to just over 11 percent.
Canadians leave almost 24 percent of per-capita GDP to be spent by various
levels of government, while Americans limit this proportion to 19 percent.

Several Measures of Income

The national income accounts include other measures of income that differ slightly in definition from GDP and GNP. It is important to be aware of the various measures because economists and the press sometimes refer to them.

We can see how the alternative measures of income relate to one another by starting with GDP and subtracting various quantities. To obtain GNP from GDP, we subtract the net income of foreigners who own factors of production employed in Canada:

GNP = GDP − Net Income of Foreigners.

To obtain *net national product (NNP)*, we subtract the depreciation of capital—the amount of the economy's stock of plants, equipment, and residential structures that wears out during the year:

NNP = GNP − Depreciation.

D = capital consumption allowances.

In the national income accounts, depreciation is called the *capital consumption allowances*. In 1993, it equaled about 13 percent of GNP. Since the depreciation of capital is a cost of producing the output of the economy, subtracting depreciation shows the net result of economic activity. For this reason, some economists believe that NNP is a better measure of economic well-being.

The next adjustment in the national income accounts is for indirect business taxes, such as sales taxes. These taxes, which make up about 15 percent of NNP, place a wedge between the price that consumers pay for a good and the price that firms receive. Because firms never receive this tax wedge, it is not part of their income. Once we subtract indirect business taxes from NNP, we obtain a measure called *national income*:

National Income = NNP − Indirect Business Taxes. *eg: Sales tax*

National income is a measure of how much everyone in the economy has earned.

The national income accounts divide national income into four components, depending on the way the income is earned. The four categories, and the percentage of national income that each comprises, in 1993, are:

- **Compensation of employees (79 percent)**   The wages and fringe benefits earned by workers
- **Corporate profits (7.5 percent)**   The income of corporations after payments to their workers and creditors
- **Nonincorporated business income (3 percent)**   The income of nonincorporate businesses, such as small farms and law partnerships, and the income that landlords receive, including the imputed rent that homeowners "pay" to themselves, less expenses, such as depreciation
- **Net interest (10.5 percent)**   The interest domestic businesses pay minus the interest they receive, plus interest earned from foreigners

A series of adjustments takes us from national income to *personal income*, the amount of income that households and noncorporate businesses receive.

Three of these adjustments are most important. First, we reduce national income by the amount corporations earn but do not pay out, either because the corporations are retaining earnings or because they are paying taxes to the government. This adjustment is made by subtracting corporate profits (which equals the sum of corporate taxes, dividends, and retained earnings) and adding back dividends. Second, we increase national income by the net amount the government pays out in transfer payments. This adjustment equals government transfers to individuals minus unemployment insurance and public pension contributions paid to the government. Third, we adjust national income to include the interest that households earn rather than the interest that businesses pay. This adjustment is made by adding personal interest income and subtracting net interest. (The difference between personal interest and net interest arises in part from the interest on the government debt.) Thus, personal income is

Personal Income = National Income
 − Corporate Profits
 − Social Insurance Contributions
 − Net Interest
 + Dividends
 + Government Transfers to Individuals
 + Personal Interest Income.

Next, if we subtract personal tax payments, we obtain *personal disposable income*:

Personal Disposable Income = Personal Income
 − Personal Tax Payments.

Personal disposable income is the amount households and noncorporate businesses have available to spend after satisfying their tax obligations to the government.

<h3>CASE STUDY</h3>

2·2 The Seasonal Cycle and Seasonal Adjustment

If we look at what happens to real GDP and other measures of income over the year, we find a regular seasonal pattern. The output of the economy rises during the year, reaching a peak in the fourth quarter (October, November, and December), and then falling in the first quarter (January, February, and March). These regular seasonal changes are substantial. From the fourth quarter to the first quarter, real GDP falls on average about 5 percent.

It is not surprising that real GDP follows a seasonal cycle. Some of these changes are attributable to changes in our ability to produce: for example, building homes is more difficult during the cold weather of winter than during other seasons. In addition, people have seasonal tastes: they have preferred times for such activities as vacations and Christmas shopping.

When economists study fluctuations in real GDP and other economic variables, they often want to eliminate the portion of fluctuations due to predictable seasonal changes. You will find that most of the economic statistics reported in the newspaper are *seasonally adjusted*—that is, statisticians have adjusted the data to remove the regular seasonal fluctuations. Therefore, when you observe a change in real GDP or any other data series, you must look beyond the seasonal cycle to explain the change.

2•2 Measuring the Cost of Living: The Consumer Price Index

A dollar today doesn't buy as much as it did 20 years ago. The cost of almost everything has gone up. This increase in the overall level of prices is called *inflation*, and it is one of the primary concerns of economists and policymakers. In later chapters we examine in detail the causes and effects of inflation. Here we discuss how economists measure changes in the cost of living.

The Price of a Basket of Goods

The most commonly used measure of the level of prices is the consumer price index (CPI). Statistics Canada has the job of computing the CPI. It begins by collecting the prices of about 500 goods and services, which its surveys suggest represent the typical purchases of Canadian households. The CPI traces the changing cost of this basket of goods. Just as GDP turns the quantities of many goods and services into a single number measuring the value of production, the CPI turns the prices of many goods and services into a single index measuring the overall level of prices.

How should economists aggregate the many prices in the economy into a single index that reliably measures the price level? They could simply compute an average of all prices. Yet this approach would treat all goods and services equally. Since people consume more chicken than caviar, the price of chicken should have a greater weight in the CPI than the price of caviar. Statistics Canada weights different items by computing the price of a basket of goods and services purchased by a typical consumer. The CPI is the price of this basket of goods and services relative to the price of the same basket in some base year.

For example, suppose that the typical consumer buys 5 apples and 2 oranges every month. That is, the basket of goods consists of 5 apples and 2 oranges. The CPI is

$$CPI = \frac{(5 \times \text{Current Price of Apples}) + (2 \times \text{Current Price of Oranges})}{(5 \times 1986 \text{ Price of Apples}) + (2 \times 1986 \text{ Price of Oranges})}.$$

In this CPI, 1986 is the base year. The index tells us how much it costs now to buy 5 apples and 2 oranges relative to how much it cost to buy the same basket of fruit in 1986.

The consumer price index is the most closely watched index of prices, but it is not the only such index. Another is the industrial products price index, which measures the price of a typical basket of goods bought by firms rather than consumers. In addition to these overall price indexes, Statistics Canada computes price indexes for specific types of goods, such as food, housing, and energy.

The CPI versus the GDP Deflator

Earlier in this chapter we discussed another measure of prices—the implicit price deflator for GDP, which is the ratio of nominal GDP to real GDP. The GDP deflator and the CPI give somewhat different information about the overall level of prices in the economy. There are three key differences between the two measures.

The first difference is that the GDP deflator measures the prices of all goods and services produced, whereas the CPI measures the prices of only a representative basket of goods and services bought by consumers. Thus, an increase in the price of goods bought by firms or the government will show up in the GDP deflator but not in the CPI.

The second difference is that the GDP deflator includes only those goods produced domestically. Imported goods are not part of GDP and do not show up in the GDP deflator. Hence, an increase in the price of a Toyota made in Japan and sold in this country affects the CPI, because the Toyota is bought by consumers, but it does not affect the GDP deflator.

The third and most subtle difference concerns how the two measures aggregate the many prices in the economy. The CPI assigns fixed weights to the prices of different goods, whereas the GDP deflator assigns changing weights. In other words, the CPI is computed using a fixed basket of goods, whereas the GDP deflator allows the basket of goods to change over time as the composition of GDP changes. To see how this works, consider an economy that produces and consumes only apples and oranges. The GDP deflator is

$$\text{GDP Deflator} = \frac{\text{Nominal GDP}}{\text{Real GDP}}.$$

$$= \frac{(P_{\text{apples}} \times Q_{\text{apples}}) + (P_{\text{oranges}} \times Q_{\text{oranges}})}{(P^{86}_{\text{apples}} \times Q_{\text{apples}}) + (P^{86}_{\text{oranges}} \times Q_{\text{oranges}})}.$$

The CPI is

$$\text{CPI} = \frac{(P_{\text{apples}} \times Q^{86}_{\text{apples}}) + (P_{\text{oranges}} \times Q^{86}_{\text{oranges}})}{(P^{86}_{\text{apples}} \times Q^{86}_{\text{apples}}) + (P^{86}_{\text{oranges}} \times Q^{86}_{\text{oranges}})}.$$

These equations show that both the CPI and the GDP deflator compare the cost of a basket of goods today with the cost of that same basket in the base year. The difference between the two measures is whether the basket changes over time. The CPI uses a fixed basket (base-year quantities), whereas the GDP deflator uses a changing basket (current quantities).

CASE STUDY

Difficulties in Measuring Inflation

From 1973 to 1976 prices in Canada rose at a very rapid pace. But exactly how much did they rise? This question was asked by public policymakers who had to judge the seriousness of the inflation problem. It was also asked by private decision makers: many private contracts, such as wage agreements and pensions, are indexed to correct for the effects of rising prices.

The magnitude of the price rise depends on which measure of prices one uses. According to the GDP deflator, prices rose an average of 10.5 percent per year during these four years. According to the CPI, prices rose 9.2 percent per year. Over the four-year period, the accumulated difference is over 5 percent.

This discrepancy is partly attributable to the large increase in the price of natural resources that occurred in the mid-1970s. A significant part of the Canadian economy involves primary commodity industries. As a result, big price increases in these commodities make a significant contribution to the overall inflation rate as measured by the GDP deflator. But since households spend a lower proportion of their incomes on these products, natural resources price increases have a smaller impact on inflation as measured by the CPI.

A similar discrepancy between the two price indexes emerged in the 1990s. At this time, the relative prices for primary commodities had fallen to their lowest levels in 60 years. This development, which was particularly hard on many individuals, such as western farmers, caused the GDP deflator to increase at a slower rate than the CPI. During the 1990–1994 period, the cumulative difference in the two measures was 6 percent.

When price indexes differ, as they did during these episodes of commodity price volatility, it is usually possible to identify the sources of the differences. Yet accounting for the differences is easier than deciding which index provides the better measure. Furthermore, which index one should use in practice is not merely a question of measurement; it also depends on one's purpose. In practice, government programs and private contracts usually use the CPI to measure the level of prices, despite the fact that we know the CPI is biased in the upward direction. The magnitude of that upward bias is in the range of one-half to one percent.[1] Thus, we should interpret an annual inflation rate for the CPI in the 0.5–1.0 range as evidence that we have reached "zero" inflation.

The following example shows how these approaches differ. Suppose that our fish stocks are completely eliminated: the quantity of fish sold therefore falls to zero, and the price of the few fish that remain in grocers' freezers is driven sky-high. Because fish are no longer part of GDP, the increase in the price of fish does not show up in the GDP deflator. But because the CPI is computed

[1] Allan Crawford, "Measuring Biases in the Canadian CPI," in *Bank of Canada Technical Report No. 64* (1993), and Pierre Fortin, "Do We Measure Inflation Correctly?" in *Zero Inflation: The Goal of Price Stability*, R.G. Lipsey, ed. (Toronto: C.D. Howe Institute, 1990).

with a fixed basket of goods that includes fish, the increase in the price of fish causes a substantial rise in the CPI.

Economists call a price index with a fixed basket of goods a *Laspeyres index* and a price index with a changing basket a *Paasche index.* Economic theorists have studied the properties of these different types of price indexes to determine which is better. The answer, it turns out, is that neither is clearly superior.

The purpose of any price index is to measure the cost of living—that is, how much it costs to maintain a given standard of living. When prices of different goods are changing by different amounts, a Laspeyres index tends to overstate the increase in the cost of living, whereas a Paasche index tends to understate it. A Laspeyres index uses a fixed basket and thus does not take into account that consumers have the opportunity to substitute less expensive goods for

Figure 2-3

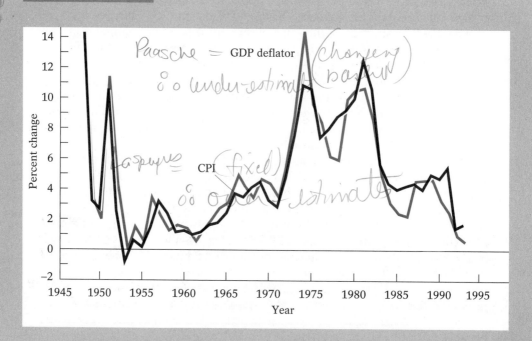

The GDP Deflator and the CPI This figure shows the percentage change in the GDP deflator and in the CPI for every year since 1948. Although these two measures of prices diverge at times, they usually tell the same story about how quickly prices are rising. Both the CPI and the GDP deflator show that prices rose slowly in most of the 1950s and 1960s, that they rose much more quickly in the 1970s, and that they rose slowly again after the 1980s.

Source: Reproduced and adapted by authority of the Minister of Industry, 1994, "Statistics Canada," *Canadian Economic Observer*, Series D20556, P484000 (Historical Statistical Supplement, 1991/92): 27, 51 and (Statistical Summary, March 1994): 22-23.

more expensive ones. By contrast, a Paasche index accounts for the substitution of alternative goods, but it does not reflect the reduction in consumers' welfare that may result from such substitutions.

The example of the depleted fish stock shows the problems with Laspeyres and Paasche price indexes. Because the CPI is a Laspeyres index, it overstates the impact of the increase in fish prices on consumers: by using a fixed basket of goods, it ignores consumers' ability to substitute chicken for fish. By contrast, because the GDP deflator is a Paasche index, it understates the impact on consumers: the GDP deflator shows no rise in prices, yet surely the high price of fish makes consumers worse off.

Luckily, the difference between the GDP deflator and the CPI is usually not large in practice. Figure 2-3 shows the percentage change in the GDP deflator and the percentage change in the CPI for each year since 1948. Both measures usually tell the same story about how quickly prices are rising.

2•3 Measuring Joblessness: The Unemployment Rate

One aspect of economic performance is how well an economy uses its resources. Since an economy's workers are its chief resource, keeping workers employed is a paramount concern of economic policymakers. The unemployment rate is the statistic that measures the percentage of those people wanting to work who do not have jobs.

Every month Statistics Canada computes the unemployment rate and many other statistics with which economists and policymakers monitor developments in the labour market. These statistics come from the Labour Force Survey of about 56,000 households. Based on survey questions, each person is

"Well, so long Eddie, the recession's over."

Drawing by M. Stevens; © 1980
The New Yorker Magazine, Inc.

placed into one of three categories: employed, unemployed, or not in the labour force. A person is employed if he or she spent most of the previous week working at a job, as opposed to keeping house, going to school, or doing something else. A person is unemployed if he or she is not employed and is waiting for the start date of a new job, is on temporary layoff, or has been looking for a job. A person who fits neither of the first two categories, such as a student or retiree, is not in the labour force. A person who wants a job but has given up looking—a *discouraged worker*—is counted as not in the labour force.

The **labour force** is defined as the sum of the employed and the unemployed, and the unemployment rate is defined as the percentage of the labour force that is unemployed. That is,

$$\text{Labour Force} = \text{Number of Employed} + \text{Number of Unemployed},$$

and

$$\text{Unemployment Rate} = \frac{\text{Number of Unemployed}}{\text{Labour Force}} \times 100.$$

A related statistic is the **labour-force participation rate**, the percentage of the adult population that is in the labour force:

$$\text{Labour-Force Participation Rate} = \frac{\text{Labour Force}}{\text{Adult Population}} \times 100.$$

Figure 2-4

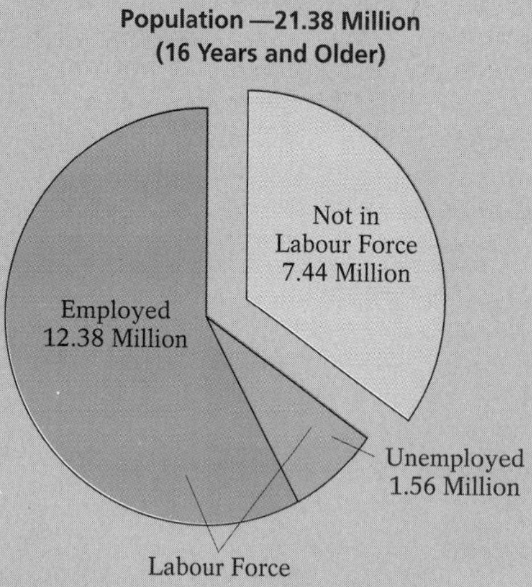

Population —21.38 Million (16 Years and Older)

Employed
12.38 Million

Not in
Labour Force
7.44 Million

Unemployed
1.56 Million

Labour Force

The Three Groups of the Population When Statistics Canada surveys the population, it places people in one of three categories: employed, unemployed, or not in the labour force. This figure shows the number of people in each category in 1993. The Canadian population was 28.8 million in 1993, while the sum of the three categories in this figure is only 21.38 million. The difference is explained by the fact that the Labour Force Survey deliberately excludes individuals in all of the following categories: (1) persons younger than 15 years old; (2) persons residing in the Yukon, the Northwest Territories, and on Native reserves; (3) full-time members of the armed forces; and (4) inmates in institutions.

Source: Reproduced and adapted by authority of the Minister of Industry, 1994, "Statistics Canada," *Canadian Economic Observer* (Statistical Summary, March 1994): 15.

Statistics Canada computes these statistics for the overall population and for groups within the population: men and women, teenagers and prime-age workers.

Figure 2-4 shows the breakdown of the population into the three categories for 1993. In that year, the labour force was

$$\text{Labour Force} = 12.38 + 1.56 = 13.94 \text{ million,}$$

the unemployment rate was

$$\text{Unemployment Rate} = (1.56/13.94) \times 100 = 11.2\%,$$

and the labour-force participation rate was

$$\text{Labour-Force Participation Rate} = (13.94/21.38) \times 100 = 65.2\%.$$

Hence, about two thirds of the adult population was in the labour force, and just over 11 percent of those in the labour force did not have a job.

CASE STUDY

2·4   Unemployment, GDP, and Okun's Law

What relationship would you expect to find between unemployment and real GDP? Since employed workers help to produce goods and services and unemployed workers do not, one would expect increases in the unemployment rate to be associated with decreases in real GDP. This negative relationship between unemployment and GDP is called **Okun's law**, after Arthur Okun, the economist who first studied it.[2]

Figure 2-5 uses annual data for Canada to illustrate Okun's law. This figure is a scatterplot—a scatter of points where each point represents one observation (in this case, the data for a particular year). The vertical axis represents the change in the unemployment rate from the previous year, and the horizontal axis represents the percentage change in real GDP. This figure shows clearly that year-to-year changes in the unemployment rate are closely associated with year-to-year changes in real GDP.

We can be more precise about the magnitude of the Okun's law relationship. The summary line drawn through the scatter of points tells us that

$$\text{Change in the Unemployment Rate} = -0.5 \left[\left(\frac{\text{Percent Change}}{\text{in Real GDP}} \right) - 4 \right]$$

On average, real GDP has grown by about 4 percent each year since 1950; this normal growth is due to population growth, capital accumulation, and technological progress. Okun's law indicates that this is roughly the amount of growth that is necessary to keep the growth in the number of jobs in pace with the growing size of the labour force—so that the unemployment rate can stay

[2] Arthur M. Okun, "Potential GNP: Its Measurement and Significance," in *Proceedings of the Business and Economics Statistics Section, American Statistical Association* (Washington, D.C.: American Statistical Association, 1962), 98–103; reprinted in Arthur M. Okun, *Economics for Policymaking* (Cambridge, Mass.: MIT Press, 1983), 145–158.

Figure 2-5

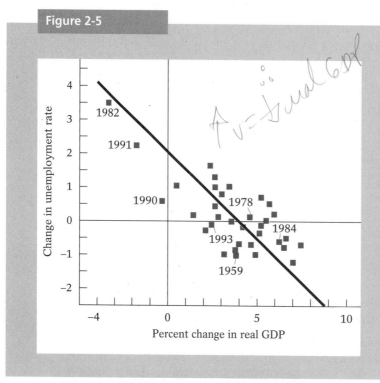

Okun's Law This figure is a scatterplot of the change in the unemployment rate on the vertical axis and the percentage change in real GDP on the horizontal axis for the last 35 years. Each point represents one year. The negative correlation between these variables shows that increases in unemployment tend to be associated with decreases in real GDP.

Source: Reproduced and adapted by authority of the Minister of Industry, 1994, Statistics Canada. For details, see source lines of Figures 1-1 and 1-3.

constant. If, however, real GDP growth is only 3 percent, this relationship tells us that the unemployment rate will rise by about one half of one percentage point.

The implications for unemployment are more dramatic in a recession (when real GDP growth is negative). For example, when real growth is − 1 percent, unemployment rises by 0.5 (1 + 4) = 2.5 percentage points. Policymakers often try to stabilize GDP growth around its long-run average value, with a view toward minimizing these disruptive swings in the unemployment rate.

2•4 Conclusion: From Economic Statistics to Economic Models

The three statistics discussed in this chapter—GDP, the CPI, and the unemployment rate—quantify the performance of the economy. Public and private decision makers use these statistics to monitor changes in the economy and to formulate appropriate policies. Economists use these statistics to develop and test theories about how the economy works.

In the chapters that follow, we examine some of these theories. Chapters 3 and 4 study GDP, Chapter 5 studies unemployment, and Chapter 6 studies inflation. We build models to help us understand how these variables are determined and how economic policy affects them. Having learned how to measure economic performance, we now learn how to explain it.

Summary

1. Gross domestic product (GDP) measures both the total output of the economy and the total expenditure on the economy's output of goods and services. GNP, which is GDP minus the net income earned by foreigners operating in Canada, measures the total income of all Canadians.

2. Nominal GDP values goods and services at current prices. Real GDP values goods and services at constant prices. Real GDP rises only when the amount of *qty* goods and services has increased, whereas nominal GDP can rise either because output has increased or because prices have increased. — *prices*

3. GDP is the sum of four categories of expenditure: consumption, investment, government purchases, and net exports. $GDP = Y = C + I + G + NX$

4. The consumer price index (CPI) measures the price of a fixed basket of goods and services purchased by a typical consumer. Like the GDP deflator, which is the ratio of nominal GDP to real GDP, the CPI measures the overall level of prices.

5. The unemployment rate shows what fraction of those who would like to work do not have a job. Increases in the unemployment rate are typically associated with decreases in real GDP. *↑U = ↓ real GDP*

KEY CONCEPTS

Gross domestic product (GDP)	GDP deflator
Consumer price index (CPI)	National income accounts identity
Unemployment rate	Consumption
Gross national product (GNP)	Investment
National income accounting	Government purchases
Stock and flow	Net exports
Value-added	Labour force
Imputed value	Labour-force participation rate
Nominal versus real GDP	Okun's law

QUESTIONS FOR REVIEW

1. List the two things that GDP measures. How can GDP measure two things at once?

2. What does the consumer price index measure?

3. List the three categories used by Statistics Canada to classify everyone in the economy. How is the unemployment rate calculated?

4. Explain Okun's law.

PROBLEMS AND APPLICATIONS

1. Look at the newspapers for the past few days. What new economic statistics have been released? How do you interpret these statistics?

2. A farmer grows wheat and sells it to a miller for $1.00. The miller turns the wheat into flour and then sells the flour to a baker for $3.00. The baker uses the flour to make bread and sells the bread to an engineer for $6.00. The engineer eats the bread. What is the value added by each person? What is GDP?

3. Suppose that a woman marries her butler. After they are married, her husband continues to wait on her as before, and she continues to support him as before (but as a husband rather than as a wage earner). How do you think the marriage affects GDP? How should it affect GDP?

4. Find data on GDP and its components and compute the percentage of GDP for the following components for 1950, 1970, and 1990.

   a. Personal consumption expenditures

   b. Gross private domestic investment

   c. Government purchases

   d. Net exports

   e. Federal government purchases

   f. Provincial and municipal government purchases

   g. Imports

Do you see any stable relationships in the data? Do you see any trends? (*Hint:* A good place to look for data is the *Historical Statistical Supplement* of the *Canadian Economic Observer*—an annual summary publication of Statistics Canada.)

5. Consider an economy that produces and consumes bread and automobiles. In the table below are data for two different years.

   a. Using the year 2000 as the base year, compute for each year nominal GDP, real GDP, the implicit price deflator for GDP, and a fixed-weight price index such as the CPI.

   b. How much have prices risen between year 2000 and year 2010? Compare the answers given by the Laspeyres and Paasche price indexes. Explain the difference.

   c. Suppose you were a member of Parliament, writing a bill to update the indexing provisions for the Canada Pension Plan. Would you use the GDP deflator or the CPI? Why?

6. In a speech that Senator Robert Kennedy gave when he was running for president of the United States in 1968, he said the following about GDP:

[It] does not allow for the health of our children, the quality of their education, or the joy of their play. It does

	Year 2000	Year 2010
Price of an automobile	$50,000	$60,000
Price of a loaf of bread	$10	$20
Number of automobiles produced	100	120
Number of loaves of bread produced	500,000	400,000

not include the beauty of our poetry or the strength of our marriages, the intelligence of our public debate or the integrity of our public officials. It measures neither our courage, nor our wisdom, nor our devotion to our country. It measures everything, in short, except that which makes life worthwhile, and it can tell us everything about America except why we are proud that we are Americans.

Was Robert Kennedy right? If so, why do we care about GDP?

The Economy in the Long Run

We are now ready to build models to explain how the economy works. In this part of the book we examine *classical* models of the economy. The key feature of classical models is that prices are assumed to be flexible. Most economists agree that this assumption describes how the economy behaves in the long run.

We proceed as follows. Chapter 3 builds the most basic classical model, which provides the benchmark for many of the models in later chapters. It discusses how much the economy produces, who gets the income from production, and how the economy's resources are allocated to alternative uses.

Whereas Chapter 3 assumes that the amounts of capital and labour are fixed, Chapters 4 and 5 look at these factors of production more closely. Chapter 4 discusses the very long run over which the economy's stock of capital can change. Chapter 5 examines the labour market in order to explain what determines the natural rate of unemployment.

Chapter 6 introduces the concept of "money" and discusses a key macroeconomic variable—the inflation rate. As we will see, the classical model and its assumption of price flexibility give a simple link between monetary policy and inflation.

Chapter 7 extends the classical model to include international aspects of the economy. It discusses exports and imports, international borrowing and lending, and the exchange rate between different currencies. Our goal is to understand how various government policies affect an open economy.

National Income: Its Production, Distribution, and Allocation

A large income is the best recipe for happiness I ever heard of.

Jane Austen

The macroeconomic variables introduced in Chapter 2 allow economists and policymakers to measure and compare various aspects of economic performance from year to year and from country to country. Our goal, however, is not merely to measure economic performance but also to explain it. That is, we want to build economic models that help us to understand the behavior of the economy, the relationships among different economic variables, and the effects of economic policy.

Perhaps the most important economic variable is gross domestic product (GDP), which measures both a nation's output of goods and services and its income. This chapter addresses four groups of questions about the sources and uses of GDP:

- How much do the firms in the economy produce? What determines a nation's total income?

- Who gets the income from production? How much goes to compensate workers and how much goes to compensate owners of capital?

- Who buys the output of the economy? How much do households purchase for consumption, how much do households and firms purchase for investment, and how much does the government buy for public purposes?

- What equilibrates the demand for goods and services and the supply? What ensures that the sum of consumption, investment, and government purchases equals the level of production?

To answer these questions, we must examine how the parts of the economy interact.

A good place to start is the circular flow diagram. In Chapter 2 we discussed the circular flow of dollars in a hypothetical economy that produced one product, bread, from labour services. Figure 3-1 more accurately reflects how real economies function. It shows the linkages among the economic actors—households, firms, and the government—and how dollars flow among them through the various markets in the economy.

Let's look at the flow of dollars from the points of view of these economic actors. Households receive income and use it to pay taxes to the government, to consume goods and services, and to save through the financial markets. Firms receive revenue from the sale of goods and services and use it to pay for the factors of production. The government receives revenue from taxes, uses it to pay for government purchases, and, if it spends more than it receives, borrows the deficit in the financial markets.

Figure 3-1

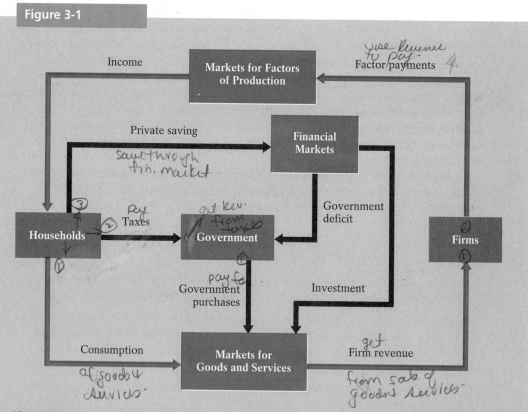

The Circular Flow of Dollars Through the Economy This figure is a more realistic version of the circular flow diagram found in Chapter 2. Each gray box represents an economic actor—households, firms, and the government. Each blue box represents a type of market—the markets for goods and services, the markets for the factors of production, and financial markets. The arrows show the flow of dollars among the economic actors through the three types of markets.

In this chapter we examine the economic interactions depicted in this diagram. We begin with firms. We look at what determines their level of production, which equals the level of national income. Then we examine how the markets for the factors of production distribute this income to households. Next, we consider how much of this income households consume and how much they save. In addition to discussing the demand for goods and services arising from the consumption of households, we discuss the demand arising from investment and government purchases. Finally, we come full circle and examine how the demand for goods and services (the sum of consumption, investment, and government purchases) and the supply of goods and services (the level of production) are brought into balance.

3•1   The Production of Goods and Services

An economy's output of goods and services—its GDP—depends on two elements: its quantity of inputs, called the factors of production, and its ability to turn inputs into output, as represented by the production function. We discuss each of these elements in turn.

The Factors of Production

Factors of production are the inputs used to produce goods and services. The two most important factors of production are capital and labour. Capital is the set of tools that workers use: the construction worker's crane, the accountant's calculator, and this book's authors' personal computers. Labour is the time people spend working. We use the symbol K to denote the amount of capital and the symbol L to denote the amount of labour.

In this chapter we take the economy's factors of production as given. In other words, to keep our analysis simple, we assume that there is a fixed amount of capital and a fixed amount of labour. We write

$$K = \bar{K}.$$
$$L = \bar{L}.$$

The bar over these variables means that they are fixed at some level. In the real world, the factors of production change over time, as we examine in Chapter 4. For now, however, we assume fixed amounts of capital and labour.

We also assume here that the factors of production are fully utilized—that is, that no resources are wasted. Again, in the real world, part of the labour force is unemployed and some capital lies idle. In Chapter 5 we examine the reasons for unemployment, but for now we assume that capital and labour are fully employed.

The Production Function

The available production technology determines how much output is produced from given amounts of capital and labour. Economists express the available technology using a **production function**, which shows how the factors of production determine the amount of output produced. Letting Y denote the amount of output, we write the production function as

$$Y = F(K, L).$$

This equation states that output is a function of the amount of capital and the amount of labour.

The production function reflects the available technology. That is, the available technology is implicit in the way this function turns capital and labour into output. If someone invents a better way to produce a good, the result is more output from the same amounts of capital and labour. Thus, technological change alters the production function.

Many production functions have a feature called **constant returns to scale**. A production function has constant returns to scale if an increase of an equal percentage in all factors of production causes an increase in output of the same percentage. If the production function has constant returns to scale, then we get 10 percent more output when we increase both capital and labour by 10 percent. Mathematically, a production function has constant returns to scale if

$$zY = F(zK, zL)$$

for any positive number z. This equation says that if we multiply both the amount of capital and the amount of labour by some amount z, the amount of output is also multiplied by z. We see in the next section that the assumption of constant returns to scale has an important implication for how the income from production is distributed.

As an example of a production function, consider production at a bakery. The kitchen and its equipment are the bakery's capital, the workers hired to make the bread are its labour, and the loaves of bread are its output. The bakery's production function shows that the number of loaves produced depends on the amount of equipment and the number of workers. The property of constant returns to scale states that if we double the amount of equipment and double the number of workers, we also double the amount of bread produced.

The Fixed Supply of Goods and Services

We can now see that the factors of production and the production function together determine the supply of goods and services, which equals the economy's output. To express this mathematically, we write

$$Y = F(\bar{K}, \bar{L})$$
$$= \bar{Y}.$$

At any point in time, the output of the economy is fixed because the supplies of capital and labour and the technology for turning capital and labour into goods and services are fixed. Over time, output changes when factor supplies change or when technology changes. The greater the amount of capital or the amount of labour, the greater the output. The better the available technology as summarized in the production function, the greater the output.

[handwritten: = National Income]
[handwritten: Y = F(K,L) = total o/p]

3.2 Distributing National Income to the Factors of Production

As we discussed in Chapter 2, the total output of an economy equals its total income. Because the factors of production and the production function together determine the total output of goods and services, they also determine national income. The circular flow diagram in Figure 3-1 shows that this national income flows from firms to households through the markets for the factors of production.

In this section we discuss how these factor markets work. Economists have long studied factor markets in order to understand the distribution of income. (For example, Karl Marx, the noted nineteenth-century economist, spent much time trying to explain the incomes of capital and labour. The political philosophy of communism was in part based on Marx's now-discredited theory.) Here we examine the modern theory of how national income is divided among the factors of production. This theory, called the *neoclassical theory of distribution*, is accepted by most economists today.

Factor Prices *[handwritten: → determines distribution of National Income.]*
[handwritten: → wages, rent etc]

The distribution of national income is determined by factor prices. **Factor prices** are the amounts paid to the factors of production—the wage workers earn and the rent the owners of capital collect. As Figure 3-2 illustrates, the price each factor of production receives for its services is in turn determined by the supply and demand for that factor. Because we have assumed that the economy's factors of production are fixed, the factor supply curve in Figure 3-2

Figure 3-2

[handwritten: ← vertical blc supply is fixed]

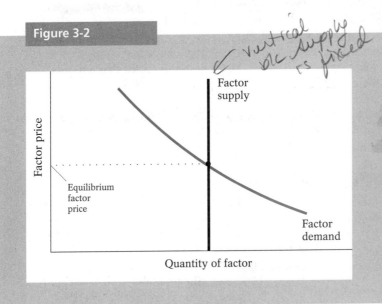

How a Factor of Production Is Compensated The price paid to any factor of production depends on the supply and demand for that factor's services. Because we have assumed that supply is fixed, the supply curve is vertical. The demand curve is downward sloping. The intersection of supply and demand determines the equilibrium factor price.

is vertical. The intersection of the downward-sloping factor demand curve and the vertical supply curve determines the equilibrium factor price.

To understand factor prices and the distribution of income, we must examine the demand for the factors of production. Factor demand arises from the thousands of firms that use capital and labour. We now look at the decisions faced by a typical firm.

The Problem Facing the Competitive Firm

The simplest assumption to make about a typical firm is that it is *competitive*. A firm that is **competitive** is small relative to the markets in which it trades, so it has little influence on market prices. For example, our firm produces a good and sells it at the market price. Because many firms produce this good, our firm can increase its sales as much as it wants without causing the price of the good to fall, or it can stop selling altogether without causing the price of the good to rise. Nor can our firm have much effect on the wages of the workers it employs, because many other local firms also employ workers. The firm has no reason to pay above the market wage and, if it tried to pay less, its workers would go elsewhere. Therefore, the competitive firm takes prices—both of its output and of its inputs—as given.

To make its product, the firm needs two factors of production, capital and labour. As we did for the aggregate economy, we represent the firm's production technology by the production function

$$Y = F(K, L),$$

where Y is the number of units produced (the firm's output), K the number of machines used (its capital), and L the number of hours worked by the firm's employees (its labour). The firm produces more output if it has more machines or if its employees work more hours.

The firm sells its output at a price P, hires workers at a wage W, and rents capital at a rate R. Notice that, when we speak of firms renting capital, we are assuming that households own the economy's stock of capital. In this analysis, households rent out their capital, just as they sell their labour. The firm obtains both factors of production from the households who own them.[1]

The goal of the firm is to maximize profit. *Profit* is revenue minus costs—it is what the owners of the firm keep after paying for the costs of production. Revenue equals $P \times Y$, the selling price of the good P multiplied by the amount of the good the firm produces Y. Costs include both labour costs and capital costs. Labour costs equal $W \times L$, the wage W times the amount of labour L.

[1] This is a simplification. In the real world, the ownership of capital is indirect, because firms own capital and households own the firms. That is, real firms have two functions: owning capital and producing output. To help us understand how the factors of production are compensated, however, we assume that firms only produce output and that households own capital directly.

Capital costs equal $R \times K$, the rental price of capital R times the amount of capital K. We can write

$$\text{Profit} = \text{Revenue} - \text{Labour Costs} - \text{Capital Costs}$$
$$= PY - WL - RK.$$

To see how profit depends on the factors of production, we use the production function $Y = F(K, L)$ to substitute for Y in this equation to obtain

$$\text{Profit} = PF(K, L) - WL - RK.$$

The equation states that profit depends on the product price P, the factor prices W and R, and the factor quantities L and K. The competitive firm takes the product price and the factor prices as given and chooses the amounts of labour and capital that maximize profit.

The Firm's Demand for Factors

We can now see how this firm decides how much labour to hire and how much capital to rent.

The Marginal Product of Labour The more labour the firm employs, the more output it produces. The **marginal product of labour (MPL)** is the extra amount of output the firm gets from one extra unit of labour. In other words, if the firm hires an additional hour of labour, its production increases by MPL units. We can express this using the production function:

$$MPL = F(K, L + 1) - F(K, L).$$

The first term is the amount of output produced with K units of capital and $L + 1$ units of labour; the second term is the amount of output produced with K units of capital and L units of labour. This equation states that the marginal product of labour is the difference between the amount of output produced with $L + 1$ units of labour and the amount produced with only L units of labour.

Most production functions have the property of **diminishing marginal product**: holding the amount of capital fixed, the marginal product of labour decreases as the amount of labour increases. For example, consider again the production of bread at a bakery. As a bakery hires more labour, it produces more bread. The MPL is the amount of extra bread produced when an extra unit of labour is hired. With each additional unit of labour, however, the MPL is smaller. Fewer additional loaves are produced because workers are less productive when the kitchen is more crowded and the ovens are already being used almost continuously. In other words, holding the size of the kitchen fixed, each additional unit of labour adds fewer loaves of bread to the bakery's output.

Figure 3-3 graphs the production function. It illustrates what happens to the amount of output when we hold the amount of capital constant and vary the amount of labour. This figure shows that the marginal product of labour is the slope of the production function. As the amount of labour increases, the production function becomes flatter, indicating diminishing marginal product.

Figure 3-3

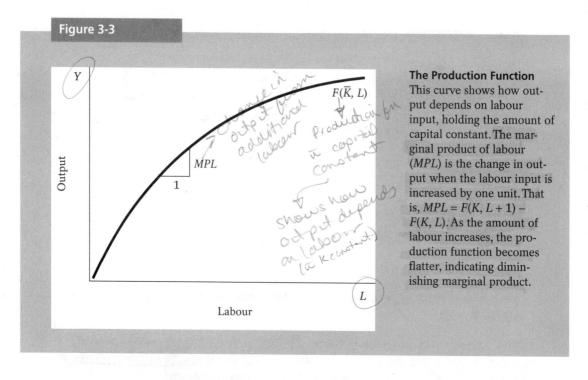

The Production Function This curve shows how output depends on labour input, holding the amount of capital constant. The marginal product of labour (*MPL*) is the change in output when the labour input is increased by one unit. That is, $MPL = F(K, L + 1) - F(K, L)$. As the amount of labour increases, the production function becomes flatter, indicating diminishing marginal product.

From the Marginal Product of Labour to Labour Demand

When the competitive, profit-maximizing firm is deciding whether to hire an additional unit of labour, it considers how that decision affects profits. It therefore compares the extra revenue from the increased production that results from the added labour to the extra cost of a higher wage bill. The increase in revenue from an additional unit of labour depends on both the marginal product of labour and the price of the output. Because an extra unit of labour produces *MPL* units of output, and each unit of output sells for *P* dollars, the extra revenue is $P \times MPL$. The extra cost from hiring one more unit of labour is the wage *W*. Thus, the change in profit from hiring an additional unit of labour is:

$$\Delta\text{Profit} = \Delta\text{Revenue} - \Delta\text{Cost}$$
$$= (P \times MPL) - W.$$

The symbol Δ (called *delta*) denotes the change in a variable.

We can now answer the question we asked at the beginning of this section: How much labour does the firm hire? The firm's manager knows that if the extra revenue $P \times MPL$ exceeds the wage *W*, an extra unit of labour increases profit. Therefore, the manager continues to hire labour until the next unit would no longer be profitable—that is, until the *MPL* falls to the point where the extra revenue equals the wage. The firm's demand for labour is determined by

$$P \times MPL = W.$$

We can write this as

$$MPL = W/P.$$

W/P is the **real wage**, the return to labour measured in units of output rather than in dollars. The real wage is the amount of purchasing power—measured as a quantity of goods and services—that the firm pays for each unit of labour. To maximize profit, the firm hires up to the point at which the marginal product of labour equals the real wage.

For example, again consider a bakery. Suppose the price of bread P is $2 per loaf, and a worker earns a wage W of $20 per hour. The real wage W/P is 10 loaves per hour. In this example, the firm keeps hiring workers until an additional worker would increase output by only 10 loaves per hour.

Figure 3-4 shows how the marginal product of labour depends on the amount of labour employed (holding the firm's capital stock constant). That is, this figure graphs the *MPL* schedule. Because the *MPL* diminishes as the amount of labour increases, this curve slopes downward. For any given real wage, the firm hires up to the point at which the *MPL* equals the real wage. Hence, the *MPL* schedule is the firm's labour demand curve.

[handwritten margin note: so hire labour until MPL = W/P.]

Figure 3-4

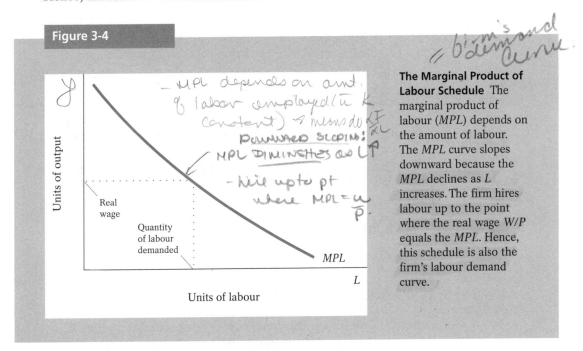

[handwritten note: firm's demand curve.]

[handwritten notes on figure: — MPL depends on amt. of labour employed (w K constant) → means do δF/δL DOWNWARD SLOPING: MPL DIMINISHES as L↑ — hire up to pt where MPL = W/P]

The Marginal Product of Labour Schedule The marginal product of labour (*MPL*) depends on the amount of labour. The *MPL* curve slopes downward because the *MPL* declines as *L* increases. The firm hires labour up to the point where the real wage *W/P* equals the *MPL*. Hence, this schedule is also the firm's labour demand curve.

The Marginal Product of Capital and Capital Demand

The firm decides how much capital to rent in the same way it decides how much labour to hire. The **marginal product of capital** (*MPK*) is the amount of extra output the firm gets from an extra unit of capital,

[handwritten note: additional capital.]

[handwritten margin note: MPL = amt. of extra output from "extra" capital]

$$\text{\textcircled{k}} \quad MPK = F(K + 1, L) - F(K, L).$$

Thus, the marginal product of capital is the difference between the amount of output produced with $K + 1$ units of capital and that produced with only K units of capital. Like labour, capital is subject to diminishing marginal product.

The increase in profit from renting an additional machine is the extra revenue from selling the output of that machine minus the machine's rental price:

[handwritten margin note: as ↑C, MPC shows diminishing marg. prod.]

Profit from extra unit of capital − rental costs

$$\Delta\text{Profit} = \Delta\text{Revenue} - \Delta\text{Cost}$$
$$= (P \times MPK) - R.$$

∵ Rent Capital until MPK = R/P.

To maximize profit, the firm continues to rent more capital until the *MPK* falls to equal the real rental price:

$$MPK = R/P. \quad = \text{real rental price of capital}$$

The **real rental price of capital** is the rental price measured in units of goods rather than in dollars.

summary

To sum up, the competitive, profit-maximizing firm follows a simple rule about how much labour to hire and how much capital to rent. *The firm demands each factor of production until that factor's marginal product falls to equal its real factor price.*   DEMAND FOR L UNTIL MPL = W/P   DEMAND FOR K UNTIL MPK = R/P

The Division of National Income   *real wage rate*   *real rental price of capital*

∵ total cost of labour = L · W/P

∵ total cost of capital = K · R/P

Having analyzed the factor demand for the individual firm, we can now explain how the markets for the factors of production distribute the economy's income. If all firms in the economy are competitive and profit-maximizing, then each factor of production is paid its marginal contribution to the production process. The real wage paid to each worker equals the *MPL*, and the real rental price paid to each owner of capital equals the *MPK*. The total real wage bill is therefore *MPL* × *L*, and the total real return to capital owners is *MPK* × *K*.

The income that remains after the firms have paid the factors of production is the **economic profit** of the owners of the firms. Real economic profit is

real wage costs   *real rental costs*

$$\text{Economic Profit} = Y - (MPL \times L) - (MPK \times K).$$

MPK

Since we want to examine the distribution of national income, we rearrange the terms as follows:

total income

$$Y = (MPL \times L) + (MPK \times K) + \text{Economic Profit}.$$

Distribution of National income

Total income is divided among the return to labour, the return to capital, and economic profit.

If we assume that the production function has the property of constant returns to scale, however, economic profit must be zero. That is, nothing is left after the factors of production are paid. This surprising conclusion follows from a famous mathematical result called *Euler's theorem*, which states that if the production function has constant returns to scale, then[2]

Production fn has Constant returns to scale

$$F(K, L) = (MPK \times K) + (MPL \times L).$$

Need this eqn for Constant Returns to scale.

If each factor of production is paid its marginal product, then the sum of these factor payments equals total output. In other words, constant returns to scale, profit maximization, and competition together imply that economic profit is zero.

[2] *Mathematical note:* To prove Euler's theorem, begin with the definition of constant returns to scale

$$zY = F(zK, zL).$$

Now differentiate with respect to *z* and evaluate at *z* = 1.

B/c Cost of each factor of production = marg. prod.
∴ Econ Profit = 0.

If economic profit is zero, how can we explain the existence of "profit" in the economy? The answer is that the term "profit" as normally used is different from economic profit. We have been assuming that there are three types of agents: labourers, owners of capital, and owners of firms. Total income is divided among wages, return to capital, and economic profit. In the real world, however, most firms own rather than rent the capital they use. Hence, the owners of firms also own the capital. The term "profit" usually includes both economic profit and the return to capital. If we call this alternative definition **accounting profit**, we can say that

when own Capital

Accounting Profit = Economic Profit + ($MPK \times K$).

Under our assumptions—constant returns to scale, profit maximization, and competition—economic profit is zero. If these assumptions approximately describe the world, then the "profit" in the national income accounts must be mostly the return to capital.

We can now answer the question posed at the beginning of this chapter about how the income of the economy is distributed from firms to households. Each factor of production is paid its marginal product, and these factor payments exhaust total output. *Total output is divided between the payments to capital and the payments to labour, depending on their marginal productivities.*

CASE STUDY

3·1

The Black Death and Factor Prices

According to the neoclassical theory of distribution, factor prices equal the marginal products of the factors of production. Because the marginal products depend on the quantities of the factors, a change in the quantity of any one factor alters the marginal products of all the factors. Therefore, a change in the supply of a factor alters equilibrium factor prices.

Fourteenth-century Europe provides a vivid example of how factor quantities affect factor prices. The outbreak of the bubonic plague—the Black Death—in 1348 reduced the population of Europe by about one-third within a few years. Because the marginal product of labour increases as the amount of labour falls, this massive reduction in the labour force raised the marginal product of labour. (The economy moved to the left along the curves in Figure 3-3 and Figure 3-4.) Real wages increased substantially—doubling, by some estimates. The peasants who were fortunate enough to survive the plague enjoyed economic prosperity.

The reduction in the labour force caused by the plague also affected the return to land, the other major factor of production in medieval Europe. With fewer workers available to farm the land, an additional unit of land produced less additional output. This fall in the marginal product of land led to a decline in real rents of 50 percent or more. While the peasant classes prospered, the landed classes suffered reduced incomes.[3]

---

[3] Carlo M. Cipolla, *Before the Industrial Revolution: European Society and Economy, 1000–1700*, 2d ed. (New York: Norton, 1980), 200–202.

3·3 The Demand for Goods and Services

We have seen what determines the level of production and how the income from production is divided between workers and owners of capital. We now continue our tour of the circular flow diagram, Figure 3-1, and examine how the output from production is used.

In Chapter 2 we discussed the four components of GDP:

- Consumption (*C*)
- Investment (*I*)
- Government purchases (*G*)
- Net exports (*NX*)

The circular flow diagram contains only the first three components. For now, to simplify the analysis, we assume a *closed economy*—a country that does not trade with other countries. Thus, net exports are always zero. We examine the macroeconomics of *open economies* in Chapter 7.

A closed economy has three uses for the goods and services it produces. These three components of GDP are expressed in the national income accounts identity:

$$Y = C + I + G.$$

Households consume some of the economy's output; firms and households use some of the output for investment; and the government buys some of the output for public purposes. We want to see how GDP is allocated among these three uses.

Consumption

When we eat food, wear clothing, or go to a movie, we are consuming some of the output of the economy. All forms of consumption together make up 60 percent of GDP. Since consumption is so large, macroeconomists have devoted much energy to studying how households decide how much to consume. Chapter 15 examines this issue in detail. Here we consider the simplest story of consumer behaviour.

Households receive income from their labour and their ownership of capital, pay taxes to the government, and then decide how much of their after-tax income to consume and how much to save. As we discussed in Section 3·2, the income that households receive equals the output of the economy *Y*. The government then taxes households an amount *T*. (Although the government imposes many kinds of taxes, such as personal and corporate income taxes and sales taxes, for our purposes we can lump all these taxes together.) We define income after the payment of all taxes, *Y* – *T*, as **disposable income**. Households divide their disposable income between consumption and saving.

[handwritten: Consumption Fn.]

We assume that the level of consumption depends directly on the level of disposable income. The higher disposable income is, the greater consumption is. Thus, *[handwritten: Consumption depends on Disp. Income]*

$$C = C(Y - T).$$

[handwritten: ↑ yd = ↑C]

This equation states that consumption is a function of disposable income. The relationship between consumption and disposable income is called the **consumption function**.

The **marginal propensity to consume (MPC)** is the amount consumption changes when disposable income increases by one dollar. The *MPC* is between zero and one: an extra dollar of income increases consumption, but by less than one dollar. Thus, if households obtain an extra dollar of income, they save a portion of it. For example, if the *MPC* is 0.7, then households spend 70 cents of each additional dollar of disposable income on consumer goods and services and save 30 cents.

Figure 3-5 illustrates the consumption function. The slope of the consumption function tells us how much consumption increases when disposable income increases by one dollar. That is, the slope of the consumption function is the *MPC*.

Figure 3-5

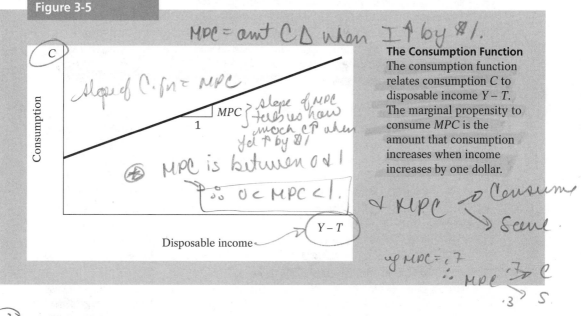

The Consumption Function
The consumption function relates consumption *C* to disposable income *Y − T*. The marginal propensity to consume *MPC* is the amount that consumption increases when income increases by one dollar.

Investment

Both firms and households purchase investment goods. Firms buy investment goods to add to their stock of capital and to replace existing capital as it wears out. Households buy new houses, which are also part of investment. Total investment in Canada averages about 16 percent of GDP.

The quantity of investment goods demanded depends on the interest rate. For an investment project to be profitable, its return must exceed its cost. Because the interest rate measures the cost of funds to finance investment, an increase in the interest rate results in fewer investment projects being profitable and, therefore, a decrease in the demand for investment goods.

For example, suppose that a firm is considering whether it should build a $1 million factory that would yield a return of $100,000 per year, or 10 percent. The firm compares this return to the cost of borrowing the $1 million. If the interest rate is below 10 percent, the firm borrows the money in financial markets and makes the investment. If the interest rate is above 10 percent, the firm forgoes the opportunity and does not build the factory.

The firm makes the same investment decision even if it already has the $1 million. The firm can always deposit the money in a bank and earn the interest rate. Building the factory is more profitable than a bank deposit if and only if the interest rate is less than the 10 percent return on the factory.

A person wanting to buy a new house faces a similar decision. The higher the interest rate, the greater is the cost of carrying a mortgage. A $100,000 mortgage costs $8,000 per year if the interest rate is 8 percent and $10,000 per year if the interest rate is 10 percent. As the interest rate rises, the cost of owning a home rises, and the demand for new homes falls.

Economists distinguish between the nominal interest rate and the real interest rate. This distinction arises during periods of inflation or deflation—that is, when prices are not stable. The **nominal interest rate** is the interest rate as the term is normally used: it is the rate of interest that investors pay to borrow money. The **real interest rate** is the nominal interest rate corrected for the effects of inflation.

To see how nominal and real interest rates differ, consider a firm that decides to build a new factory and borrows the money from a bank at an interest rate of 8 percent. The nominal interest rate is therefore 8 percent—that is, the amount the firm owes to the bank grows by 8 percent per year. But if prices are rising, say by 5 percent per year, the dollars with which the firm will repay the bank are losing 5 percent of their value per year. Each year the firm owes 8 percent more dollars, but the dollars are worth 5 percent less. Since the firm got to spend the original dollars and then only has to pay back dollars with lower purchasing power, the real burden to the firm is only growing at 3 percent. Thus, the real interest rate is 3 percent, the difference between the nominal interest rate and the rate of inflation.

In Chapter 6 we discuss the relation between nominal and real interest rates in more detail. Here it is sufficient to note that the real interest rate measures the true cost of borrowing. We therefore expect investment to depend on the real rather than the nominal interest rate.

The link between the real interest rate r and investment I can be expressed as

$$I = I(r).$$

This equation states that investment depends on the interest rate. Figure 3-6 shows this investment function. It slopes downward, because as the interest rate rises, the quantity of investment demanded falls.

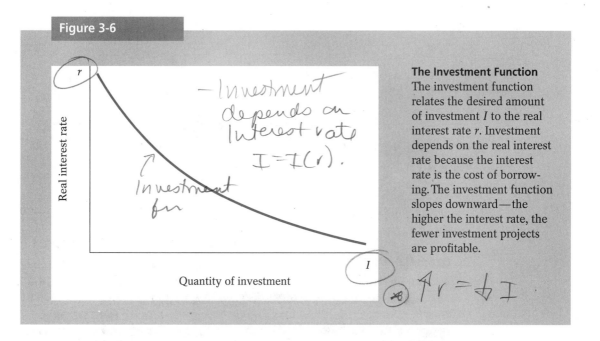

Figure 3-6

r (vertical axis: Real interest rate)

Quantity of investment (horizontal axis)

I

—Investment depends on interest rate $I = I(r)$.

Investment fn

$\uparrow r = \downarrow I$.

The Investment Function
The investment function relates the desired amount of investment I to the real interest rate r. Investment depends on the real interest rate because the interest rate is the cost of borrowing. The investment function slopes downward—the higher the interest rate, the fewer investment projects are profitable.

Government Purchases

3 types: ① Roads, Gov't employees, Public works; ② transfer payments ③ Not included in G.

Government purchases are the third component of the demand for goods and services. The federal government buys helicopters, computers, and the services of government employees. Provincial and municipal governments buy library books, build schools and hospitals, and hire teachers and doctors. Governments at all levels build roads and other public works. All these transactions make up government purchases of goods and services, which account for about 23 percent of GDP in Canada.

These purchases are only one type of government spending. The other type is transfer payments to households, such as welfare for the poor and Canada Pension payments for the elderly. Unlike government purchases, transfer payments do not directly use the economy's output of goods and services. Therefore, they are not included in the variable G.

Transfer payments do affect the demand for goods and services indirectly. Transfer payments are the opposite of taxes: they increase households' disposable income, just as taxes reduce disposable income. Thus, an increase in transfer payments financed by an increase in taxes leaves disposable income unchanged. We can now revise our definition of T to taxes minus transfer payments. Disposable income, $Y - T$, includes both the negative impact of taxes and the positive impact of transfer payments.

If government purchases equal taxes minus transfers, then $G = T$, and the government has a *balanced budget*. If G exceeds T, the government runs a *budget deficit*, which it funds by issuing government debt—that is, by borrowing in the financial markets. If G is less than T, the government runs a *budget surplus*, which it can use to repay some of its outstanding loans and reduce its debt.

↑transpayments
↑yd

↑trans $ financed by ↑taxes is No change in yd.

when G = T ∴ Balanced Budget, when G > T ∴ Deficit ∴ borrow when G < T ∴ Surplus ∴ Pays debt

The Many Different Interest Rates

If you look in the business section of a newspaper, you will find many different interest rates reported. By contrast, throughout this book, we will talk about "the" interest rate, as if there were only one interest rate in the economy. The only distinction we will make is between the nominal interest rate (which is not corrected for inflation) and the real interest rate (which is corrected for inflation). All the interest rates reported in the newspaper are nominal.

Why are there so many interest rates in the newspaper? The various interest rates differ in three ways:

- **Term**   Some loans in the economy are for short periods of time, even as short as overnight. Other loans are for as long as 30 years. The interest rate on a loan depends on its term. Long-term interest rates are usually, but not always, higher than short-term interest rates.

- **Credit risk**   In deciding whether to make a loan, a lender must take into account the probability that the borrower will repay. The law allows borrowers to default on their loans by declaring bankruptcy. The higher the perceived probability of default, the higher the interest rate. The safest credit risk is the government, and so government bonds tend to pay a low interest rate. At the other extreme, financially shaky corporations can raise funds only by issuing *junk bonds*, which pay a high interest rate.

- **Currency denomination**   A lender must be concerned about possible changes in international exchange rates. For example, an American who lends money to a provincial government by buying a bond denominated in Canadian dollars will form expectations concerning the likely change in the value of the Canadian dollar over the period she is making this loan. If the Canadian dollar is expected to fall in value, perhaps due to uncertainty concerning Quebec separation, Canadian borrowers have to pay a higher interest rate than do borrowers in the United States. Thus, the spread between Canadian and American interest rates widens whenever the Canadian dollar is perceived as "weak."

When you see two different interest rates in the newspaper, you can almost always explain the difference by considering the term, credit risk, and currency denomination of the loan.

Although there are many different domestic interest rates, macroeconomists can usually ignore these distinctions. The various interest rates tend to move up and down together. The assumption that there is only one domestic interest rate is, for our purposes, a useful simplification.

Here we do not try to explain the political process that leads to a particular fiscal policy—that is, to the level of government purchases and taxes. Instead, we take government purchases and taxes as exogenous variables. To denote that these variables are fixed outside of the model, we write

$$G = \bar{G}.$$
$$T = \bar{T}.$$

We do, however, want to examine the impact of fiscal policy on the variables determined within the model, the endogenous variables. The endogenous variables here are consumption, investment, and the interest rate.

To see how the exogenous variables affect the endogenous variables, we must solve our model. This is the subject of the next section.

3•4 Equilibrium and the Interest Rate

We have now come full circle in the circular flow diagram, Figure 3-1. We began by examining the supply of goods and services, and we have just discussed the demand for them.

How can we be certain that all these flows balance? In other words, what ensures that the sum of consumption, investment, and government purchases equals the amount of output produced? We will see that the interest rate has the crucial role of equilibrating supply and demand.

Equilibrium in the Market for Goods and Services: The Supply and Demand for the Economy's Output

The following equations summarize the discussion in Section 3•3 of the demand for goods and services:

$$Y = C + I + G$$
$$C = C(Y - T)$$
$$I = I(r)$$
$$G = \bar{G}$$
$$T = \bar{T}.$$

The demand for the economy's output comes from consumption, investment, and government purchases. Consumption depends on disposable income; investment depends on the real interest rate; and government purchases and taxes are the exogenous fiscal policy variables.

In addition to the demand for goods and services, we now consider the supply. As we discussed in Section 3•1, the factors of production and the production function determine the amount of output:

$$Y = F(\bar{K}, \bar{L})$$
$$= \bar{Y}.$$

Now let's combine these equations describing the supply and demand for output. If we substitute the consumption function and the investment function into the national income accounts identity, we obtain

$$Y = C(Y - T) + I(r) + G.$$

Since the variables G and T are fixed by policy, and the level of output Y is fixed by the availability of the factors of production and the production function, we can write:

$$\bar{Y} = C(\bar{Y} - \bar{T}) + I(r) + \bar{G}.$$

This equation states that the supply of output equals its demand, which is the sum of consumption, investment, and government purchases.

Now you can see why the interest rate r plays a key role: it must adjust to ensure that the demand for goods equals the supply. The greater the interest rate, the lower the level of investment, and thus the lower the demand for goods and services, $C + I + G$. If the interest rate is too high, investment is too low, and the demand for output falls short of the supply. If the interest rate is too low, investment is too high, and the demand exceeds the supply. *At the equilibrium interest rate, the demand for goods and services equals the supply.*

Equilibrium in the Financial Markets: The Supply and Demand for Loanable Funds

Because the interest rate is the cost of borrowing and the return to lending in financial markets, we can better understand the role of the interest rate by thinking about the financial markets. To do this, rewrite the national income accounts identity as

$$Y - C - G = I.$$

The term $Y - C - G$, called **national saving** or simply **saving (S)**, is the output that remains after the demands of consumers and the government have been satisfied. In this form, the national income accounts identity states that saving equals investment.

We can split national saving into two parts to separate the saving of households from that of the government:

$$(Y - T - C) + (T - G) = I.$$

The term $Y - T - C$ is disposable income minus consumption, which is **private saving**. The term $T - G$ is government revenue minus government spending, which is **public saving**. (If government spending exceeds government revenue, the government runs a budget deficit, and public saving is negative.) National saving is the sum of private and public saving. The circular flow diagram in Figure 3-1 reveals an interpretation of this equation: this equation states that the flows into and out of the financial markets must balance.

To see the role of the interest rate in equilibrating financial markets, substitute the consumption function and the investment function into the national income accounts identity:

$$Y - C(Y - T) - G = I(r).$$

Next, make G and T fixed by policy and Y fixed by the factors of production and the production function:

$$\bar{Y} - C(\bar{Y} - \bar{T}) - \bar{G} = I(r)$$
$$\bar{S} = I(r).$$

[handwritten: ∴ NATIONAL SAVINGS depends on Investment @ Invest. or r) & invest. or r).]

The left-hand side of this equation shows that national saving depends on income, Y, and the fiscal policy variables, G and T. For fixed values of Y, G, and T, national saving S is also fixed. The right-hand side of the equation shows that investment depends on the interest rate.

Figure 3-7 is a graph of both saving and investment as a function of the interest rate. The saving function is a vertical line, because in this model saving does not depend on the interest rate (although we relax this assumption later). The investment function slopes downward: the higher the interest rate, the fewer investment projects are profitable.

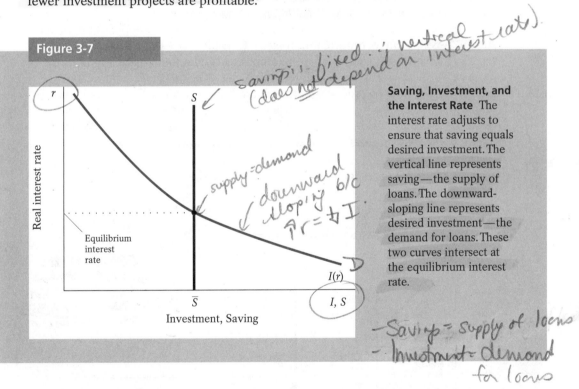

Figure 3-7

[handwritten: Saving is fixed ∴ vertical on interest rate). (does not depend on interest rate).]

[handwritten: supply = demand]

[handwritten: downward sloping b/c ↑r = ↓I.]

Equilibrium interest rate

$\bar{S}$

$I(r)$

Investment, Saving

[handwritten circled: I, S]

Saving, Investment, and the Interest Rate The interest rate adjusts to ensure that saving equals desired investment. The vertical line represents saving—the supply of loans. The downward-sloping line represents desired investment—the demand for loans. These two curves intersect at the equilibrium interest rate.

[handwritten: - Saving = supply of loans - Investment = demand for loans]

From a quick glance at Figure 3-7, one might think it was a supply and demand diagram for a particular good. In fact, saving and investment can be interpreted in terms of supply and demand. In this case, the "good" is **loanable funds**, and its "price" is the interest rate. Saving is the supply of loans—individuals lend their saving to investors or they deposit their saving in a bank that makes the loans for them. Investment is the demand for loans—investors borrow from the public directly by selling bonds or indirectly by borrowing from banks. Since investment depends on the interest rate, the demand for these loans also depends on the interest rate.

[handwritten margin: supply (loans) Bank deposits — demand by selling bonds, borrow from Bank]

[handwritten margin notes: "r adjusts until I=S.", "when r>S ∴ ↓r", "when r<S ∴ ↑r", "when D=S @ equilib ∴ S=I"]

The interest rate adjusts until investment equals saving. If the interest rate is too low, investors want more of the economy's output than individuals want to save. Equivalently, the demand for loans exceeds the supply. When this happens, the interest rate rises. Conversely, if the interest rate is too high, saving exceeds investment; because the supply of loans is greater than the demand, the interest rate falls. The equilibrium interest rate is found where the two curves cross. *At the equilibrium interest rate, saving equals investment, and the supply of loans equals the demand.*

Changes in Saving: The Effects of Fiscal Policy

[handwritten: "– has direct Impact ∴ alters S, I & r. & National Savip."]

We can use our model to show how fiscal policy—changes in government purchases or taxes—affects the economy. Fiscal policy has a direct impact on the demand for the economy's output of goods and services. It thereby alters national saving, investment, and the equilibrium interest rate.

An Increase in Government Purchases   Consider first the effects of an increase in government purchases of an amount ΔG. The immediate impact is to increase the demand for goods and services by ΔG. But since total output is fixed by the factors of production, the increase in government purchases must be met by a decrease in some other category of demand. Since disposable income $Y - T$ is unchanged, consumption C is unchanged. The increase in government purchases must be met by an equal decrease in investment.

[handwritten: "↑G ⇒ ↑r to ↓I ∴ "G" crowds out "I""]

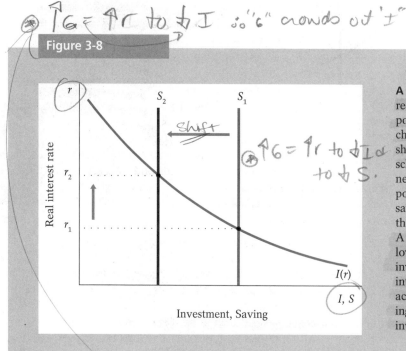

Figure 3-8

A Reduction in Saving A reduction in saving, possibly the result of a change in fiscal policy, shifts the vertical saving schedule to the left. The new equilibrium is the point at which the new saving schedule crosses the investment schedule. A reduction in saving lowers the amount of investment and raises the interest rate. Fiscal policy actions that reduce saving are said to crowd out investment.

[handwritten on figure: "Shift", "↑G = ↑r to ↓Id to ↓S."]

[handwritten below figure: "An ↓S = ↓I ∴↑r ∴ "S" crowdsout "I""]

To induce investment to fall, the interest rate must rise. Hence, the increase in government purchases causes the interest rate to increase and investment to decrease, in which case government purchases are said to be **crowding out** investment.

To grasp the effects of an increase in government purchases, consider the market for loanable funds. Since the increase in government purchases is not accompanied by an increase in taxes, the government finances the additional spending by borrowing—that is, by reducing public saving. Since private saving is unchanged, this government borrowing reduces national saving. As Figure 3-8 shows, a reduction in national saving is represented by a leftward shift in the supply of loanable funds available for investment. At the initial interest rate, the demand for loans exceeds the supply. The equilibrium interest rate rises to the point where the investment schedule crosses the new saving schedule. Thus, an increase in government purchases causes the interest rate to rise.

↑G, ↓ Public Savings (T−G) (B/c Borrows). ∴ ↓ National Savings. I.

CASE STUDY

3·2 **Wars and Interest Rates in the United Kingdom, 1730–1920**

Wars are traumatic—both for those who fight them and for a nation's economy. Because the economic changes accompanying them are often large, wars provide a natural experiment with which economists can test their theories. We can learn about the economy by seeing how in wartime the endogenous variables respond to the major changes in the exogenous variables.

One exogenous variable that changes substantially in wartime is the level of government purchases. Figure 3-9 shows military spending as a percentage of GDP for the United Kingdom from 1730 to 1919. This graph shows, as one would expect, that government purchases rose suddenly and dramatically during the eight wars of this period.

Our model predicts that this wartime increase in government purchases—and the increase in government borrowing to finance the wars—should have raised the demand for goods and services, reduced the supply of loanable funds, and raised the interest rate. To test this prediction, Figure 3-9 also shows the interest rate on long-term government bonds, called *consols* in the United Kingdom. A positive association between military purchases and interest rates is apparent in this figure. These data support the model's prediction: interest rates do tend to rise when government purchases increase.[4]

One of the problems with using wars to test theories is that many things may be happening to the economy at the same time. For example, in World War II, while government purchases increased dramatically, rationing also restricted

War = ↑G. ∴ ↑ demand for goods & services ∴ ↓ supply of loanable funds ∴ ↑r. ⓧ ↑G = ↑r.

[4] Daniel K. Benjamin and Levis A. Kochin, "War, Prices, and Interest Rates: A Martial Solution to Gibson's Paradox," in M. D. Bordo and A. J. Schwartz, eds., *A Retrospective on the Classical Gold Standard, 1821–1931* (Chicago: University of Chicago Press, 1984), 587–612; Robert J. Barro, "Government Spending, Interest Rates, Prices, and Budget Deficits in the United Kingdom, 1701–1918," *Journal of Monetary Economics* 20 (September 1987): 221–248.

Figure 3-9

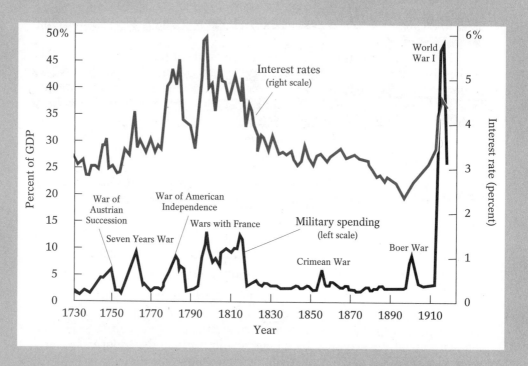

Military Spending and the Interest Rate in the United Kingdom This figure shows military spending as a percentage of GDP in the United Kingdom from 1730 to 1919. Not surprisingly, military spending rose substantially during each of the eight wars of this period. This figure also shows that the interest rate (here the rate on a government bond called a *consol*) tended to rise when military spending rose.

Source: Series constructed from various sources described in Robert J. Barro, "Government Spending, Interest Rates, Prices, and Budget Deficits in the United Kingdom, 1701–1918," *Journal of Monetary Economics* 20 (September 1987): 221–248.

consumption of many goods. In addition, the risk of losing the war and of the government's defaulting on its debt presumably increases the interest rate the government must pay. Economic models predict what happens when one exogenous variable changes and all the other exogenous variables remain constant. In the real world, however, many different exogenous variables may change at once. Unlike controlled laboratory experiments, the natural experiments on which economists must rely are not always easy to interpret.

A Decrease in Taxes   Now consider a reduction in taxes of ΔT. The immediate impact of the tax cut is to raise disposable income and thus to raise consumption. Disposable income rises by ΔT, and consumption rises by ΔT times the marginal propensity to consume. The higher the MPC, the greater is the impact of the tax cut on consumption.

Since the economy's output is fixed by the supplies of the factors of production, and the level of government purchases is fixed by the government, the increase in consumption must be met by a decrease in investment. For investment to fall, the interest rate must rise. Hence, a reduction in taxes, like an increase in government purchases, crowds out investment and raises the interest rate.

We can also analyze the effect of a tax cut by looking at saving and investment. Since the tax cut raises disposable income by ΔT, consumption goes up by the $MPC \times \Delta T$. National saving, which is $Y-C-G$, falls by the same amount as consumption rises. As in Figure 3-8, the reduction in saving shifts the supply of loanable funds to the left, which increases the equilibrium interest rate and crowds out investment.

CASE STUDY

3·3   Fiscal Policy in the 1980s

One of the most dramatic economic events in recent history was the large change in the fiscal policies of most western countries in the late 1970s and in the 1980s. Before this period, all governments had run deficits during numerous short intervals of time. But governments had often run surpluses as well, so that, over the longer run, there was not a large increase in their national debts. Starting in the mid-1970s, however, the excess of government spending over tax revenues increased by a wide margin, and this gap became a permanent fixture of fiscal policy.

As our model predicts, this change in fiscal policy led to higher world interest rates and lower levels of saving. In Canada's case, the real interest rate (the difference between the yield on government bonds and the inflation rate) rose from 0.8 percent in the 1960–1975 period to 3.9 percent since 1975. Total saving in Canada averaged 10 percent of national income in the 1960–1975 period, and only 2 percent in 1992.[5] The change in fiscal policy in the 1980s certainly had the effects that our simple model of the economy predicts.

---

[5] See William B.P. Robson, "Digging Holes and Hitting Walls: Canada's Fiscal Prospects in the Mid-1990s," *Commentary No.* 56 (Toronto: C.D. Howe Institute, 1994).

Changes in Investment Demand

Thus far, we have discussed how fiscal policy can change national saving. We can also use the model to examine the other side of the market—the demand for investment. In this section we look at the causes and effects of changes in investment demand.

One reason that investment demand might increase is technological innovation. Suppose, for example, that someone invents a new technology, such as the railroad or the computer. Before a firm or household can use the innovation, it must buy investment goods. The invention of the railroad had no value until railroad cars were produced and tracks were laid. The idea of the computer was not productive until computers were manufactured. Thus, technological innovation leads to an increase in investment demand.

Investment demand may also change because the government encourages or discourages investment through the tax laws. For example, suppose that the

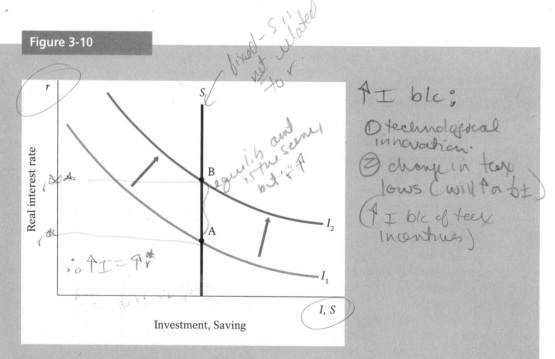

Figure 3-10

An Increase in Desired Investment An increase in the demand for investment goods, perhaps because of technological innovation or tax incentives for investment, shifts the investment schedule outward. At any given interest rate, the desired amount of investment is greater. The new equilibrium is the point where the new investment schedule crosses the vertical saving schedule. Because the amount of saving is fixed, the increase in investment demand raises the interest rate while leaving the equilibrium amount of investment unchanged.

government increases personal income taxes and uses the extra revenue to provide tax cuts for those who invest in new capital. Such a change in the tax laws makes more investment projects profitable and, like a technological innovation, increases the demand for investment goods.

Figure 3-10 shows the effects of an increase in investment demand. At any given interest rate, the demand for investment goods (and also for loans) is higher—this is represented by a shift in the investment schedule to the right. The economy moves from the old equilibrium, point A, to the new equilibrium, point B.

The surprising implication of Figure 3-10 is that the equilibrium amount of investment is unchanged. Under our assumptions, the fixed level of saving determines the amount of investment; in other words, there is a fixed supply of loans. An increase in investment demand merely raises the equilibrium interest rate.

We would reach a different conclusion, however, if we modified our simple consumption function and allowed consumption to depend on the interest rate. Since the interest rate is the return to saving (as well as the cost of borrowing), a higher interest rate might reduce consumption and increase saving. If so, the saving schedule would be upward-sloping, as it is in Figure 3-11, rather than vertical.

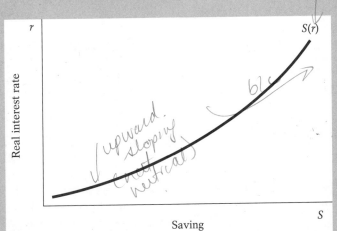

Figure 3-11

Saving as a Function of the Interest Rate
Here saving is positively related to the interest rate. A positive relation occurs if a higher interest rate induces people to consume less and save more.

The Identification Problem

In our model, investment depends on the interest rate. The higher the interest rate, the fewer investment projects are profitable. The investment schedule therefore slopes downward.

Economists who look at macroeconomic data, however, usually fail to find an obvious association between investment and interest rates. In years when interest rates are high, investment is not always low. In years when interest rates are low, investment is not always high.

How do we interpret this finding? Does it mean that investment does not depend on the interest rate? Does it suggest that our model of the economy is inconsistent with how the economy actually functions?

Luckily, we do not have to discard our model. The inability to find an empirical relationship between investment and interest rates is an example of what is called the *identification problem*. The identification problem arises when variables are related in more than one way. When we look at data, we are observing a combination of these different relationships, and it is difficult to "identify" any one of them.

To understand this problem more concretely, consider the relationships among saving, investment, and the interest rate. Suppose, on the one hand, that all changes in the interest rate resulted from changes in saving—that is, from shifts in the saving schedule. Then, as shown in the left-hand side of Panel (a) in Figure 3-12, all changes would represent movement *along* the investment schedule. We would observe a negative relationship between investment and interest rates. As the right-hand side of Panel (a) shows, the data would trace out the investment schedule; that is, we would "identify" the investment schedule.

Suppose, on the other hand, that all changes in the interest rate resulted from technological innovations—that is, from shifts in the investment schedule. Then, as shown in Panel (b), all changes would represent movements in the investment schedule. We would observe a positive relationship between investment and interest rates. As the right-hand side of Panel (b) shows, when we plot the data, we would "identify" the saving schedule.

More realistically, interest rates change sometimes because of shifts in the saving schedule and sometimes because of shifts in the investment schedule. In this mixed case, as shown in Panel (c), a plot of the data would reveal no recognizable relation between interest rates and the quantity of investment, just as economists observe in actual data. The moral of the story is simple and is applicable to many other situations: the empirical relationship we expect to observe depends crucially on which exogenous variables we think are changing.

Figure 3-12

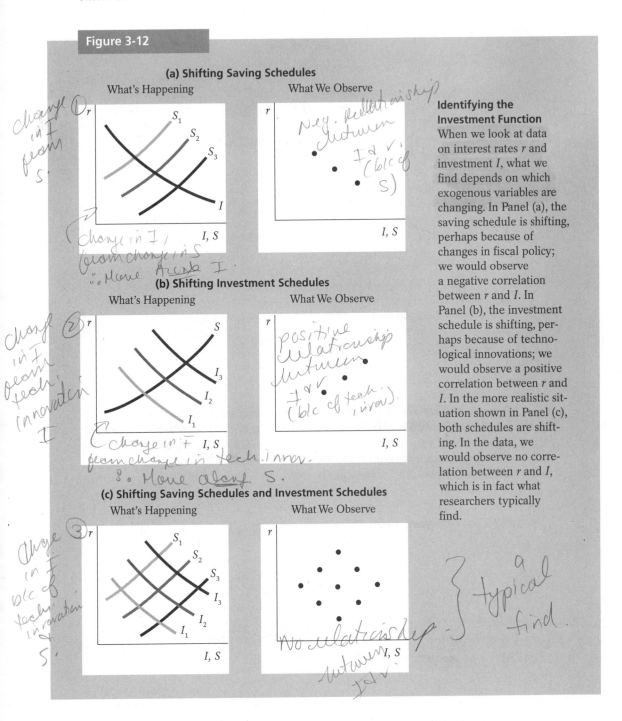

(a) Shifting Saving Schedules

What's Happening

What We Observe

(b) Shifting Investment Schedules

What's Happening

What We Observe

(c) Shifting Saving Schedules and Investment Schedules

What's Happening

What We Observe

Identifying the Investment Function
When we look at data on interest rates r and investment I, what we find depends on which exogenous variables are changing. In Panel (a), the saving schedule is shifting, perhaps because of changes in fiscal policy; we would observe a negative correlation between r and I. In Panel (b), the investment schedule is shifting, perhaps because of technological innovations; we would observe a positive correlation between r and I. In the more realistic situation shown in Panel (c), both schedules are shifting. In the data, we would observe no correlation between r and I, which is in fact what researchers typically find.

[Handwritten annotations: "change in I from peons S."; "Neg. Relationship between I & r (b/c of S)"; "change in I from change in S :. More About I."; "change in I from peons tech innovation I"; "positive relationship between I & r (b/c of tech innov.)"; "change in I from change in tech innov. :. More about S."; "change in I b/c of tech innovation in S."; "No relationship between I & r"; "a typical find."]

Figure 3-13

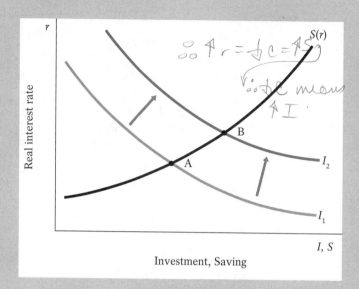

An Increase in Desired Investment When Saving Depends on the Interest Rate If saving depends on the interest rate, then a shift outward in the investment schedule increases the interest rate and the amount of investment. The higher interest rate induces people to increase saving, which in turn allows investment to increase.

With an upward-sloping saving schedule, an increase in investment demand would raise both the equilibrium interest rate and the equilibrium quantity of investment. Figure 3-13 shows such a change. The increase in the interest rate causes households to consume less and save more. The decrease in consumption frees resources for investment.

3•5 Conclusion

In this chapter we have developed a model that explains the production, distribution, and allocation of the economy's output of goods and services. Because the model incorporates all the interactions illustrated in the circular flow diagram, Figure 3-1, it is sometimes called a *general equilibrium model*. The model emphasizes how prices adjust to equilibrate supply and demand. Factor prices equilibrate factor markets. The interest rate equilibrates the supply and demand for goods and services (or, equivalently, the supply and demand for loanable funds).

Throughout the chapter, we have discussed various applications of the model. The model can explain how income is divided among the factors of production and how factor prices depend on factor supplies. We have also used the model to discuss how fiscal policy alters the allocation of output among its alternative uses—consumption, investment, and government purchases—and how it affects the equilibrium interest rate.

At this point it is useful to review some of the simplifying assumptions we have made in this chapter. In the following chapters we relax some of these assumptions in order to address a greater range of questions.

- We have assumed that the capital stock, the labour force, and the production technology are fixed. In Chapter 4 we see how changes over time in each of these lead to growth in the economy's output of goods and services.

- We have assumed that the labour force is fully employed. In Chapter 5 we examine the reasons for unemployment, and we see how public policy influences the level of unemployment.

- We have ignored the role of money, the asset with which goods and services are bought and sold. In Chapter 6 we discuss how money affects the economy and the influence of monetary policy.

- We have assumed that there is no trade with other countries. In Chapter 7 we consider how international interactions affect our conclusions.

- We have ignored the role of short-run sticky prices. In Chapters 8, 9, 10, and 11 we develop a model of short-run fluctuations that includes sticky prices. We then discuss how the model of short-run fluctuations relates to the model of national income developed in this chapter.

Before going on to these chapters, go back to the beginning of this one and make sure you can answer the four groups of questions about national income that begin the chapter.

Summary

1. The factors of production and the production technology determine the economy's output of goods and services. An increase in one of the factors of production or a technological advance raises output.

2. Competitive, profit-maximizing firms hire labour until the marginal product of labour (MPL) equals the real wage. Similarly, these firms hire capital until the marginal product of capital (MPK) equals the real rental price. Therefore, each factor of production is paid its marginal product. If the production function has constant returns to scale, all output is used to compensate the inputs.

3. The economy's output is used for consumption, investment, and government purchases. Consumption depends positively on disposable income. Investment depends negatively on the real interest rate. Government purchases and taxes are the exogenous variables of fiscal policy.

4. The real interest rate adjusts to equilibrate the supply and demand for the economy's output—or, equivalently, to equilibrate the supply of loanable funds (saving) and the demand for loanable funds (investment). A decrease in national saving, perhaps because of an increase in government purchases or a de-

crease in taxes, reduces the equilibrium amount of investment and raises the interest rate. An increase in investment demand, perhaps because of a techno-logical innovation or a tax incentive for investment, also raises the interest rate. An increase in investment demand increases the quantity of investment only if higher interest rates stimulate additional saving.

KEY CONCEPTS

Factors of production

Production function

Constant returns to scale

Factor prices

Competition

Marginal product of labour (*MPL*)

Diminishing marginal product

Real wage

Marginal product of capital (*MPK*)

Real rental price of capital

Economic profit

Accounting profit

Disposable income

Consumption function

Marginal propensity to consume (*MPC*)

Nominal interest rate

Real interest rate

National saving (saving)

Private saving

Public saving

Loanable funds

Crowding out

QUESTIONS FOR REVIEW

1. What determines the amount of out-put an economy produces?

2. Explain how a competitive, profit-maximizing firm decides how much of each factor of production to demand.

3. What is the role of constant returns to scale in the distribution of income?

4. What determines consumption and in-vestment?

5. Explain the difference between gov-ernment purchases and transfer pay-ments. Give two examples of each.

6. What makes the demand for the econ-omy's output of goods and services equal the supply?

7. Explain what happens to consump-tion, investment, and the interest rate when the government increases taxes.

PROBLEMS AND APPLICATIONS

1. Use the neoclassical theory of distrib-ution to predict the impact on the real wage and the real rental price of capital of each of the following events:

a. A wave of immigration increases the labour force.

b. An earthquake destroys some of the capital stock.

c. A technological advance improves the production function.

2. If a 10 percent increase in both capital and labour causes output to increase by less than 10 percent, the production function is said to exhibit *decreasing returns to scale*. If it causes output to increase by more than 10 percent, the production function is said to exhibit *increasing returns to scale*. Why might a production function exhibit decreasing or increasing returns to scale?

3. According to the neoclassical theory of distribution, the real wage earned by any worker equals that worker's marginal productivity. Let's use this insight to examine the incomes of two groups of workers: farmers and barbers.

a. Over the past century, the productivity of farmers has risen substantially because of technological progress. According to the neoclassical theory, what should have happened to their real wage?

b. In what units is the real wage discussed in part (a) measured?

c. Over the same period, the productivity of barbers has remained constant. What should have happened to their real wage?

d. In what units is the real wage in part (c) measured?

e. Suppose workers can move freely between being farmers and being barbers. What does this mobility imply for the wages of farmers and barbers?

f. What do your previous answers imply for the price of haircuts relative to the price of food?

g. Who benefits from technological progress in farming—farmers or barbers?

4. The government raises taxes by $100 billion. If the marginal propensity to consume is 0.6, what happens to

a. Public saving?

b. Private saving?

c. National saving?

d. Investment?

5. Suppose that an increase in consumer confidence raises consumers' expectations of future income and thus the amount they want to consume today. This might be interpreted as an upward shift in the consumption function. How does this shift affect investment and the interest rate?

6. Suppose that the government increases taxes and government purchases by equal amounts. What happens to the interest rate and investment in response to this balanced budget change? Does your answer depend on the marginal propensity to consume?

7. If consumption depended on the interest rate, how would that affect the conclusions reached in this chapter about the effects of fiscal policy?

The Cobb-Douglas Production Function

What production function describes how actual economies turn capital and labour into GDP? The answer to this question came from a historic collaboration between a U.S. senator and a mathematician.

Paul Douglas was a U.S. senator from Illinois from 1949 to 1966. In 1927, however, when he was still a professor of economics, he noticed a surprising fact: the division of national income between capital and labour had been roughly constant over a long period. In other words, as the output of the economy grew, workers and the owners of capital shared equally in the greater prosperity. This observation caused Douglas to wonder what conditions lead to constant factor shares.

Douglas asked Charles Cobb, a mathematician, what production function, if any, would produce constant factor shares if factors always earned their marginal products. The production function would need to have the property that

$$\text{Capital Income} = MPK \times K = \alpha Y,$$

and

$$\text{Labour Income} = MPL \times L = (1 - \alpha)\,Y,$$

where α is a constant between zero and one that measures capital's share of income. That is, α determines what share of income goes to capital and what share goes to labour. Cobb showed that the function with this property is

$$Y = F(K, L) = AK^{\alpha}L^{1-\alpha},$$

Cobb–Douglas Production fn

where A is a parameter greater than zero that measures the productivity of the available technology. This became known as the *Cobb-Douglas production function*.

Let's take a closer look at some of the properties of this production function. First, the Cobb-Douglas production function has constant returns to scale. That is, if capital and labour are increased by the same proportion, then output increases by that proportion as well.[6]

---

[6] *Mathematical note:* To prove that the Cobb-Douglas production function has constant returns to scale, examine what happens when we multiply capital and labour by a constant z:

$$F(zK, zL) = A(zK)^{\alpha}(zL)^{1-\alpha}.$$

Expanding terms on the right,

$$F(zK, zL) = Az^{\alpha}K^{\alpha}z^{1-\alpha}L^{1-\alpha}.$$

Rearranging to bring like terms together, we get

$$F(zK, zL) = z^{\alpha}z^{1-\alpha}AK^{\alpha}L^{1-\alpha}.$$

Since $z^{\alpha}z^{1-\alpha} = z$, our function becomes

$$F(zK, zL) = zAK^{\alpha}L^{1-\alpha}.$$

But $AK^{\alpha}L^{1-\alpha} = F(K, L)$. Thus,

$$F(zK, zL) = zF(K, L) = zY.$$

Hence, the amount of output Y increases by the same factor z, which implies that this production function has constant returns to scale.

Next, consider the marginal products for the Cobb-Douglas production function. The marginal product of labour is[7]

$$MPL = (1 - \alpha)AK^{\alpha}L^{-\alpha},$$

and the marginal product of capital is

$$MPK = \alpha AK^{\alpha-1}L^{1-\alpha}.$$

for Cobb-Douglas:
$\partial AK = \partial MPL \times \partial MPK$
$\partial AK = \partial MPL \times \partial MPK$
$\partial AL = \partial MPL \times \partial MPK$

From these equations, recalling that α is between zero and one, we can see what causes the marginal products of the two factors to change. An increase in the amount of capital raises the *MPL* and reduces the *MPK*. Similarly, an increase in the amount of labour reduces the *MPL* and raises the *MPK*. A technological advance that increases the parameter A raises the marginal product of both factors proportionately.

The marginal products for the Cobb-Douglas production function can also be written as[8]

$$MPL = (1 - \alpha)Y/L,$$
$$MPK = \alpha Y/K.$$

$\frac{Y}{L} = $ *average labour productivity*

$\frac{Y}{K} = $ *average capital productivity*

The *MPL* is proportional to output per worker, and the *MPK* is proportional to output per unit of capital. Y/L is called *average labour productivity*, and Y/K is called *average capital productivity*. If the production function is Cobb-Douglas, then the marginal productivity of a factor is proportional to its average productivity.

We can now verify that, if factors earn their marginal products, then the parameter α indeed tells us how much income goes to labour and how much goes to capital. The total wage bill, which we have seen is $MPL \times L$, is simply $(1 - \alpha)Y$. Therefore, $(1 - \alpha)$ is labour's share of output. Similarly, the total return to capital, $MPK \times K$, is αY, and α is capital's share of output. The ratio of labour income to capital income is a constant, $(1 - \alpha)/\alpha$, just as Douglas observed. The factor shares depend only on the parameter α, not on the amounts of capital or labour or on the state of technology as measured by the parameter A.

More recent data are also consistent with the Cobb-Douglas production function. Figure 3-14 shows the ratio of labour income to total income in Canada from 1945 to 1993. Despite the many changes in the economy over the past four decades, this ratio has remained about 0.67. This division of income is easily explained by a Cobb-Douglas production function in which the parameter α is about 0.33.

— wage Bill: $MPL \times L = (1-\alpha)Y$ ∴ $(1-\alpha) =$ labour's share of output

— return to capital: $MPK \times K = \alpha Y$ ∴ $\alpha =$ capital's share of output.

---

[7] *Mathematical note:* Obtaining the formulas for the marginal products from the production function requires a bit of calculus. To find the *MPL*, differentiate the production function with respect to L. This is done by multiplying by the exponent $(1 - \alpha)$, and then subtracting one from the old exponent to obtain the new exponent, $-\alpha$. Similarly, to obtain the *MPK*, differentiate the production function with respect to K.

[8] *Mathematical note:* To check these expressions for the marginal products, substitute in the production function for Y to show that these expressions are equivalent to the earlier formulas for the marginal products.

Figure 3-14

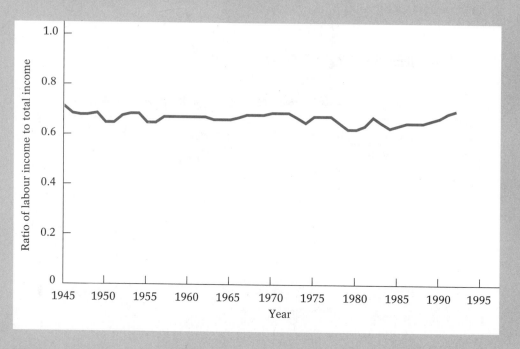

The Ratio of Labour Income to Total Income
Labour income has remained about 0.67 of total income over a long period of time. This approximate constancy of factor shares is evidence for the Cobb-Douglas production function. (This figure is produced from Canadian national income accounts data.

Labour income is wages, salaries, and supplementary income. Total income is the sum of labour income, corporate profits before taxes, interest and investment income, and depreciation.

Source: Reproduced and adapted by authority of the Minister of Industry, 1994, "Statistics Canada," *Canadian Economic Observer*, Series D20002, D20003, D20004, D20009 (Historical Statistical Supplement, 1991/92): 2-3 and (Statistical Summary, March 1994): 3.

MORE PROBLEMS AND APPLICATIONS

1. Suppose that the production function is Cobb-Douglas with parameter $\alpha = 0.3$.

   a. What fractions of income do capital and labour receive?

   b. Suppose that the labour force increases by 10 percent (for example, because of immigration). What happens to total output (in percent)? The rental price of capital? The real wage?

CHAPTER 4

Economic Growth

*The question of growth is nothing new but a new disguise for an
age-old issue, one which has always intrigued and preoccupied
economics: the present versus the future.*

James Tobin

Over the past century, most countries in the world have enjoyed substantial
economic growth. Real incomes have risen from generation to generation, and
these higher incomes have allowed people to consume greater quantities of
goods and services. Higher levels of consumption have led to a higher standard
of living.

To measure economic growth, economists use data on gross domestic
product, which measures the total income of everyone in the economy. The real
GDP of Canada in 1993 was 5.5 times its 1950 level, and real GDP per person
was 2.6 times its 1950 level. In any given year, we can also observe large differences in the standard of living among countries. Table 4-1 shows income per
person in 1990 for Canada and the 12 most populous countries in the world.
The United States tops the list with an income of $22,063 per person. Nigeria
has an income per person of only $929—less than 5 percent of the figure for
the United States.

Our goal in this chapter is to understand these differences in income over
time and across countries. In Chapter 3 we identified the factors of production—
capital and labour—and the production technology as the sources of the economy's output and, thus, of its income. Differences in income must come from
differences in capital, labour, and technology.

Our primary task is to develop a model of economic growth called the
Solow growth model. Our analysis in Chapter 3 enabled us to describe the production, distribution, and allocation of the economy's output at a point in time.
The analysis was static—a snapshot of the economy. To explain rising living
standards, we must refine our analysis so that it describes changes in the economy over time. We want to make our analysis dynamic, so that it is more like a
movie than a photograph. The **Solow growth model** shows how saving, population growth, and technological progress affect the growth of output over time.
The model also identifies some of the reasons that countries vary so widely in
their standards of living.[1]

---

[1] The Solow growth model is named after economist Robert Solow and was developed in the 1950s
and 1960s. In 1987 Solow won the Nobel Prize in Economics for his work in economic growth. The
model was introduced in Robert M. Solow, "A Contribution to the Theory of Economic Growth,"
Quarterly Journal of Economics (February 1956): 65–94.

Table 4-1	International Differences in the Standard of Living, 1990	
Country		Income per Person (in U.S. dollars)
United States		$22,063
Canada		19,576
Japan		17,791
West Germany		17,385
Mexico		6,450
Soviet Union (1989)		6,272
Brazil		4,684
China		2,671
Indonesia		2,329
Pakistan		1,631
Bangladesh		1,447
India		1,280
Nigeria		929

Note: Many analysts believe that faulty reporting of data in the Soviet Union and China render the statistics from those countries unreliable and that actual income per person is much lower than reported.

Source: Robert Summers and Alan Heston, Supplement (Mark 5.5) to "The Penn World Table (Mark 5): An Expanded Set of International Comparisons 1950–1988," *Quarterly Journal of Economics* (May 1991): 327–368.

Our second task is to examine how economic policy can influence the level and growth of the standard of living. Our model provides a framework with which we can address one of the most important questions in economics: How much of the economy's output should be consumed today and how much should be saved for the future? Since an economy's saving equals its investment, saving determines the amount of capital an economy will have for future production. National saving is influenced directly and indirectly by government policies. Evaluating these policies requires an understanding of the costs and benefits to society of alternative rates of saving.

4•1   The Accumulation of Capital

The Solow growth model shows how growth in the capital stock, growth in the labour force, and advances in technology interact, and how they affect output. As our first step in building the model, we examine how the supply and demand for goods determine the accumulation of capital. To do this, we hold the labour force and technology fixed. Later, we relax these assumptions, first by introducing changes in the labour force and then by introducing changes in technology.

The Supply and Demand for Goods

The supply and demand for goods played a central role in our static model of the economy in Chapter 3. The same is true in the Solow growth model. As in Chapter 3, the supply of goods determines how much output is produced at any given point in time, and the demand determines how this output is allocated among alternative uses.

The Supply of Goods and the Production Function   The supply of goods in the Solow model is based on the now familiar production function:

$$Y = F(K, L).$$

Output depends on the capital stock and the labour force. The Solow growth model assumes that the production function has constant returns to scale. Recall that a production function has constant returns to scale if

$$zY = F(zK, zL)$$

for any positive number z. That is, if we multiply both capital and labour by z, we also multiply the amount of output by z.

To keep the analysis simple, we express all quantities relative to the size of the labour force. Production functions with constant returns to scale are convenient for this purpose because output per worker depends only on the amount of capital per worker. To see that this is true, set $z = 1/L$ in the equation above to obtain

$$Y/L = F(K/L, 1).$$

This equation states that output per worker Y/L is a function of capital per worker K/L.

We use lowercase letters to denote quantities per worker. Thus, $y = Y/L$ is output per worker, and $k = K/L$ is capital per worker. We can write the production function as

$$y = f(k),$$

where we define $f(k) = F(k, 1)$. It is more convenient to analyze the economy using this production function relating capital per worker to output per worker. Figure 4-1 illustrates the production function.

The slope of this production function shows how much extra output per worker is produced from an extra unit of capital per worker. This amount is the marginal product of capital MPK. Mathematically, we write

$$MPK = f(k + 1) - f(k).$$

Note that in Figure 4-1, as the amount of capital increases, the production function becomes flatter. The production function exhibits diminishing marginal product of capital: each incremental unit of capital produces less output than did the preceding unit. When there is only a little capital, an extra unit of capital is very useful and produces much additional output. When there is a lot of capital, an extra unit is less useful and produces less additional output.

Figure 4-1

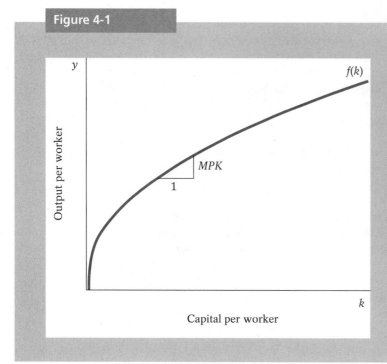

The Production Function The production function shows how the amount of capital per worker k determines the amount of output per worker $y = f(k)$. The slope of the production function is the marginal product of capital: if k increases by 1 unit, y increases by MPK units. The production function becomes flatter as k increases, indicating diminishing marginal product.

The Demand for Goods and the Consumption Function   The demand for goods in the Solow model comes from consumption and investment. In other words, output per worker y is divided between consumption per worker c and investment per worker i:

$$y = c + i.$$

This equation is the national income accounts identity for the economy. It differs slightly from the identity in Chapter 3 because it omits government purchases (which for present purposes we can ignore) and because it expresses y, c, and i as quantities per worker.

The Solow model assumes that the consumption function takes the simple form

$$c = (1 - s)y,$$

where s, the saving rate, is a number between zero and one. This consumption function states that consumption is proportional to income. Each year a fraction $(1 - s)$ of income is consumed, and a fraction s is saved.

To see what this consumption function implies, substitute $(1 - s)y$ for c in the national income accounts identity:

$$y = (1 - s)y + i.$$

Rearrange the terms to obtain

$$i = sy.$$

This equation states that investment, like consumption, is proportional to income. Since investment equals saving, the rate of saving s is also the fraction of output devoted to investment.

The Evolution of Capital and the Steady State

Having introduced the two main ingredients of the Solow model—the production function and the consumption function—we can now examine how increases in the capital stock over time result in economic growth. Two forces cause the capital stock to change:

- **Investment** The capital stock rises as firms buy new plants and equipment.
- **Depreciation** The capital stock falls as some of the old capital wears out.

To understand how the capital stock changes, we must understand the determinants of investment and depreciation.

We noted previously that investment per worker is a fraction of output per worker, sy. By substituting the production function for y, we can express investment per worker as a function of the capital stock per worker:

$$i = sf(k).$$

The higher the level of capital k, the greater the levels of output $f(k)$ and investment i. This equation, which incorporates both the production and consumption functions, relates the existing stock of capital k to the accumulation of new capital i. Figure 4-2 shows how the saving rate determines the allocation of output between consumption and investment for every value of k.

Figure 4-2

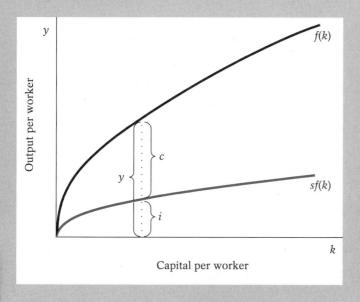

Output, Consumption, and Investment The saving rate s determines the allocation of output between consumption and investment. At any level of capital k, output is $f(k)$, investment is $sf(k)$, and consumption is $f(k) - sf(k)$.

To incorporate depreciation into the model, we assume that a certain fraction δ of the capital stock wears out each year. We call δ the *depreciation rate*. For example, if capital lasts an average of 25 years, then the depreciation rate is 4 percent per year (δ = 0.04). The amount of capital that depreciates each year is δk. Figure 4-3 shows how depreciation depends on the capital stock.

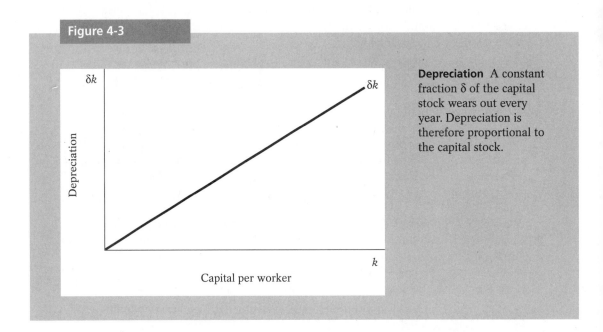

Figure 4-3

Depreciation A constant fraction δ of the capital stock wears out every year. Depreciation is therefore proportional to the capital stock.

We can express the impact of investment and depreciation on the capital stock with this adjustment equation:

$$\text{Change in Capital Stock} = \text{Investment} - \text{Depreciation}$$
$$\Delta k \qquad = \qquad i \qquad - \qquad \delta k,$$

where Δk is the change in the capital stock between one year and the next. Because investment equals saving, we can write the change in the capital stock as

$$\Delta k = sf(k) - \delta k.$$

This equation states that the change in the capital stock equals investment $sf(k)$ minus the depreciation of existing capital δk.

Figure 4-4 graphs investment and depreciation for different levels of the capital stock k. The higher the capital stock, the greater the amounts of output and investment. Yet the higher the capital stock, the greater also the amount of depreciation.

Figure 4-4 shows that there is a single capital stock at which the amount of investment equals the amount of depreciation. If the economy has this capi-

Figure 4-4

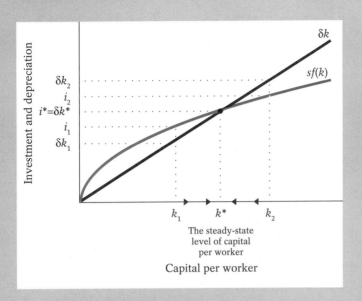

The steady-state
level of capital
per worker

Capital per worker

Investment, Depreciation, and the Steady State Since the saving rate s is constant and saving equals investment, the amount of investment is $sf(k)$. Since capital depreciates at a constant rate δ, the amount of depreciation is δk. The steady-state level of capital k^* is the level at which investment equals depreciation; at k^* the two curves cross. Below k^* investment exceeds depreciation, so the capital stock grows. Above k^* investment is less than depreciation, so the capital stock shrinks.

tal stock, the capital stock will not change over time because the two forces acting to change it—investment and depreciation—just balance. That is, at this level of the capital stock, $\Delta k = 0$. We call this outcome the **steady-state level of capital** and designate it as k^*.

Approaching the Steady State

The steady state represents the long-run equilibrium of the economy. The economy ends up with the steady-state level of capital, regardless of the level of capital with which it begins.

Suppose that the economy starts with less than the steady-state level of capital, such as level k_1 in Figure 4-4. In this case, the level of investment exceeds the amount of depreciation. Over time, the capital stock will rise and will continue to grow—along with output—until it approaches the steady state k^*.

Similarly, suppose that the economy starts with more than the steady-state level of capital, such as level k_2. In this case, investment is less than depreciation: capital is wearing out faster than it is being replaced. The capital stock will fall, again approaching the steady-state level. Once the capital stock reaches the steady state, investment equals depreciation, and the capital stock neither increases nor decreases.

Approaching the Steady State: A Numerical Example

Let's use a numerical example to see how the Solow model works and how the economy approaches the steady state. For this example, we assume that the production function is[2]

$$Y = K^{1/2} L^{1/2}.$$

To derive the per-worker production function $f(k)$, divide both sides of the production function by L:

$$\frac{Y}{L} = \frac{K^{1/2} L^{1/2}}{L}.$$

Substitute y for Y/L, and rearrange to obtain

$$y = \left(\frac{K}{L}\right)^{1/2}.$$

Since $k = K/L$, this becomes

$$y = k^{1/2}.$$

This equation can also be written as

$$y = \sqrt{k}.$$

Output per worker is the square root of capital per worker.

To complete the example, we assume that 30 percent of output is saved ($s = 0.3$), that 10 percent of the capital stock depreciates every year ($\delta = 0.1$), and that the economy starts off with 4 units of capital per worker ($k = 4$). We can now examine what happens to this economy over time.

We begin by looking at the production and allocation of output in the first year. According to the production function, the 4 units of capital per worker produce 2 units of output per worker. Since 70 percent of output is consumed and 30 percent is saved and invested, $c = 1.4$ and $i = 0.6$. Also, since 10 percent of the capital stock depreciates, $\delta k = 0.4$. With investment of 0.6 and depreciation of 0.4, the change in the capital stock is $\Delta k = 0.2$. The second year begins with 4.2 units of capital per worker.

Table 4-2 shows how the economy progresses year by year. Every year new capital is added, and output grows. Over many years, the economy approaches a steady state with 9 units of capital per worker. In this steady state, investment of 0.9 exactly offsets depreciation of 0.9, so that the capital stock and output are no longer growing.

---

[2] If you read the appendix to Chapter 3, you will recognize this as the Cobb-Douglas production function with the parameter α equal to 1/2.

Table 4-2

Approaching the Steady State: A Numerical Example

	Assumptions: $y = \sqrt{k}$		$s = 0.3$	$\delta = 0.1$	Initial $k = 4.0$	$\Delta k = c - \delta(k)$.
Year	k	y	$c = (1-s)y$	$i = s \cdot f(k)$	δk	
1	4.000	2.000	1.400	0.600	0.400	0.200
2	4.200	2.049	1.435	0.615	0.420	0.195
3	4.395	2.096	1.467	0.629	0.440	0.189
4	4.584	2.141	1.499	0.642	0.458	0.184
5	4.768	2.184	1.529	0.655	0.477	0.178
⋮						
10	5.602	2.367	1.657	.0.710	0.560	0.150
⋮						
25	7.321	1.706	1.894	0.812	0.732	0.080
⋮						
100	8.962	2.994	2.096	0.898	0.896	0.002
⋮						
∞	9.000	3.000	2.100	0.900	0.900	0.000

S.S.
$\Delta k = 0$.

Following the progress of the economy for many years is one way to find the steady-state capital stock, but another way requires fewer calculations. Recall that

$$\Delta k = sf(k) - \delta k.$$

This equation shows how k evolves over time. Since $\Delta k = 0$ in the steady state, we know that

$$0 = sf(k^*) - \delta k^*,$$

or, equivalently,

$$\frac{k^*}{f(k^*)} = \frac{s}{\delta}.$$

This equation provides a way of finding the steady-state level of capital per worker, k^*. Substituting in our example, we obtain

$$\frac{k^*}{\sqrt{k^*}} = \frac{0.3}{0.1}.$$

Now square both sides of this equation to find

$$k^* = 9.$$

The steady-state capital stock is 9 units per worker. This result confirms the calculation of the steady state in Table 4-2.

CASE STUDY

4·1

The Miracle of Japanese and German Growth

Japan and Germany are two success stories of economic growth. Although today they are economic superpowers, in 1945 the economies of both countries were in shambles. World War II had destroyed much of their capital stocks. In the decades after the war, however, these two countries experienced some of the most rapid growth rates on record. Between 1948 and 1972, output per person grew at 8.2 percent per year in Japan and 5.7 percent per year in Germany, compared to only 4.1 percent per year in Canada and only 2.2 percent per year in the United States.

Are the postwar experiences of Japan and Germany so surprising from the standpoint of the Solow growth model? Consider an economy in steady state. Now suppose that a war destroys some of the capital stock. (In Figure 4-4, the capital stock falls from k^* to k_1.) Not surprisingly, the level of output immediately falls. But if the saving rate—the fraction of output devoted to saving and investment—is unchanged, the economy will then experience a period of high growth. Output grows because, at the lower capital stock, more capital is added by investment than is removed by depreciation. This high growth continues until the economy approaches its former steady state. Hence, although destroying part of the capital stock immediately reduces output, it is followed by higher than normal growth. The "miracle" of rapid growth in Japan and Germany, as it is often described in the business press, is what the Solow model predicts for countries in which war has greatly reduced the capital stock.

The explanation of Japanese and German growth is not this simple, however. There is another important difference between these countries and those in North America that is key to their economic performance. Both Japan and Germany save and invest a higher fraction of their output. They are, therefore, approaching a different steady state. To understand more fully the differences among countries, we must consider the effects of different saving rates.

Changes in the Saving Rate

Consider what happens to an economy when the saving rate increases. Figure 4-5 shows such a change. We assume that the economy begins in a steady state with saving rate s_1 and capital stock k_1^*. The saving rate then increases from s_1 to s_2, causing an upward shift in the $sf(k)$ curve. At the initial saving rate s_1 and the initial capital stock, k_1^*, the amount of investment just offset the amount of depreciation. The moment after the saving rate rises, investment is higher, but the capital stock and depreciation are unchanged. Therefore, investment exceeds depreciation. The capital stock will gradually rise until the economy reaches the new steady state, k_2^*, with a higher capital stock and a higher level of output than the old steady state.

Figure 4-5

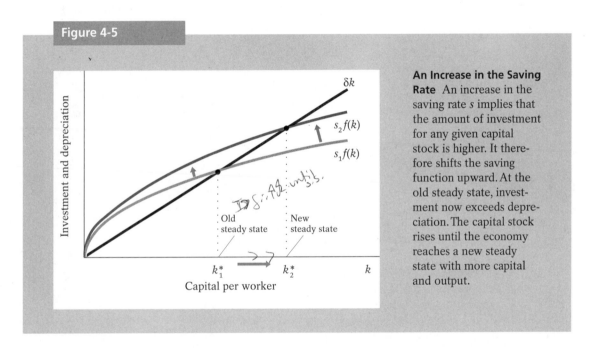

An Increase in the Saving Rate An increase in the saving rate s implies that the amount of investment for any given capital stock is higher. It therefore shifts the saving function upward. At the old steady state, investment now exceeds depreciation. The capital stock rises until the economy reaches a new steady state with more capital and output.

The Solow growth model shows that the saving rate is a key determinant of the steady-state capital stock. If the saving rate is high, the economy will have a large capital stock and a high level of output. If the saving rate is low, the economy will have a small capital stock and a low level of output.

What is the relationship between saving and economic growth? Higher saving leads to faster growth, but only in the short run. An increase in the rate of saving raises growth until the economy reaches the new steady state. If the economy maintains a high saving rate, it will also maintain a large capital stock and a high level of output, but it will not maintain a high rate of growth forever.

CASE STUDY

4·2   Saving and Investment in Rich and Poor Countries

According to the Solow growth model, if a nation devotes a high fraction of its income to saving and investment, it will have a high steady-state capital stock and a high level of income. This theoretical conclusion has important practical implications. Indeed, it can help explain the large international variation in standards of living.

Figure 4-6 is a scatterplot of data from 113 countries. The figure includes most of the world's economies. (It excludes some oil-producing countries and countries that were communist during this period.) The data show a positive relationship between the fraction of output devoted to investment and the level of income per person. That is, countries with high rates of investment, such as Canada and Japan, usually have high incomes, whereas countries with low

Figure 4-6

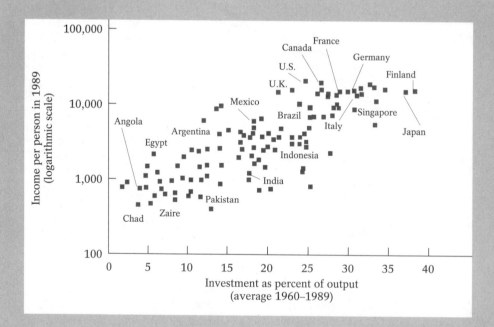

International Evidence on Investment Rates and Income per Person This scatterplot shows the experience of 113 countries, each represented by a single point. The horizontal axis shows each country's rate of investment, and the vertical axis shows each country's income per person. High investment is associated with high income per person, as the Solow model predicts.

Source: Robert Summers and Alan Heston, Supplement (Mark 5.5) to "The Penn World Table (Mark 5): An Expanded Set of International Comparisons 1950–1988," *Quarterly Journal of Economics* (May 1991): 327–368.

rates of investment, such as Zaire and Chad, have low incomes. As the Solow model suggests, the investment rate is a key determinant of whether a country is rich or poor.

Although the association in this figure is strong, it is not perfect. There must be other determinants of income per person beyond saving and investment. We return to the international differences later in the chapter to see what other variables enter the picture.

4·2 The Golden Rule Level of Capital   *omit section 4.2*

Now that we have examined the link between the rate of saving and the steady-state levels of capital and income, we can discuss what amount of capital accumulation is optimal. Later, in Section 4·5, we describe how government policies alter the saving rate. But first, in this section, we present the theory behind these policy decisions. To keep our analysis as simple as possible, we assume that a policymaker can set the economy's saving rate at any level. By setting the saving rate, the policymaker determines the economy's steady state. We consider what steady state the policymaker should choose.

Comparing Steady States

When choosing a steady state, the policymaker's goal is to maximize the well-being of the individuals who make up the society. Individuals themselves do not care about the amount of capital in the economy, or even the amount of output. They care about the amount of goods and services they can consume. Thus, a benevolent policymaker would want to choose the steady state with the highest level of consumption. The steady state with the highest consumption is called the **Golden Rule level of capital accumulation** and is denoted k^*_{gold}.[3]   *omit*

How can we tell whether an economy is at the Golden Rule level? To answer this question, we must first determine steady-state consumption per worker. Then we can see which steady state provides the most consumption.

To find steady-state consumption per worker, we begin with the national income accounts identity

$$y = c + i,$$

and rearrange it as

$$c = y - i.$$

Consumption is simply output minus investment. Since we want to find steady-state consumption, we substitute steady-state values for output and investment. Steady-state output per worker is $f(k^*)$, where k^* is the steady-state capital

---

[3] Edmund Phelps, "The Golden Rule of Accumulation: A Fable for Growthmen," *American Economic Review* 51 (September 1961): 638–643.

stock per worker. Furthermore, since the capital stock is not changing in the steady state, investment is equal to depreciation, δk^*. Substituting $f(k^*)$ for y and δk^* for i, we can write steady-state consumption per worker as

$$c^* = f(k^*) - \delta k^*.$$

This equation states that steady-state consumption is the difference between steady-state output and steady-state depreciation. It shows that increased capital has two effects on steady-state consumption: it causes greater output, but more output must be used to replace depreciating capital.

Figure 4-7 graphs steady-state output and steady-state depreciation as a function of the steady-state capital stock. Steady-state consumption is the gap between output and depreciation. This figure shows that there is one level of the capital stock—the Golden Rule level k^*_{gold}—that maximizes consumption.

When we compare steady states, we must take into account the effects of higher capital on both output and depreciation. If the capital stock is below the Golden Rule level, an increase in the capital stock raises output more than depreciation, so that consumption rises. In this case, the production function is steeper than the δk^* line, so the gap between these two curves—which equals consumption—grows as k^* rises. By contrast, if the capital stock is above the Golden Rule level, an increase in the capital stock reduces consumption, since the increase in output is smaller than the increase in depreciation. In this case, the production function is flatter than the δk^* line, so the gap between the curves—consumption—shrinks as k^* rises. At the Golden Rule level of capital,

Figure 4-7

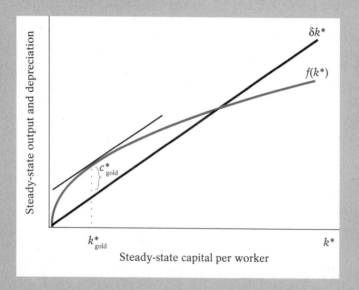

Steady-State Consumption The economy's output is used for consumption or investment. In the steady state, investment equals depreciation. Therefore, steady state consumption is the difference between output $f(k^*)$ and depreciation δk^*. The steady state that maximizes steady-state consumption is called the Golden Rule. The Golden Rule capital stock is denoted k^*_{gold}, and the Golden Rule consumption is denoted c^*_{gold}.

the production function and the δk^* line have the same slope, and consumption is at its greatest level.

To make the point somewhat differently, suppose that the economy starts at some capital stock k^* and that the policymaker is considering increasing the capital stock to $k^* + 1$. The amount of extra output would then be $f(k^* + 1) - f(k^*)$, which is the marginal product of capital MPK. The amount of extra depreciation from having to maintain one more unit of capital is the depreciation rate δ. The net effect of this extra unit of capital on consumption is then $MPK - \delta$, which is the marginal product of capital less the depreciation rate. If the steady-state capital stock is below the Golden Rule level, increases in capital increase consumption because the marginal product of capital is greater than the depreciation rate. If the steady-state capital stock exceeds the Golden Rule level, increases in capital reduce consumption because the marginal product of capital is less than the depreciation rate. Therefore, the following condition describes the Golden Rule:

$$MPK = \delta.$$

At the Golden Rule level of capital, the marginal product of capital equals the rate of depreciation. In other words, at the Golden Rule, the marginal product net of depreciation, $MPK - \delta$, equals zero.

Keep in mind that the economy does not automatically gravitate toward the Golden Rule steady state. The choice of a particular steady-state capital stock, such as the Golden Rule, implies a choice of a particular saving rate. Figure 4-8 shows the steady-state if the saving rate is set to produce the Golden Rule level of capital. If the saving rate is higher than the one used in this figure, the steady-state capital stock will be too high. If the saving rate is lower, the steady-state capital stock will be too low.

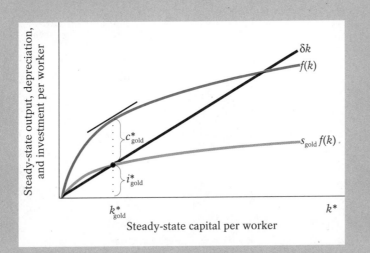

Figure 4-8

The Saving Rate and the Golden Rule There is one saving rate that produces the Golden Rule level of capital k^*_{gold}. A change in the saving rate would shift the $sf(k)$ curve, which would move the economy to a steady state with a lower level of consumption.

Comparing Steady States: A Numerical Example

Consider the decision of a policymaker choosing a steady state in the following economy. The production function is the same as in our earlier example:

$$y = \sqrt{k}.$$

Output per worker is the square root of capital per worker. Depreciation is again 10 percent of capital. This time, the policymaker chooses the saving rate s and thus the economy's steady state.

To see the outcomes available to the policymaker, recall that the following equation holds in the steady state:

$$\frac{k^*}{f(k^*)} = \frac{s}{\delta}.$$

In this economy, this equation becomes

$$\frac{k^*}{\sqrt{k^*}} = \frac{s}{0.1}.$$

Squaring both sides of this equation yields a solution for the steady-state capital stock. We find

$$k^* = 100s^2.$$

Using this result, we can compute the steady-state capital stock for any saving rate.

Table 4-3 presents calculations showing the steady states that result from various saving rates. We see that higher saving leads to higher capital, which in

Table 4-3

Comparing Steady States: A Numerical Example

Assumptions: $y = \sqrt{k}$ $\delta = 0.1$

s	k^*	y^*	δk^*	c^*	MPK	$MPK - \delta$
0.0	0.0	0.0	0.0	0.0	∞	∞
0.1	1.0	1.0	0.1	0.9	0.500	0.400
0.2	4.0	2.0	0.4	1.6	0.250	0.150
0.3	9.0	3.0	0.9	2.1	0.167	0.067
0.4	16.0	4.0	1.6	2.4	0.125	0.025
0.5	25.0	5.0	2.5	2.5	0.100	0.000
0.6	36.0	6.0	3.6	2.4	0.083	−0.017
0.7	49.0	7.0	4.9	2.1	0.071	−0.029
0.8	64.0	8.0	6.4	1.6	0.062	−0.038
0.9	81.0	9.0	8.1	0.9	0.056	−0.044
1.0	100.0	10.0	10.0	0.0	0.050	−0.050

turn leads to higher output and higher depreciation. Steady-state consumption, the difference between output and depreciation, first rises with higher saving rates and then declines. Consumption is highest when the saving rate is 0.5. Hence, a saving rate of 0.5 produces the Golden Rule steady state.

Another way to identify the Golden Rule steady state is from the marginal product of capital. For this production function, the marginal product is [4]

$$MPK = \frac{1}{2\sqrt{k}}.$$

Using this formula, the last two columns of Table 4-3 present the value of $MPK - \delta$ in the different steady states. Note again that in the Golden Rule steady state, the marginal product of capital net of depreciation equals zero.

The Transition to the Golden Rule Steady State

Let's now make our policymaker's problem more realistic. So far, we have been assuming that the policymaker can simply choose the economy's steady state. In this case, the policymaker would choose the steady state with highest consumption—the Golden Rule steady state. But now suppose that the economy has reached a steady state other than the Golden Rule. What happens to consumption, investment, and capital when the economy makes the transition between steady states? Might the impact of the transition deter the policymaker from trying to achieve the Golden Rule?

We must consider two cases: the economy might begin with more capital than in the Golden Rule steady state, or with less. The second case—too little capital—presents far greater difficulties; it forces the policymaker to evaluate the benefits of current consumption relative to future consumption. As we see in Section 4•5, this situation describes actual economies, including that of Canada.

Starting With More Capital Than in the Golden Rule   We first consider the case in which the economy begins with more capital than it would have in the Golden Rule steady state. In this case, the policymaker should pursue policies aimed at reducing the rate of saving in order to reduce the steady-state capital stock. Suppose that these policies succeed and that, at some point in time—call it t_0—the saving rate falls to the level that will eventually lead to the Golden Rule steady state.

Figure 4-9 shows what happens to output, consumption, and investment when the saving rate falls. The reduction in the saving rate causes an immediate increase in the level of consumption and a decrease in the level of investment. Investment is now less than depreciation, so the economy is no longer in a steady state. Gradually, as the capital stock falls, output, consumption, and investment also fall to the new steady state. Because the new steady state is the

---

[4] *Mathematical note*: To prove this formula, note that the marginal product of capital is the derivative of the production function with respect to k.

Figure 4-9

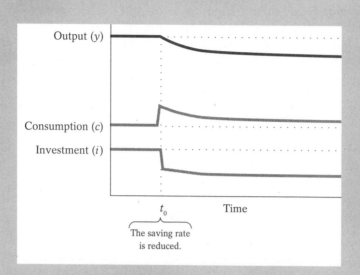

Reducing Saving When Starting With More Capital Than in the Golden Rule Steady State This figure shows what happens over time to output, consumption, and investment when the economy begins with more capital than the Golden Rule and the saving rate is reduced. The reduction in the saving rate (at time t_0) causes an immediate increase in consumption and an equal decrease in investment. Over time, as the capital stock falls, output, consumption, and investment fall together. Since the economy began with too much capital, the new steady state has a higher level of consumption than the initial steady state.

Golden Rule steady state, we know that the level of consumption is now higher than it was before the change in the saving rate, even though output and investment are lower.

Note that, compared to the old steady state, consumption is higher not just in the new steady state but also along the entire path to it. When the capital stock exceeds the Golden Rule level, reducing saving is clearly a good policy, for it increases consumption at every point in time.

Starting With Less Capital Than in the Golden Rule When the economy begins with less capital than in the Golden Rule steady state, the policymaker must raise the saving rate to reach the Golden Rule. Figure 4-10 shows what happens. The increase in the saving rate at time t_0 causes an immediate fall in consumption and a rise in investment. Over time, higher investment causes the capital stock to rise. As capital accumulates, output, consumption, and investment gradually increase, eventually approaching the new steady-state levels. Because the initial steady state was below the Golden Rule, the increase in saving eventually leads to a higher level of consumption than that which prevailed initially.

Figure 4-10

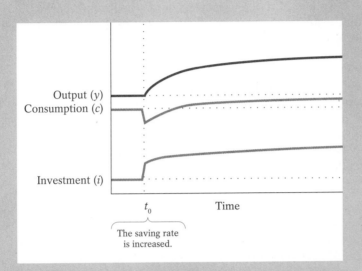

Increasing Saving When Starting With Less Capital Than in the Golden Rule Steady State This figure shows what happens over time to output, consumption, and investment when the economy begins with less capital than the Golden Rule, and the saving rate is increased. The increase in the saving rate (at time t_0) causes an immediate drop in consumption and an equal jump in investment. Over time, as the capital stock grows, output, consumption, and investment increase together. Since the economy began with less capital than the Golden Rule, the new steady state has a higher level of consumption than the initial steady state.

Does the increase in saving that leads to the Golden Rule steady state raise economic welfare? Eventually it does, because the steady-state level of consumption is higher. But achieving that new steady state requires an initial period of reduced consumption, which can last for many years. Note the contrast to the case in which the economy begins above the Golden Rule. *When the economy begins above the Golden Rule, reaching the Golden Rule produces higher consumption at all points in time. When the economy begins below the Golden Rule, reaching the Golden Rule requires reducing consumption today to increase consumption in the future.*

Deciding whether to try to reach the Golden Rule steady state is especially difficult because the population of consumers changes over time. Reaching the Golden Rule achieves the highest steady-state level of consumption and thus benefits future generations. But, when the economy is below the Golden Rule, reaching the Golden Rule requires raising investment and thus lowering the consumption of current generations.

When choosing whether to increase capital accumulation, the policy-maker must compare the welfare of different generations. A policymaker who cares more about current generations than about future generations may decide not to pursue policies to reach the Golden Rule steady state. By contrast, a policymaker who cares about all generations equally will choose to reach the Golden Rule. Even though current generations will consume less, an infinite number of future generations will benefit by moving to the Golden Rule.

Thus, optimal capital accumulation depends crucially on how we weigh the interests of current and future generations. The biblical Golden Rule tells us to "do unto others as you would have them do unto you." If we heed this advice, we give all generations equal weight. In this case, it is optimal to reach the Golden Rule level of capital—which is why it is called the "Golden Rule."

4·3 Population Growth

The basic Solow growth model shows that capital accumulation, by itself, cannot explain sustained economic growth. High rates of saving lead to high growth temporarily, but the economy eventually approaches a steady state in which capital and output are constant. To explain the sustained economic growth that we observe in most parts of the world, we must expand the Solow model to incorporate the other two sources of economic growth: population growth and technological progress. In this section we add population growth to the model.

Instead of assuming that the population is fixed, as we did in Sections 4·1 and 4·2, we now suppose that the population and the labour force grow at a constant rate n. For example, in Canada during the last 70 years, the population grew about 1.6 percent per year, so $n = 0.016$. This means that if 13 million people are working one year, then 13.2 million (1.016×13) are working the next year, and 13.41 million (1.016×13.2) the year after that, and so on.

The Steady State With Population Growth

How does population growth affect the steady state? To answer this question, we must discuss how population growth, along with investment and depreciation, influences the accumulation of capital per worker. As we noted before, investment raises the capital stock, and depreciation reduces it. But now there is a third force acting to change the amount of capital per worker: the growth in the number of workers causes capital per worker to fall.

We continue to let lowercase letters stand for quantities per worker. Thus, $k = K/L$ is capital per worker, and $y = Y/L$ is output per worker. Keep in mind, however, that the number of workers is growing over time.

The change in the capital stock per worker is

$$\Delta k = i - (\delta + n)k.$$

This equation shows how new investment, depreciation, and population growth influence the per-worker capital stock. New investment increases k, whereas depreciation and population growth decrease k. We have seen this equation before in the special case of a constant population ($n = 0$).

We can think of the term $(\delta + n)k$ as *break-even investment*: the amount of investment necessary to keep the capital stock per worker constant. Break-even investment includes the depreciation of existing capital, which equals δk. It also includes the amount of investment necessary to provide new workers with capital. The amount of investment necessary for this purpose is nk, because there are n new workers for each existing worker, and because k is the amount of capital for each worker. The equation shows that population growth reduces the accumulation of capital per worker much the way depreciation does. Depreciation reduces k by wearing out the capital stock, whereas population growth reduces k by spreading the capital stock more thinly among a larger population of workers.

To make use of this equation, substitute $sf(k)$ for i. The equation can then be written as

$$\Delta k = sf(k) - (\delta + n)k.$$

To see what determines the steady-state level of capital per worker, we use Figure 4-11, which extends the analysis of Figure 4-4 to include the effects of population growth. An economy is in a steady state if capital per worker k is unchanging. We designate the steady-state value of k as k^*. If k is less than k^*, investment is greater than break-even investment, so k rises. If k is greater than k^*, investment is less than break-even investment, so k falls.

Figure 4-11

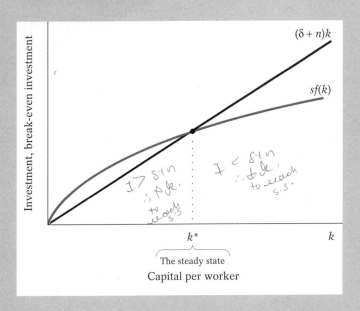

Population Growth in the Solow Model Like depreciation, population growth is one reason the capital stock per worker shrinks. If n is the rate of population growth and δ is the rate of depreciation, then $(\delta + n)k$ is the amount of investment necessary to keep constant the capital stock per worker k. For the economy to be in a steady state, investment $sf(k)$ must offset the effects of depreciation and population growth $(\delta + n)k$. This is represented by the crossing of the two curves.

In the steady state, the positive effect of investment on the capital stock per worker just balances the negative effects of depreciation and population growth. That is, at k^*, $\Delta k = 0$ and $i^* = \delta k^* + nk^*$. Once the economy is in the steady state, investment has two purposes. Some of it (δk^*) replaces the depreciated capital, and the rest (nk^*) provides the new workers with the steady-state amount of capital.

The Effects of Population Growth

Population growth alters the basic Solow model in three ways. First, it brings us closer to explaining sustained economic growth. In the steady state with population growth, capital per worker and output per worker are unchanging. Because the number of workers is growing at rate n, total capital and total output are also growing at the rate n. Hence, population growth cannot explain sustained growth in standards of living, because output per worker is constant in the steady state. But population growth can explain sustained growth in total output.

Figure 4-12

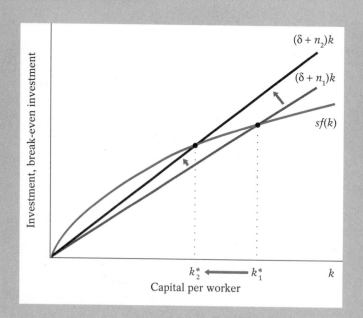

The Impact of Population Growth An increase in the rate of population growth n shifts the line representing population growth and depreciation upward. The new steady state has a lower level of capital per worker. Thus, the Solow model predicts that economies with higher rates of population growth will have lower levels of capital per worker and therefore lower incomes.

Second, population growth gives us another explanation for why some countries are rich and others are poor. Consider the effects of an increase in population growth. Figure 4-12 shows that an increase in the rate of population growth from n_1 to n_2 reduces the steady-state level of capital per worker from k_1^* to k_2^*. Since k^* is lower, and since $y^* = f(k^*)$, the level of output per worker y^* is also lower. Thus, the Solow model predicts that countries with higher population growth will have lower levels of GDP per person.

Finally, population growth affects our condition for determining the Golden Rule level of capital accumulation. To find this condition in an economy with population growth, we proceed as we did previously. Consumption per worker is

$$c = y - i.$$

Since steady-state output is $f(k^*)$ and steady-state investment is $(\delta + n)k^*$, we can write steady-state consumption as

$$c^* = f(k^*) - (\delta + n)k^*.$$

Using an argument largely the same as before, we conclude that the level of k^* that maximizes consumption is the one at which

$$MPK = \delta + n,$$

or equivalently,

$$MPK - \delta = n.$$

In the Golden Rule steady state, the marginal product of capital net of depreciation equals the rate of population growth.

CASE STUDY

4•3 Population Growth in Rich and Poor Countries

According to the Solow model, a nation with a high rate of population growth will have a low steady-state capital stock per worker and thus also a low level of income per worker. In other words, high population growth tends to impoverish a country, because it is hard to maintain a high level of capital per worker when the number of workers is growing quickly. To see whether the evidence supports this conclusion, we again turn to international data.

Figure 4-13 is a scatterplot of data for the same 113 countries examined in Case Study 4•2. The figure shows that countries with high rates of population

Figure 4-13

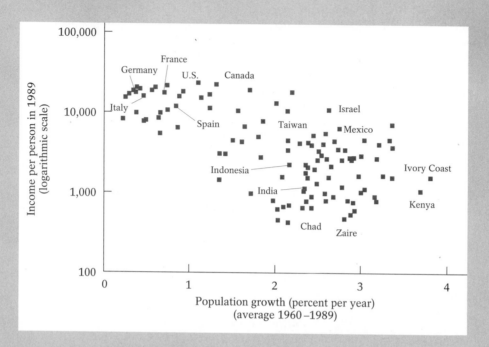

International Evidence on Population Growth and Income per Person This figure is a scatterplot of 113 countries showing that countries with high rates of population growth tend to have low levels of income per person, as the Solow model predicts.

Source: Robert Summers and Alan Heston, Supplement (Mark 5.5) to "The Penn World Table (Mark 5): An Expanded Set of International Comparisons 1950–1988," *Quarterly Journal of Economics* (May 1991): 327–368.

growth tend to have low levels of income per person. The international evidence is consistent with the Solow model's prediction that the rate of population growth is one determinant of a country's standard of living.

4•4 Technological Progress

We now incorporate technological progress, the third source of economic growth, into the Solow model. So far, our model has assumed an unchanging relationship between the inputs of capital and labour and the output of goods and services. Yet the model can be modified to allow for exogenous increases in society's ability to produce.

The Efficiency of Labour

To incorporate technological progress, we must return to the production function that relates total capital K and total labour L to total output Y. Thus far, the production function has been

$$Y = F(K, L).$$

We now write the production function as

$$Y = F(K, L \times E),$$

where E is a new variable called the efficiency of labour. The **efficiency of labour** reflects society's knowledge about production methods: as the available technology improves, the efficiency of labour rises. The efficiency of labour may also reflect the health, education, and skills of the labour force.

The term $L \times E$ is the labour force measured in efficiency units. **Efficiency units of labour** take into account the number of workers L and the efficiency of each worker E. This new production function states that total output Y depends on the number of units of capital K and on the number of efficiency units of labour, $L \times E$.

The simplest assumption about technological progress is that it causes the efficiency of labour E to grow at some constant rate g. For example, if $g = 0.02$, then each unit of labour becomes 2 percent more efficient each year: output increases as if the labour force had increased by an additional 2 percent. This form of technological progress is called labour-augmenting, and g is called the rate of **labour-augmenting technological progress**. Since the labour force L is growing at rate n, and the efficiency of each unit of labour E is growing at rate g, the number of efficiency units of labour $L \times E$ is growing at rate $n + g$.

The Steady State With Technological Progress

Expressing technological progress as labour-augmenting makes it analogous to population growth. Just as we have been analyzing the economy in terms of quantities per worker, we now analyze it in terms of quantities per efficiency unit of labour. Let $k = K/(L \times E)$ stand for capital per efficiency unit, and $y = Y/(L \times E)$ stand for output per efficiency unit. With these definitions, we can again write $y = f(k)$.

Our analysis of the economy proceeds just as it did when we examined population growth. The equation showing the evolution of k over time now changes to

$$\Delta k = sf(k) - (\delta + n + g)k.$$

The new term involving g, the rate of technological progress, arises because k is the amount of capital per efficiency unit of labour. If g is high, then the number of efficiency units is growing quickly, and the amount of capital per efficiency unit tends to fall.

As shown in Figure 4-14, the inclusion of technological progress does not substantially alter our analysis of the steady state. There is one level of k, denoted k^*, at which capital per efficiency unit and output per efficiency unit are constant. This steady state represents the long-run equilibrium of the economy.

Figure 4-14

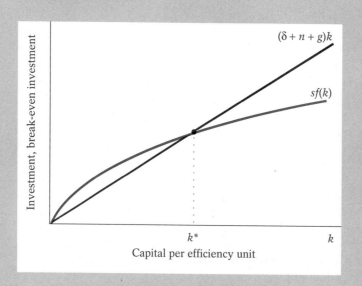

Capital per efficiency unit

Introducing Technological Progress Including labour-augmenting technological progress at rate g affects our analysis in much the same way as did population growth. Now that k is defined as the amount of capital per efficiency unit of labour, increases in the number of efficiency units because of technological progress tend to decrease k. In the steady state, investment $sf(k)$ offsets the reductions in k due to depreciation, population growth, and technological progress.

The Effects of Technological Progress

Table 4-4 shows how four key variables behave in the steady state with technological progress. As we have just seen, capital per efficiency unit k is constant in the steady state. Since $y = f(k)$, output per efficiency unit is also constant. Remember, though, that the number of efficiency units per worker is growing at rate g. Hence, output per worker ($Y/L = y \times E$) also grows at rate g. Total output [$Y = y \times (E \times L)$] grows at rate $n + g$.

With the addition of technological progress, our model can finally explain the sustained increases in standards of living that we observe. That is, we have shown that technological progress can lead to sustained growth in output per worker. By contrast, a high rate of saving leads to a high rate of growth only until the steady state is reached. Once the economy is in steady state, the rate of growth of output per worker depends only on the rate of technological

Table 4-4	Steady-State Growth Rates in the Solow Model With Technological Progress	
Variable	Symbol	Growth Rate
Capital per efficiency unit	$k = K/(E \times L)$	0
Output per efficiency unit	$y = Y/(E \times L) = f(k)$	0
Output per worker	$Y/L = y \times E$	g
Total output	$Y = y \times (E \times L)$	$n + g$

progress. *The Solow growth model shows that only technological progress can explain persistently rising living standards.*

The introduction of technological progress also modifies the condition for the Golden Rule. The Golden Rule level of capital accumulation is defined as the steady state that maximizes consumption per efficiency unit of labour. Following the same arguments that we have used before, we can show that steady-state consumption per efficiency unit is

$$c^* = f(k^*) - (\delta + n + g)k^*.$$

Steady-state consumption is maximized if

$$MPK = \delta + n + g,$$

or

$$MPK - \delta = n + g.$$

That is, at the Golden Rule level of capital, the net marginal product of capital, $MPK - \delta$, equals the rate of growth of total output, $n + g$. Because actual economies experience both population growth and technological progress, we must use this condition to evaluate whether they have more or less capital than at the Golden Rule steady state.

CASE STUDY

4·4   Steady-State Growth in Canada

Now that we have introduced technological progress into the Solow model and explained sustained growth in standards of living, we should ask how well our theory fits the facts. The Solow growth model predicts that technological progress causes many variables to grow together. In the steady state, output per worker and the capital stock per worker both grow at the rate of technological progress. Data for Canada over the past 40 years show that output per worker and the capital stock per worker have in fact grown at approximately the same rate—about 2.2 percent per year.

Technological progress also affects factor prices. Problem 8(d) at the end of the chapter asks you to show that, in the steady state, the real wage grows at the rate of technological progress. The real rental price of capital, however, is constant over time. Again, these predictions hold true for Canada. Over the past 40 years, the real wage has increased about 2.4 percent per year—about the same amount as real GDP per worker. Yet the real rental price of capital (measured as real capital income divided by the capital stock) has remained essentially constant. Given the vast changes in the Canadian economy during this 40-year period (fewer workers in the agricultural industry and many more in the service sector), it is impressive that a simple model that ignores all these sectoral shifts can do so well.

The Solow growth model's prediction about factor prices—and the success of this prediction—is especially noteworthy when contrasted with Karl Marx's theory of the development of capitalist economies. Marx predicted that the return to capital would decline over time and that this would lead to economic and political crisis. Economic history has not supported Marx's prediction, which partly explains why we now study Solow's theory of growth rather than Marx's.

CASE STUDY

4·5   The Aging of Canada

Over the next 40 years, the ratio of the Canadian labour force to the Canadian population is expected to fall from 0.525 to 0.475—a 10 percent reduction. As a result, a higher proportion of Canadians will be dependent on a smaller group of workers. The main reason for this development is that the "baby boom" generation is growing older. We can use the Solow growth model to get some idea about how much stress this demographic change will cause for Canadians.

Let β and LS stand for the proportion of the population that is working, and the living standard of the average citizen. Since we have used c to denote consumption per efficiency unit of labour, then

$$LS = \frac{\text{Total Consumption}}{\text{Population}} = \frac{\text{Consumption per Worker}}{\text{Population per Worker}} = c\beta.$$

If the level of c is independent of β, this equation implies that

$$\Delta LS/LS = \Delta \beta/\beta.$$

That is, the living standard of the average person falls by the same percentage as does the proportion of the population that is working.[5] We have already learned that the steady-state values of consumption and capital (defined in pro-

---

[5] To help in understanding this relationship, see the primer on products and percentage changes on page 162.

portion to labour measured in efficiency units), c^* and k^*, are determined by the following equations (which do not involve β):

$$sf(k^*) = (\delta + n + g)k^*$$
$$c^* = f(k^*) - (\delta + n + g)k^*$$

As a result, the steady-state value of c *is* independent of β.

As noted, Canada's β will fall by 10 percent over the next 40 years. According to the Solow growth model, this development will lower the average living standard to a level that is 10 percent below what it would otherwise have reached. This is a large change in living standards, so it is no wonder that more Canadians are becoming concerned about how social policies can be redesigned to cope with this development.

4•5 Saving, Growth, and Economic Policy

Having used the Solow growth model to uncover the relationships among the different sources of economic growth, we can now use the theory to help guide our thinking about economic policy. Here we address four policy questions:

1. Should our society save more or save less?

2. How can policy influence the rate of saving?

3. Are there particular types of investment that policy should especially encourage?

4. How can policy influence the rate of technological progress?

Evaluating the Rate of Saving

The Solow growth model shows how the saving rate determines the steady-state levels of capital and output. One particular saving rate produces the Golden Rule steady state, which maximizes consumption per worker and thus economic well-being. These results help us address the first question for economic policy: Is the rate of saving in the economy too low, too high, or about right?

If the marginal product of capital net of depreciation is greater than the growth rate, the economy is operating with less capital than in the Golden Rule steady state. In this case, increasing the rate of saving will eventually lead to a steady state with higher consumption. On the other hand, if the net marginal product of capital is below the growth rate, the economy is operating with too much capital, and the rate of saving should be reduced. To evaluate a nation's rate of capital accumulation, one needs to compare the growth rate and the net return to capital.

This comparison requires an estimate of the growth rate $(n + g)$ and an estimate of the net marginal product of capital $(MPK - \delta)$. Real GDP in Canada has grown at 4 percent per year since 1950, so $n + g = 0.04$. We can estimate the net marginal product of capital from the following three facts:

1. The capital stock is about 3 times one year's GDP.
2. Depreciation of capital is about 10 percent of GDP.
3. Capital's share in output is about 33 percent.

Fact 1 states that $k = 3y$, and fact 2 states that $\delta k = 0.1y$. Therefore,

$$\delta = (\delta k)/k$$
$$= (0.1y)/(3y)$$
$$= 0.033.$$

That is, about 3.3 percent of the capital stock depreciates each year. To obtain the marginal product of capital from facts 1 and 3, recall our conclusion in Chapter 3 that capital is paid its marginal product. Therefore,

$$\text{Capital's Share} = (MPK \times K)/Y$$
$$= MPK \times (K/Y).$$

Now substitute the numbers from facts 1 and 3 into this equation,

$$0.33 = MPK \times 3.$$

This implies that

$$MPK = 0.33/3 = 0.11.$$

Thus, the marginal product of capital is about 11 percent per year. The net marginal product of capital ($MPK - \delta$) is 0.77 (0.11 − 0.033), or about 7.7 percent per year, well in excess of the average growth rate of 4 percent per year.

The high return to capital implies that the capital stock in the Canadian economy is well below the Golden Rule level. This finding suggests that policymakers should want to increase the rate of saving and investment. In fact, for many years, increasing capital formation has been a high priority of economic policy.

Changing the Rate of Saving

Public policy influences national saving in two ways: directly through public saving, and indirectly through the incentives it gives for private saving.

Public saving is the difference between government revenue and government spending. If the government spends more than it raises in revenue, it runs a budget deficit, which represents negative saving. As we saw in Chapter 3, the budget deficit crowds out investment. The reduced capital stock that results is part of the burden of the national debt on future generations. On the other hand, if the government spends less than it raises in revenue, it runs a budget surplus. It can then retire some of the national debt and stimulate investment.

Private saving is affected by various government policies. Although not included in the Solow model, the saving decisions of households depend on the rate of return; the greater the return to saving, the more attractive saving becomes. High tax rates on capital income discourage private saving by reducing the rate of return. Various tax provisions, such as tax-exempt registered retirement savings plans (RRSPs), are designed to raise the rate of return and encourage private saving. Economists differ in their views about how much private saving responds to these incentives.

CASE STUDY

4·6 Tax Incentives for Saving and Investment

The Canadian government has long believed that Canada's capital/labour ratio is below the Golden Rule value. This has been the motivation behind a series of policies that were designed to raise domestic saving and to make investment more profitable for firms.

On the saving side, we have had RRSPs, the new goods and services tax (GST), and the capital gains exemption from income taxes. All savings that are deposited within an RRSP involve two tax breaks. First, the amount contributed can be deducted from taxable income (so individuals in a 50 percent tax bracket are effectively earning interest on twice the funds that they would have without an RRSP). Second, all interest earned within the plan is tax deferred. Eventually, when the RRSP is closed out, the individuals must pay taxes on all funds withdrawn. But this does not remove the tax advantage. For one thing, the tax rate is often lower during one's retirement. For another thing, even when this is not the case, people prefer to pay taxes later. By allowing people to defer taxes, RRSPs involve the government in extending an interest-free loan to individuals (for many years). The government has been willing to give up all the associated revenue in an attempt to increase national saving.

The GST was introduced in 1988. One rationale for this tax is that sales taxes stimulate saving (compared to income taxes). With an income tax, individuals pay taxes whether they spend their income on consumption or saving. With a sales tax, people can avoid the tax by saving, since the tax is only levied when people spend.

The tax exemption on capital gains income was removed in the 1994 federal budget. With the government budget deficit running out of control, the government felt it had no option but to end this tax incentive. But its original intent was the same as with RRSPs. Prior to the 1994 budget, all individuals were exempt from tax on the first $100,000 of capital gains they had received on their savings. By removing all gains from real estate holdings (except one's family home) from this provision in an earlier budget, it was clear that the government was trying to make more funds available to firms for investment.

The government also gives interest-free loans directly to firms, in the form of "accelerated depreciation allowances." Again, the purpose is to increase capital accumulation in the economy. When firms fill out their corporate tax forms, they deduct expenses from gross sales to calculate their tax base (profits). One aspect of these calculations is particularly arbitrary—how the expenses of the firms' machines and equipment are treated. Firms would like to claim (for tax purposes) that equipment fully wears out (depreciates) during the purchase year. Firms can then claim the entire cost of the equipment immediately. This makes recorded profits low, and so keeps initial tax payments low. In fact, equipment wears out over a period of years. By having no equipment-purchase expenses left to claim in those later years, firms have bigger tax obligations later on. But, as with households, firms like paying taxes later, since by doing so they have received an interest-free loan from the government.

Vast amounts of tax revenue are forgone because of these tax incentives, so it should not be surprising to learn that some have been controversial. One class of policies that is particularly "expensive" is the set of corporate tax breaks that are available to all firms operating in Canada, whether or not they are branch plants of multinational companies. International tax agreements make our tax initiatives useless for these firms. Multinationals are allowed a tax credit for taxes already paid in other countries when they calculate their corporate tax obligations in the country where the parent company is based. For example, a company based in the United States is allowed to deduct the taxes its affiliate has already paid in Canada from what taxes it would otherwise owe to the U.S. government. Thus, a tax break offered by the Canadian government makes the tax credit in the United States precisely that much smaller. The Canadian government is simply transferring revenue to the U.S. government. Since these firms are no better off as a result of the Canadian government's generosity, we cannot expect the policy to stimulate investment spending on the part of these firms.

This is not the place to evaluate more fully the Canadian attempts to raise saving and investment. However successful these schemes have been, the main point to be appreciated is *why* these initiatives were taken. The purpose has been to move Canada closer to the Golden Rule outcome.

Allocating the Economy's Investment

The Solow growth model makes the simplifying assumption that there is only one type of capital. In the world, of course, there are many types. Private businesses invest in traditional types of capital, such as bulldozers and steel plants, and newer types of capital, such as computers and robots. The government invests in various forms of public capital, called *infrastructure*, such as roads, bridges, and sewer systems.

In addition, there is *human capital*—the knowledge and skills that workers acquire through education, from early childhood programs to on-the-job training for adults in the labour force. Although the basic Solow model includes only physical capital and does not try to explain the efficiency of labour, in many ways human capital is analogous to physical capital. Like physical capital, human capital raises our ability to produce goods and services. Raising the level of human capital requires investment in the form of teachers, libraries, and student time. Recent research on economic growth has emphasized that human capital is at least as important as physical capital in explaining international differences in standards of living.[6]

Policymakers trying to stimulate economic growth must confront the issue of what kinds of capital the economy needs most. In other words, what kinds of capital yield the highest marginal products? To a large extent, policymakers can rely on the marketplace to allocate the pool of saving to alternative types of investment. Those industries with the highest marginal products of capital will naturally be most willing to borrow at market interest rates to finance new investment. Many economists advocate that the government should merely create a "level playing field" for different types of capital—for example, by ensuring that the tax system treats all forms of capital equally. The government can then rely on the market to allocate capital efficiently.

Other economists have suggested that the government should actively encourage particular forms of capital. They argue that technological advance occurs as a beneficial by-product of certain economic activities. Such a by-product is called an *externality*. For example, new and improved production processes may be devised during the process of accumulating capital. If this speculation is correct, then the benefits of capital accumulation to society may be greater than the Solow growth model suggests.[7] Moreover, some types of capital accumulation may yield greater externalities than others. If, for example, installing robots yields greater technological externalities than building a new steel mill, then perhaps the government should use the tax laws to encourage investment in robots. The success of such an *industrial policy*, as it is called, requires that the government be able to measure the externalities of different economic activities. Most economists are skeptical about such policies because the measurement problem is so difficult.

One type of capital that necessarily involves the government is public capital. Municipal, provincial, and federal governments are always deciding whether to borrow to finance new roads, bridges, and transit systems. During the federal election campaign of 1993, Prime Minister Jean Chrétien argued that Canada had been investing too little in infrastructure. He claimed that a higher level of infrastructure investment would make the economy substantially more productive. Among economists, this claim has had both defenders and critics. Yet all of them agree that measuring the marginal product of public capital is difficult. Private capital generates an easily measured rate of profit for the firm owning the capital, whereas the benefits of public capital are more diffuse.

---

[6] Robert E. Lucas, Jr., "On the Mechanics of Economic Development," *Journal of Monetary Economics* 22 (1988): 3–42; N. Gregory Mankiw, David Romer, and David N. Weil, "A Contribution to the Empirics of Economic Growth," *Quarterly Journal of Economics* (May 1992): 407–437.

[7] Paul Romer, "Crazy Explanations for the Productivity Slowdown," *NBER Macroeconomics Annual* 2 (1987): 163–201.

Encouraging Technological Progress

The Solow growth model shows that sustained growth in income per worker must come from technological progress. The Solow growth model, however, takes technological progress as exogenous; it does not explain it. Unfortunately, the determinants of technological progress are not well understood.

Despite this limited understanding, many public policies are designed to stimulate technological progress. Most of these policies encourage individuals to devote resources to technological innovation. The patent system gives a temporary monopoly to inventors of new products. The tax code offers tax breaks for research and development. Government funding agencies directly subsidize basic research. Finally, as discussed above, proponents of industrial policy argue that the government should take a more active role in promoting specific industries that are key for rapid technological progress.

CASE STUDY

4·7

The Worldwide Slowdown in Economic Growth

One of the most perplexing problems that policymakers have faced over the past 20 years is the worldwide slowdown in economic growth that began in the early 1970s. Table 4-5 presents data on the growth in real GDP per person for the seven major world economies. Growth in Canada fell from 2.9 percent to 2.3 percent. (Note that Table 4-5 focuses on growth in output *per person*. Since Canada's population has grown more rapidly than our real GDP, these growth rates are lower than the 4 percent output growth rate discussed earlier.) Other countries experienced similar or more severe declines in growth rates.

Table 4-5		
The Slowdown in Growth Around the World		
	Growth in Output per Person (percent per year)	
Country	1948–1972	1972–1991
Canada	2.9	2.3
France	4.3	2.1
West Germany	5.7	2.3
Italy	4.9	2.8
Japan	8.2	3.6
United Kingdom	2.4	1.9
United States	2.2	1.7

Source: Angus Maddison, *Phases of Capitalist Development* (Oxford: Oxford University Press, 1992); *International Financial Statistics.*

Studies have shown that the slowdown in growth is attributable to a slowdown in the rate at which the production function is improving over time. The appendix to this chapter explains how economists measure changes in the production function with a variable called *total factor productivity*, which is closely related to the efficiency of labour in the Solow model. Accumulated over many years, even a small change in productivity growth has a large effect on economic welfare. Real income in Canada today is more than 20 percent lower than it would have been if productivity growth had remained at its previous level.

Many economists have attempted to explain this adverse change. Here are some of their explanations:

- The composition of the labour force has been changing. The entrance of the younger baby-boom generation into the labour force beginning in the 1970s lowered the average level of experience and, therefore, the productivity of labour.

- An increase in government regulations, such as those to protect the environment, requires firms to use less productive production methods. The regulations reduce growth in productivity and incomes (even if they are socially desirable).

- Large changes in oil prices in the 1970s caused by OPEC, the oil cartel, made some of the capital stock prematurely obsolete. Firms may have retired some of their machinery that was heavily dependent on fuel.

- The world has started to run out of new ideas about how to produce. We have entered an age of slower technological progress.

Which of these suspects is the culprit? All of them are plausible, but it is difficult to prove beyond a reasonable doubt that any one of them is guilty. The widespread slowdown in economic growth remains a mystery.[8]

Part of the support for a more active industrial policy stems from the fact that many other countries, including Japan and several Western European countries, have had higher growth rates than Canada in the last 30 years. Some policymakers think that Canada should be able to duplicate the outcomes in these other countries. But many economists argue that there is a natural growth-rate convergence process that is ongoing among countries. This process suggests that Canada's relative performance is quite predictable, and that it may be difficult to do anything about it.

The essence of the convergence process is that the high-productivity countries can be copied easily by other counties and that the less productive countries have less to offer in exchange (for the existing leaders to copy). Since Canada has been (and will likely remain) one of the leaders in the *level* of productivity, it is natural to expect that others will converge gradually to Canada's level by growing at a more rapid rate.

---

[8] For various views on the growth slowdown, see "Symposium: The Slowdown in Productivity Growth," *The Journal of Economic Perspectives* 2 (Fall 1988): 3–98.

4•6 Conclusion: Beyond the Solow Growth Model

Although the Solow growth model provides the best framework with which to start studying economic growth, it is only a beginning. The model simplifies many aspects of the world, and it omits many others altogether. Economists who study economic growth try to build more sophisticated models that allow them to address a broader range of questions.

These advanced models usually turn one of the exogenous variables in the Solow growth model into an endogenous variable. For example, the Solow growth model takes the rate of saving as exogenous. As we see in Chapter 15, consumption arises from the decisions of households about how much to consume today and how much to save for the future. More sophisticated growth models replace the consumption function of the Solow model with an explicit theory of household behaviour.

Perhaps most important, economists have tried to build models to explain the level and growth of the efficiency of labour. The Solow growth model shows that sustained growth in standards of living can arise only from technological progress. Our understanding of economic growth will not be complete until we understand how private decisions and public policy affect technological progress. This is one of the greatest challenges facing economists today.

Summary

1. The Solow growth model shows that, in the long run, an economy's rate of saving determines the size of its capital stock and thus its level of production. The higher the rate of saving, the higher the stock of capital and the higher the level of output.

2. An increase in the rate of saving causes a period of high growth until the new steady state is reached. In the long run, the saving rate does not affect the growth rate. Sustained growth of output per worker depends on technological progress.

3. The level of capital that maximizes consumption is called the Golden Rule level. At this level, the net marginal product of capital equals the growth rate of output. Estimates for actual economies, such as Canada, suggest that the capital stock is well below the Golden Rule level. To reach the Golden Rule requires increased investment and thus lower consumption for current generations.

4. Economic policymakers often claim that the rate of capital accumulation should be increased. Increased public saving and tax incentives for private saving are two ways to encourage capital accumulation.

5. The Solow growth model shows that an economy's rate of population growth is another long-run determinant of the standard of living. The higher the rate of population growth, the lower the level of output per worker.

6. In the early 1970s, the rate of growth fell substantially in most industrialized countries. The cause of this slowdown is not well understood.

KEY CONCEPTS

Solow growth model

Steady-state level of capital accumulation

Golden Rule level of capital accumulation

Efficiency of labour

Efficiency units of labour

Labour-augmenting technological progress

QUESTIONS FOR REVIEW

1. In the Solow growth model, how does the saving rate affect the steady-state level of income? How does it affect the steady-state rate of growth?

2. Why might an economic policymaker choose the Golden Rule level of capital?

3. Might a policymaker choose a steady state with more capital than in the Golden Rule steady state? With less capital than in the Golden Rule steady state?

4. In the Solow growth model, how does the rate of population growth affect the steady-state level of income? How does it affect the steady-state rate of growth?

5. What determines the steady-state rate of growth of income per worker?

6. How can economic policy influence the saving rate?

7. What has happened to the rate of growth over the past 40 years? How might you explain this phenomenon?

PROBLEMS AND APPLICATIONS

1. Country A and country B both have the production function

$$Y = F(K, L) = K^{1/2}L^{1/2}.$$

a. Does this production function have constant returns to scale? Explain.

b. What is the per-worker production function, $y = f(k)$?

c. Assume that neither country has population growth or technological progress and that 5 percent of capital depreciates each year. Assume further that country A saves 10 percent of output each year and country B saves 20 percent of output each year. Use your answer from part (b) and the steady-state condition that investment equals depreciation to find the steady-state level of capital per worker for each country. Then find the steady-

state levels of income per worker and consumption per worker.

d. Suppose that both countries start off with a capital stock per worker of 2. What are the levels of income per worker and consumption per worker? Remembering that the change in the capital stock is investment less depreciation, use a calculator to show how the capital stock per worker will evolve over time in both countries. For each year, calculate income per worker and consumption per worker. How many years will it be before the consumption in country B is higher than the consumption in country A?

2. In the discussion of German and Japanese postwar growth, the text describes what happens when part of the capital stock is destroyed in a war. By

contrast, suppose that a war does not directly affect the capital stock, but that casualties reduce the labour force.

a. What is the immediate impact on total output and on output per person?

b. Assuming that the saving rate is unchanged and that the economy was in a steady state before the war, what happens subsequently to output per worker in the postwar economy? Is the growth rate of output per worker after the war smaller or greater than normal?

3. "Devoting a larger share of national output to investment would help restore rapid productivity growth and rising living standards." Do you agree with this claim? Explain.

4. Suppose the production function is

$$y = \sqrt{k}.$$

a. Solve for the steady-state value of y as a function of s, n, g, and δ.

b. A developed country has a saving rate of 28 percent and a population growth rate of 1 percent per year. A less-developed country has a saving rate of 10 percent and a population growth rate of 4 percent per year. In both countries, $g = 0.02$ and $\delta = 0.04$. Find the steady-state value of y for each country.

c. What policies might the less-developed country pursue to raise its level of income?

5. In Canada, gross capital income is about 30 percent of GDP; the average growth in output for the last 25 years is about 3 percent per year; the depreciation rate is about 4 percent per year; and the capital–output ratio is about 2.5. Suppose that the production function is Cobb-Douglas, so that the capital share in output is constant, and that Canada

has been in a steady state. (For a discussion of the Cobb-Douglas production function, see the appendix to Chapter 3.)

a. What must the saving rate be in the initial steady state? [*Hint:* Use the steady-state savings equals investment rule, $sy = (\delta + n + g)k$.]

b. What is the marginal product of capital in the initial steady state?

c. Suppose that public policy raises the saving rate so that the economy reaches the Golden Rule level of capital. What will the marginal product of capital be at the Golden Rule steady state? Compare the marginal product at the Golden Rule steady state to the marginal product in the initial steady state. Explain.

d. What will the capital-output ratio be at the Golden Rule steady state? (*Hint:* For the Cobb-Douglas production function, the capital-output ratio is simply related to the marginal product of capital.)

e. What must the saving rate be to reach the Golden Rule steady state?

6. One view of the consumption function, sometimes advocated by Marxist economists, is that workers have high propensities to consume and capitalists have low propensities to consume. To explore the implications of this view, suppose an economy consumes all wage income and saves all capital income. Show that if the factors of production earn their marginal product, this economy reaches the Golden Rule level of capital accumulation. (*Hint:* Begin with the identity that saving equals investment. Then use the steady-state condition that investment is just enough to keep up with depreciation, population growth, and technological progress, along with the fact that saving equals capital income in this economy.)

7. Many demographers predict that Canada will have zero population growth in the twenty-first century, in contrast to average population growth of well over 1 percent per year in the twentieth century. Use the Solow growth model to forecast the effect of this slowdown in population growth on the growth of total output and the growth of output per person. Consider the effects both in the steady state and in the transition between steady states.

8. Prove each of the following statements about the steady state with population growth and technological progress.

a. The capital-output ratio is constant.

b. The capital and labour shares of income are constant. [*Hint:* Recall the definition $MPK = f(k + 1) - f(k)$.]

c. Total capital income and total labour income both grow at the rate of population growth plus the rate of technological progress ($n + g$).

d. The real rental price of capital is constant, and the real wage grows at the rate of technological progress g. (*Hint:* The real rental price of capital equals total capital income divided by the capital stock, and the real wage equals total labour income divided by the labour force.)

9. The amount of education the typical person receives varies substantially among countries. Suppose you were to compare a country with a highly educated labour force and a country with a less educated labour force. Assume that the countries have the same saving rate, the same population growth rate, and the same rate of technological progress. Using the Solow growth model, what would you predict for the following variables?

a. The rate of growth of total income

b. The level of income per worker

c. The real rental price of capital

d. The real wage

10. In the Solow growth model, population growth leads to growth in total output, but not in output per worker. Do you think this would still be true if the production function exhibited increasing or decreasing returns to scale? Explain. (For the definitions of increasing and decreasing returns to scale, see Chapter 3, "Problems and Applications," number 2.)

11. Suppose that the production function does not exhibit diminishing marginal product of capital and that, instead, the production function is

$$y = Ak,$$

where A is a positive constant.

a. Show that this production function implies that the marginal product of capital is constant.

b. Show that, in this case, a higher saving rate leads to a permanently higher growth rate. (Remember that growth in a variable X is defined to be $\Delta X/X$.)

c. Why does this conclusion differ from that in the Solow model?

d. Do you think this production function is reasonable? Explain.

Accounting for the Sources of Economic Growth

Real GDP in Canada has grown an average of 4 percent per year over the past 40 years. What accounts for this growth? In Chapter 3 we linked the output of the economy to the factors of production—capital and labour—and to the production technology. Here we divide the growth in output into three different sources: increases in capital, increases in labour, and advances in technology. This breakdown provides us with a measure of the rate of technological change.

Increases in the Factors of Production

We first examine how increases in the factors of production contribute to increases in output. We assume there is no technological change. Therefore, the production function relating output Y to capital K and labour L does not change over time:

$$Y = F(K, L).$$

In this case, the amount of output changes only because the amount of capital or labour changes.

Increases in Capital First, consider changes in capital. If the amount of capital increases by ΔK units, how much does the amount of output increase? To answer this question, we need to recall the definition of the marginal product of capital MPK:

$$MPK = F(K + 1, L) - F(K, L).$$

The marginal product of capital tells us how much output increases when capital increases by one unit. Therefore, when capital increases by ΔK units, output increases by approximately $MPK \times \Delta K$.[9]

For example, suppose that the marginal product of capital is 1/5; that is, an additional unit of capital increases the amount of output produced by one fifth of a unit. If we increase the amount of capital by 10 units, we can compute the

---

[9] Note the word "approximately" here. This answer is only an approximation because the marginal product of capital varies: it falls as the amount of capital increases. An exact answer would take into account that each unit of capital has a different marginal product. If the change in K is not too large, however, the approximation of a constant marginal product is very accurate.

amount of additional output as follows:

$$\Delta Y = MPK \times \Delta K$$
$$= 1/5 \frac{\text{Output}}{\text{Capital}} \times 10 \text{ Units of Capital}$$
$$= 2 \text{ Units of Output.}$$

By increasing capital by 10 units, we obtain 2 more units of output per year. Thus, we use the marginal product of capital to convert changes in capital into changes in output.

Increases in Labour Next, consider changes in labour. If the amount of labour increases by ΔL units, how much does output increase? We answer this question the same way we answered the question about capital. The marginal product of labour MPL tells us how much output changes when labour increases by one unit—that is,

$$MPL = F(K, L + 1) - F(K, L).$$

Therefore, when the amount of labour increases by ΔL units, output increases by approximately $MPL \times \Delta L$.

For example, suppose that the marginal product of labour is 2; that is, an additional unit of labour increases the amount of output produced by 2 units. If we increase the amount of labour by 10 units, we can compute the amount of additional output as follows:

$$\Delta Y = MPL \times \Delta L$$
$$= 2 \frac{\text{Output}}{\text{Labour}} \times 10 \text{ Units of Labour}$$
$$= 20 \text{ Units of Output.}$$

By increasing labour by 10 units, we obtain 20 more units of output per year. Thus, we use the marginal product of labour to convert changes in labour into changes in output.

Increases in Capital and Labour Finally, let's consider the more realistic case in which both factors of production change. Suppose that the amount of capital increases by ΔK and the amount of labour increases by ΔL. The increase in output, then, comes from two sources: more capital and more labour. We can divide this increase into the two sources using the marginal products of the two inputs:

$$\Delta Y = (MPK \times \Delta K) + (MPL \times \Delta L).$$

The first term in parentheses is the increase in output resulting from the increase in capital, and the second term in parentheses is the increase in output resulting from the increase in labour. This equation shows us how to attribute growth to each factor of production.

We now want to convert this last equation into a form that is easier to interpret and apply to the available data. First, with some algebraic rearrangement, the equation becomes[10]

$$\frac{\Delta Y}{Y} = \left(\frac{MPK \times K}{Y}\right)\frac{\Delta K}{K} + \left(\frac{MPL \times L}{Y}\right)\frac{\Delta L}{L}.$$

This form of the equation relates the growth rate of output, $\Delta Y/Y$, to the growth rate of capital, $\Delta K/K$, and the growth rate of labour, $\Delta L/L$.

Next, we need to find some way to measure the terms in parentheses in the last equation. In Chapter 3 we showed that the marginal product of capital equals its real rental price. Therefore, $MPK \times K$ is the total return to capital, and $(MPK \times K)/Y$ is capital's share of output. Similarly, the marginal product of labour equals the real wage. Therefore, $MPL \times L$ is the total compensation that labour receives, and $(MPL \times L)/Y$ is labour's share of output. Under the assumption that the production function has constant returns to scale, Euler's theorem tells us that these two shares sum to one. In this case, we can write

$$\frac{\Delta Y}{Y} = \alpha\frac{\Delta K}{K} + (1-\alpha)\frac{\Delta L}{L},$$

where α is capital's share and $(1-\alpha)$ is labour's share.

This last equation gives us a simple formula for showing how changes in inputs lead to changes in output. In particular, we must weight the growth rates of the inputs by the factor shares. As we discussed in Chapter 3, capital's share in Canada is about 33 percent—that is, $\alpha = 0.33$. Therefore, a 10 percent increase in the amount of capital ($\Delta K/K = 0.10$) leads to a 3.3 percent increase in the amount of output ($\Delta Y/Y = 0.033$). Similarly, a 10 percent increase in the amount of labour ($\Delta L/L = 0.10$) leads to a 6.7 percent increase in the amount of output ($\Delta Y/Y = 0.067$).

Technological Progress

Thus far in our analysis of the sources of growth, we have been assuming that the production function does not change over time. In practice, of course, technological progress improves the production function. For the same amount of inputs, we get more output today than we did in the past. We now extend the analysis to allow for technological progress.

We include the effects of the changing technology by writing the production function as

$$Y = AF(K, L),$$

[10] *Mathematical note:* To see that this is equivalent to the previous equation, note that we can multiply both sides of this equation by Y and thereby cancel Y from three places in which it appears. We can cancel the K in the top and bottom of the first term on the right-hand side and the L in the top and bottom of the second term on the right-hand side. These algebraic manipulations turn this equation into the previous one.

where A is a measure of the current level of technology called *total factor productivity*. Output now increases not only because of increases in capital and labour but also because of increases in total factor productivity. If total factor productivity increases by 1 percent and if the inputs are unchanged, then output increases by 1 percent.

Allowing for a changing technology adds an additional term to our equation accounting for economic growth:

$$\frac{\Delta Y}{Y} = \alpha \frac{\Delta K}{K} + (1 - \alpha)\frac{\Delta L}{L} + \frac{\Delta A}{A}$$

Growth in = Contribution + Contribution + Growth in Total
Output   of Capital   of Labour   Factor Productivity.

This is the key equation of growth accounting. It identifies and allows us to measure the three sources of growth: changes in the amount of capital, changes in the amount of labour, and changes in total factor productivity.

Because total factor productivity is not observable directly, it is measured indirectly. We have data on the growth in output, capital, and labour; we also have data on capital's share of output. From these data and the growth-accounting equation, we can compute the growth in total factor productivity to make sure that everything adds up:

$$\frac{\Delta A}{A} = \frac{\Delta Y}{Y} - \alpha \frac{\Delta K}{K} - (1 - \alpha)\frac{\Delta L}{L}.$$

$\Delta A/A$ is the change in output that cannot be explained by changes in inputs. Thus, the growth in total factor productivity is computed as a residual—that is, as the amount of output growth that remains after we have accounted for the determinants of growth that we can measure. Indeed, $\Delta A/A$ is sometimes called the *Solow residual*, after Robert Solow, who first showed how to compute it.[11]

Total factor productivity can change for many reasons. Changes most often arise because of increased knowledge about production methods. The Solow residual is often used as a measure of technological progress. Yet other factors, such as education and government regulation, can affect total factor productivity as well. For example, if higher public spending raises the quality of education, then workers may become more productive and output may rise, which implies higher total factor productivity. As another example, if government regulations require firms to purchase capital to reduce pollution or increase worker safety, then the capital stock may rise without any increase in measured output, which implies lower total factor productivity. *Total factor productivity captures anything that changes the relation between measured inputs and measured output.*

---

[11] Robert M. Solow, "Technical Change and the Aggregate Production Function," *Review of Economics and Statistics* 39 (1957): 312–320. One might ask how growth in labour efficiency E relates to growth in total factor productivity. One can show that $\Delta A/A = (1 - \alpha)\Delta E/E$, where α is capital's share.

The Sources of Growth in Canada

Having learned how to measure the sources of economic growth, we now consider the data. On average, since the start of this century, Canadian output has grown at an annual rate of approximately 3 percent. Roughly speaking, over the same period, labour and capital have annually grown at 1 percentage point and 3 percentage points, respectively. Taking α at 0.33, we can provide rough estimates of the contribution to output growth of its three main determinants—growth in the labour input, growth in the capital input, and technological change. (The contribution of the latter is calculated as the residual.) Table 4-1A shows the results.

We see that about 44 percent of the increase in Canadian output has been due to increases in productivity. More detailed estimates of this breakdown and evidence for subperiods within the century are available.[12] These studies show that the contribution of increased productivity to growth has been as low as 23 percent and as high as 69 percent (in particular periods), but the average is the 44 percent that we have calculated above. It is in recent decades that the contribution of productivity growth has been the smallest. This means that Canada's slower average growth rate during the last quarter-century has more to do with slower productivity growth than it does with a drop in the level of investment in new capital equipment. This fact makes it difficult to argue that all Canada needs to return to more rapid growth is to increase the rate of saving and investment spending.

Table 4-1A	Accounting for Economic Growth in Canada		
			Output Growth
Sources of Growth	$(\Delta Y/Y)$	3.00	3.00
Labour	$(1-\alpha)\,(\Delta L/L)$	(0.067) (1)	0.67
Capital	$\alpha(\Delta K/K)$	(0.33) (3)	0.99
Total Factor Productivity	$(\Delta A/A)$	(3.00 − 0.67 − 0.99)	1.34

Source: Authors' calculations.

[12] Michael Denny and Thomas Wilson, "Productivity and Growth: Canada's Competitive Roots," in *The Bell Canada Papers on Economic and Public Policy,* Vol. 1 (Kingston: John Deutsch Institute, 1993), 7–58; *Aggregate Productivity Measures* (Ottawa: Statistics Canada, 1989).

PROBLEMS AND APPLICATIONS

1. In the economy of Solovia, the owners of capital get two thirds of national income, and the workers receive one third.

   a. The men of Solovia stay at home performing household chores, while the women work in factories. If some of the men decided to start working outside of the home so that the labour force increased by 5 percent, what would happen to the measured output of the economy? Does labour productivity—defined as output per worker—increase, decrease, or stay the same? Does total factor productivity increase, decrease, or stay the same?

   b. In year 1, the capital stock was 6, the labour input was 3, and output was 12. In year 2, the capital stock was 7, the labour input was 4, and output was 14. What happened to total factor productivity between the two years?

2. Labour productivity is defined as Y/L, the amount of output divided by the amount of labour input. Start with the growth-accounting equation and show that the growth in labour productivity depends on growth in total factor productivity and growth in the capital–labour ratio. In particular, show that

$$\frac{\Delta(Y/L)}{Y/L} = \frac{\Delta A}{A} + \alpha \frac{\Delta(K/L)}{K/L}.$$

Hint: You may find the following mathematical trick helpful. If $z = wx$, then the growth rate of z is approximately the growth rate of w plus the growth rate of x. That is,

$$\Delta z/z \approx \Delta w/w + \Delta x/x.$$

3. Suppose an economy described by the Solow model is in a steady state with population growth n of 1.0 percent per year and technological progress g of 2.0 percent per year. Total output and total capital grow at 3.0 percent per year. Suppose further that the capital share of output is 0.3. If you used the growth-accounting equation to divide output growth into three sources—capital, labour, and total factor productivity—how much would you attribute to each source? Compare your results to the figures we found for Canada in Table 4-1A.

CHAPTER 5

Unemployment

Unemployed labour means human want in the midst of plenty.
This is the most challenging paradox of modern times.

Henry Wallace

Unemployment is the macroeconomic problem that affects individuals most directly and severely. For most people, the loss of a job means a reduced living standard and psychological distress. It is therefore no surprise that unemployment is a frequent topic of political debate. Some policymakers have used the "misery index"—the sum of the inflation and unemployment rates—to measure the health of the economy and the success or failure of economic policies.

Economists study unemployment to identify its causes and to help improve the public policies that affect the unemployed. Some of these policies, such as job training programs, assist people in regaining employment. Others, such as unemployment insurance, alleviate some of the economic hardships that the unemployed face. Still other policies affect the prevalence of unemployment inadvertently. For example, most economists believe that laws prescribing a high minimum wage lead to greater unemployment. By pointing out a policy's unintended side effects, economists can help policymakers to evaluate the various options.

In our previous discussion of the labour market, we ignored unemployment. In our study of national income in Chapter 3 and economic growth in Chapter 4, we simply assumed that the economy reaches full employment. In reality, of course, not everyone in the labour force has a job all the time: all free-market economies experience some unemployment.

Figure 5-1 presents the rate of unemployment—the percentage of the labour force unemployed—in Canada since 1950. The figure shows that there is always some unemployment, although the amount fluctuates from year to year. In this chapter we begin our study of unemployment by discussing why there is unemployment and what determines its level. We do not study the year-to-year fluctuations in the rate of unemployment until Part Three of this book, which examines short-run economic fluctuations. Here we examine the determinants of the **natural rate of unemployment**—the average rate of unemployment around which the economy fluctuates.

Figure 5-1

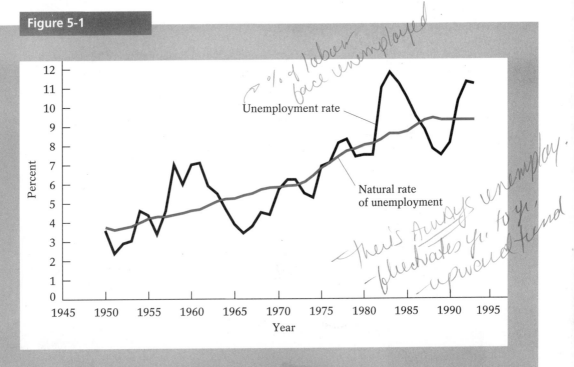

% of labour force unemployed

- there's always unemploy.
- fluctuates yr. to yr.
- upward trend

The Unemployment Rate and the Natural Rate of Unemployment in Canada There is always some unemployment. The natural rate of unemployment is the average level around which the unemployment rate fluctuates. (The natural rate of unemployment for any particular year is estimated here by averaging all the unemployment rates from 10 years earlier to 10 years later.)

Source: Reproduced and adapted by authority of the Minister of Industry, 1994, Statistics Canada. For details, see source line of Figure 1-3.

5•1 Job Loss, Job Finding, and the Natural Rate of Unemployment

Every day some workers lose or quit their jobs, and some unemployed workers are hired. This perpetual ebb and flow determines the fraction of the labour force that is unemployed. In this section we develop a model of labour force dynamics that shows what determines the natural rate of unemployment.[1]

Let L denote the labour force, E the number of employed workers, and U the number of unemployed workers. Because every worker is either employed or unemployed,

$$L = E + U.$$

LABOUR FORCE = EMPLOYED + UNEMPLOYED

[1] Robert E. Hall, "A Theory of the Natural Rate of Unemployment and the Duration of Unemployment," *Journal of Monetary Economics* 5 (April 1979): 153–169.

⊛ $\frac{U}{L}$ = unemploy rate

The labour force is the sum of the employed and the unemployed. The rate of unemployment is U/L.

To focus on the determinants of unemployment, we assume that the size of the labour force is fixed. The transition of individuals between employment and unemployment is illustrated in Figure 5-2. Let s denote the rate of job separation, the fraction of employed individuals who lose their job each month. Let f denote the rate of job finding, the fraction of unemployed individuals who find a job each month. We assume that both these rates are constant, and we see how together they determine the rate of unemployment.

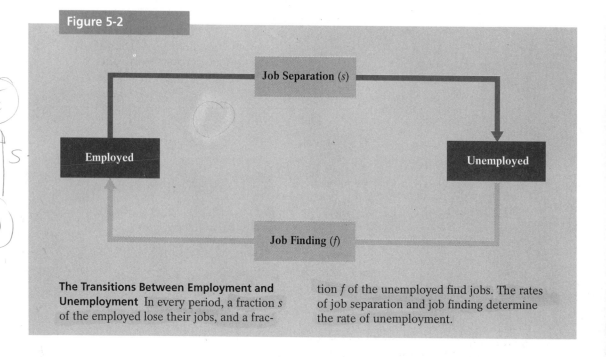

Figure 5-2

The Transitions Between Employment and Unemployment In every period, a fraction s of the employed lose their jobs, and a fraction f of the unemployed find jobs. The rates of job separation and job finding determine the rate of unemployment.

If the rate of unemployment is neither rising nor falling—that is, if the labour market is in a steady state—then the number of people finding jobs must equal the number of people losing jobs. Because fU is the number of people finding jobs and sE the number of people losing jobs, these two values must be equal:

$$fU = sE.$$

We can rearrange this equation to find the steady-state unemployment rate. Note that $E = L - U$, that is, the number of employed equals the labour force minus the number of unemployed. This implies that

$$fU = s(L - U).$$

⊛ $E = L - U$.

Divide both sides of this equation by L to obtain

$$f\frac{U}{L} = s\left(1 - \frac{U}{L}\right).$$

Then solve for U/L to find

[handwritten: Steady state unemployment]

$$\frac{U}{L} = \frac{s}{s+f}.$$

[handwritten: $\uparrow s = \uparrow \frac{U}{L}$ $\uparrow f = \downarrow U/L$]

This equation states that the rate of unemployment U/L depends on the rates of job separation s and job finding f. The higher the rate of job separation, the higher the unemployment rate. The higher the rate of job finding, the lower the unemployment rate.

Here's a numerical example. Suppose that 1 percent of the employed lose their jobs each month ($s = 0.01$), which implies that the average job lasts 100 months, or about 8 years. Suppose further that about 20 percent of the unemployed find a job each month ($f = 0.20$), which implies that the average spell of unemployment lasts 5 months. In this case, the steady-state rate of unemployment is:

$$\frac{U}{L} = \frac{0.01}{0.01 + 0.20}$$

$$= 0.0476.$$

The rate of unemployment in this example is about 5 percent.

This model of the natural rate of unemployment has an obvious but important implication for public policy. *Any policy aimed at lowering the natural rate of unemployment must either reduce the rate of job separation or increase the rate of job finding. Similarly, any policy that affects the rate of job separation or job finding also changes the natural rate of unemployment.*

[margin handwritten: ∴ any policy that wants to lower U/L must either ① ↓ s a ② ↑ f, (not instantaneous)]

Although this model is useful in relating the unemployment rate to job separation and job finding, it does not answer a central question: Why is there unemployment in the first place? If a person could always find a job quickly, then the rate of job finding would be very high, and the rate of unemployment would be near zero. This model of the unemployment rate assumes that job finding is not instantaneous, but it fails to explain why. In the next two sections, we examine two underlying reasons for unemployment: job search and wage rigidity.

[handwritten: 2 Reasons for Unemployment ① job search ② wage rigidity.]

5·2 Job Search and Frictional Unemployment

One reason for unemployment is that it takes time to match workers and jobs. The equilibrium model of the aggregate labour market discussed in Chapter 3 assumes that all workers and all jobs are identical, and therefore that all workers are equally well suited for all jobs. If this were really true and the labour market were in equilibrium, then a job loss would not cause unemployment: a laid-off worker would immediately find a new job at the market wage.

In fact, workers have different preferences and abilities, and jobs have different attributes. Furthermore, the flow of information about job candidates and job vacancies is imperfect, and the geographic mobility of workers is not instantaneous. Searching for an appropriate job takes time and effort. Indeed, because different jobs require different skills and pay different wages, unemployed workers may not accept the first job offer they receive. The unemployment caused by the time it takes workers to search for a job is called **frictional unemployment**.

Some frictional unemployment is inevitable in a changing economy. For numerous reasons, the types of goods that firms and households demand vary over time. As the demand for goods shifts, so does the demand for the labour that produces those goods. The invention of the personal computer, for example, reduced the demand for typewriters and, as a result, for labour by typewriter manufacturers. At the same time, it increased the demand for labour in the electronics industry. Similarly, because different regions produce different goods, the demand for labour may be rising in one part of the country while it is falling in another. An increase in the price of oil may cause the demand for labour to rise in an oil-producing province such as Alberta and fall in an auto-producing province such as Ontario. Economists call such a change in the composition of demand among industries or regions a **sectoral shift**. Because sectoral shifts are always occurring, and because it takes time for workers to change sectors, there is always frictional unemployment.

Sectoral shifts are not the only cause of job separation and frictional unemployment. In addition, workers find themselves unexpectedly out of work when their firm fails, when their job performance is deemed unacceptable, or when their particular skills are no longer needed. Workers also may quit their jobs to change careers or to move to different parts of the country. As long as the supply and demand for labour among firms is changing, frictional unemployment is unavoidable.

Public Policy and Frictional Unemployment

Many public policies seek to decrease the natural rate of unemployment by reducing frictional unemployment. Government employment agencies disseminate information about job vacancies in order to match jobs and workers more efficiently. Public retraining programs are designed to ease the transition of workers from declining to growing industries. To the extent that these programs increase the rate of job finding, they decrease the natural rate of unemployment.

Other government programs inadvertently increase the amount of frictional unemployment. One of these is **unemployment insurance**. Under this program, unemployed workers can collect a fraction of their wages for a certain period after losing their jobs. Although the precise terms of the program differ from year to year and from region to region, a typical worker covered by unemployment insurance in Canada has received about 57 percent of his or her former wages for up to one year. Canada's insurance system has been one of the most generous in the world.

[handwritten margin note top: ↓ UI ↑ frictional unemployment blc: a) ↓ hardship of unemply b) less pressed to search for new jobs c) more likely to turn down unattractive jobs d) less likely to seek guaranteed jobs (blc have UI) ∴ ↑ S.]

By softening the economic hardship of unemployment, unemployment insurance increases the amount of frictional unemployment and raises the natural rate. The unemployed who receive unemployment-insurance benefits are less pressed to search for new employment, and they are more likely to turn down unattractive job offers. This reduces the rate of job finding. In addition, when negotiating employment agreements, workers are less likely to seek guarantees of job security, because they know that unemployment insurance will partially protect their incomes. This raises the rate of job separation.

[handwritten margin note left: Benefits: But ↓ uncertainty ↑ helps find better job match by inducing workers to reject 1st offered job]

That unemployment insurance raises the natural rate of unemployment does not necessarily imply that the policy is undesirable. The program has the benefit of reducing workers' uncertainty about their income. Moreover, inducing workers to reject unattractive job offers may lead to a better matching between workers and jobs. Evaluating the costs and benefits of different systems of unemployment insurance is a difficult task that continues to be a topic of much research.

Economists who study unemployment insurance often propose ways to reform the system in order to reduce the amount of unemployment. One common proposal is to require a firm that lays off a worker to pay for that worker's unemployment benefits in full. Such a system is called *100 percent experience rated*, because the rate that each firm pays for unemployment insurance fully reflects the unemployment experience of its own workers. The programs in many countries are *partially experience rated*. Under this system, when a firm lays off a worker, it is charged only part of the worker's unemployment benefits; the remainder comes from the program's general revenue. Because a firm pays only a fraction of the cost of the unemployment it causes, it has an incentive to lay off workers when its demand for labour is temporarily low. Canada's system has no experience rating, so this incentive problem is acute. By reducing that incentive, the proposed reform may reduce the prevalence of temporary layoffs.

CASE STUDY

5·1 Interwar British Unemployment

Between World War I and World War II, Britain experienced persistently high unemployment. From 1920 to 1938 the unemployment rate in Britain averaged 14 percent and never fell below 9 percent.

Economists Daniel Benjamin and Levis Kochin have suggested that Britain's generous unemployment benefits can largely explain this high rate of unemployment. They cite three pieces of evidence to support their view. First, during this period, increases in British unemployment benefits coincided with increases in the economy's unemployment rate. Second, teenagers, who received few or no unemployment benefits, had much lower unemployment rates than adults. Third, when the benefits for married women were reduced in 1932, their unemployment rate dropped significantly relative to that for men. All three pieces of evidence suggest a connection between unemployment benefits and unemployment rates.

This explanation of interwar British unemployment is controversial among economists who study this period. One difficulty in interpreting the evidence is that the data on unemployment benefits and unemployment rates may reflect two different relationships—one economic and one political. On the one hand, the higher the level of benefits, the more likely it is that an unemployed person will turn down an unattractive job offer, and the higher the level of frictional unemployment. On the other hand, the higher the rate of unemployment, the more pressing unemployment becomes as a political issue, and the higher the level of benefits the government chooses to offer. Hence, high unemployment rates may have caused high unemployment benefits, rather than the other way around. When we observe an empirical relationship between unemployment rates and unemployment benefits, we cannot tell whether we have identified an economic connection, a political connection, or some combination of the two.[2]

CASE STUDY

5·2

Unemployment Insurance and the Rate of Job Finding

Another way to demonstrate the effect of unemployment insurance on job search is to examine how the economic incentives facing unemployed workers influence their rate of job finding. To do this, one needs to examine data on unemployed individuals, rather than data on economy-wide rates of unemployment. Individual data sometimes provide evidence that is less open to alternative interpretations.

One finding from individual data is that when unemployed workers become ineligible for unemployment insurance, the probability of their finding a new job rises markedly. Canadian evidence shows that the probability of an unemployed person finding employment varies—depending on how many weeks that person has been unemployed and how many weeks of unemployment insurance benefits remain. In the first few weeks after becoming unemployed, the probability of being employed is about 15 percent. Then, if the person remains unemployed, the probability of a job falls to quite a low number—3 percent or 4 percent after 20–25 weeks of unemployment. As the unemployment spell lasts even longer, however, the probability of work rises again—to the 12–13 percent range—as the exhaustion of unemployment insurance benefits is approached. Many economists interpret this evidence as verifying that at least some part of recorded unemployment is voluntary.[3]

More evidence in this vein comes from considering the regional dimensions of the Canadian unemployment system. The Canadian unemployment insurance program has been substantially more generous in the high-unemployment

---

[2] Daniel Benjamin and Levis Kochin, "Searching for an Explanation of Unemployment in Interwar Britain," *Journal of Political Economy* 87 (June 1979): 441–478. For critical comments on this article and a reply by the authors, see *Journal of Political Economy* 90 (April 1982): 369–436.

[3] Miles Corak, "Unemployment Insurance, Work Disincentives, and the Canadian Labour Market: An Overview," *Unemployment Insurance: How to Make It Work* (Toronto: C.D. Howe Institute, 1994): 117.

regions of the country. These differences have been mainly due to differences in what is called the *duration ratio*—the maximum number of weeks one can collect benefits relative to the minimum number of insurable earnings necessary to become eligible for any benefits. This ratio has varied between 26/14 in relatively low-unemployment provinces like Saskatchewan to 42/10 in relatively high-unemployment provinces like Newfoundland. Multiplying these duration ratios by the proportion of a worker's wage that could be received through unemployment insurance (0.57) generates an estimated wage subsidy that varies between 1.06 and 2.39. These values indicate the number of weeks of insurance benefits and leisure (at full pay) to which Canadians were entitled, for each week of work completed up to the minimum qualifying value (of 10 weeks or 14 weeks). Clearly, work disincentives were much greater in high-unemployment provinces. Many economists have concluded that the Canadian unemployment insurance system has exacerbated regional unemployment disparities by discouraging the migration of labour from high- to low-unemployment rate regions.

Additional evidence on how economic incentives affect job search comes from an American experiment that the state of Illinois ran in 1985. Randomly selected new claimants for unemployment insurance were each offered a $500 bonus if they found employment within 11 weeks. The subsequent experience of this group was compared to that of a control group not offered the incentive. The average duration of unemployment for the group that was offered the $500 bonus was 17.0 weeks, compared to 18.3 weeks for the control group. Thus, the bonus reduced the average spell of unemployment by 7 percent, suggesting that more effort was devoted to job search. This experiment shows clearly that the incentives provided by the unemployment-insurance system affect the rate of job finding.[4]

5•3 Real-Wage Rigidity and Wait Unemployment

A second reason for unemployment is **wage rigidity**—the failure of wages to adjust until labour supply equals labour demand. In the equilibrium model of the labour market, as outlined in Chapter 3, the real wage adjusts to equilibrate supply and demand. Yet wages are not always flexible. Sometimes the real wage is stuck above the market-clearing level.

Figure 5-3 shows why wage rigidity leads to unemployment. When the real wage is above the level that equilibrates supply and demand, the quantity of labour supplied exceeds the quantity demanded. Firms must in some way ration the scarce jobs among workers. Real-wage rigidity reduces the rate of job finding and raises the level of unemployment.

4 Stephen A. Woodbury and Robert G. Spiegelman, "Bonuses to Workers and Employers to Reduce Unemployment: Randomized Trials in Illinois," *American Economic Review* 77 (September 1987): 513–530.

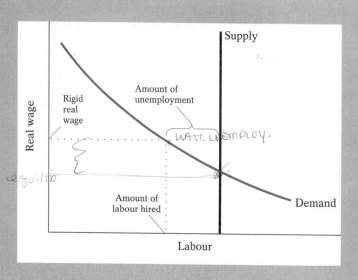

Real-Wage Rigidity Leads to Job Rationing If the real wage is stuck above the equilibrium level, then the supply of labour exceeds the demand. The result is unemployment.

(handwritten annotation in figure: WAIT. UNEMPLOY.; equilib)

The unemployment resulting from wage rigidity and job rationing is called **wait unemployment**. Workers are unemployed not because they are actively searching for the jobs that best suit their individual skills but because, at the going wage, the supply of labour exceeds the demand. These workers are simply waiting for jobs to become available.

To understand wage rigidity and wait unemployment, we must examine why the labour market does not clear. When the real wage exceeds the equilibrium level and the supply of workers exceeds the demand, we might expect firms to lower the wages they pay. Wait unemployment arises because firms fail to reduce wages despite an excess supply of labour. We now turn to three causes of this wage rigidity: minimum-wage laws, the monopoly power of unions, and efficiency wages.

(handwritten: ∴ Have wait Unemploy. blc don't ↓ wage. (3 causes) a) Min wge b) unions c) efficiency wages.)

Minimum-Wage Laws

The government causes wage rigidity when it prevents wages from falling to equilibrium levels. Minimum-wage laws set a legal minimum on the wages that firms pay their employees. For most workers, this minimum wage is not binding, because they earn well above the minimum. Yet for some workers, especially the unskilled and inexperienced, the minimum wage raises their wage above its equilibrium level. It therefore reduces the quantity of their labour that firms demand.

The minimum wage is often thought to have its greatest impact on teenage unemployment. The equilibrium wages of teenagers tend to be low for two reasons. First, because teenagers are among the least skilled and least experienced members of the labour force, they tend to have low marginal productivity. Second, teenagers often take some of their "compensation" in the

(handwritten margin notes, left side: supply > demand ∴ waiting for jobs @ real wage level (blc higher than equilib); Gov't sets wage rate. ∴ ↓ demand for labour by firms)

Min-wage has least greatest effect or few

form of on-the-job training rather than direct pay. An apprenticeship is a classic example of this. For both these reasons, the wage at which the supply of teenage workers equals the demand is low. The minimum wage is therefore more often binding for teenagers than for others in the labour force.

Many economists have studied the impact of the minimum wage on teenage employment. These researchers compare the variation in the minimum wage over time with the variation in the number of teenagers with jobs. These studies find that a 10 percent increase in the minimum wage reduces teenage employment by 1 to 3 percent.[5]

Canadian studies have reached similar conclusions. Estimates reported by the Ontario Ministry of Labour in 1989 showed that a 10 percent increase in the minimum wage eliminated 25,000 jobs. Also, economist Walter Block performed a cross-sectional study of provincial minimum-wage laws.[6] Back in 1985 when the study was done, Manitoba and Saskatchewan had the highest minimum-wage laws—some 15 percent above those provinces (British Columbia and Alberta) with the lowest legal minimums. Block compared all provinces according to the ratio of their youth unemployment rate to that of their prime-aged residents (those over 24 years old). By comparing this ratio of unemployment rates, rather than just youth unemployment rates directly, Block was trying to ensure that he was not focusing inadvertently on the differences across provinces that were due to influences other than the minimum wage. Block found that Manitoba and Saskatchewan had the highest youth unemployment ratios (2.9 times and 2.6 times the unemployment rate for prime-aged labour), while British Columbia and Alberta had the lowest youth unemployment ratios (1.9 times and 1.8 times the unemployment rate for prime-aged workers).

To mitigate the effects on teenage unemployment, some economists and policymakers have advocated exempting young workers from the regular minimum wage. This would permit a lower wage for teenagers, thereby reducing their unemployment and enabling them to get training and job experience. Opponents of this exemption argue that it gives firms an incentive to substitute teenagers for unskilled adults, thereby raising unemployment among that group.

CASE STUDY

5·3 **The Minimum Wage and the Working Poor**

The minimum wage is a perennial source of political debate. Advocates of a higher minimum wage view it as a means of raising the income of the working poor. Certainly, the minimum wage provides only a meager standard of living. In most provinces, a full-time worker receiving the minimum wage earns an income that is below the official poverty line.

---

[5] Charles Brown, "Minimum Wage Laws: Are They Overrated?" *Journal of Economic Perspectives* 2 (Summer 1988): 133–146.

[6] Walter Block, *The Fraser Forum* (Vancouver: The Fraser Institute August 1985): 4–5.

Opponents of a higher minimum wage argue that it is not the best way to help the working poor. They contend not only that the increased labour costs would raise unemployment, but also that the minimum wage is poorly targeted. Many minimum-wage earners are teenagers from middle-class homes working for discretionary spending money. Many economists and policymakers believe that tax credits provide a better way to help the working poor. A *refundable income tax credit* is an amount that poor working families are allowed to subtract from the taxes they owe. For a family with a very low income, the credit exceeds its taxes, and the family receives a payment from the government. Unlike the minimum wage, the refundable income tax credit does not raise labour costs to firms and, therefore, does not reduce the quantity of labour that firms demand. It has the disadvantage, however, of reducing the government's tax revenue.

Unions and Collective Bargaining

A second cause of wage rigidity is the monopoly power of unions. Table 5-1 shows the importance of unions in 12 major countries. In Canada, about one third of workers belong to unions. This rate of union membership is about twice that of the United States, but unions play a greater role in many European countries.

The wages of unionized workers are determined not by the equilibrium of supply and demand but by collective bargaining between union leaders and firm management. Often, the final agreement raises the wage above the equilibrium level and allows the firm to decide how many workers to employ. The

Table 5-1	Union Membership as a Percentage of Employment
Sweden	84
Denmark	75
Italy	47
United Kingdom	41
Australia	34
Canada	33
Germany	33
Netherlands	28
Switzerland	28
Japan	26
United States	16
France	11

Source: Clara Chang and Constance Sorrentino, "Union Membership Statistics in 12 Countries," *Monthly Labour Review* (December 1991): 46–53.

result is a reduction in the number of workers hired and an increase in wait un-employment.

Some evidence on the effects of unionization comes from comparing un-employment in different states south of the border. As one might expect, states with a more highly unionized labour force tend to have higher rates of unem-ployment. According to a study of data for 1985, an increase of 10 percentage points in the proportion of the labour force that is unionized increases the un-employment rate by 1.2 percentage points.[7]

Unions can also influence the wages paid by firms whose work forces are not unionized because the threat of unionization can keep wages above the equilibrium level. Most firms dislike unions. Unions not only raise wages but they also increase the bargaining power of labour on many other issues, such as hours of employment and working conditions. A firm may choose to pay its workers high wages to keep them happy in order to discourage them from forming a union.

The unemployment caused by unions and by the threat of unionization is an instance of conflict between different groups of workers—insiders and out-siders. Those workers already employed by a firm, the **insiders**, typically try to keep their firm's wages high. The unemployed, the **outsiders**, bear part of the cost of higher wages because at a lower wage they might have been hired. These two groups inevitably have conflicting interests. The effect of any bar-gaining process on wages and employment depends crucially on the relative in-fluence of each group.

The conflict between insiders and outsiders is resolved differently in dif-ferent countries. In some countries, such as in North America, wage bargaining takes place at the level of the firm or plant. In other countries, such as Sweden, wage bargaining takes place at the national level—with the government often playing a key role. Despite a highly unionized labour force, Sweden has had low unemployment at least until the 1990s. One possible explanation is that the centralization of wage bargaining and the role of the government in the bargaining process gives more influence to the outsiders, which keeps wages closer to the equilibrium level.[8]

CASE STUDY

5·4 **Unemployment in the United States and Canada**

Throughout the 1960s the United States and Canada had similar labour mar-kets. The rates of unemployment in the two countries were about the same on average, and they fluctuated together. In the mid-1970s, the experiences of the two countries began to diverge. Unemployment became much more prevalent in Canada than in the United States. Over the past decade, the Canadian un-employment rate has been about 2 to 3 percentage points above the U.S. un-

---

[7] Lawrence H. Summers, "Why Is the Unemployment Rate So Very High Near Full Employment?" *Brookings Papers on Economic Activity* (1986:2): 339–383.

[8] Michael Bruno and Jeffrey Sachs, *Economics of Worldwide Stagflation* (Cambridge, Mass.: Harvard University Press, 1985).

employment rate, and as this book goes to press, the gap has widened to 4 percentage points.

The changing roles of unions in the two countries is one possible explanation for this divergence. In the 1960s, about 30 percent of the labour force was unionized in each country. But Canadian labour laws did more to foster unionization than U.S. laws did. Unionization fell in the United States, while it did not in Canada.

As one might have predicted, changes in real wages accompanied the change in unionization. The real wage in Canada increased by about 30 percent relative to the real wage in the United States. This evidence suggests that unions in Canada have maintained the real wage further above the equilibrium level, leading to more wait unemployment.

The divergence in the two unemployment rates may also be attributable to the increase in the availability of unemployment-insurance benefits in Canada. Not only does unemployment insurance raise search times and the amount of frictional unemployment, but it also interacts with the effects of unionization

Figure 5-4

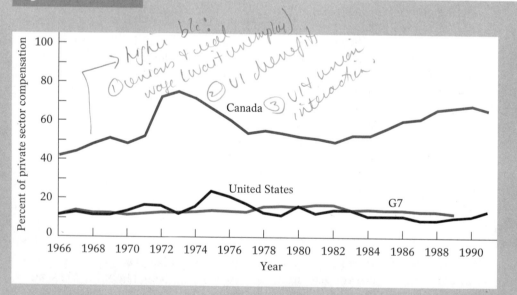

Generosity of Unemployment Benefits in the G7 Countries This graph shows what percent of a person's wages can be made up by unemployment insurance in several countries. Canada's unemployment insurance system is far more generous than the programs available in other G7 countries. (The G7 countries include the United States, Japan, Great Britain, France, Germany, Italy, and Canada.)

Source: *Canada's Economic Challenge: Background* (Ottawa: Department of Finance, 1994): 33.

in two ways. First, unemployment insurance makes unemployed workers more willing to wait for a high-wage job in a unionized firm, rather than take a lower-wage job in a nonunion firm. Second, since unemployment insurance partially protects the incomes of unemployed workers, it makes unions more willing to press for high wages at the expense of lower employment.[9]

The relative generosity of Canada's unemployment insurance system is shown in Figure 5-4. The data in this graph give conflicting messages concerning the role played by unemployment insurance in determining unemployment. On the one hand, Canada's insurance scheme is dramatically more generous than that of the United States. This fact is consistent with the proposition that the availability of unemployment insurance raises unemployment (since the U.S. unemployment rate is much lower than Canada's). On the other hand, Canada's insurance scheme is far more generous than that of the other Group of 7 (G7) countries (the United States, Japan, Great Britain, France, Germany, Italy, and Canada) as well, and the unemployment rate in the European countries of this group is just as high as it is in Canada.

Efficiency Wages (high wages make workers more production)

Efficiency-wage theories propose a third cause of wage rigidity in addition to minimum-wage laws and unionization. These theories hold that high wages make workers more productive. The influence of wages on worker efficiency may explain the failure of firms to cut wages despite an excess supply of labour. Even though a wage reduction would lower a firm's wage bill, it would also—if these theories are correct—lower worker productivity and the firm's profits.

There are various theories about how wages affect worker productivity. One efficiency-wage theory, which is applied mostly to poorer countries, holds that wages influence nutrition. Better-paid workers can afford a more nutritious diet, and healthier workers are more productive. A firm may decide to pay a wage above the equilibrium level to maintain a healthy work force. Obviously, this consideration is not important for employers in wealthy countries, such as Canada, the United States, and most of Europe, since the equilibrium wage is well above the level necessary to maintain good health.

A second efficiency-wage theory, which is more relevant for developed countries, holds that high wages reduce labour turnover. Workers quit jobs for many reasons—to accept better positions at other firms, to change careers, or to move to other parts of the country. The more a firm pays its workers, the greater their incentive to stay with the firm. By paying a high wage, a firm reduces the frequency of quits, thereby decreasing the time spent hiring and training new workers.

---

[9] Herbert G. Grubel, "Drifting Apart: Canadian and U.S. Labour Markets," *Contemporary Policy Issues* 6 (January 1988): 39–55, also in *Journal of Economic and Monetary Affairs* 2 (Winter 1988): 59–75.

↑ wages =
adverse
selection

   A third efficiency-wage theory holds that the average quality of a firm's
work force depends on the wage it pays its employees. If a firm reduces its
wage, the best employees may take jobs elsewhere, leaving the firm with inferior employees who have fewer alternative opportunities. Economists call
this unfavourable sorting *adverse selection*. By paying a wage above the equilibrium level, the firm may reduce adverse selection, improve the average quality of its work force, and thereby increase productivity.

↑ wage =
↑ workers
effort.

   A fourth efficiency-wage theory holds that a high wage improves worker
effort. This theory posits that firms cannot perfectly monitor their employees'
work effort, and that employees must themselves decide how hard to work.
Workers can choose to work hard, or they can choose to shirk and risk getting
caught and fired. Economists call this possibility of dishonest behaviour *moral
hazard*. The firm can reduce the problem of moral hazard by paying a high

↓ wage =
moral
hazard
(shirking)

wage. The higher the wage, the greater the cost to the worker of getting fired.
By paying a higher wage, a firm induces more of its employees not to shirk and
thus increases their productivity.

   All these efficiency-wage theories share the theme that the firm operates
more efficiently if it pays its workers a high wage. These theories imply that it is
sometimes in the firm's interest to keep wages above the equilibrium level. The
result of this wage rigidity is wait unemployment.[10]

CASE STUDY

5·5   Henry Ford's $5 Workday

In 1914 the Ford Motor Company started paying its workers $5 a day. Since
the prevailing wage at the time was between $2 and $3 a day, Ford's wage was
well above the equilibrium level. Not surprisingly, long lines of job-seekers
waited outside the Ford plant gates hoping for a chance to earn this high wage.

   What was Ford's motive? Henry Ford later wrote, "We wanted to pay
these wages so that the business would be on a lasting foundation. We were
building for the future. A low wage business is always insecure. . . . The payment of five dollars a day for an eight hour day was one of the finest cost cutting moves we ever made."

   From the standpoint of traditional economic theory, Ford's explanation
seems peculiar. He was suggesting that *high* wages imply *low* costs. But perhaps Ford had discovered efficiency-wage theory. Perhaps he was using the
high wage to increase worker productivity.

   Evidence suggests that paying such a high wage did benefit the company.
According to an engineering report written at the time, "The Ford high wage
does away with all the inertia and living force resistance. . . . The workingmen
are absolutely docile, and it is safe to say that since the last day of 1913, every

---

[10] For more extended discussions of efficiency wages, see Janet Yellen, "Efficiency Wage Models of Unemployment," *American Economic Review Papers and Proceedings* (May 1984): 200–205; Lawrence
Katz, "Efficiency Wages: A Partial Evaluation," *NBER Macroeconomics Annual* (1986): 235–276.

single day has seen m̲   ̲nteeism
fell by 75 percent, su̲   ̲evins, a
historian who studied   ̲d his as-
sociates freely decla̲   ̲licy had
turned out to be goo   ̲ved the
discipline of the worl   ̲stitution,
and raised their perso

[handwritten note: PF 139-145 Pattern of Unemployment not in fact → But Considered as part of required material]

5•4   Patterns o

We now turn to ̲   ̲facts will
help us to evaluate c̲.. ..̲   ̲ policies
aimed at reducing it.

The Duration of Unemployment

When a person becomes unemployed, is the spell of unemployment likely to be short or long? The answer to this question is important because it indicates the reasons for the unemployment and what policy response is appropriate. On the one hand, if most unemployment is short-term, one might argue that it is frictional and, perhaps, unavoidable. Unemployed workers may need some time to search for the job that is best suited to their skills and tastes. On the other hand, long-term unemployment cannot easily be attributed to the time it takes to match jobs and workers: we would not expect this matching process to take many months. Long-term unemployment is more likely to be wait unemployment. Thus, data on the duration of unemployment can affect our view about the reasons for unemployment.

[handwritten margin note: Short term = frictional unemploy]

In any one month, a lot of action takes place within Canada's labour market. Over the last 20 years, during an average month, about 1.1 million Canadians were unemployed. About 22 percent of these individuals became employed the next month, and another 17 percent left the labour force altogether. Of the two thirds that remained unemployed, it was typical for about one third of these to remain unemployed six months later. But changes have occurred in the makeup of the unemployed during this 20-year period. Compared to earlier times, a smaller proportion of unemployment is due to short unemployment spells spread across a large number of people, and a bigger proportion of the problem is due to a particular group of individuals' remaining unemployed longer. Policymakers speak in terms of the "incidence" of unemployment

[handwritten margin note: Long term = wait unemploy]

[11]   Jeremy I. Bulow and Lawrence H. Summers, "A Theory of Dual Labour Markets With Application to Industrial Policy, Discrimination, and Keynesian Unemployment," *Journal of Labour Economics* 4 (July 1986): 376–414; Daniel M. G. Raff and Lawrence H. Summers, "Did Henry Ford Pay Efficiency Wages?" *Journal of Labour Economics* 5 (October 1987, Part 2): S57–S86.

across the population being reduced but the "duration" of each unemployment spell having been increased. Canadian data for both incidence and duration are given in Figure 5-5. Statistics Canada estimates that about two thirds of an increase in unemployment rate is due to longer duration, and one third to higher incidence.[12]

Figure 5-5

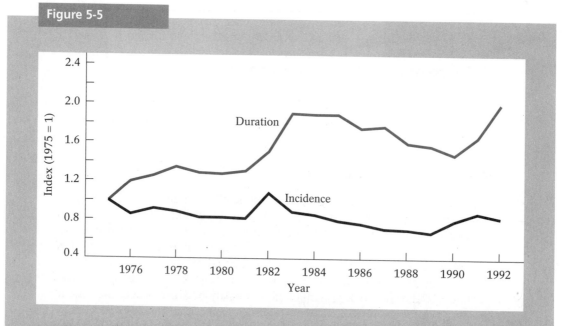

Duration and Incidence of Unemployment
Compared to earlier periods, a smaller proportion of unemployment in the 1990s is due to short spells of unemployment spread across many people, and a bigger proportion of unemployment is due to individuals' remaining out of work for a longer period.

Source: Canada's Economic Challenge: Background (Ottawa: Department of Finance, 1994): 31.

This evidence on the duration of unemployment has an important implication for public policy. If the goal is to lower substantially the rate of unemployment, policies must aim at the long-term unemployed, because these individuals are accounting for a larger amount of unemployment. Yet policies must be carefully targeted, because the long-term unemployed still constitute a minority of those who become unemployed at some point during the year. It is still the case that most people who become unemployed find work within a fairly short time.

[12] Mike Corak, "The Duration of Unemployment During Boom and Bust," *Canadian Economic Observer* (September 1993): 4.9.

Variation in the Unemployment Rate Across Age Groups and Regions

The rate of unemployment varies substantially across different groups within the population. Table 5-2 presents the unemployment rates for different age groups during the fall of 1992, the recent peak year for unemployment. While the country's overall unemployment rate was 11.3 percent in 1992, this unemployment was not equally distributed by age. The unemployment rate for teenagers was a full two-and-one-half times that of people in the 45–54 age category. Not surprisingly, education affects employment prospects as well. Over the last 20 years, the unemployment rate for those with only primary-level education has been 2.75 times that facing those with a university education. Most analysts expect this gap to widen in years to come.

Table 5-2	
Unemployment by Age Groups: October 1992	
Age	Unemployment Rate (%)
15–19	19.0
20–24	14.2
25–34	11.4
35–44	8.6
45–54	7.5
55–64	8.9
65 and over	5.4

Source: Statistics Canada, *Catalogue 71–001* (October 1992): B7.

To explain the differences in unemployment across age groups, recall our model of the natural rate of unemployment. The model isolates two possible causes for a high rate of unemployment: a low rate of job finding, or a high rate of job separation. When economists study data on the transition of individuals between employment and unemployment, they find that those groups with high unemployment tend to have high rates of job separation. They find less variation across groups in the rate of job finding.

These findings help explain the higher unemployment rates for younger workers. Younger workers have only recently entered the labour market, and they are often uncertain about their career plans. It may be best for them to try different types of jobs before making a long-term commitment to a specific occupation. If so, we should expect a higher rate of job separation and a higher rate of frictional unemployment for this group.

Varies a lot from above.

Finally, unemployment varies significantly across the Canadian regions, as is shown in Figure 5-6. This regional variation helps explain why it is difficult to reform the unemployment system, so that it operates as a true insurance policy, instead of being just a means for performing *ongoing* income redistribution. Without some other policies to support those in the depressed regions, many policymakers oppose changes and cuts in the current unemployment insurance system. There is a certain irony in this outcome. It is concern for the welfare of Canadians living in the depressed regions in the *short run* that keeps reforms to unemployment insurance from being implemented. Nevertheless, it hurts the welfare of those same individuals in the *long run* if unemployment insurance is not reformed. Without reform, these regions can never escape the long-run dependency trap.

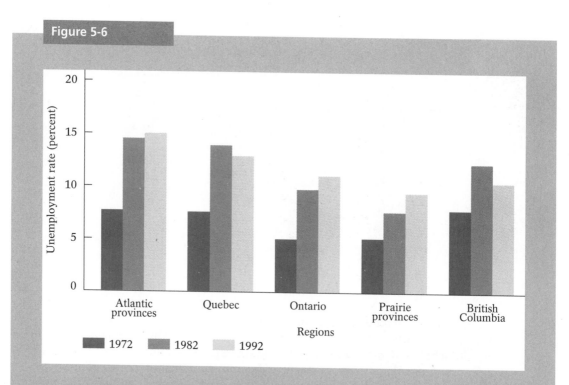

Figure 5-6

Unemployment Rate by Region: 1972 to 1992 Unemployment is much higher in the Atlantic provinces than it is in the rest of the country.

Source: Canada's Economic Challenge: Background (Ottawa: Department of Finance, 1994): 32.

The Upward Drift in Unemployment

Over the past 45 years, the rate of unemployment in Canada has drifted upward. As Figure 5-7 shows, unemployment averaged well below 5 percent in the 1950s and 1960s, and 8 percent in the 1970s and 1980s. In the early 1990s, the unemployment rate has averaged over 10 percent. Although economists do not have a conclusive explanation for this trend, they have proposed various hypotheses.

Figure 5-7

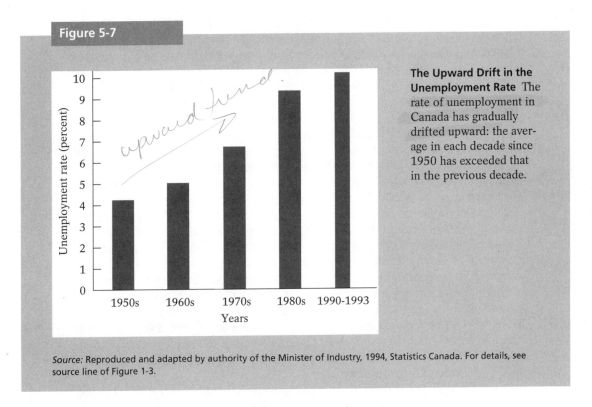

The Upward Drift in the Unemployment Rate The rate of unemployment in Canada has gradually drifted upward: the average in each decade since 1950 has exceeded that in the previous decade.

Source: Reproduced and adapted by authority of the Minister of Industry, 1994, Statistics Canada. For details, see source line of Figure 1-3.

One explanation stresses the changing composition of the Canadian labour force. After World War II, birth rates rose dramatically, producing a baby-boom generation that began entering the labour force around 1970. Because younger workers have higher unemployment rates, this influx of baby-boomers into the labour force increased the average level of unemployment. At roughly the same time, the participation of women in the labour force also was increasing significantly. Since 1966, the labour-force participation rate for women has risen from 35 percent to 58 percent. Since women historically have had higher unemployment rates than men (a difference that has disappeared since the early 1980s), the increasing proportion of women in the labour force may have raised the average unemployment rate, at least in the 1970s.

These two demographic changes, however, cannot fully explain the upward trend in unemployment because the trend also was apparent for fixed demographic groups. For example, for prime-aged males (men aged 25 years or more), the average unemployment rate rose from below 3 percent in the 1950s and 1960s to 4.2 percent in the 1970s, 7.1 percent in the 1980s, and 9.1 percent in the 1990s.

Another point to bear in mind is that some of the demographic shifts and microeconomic rigidities that can explain rising unemployment in the 1970s have since reversed—without a corresponding decrease in unemployment. For example, as a proportion of the population, the 15–24 age group has dropped from 26 percent of the population in the mid-1970s to under 18 percent in 1992. Also the *ratio* of the minimum wage to the average hourly wage available in Canada has *fallen* by 15 percent over this same period.[13]

A second possible explanation for the upward trend in unemployment is that sectoral shifts have become more prevalent. The greater the amount of sectoral reallocation, the greater the rate of job separation and the higher the level of frictional unemployment.[14] One source of sectoral shifts has been the increased pace of technological change involving robotics and major breakthroughs in the methods of information storage and transfer. Another series of sectoral shifts has resulted from the major shifts in natural resource prices. The world price of oil has been *far* more volatile since the mid-1970s, and the relative price of most of the natural resources that Canada exports has fallen by a factor of 50 percent since 1981. This vast deterioration in the terms of trade for all parts of the country except central Canada has very much hurt the profits of Canadian firms, and so limited their ability to create jobs. It is interesting to note that central Canada recovered from the recession of the 1980s almost as rapidly as did the United States. Canada's higher unemployment problem overall is concentrated in the rest of the country where the problem of sectoral shifts has been more pronounced.

In the end, the upward drift in the unemployment rate is probably the result of all these unrelated developments operating at the same time.

Transitions Into and Out of the Labour Force

So far we have been ignoring an important aspect of labour market dynamics: the movement of individuals into and out of the labour force. Our model of the

---

[13] Pierre Fortin, "Slow Growth, Unemployment and Debt: What Happened? What Can We Do?" in *The Bell Canada Papers on Economic and Public Policy* (Kingston: John Deutsch Institute for the Study of Economic Policy, 1994).

[14] David M. Lilien, "Sectoral Shifts and Cyclical Unemployment," *Journal of Political Economy* 90 (August 1982): 777–793.

natural rate of unemployment assumes that the labour force is fixed. In this case, the sole reason for unemployment is job separation, and the sole reason for leaving unemployment is job finding.

In fact, changes in the labour force are important. The fact that individuals enter and leave the labour force makes the unemployment statistics more difficult to interpret. On the one hand, some individuals calling themselves unemployed may not be seriously looking for a job and perhaps should best be viewed as out of the labour force. Their "unemployment" may not represent a social problem. On the other hand, some individuals, called **discouraged workers**, may want a job but, after an unsuccessful search, have given up looking. These discouraged workers are counted as being out of the labour force and do not show up in unemployment statistics. Even though their joblessness is unmeasured, it may nonetheless be a social problem.

It is important to have some idea of the magnitude of these unemployed who do not usually get measured. Periodically, Statistics Canada does a study that is much more extensive than the usual monthly labour force survey. Through these interviews, they can estimate the number of discouraged workers. Officials find that when these discouraged individuals are transferred from the "not in the labour force" category to the "unemployed" category, the unemployment rate rises by 1 percentage point. A further dimension adds to the "disguised unemployment" problem. All individuals who want to work full-time but who only have part-time jobs are counted as employed. One adjustment of the figures that can be made to accommodate this practice is to count half of these involuntary part-timers as unemployed. When this adjustment to the figures is made, it adds another full percentage point to the unemployment rate.

5•5 Conclusion

Unemployment represents wasted resources. Unemployed workers have the potential to contribute to national income but are not doing so. Those searching for jobs to suit their skills are happy when the search is over, and those waiting for jobs in firms that pay above-equilibrium wages are happy when positions open up.

Unfortunately, neither search unemployment nor wait unemployment can be easily reduced. The government cannot make job search instantaneous, nor can it easily bring wages closer to equilibrium levels. Zero unemployment is not a plausible goal for free-market economies.

Yet public policy is not powerless in the fight to reduce unemployment. Job-training programs, the unemployment-insurance system, the minimum wage, and the laws governing collective bargaining are often topics of political debate. The policies we choose are likely to have important effects on the prevalence of unemployment.

Summary

1. The natural rate of unemployment is the steady-state rate of unemployment. It depends on the rate of job separation and the rate of job finding.

2. Because it takes time for workers to search for the job that best suits their individual skills and tastes, some frictional unemployment is inevitable. Various government policies, such as unemployment insurance, alter the amount of frictional unemployment.

3. Wait unemployment results when the real wage remains above the level that equilibrates labour supply and labour demand. Minimum-wage legislation is one cause of wage rigidity. Another cause is unions and the threat of unionization. Finally, efficiency-wage theories suggest that, for various reasons, firms may find it profitable to keep wages high despite an excess supply of labour.

4. Whether we conclude that most unemployment is short-term or long-term depends on how we look at the data. Most spells of unemployment are short. Yet most weeks of unemployment are attributable to the small number of long-term unemployed.

5. The unemployment rates among demographic groups and among Canada's regions differ substantially. In particular, the unemployment rates for younger workers are much greater than for older workers. This difference results from a difference in the rate of job separation rather than from a difference in the rate of job finding. Unemployment in the Maritimes is very high, and this is largely due to a lower rate of job finding.

6. The unemployment rate has gradually drifted upward over the past 40 years. Various explanations have been proposed, including the changing demographic composition of the labour force and an increase in sectoral shifts.

KEY CONCEPTS

Natural rate of unemployment	Wait unemployment
Frictional unemployment	Insiders versus outsiders
Sectoral shift	Efficiency wage
Unemployment insurance	Discouraged workers
Wage rigidity	

QUESTIONS FOR REVIEW

1. What determines the natural rate of unemployment?

2. Describe the difference between frictional unemployment and wait unemployment.

3. Give three explanations for why the real wage may remain above the level that equilibrates labour supply and labour demand.

4. Is most unemployment long-term or short-term? Explain your answer.

5. How do economists explain the up-ward drift in the rate of unemployment over the past 40 years?

PROBLEMS AND APPLICATIONS

1. Answer the following questions about your own experience in the labour force:

a. When you or one of your friends is looking for a part-time job, how many weeks does it typically take? After you find a job, how many weeks does it typically last?

b. From your estimates, calculate (in a rate per week) your rate of job finding f and your rate of job separation s. (*Hint:* If f is the rate of job finding, then the average spell of unemployment is $1/f$.)

c. What is the natural rate of unemployment for the population you represent?

2. In this chapter we saw that the steady-state rate of unemployment is $U/L = s/(s + f)$. Suppose that the unemployment rate does not begin at this level. Show that unemployment will evolve over time and reach this steady state. (*Hint:* Express the change in the number of unemployed as a function of s, f, and U. Then show that if unemployment is above the natural rate, unemployment falls, and if unemployment is below the natural rate, unemployment rises.)

3. Some economists who have studied differences across countries in labour markets have suggested that the relationship between unemployment and unionization resembles an inverted letter "U." That is, they find that the natural rate of unemployment is low if unionization is very low or very high, and that intermediate levels of unionization lead to the highest rates of unemployment. Why might this be true?

4. Suppose that a country experiences a reduction in productivity—that is, an adverse shock to the production function.

a. What happens to the labour demand curve?

b. How would this change affect the labour market—that is, employment, unemployment, and real wages—if the labour market were always in equilibrium?

c. How would this change affect the labour market if unions constrained real wages to remain unaltered?

5. In any city at any time, some of the stock of usable office space is vacant. This vacant office space is unemployed capital. How would you explain this phenomenon? Is it a social problem?

CHAPTER 6

Money and Inflation

*Lenin is said to have declared that the best way to destroy the Capi-
talist System was to debauch the currency. . . . Lenin was certainly
right. There is no subtler, no surer means of overturning the existing
basis of society than to debauch the currency. The process engages
all the hidden forces of economic law on the side of destruction, and
does it in a manner which not one man in a million is able to diagnose.*

John Maynard Keynes

In 1950, a shopping cart of groceries could be purchased for $25 and the aver-
age wage in Canada was $1.04 per hour. In 1991, that same cart of groceries
cost $147 and the average wage had climbed to over $13 per hour.[1] This overall increase in prices is called **inflation**, and it is the subject of this chapter.

The rate of inflation—the percentage change in the overall level of prices—
varies substantially over time and across countries. In Canada, prices rose an
average of 2.9 percent per year in the 1960s, 7.8 percent per year in the 1970s,
and 5.7 percent per year in the 1980s. Inflation in Canada has, by international
standards, been moderate. In Israel in the early 1980s, prices increased over
100 percent every year. In Germany between December 1922 and December
1923, prices rose an average of 500 percent per month. Such an episode of extraordinarily high inflation is called a **hyperinflation**.

Many people consider inflation a major social problem. In this chapter we
examine the causes, effects, and social costs of inflation. Because inflation is
the increase in the price level, we begin our study by examining how prices are
determined. A price is the rate at which money is exchanged for a good or a
service. To understand prices, we must understand money—what it is, what affects its supply and demand, and what influence it has on the economy. This
chapter is an introduction to a branch of economics called *monetary economics.*

The "hidden forces of economic law" that lead to inflation are not as
mysterious as suggested in the quotation that opens this chapter. Section 6•1
begins our analysis of inflation by discussing the economist's concept of
"money" and how, in our economy, the government controls the number
of dollars in the hands of the public. Section 6•2 shows that the quantity of
money determines the price level, and that the rate of growth in the quantity
of money determines the rate of inflation.

Inflation in turn has numerous effects of its own on the economy. Section

[1] Patrick Luciani, *Economic Myths: Making Sense of Canadian Policy Issues* (Toronto: Addison-Wesley
Publishers, 1991): 196.

6•3 discusses the revenue that the government raises by printing money, sometimes called the *inflation tax*. Section 6•4 examines how inflation affects the nominal interest rate. Section 6•5 discusses how the nominal interest rate in turn affects the quantity of money people wish to hold and, thereby, the price level. All of these issues come into play when a government faces the formidable task of ending a hyperinflation.

After completing our analysis of the causes and effects of inflation, in Section 6•6 we address what is perhaps the most important question about inflation: Is it a major social problem? Does inflation really amount to "overturning the existing basis of society"?

6•1   What Is Money?

When we say that a person has a lot of money, we usually mean that he or she is wealthy. By contrast, economists use the term **money** in a more specialized way. To an economist, money does not refer to all wealth but only to one type of it. *Money is the stock of assets that can be readily used to make transactions*. Roughly speaking, the dollars in the hands of the public make up the nation's stock of money.

The Functions of Money

Money has three purposes. It is a store of value, a unit of account, and a medium of exchange.

As a **store of value,** money is a way to transfer purchasing power from the present to the future. If I work today and earn $100, I can hold the money and spend it tomorrow, next week, or next month. Of course, money is an imperfect store of value: if prices are rising, the real value of money is falling. Even so, people hold money because they can trade the money for goods and services at some time in the future.

As a **unit of account,** money provides the terms in which prices are quoted and debts are recorded. Microeconomics teaches us that resources are allocated according to relative prices—the prices of goods relative to other goods—yet stores post their prices in dollars and cents. A car dealer tells you that a car costs $12,000, not 400 shirts (even though it may amount to the same thing). Similarly, most debts require the debtor to deliver a specified number of dollars in the future, not a specified amount of some commodity. Money is the yardstick with which we measure economic transactions.

As a **medium of exchange,** money is what we use to buy goods and services. "This note is legal tender" is printed on Canadian bills. When we walk into stores, we are confident that the shopkeepers will accept our money in exchange for the items they are selling.

To better understand the functions of money, try to imagine an economy without it: a barter economy. In such a world, trade requires the **double coincidence of wants**—the unlikely happenstance of two people each having a good that the other wants at the right time and place to make an exchange. A barter economy permits only simple transactions.

Money makes more indirect transactions possible. A professor uses her salary to buy books; the book publisher uses its revenue from the sale of books to buy paper; the paper company uses its revenue from the sale of paper to pay the lumberjack; the lumberjack uses his income to send his child to university; and the university uses its tuition receipts to pay some of the professor's salary. In a complex, modern economy, trade is usually indirect and requires the use of money.

The Types of Money

Money takes many forms. In the Canadian economy we make transactions with an item whose sole function is to act as money: dollars. These coins and pieces of paper would have little value if they were not widely accepted as money. Money that has no intrinsic value is called **fiat money**, since it is established as money by government decree.

Although fiat money is the norm in most economies today, historically most societies have used for money a commodity with some intrinsic value, called **commodity money**.

Gold is the most widespread example of commodity money. An economy in which gold serves as money is said to be on a **gold standard**. Gold is a form of commodity money because it can be used for various purposes—jewelry, dental fillings, etc.—as well as for transactions. The gold standard was common throughout the world during the late nineteenth century.

"And how would you like your funny money?"

Drawing by Bernard Schoenbaum; © 1979
The New Yorker Magazine, Inc.

CASE STUDY

6•1   Money in a POW Camp

An unusual form of commodity money developed in the Nazi prisoner of war (POW) camps during World War II. The Red Cross supplied the prisoners with various goods—food, clothing, cigarettes, and so on. Yet these rations were allocated without close attention to personal preferences, so naturally the allocations were often inefficient. One prisoner may have preferred chocolate, while another may have preferred cheese, and a third may have wanted a new shirt. The differing tastes and endowments of the prisoners led them to trade with one another.

Barter proved to be an inconvenient way to allocate these resources, however, because it required the double coincidence of wants. In other words, a barter system was not the easiest way to ensure that each prisoner received the goods he valued most. Even the limited economy of the POW camp needed some form of money to facilitate transactions.

Eventually, cigarettes became the established "currency" in which prices were quoted and with which trades were made. A shirt, for example, cost about 80 cigarettes. Services were also quoted in cigarettes: some prisoners offered to do other prisoners' laundry for 2 cigarettes per garment. Even nonsmokers were happy to accept cigarettes in exchange, knowing they could trade the cigarettes in the future for some good they did enjoy. Within the POW camp the cigarette became the store of value, the unit of account, and the medium of exchange.[2] The use of cigarettes as money is not limited to this example. In the Soviet Union in the late 1980s, packs of Marlboros were preferred to the ruble in the large underground economy.

How Fiat Money Evolves

It is not surprising that some form of commodity money arises to facilitate exchange: people are willing to accept a commodity currency such as gold because it has intrinsic value. The development of fiat money, however, is more perplexing. What would make people begin to value something that is intrinsically useless?

To understand how the evolution from commodity money to fiat money takes place, imagine an economy in which people carry around bags of gold. When a purchase is made, the buyer measures out the appropriate amount of gold. If the seller is convinced that the weight and purity of the gold are right, the buyer and seller make the exchange.

The government first intervenes to reduce transaction costs. Using raw gold as money is costly because it takes time to verify the purity of the gold and to measure the correct quantity. To help reduce these costs, the government mints gold coins of known purity and weight. The coins are easier to use than gold bullion because their values are widely recognized. The next step is for the government to issue gold certificates—pieces of paper that can be redeemed for a certain quantity of gold. If people believe the government's promise to pay, these bills are just as valuable as the gold itself. In addition, because the bills are lighter than the gold, they are easier to use in transactions. Eventually, no one carries gold around at all, and these gold-backed government bills become the monetary standard.

Finally, the gold backing becomes irrelevant. If no one ever bothers to redeem the bills for gold, no one cares if the option is abandoned. As long as everyone continues to accept the paper bills in exchange, they will have value and serve as money. Thus, the system of commodity money evolves into a system of fiat money.

---

[2] R.A. Radford, "The Economic Organization of a P.O.W. Camp," *Economica* (November 1945): 189–201.

CASE STUDY

6•2

Money on the Island of Yap

The economy of Yap, a small island in the Pacific, once had a type of money that was something between commodity and fiat money. The traditional medium of exchange in Yap was *fei*, stone wheels up to 12 feet in diameter. These stones had holes in the center so that they could be carried on poles and used for exchange.

Large stone wheels are not a convenient form of money. The stones were heavy, so it took substantial effort for a new owner to take his *fei* home after completing a bargain. Although the monetary system facilitated exchange, it did so at great cost.

Eventually, it became common practice for the new owner of the *fei* not to bother to take physical possession of the stone. Instead, the new owner merely accepted a claim to the *fei* without moving it. In future bargains, he traded this claim for goods that he wanted. Having physical possession of the stone became less important than having legal claim to it.

This practice was put to a test when an extremely valuable stone was lost at sea during a storm. Because the owner lost his money by accident rather than through negligence, it was universally agreed that his claim to the *fei* remained valid. Even generations later, when no one alive had ever seen this stone, the claim to this *fei* was still valued in exchange.[3]

How the Quantity of Money Is Controlled

The quantity of money available is called the **money supply**. In an economy that uses commodity money, the money supply is the quantity of that commodity. In an economy that uses fiat money, such as most economies today, the government controls the supply of money: legal restrictions give the government a monopoly on the printing of money. Just as the level of taxation and the level of government purchases are policy instruments of the government, so is the supply of money.

In Canada and many other countries, the control of the money supply is delegated to a partially independent institution called the **central bank**. The central bank of Canada is the **Bank of Canada**. If you look at Canadian paper currency, you will see that each bill is signed by the Governor of the Bank of Canada, who is appointed by the federal cabinet for a term of seven years. The Governor and the Minister of Finance together decide on the money supply. The control of the money supply is called **monetary policy**.

Ultimately, the power to make monetary policy decisions rests with the federal cabinet. The Minister of Finance communicates the overall desires of the government to the Governor of the Bank, and the Governor is left to implement those broad instructions on a day-to-day basis. If the Governor feels

---

[3] Norman Angell, *The Story of Money* (New York: Frederick A. Stokes Company, 1929): 88–89.

that the government's instructions represent an inappropriate policy that he or she does not wish to implement, the Governor must resign. But the Governor has significant power, since the resignation must be preceded by a formal directive—a written document in which the government makes quite explicit what it wants done. Thus, both the resignation and the details of the disagreement between the government and a respected banker become very public. Governments do not want to force a Governor's resignation unless they are sure that they can defend their views on monetary policy under heavy scrutiny. The Governor of the Bank can use this power to influence policy.

The primary way in which the Bank of Canada controls the supply of money is through **open-market operations**—the purchase and sale of government bonds (mostly short-term bonds called treasury bills). To increase the supply of money, the Bank of Canada uses dollars to buy government bonds from the public. This purchase increases the quantity of dollars in circulation. To decrease the supply of money, the Bank of Canada sells some of its government bonds. This open-market sale of bonds takes some dollars out of the hands of the public.

In Chapter 18 we discuss in detail how the Bank of Canada controls the supply of money by influencing the chartered banking system. In addition to buying and selling bonds, the Bank of Canada adjusts the size of the government's deposits at chartered banks. But for our current discussion, these details are not crucial. It is sufficient to assume that the Bank of Canada directly controls the supply of money.

How the Quantity of Money Is Measured

One of the goals of this chapter is to determine how the money supply affects the economy; we turn to that problem in the next section. As a background for that analysis, let's first discuss how economists measure the quantity of money.

Because money is the stock of assets used for transactions, the quantity of money is the quantity of those assets. In simple economies, this quantity is easily measured. In the POW camp, the quantity of money was the quantity of cigarettes in the camp. But how can we measure the quantity of money in more complex economies such as ours? The answer is not obvious, because no single asset is used for all transactions. People can use various assets to make transactions, although some assets are more convenient than others. This ambiguity leads to numerous measures of the quantity of money.

① The most obvious asset to include in the quantity of money is **currency**, the sum of outstanding paper money and coins. Most day-to-day transactions use currency as the medium of exchange.

② A second type of asset used for transactions is **demand deposits**, the funds people hold in their chequing accounts in chartered banks and other financial institutions, such as trust companies. If most sellers accept personal cheques, assets in a chequing account are almost as convenient as currency. In both cases, the assets are in a form ready to facilitate a transaction. Demand deposits are therefore added to currency when measuring the quantity of money.

Once we admit the logic of including demand deposits in the measured money stock, many other assets become candidates for inclusion. Funds in chartered bank savings accounts, for example, can be easily transferred into chequing accounts; these assets are almost as convenient for transactions. Further, funds in similar accounts in trust companies and the Caisses Populaires in Quebec can be easily used for transactions. Thus, they could be included in the quantity of money.

Table 6-1

The Measures of Money

Symbol	Assets Included	Amount in January 1994 (billions of dollars)
B	Currency plus chartered bank deposits at the Bank of Canada	$ 24.8
$M1$	Sum of currency in circulation, demand deposits, and other chequing deposits at chartered banks	54.0
$M2$	Sum of $M1$ plus personal savings deposits and nonpersonal notice deposits at chartered banks	344.1
$M3$	Sum of $M2$ plus fixed-term deposits of firms at chartered banks	409.3
$M2+$	Sum of $M2$ plus all deposits and shares at trust companies, mortgage loan companies, credit unions, and caisses populaires	578.8

Source: *Review* (Ottawa: Bank of Canada), Tables B1 and E1.

Since it is unclear exactly which assets should be included in the money stock, various measures are available. Table 6-1 presents the five measures of the money stock that the Bank of Canada calculates for the Canadian economy. Listed from the smallest to the largest, they are designated B, $M1$, $M2$, $M3$, and $M2+$. The most commonly used measures for studying the effects of money on the economy are $M1$ and $M2$. There is no consensus, however, about which measure of the money stock is best. Disagreements about monetary policy sometimes arise because different measures of money are moving in different directions. Luckily, the different measures normally move together and so tell the same story about whether the quantity of money is growing quickly or slowly.

6•2 The Quantity Theory of Money

Having defined what money is and described how it is controlled and measured, we can now examine how the quantity of money affects the economy. To do this, we must see how the quantity of money is related to other economic variables.

Transactions and the Quantity Equation

People hold money to buy goods and services. The more money they need for such transactions, the more money they hold. Thus, the quantity of money in the economy is closely related to the number of dollars exchanged in transactions.

The link between transactions and money is expressed in the following equation, called the **quantity equation:** *IDENTITY.*

$$\text{Money} \times \text{Velocity} = \text{Price} \times \text{Transactions}$$
$$M \quad \times \quad V \quad = \quad P \quad \times \quad T.$$

PT = # of dollars exchanged in 1 yr.

MV = amt. of money needed to make more transactions

Let's examine each of the four variables in this equation.

The right-hand side of the quantity equation tells us about transactions. T represents the total number of transactions during some period of time, say, a year. In other words, T is the number of times in a year that goods or services are exchanged for money. P is the price of a typical transaction—the number of dollars exchanged. The product of the price of a transaction and the number of transactions, PT, equals the number of dollars exchanged in a year.

The left-hand side of the quantity equation tells us about the money used to make the transactions. M is the quantity of money, and for this discussion, we do not need to be specific on how the money supply is measured. V is called the **transactions velocity of money** and measures the rate at which money circulates in the economy. In other words, velocity tells us the number of times a dollar bill changes hands in a given period of time.

For example, suppose that 60 loaves of bread are sold in a given year at $0.50 per loaf. Then T equals 60 loaves per year, and P equals $0.50 per loaf. The total number of dollars exchanged is

$$PT = \$0.50/\text{loaf} \times 60 \text{ loaves/year} = \$30.00/\text{year}.$$

The right-hand side of the quantity equation equals $30 per year, which is the dollar value of all transactions.

Suppose further that the quantity of money in the economy is $10. Then we can compute velocity as

$$V = PT/M$$
$$= (\$30/\text{year})/(\$10)$$
$$= 3 \text{ times per year}.$$

That is, for $30 of transactions per year to take place with $10 of money, each dollar must change hands 3 times per year.

The quantity equation is an *identity*: the definitions of the four variables make it true. The equation is useful because it shows that if one of the variables changes, one or more of the others must also change to maintain the equality. For example, if the quantity of money increases and the velocity of money stays unchanged, then either the price or the number of transactions must rise.

From Transactions to Income

Economists usually use a slightly different version of the quantity equation than the one just introduced. The problem with the first equation is that the number of transactions is difficult to measure. To solve this problem, the number of transactions T is replaced by the total output of the economy Y.

Transactions and output are closely related, because the more the economy produces, the more goods are bought and sold. They are not the same, however. When one person sells a used car to another person, for example, they make a transaction using money, even though the used car is not part of current output. Nonetheless, the dollar value of transactions is roughly proportional to the dollar value of output.

If Y denotes the amount of output and P denotes the price of one unit of output, then the dollar value of output is PY. We encountered measures for these variables when we discussed the national income accounts in Chapter 2: Y is real GDP, P the GDP deflator, and PY nominal GDP. The quantity equation becomes

$$\text{Money} \times \text{Velocity} = \text{Price} \times \text{Output}$$
$$M \times V = P \times Y.$$

Because Y is also total income, V in this version of the quantity equation is called the **income velocity of money**. The income velocity of money tells us the number of times a dollar bill enters someone's income in a given period of time. This version of the quantity equation is the most common, and it is the one we use from now on.

The Money Demand Function and the Quantity Equation

When analyzing how money affects the economy, it is often convenient to express the quantity of money in terms of the quantity of goods and services it can buy. This amount is M/P and is called **real money balances**.

Real money balances measure the purchasing power of the stock of money. For example, consider an economy that produces only bread. If the quantity of money is $10, and the price of a loaf is $0.50, then real money balances are 20 loaves of bread. That is, the stock of money in the economy is able to buy 20 loaves at current prices.

A **money demand function** is an equation that shows what determines the quantity of real money balances people wish to hold. A simple money demand function is

$$(M/P)^{\mathrm{d}} = kY,$$

where k is a constant. This equation states that the quantity of real balances demanded is proportional to real income.

The money demand function is like the demand function for a particular good. Here the "good" is the convenience of holding real money balances. Just as owning an automobile makes it easier for a person to travel, holding money makes it easier to make transactions. Therefore, just as higher income leads to a greater demand for automobiles, higher income also leads to a greater demand for real money balances.

From this money demand function, we can derive the quantity equation. To do so we add the condition that the demand for real balances $(M/P)^d$ must equal the supply M/P. Therefore,

$$M/P = kY.$$

A simple rearrangement of terms changes this equation into

$$M(1/k) = PY,$$

which can be written as

$$MV = PY,$$

where $V = 1/k$. Hence, when we use the quantity equation, we are assuming that the supply of real money balances equals the demand and that the demand is proportional to income.

The Assumption of Constant Velocity

We can view the quantity equation as merely defining velocity as the ratio of nominal GDP to the quantity of money. Yet we can turn the equation into a useful theory—called the **quantity theory of money**—by making the additional assumption that velocity is constant.

As with many of the assumptions in economics, we can justify the assumption of constant velocity only as an approximation. Velocity does change if the money demand function changes. For example, the introduction of the automatic teller machine allows people to reduce their average money holdings, which reduces the money demand parameter k; the machines raise the rate at which money circulates in the economy, which implies greater velocity V. Nonetheless, the assumption of constant velocity provides a good approximation in many situations. Let's therefore assume that velocity is constant and see what this assumption implies about the effects of the money supply on the economy.

Once we assume that velocity is constant, the quantity equation can be seen as a theory of nominal GDP. The quantity equation says

$$M\bar{V} = PY,$$

where the bar over V means that velocity is fixed. Therefore, a change in the quantity of money (M) must cause a proportionate change in nominal GDP (PY). That is, the quantity of money determines the dollar value of the economy's output.

Money, Prices, and Inflation

We now have a theory to explain what determines the economy's overall level of prices. The theory has three building blocks:

1. The factors of production and the production function determine the level of output Y. We borrow this conclusion from Chapter 3.

2. The money supply determines the nominal value of output PY. This conclusion follows from the quantity equation and the assumption that the velocity of money is fixed.

3. The price level P is then the ratio of the nominal value of output PY to the level of output Y.

In other words, the productive capability of the economy determines real GDP; the quantity of money determines nominal GDP; and the GDP deflator is the ratio of nominal GDP to real GDP.

This theory explains what happens when the Bank of Canada changes the supply of money. Because velocity is fixed, any change in the supply of money leads to a proportionate change in nominal GDP. Because the factors of production and the production function have already determined real GDP, the change in nominal GDP must represent a change in the price level. Hence, the quantity theory implies that the price level is proportional to the money supply.

Because the inflation rate is the percentage change in the price level, this theory of the price level is also a theory of the inflation rate. The quantity equation, written in percentage-change form, is

% Change in M + % Change in V = % Change in P + % Change in Y.

Consider each of these four terms. First, the percentage change in the quantity of money is under the control of the central bank. Second, the percentage change in velocity reflects shifts in money demand; we have assumed velocity is constant, so the percentage change in velocity is zero. Third, the percentage change in the price level is the rate of inflation; this is the variable in the equation that we would like to explain. Fourth, the percentage change in output depends on growth in the factors of production and on technological progress, which for our present purposes we can take as given. This analysis tells us that (except for a constant that depends on exogenous growth in real output) the growth in the money supply determines the rate of inflation.

Thus, the quantity theory of money states that the central bank, which controls the money supply, has the ultimate control over the rate of inflation. If the central bank keeps the money supply stable, the price level will be stable. If the central bank increases the money supply quickly, the price level will rise quickly.

CASE STUDY

6·3   **Inflation and Money Growth**

"Inflation is always and everywhere a monetary phenomenon." So wrote Milton Friedman, the great monetary economist who won the Nobel Prize for economics in 1976. The quantity theory of money leads us to agree that the growth in the quantity of money is the primary determinant of the inflation rate. Yet Friedman's claim is empirical, not theoretical. To evaluate his claim, and to judge the usefulness of our theory, we need to look at data on money and prices.

Friedman, together with fellow economist Anna Schwartz, wrote two treatises on monetary history that documented the sources and effects of changes in the quantity of money over the past century.[4]

Figure 6-1 uses some of their data and plots the average rate of money growth and the average rate of inflation in the United States over each decade

Figure 6-1

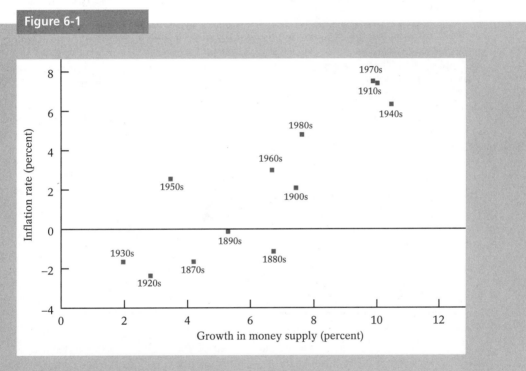

Historical Data on Inflation and Money Growth In this scatterplot of money growth and inflation, each point represents a decade. The horizontal axis shows the average growth in the money supply (as measured by *M*2) over the decade, and the vertical axis shows the average rate of inflation (as measured by the GDP deflator). The positive correlation between money growth and inflation is evidence for the quantity theory's prediction that high money growth leads to high inflation.

Source: For the data through the 1960s: Milton Friedman and Anna J. Schwartz, *Monetary Trends in the United States and the United Kingdom: Their Relation to Income, Prices, and Interest Rates 1867–1975* (Chicago: University of Chicago Press, 1982). For recent data: U.S. Department of Commerce, Federal Reserve Board.

---

[4] Milton Friedman and Anna J. Schwartz, *A Monetary History of the United States, 1867–1960* (Princeton, N.J.: Princeton University Press, 1963); Milton Friedman and Anna J. Schwartz, *Monetary Trends in the United States and the United Kingdom: Their Relation to Income, Prices, and Interest Rates, 1867–1975* (Chicago: University of Chicago Press, 1982).

since the 1870s. The data verify the link between growth in the quantity of money and inflation. Decades with high money growth tend to have high inflation, and decades with low money growth tend to have low inflation.

Figure 6-2 examines the same question with data from many more countries. It shows the average rate of inflation and the average rate of money growth in the decade of the 1980s in 34 countries. Again, the link between money growth and inflation is clear. Countries with high money growth tend to have high inflation, and countries with low money growth tend to have low inflation.

If we looked at monthly data on money growth and inflation, rather than decadal data, we would not see as close a connection between these two vari-

Figure 6-2

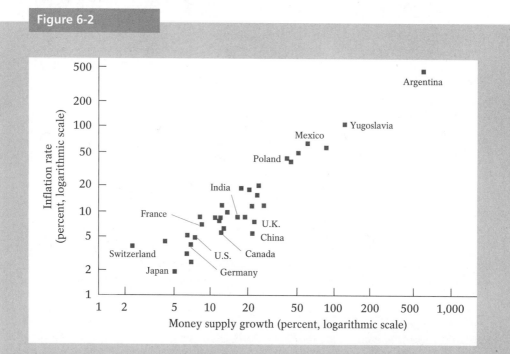

International Data on Inflation and Money Growth In this scatterplot, each point represents a country. The horizontal axis shows the average growth in the money supply (as measured by currency plus demand deposits) during the 1980s, and the vertical axis shows the average rate of inflation (as measured by the GDP deflator). Once again, the positive correlation is evidence for the quantity theory's prediction that high money growth leads to high inflation.

Source: International Financial Statistics.

Figure 6-3

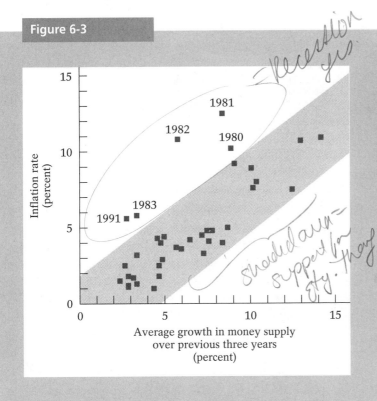

Annual Inflation and Money Growth Over the Previous Three Years In this scatterplot, each point represents an annual observation on both the percentage change in the CPI and the average growth in *M1* over the previous three years (Canadian data, 1957–1993). In all but the severe recession years of the early 1980s and 1990s, the fairly tight positive correlation is evidence that supports the quantity theory of inflation (even within quite a short time interval).

Source: Review (Ottawa: Bank of Canada).

ables. This is because real GDP is not independent of the money supply in the short run. Nevertheless, even when we graph the annual rate of inflation and the average rate of money growth in the previous three years (as in Figure 6-3), the longer-run relationship between money growth and inflation is clearly visible. Figure 6-3 is a scatter diagram showing Canadian data since 1957. Almost all of the annual observations are within the shaded region, indicating support for the quantity theory. The five observations that lie outside this region are the recession years of the early 1980s and early 1990s. We will learn in Part Three of this book that inflation tends to fall only *after* a recession proceeds for a year or two. This is because prices tend to be particularly sticky in the downward direction, and this tendency makes money supply changes affect real GDP more strongly than inflation during this phase of the business cycle. Thus, the quantity theory of inflation works best in the long run, not in the short run. We examine the short-run impact of changes in the quantity of money in much more detail when we turn to economic fluctuations in Part Three of this book.

FYI

Products and Percentage Changes

For manipulating the quantity equation and many other relationships in economics, there is an arithmetic trick that is useful to know: *the percentage change of a product of two variables is approximately the sum of the percentage changes in each of the variables.* We used this trick when we wrote the quantity equation in percentage changes.

To see how this trick works, let's apply it to the GDP deflator (P), real GDP (Y), and nominal GDP ($P \times Y$). The trick states that

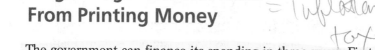

$$\% \text{ Change in } (P \times Y) \approx (\% \text{ Change in } P) + (\% \text{ Change in } Y).$$

For example, suppose that in one year, real GDP is 100 and the GDP deflator is 2; the next year real GDP is 103 and the GDP deflator is 2.1. We can calculate that real GDP rose by 3 percent, and the GDP deflator rose by 5 percent. Nominal GDP rose from 200 the first year to 216.3 the second year, an increase of 8.15 percent. Notice that the growth in nominal GDP (8.15 percent) is approximately the sum of the growth in the GDP deflator (5 percent) and the growth in real GDP (3 percent).

6·3 Seigniorage: The Revenue From Printing Money

The government can finance its spending in three ways. First, it can raise revenue through taxes, such as personal and corporate income taxes. Second, it can borrow from the public. Third, it can simply print money.

The revenue raised through the printing of money is called **seigniorage**. The term comes from *seigneur*, the French word for feudal lord. In the Middle Ages, the lord had the exclusive right on his manor to coin money. Today this right belongs to the federal government, and it is one source of revenue.

When the government prints money to finance expenditure, it increases the money supply. The increase in the money supply, in turn, causes inflation. Printing money to raise revenue is like imposing an *inflation tax.*

At first it may not be obvious that inflation can be viewed as a tax. After all, no one receives a bill for this tax—the government merely prints the money it needs. Who then pays the inflation tax? The answer is: the holders of money. As prices rise, the real value of your money falls. When the government prints new money for its use, it makes the old money in the hands of the public less valuable. Thus, inflation is a tax on holding money.

The amount raised by printing money varies substantially from country to country. In Canada, the amount has been small: seigniorage has usually accounted for only about 1 percent of government revenue. In Italy and Greece, seigniorage has often been over 10 percent of government revenue.[5] In countries experiencing hyperinflation, seigniorage is often the government's chief source of revenue—indeed, the need to print money to finance expenditure is a primary cause of hyperinflation.

CASE STUDY

6•4 **American and Russian Inflations**

Although seigniorage has not been a major source of revenue for either the Canadian or the American governments in recent history, the situation was very different two centuries ago in the United States, and it has been very different in Russia quite recently. We consider first the American history.

Beginning in 1775 the Continental Congress needed to find a way to finance the American Revolution, but it had limited ability to raise revenue through taxation. It therefore relied heavily on the printing of fiat money to help pay for the war. The Continental Congress's reliance on seigniorage increased over time. In 1775 new issues of continental currency were approximately $6 million. This amount increased to $19 million in 1776, $13 million in 1777, $63.4 million in 1778, and $124.8 million in 1779.

Not surprisingly, this rapid growth in the money supply led to massive inflation. At the end of the war, the price of gold measured in continental dollars was more than 100 times its level of only a few years earlier. The large quantity of the continental currency made the continental dollar nearly worthless. Even today the expression "not worth a continental" means that something has little real value.

The Russian ruble is another currency that has fallen precipitously in value. During the early 1990s, the former system of central planning was abandoned. But without a well-developed market system that already was flourishing and without the trade that had taken place earlier with the other former Soviet republics, many factories found that there was no demand for their output. To avoid massive layoffs, the government simply printed up vast quantities of money to subsidize the operation of the factories. As the quantity theory predicts, prices began to soar. In the final months of 1992, inflation was running at a rate of 13 hundred percent per year.

---

[5] William Scarth, "A Note on the Desirability of a Separate Quebec Currency," in David Laidler and William Robson, *Two Nations, One Money*? (Toronto: C.D. Howe Institute 1991): 76; Stanley Fischer, "Seigniorage and the Case for a National Money," *Journal of Political Economy* 90 (April 1982): 295–313.

6·4   Inflation and Interest Rates

So far we have examined the link between money growth and inflation. We now discuss the link between inflation and interest rates.

Two Interest Rates: Real and Nominal

Suppose you deposit your savings in a bank account that pays 8 percent interest annually. Next year, you withdraw your savings and the accumulated interest. Are you 8 percent richer than you were when you made the deposit a year earlier?

The answer depends on what "richer" means. Certainly, you have 8 percent more dollars than you had before. But if prices have risen, so that each dollar buys less, then your purchasing power has not risen by 8 percent. If the inflation rate was 5 percent, then the amount of goods you can buy has increased by only 3 percent. And if the inflation rate was 10 percent, then your purchasing power actually fell by 2 percent.

Economists call the interest rate that the bank pays the **nominal interest rate** and the increase in your purchasing power the **real interest rate**. If i denotes the nominal interest rate, r the real interest rate, and π the rate of inflation, then the relationship among these three variables can be written as

$$r = i - \pi.$$

The real interest rate is the difference between the nominal interest rate and the rate of inflation.

The Fisher Effect

Rearranging terms in our equation for the real interest rate, we can show that the nominal interest rate is the sum of the real interest rate and the inflation rate:

$$i = r + \pi.$$

The equation written in this way is called the **Fisher equation**, after economist Irving Fisher (1867–1947). It shows that the nominal interest rate can change for two reasons: because the real interest rate changes or because the inflation rate changes.

Once we separate the nominal interest rate into these two parts, we can use this equation to develop a theory of the nominal interest rate. Chapter 3 showed that the real interest rate adjusts to equilibrate saving and investment. The quantity theory of money shows that the rate of money growth determines the rate of inflation. The Fisher equation then tells us to add the real interest rate and the inflation rate together to determine the nominal interest rate.

The quantity theory and the Fisher equation together tell us how money growth affects the nominal interest rate. *According to the quantity theory, an increase in the rate of money growth of 1 percent causes a 1 percent increase in the rate of inflation. According to the Fisher equation, a 1 percent increase in the rate of inflation in turn causes a 1 percent increase in the nominal interest rate.* The one-for-one relation between the inflation rate and the nominal interest rate is called the **Fisher effect**.

[handwritten: Effects: $\bar{M}V = PY$ ↑ causes ↑ π causes ↑ $i = r + π$; 1:1 relation between π & i = Fisher effect.]

CASE STUDY

6•5 Inflation and Nominal Interest Rates

How useful is the Fisher effect in explaining interest rates? To answer this question we look at two types of data on inflation and nominal interest rates.

Figure 6-4 shows the variation over time in the nominal interest rate and the inflation rate in Canada. You can see that, over the past 40 years, the Fisher effect has worked fairly well. When inflation is high, nominal interest rates also tend to be high.

Figure 6-4

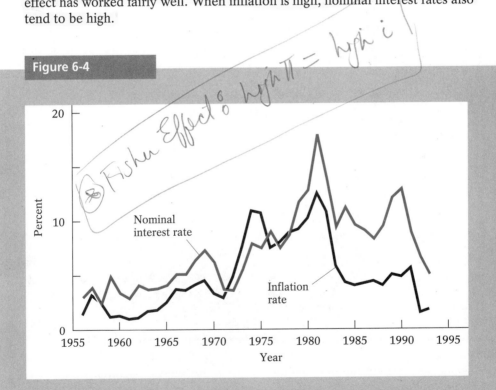

[handwritten: Fisher Effect: high π = high i]

Inflation and Nominal Interest Rates Over Time This figure plots the nominal interest rate (on three-month Treasury bills) and the inflation rate (as measured by the CPI) in Canada since 1956. It shows the Fisher effect: higher inflation leads to a higher nominal interest rate.

Source: Canadian Economic Observer (Ottawa: Statistics Canada).

Figure 6-5 examines the variation across countries in the nominal interest rate and the inflation rate at a single point in time. Once again, the inflation rate and nominal interest rate are closely related. Countries with high inflation tend to have high nominal interest rates as well.

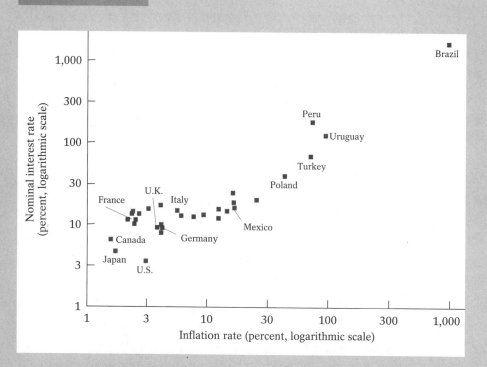

Inflation and Nominal Interest Rates Across Countries This scatterplot exhibits the three-month nominal interest rate and the inflation rate (during the previous year) in 28 countries in 1992. This figure also shows the positive correlation between the inflation rate and the nominal interest rate.

Source: International Financial Statistics.

The link between inflation and interest rates is well known to investment firms. Since bond prices move inversely with interest rates, one can get rich by predicting correctly the direction in which interest rates will move. Many investment firms hire *central bank watchers* to monitor monetary policy and news about inflation in order to anticipate changes in interest rates.

Two Real Interest Rates: *Ex Ante* and *Ex Post*

When a borrower and lender agree on a nominal interest rate, they do not know what the inflation rate over the term of the loan will be. Therefore, we must distinguish between two concepts of the real interest rate: the real interest rate the borrower and lender expect when the loan is made, called the *ex ante* **real interest rate**, and the real interest rate actually realized, called the *ex post* **real interest rate**.

Although borrowers and lenders cannot predict future inflation with certainty, they do have some expectation of the inflation rate. Let π denote actual future inflation and π^e the expectation of future inflation. The *ex ante* real interest rate is $i - \pi^e$, and the *ex post* real interest rate is $i - \pi$. The two real interest rates differ when actual inflation π differs from expected inflation π^e.

How does this distinction between actual and expected inflation modify the Fisher effect? Clearly, the nominal interest rate cannot adjust to actual inflation, because actual inflation is not known when the nominal interest rate is set. The nominal interest rate can adjust only to expected inflation. The Fisher effect is more precisely written as

$$i = r + \pi^e.$$

The *ex ante* real interest rate r is determined by equilibrium in the market for goods and services, as described by the model in Chapter 3. The nominal interest rate i moves one-for-one with changes in expected inflation π^e.

CASE STUDY

6•6 Nominal Interest Rates in the Nineteenth Century

Although recent data show a positive relationship between nominal interest rates and inflation rates, this finding is not universal. In data from the late nineteenth and early twentieth centuries, high nominal interest rates did not accompany high inflation. The apparent absence of any Fisher effect during this time puzzled Irving Fisher. He suggested that inflation "caught merchants napping."

How should we interpret the absence of an apparent Fisher effect in nineteenth-century data? Does this period of history provide evidence against the adjustment of nominal interest rates to inflation? Recent research suggests that this period has little to tell us about the validity of the Fisher effect. The reason is that the Fisher effect relates the nominal interest rate to expected inflation and, according to this research, inflation at this time was largely unexpected.

Although expectations are not directly observable, we can draw inferences about them by examining the persistence of inflation. In recent experience, inflation has been highly persistent: when it is high one year, it tends to be high the next year as well. Therefore, when people have observed high inflation, it has been rational for them to expect high inflation in the future. By contrast, during the nineteenth century, when the gold standard was in effect, inflation had little persistence. High inflation in one year was just as likely to be followed the next year by low inflation as by high inflation. Therefore, high inflation did not imply high expected inflation and did not lead to high nominal interest rates. So, in a sense, Fisher was right to say that inflation "caught merchants napping."[6]

6•5 The Nominal Interest Rate and the Demand for Money

The quantity theory is based on a simple money demand function: it assumes that the demand for real money balances is proportional to income. Although the quantity theory is a good place to start when analyzing the role of money, it is not the whole story. Here we add another determinant of the quantity of money demanded—the nominal interest rate.

The Cost of Holding Money

The money you hold in your wallet does not earn interest. If instead of holding that money you used it to buy government bonds or deposited it in a savings account, you would earn the nominal interest rate. The nominal interest rate is what you give up by holding money rather than bonds: it is the opportunity cost of holding money.

Another way to see that the cost of holding money equals the nominal interest rate is by comparing the real returns on alternative assets. Assets other than money, such as government bonds, earn the real return r. Money earns an expected real return of $-\pi^e$, since its real value declines at the rate of inflation. When you hold money, you give up the difference between these two returns. Thus, the cost of holding money is $r - (-\pi^e)$, which the Fisher equation tells us is the nominal interest rate i.

Just as the quantity of bread demanded depends on the price of bread, the quantity of money demanded depends on the price of holding money. Hence, the demand for real balances depends both on the level of income and on the nominal interest rate. We write the general money demand function as

$$(M/P)^d = L(i, Y).$$

The letter L is used to denote money demand, because money is the liquid asset—the asset most easily used to make transactions. This equation states that the demand for the liquidity of real money balances is a function of income and the nominal interest rate. The higher the level of income Y, the greater the demand for real balances. The higher the nominal interest rate i, the lower the demand for real balances.

---

[6] Robert B. Barsky, "The Fisher Effect and the Forecastability and Persistence of Inflation," *Journal of Monetary Economics* 19 (January 1987): 3–24.

Future Money and Current Prices

Consider how this general money demand function affects our theory of the price level. First, equate the supply of real balances M/P to the demand $L(i, Y)$:

supply of real money $M/P = L(i, Y).$ *demand*

Next, use the Fisher equation to write the nominal interest rate as the sum of the real interest rate and expected inflation:

$$M/P = L(r + \pi^e, Y).$$

Fisher equation $i = r + \pi^e$

This equation states that the level of real balances depends on the expected rate of inflation.

The general money demand equation tells a more sophisticated story than the quantity theory about the determination of the price level. The quantity theory of money says that today's money supply determines today's price level. This conclusion remains partly true: if the nominal interest rate and the level of output are held constant, the price level moves proportionately with the money supply. Yet the nominal interest rate is not constant; it depends on expected inflation, which in turn depends on money growth. The presence of the nominal interest rate in the money demand function yields an additional channel through which money supply affects the price level.

This general money demand equation implies that the price level depends not just on today's money supply but also on the money supply expected in the future. To see why, suppose the Bank of Canada announces that it will raise the money supply in the future but does not change the money supply today. This announcement causes people to expect higher money growth and higher inflation. Through the Fisher effect, this increase in expected inflation raises the nominal interest rate. The higher nominal interest rate immediately reduces the demand for real money balances. Because the quantity of money has not changed, the reduced demand for real balances leads to a higher price level. Hence, higher expected money growth in the future leads to a higher price level today.

The effect of money on prices is fairly complex. The appendix to this chapter works out the mathematics relating the price level to current and future money. The conclusion of the analysis is that the price level depends on a weighted average of the current money supply and the money supply expected to prevail in the future.

CASE STUDY

◆ 6•7 **Canadian Monetary Policy**

Given the fact that the price level depends on the money supply that is expected to prevail in the future, it is not surprising that Gordon Thiessen, the current Governor of the Bank of Canada, stresses in every speech he makes his commitment to maintaining low inflation. Indeed, when Mr. Thiessen was appointed on February 1, 1994, the government published five-year inflation targets—a commitment that the Bank of Canada will keep inflation within the range of 1–3 percent for five years. The point of making this announcement and drawing so much attention to it is to try to convince individuals and firms that the Bank of Canada really will keep money growth limited for the foreseeable future. Clearly, the officials in both the Department of Finance and the Bank of Canada believe that inflation *now* depends very much on the rate that private agents *expect* the Bank will issue money in the *future*. Policy is based on the view that the Bank of Canada's "credibility" must be maintained, and that this stance involves convincing private individuals that money growth will not be excessive.

In the debates on constitutional change in 1992, one of the federal government's proposals was that the Bank of Canada Act be changed to make the maintenance of price stability the *sole* objective of monetary policy. The government wanted to dispell any notions people might have that the Bank would give up its commitment to price stability if some other crisis, such as a deep recession, emerged. Clearly, officials believe that the analysis we have just summarized is directly relevant to the Canadian policy challenge.

How to Stop a Hyperinflation

The sensitivity of real money balances to the nominal interest rate complicates the problem of stopping a hyperinflation. If the quantity theory were completely true and the nominal interest rate did not affect money demand, then stopping a hyperinflation would be easy: the central bank would merely need to stop printing money. As soon as the quantity of money stabilized, the price level would stabilize.

But if money demand depends on the nominal interest rate, ending a hyperinflation is more complicated. The fall in inflation will lead to a fall in the cost of holding money and, therefore, an increase in real money balances. If the central bank merely stops printing money (that is, keeps M constant), the increase in real balances (M/P) necessitates a fall in prices. Hence, the apparently simple task of ending a hyperinflation will, if the central bank is not careful, lead to a falling price level. In this case, the central bank will not have achieved its goal of price stability.

What monetary policy should the central bank pursue to achieve stable prices? That is, what path should the money supply follow to end the inflation without causing deflation? To answer this question, we work backwards. We begin with the goal of price stabilization and find the path of the money supply that is consistent with that objective. Figure 6-6 shows the five steps to determining the path of the money supply.

1. The desired path of the price level is at the top of the figure. The price level is rising during the hyperinflation. Then the new monetary policy goes into effect and prices stabilize.

2. Next is the rate of inflation π, which is the growth in the price level. It is high until the period of price stability, when it drops to zero.

3. The nominal interest rate i adjusts one-for-one with the rate of inflation. This is required by the Fisher effect. Thus, the nominal interest rate also is high until prices stabilize, and then falls to a lower level.

4. This fall in the nominal interest rate leads to a jump up in real balances, because the cost of holding money has declined.

Figure 6-6

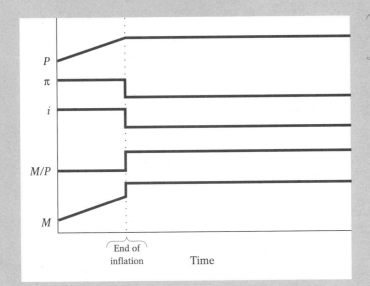

Handwritten note in top margin: 5 steps to determine the path of money supply?

How to Stop Inflation When Real Balances Depend on the Nominal Interest Rate By examining the paths we expect the key monetary variables to follow, we can derive the path that the money supply must follow to end an inflation. (1) At the top is the desired path of the price level P. (2) Next is the rate of inflation π, which is high until the period of price stability, when it drops to zero. (3) The nominal interest rate i adjusts one-for-one with the rate in inflation. (4) The fall of the nominal interest rate leads to a jump up in real balances M/P. (5) The path of the money supply M then depends on the path of the price level P and the path of real balances M/P.

Note: Each variable is drawn on its own scale.

5. Since we now know the path of the price level P and the path of real balances M/P, we can infer the required path of money M. At the moment the hyperinflation ends, the money supply must jump up to accommodate the increase in real balances. After the jump, the money supply stays constant to ensure price stability.

An important issue that this analysis does not address is the central bank's credibility. For expected inflation and the nominal interest rate to fall, people must believe that the central bank will stop printing so much money. This expectation is hard to create in the midst of a hyperinflation. Indeed, if the central bank follows our advice and makes the money supply jump up, it may have trouble convincing the public that the hyperinflation is over. And if the central bank does not achieve credibility, expected inflation and the nominal interest rate will not fall, real balances will not rise, and the jump in the money supply will lead to more inflation.

In practice, the central bank usually achieves credibility by removing the underlying cause of the hyperinflation: the need for seigniorage. Most hyperinflations begin when the government prints money to finance its spending. As long as the government needs the revenue from seigniorage, the public is not likely to believe the central bank's announcements about price stability. For this reason, the ends of hyperinflations usually coincide with fiscal reforms—reductions in government spending and increases in taxes—that reduce the need for seigniorage. Hence, even if inflation is always and everywhere a monetary phenomenon, the end of hyperinflation is often a fiscal phenomenon as well.[7]

CASE STUDY

6•8 Hyperinflation in Interwar Germany

After World War I, Germany experienced one of history's most spectacular examples of hyperinflation. At the war's end, the Allies demanded that Germany pay substantial reparations. These payments led to fiscal deficits in Germany, which the German government eventually financed by printing large quantities of money.

Figure 6-7

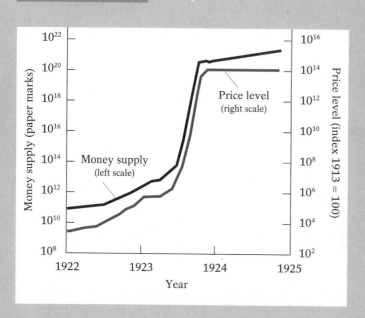

Money and Prices in Interwar Germany
This figure shows the money supply and the price level in Germany from January 1922 to December 1924. The immense increases in the money supply and the price level provide one of the most dramatic illustrations of the effects of printing large amounts of money.

Source: Adapted from Thomas J. Sargent, "The End of Four Big Inflations," in Robert Hall, ed., *Inflation* (Chicago: University of Chicago. Press, 1983): 41–98.

[7] Thomas J. Sargent, "The End of Four Big Inflations," in Robert Hall, ed., *Inflation* (Chicago: University of Chicago Press, 1983), 41–98; Rudiger Dornbusch and Stanley Fischer, "Stopping Hyperinflations: Past and Present," *Weltwirtschaftliches Archiv* 122 (April 1986): 1–47.

Figure 6-7 shows the quantity of money and the general price level in Germany from January 1922 to December 1924. During this period both money and prices rose at an amazing rate. For example, the price of a daily newspaper rose from 0.30 marks in January 1921 to 1 mark in May 1922, to 8 marks in October 1922, to 100 marks in February 1923, and to 1,000 marks in September 1923. Then, in the fall of 1923, prices really took off: the newspaper sold for 2,000 marks on October 1, 20,000 marks on October 15, 1 million marks on October 29, 15 million marks on November 9, and 70 million marks on November 17. In December 1923 the money supply and prices abruptly stabilized.[8]

Just as fiscal problems caused the German hyperinflation, a fiscal reform ended it. At the end of 1923, the number of government employees was cut by one-third, and the reparations payments were temporarily suspended and eventually reduced. At the same time, a new central bank, the Rentenbank, replaced the old central bank, the Reichsbank. The Rentenbank was committed to not financing the government by printing money.

According to our theoretical analysis, an end to a hyperinflation should lead to an increase in real money balances. Figure 6-8 shows that real balances

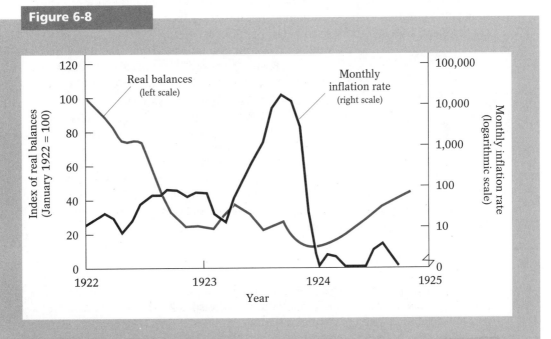

Figure 6-8

Inflation and Real Balances in Interwar Germany This figure shows inflation and real balances in Germany from January 1922 to December 1924. As inflation rose, real balances fell. When the inflation ended, real balances rose.

Source: Adapted from Thomas J. Sargent, "The End of Four Big Inflations," in Robert Hall, ed., *Inflation* (Chicago: University of Chicago Press, 1983): 41–93.

---

[8] The data on newspaper prices are from Michael Mussa, "Sticky Individual Prices and the Dynamics of the General Price Level," *Carnegie-Rochester Conference on Public Policy* 15 (Autumn 1981): 261–296.

in Germany did fall as inflation increased, and then increased again as inflation fell. Yet in contrast to our theory, the increase in real balances was not immediate. Perhaps the adjustment of real balances to the cost of holding money is a gradual process. Or perhaps it took time for people in Germany to believe that the inflation had really ended, so that expected inflation fell more gradually than actual inflation.

6•6   The Social Costs of Inflation

Our discussion of the causes and effects of inflation does not tell us much about the social problems that result from inflation. We turn to those problems now.

If you ask the average person why inflation is a social problem, she will probably answer that inflation makes her poorer. "Each year my boss gives me a raise, but prices go up and that takes some of my raise away from me." The implicit assumption in this statement is that if there were no inflation, she would get the same raise and be able to buy more goods.

This complaint about inflation is a common fallacy. From Chapters 3 and 4, we know that increases in the purchasing power of labour come from capital accumulation and technological progress. In particular, the real wage does not depend on how much money the government chooses to print. If the government slowed the rate of money growth, prices would not rise as quickly. But workers would not see their real wage increasing more rapidly. Instead, when inflation slowed, they would get smaller raises each year.

Why then is inflation a social problem? It turns out that the costs of inflation are subtle. Indeed, economists disagree about the size of the social costs. To the surprise of many laymen, some economists argue that the costs of inflation are small—at least for the moderate rates of inflation that most countries have experienced in recent years.[9]

Expected Inflation

Consider first the case of expected inflation. Suppose that every month the price level rose by 1 percent. What would be the social costs of such a steady and predictable 12 percent annual inflation?

One cost is the distortion of the inflation tax on the amount of money people hold. As we have already discussed, a higher inflation rate leads to a

---

[9]   See, for example, Robert York, ed., *Taking Aim: The Debate on Zero Inflation* (Toronto: C.D. Howe Institute, 1990).

higher nominal interest rate, which in turn leads to lower real money balances. If people are to hold lower money balances on average, they must make more frequent trips to the bank to withdraw money—for example, they might withdraw $50 twice a week rather than $100 once a week. The inconvenience of reducing money holding is metaphorically called the **shoeleather cost** of inflation, because walking to the bank more often causes one's shoes to wear out more quickly.

A second cost of inflation, called **menu cost,** arises because high inflation induces firms to change their posted prices more often. Changing prices is sometimes costly: for example, it may require printing and distributing a new catalogue. These costs are called menu costs, because the higher the rate of inflation, the more often restaurants have to print new menus.

A third cost of inflation arises because firms facing menu costs change prices infrequently; therefore, the higher the rate of inflation, the greater the variability in relative prices. For example, suppose a firm issues a new catalogue every January. If there is no inflation, then the firm's prices relative to overall price level are constant over the year. Yet if inflation is 1 percent per month, then from the beginning to the end of the year the firm's relative prices fall by 12 percent. Thus, inflation induces variability in relative prices. Since free-market economies rely on relative prices to allocate resources efficiently, inflation leads to microeconomic inefficiencies.

A fourth cost of inflation results from the tax laws. Many provisions of the tax code do not take into account the effects of inflation. Inflation can alter individuals' tax liability, often in ways that lawmakers did not intend.

One example of the failure of the tax code to deal with inflation is the tax treatment of capital gains. Suppose you buy some stock today and sell it a year from now at the same real price. It would seem reasonable for the government not to levy a tax, since you have earned no real income from this investment. Indeed, if there is no inflation, a zero tax liability would be the outcome. But suppose the rate of inflation is 12 percent and you initially paid $100 per share for the stock; for the real price to be the same a year later, you must sell the stock for $112 per share. In this case the tax code, which ignores the effects of inflation, says that you have earned $12 per share in income, and the government taxes you on this capital gain. The problem, of course, is that the tax code measures income as the nominal rather than the real capital gain.

A similar problem occurs with interest-income taxes. Because the Canadian tax system was designed for a zero-inflation environment, it does not work well when inflation occurs. It turns out that when inflation and the tax system interact, the result is a powerful disincentive to save and invest. And worse still, this problem occurs even for mild inflations and even when all individuals anticipate inflation perfectly. Let us see how this problem develops, by adding interest-income taxes to our discussion of the Fisher equation.

If t stands for the tax rate that an individual must pay on her interest income, the *after-tax* real yield is

$$\text{After-tax } r = i\,(1 - t) - \pi.$$

Consider what happens to this effective yield on savings if inflation rises from 0 percent to 10 percent. Assume that the nominal interest rate rises by the same 10 percentage points—enough to compensate lenders fully for the inflation, if it were not for the tax system. The revised Fisher equation makes clear that the after-tax real yield must fall by t times 10 percent in this case. If the individual's marginal tax rate is 50 percent, the reduction in the real return to saving is a full $t\pi = .5$ percentage points. Most economists believe that this represents a significant disincentive to save, and so inflation reduces capital accumulation and future living standards.

The problem is that the tax system taxes nominal interest income instead of real interest income. During an inflationary time, much of an individual's nominal interest receipts are just a compensation for the fact that the loan's principal value is shrinking. Since that "inflation premium" part of interest is not income at all, it should not be taxed. If the tax system were fully indexed, it would not be taxed. In that case, the after-tax real yield would be given by

$$\text{After-tax } r = (i - \pi)(1 - t).$$

In this case, as long as the nominal interest rate rises one-for-one with inflation (as we discussed in the non-indexed tax case), the after-tax real yield is *not* reduced at all by inflation. The disincentive for saving and investment is removed.

Nevertheless, because our tax system is not indexed, one of the central costs of inflation is that it lowers the economy's accumulation of capital, and so it reduces the standard of living for all members of future generations.

A fifth cost of inflation is the inconvenience of living in a world with a changing price level. Money is the ruler with which we measure economic transactions. When there is inflation, that ruler is changing in length. To continue the analogy, suppose that Parliament passed a law specifying that a metre would equal 39 inches in 1995, 37 inches in 1996, 35 inches in 1997, and so on. Although the law would result in no ambiguity, it would be highly inconvenient. When someone measured a distance in metres, it would be necessary to specify whether the measurement was in 1995 metres or 1996 metres; to compare distances measured in different years, one would need to make an "inflation" correction. Similarly, the dollar is a less useful measure when its value is always changing.

For example, a changing price level complicates personal financial planning. One important decision that all households face is how much of their income to consume today and how much to save for retirement. A dollar saved today and invested at a fixed nominal interest rate will yield a fixed dollar amount in the future. Yet the real value of that dollar amount—which will determine the retiree's living standard—depends on the future price level. Deciding how much to save would be much simpler if people could count on the price level in 30 years being similar to its level today.

CASE STUDY

6•9   Life During the Bolivian Hyperinflation

The costs of inflation are most apparent when inflation reaches extreme levels. The following article from *The Wall Street Journal* shows what life was like during the hyperinflation in Bolivia in 1985. Note the costs of inflation that the article emphasizes. Does the Bolivian experience conform to the assessment by Lenin and Keynes in the quotation that began this chapter?

Precarious Peso—Amid Wild Inflation,
Bolivians Concentrate on Swapping Currency

LA PAZ, Bolivia—When Edgar Miranda gets his monthly teacher's pay of 25 million pesos, he hasn't a moment to lose. Every hour, pesos drop in value. So, while his wife rushes to market to lay in a month's supply of rice and noodles, he is off with the rest of the pesos to change them into black-market dollars.

Mr. Miranda is practicing the First Rule of Survival amid the most out-of-control inflation in the world today. Bolivia is a case study of how runaway inflation undermines a society. Price increases are so huge that the figures build up almost beyond comprehension. In one six-month period, for example, prices soared at an annual rate of 38,000%. By official count, however, last year's inflation reached 2,000%, and this year's is expected to hit 8,000%—though other estimates range many times higher. In any event, Bolivia's rate dwarfs Israel's 370% and Argentina's 1,100%—two other cases of severe inflation.

It is easier to comprehend what happens to the 38-year-old Mr. Miranda's pay if he doesn't quickly change it into dollars. The day he was paid 25 million pesos, a dollar cost 500,000 pesos. So he received $50. Just days later, with the rate at 900,000 pesos, he would have received $27.

"We think only about today and converting every peso into dollars," says Ronald MacLean, the manager of a gold-mining firm. "We have become myopic."

And intent on survival. Civil servants won't hand out a form without a bribe. Lawyers, accountants, hairdressers, even prostitutes have almost given up working to become money-changers in the streets. Workers stage repeated strikes and steal from their bosses. The bosses smuggle production abroad, take out phony loans, duck taxes—anything to get dollars for speculation.

The production at the state mines, for example, dropped to 12,000 tons last year from 18,000. The miners pad their wages by smuggling out the richest ore in their lunch pails, and the ore goes by a contraband network into neighboring Peru. Without a major tin mine, Peru now exports some 4,000 metric tons of tin a year.

"We don't produce anything. We are all currency speculators," a heavy-equipment dealer in La Paz says. "People don't know what's good and bad anymore. We have become an amoral society. . . ."

It is an open secret that practically all of the black-market dollars come from the illegal cocaine trade with the U.S. Cocaine traffickers earn an estimated $1 billion a year. . . .

But meanwhile the country is suffering from inflation largely because the government's revenues cover a mere 15% of its expenditures and its deficit has widened to nearly 25% of the country's total annual output. The revenues are hurt by a lag in tax payments, and taxes aren't being collected largely because of widespread theft and bribery.

Source: Reprinted by permission of *The Wall Street Journal,* © August 13, 1985, page 1, Dow Jones & Company, Inc. All Rights Reserved Worldwide.

Unexpected Inflation

Unexpected inflation has an effect that is more pernicious than any of the costs of steady, anticipated inflation: it arbitrarily redistributes wealth among individuals. You can see how this works by examining long-term loans. Loan agreements typically specify a nominal interest rate, which is based on the expected rate of inflation. If inflation turns out differently from what was expected, the *ex post* real return that the debtor pays to the creditor differs from what both parties anticipated. On the one hand, if inflation turns out to be higher than expected, the debtor wins and the creditor loses because the debtor repays the loan with less valuable dollars. On the other hand, if inflation turns out to be lower than expected, the creditor wins and the debtor loses because the repayment is worth more than the two parties anticipated.

Unanticipated inflation also hurts individuals on fixed pensions. Workers and firms often agree on a fixed nominal pension when the worker retires (or even earlier). Since the pension is deferred earnings, the worker is essentially providing the firm a loan: the worker provides labour services to the firm while young but does not get fully paid until old age. Like any creditor, the worker is hurt when inflation is higher than anticipated. Like any debtor, the firm is hurt when inflation is lower than anticipated. The magnitudes involved in these arbitrary redistributions of income can be very large. For example, with inflation of just 5 percent per year (an amount nowhere near the hyperinflations we have discussed in the chapter), the purchasing power of money *halves* in value in fewer than 15 years. So in a period when inflation is underpredicted by 5 percent, pensioners' real income is cut in half well before they are expected to die. This reduction in real income can be devastating.

These situations provide a clear argument against highly variable inflation. The more variable the rate of inflation, the greater the uncertainty that both debtors and creditors face. Since most people are *risk averse*—they dislike uncertainty—the unpredictability caused by highly variable inflation hurts almost everyone.

Given these effects of inflation uncertainty, it is puzzling that nominal contracts are so prevalent. One might expect debtors and creditors to protect themselves from this uncertainty by writing contracts in real terms—that is, by indexing to some measure of the price level. In economies with extremely high and variable inflation, indexation is often widespread; sometimes this indexation takes the form of writing contracts using a more stable foreign currency. In economies that have experienced more moderate inflation, such as Canada, indexation is less common. Yet even in Canada, some long-term obligations are indexed: for example, Canada Pension benefits for the elderly are adjusted annually in response to changes in the consumer price index.

CASE STUDY

6•10 The Wizard of Oz

The redistributions of wealth caused by unexpected changes in the price level are often a source of political turmoil, as evidenced by the Free Silver movement in the late nineteenth century in the United States. From 1880 to 1896 the price level in the United States fell 23 percent. This deflation was good for creditors—the bankers of the Northeast—but it was bad for debtors—the farmers of the South and West. One proposed solution to this problem was to replace the gold standard with a bimetallic standard, under which both gold and silver could be minted into coin. The move to a bimetallic standard would increase the money supply and stop the deflation.

The silver issue dominated the presidential election of 1896. William McKinley, the Republican nominee, campaigned on a platform of preserving the gold standard. William Jennings Bryan, the Democratic nominee, supported the bimetallic standard. In a famous speech, Bryan proclaimed, "You shall not press down upon the brow of labour this crown of thorns, you shall not crucify mankind upon a cross of gold." Not surprisingly, McKinley was the candidate of the conservative eastern establishment, while Bryan was the candidate of the southern and western populists.

This debate over silver found its most memorable expression in a children's book, *The Wizard of Oz*. Written by a midwestern journalist, Frank Baum, just after the 1896 election, it tells the story of Dorothy, a girl lost in a strange land far from her home in Kansas. Dorothy (representing traditional American values) makes three friends: a scarecrow (the farmer), a tin woodman (the industrial worker), and a lion whose roar exceeds his might (William Jennings Bryan). Together, the four of them make their way along a perilous yellow brick road (the gold standard), hoping to find the Wizard who will help Dorothy return home. Eventually they arrive in Oz (Washington), where everyone sees the world through green glasses (money). The Wizard (William McKinley) tries to be all things to all people but turns out to be a fraud. Dorothy's problem is solved only when she learns about the magical power of her silver slippers.[10]

---

[10] The movie made 40 years later hid much of the allegory by changing Dorothy's slippers from silver to ruby. For more on this topic, see Henry M. Littlefield, "*The Wizard of Oz*: Parable on Populism," *American Quarterly* 16 (Spring 1964): 47–58; Hugh Rockoff, "*The Wizard of Oz* as a Monetary Allegory," *Journal of Political Economy* 89 (August 1990): 739–760

Although the Republicans won the election of 1896 and the United States stayed on a gold standard, the Free Silver advocates got what they ultimately wanted: inflation. Around the time of the election, gold was discovered in Alaska, Australia, and South Africa. In addition, gold refiners devised the cyanide process, which facilitated the extraction of gold from ore. These developments led to increases in the money supply and in prices. From 1896 to 1910 the price level rose 35 percent.

The Level and Variability of Inflation

No discussion of inflation would be complete without noting an important but little understood fact: high inflation is variable inflation. That is, countries with high average inflation also tend to have inflation rates that change greatly from one year to the next. The implication is that if a country decides to pursue a high-inflation monetary policy, it will likely have to accept highly variable inflation as well. For the reasons discussed previously, highly variable inflation increases uncertainty for both creditors and debtors by subjecting them to arbitrary and potentially large redistributions of wealth. The social cost of this uncertainty is hard to evaluate, but it is most likely substantial.

6•7 Conclusion: The Classical Dichotomy

We have finished our discussion of money and inflation. Let's now step back and examine a key assumption that has been implicit in our discussion.

In Chapters 3, 4, and 5, we explained many macroeconomic variables, such as real GDP, the capital stock, the real wage, and the real interest rate. These variables fall into two categories. The first category is *quantities.* For example, real GDP is the quantity of goods produced in a given year; the capital stock is the amount of capital available at a given time. The second category is *relative prices.* For example, the real wage is the relative price of consumption and leisure; the real interest rate is the price of output today relative to output tomorrow. Together these two categories—quantities and relative prices—are called **real variables**.

In this chapter we examined nominal variables. **Nominal variables** are expressed in terms of money. There are many nominal variables: the price level, the inflation rate, the nominal wage a person earns (the number of dollars received for working).

At first it may seem surprising that we were able to explain real variables without introducing nominal variables or the existence of money. In previous chapters we studied the level and allocation of the economy's output without mentioning the rate of inflation. Our theory of the labour market explained the real wage without explaining the nominal wage.

Economists call this theoretical separation of real and nominal variables the **classical dichotomy**. It is the hallmark of classical macroeconomic theory.

The classical dichotomy is an important insight, because it greatly simplifies economic theory. In particular, it allows us to examine real variables, as we have done, while ignoring nominal variables. The classical dichotomy arises because, in classical theory, changes in the money supply do not influence real variables. This irrelevance of money for real variables is called **monetary neutrality**. For many purposes—in particular for studying long-run issues—monetary neutrality is approximately correct.

Monetary neutrality is only approximately correct, however, since, as we have seen, inflation impedes the transaction process—especially when transactions involve a long-term contract, as with loans. One key dimension of the problem is that inflation (and therefore money growth) becomes a real variable, because inflation interacts with a tax system that is not indexed. In that case, inflation is equivalent to an increase in the rate of tax that is levied on interest income. Thus, higher inflation becomes a disincentive to save and invest, and it takes the economy further away from the Golden Rule level of capital accumulation.

Monetary neutrality is also incomplete in shorter-run time horizons during which nominal prices can be sticky. Beginning in Chapter 8, we discuss this and other departures from the classical model and monetary neutrality. These departures are crucial for understanding many macroeconomic phenomena, such as short-run economic fluctuations.

Summary

1. Money is the stock of assets used for transactions. It serves as a store of value, a unit of account, and a medium of exchange. Different sorts of assets are used as money: commodity money systems use an asset with intrinsic value, whereas fiat money systems use an asset whose sole function is to serve as money. In modern economies, a central bank such as the Bank of Canada has the responsibility for controlling the supply of money.

2. The quantity theory of money states that nominal GDP is proportional to the stock of money. Because the factors of production and the production function determine real GDP, the quantity theory implies that the price level is proportional to the quantity of money. Therefore, the rate of growth in the quantity of money determines the inflation rate.

3. Seigniorage is the revenue that the government raises by printing money. It is a tax on money holding. Although seigniorage is quantitatively small in most economies, it is often a major source of government revenue in economies experiencing hyperinflation.

4. The nominal interest rate is the sum of the real interest rate and the inflation rate. Abstracting from taxes, the Fisher effect says that the nominal interest rate moves one-for-one with expected inflation.

5. The nominal interest rate is the cost of holding money. Thus, one might expect the demand for money to depend on the nominal interest rate. If it does,

stopping inflation is a tricky task because real money balances will rise when inflation stops.

6. The costs of expected inflation include shoeleather costs, menu costs, the cost of relative price variability, tax distortions (such as the distinctive to save and invest), and the inconvenience of making inflation corrections. The cost of unexpected inflation is the arbitrary redistribution of wealth between debtors and creditors.

7. According to classical economic theory, money is neutral: the money supply does not affect real variables. Therefore, classical theory allows us to study how real variables are determined without any reference to the money supply. The equilibrium in the money market then determines the price level and, as a result, all other nominal variables. This theoretical separation of real and nominal variables is called the classical dichotomy.

KEY CONCEPTS

Inflation	Demand deposits
Hyperinflation	Quantity equation
Money	Transactions velocity of money
Store of value	Income velocity of money
Unit of account	Real money balances
Medium of exchange	Money demand function
Double coincidence of wants	Quantity theory of money
Fiat money	Seigniorage
Commodity money	Nominal and real interest rates
Gold standard	Fisher equation and Fisher effect
Money supply	*Ex ante* and *ex post* real interest rates
Central bank	Shoeleather costs
Bank of Canada	Menu costs
Monetary policy	Real and nominal variables
Open-market operations	Classical dichotomy
Currency	Monetary neutrality

QUESTIONS FOR REVIEW

1. List the functions of money.

2. What is fiat money? What is commodity money?

3. Who controls the money supply and how?

4. Write down the quantity equation and explain it.

5. What does the assumption of constant velocity imply?

6. Who pays the inflation tax?

7. If inflation rises from 6 to 8 percent, what happens to real and nominal interest rates according to the Fisher effect?

8. Explain what happens to real balances at the end of a hyperinflation.

9. List all the costs of inflation you can think of, and rank them according to how important you think they are.

PROBLEMS AND APPLICATIONS

1. What are the three functions of money? Which of the functions do the following items satisfy? Which do they not satisfy?

a. A credit card

b. A Rembrandt painting

c. A subway token

2. Suppose you are advising a small country (such as Bermuda) on whether to print its own money or to use the money of its larger neighbour (such as the United States). What are the costs and benefits of a national money? You could also think of advising a sovereign Quebec, after separation from the rest of Canada. Should a separate Quebec use the Canadian dollar? Should the rest of Canada permit Quebec to use its currency? Does the relative political stability of the two countries have any role in this decision?

3. During World War II, both Germany and England had plans for a paper weapon: they each printed the other's currency with the intention of dropping large quantities by airplane. Why might this have been an effective weapon?

4. Calvin Coolidge once said that "inflation is repudiation." What might he have meant by this? Do you agree? Why or why not? Does it matter whether the inflation is expected or unexpected?

5. Some economic historians have noted that during the period of the gold standard, gold discoveries were most likely to occur after a long deflation. (The discoveries of 1896 are an example.) Why might this be true?

6. Suppose that consumption depends on the level of real balances (on the grounds that real balances are part of wealth). Show that if real balances depend on the nominal interest rate, then an increase in the rate of money growth now affects consumption, investment, and the real interest rate. Does the nominal interest rate adjust more than one-for-one or less than one-for-one to expected inflation? This deviation from the classical dichotomy and the Fisher effect is called the *Mundell-Tobin effect*. How might you decide whether the Mundell-Tobin effect is important in practice?

The Impact of Current and Future Money on the Price Level

In this chapter we showed that if the quantity of real balances demanded depends on the cost of holding money, the price level depends both on the current money supply and on the future money supply. We now examine more explicitly how this works.

To keep the math as simple as possible, we posit a money demand function that is linear in the natural logarithms of all the variables. The money demand function is

$$m_t - p_t = -\gamma(p_{t+1} - p_t), \tag{A1}$$

where m_t is the log of the quantity of money at time t, p_t is the log of the price level at time t, and γ is a parameter which governs the sensitivity of money demand to the rate of inflation. By the property of logarithms, $m_t - p_t$ is the log of real balances, and $p_{t+1} - p_t$ is the inflation rate between period t and period $t + 1$. This equation states that if inflation goes up by one percentage point, real balances fall by γ percent.

We have made a number of assumptions in writing the money demand function in this way. First, by excluding the level of output as a determinant of money demand, we are implicitly assuming that it is constant. Second, by including the rate of inflation rather than the nominal interest rate, we are assuming that the real interest rate is constant. Third, by including actual inflation rather than expected inflation, we are assuming perfect foresight. All of these assumptions are for simplification.

We want to solve Equation A1 to express the price level as a function of current and future money. To do this, note that Equation A1 can be written as

$$p_t = \left(\frac{1}{1+\gamma}\right)m_t + \left(\frac{\gamma}{1+\gamma}\right)p_{t+1}. \tag{A2}$$

This equation states that the current price level is a weighted average of the current money supply and next period's price level. Next period's price level will be determined the same way as this period's price level:

$$p_{t+1} = \left(\frac{1}{1+\gamma}\right)m_{t+1} + \left(\frac{\gamma}{1+\gamma}\right)p_{t+2}. \tag{A3}$$

Use this equation to substitute for p_{t+1} in Equation A2 to obtain

$$p_t = \frac{1}{1 + \gamma} m_t + \frac{\gamma}{(1 + \gamma)^2} m_{t+1} + \frac{\gamma^2}{(1 + \gamma)^2} p_{t+2}. \tag{A4}$$

This equation states that the current price level is a weighted average of the current money supply, the next period's money supply, and the following period's price level. Once again, the price level in $t + 2$ is determined as in Equation A2:

$$p_{t+2} = \left(\frac{1}{1 + \gamma}\right) m_{t+2} + \left(\frac{\gamma}{1 + \gamma}\right) p_{t+3}. \tag{A5}$$

Now use Equation A5 to substitute into Equation A4 to obtain

$$p_t = \frac{1}{1 + \gamma} m_t + \frac{\gamma}{(1 + \gamma)^2} m_{t+1} + \frac{\gamma^2}{(1 + \gamma)^3} m_{t+2} + \frac{\gamma^3}{(1 + \gamma)^3} p_{t+3}. \tag{A6}$$

By now you see the pattern. We can continue to use Equation A2 to substitute for the future price level. If we do this an infinite number of times, we find

$$p_t = \left(\frac{1}{1 + \gamma}\right) \left[m_t + \left(\frac{\gamma}{1 + \gamma}\right) m_{t+1} + \left(\frac{\gamma}{1 + \gamma}\right)^2 m_{t+2} + \left(\frac{\gamma}{1 + \gamma}\right)^3 m_{t+3} \ldots \right], \tag{A7}$$

where ". . ." indicates an infinite number of analogous terms. According to Equation A7, the current price level is a weighted average of the current and all future money supplies.

Note the importance of γ, the parameter governing the sensitivity of real balances to inflation. The weights on the future money supplies decline geometrically at rate $\gamma/(1 + \gamma)$. If γ is small, then $\gamma/(1 + \gamma)$ is small, and the weights decline quickly. In this case, the current money supply is the primary determinant of the price level. (Indeed, if γ equals zero, then we obtain the quantity theory of money: the price level is proportional to the current money supply, and the future money supplies do not matter at all.) If γ is large, then $\gamma/(1 + \gamma)$ is close to 1, and the weights decline slowly. In this case, the future money supplies play a key role in determining today's price level.

Finally, let's relax the assumption of perfect foresight. If the future is not known with certainty, then we should write the money demand function as

$$m_t - p_t = -\gamma(E p_{t+1} - p_t), \tag{A8}$$

where $E p_{t+1}$ is the expected price level. Equation A8 states that real balances depend on expected inflation. By following steps similar to those above, we can show that

$$p_t = \left(\frac{1}{1 + \gamma}\right) \left[m_t + \left(\frac{\gamma}{1 + \gamma}\right) E m_{t+1} + \left(\frac{\gamma}{1 + \gamma}\right)^2 E m_{t+2} + \left(\frac{\gamma}{1 + \gamma}\right)^3 E m_{t+3} + \ldots \right]. \tag{A9}$$

Equation A9 states that the price level depends on current and future expected money.

Equation A9 is relevant to our discussion of stopping hyperinflations. When a hyperinflation ends, individuals revise downward their expectations of future money; this tends to reduce the current price level. To offset this downward effect of future money on current prices, the current money supply can rise even as prices stabilize.

The Open Economy

No nation was ever ruined by trade.

Benjamin Franklin

Many of the goods and services we enjoy are produced abroad. We eat oranges from Florida as well as apples from British Columbia, drive cars made in Japan as well as Oshawa, and vacation in Mexico as well as the Maritimes. The freedom to import and export benefits the citizens of all countries. Trade allows each country to specialize in what it produces best, and it provides everyone with a greater variety of goods and services.

Over the past four decades the volume of international trade has been increasing, making the economies of the world more interdependent. Canada has signed free trade agreements with the United States and Mexico, and Canadian exports, as a percentage of GDP, have risen from 21 percent in 1950 to 29 percent in 1993. While trade is more important for Canada than for many other countries, all of the G7 countries have become heavily involved in trade, as Figure 7-1 shows. In all countries, then, international trade is central to analyzing economic developments and formulating economic policies.

In previous chapters we simplified our analysis by assuming that the economy does not trade internationally. That is, we assumed a closed economy. As we have just seen, however, actual economies export goods and services abroad, and they import goods and services from abroad. In this chapter we begin our study of open-economy macroeconomics.

We begin in Section 7·1 with questions of measurement. To understand how the open economy works, we must understand the key macroeconomic variables that measure the interactions among countries. Accounting identities reveal a key insight: the flow of goods and services across national borders is closely related to the flow of funds to finance capital accumulation.

In Section 7·2 we examine the determinants of these international flows. We develop a model of the small open economy that corresponds to our model of the closed economy in Chapter 3. The model shows what determines whether a country is a borrower or lender in world markets, and how policies at home and abroad affect the flows of capital and goods.

In Section 7·3 we discuss the prices at which a country makes exchanges in world markets. We examine what determines the price of domestic goods relative to foreign goods. We also examine what determines the rate at which the domestic currency trades for foreign currencies. Our model shows how protectionist trade policies—policies designed to protect domestic industries from foreign competition—influence the amount of international trade and the rate of exchange.

187

Figure 7-1

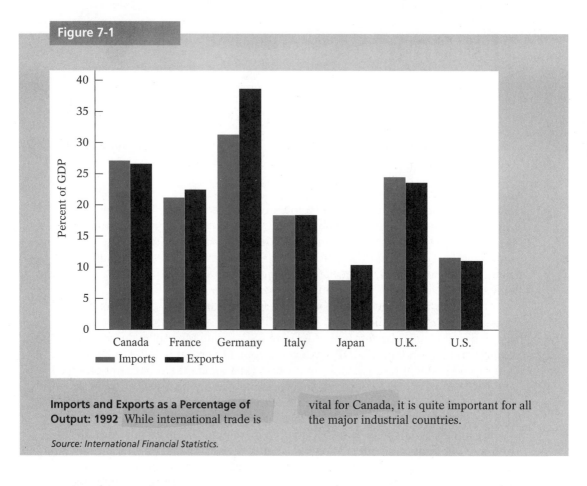

Imports and Exports as a Percentage of Output: 1992 While international trade is vital for Canada, it is quite important for all the major industrial countries.

Source: *International Financial Statistics.*

7•1   The International Flows of Capital and Goods

We begin our study of open-economy macroeconomics by taking another look at national income accounting, which we first discussed in Chapter 2.

The Role of Net Exports

Consider the expenditure on an economy's output of goods and services. In a closed economy, all output is sold domestically, and expenditure is divided into three components: consumption, investment, and government purchases. In an open economy, some output is sold domestically, and some is exported to be sold abroad. We can divide expenditure on an open economy's output Y into four components:

- Consumption of domestic goods and services—C^d
- Investment spending on domestic goods—I^d

• Government purchases of domestic goods and services—G^d

• Exports of domestic goods and services—EX

The division of expenditure into these components is expressed in the identity

$$Y = C^d + I^d + G^d + EX.$$

The sum of the first three terms, $C^d + I^d + G^d$, is domestic spending on domestic goods and services. The fourth term, EX, is foreign spending on domestic goods and services.

We now want to make this identity more useful. To do this, note that domestic spending on all goods and services is the sum of domestic spending on domestic goods and services and on foreign goods and services. Hence, total consumption C equals consumption of domestic goods and services C^d plus consumption of foreign goods and services C^f; total investment I equals investment of domestic goods and services I^d plus investment of foreign goods and services I^f; and total government purchases G equals government purchases of domestic goods and services G^d plus government purchases of foreign goods and services G^f. We write this as:

$$C = C^d + C^f.$$
$$I = I^d + I^f.$$
$$G = G^d + G^f.$$

We substitute these three equations into the identity above:

$$Y = (C - C^f) + (I - I^f) + (G - G^f) + EX.$$

We can rearrange to obtain

$$Y = C + I + G + EX - (C^f + I^f + G^f).$$

The sum of domestic spending on foreign goods and services $(C^f + I^f + G^f)$ is expenditure on imports (IM). We can thus write the national income accounts identity as

$$Y = C + I + G + EX - IM.$$

Because spending on imports is included in domestic spending $(C + I + G)$, and because goods and services imported from abroad are not part of a country's output, this equation subtracts spending on imports. Defining **net exports** to be exports minus imports $(NX = EX - IM)$, the identity becomes

$$Y = C + I + G + NX.$$

This equation states that expenditure on domestic output is the sum of consumption, investment, government purchases, and net exports. This form of the national income accounts identity is the most common; it should be familiar from Chapter 2.

The national income accounts identity shows how domestic output, domestic spending, and net exports are related. In particular,

$$NX = Y - (C + I + G)$$

Net Exports = Output − Domestic Spending.

If output exceeds domestic spending, we export the difference: net exports are positive. If output falls short of domestic spending, we import the difference: net exports are negative.

[handwritten: IF y > (C+I+G) ∴ EXPORT THE DIFFERENCE (NX POSITIVE).]

Net Foreign Investment and the Trade Balance

In an open economy, as in the closed economy we discussed in Chapter 3, financial markets and goods markets are closely related. To see the relationship, we must rewrite the national income accounts identity in terms of saving and investment. Begin with the identity

$$Y = C + I + G + NX.$$

[handwritten: Rewrite in terms of S + I]

Subtract C and G from both sides to obtain

$$Y - C - G = I + NX.$$

Recall from Chapter 3 that $Y - C - G$ is national saving (S), the sum of private saving ($Y - T - C$), and public saving ($T - G$). Therefore,

[handwritten: S = Sₚ + S_G, (T−G) (Y−T−C)]

$$S = I + NX.$$

Subtracting I from both sides of the equation, we can write the national income accounts identity as

$$S - I = NX.$$

[handwritten: ∴ NATIONAL INCOME ACCOUNTS IDENTITY]

This form of the national income accounts identity shows the relationship between the international flow of funds for capital accumulation ($S - I$) and the international flow of goods and services (NX).

Let's look more closely at each part of this identity. $S - I$ is called **net foreign investment**, which is the excess of domestic saving over domestic investment; it is equal to the amount that domestic residents are lending abroad minus the amount that foreigners are lending to us. The second part of this identity, NX, is called the **trade balance**, which is another name for our net export of goods and services.

The national income accounts identity says that net foreign investment always equals the trade balance. That is,

Net Foreign Investment = Trade Balance

$$S - I = NX.$$

[handwritten: ALWAYS]

If $S - I$ and NX are positive, we have a *trade surplus*. In this case, we are net

[handwritten: if pos = trade surplus]

lenders in world financial markets, and we are exporting more goods than we are importing. If *S − I* and *NX* are negative, we have a *trade deficit*. In this case, we are net borrowers in world financial markets, and we are importing more goods than we are exporting.

The national income accounts identity shows that the international flow of funds to finance capital accumulation and the international flow of goods and services are two sides of the same coin. On the one hand, if our saving exceeds our investment, the saving that is not invested domestically is used to make loans to foreigners. Foreigners require these loans because we are providing them with more goods and services than they are providing us. That is, we are running a trade surplus. On the other hand, if our investment exceeds our saving, the extra investment must be financed by borrowing from abroad. These foreign loans enable us to import more goods and services than we export. That is, we are running a trade deficit.

Note that the international flow of capital can take many forms. It is easiest to assume—as we have done so far—that when we run a trade deficit, foreigners make loans to us. This happens, for example, when Americans buy the debt issued by Canadian corporations or by provincial governments. But, equivalently, the flow of capital can take the form of foreigners buying domestic assets. For example, when Japanese investors buy an apartment building in Vancouver, that transaction reduces net foreign lending by Canadians. In both the case of foreigners buying domestically issued debt and the case of foreigners buying domestically owned assets, foreigners are obtaining a claim to the future returns to domestic capital. In other words, in both cases, foreigners end up owning some of the domestic capital stock.

7•2 Saving and Investment in a Small Open Economy

So far, our discussion of the international flows has merely involved accounting identities. That is, we have defined some of the variables that measure transactions in an open economy, and we have shown the links among these variables that follow from their definitions. Our next step is to develop a model that explains the behaviour of these variables. We then use the model to answer questions such as how the trade balance responds to changes in policy.

Here we present a model of the international flows of capital and goods. Since net foreign investment is domestic saving minus domestic investment, our model explains net foreign investment by explaining these two variables. The model also explains the trade balance, because the trade balance must equal net foreign investment.

To develop this model, we use some of the elements of the model of national income in Chapter 3. In contrast to the model in Chapter 3, however, we do not assume that the real interest rate equilibrates saving and investment. Instead, we allow the economy to run a trade deficit and borrow from other countries, or to run a trade surplus and lend to other countries.

Assume instead is SMALL OPEN ECON ○○ Interest rate = wald Interest rate r ✷

If the real interest rate does not equilibrate saving and investment in this model, what does determine the real interest rate? The simplest assumption is that the economy we are examining is a **small open economy** with perfect capital mobility. By "small" we mean that this economy is a small part of the world market and thus, by itself, can have only a negligible effect on the world interest rate. By "perfect capital mobility" we mean that residents of the country have full access to world financial markets. In particular, the government does not impede international borrowing or lending. Thus, the interest rate in a small open economy equals the **world interest rate** r^*, the real interest rate prevailing in world financial markets, plus the risk premium γ associated with that particular economy. We write

$$r = r^* + \gamma. \quad \leftarrow \text{risk premium. associated w} \atop \text{econ.}$$

The small open economy takes the world real rate of interest as given, but its policies can have some effect on the risk premium.

Risk premium demanded by foreign lenders in case in con's t.

Foreign lenders demand a risk premium when lending funds to Canadian firms and governments if they anticipate that the Canadian dollar may fall in value while the loan is outstanding. If that happens, foreign lenders will suffer a capital loss when they turn their earnings back into their own currency after the loan is repaid. To be compensated for that expected capital loss, lenders demand a yield that exceeds the world interest rate.

Figure 7-2 shows data for Canadian and American interest rates since 1962. Because we can interpret the U.S. interest rate as the "world" interest rate in our theoretical analysis, we see that the Canadian risk premium was quite small (and sometimes even negative) before 1975. More recently, the risk premium has widened somewhat, and many analysts attribute this to the fact that foreign lenders have become uneasy about both the size of Canadian government budget deficits and the prospect of prolonged political uncertainty surrounding the question of Quebec separation. Both these problems are expected to decrease the government's resolve in maintaining zero inflation. If Canada begins to inflate at a more rapid rate than other countries, the Canadian dollar will have to fall in value to keep Canada's exports from being priced out of foreign markets.

Bic of yield differentials there are short-run departures from Eqn 1-6

The interest rate differential shown in Figure 7-2 involves many short-run variations. These variations cannot be explained by longer-run issues, such as trends in political uncertainty. Instead, they are a result of the fact that it takes some time for international lenders to react to yield differentials. For example, if the Canadian interest rate rises above the American yield, it takes some time for lenders to notice that there is a substantial payoff to rearranging their bond holdings. Then, they must sell bonds in the rest of the world to obtain the funds necessary to buy Canadian bonds. Only after enough lenders have made this switch will the price paid for Canadian bonds be bid up sufficiently to force the effective yield earned by new buyers back down to equality with opportunities elsewhere. It is not surprising, therefore, that there are short-run departures from the equilibrium relationship.

For much of our discussion, we abstract from issues of political uncertainty, and so we set the risk premium, γ, equal to 0. In other words, given the longer-run focus in this chapter, we give little emphasis to the temporary de-

Figure 7-2

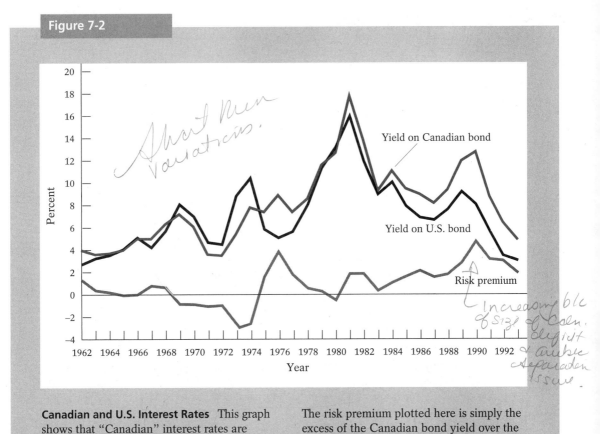

[handwritten: Short Run Variations.]

[handwritten right margin: Increasing b/c of size of Cdn. deficit & double separation issue.]

Canadian and U.S. Interest Rates This graph shows that "Canadian" interest rates are largely determined in the rest of the world.

The risk premium plotted here is simply the excess of the Canadian bond yield over the U.S. bond yield.

Source: Review (Ottawa: Bank of Canada), various issues, Table F1.

partures from the equal yield relationship, and we assume

[handwritten: Instead assume this b/c dealing w long run i.e. Y=0.]

$$r = r^*.$$

The small open economy takes its interest rate as given by the world real interest rate.

Let us discuss for a moment what determines the world real interest rate. In a closed economy, the equilibrium of saving and investment determines the interest rate. Surely, the world economy—barring interplanetary trade—is a closed economy. Therefore, the equilibrium of world saving and world investment determines the world interest rate. Canada's small open economy has a negligible effect on the world real interest rate because, being a small part of the world, it has a negligible effect on world saving and world investment.

[handwritten right margin: Small open econ has negligable effect on S & I]

The Model

To build the model of the longer-run developments in a small open economy, we take three assumptions from Chapter 3:

- The output of the economy Y is fixed by the factors of production and the production function. We write this as

$$Y = \bar{Y} = F(\bar{K}, \bar{L}).$$

- Consumption C is positively related to disposable income $Y - T$. We write the consumption function as

$$C = C(Y - T).$$

- Investment I is negatively related to the real interest rate r. We write the investment function as

$$I = I(r).$$

These are the three key elements of our model. If you do not understand them, review Chapter 3 before continuing.

We can now return to the accounting identity and write it as

$$NX = (Y - C - G) - I$$
$$NX = S - I.$$

Substituting our three assumptions from Chapter 3 and the condition that the interest rate equals the world interest rate, we obtain

$$NX = [\bar{Y} - C(\bar{Y} - T) - G] - I(r^*)$$
$$= \quad\quad \bar{S} \quad\quad\quad - I(r^*).$$

This equation shows what determines saving (S) and investment (I)—and thus the trade balance (NX). Remember that saving depends on fiscal policy (G and T): lower government purchases or higher taxes raise national saving. Investment depends on the world real interest rate (r^*): high interest rates make some investment projects unprofitable. Therefore, the trade balance depends on these variables as well. We can use this equation to examine how the trade balance responds to changes in the economy, such as changes in fiscal policy.

In Chapter 3 we graphed saving and investment as we see in Figure 7-3. In the closed economy of that chapter, the real interest rate adjusts to equilibrate saving and investment—that is, the real interest rate is found where the saving and investment curves cross. In the small open economy, however, the real interest rate equals the world real interest rate. *The trade balance is determined by the difference between saving and investment at the world interest rate.*

At this point, one might wonder about the mechanism that causes the trade balance to equal net foreign investment. The determinants of net foreign investment are easy to understand. When domestic saving falls short of domestic investment, investors borrow from abroad; when saving exceeds investment, the excess is lent to other countries. But what causes those who import and export to behave in a way that ensures that the international flow of goods exactly balances this international flow of capital? For now we leave this question unanswered, but we return to it later in the chapter when we discuss exchange rates.

Figure 7-3

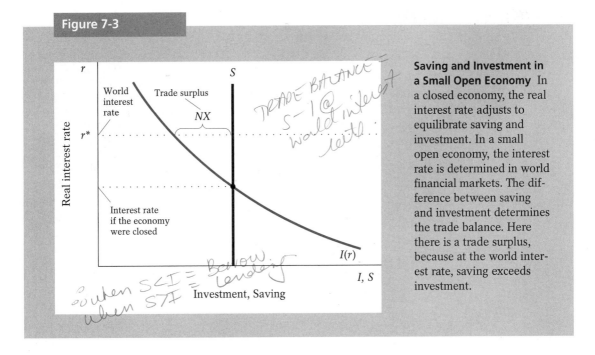

Handwritten notes on figure: TRADE BALANCE = S − I @ world interest rate

when S<I = Borrow / lending
when S>I

oo when S<I = Borrow / lending when S>I

Saving and Investment in a Small Open Economy In a closed economy, the real interest rate adjusts to equilibrate saving and investment. In a small open economy, the interest rate is determined in world financial markets. The difference between saving and investment determines the trade balance. Here there is a trade surplus, because at the world interest rate, saving exceeds investment.

How Policies Influence the Trade Balance

Suppose that the economy begins in a position of balanced trade. That is, at first, its exports exactly balance its imports, so net exports NX equal zero, and investment I equals saving S. Let's use our model to predict the effects of government policies at home and abroad.

Fiscal Policy at Home Consider first what happens to the small open economy if the government expands domestic spending by increasing government purchases without increasing taxes. The increase in G reduces national saving, because $S = Y - C - G$. With an unchanged world real interest rate, investment remains the same. Therefore, saving falls below investment, and some investment must now be financed by borrowing from abroad. Since $NX = S - I$, the fall in S implies a fall in NX. The economy now runs a trade deficit.

The same logic applies to a decrease in taxes T. A tax cut raises disposable income $Y - T$, stimulates consumption, and reduces national saving. (Even though some of the tax cut finds its way into private saving, public saving falls by the full amount of the tax cut; in total, saving falls.) Since $NX = S - I$, the reduction in national saving in turn lowers NX.

Figure 7-4 illustrates these effects. A fiscal policy change that increases private consumption C or public consumption G reduces national saving $(Y - C - G)$ and, therefore, shifts to the left the vertical line that represents saving. Because NX is the distance between the saving schedule and the investment schedule at the world interest rate, this shift reduces NX. *Hence, starting from balanced trade, a change in fiscal policy that reduces national saving leads to a trade deficit.*

Handwritten margin notes:
when G↑

↑G = ↓S: b/c r is same, I is same, S<I = Borrow ↓ ↓NX

∴ ↑G = ↓S = ↓NX trade deficit

↓T = ↑Yd ∴ ↑C ∴ ↓S ∴ ↓NX.

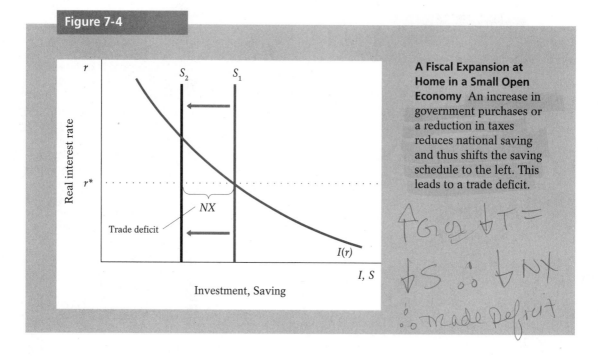

Figure 7-4

A Fiscal Expansion at Home in a Small Open Economy An increase in government purchases or a reduction in taxes reduces national saving and thus shifts the saving schedule to the left. This leads to a trade deficit.

CASE STUDY

7·1 **The Twin Deficits**

Government budget deficits and trade deficits are linked by the fundamental accounting identity: the trade surplus equals the excess of national saving over domestic investment. Since national saving is the sum of private saving $(Y - T - C)$ and public saving $(T - G)$, this fundamental identity can be rephrased as

 Trade Deficit = Government Budget Deficit + The Excess of Investment Over Private Saving.

Many governments have run up large budget deficits in recent years without a corresponding increase in private saving relative to investment. Given these developments, we should expect to see these countries with large trade deficits. Moreover, it should be the case that the larger a country's government budget deficit, the larger its trade deficit.

   A country's trade with other countries is recorded in what are called the *balance of payments* accounts. Trades in goods and services are listed in the *current account* of this table, while trades in financial assets are listed in the *capital account* section. The twin deficits relationship that we have just noted should be evident if we compare government budget deficits and current account deficits (from the balance of payments records) across countries.

   This comparison is given in Figure 7-5. This scatterplot shows the joint observation (in 1992) on the twin deficits for all G7 countries. The positive correlation is evident in the graph. It follows that no country can "solve" its trade deficit "problem" without achieving some combination of reducing its govern-

Figure 7-5

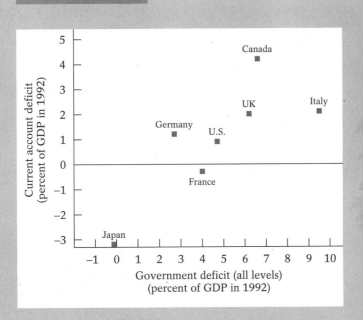

The Twin Deficits This scatterplot shows the joint observation on the twin deficits for all G7 countries in 1992. The positive correlation is evident from the graph, and this supports the basic proposition that if a country's citizens "spend beyond their means," they must increase their indebtedness with the rest of the world.

Source: Canada's Economic Challenge: Background (Ottawa: Department of Finance, 1994): 40, 43.

ment budget deficit, increasing its rate of private saving, and decreasing its rate of investment spending.

It is interesting to interpret the rhetoric on both sides concerning the massive trade imbalance between the Japanese and the Americans. Japan needs a trading surplus in manufactured goods to finance its trade deficit in the area of primary commodities (which Japan must import, given its natural geography). But the United States is concerned about the large magnitude of the net surplus Japan has in the trade between the two nations. American politicians argue that the Japanese should raise government spending to stimulate Japanese imports from the United States and to force a government budget deficit there. Given the connection between the twin deficits, this would help reduce the U.S. trade deficit, without the Americans' having to make painful choices themselves. Like everyone else, the Americans find it difficult to make large cuts in their own government budget deficit or to make cuts in domestic investment (since these cuts lower capital accumulation and future living standards within the country). Knowledge of the twin deficits relationship allows us to understand the logic behind these trade disputes.

Fiscal Policy Abroad Consider now what happens to a small open economy when foreign governments increase their government purchases. If these foreign countries are a small part of the world economy, then their fiscal change has a negligible impact on other countries. But if these foreign countries are a large part of the world economy, their increase in government purchases reduces world saving and causes the world interest rate to rise.

The increase in the world interest rate in turn reduces investment in the small open economy. Because there has been no change in domestic saving, saving S now exceeds investment I. Some of the saving begins to flow abroad. Since $NX = S - I$, the reduction in I must also increase NX. Hence, reduced saving abroad leads to a trade surplus at home.

Figure 7-6 illustrates how a small open economy starting from balanced trade responds to a foreign fiscal expansion. Because the policy change is occurring abroad, the domestic saving and investment schedules remain the same. The only change is an increase in the world interest rate. Since the trade balance is the difference between the two schedules, the increase in the interest rate leads to a trade surplus. *Hence, an increase in the world interest rate due to a fiscal expansion abroad leads to a trade surplus.*

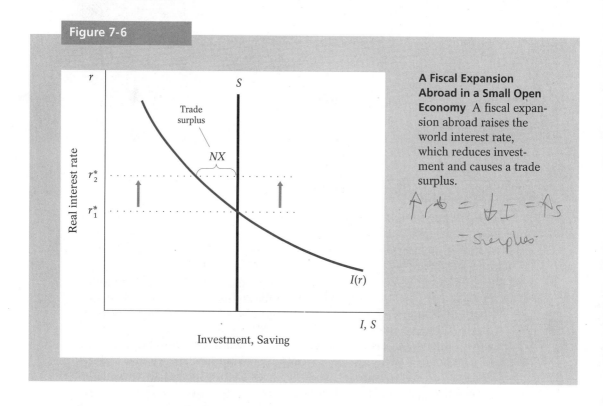

Figure 7-6

A Fiscal Expansion Abroad in a Small Open Economy A fiscal expansion abroad raises the world interest rate, which reduces investment and causes a trade surplus.

Shifts in Investment Demand Consider what happens to the small open economy if its investment schedule shifts outward. This shift would occur if, for example, the government changed the tax laws to encourage domestic investment by providing an investment tax credit. Figure 7-7 illustrates the impact of a shift in the investment schedule. At a given world interest rate, investment is now higher. Because saving is unchanged, some investment must now be financed by borrowing from abroad. Of course, $NX = S - I$, so the increase in I implies a decrease in NX. Hence, *an outward shift in the investment schedule causes a trade deficit.*

Figure 7-7

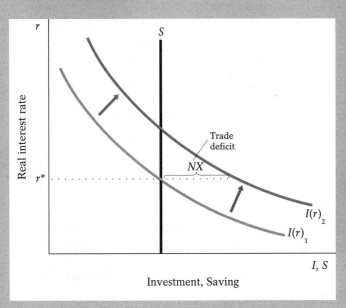

A Shift in the Investment Schedule in a Small Open Economy An outward shift in the investment schedule leads to a trade deficit.

[handwritten: I shifts ∴ ↑I=↓NX deficit]

CASE STUDY

7·2 Fiscal Policy and the Canadian Economy

Several instances of major fiscal expansion in the rest of the world have occurred in the last 15 years. For example, the United States ran a large government budget deficit throughout the 1980s, as President Ronald Reagan introduced major tax cuts without, at the same time, persuading Congress to make similar reductions in government spending. Also in the late 1980s, the reunification of Germany led that country's government to run up a series of large fiscal deficits, as officials tried to raise opportunities for those living in the former East Germany in just a few years.

These events pushed up the general level of world interest rates, but they did not produce a trade surplus for Canada, because these events were dominated (in Canada) by the large increase in Canadian government budget deficits. By raising world interest rates, the international developments did reduce investment spending in Canada. Overspending by the Canadian governments, however, decreased national saving by an even bigger amount, so Canada's trade balance deteriorated.

Evaluating Economic Policy

The central message of our model of the open economy is that the flow of goods and services measured by the trade balance is inextricably connected to the flow of funds for capital accumulation measured by net foreign investment.

Net Foreign Investment = $S^d - I^d$. domestic

Policies that: ↑I or ↓S = TRADE DEFICIT ↓I for ↑S = trade surplus.

Net foreign investment is the difference between domestic saving and domestic investment. Thus, the impact of economic policies on the trade balance can always be found by examining their impact on saving and investment. Policies that increase investment or decrease saving tend to cause a trade deficit, and policies that decrease investment or increase saving tend to cause a trade surplus.

Our analysis of the open economy has been positive, not normative. That is, our analysis of how economic policies influence the international flows of capital and goods does not tell us whether these policies are desirable. Evaluating economic policies and their impact on the open economy is a frequent topic of debate among economists and policymakers.

When a country runs a trade deficit, policymakers must confront the question of whether the trade deficit represents a national problem. Most economists view a trade deficit not as a problem in itself, but perhaps as a symptom of a problem. Trade deficits typically reflect a low saving rate. A low saving rate means that we are putting away less for the future. In a closed economy, low saving leads to low investment and a smaller future capital stock. In an open economy, low saving leads to a trade deficit and a growing foreign debt, which eventually must be repaid. In both cases, high current consumption leads to lower future consumption, implying that future generations bear the burden of low national saving.

Yet trade deficits are not always a reflection of economic malady. When poor rural economies develop into modern industrial economies, they often finance high investment by foreign borrowing. Thus, trade deficits are sometimes a sign of economic development. One cannot judge economic performance from the trade balance alone. Instead, one must look at the underlying causes of the international flows.

7•3 Exchange Rates

Having built a model of the international flows of capital and of goods and services, we now examine the prices that apply to these transactions. The *exchange rate* between two countries is the price at which exchanges between them take place. In this section we first examine precisely what the exchange rate measures, and then discuss how exchange rates are determined.

Nominal and Real Exchange Rates

Economists distinguish between two exchange rates: the nominal exchange rate and the real exchange rate. Let's discuss each in turn and see how they are related.

The Nominal Exchange Rate The **nominal exchange rate** is the relative price of the currency of two countries. For example, if the exchange rate between the Canadian dollar and the Japanese yen is 75 yen per dollar, then you can exchange one dollar for 75 yen in world markets for foreign currency. A Japanese who wants to obtain dollars would pay 75 yen for each dollar he or she bought. A Canadian who wants to obtain yen would get 75 yen for each dollar he or she paid. When people refer to "the exchange rate" between two countries, they usually mean the nominal exchange rate.

The Real Exchange Rate The **real exchange rate** is the relative price of the goods of two countries. That is, the real exchange rate tells us the rate at which we can trade the goods of one country for the goods of another. The real exchange rate is sometimes called the *terms of trade*.

To see the relation between the real and nominal exchange rates, consider a single good produced in many countries: cars. Suppose a Canadian car costs $10,000 and a similar Japanese car costs 1.5 million yen. To compare the prices of the two cars, we must convert them into a common currency. If a Canadian dollar is worth 75 yen, then the Canadian car costs 750,000 yen. Comparing the price of the Canadian car (750,000 yen) and the price of the Japanese car (1.5 million yen), we conclude that the Canadian car costs one half of what the Japanese car costs. In other words, at current prices, we can exchange 2 Canadian cars for 1 Japanese car.

We can summarize our calculation above as follows:

$$\frac{\text{Real Exchange}}{\text{Rate}} = \frac{(75 \text{ Yen/Dollar}) \times (10{,}000 \text{ Dollars/Canadian Car})}{(1.5 \text{ Million Yen/Japanese Car})}$$

$$= 0.5 \text{ Canadian Car/Japanese Car.}$$

At these prices and this exchange rate, we obtain one half of a Japanese car per Canadian car. More generally, we can write this calculation as

$$\frac{\text{Real Exchange}}{\text{Rate}} = \frac{\text{Nominal Exchange Rate} \times \text{Price of Domestic Good}}{\text{Price of Foreign Good}}.$$

The rate at which we exchange foreign and domestic goods depends on the prices of the goods in the local currencies and on the rate at which the currencies are exchanged.

This calculation of the real exchange rate for a single good suggests how we should define the real exchange rate for a broader basket of goods. Let e be the nominal exchange rate (the number of yen per dollar), P be the price level in Canada (measured in dollars), and P^* be the price level in Japan (measured in yen). Then the real exchange rate ε is

Real	Nominal	Ratio of
Exchange =	Exchange ×	Price
Rate	Rate	Levels
ε =	e	× (P/P^*).

The real exchange rate between two countries is computed from the nominal exchange rate and the price levels in the two countries. *If the real exchange rate is high, foreign goods are relatively cheap and domestic goods are relatively expensive. If the real exchange rate is low, foreign goods are relatively expensive and domestic goods are relatively cheap.*

How Newspapers Report the Exchange Rate

FYI

You can find exchange rates reported daily in many newspapers. Here's how they are reported in the Toronto *Globe and Mail*.

Notice in the top line that the Canada–United States exchange rate is reported in two ways. On this Friday, a Canadian dollar bought $0.7255 U.S., and a U.S. dollar bought $1.38 Canadian currency. We can say the exchange rate is 1.38 Canadian dollars per U.S. dollar, or we can say the exchange rate is 0.7255 U.S. dollars per Canadian dollar. Since 1.38 equals 1/0.7255, these two ways of expressing the exchange rate are equivalent. This book always expresses the exchange rate in units of foreign currency per Canadian dollar—the opposite of most of the entries in the *Globe and Mail* table.

Near the very bottom of the table, it is indicated that the U.S. dollar traded at a slightly lower value compared to the previous day. That means that the Canadian dollar had increased in value somewhat. Since we are defining the value of the Canadian dollar as our exchange rate, such a fall in the exchange rate is called a *depreciation* of our dollar; a rise in the exchange rate is called an *appreciation*.

Mid-market rates in Toronto at noon, April 22, 1994. Prepared by the Bank of Montreal Treasury Group.

		$1 U.S. in Cdn.$ =	$1 Cdn. in U.S.$ =
U.S./Canada spot		1.3783	0.7255
1 month forward		1.3804	0.7244
2 months forward		1.3826	0.7233
3 months forward		1.3844	0.7223
6 months forward		1.3904	0.7192
12 months forward		1.3988	0.7149
3 years forward		1.4278	0.7004
5 years forward		1.4533	0.6881
7 years forward		1.4858	0.6730
10 years forward		1.5483	0.6459
Canadian dollar	High	1.3083	0.7644
in 1994:	Low	1.3990	0.7148
	Average	1.3503	0.7406

Country	Currency	Cdn. $ per unit	U.S. $ per unit
Britain	Pound	2.0509	1.4880
1 month forward		2.0518	1.4864
2 months forward		2.0534	1.4852
3 months forward		2.0549	1.4843
6 months forward		2.0610	1.4823
12 months forward		2.0709	1.4805
Germany	Mark	0.8139	0.5905
1 month forward		0.8140	0.5897
3 months forward		0.8150	0.5887
6 months forward		0.8179	0.5882
12 months forward		0.8249	0.5897
Japan	Yen	0.013300	0.009650
1 month forward		0.013320	0.009650
3 months forward		0.013359	0.009650
6 months forward		0.013418	0.009651
12 months forward		0.013501	0.009652
Algeria	Dinar	0.0460	0.0333
Argentina	Peso	1.37734	0.99930
Australia	Dollar	0.9903	0.7185
Austria	Schilling	0.11577	0.08400
Barbados	Dollar	0.6858	0.4975
Belgium	Franc	0.03958	0.02872
Brazil	Cruzeiro	0.00116	0.00084
Bulgaria	Lev	0.0260	0.0189
Chile	Peso	0.003247	0.002356
China	Renminbi	0.1586	0.1150
Czech Rep.	Koruna	0.0463	0.0336

Country	Currency	Cdn. $ per unit	U.S. $ per unit
Denmark	Krone	0.2076	0.1506
Egypt	Pound	0.4076	0.2957
Finland	Markka	0.2515	0.1824
France	Franc	0.2374	0.1722
Greece	Drachma	0.00555	0.00403
Hong Kong	Dollar	0.1784	0.1294
Hungary	Forint	0.01330	0.00965
Iceland	Krona	0.01918	0.01391
India	Rupee	0.04434	0.03217
Ireland	Punt	1.9922	1.4454
Israel	N. Shekel	0.4608	0.3343
Italy	Lira	0.000851	0.000617
Lebanon	Pound	0.000815	0.000591
Malaysia	Ringgit	0.5123	0.3717
Mexico	N Peso	0.4093	0.2970
New Zealand	Dollar	0.7896	0.5729
Norway	Krone	0.1878	0.1363
Pakistan	Rupee	0.04526	0.03284
Philippines	Peso	0.05012	0.03636
Poland	Zloty	0.0000615	0.0000446
Romania	Leu	0.0008	0.0006
Russia	Ruble	0.000761	0.000552
Saudi Arabia	Riyal	0.3675	0.2666
Singapore	Dollar	0.8836	0.6411
Slovakia	Koruna	0.0418	0.0303
South Africa	Rand	0.3827	0.2777
South Korea	Won	0.001707	0.001239
Spain	Peseta	0.00999	0.00725
Sweden	Krona	0.1748	0.1268
Switzerland	Franc	0.9585	0.6954
Taiwan	Dollar	0.0525	0.0381
Thailand	Baht	0.0548	0.0398
Trinidad, Tobago	Dollar	0.2477	0.1797
Zambia	Kwacha	0.002120	0.001538
European Currency Unit		1.5733	1.1415
Special Drawing Right		1.9359	1.4045

The U.S. dollar closed at $1.3784 in terms of Canadian funds, down $0.0003 from Thursday. The pound sterling closed at $2.0517, down $0.0033.

In New York, the Canadian dollar closed up $0.0002 at $0.7255 in terms of U.S. funds. The pound sterling was down $0.0020 to $1.4885.

Source: The Globe and Mail, April 23, 1994, p. B 12.

The Real Exchange Rate and Net Exports

Just as the price of bread affects the demand for bread, the relative price of domestic and foreign goods affects the demand for these goods. If the real exchange rate is low so that domestic goods are relatively cheap, domestic residents will purchase few imported goods: they will buy Fords rather than Toyotas, drink Coors rather than Heineken, and go to Canada's Wonderland instead of America's Disney World. For the same reason, foreigners will buy many Canadian goods. Therefore, Canadian net exports will be high.

The opposite occurs if the real exchange rate is high and, therefore, domestic goods are expensive relative to foreign goods. Domestic residents will buy many imported goods, and foreigners will buy few Canadian goods. Therefore, Canadian net exports will be low.

We write this relationship between the real exchange rate and net exports as

$$NX = NX(\varepsilon).$$

NX is a fcn of ε

high ε = low NX
low ε = high NX

This equation states that net exports are a function of the real exchange rate. Figure 7-8 illustrates this negative relationship between the trade balance and the real exchange rate.

Figure 7-8

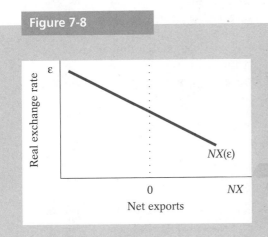

Net Exports and the Real Exchange Rate The figure shows the relationship between the real exchange rate and net exports: the lower the real exchange rate, the less expensive domestic goods are relative to foreign goods, and thus the greater our net exports are. Note that a portion of the horizontal axis measures negative values of *NX*: because imports can exceed exports, net exports can be less than zero.

CASE STUDY

7•3 Traders Respond to the Exchange Rate

The value of the Canadian dollar has fluctuated rather dramatically in recent years. Back in 1986, the Canadian dollar bought only $0.72 U.S. By 1991, Canadian currency had so increased in value that it bought $0.87 U.S. Then, by April 1994, the Canadian dollar had dropped again, and (as in 1986) it could only bring $0.72 U.S. in trades on the foreign exchange market. Given this pattern, it is not surprising that trade across the Canada–United States border was affected during this period.

The phenomenon of "cross-border shopping" was widely discussed in the media. While the Canadian dollar was high in value, many Canadians made one-day trips to border towns in the United States to capitalize on the bargains that could be had in the "warehouse malls" there. On weekend days, there were tremendous traffic jams at the border, as cross-border shoppers swamped the facilities at the customs points. Canadian retailers pleaded with governments to "do something" to help keep their businesses from failing (and many did fail). By 1994, the cross-border shopping "problem" had all but disappeared. Indeed, the media carried stories about how the traffic had started to go the other way. Americans had started to realize how much their currency then could buy in Canada. These developments are perfectly predictable, given the large changes in the exchange rate. Cross-border shopping is just one more instance of households and firms choosing to consume more of the items that are available at lower relative prices.

The variation in the Canada–United States exchange rate during this period also caused controversy regarding the Canada–U.S. Free Trade Agreement, which came into effect in January 1989. From Canada's point of view, one of the purposes of the deal was to allow Canadian firms to gain better access to the large U.S. market (for selling Canadian goods). But there were competing effects on the competitiveness of Canadian firms. The removal of U.S. tariffs that formed part of the Free Trade Agreement made Canadian firms more competitive, but the fact that the Canadian dollar was so much more expensive to buy in 1989 (than it was in 1986) made Canadian firms less competitive. Many analysts argue that the high value of the Canadian exchange rate at that time delayed the benefits that Canada should have obtained from signing the trade deal.

It is not just trade with the United States that is affected by exchange-rate changes. In 1990, one Canadian dollar bought 123 Japanese yen. By 1994, the Canadian dollar had fallen to the point where it could only buy 75 yen. Consumers responded in the obvious way. Back in 1990, North American car manufacturers were suffering losses in sales and were offering large "cashbacks" to attract customers. North American sales of Japanese cars, on the other hand, were booming. Then, by 1994, the Japanese manufacturers were suffering large drops in car sales, and the North American car sales had recovered.

The point of these stories is that the negative slope we have shown for the net export schedule in Figure 7-7 should not be controversial.

The Determinants of the Real Exchange Rate

To construct a model of the real exchange rate, we combine the relationship between net exports and the real exchange rate with our model of the trade balance. We find that two forces determine the real exchange rate:

- The real exchange rate is related to net exports. The lower the real exchange rate is, the less expensive domestic goods are relative to foreign goods, and the greater the demand for net exports is.

- The trade balance must equal net foreign investment, which implies that net exports equal saving minus investment. Saving is fixed by the consumption function and fiscal policy; investment is fixed by the investment function and the world interest rate.

Figure 7-9 illustrates these two conditions. The line showing the relationship between net exports and the real exchange rate slopes downward because a low real exchange rate—a "competitive" domestic economy—makes domestic goods relatively inexpensive. The line representing the excess of saving over investment, $S - I$, is vertical because neither saving nor investment depends on the real exchange rate. The crossing of these two lines determines the equilibrium exchange rate.

Figure 7-9 looks like an ordinary supply-and-demand diagram. In fact, you can think of this diagram as representing the supply and demand for foreign-currency exchange. The vertical line, $S - I$, represents the excess of our saving over our investment, and thus the supply of dollars to be exchanged into foreign currency and invested abroad. The downward-sloping line, NX, represents the net demand for Canadian dollars coming from foreigners who want Canadian dollars to buy Canadian goods. *At the equilibrium real exchange rate, the supply of Canadian dollars available for net foreign investment balances the demand for dollars by foreigners buying our net exports.*

Figure 7-9

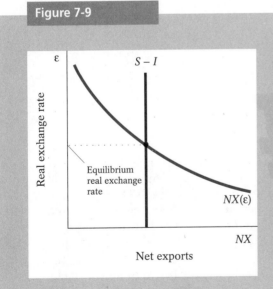

How the Real Exchange Rate Is Determined The real exchange rate is determined by the crossing of the vertical line representing saving minus investment and the downward-sloping net-exports schedule. At this intersection, the quantity of Canadian dollars supplied for net foreign investment equals the quantity of dollars demanded for the net export of goods and services.

How Policies Influence the Real Exchange Rate

We can use this model to show how the changes in economic policy we discussed earlier affect the real exchange rate.

Fiscal Policy at Home

Fiscal Policy at Home   What happens to the real exchange rate if the government reduces national saving by increasing government purchases or cutting taxes? As we discussed earlier, this reduction in saving lowers $S - I$ and thus NX. That is, the reduction in saving causes a trade deficit.

Figure 7-10 shows how the equilibrium real exchange rate adjusts to ensure that NX falls. The change in policy shifts the vertical $S - I$ line to the left, lowering the supply of Canadian dollars to be invested abroad. The lower supply causes the equilibrium real exchange rate to rise—that is, the dollar becomes more valuable. Because of the rise in the value of the dollar, domestic goods become more expensive relative to foreign goods, which causes exports to fall and imports to rise.

Figure 7-10

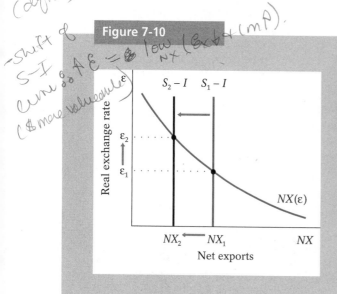

The Impact of Expansionary Fiscal Policy at Home on the Real Exchange Rate
Expansionary fiscal policy at home reduces national saving, which reduces the supply of Canadian dollars and raises the equilibrium real exchange rate.

Fiscal Policy Abroad   What happens to the real exchange rate if foreign governments increase government purchases or cut taxes? This change in fiscal policy reduces world saving and raises the world interest rate. The increase in the world interest rate reduces domestic investment I, which raises $S - I$ and thus NX. That is, the increase in the world interest rate causes a trade surplus.

Figure 7-11 shows that this change in policy shifts the vertical $S - I$ line to the right, raising the supply of Canadian dollars to be invested abroad. The equilibrium real exchange rate falls. That is, the dollar becomes less valuable, and domestic goods become less expensive relative to foreign goods.

Shifts in Investment Demand   What happens to the real exchange rate if investment demand at home increases, perhaps because the Canadian government introduces an investment tax credit? At the given world interest rate, the increase in investment demand leads to higher investment. A higher value of I means lower values of $S - I$ and NX. That is, the increase in investment demand causes a trade deficit.

Figure 7-11

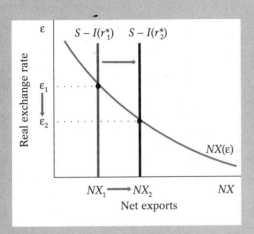

The Impact of Expansionary Fiscal Policy Abroad on the Real Exchange Rate Expansionary fiscal policy abroad reduces world saving, raises the world interest rate, and therefore reduces investment at home. The reduction in investment raises the supply of Canadian dollars and lowers the equilibrium real exchange rate.

Figure 7-12 shows that the increase in investment demand shifts the vertical $S - I$ line to the left, reducing the supply of Canadian dollars to be invested abroad. The equilibrium real exchange rate rises. Hence, when the investment tax credit makes investing in Canada more attractive, it also makes the Canadian dollars necessary to make these investments more valuable. The appreciation of the Canadian dollar makes domestic goods become more expensive relative to foreign goods, which reduces net exports.

Figure 7-12

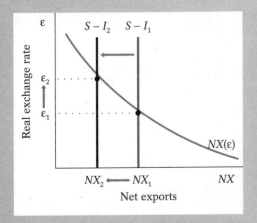

The Impact of an Outward Shift of Investment Demand on the Real Exchange Rate An increase in investment demand raises the quantity of domestic investment. It therefore reduces $S - I$, which reduces the supply of Canadian dollars and raises the equilibrium real exchange rate.

The Effects of Trade Policies

Now that we have a model that explains the trade balance and the real exchange rate, we have the tools to examine the longer-run macroeconomic effects of trade policies. Trade policies are, broadly defined, policies designed to influence directly the amount of goods and services exported or imported. Most often, trade policies take the form of protecting domestic industries from foreign competition—either by placing a tax on foreign imports (a tariff) or restricting the amount of goods and services that can be imported (a quota).

As an example of a protectionist trade policy, consider what would happen if the government prohibited the import of foreign cars. For any given real exchange rate, imports would now be lower, implying that net exports (exports minus imports) would be higher. Thus, the net-exports schedule shifts outward, as in Figure 7-13. In the new equilibrium, the real exchange rate is higher, and net exports are unchanged.

Eg:
NO Imports =
↓ Im ∴ ↑NX.
upward shift
NX(€) curve
∴ ↑ €.

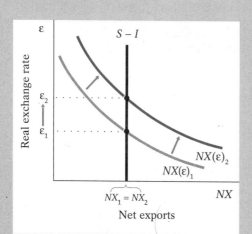

Figure 7-13

The Impact of Protectionist Trade Policies on the Real Exchange Rate A protectionist trade policy, such as a ban on imported cars, raises the demand for net exports and thus raises the real exchange rate.

∴ Protectionist trade policies Don't affect trade Balance; Do not affect our trade

This analysis shows that protectionist trade policies do not affect the trade balance. This surprising conclusion is often overlooked in the popular debate over trade policies. Since a trade deficit reflects an excess of imports over exports, one might guess that reducing imports—such as by prohibiting the import of foreign cars—would reduce a trade deficit. Yet our model shows that protectionist policies lead only to an appreciation of the real exchange rate. The increase in the price of domestic goods relative to foreign goods tends to lower net exports, offsetting the increase in net exports that is directly attributable to the trade restriction. Because protectionist policies do not alter either investment or saving, they cannot alter the trade balance.

Protectionist policies do affect the amount of trade, however. As we have seen, because the real exchange rate appreciates, the goods and services we produce become more expensive relative to foreign goods and services. We therefore export less in the new equilibrium. Since net exports are unchanged, we must import less as well. Thus, protectionist policies reduce both the quantity of imports and the quantity of exports.

This reduction in the total amount of trade is the reason economists almost always oppose protectionist policies. International trade benefits all countries by allowing each country to specialize in what it produces best and by providing each country with a greater variety of goods and services. Protectionist policies diminish these gains from trade. Although these policies benefit certain groups within society—for example, a ban on imported cars helps domestic car producers—society on average is worse off when policies reduce the amount of international trade.

Don't like protectionist policies b/c ↓ trade.

CASE STUDY

7•4 The Conservative Policy Agenda in the 1980s and 1990s

During the 1984–1993 period, Canada's Conservative government had an economic plan that involved four key elements:

- Tax reform
- Deficit reduction
- Disinflation
- Free trade

It is instructive to evaluate this package of initiatives using the analysis of this chapter.

The broad principle underlying tax reform was a move toward sales taxes and away from income taxes. This general move took several forms: (1) the introduction of the goods and services tax (GST), (2) the introduction of the capital gains tax exemption, and (3) the increase in the allowed contributions to registered retirement savings plans. All these initiatives were intended to stimulate private saving. Deficit reduction by the government itself is also a direct move toward higher national saving (since overall saving in the country is the excess of private saving over the government budget deficit). The reduction of inflation was also geared to stimulating saving, since (as we noted in Chapter 6) with nominal (not real) interest income subject to tax in Canada, lower inflation is equivalent to a cut in interest-income taxes.

wanted to stimulate Sp (private) ↓↓ ↓G (deficit) - ↓π.

Thus, the first three government initiatives were intended to shift the $S - I$ line to the right, and so to lower the real exchange rate and decrease the trade deficit. By decreasing the rate at which Canadians become more indebted to foreigners, this policy package was intended to increase the standard of living for future generations.

∴ wanted shift (S−I) curve right ∴ ↓ε & ↓ deficit (∴ ↓ debt & ↑ standard living)

The fourth policy initiative—free trade—has a less obvious effect on the trade balance. The Free Trade Agreement with the United States involved both countries dropping their tariffs by essentially the same amount. Thus, it involved at most a small net shift in the position of the net exports schedule. But one of the expected outcomes was an increased level of investment spending in Canada. With access to the large U.S. market guaranteed (for firms located in Canada), it was expected that plants in Canada would expand. They no longer had to limit their operations to serve the small Canadian market. Such an increase in investment spending in Canada shifts the $S - I$ line to the left. Thus, free trade involves competing effects on welfare: individuals can consume more goods at lower prices, but the investment effect leads to a larger trade deficit, and so (other things equal) to an increased level of foreign indebtedness in the future. The government was confident that the benefits would exceed the costs in this trade-off for two reasons. First, the return on the extra capital employed in Canada should generate enough extra Canadian income for Canadians to be able to afford higher interest payments to foreigners. Second, the other three initiatives within the policy package were intended to increase domestic saving more than free trade increased investment. Thus, the net effect of the package was expected to be a reduction in the trade deficit.

While this policy package can be rationalized easily within our analytical framework, it turned out that there were several slips between the design and the execution of these measures. First, the attempt to reduce the government's budget failed; indeed, government deficits increased during this period. Second, changes to the tax system have been only partial. The GST turned out to be an administrative headache, and it raised much less revenue than was expected. Also, the capital gains exemption was reduced and then was eliminated in 1994. As a result, disinflation was the only policy (of the first three listed above) that was fully and successfully implemented. Thus, much of what was to shift the $S - I$ line to the right did not materialize. As a result, the current account deficit (the negative value for Canadian NX) did not shrink appreciably. Unfortunately, for future generations of Canadians, the rate of foreign debt accumulation was not decreased.

This fact was not only a concern for future generations. Without the intended increase in national saving, the exchange rate remained higher in the late 1980s and early 1990s than had been the government's intention. The high value of the Canadian dollar removed the competitive advantage that Canadian firms were getting through the reduction of U.S. tariffs. In the end, the fact that the government succeeded with respect to its monetary policy objective (disinflation) but failed with respect to its fiscal policy objective (deficit reduction) meant that the overall outcome for both current and future generations was far less than was possible given the basic consistency of the overall package of intended policies.

The Determinants of the Nominal Exchange Rate

We now turn our attention from the real exchange rate to the nominal exchange rate—the rate at which the currencies of two countries trade. Recall the relationship between the real and the nominal exchange rate:

$$\begin{array}{ccccc}
\text{Real} & & \text{Nominal} & & \text{Ratio of} \\
\text{Exchange} & = & \text{Exchange} & \times & \text{Price} \\
\text{Rate} & & \text{Rate} & & \text{Levels} \\
\varepsilon & = & e & \times & (P/P^*).
\end{array}$$

We can write the nominal exchange rate as

$$e = \varepsilon \times (P^*/P).$$

This equation shows that the nominal exchange rate depends on the real exchange rate and the price levels in the two countries. If the domestic price level P rises, then the nominal exchange rate e will fall: because a Canadian dollar is worth less, a dollar will buy fewer yen. On the other hand, if the Japanese price level P^* rises, then the nominal exchange rate will increase: because the yen is worth less, a dollar will buy more yen.

It is instructive to consider changes in exchange rates over time. The exchange rate equation can be written

% Change in e = % Change in ε + % Change in P^* − % Change in P.

The percentage change in ε is the change in the real exchange rate. The percentage change in P is our inflation rate π and the percentage change in P^* is the foreign country's inflation rate π^*. Thus, the percentage change in the nominal exchange rate is

$$\begin{array}{ccccc}
\text{\% Change in } e & = & \text{\% Change in } \varepsilon & + & (\pi^* - \pi) \\
\text{Percent Change in} & & \text{Percent Change in} & & \text{Difference in} \\
\text{Nominal Exchange Rate} & = & \text{Real Exchange Rate} & + & \text{Inflation Rates.}
\end{array}$$

This equation states that the change in the nominal exchange rate between the currencies of two countries equals the change in the real exchange rate plus the difference in their inflation rates. *If a country has a high rate of inflation relative to Canada, a Canadian dollar will buy an increasing amount of the foreign currency over time. If a country has a low rate of inflation relative to Canada, a Canadian dollar will buy a decreasing amount of the foreign currency over time.*

This analysis shows how monetary policy affects the nominal exchange rate. We know from Chapter 6 that high growth in the money supply leads to high inflation. One consequence of high inflation is a depreciating currency: high π implies falling e. In other words, just as growth in the amount of money raises the price of goods measured in terms of money, it also tends to raise the price of foreign currencies measured in terms of the domestic currency.

CASE STUDY

◆ 7•5   **Inflation and Nominal Exchange Rates**

If we look at data on exchange rates and price levels of different countries, we quickly see the importance of inflation for explaining changes in the nominal exchange rate. The most dramatic examples come from periods of hyperinflation. For example, the price level in Mexico rose by 2,300 percent from 1983 to 1988. Because of this inflation, the number of pesos a person could buy with a U.S. dollar rose from 144 in 1983 to 2,281 in 1988.

The same relationship holds true for countries with more moderate inflation. Figure 7-14 is a scatterplot showing the relationship between inflation and the exchange rate for 11 countries. On the horizontal axis is the difference between each country's average inflation rate and the average inflation rate of the United States, our base for comparison. On the vertical axis is the average percent change in the exchange rate between each country's currency and the U.S. dollar. The positive relationship between these two variables is clear in this figure. Countries with relatively high inflation tend to have depreciating currencies, and countries with relatively low inflation tend to have appreciating currencies.

Figure 7-14

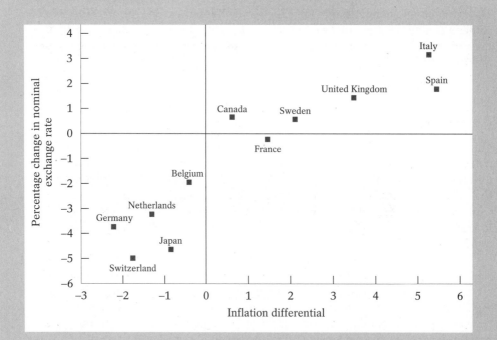

Inflation Differentials and the Exchange Rate This scatterplot shows the relationship between inflation and the nominal exchange rate. The horizontal axis shows the country's average inflation rate minus the U.S. average inflation rate over the period 1970–1991. The vertical axis is the average percentage change in the country's exchange rate (per U.S. dollar) over that period. This figure shows that countries with relatively high inflation tend to have depreciating currencies and that countries with relatively low inflation tend to have appreciating currencies.

Source: International Financial Statistics.

As an example, consider the exchange rate between German marks and U.S. dollars. Both Germany and the United States have experienced inflation over the past 20 years, so both the mark and the dollar buy fewer goods than they once did. But, as Figure 7-14 shows, inflation in Germany has been lower than inflation in the United States. This means that the value of the mark has fallen less than the value of the dollar. Therefore, the number of German marks one can buy with a U.S. dollar has been falling over time.

The Special Case of Purchasing-Power Parity

Not on EXAM

A basic tenet in economics, called the *law of one price*, says that the same good cannot sell for different prices in different locations at the same time. If a bushel of wheat sold for less in Calgary than in Winnipeg, it would be profitable to buy wheat in Calgary and then sell it in Winnipeg. Always ready to take advantage of such opportunities, astute arbitrageurs would increase the demand for wheat in Calgary and increase the supply in Winnipeg. This would drive the price up in Calgary and down in Winnipeg—thereby ensuring that prices are equalized in the two markets.

The law of one price applied to the international marketplace is called **purchasing-power parity**. It states that if international arbitrage is possible, then a dollar (or any other currency) must have the same purchasing power in every country. The argument goes as follows. If a dollar could buy more wheat domestically than abroad, there would be opportunities to profit by buying wheat domestically and selling it abroad. Profit-seeking arbitrageurs would drive up the domestic price of wheat relative to the foreign price. Similarly, if a dollar could buy more wheat abroad than domestically, the arbitrageurs would buy wheat abroad and sell it domestically, driving down the domestic price relative to the foreign price. Thus, profit-seeking by international arbitrageurs drives international wheat prices to equality.

Omit

We can interpret the doctrine of purchasing-power parity using our model of the real exchange rate. The quick action of these international arbitrageurs implies that net exports are highly sensitive to small movements in the real exchange rate. A small decrease in the price of domestic goods relative to foreign goods—that is, a small decrease in the real exchange rate—causes arbitrageurs to buy goods domestically and sell them abroad. Similarly, a small increase in the relative price of domestic goods causes arbitrageurs to import goods from abroad. Therefore, as in Figure 7-15, the net-exports schedule is very flat at the real exchange rate that equalizes purchasing power among countries: any small movement in the real exchange rate leads to a large change in net exports. This extreme sensitivity of net exports guarantees that the equilibrium real exchange rate is always close to the level ensuring purchasing-power parity.

Purchasing-power parity has two important implications. First, since the net-exports schedule is flat, changes in saving or investment do not influence the real or nominal exchange rate. Second, since the real exchange rate is fixed, all changes in the nominal exchange rate result from changes in price levels.

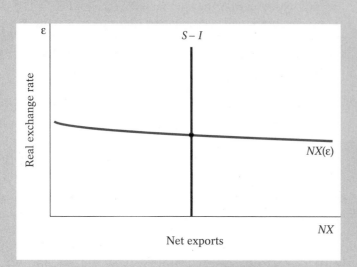

Purchasing-Power Parity The law of one price applied to the international marketplace suggests that net exports are highly sensitive to small movements in the real exchange rate.

Is this doctrine of purchasing-power parity realistic? Most economists believe that, despite its appealing logic, purchasing-power parity does not provide a completely accurate description of the world. First, many goods are not easily traded. A haircut can be more expensive in Tokyo than in Toronto, yet there is no room for international arbitrage since it is impossible to transport haircuts. Second, even tradable goods are not always perfect substitutes. Some consumers prefer Toyotas, and others prefer Fords. Thus, the relative price of Toyotas and Fords can vary to some extent without leaving any profit opportunities. For these reasons, real exchange rates do in fact vary over time.

Although the doctrine of purchasing-power parity does not describe the world perfectly, it does provide a reason to expect limited movement in the real exchange rate. There is much validity to its underlying logic: the farther the real exchange rate drifts from the level predicted by purchasing-power parity, the greater the incentive for individuals to engage in international arbitrage in goods. Although we cannot rely on purchasing-power parity to eliminate all movements in the real exchange rate, this doctrine does provide a reason to expect that movements in the real exchange rate will typically be small or temporary.

CASE STUDY

The Big Mac Around the World

The doctrine of purchasing-power parity says that, after adjusting for exchange rates, goods should sell for the same price everywhere. Conversely, it says that the exchange rate between two currencies should depend on the price levels in the two countries.

Table 7-1

Big Mac Prices and the Exchange Rate: An Application of Purchasing-Power Parity

Country	Currency	Price of a Big Mac	Exchange Rate (per U.S. Dollar)	
			Predicted	Actual
Argentina	Peso	3.60	1.58	1.00
Australia	Dollar	2.45	1.07	1.39
Belgium	Franc	109.00	47.81	32.45
Brazil	Cruzeiro	77,000.00	33,772.00	27,521.00
Britain	Pound	1.79	1.27	1.56
Canada	Dollar	2.76	1.21	1.26
China	Yuan	8.50	3.73	5.68
Denmark	Crown	25.75	11.29	6.06
France	Franc	18.50	8.11	5.34
Germany	Mark	4.60	2.02	1.58
Hong Kong	Dollar	9.00	3.95	7.73
Hungary	Forint	157.00	68.86	88.18
Ireland	Pound	1.48	1.54	1.54
Italy	Lira	4,500.00	1,974.00	1,523.00
Japan	Yen	391.00	171.00	113.00
Malaysia	Ringgit	3.35	1.47	2.58
Mexico	Peso	7.09	3.11	3.10
Netherlands	Guilder	5.45	2.39	1.77
Russia	Ruble	780.00	342.00	686.00
South Korea	Won	2,300.00	1,009.00	796.00
Spain	Peseta	325.00	143.00	114.00
Sweden	Crown	25.50	11.18	7.43
Switzerland	Franc	5.70	2.50	1.45
Thailand	Baht	48.00	21.05	25.16
United States	Dollar	2.28	1.00	1.00

Note: The predicted exchange rate is the exchange rate that would make the price of a Big Mac in that country equal to its price in the United States.

Source: The Economist, April 17, 1993, p. 79.

To see how well this doctrine works, *The Economist,* an international news magazine, regularly collects data on the price of a good sold in many countries: the McDonald's Big Mac hamburger. According to purchasing-power parity, the price of a Big Mac should be closely related to the country's nominal exchange rate. The higher the price of a Big Mac in the local currency, the higher the exchange rate (measured per U.S. dollar) should be.

Table 7-1 presents the international prices in 1993, when a Big Mac sold for $2.28 in the United States. With these data one can use the doctrine of purchasing-power parity to predict nominal exchange rates. For example, since a Big Mac cost 391 yen in Japan, one would predict that the exchange rate between the dollar and the yen was 391/2.28, or 171, yen per dollar. At this exchange rate, a Big Mac would have cost the same in Japan and the United States.

Table 7-1 shows the predicted and actual exchange rates for 24 countries. You can see that the evidence on purchasing-power parity is mixed. In some cases, the predicted and actual exchange rates differed substantially. For example, the predicted exchange rate of 171 yen per dollar was quite different from the actual rate of 113 yen per dollar. Yet, for most countries, the predicted and actual exchange rates were in the same ballpark. In some cases, such as Canada and Mexico, the predicted and actual exchange rates were very close. Although not exact, purchasing-power parity does provide a rough guide to the level of exchange rates.

7•4 Small versus Large Open Economies

In this chapter we have seen how a small open economy works. We have examined the determinants of the international flow of funds for capital accumulation and the international flow of goods and services. We have also examined the determinants of a country's real and nominal exchange rates. Our analysis shows how various policies—monetary policies, fiscal policies, and trade policies—affect the trade balance and the exchange rate.

The economy we have studied is "small" in the sense that its interest rate is fixed by world financial markets. That is, we have assumed that this economy does not affect the world interest rate, and that the economy can borrow and lend at the world interest rate in unlimited amounts. This assumption contrasts with the assumption we made when we studied the closed economy in Chapter 3. In the closed economy, the domestic interest rate equilibrates domestic saving and domestic investment, implying that policies that influence saving or investment alter the equilibrium interest rate.

The small-open-economy specification is directly applicable to Canada. But which of our earlier analyses should one apply to an economy like the United States? The answer is a little of both. On the one hand, the United States is not so large or so isolated that it is immune to developments occurring abroad. The large U.S. trade deficits of the 1980s and early 1990s show the importance of international financial markets for funding U.S. investment. Hence, the closed-economy analysis of Chapter 3 cannot by itself fully explain the impact of policies on the U.S. economy.

On the other hand, the U.S. economy is not so small and so open that the analysis of this chapter applies perfectly either. First, the United States is large enough that it can influence world financial markets. Indeed, U.S. fiscal policy was blamed for the high real interest rates that prevailed throughout the world in the 1980s. Second, capital may not be perfectly mobile among countries. If individuals prefer holding their wealth in domestic rather than foreign assets, funds for capital accumulation will not flow freely to equate interest rates in all countries. For these two reasons, we cannot directly apply our model of the small open economy to the United States.

When analyzing policy for a country like the United States, we need to combine the closed-economy logic of Chapter 3 and the small-open-economy logic of this chapter. The appendix to this chapter builds a model of an economy between these two extremes. In this intermediate case, there is international borrowing and lending, but the interest rate is not fixed by world financial markets. Instead, the more the economy borrows from abroad, the higher the interest rate it must offer foreign investors. The results, not surprisingly, are a mixture of the two polar cases we have already examined.

Consider, for example, a reduction in national saving due to a fiscal expansion. As in the closed economy, this policy raises the interest rate and crowds out investment. As in the small open economy, it also causes a trade deficit and an appreciation of the exchange rate. Hence, although the model of the small open economy examined here does not precisely describe an economy like the United States, it does provide approximately the right answer to how policies affect the trade balance and the exchange rate.

Summary

1. Net exports are the difference between exports and imports. They are equal to the difference between what we produce and what we demand for consumption, investment, and government purchases.

2. Net foreign investment is the excess of domestic saving over domestic investment. The trade balance is the amount received for our net exports of goods and services. The national income accounts identity shows that net foreign investment always equals the trade balance.

3. The impact of any policy on the trade balance can be determined by examining its impact on saving and investment. Policies that raise saving or lower investment lead to a trade surplus, and policies that lower saving or raise investment lead to a trade deficit.

4. The nominal exchange rate is the rate at which one can exchange the currency of one country for the currency of another country. The real exchange rate is the rate at which one can exchange the goods produced by the two countries. The real exchange rate equals the nominal exchange rate multiplied by the ratio of the price levels in the two countries.

5. The higher our real exchange rate, the lower the demand for our net exports. The equilibrium real exchange rate is the rate at which the quantity of net exports demanded equals net foreign investment.

6. The nominal exchange rate is determined by the real exchange rate and the price levels in the two countries. Other things equal, a high rate of inflation leads to a depreciating currency.

KEY CONCEPTS

Net exports

Net foreign investment

Trade balance

Small open economy

World interest rate

Nominal exchange rate

Real exchange rate

Purchasing-power parity

QUESTIONS FOR REVIEW

1. What are net foreign investment and the trade balance? Explain how they are related.

2. Define the nominal exchange rate and the real exchange rate.

3. If a small open economy cuts defense spending, what happens to saving, investment, the trade balance, the interest rate, and the exchange rate?

4. If a small open economy bans the import of Japanese VCRs, what happens to saving, investment, the trade balance, the interest rate, and the exchange rate?

5. If Germany has low inflation and Italy has high inflation, what will happen to the exchange rate between the German mark and the Italian lira?

PROBLEMS AND APPLICATIONS

1. Use the model of the small open economy to predict what would happen to the trade balance, the real exchange rate, and the nominal exchange rate in response to each of the following events.

   a. A fall in consumer confidence about the future induces consumers to spend less and save more.

   b. The introduction of a stylish line of Toyotas makes some consumers prefer foreign cars over domestic cars.

   c. The introduction of automatic teller machines reduces the demand for money.

2. What will happen in a small open economy to the trade balance and the real exchange rate when government purchases increase, such as during a war? Does your answer depend on whether this is a local war or a world war?

3. Suppose that some foreign countries begin to subsidize investment by instituting an investment tax credit.

   a. What happens to world investment demand as a function of the world interest rate?

   b. What happens to the world interest rate?

   c. What happens to investment in our small open economy?

   d. What happens to our trade balance?

   e. What happens to our real exchange rate?

4. "Traveling in Italy is much cheaper now than it was 10 years ago," says a friend. "Ten years ago, one dollar bought 1,000 lire; this year, one dollar buys 1,500 lire."

   Is your friend right or wrong? Given

that total inflation over this period was 40 percent in the Canada and 100 percent in Italy, has it become more or less expensive to travel in Italy? Write your answer using a concrete example—like a cup of Canadian coffee versus a cup of Italian espresso—that will convince your friend.

5. The newspaper reports that the nominal interest rate is 12 percent per year in Canada and 8 percent per year in the United States. Suppose that the real interest rates are equalized in the two countries and that purchasing-power parity holds.

a. Using the Fisher equation, which was discussed in Chapter 6, what can you infer about expected inflation in Canada and in the United States?

b. What can you infer about the expected change in the exchange rate between the Canadian dollar and the U.S. dollar?

c. A friend proposes a get-rich-quick scheme: borrow from a U.S. bank at 8 percent, deposit the money in a Canadian bank at 12 percent, and make a 4 percent profit. What's wrong with this scheme?

The Large Open Economy

Because Canada is so heavily influenced by economic events in the United States, many individuals value an analysis that is appropriate for that country. To provide that analysis, we need to combine the closed-economy logic in Chapter 3 and the small-open-economy logic in this chapter. In this appendix we build a model of an economy between these two extremes, called the *large open economy*. Our interpretation is from the American perspective, so, for the purposes of this appendix, words like "domestic" refer to the United States.

Net Foreign Investment

The key difference between the small and large open economies is the behaviour of net foreign investment. In the model of the small open economy, capital flows freely into or out of the economy at a fixed world interest rate r^*. The model of the large open economy makes a different assumption about international capital flows. To understand that assumption, keep in mind that net foreign investment is the amount that domestic investors lend abroad minus the amount that foreign investors lend here.

Imagine that you are a domestic investor—such as the portfolio manager of a university endowment—deciding where to invest your funds. You could invest domestically (by, for example, making loans to U.S. companies), or you could invest abroad (by making loans to foreign companies). Many factors may affect your decision, but surely one of them is the interest rate you can earn. The higher the interest rate you can earn domestically, the less attractive you would find foreign investment.

Investors abroad face a similar decision. They have a choice between investing in their home country, or lending to the United States. The higher the interest rate in the United States, the more willing foreigners are to lend to U.S. companies and to buy U.S. assets.

Thus, because of the behaviour of both domestic and foreign investors, net foreign investment NFI is negatively related to the domestic interest rate r. As the interest rate rises, less of our saving flows abroad, and more funds for capital accumulation flow in from other countries. We write this as

$$NFI = NFI(r).$$

This equation states that net foreign investment is a function of the domestic interest rate. Figure 7-16 illustrates this relationship. Notice that NFI can be either positive or negative, depending on whether the economy is a lender or borrower in world financial markets.

To see how this NFI function relates to our previous models, consider Figure 7-17. This figure shows two special cases: a vertical NFI function and a horizontal NFI function.

Figure 7-16

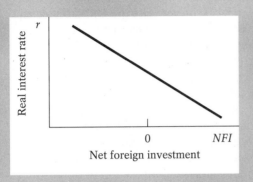

How Net Foreign Investment Depends on the Interest Rate A higher domestic interest rate discourages domestic investors from lending abroad and encourages foreign investors to lend here. Therefore, net foreign investment is negatively related to the interest rate.

The closed economy is the special case in Figure 7-17(a). In the closed economy, $NFI = 0$ at all interest rates. This situation would arise if investors here and abroad were unwilling to hold foreign assets, regardless of the return. It might also arise if the government prohibited its citizens from transacting in foreign financial markets, as some governments do. In the closed economy, there is no international borrowing or lending, and the interest rate adjusts to equilibrate domestic saving and investment.

The small open economy with perfect capital mobility is the special case in Figure 7-17(b). In this case, capital flows freely into and out of the country at the fixed world interest rate, r^*. This situation would arise if investors here and abroad bought whatever asset yielded the highest return, and if this economy

Figure 7-17

(a) The Closed Economy

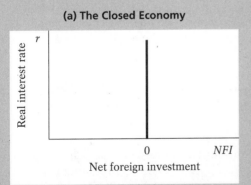

(b) The Small Open Economy With Perfect Capital Mobility

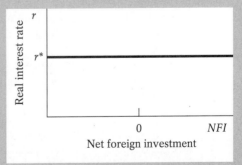

Two Special Cases In the closed economy [Panel (a)], net foreign investment is zero for all interest rates. In the small open economy with perfect capital mobility [Panel (b)], net foreign investment is perfectly elastic at the world interest rate r^*.

were too small to affect the world interest rate. The economy's interest rate would be fixed at the interest rate prevailing in world financial markets.

Why isn't the interest rate of a large open economy like the United States fixed by the world interest rate? There are two reasons. The first is that the United States is large enough to influence world financial markets. The more the United States lends abroad, the greater is the supply of loans in the world economy, and the lower interest rates become around the world. The more the United States borrows from abroad (that is, the more negative *NFI* becomes), the higher world interest rates are. We use the label "large open economy" because this model applies to an economy large enough to affect world interest rates.

There is, however, a second reason that the interest rate in an economy may not be fixed by the world interest rate: capital may not be perfectly mobile. That is, investors here and abroad prefer holding their wealth in domestic rather than foreign assets. Such a preference for domestic assets could arise because of imperfect information about foreign assets or because of government impediments to international borrowing and lending. In either case, funds for capital accumulation will not flow freely to equalize interest rates in all countries. Instead, net foreign investment will depend on domestic interest rates relative to foreign interest rates. U.S. investors will lend abroad only if U.S. interest rates are comparatively low, and foreign investors will lend in the United States only if U.S. interest rates are comparatively high. The large-open-economy model, therefore, may be applied even to a small economy if capital does not flow freely into and out of the economy.

Hence, either because the large open economy affects world interest rates, or because capital is imperfectly mobile, or perhaps for both reasons, the *NFI* function slopes downward. Except for this new *NFI* function, the model of the large open economy resembles the model of the small open economy. We put all the pieces together in the next section.

The Model

To understand how the large open economy works, we need to consider two key markets: the market for loanable funds and the market for foreign exchange. We discuss each in turn.

The Market for Loanable Funds   An open economy's saving S is used in two ways: to finance domestic investment I and to finance net foreign investment *NFI*. We can write

$$S = I + NFI.$$

Consider how these three variables are determined. National saving is fixed by the level of output, fiscal policy, and the consumption function. Investment and net foreign investment both depend on the interest rate. We can write

$$\overline{S} = I(r) + NFI(r).$$

Figure 7-18 shows the market for loanable funds. The supply of loans is national saving. The demand for loans is the sum of the demand for domestic investment and the demand for net foreign investment. The interest rate adjusts to equilibrate supply and demand.

Figure 7-18

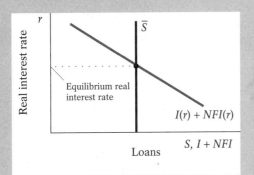

The Market for Loanable Funds in the Large Open Economy At the equilibrium interest rate, the supply of loans from saving (S) balances the demand for loans from domestic investment (I) and net foreign investment (NFI).

The Market for Foreign Exchange Next, consider the relationship between net foreign investment and the trade balance. The national income accounts identity tells us

$$NX = S - I.$$

Since NX is a function of the exchange rate, and since $NFI = S - I$, we can write

$$NX(\varepsilon) = NFI.$$

Figure 7-19 shows the equilibrium in the market for foreign exchange. Once again, the real exchange rate is the price that equilibrates the trade balance and net foreign investment.

The last variable we should consider is the nominal exchange rate. As before, the nominal exchange rate is the real exchange rate times the ratio of the price levels:

$$e = \varepsilon \times (P^*/P).$$

The real exchange rate is determined as in Figure 7-19, and the price levels are

Figure 7-19

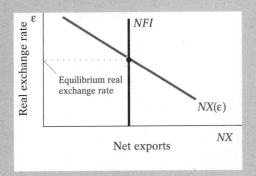

The Market for Foreign Currency Exchange in the Large Open Economy At the equilibrium exchange rate, the supply of dollars from net foreign investment balances the demand for dollars from our net exports of goods and services.

determined by monetary policies here and abroad, as we discussed in Chapter 6. Forces that move the real exchange rate or the price levels also move the nominal exchange rate.

Policies in the Large Open Economy

We can now consider how economic policies influence the large open economy. Figure 7-20 shows the three diagrams we need for the analysis: the equilibrium in the market for loanable funds [Panel (a)], the relationship between the equilibrium interest rate and net foreign investment [Panel (b)], and the equilibrium in the market for foreign exchange [Panel (c)].

Fiscal Policy at Home   Consider the effects of expansionary fiscal policy—an increase in government purchases or a decrease in taxes. Figure 7-21 shows what happens. The policy reduces national saving S, thereby reducing the supply of loans and raising the equilibrium interest rate r. The higher interest rate

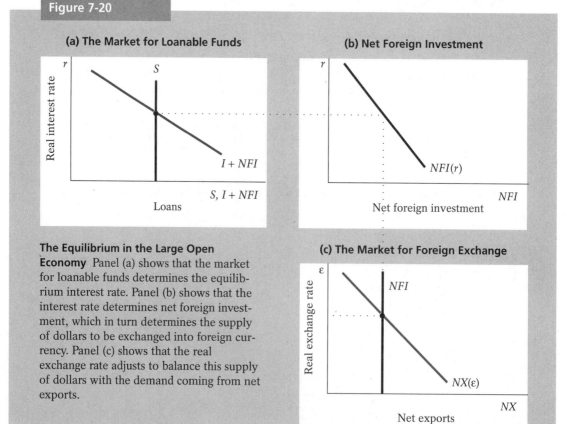

Figure 7-20

(a) The Market for Loanable Funds

(b) Net Foreign Investment

(c) The Market for Foreign Exchange

The Equilibrium in the Large Open Economy Panel (a) shows that the market for loanable funds determines the equilibrium interest rate. Panel (b) shows that the interest rate determines net foreign investment, which in turn determines the supply of dollars to be exchanged into foreign currency. Panel (c) shows that the real exchange rate adjusts to balance this supply of dollars with the demand coming from net exports.

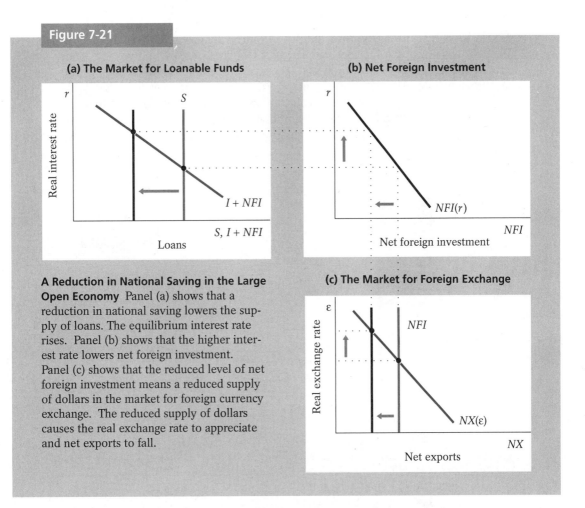

Figure 7-21

(a) The Market for Loanable Funds

(b) Net Foreign Investment

A Reduction in National Saving in the Large Open Economy Panel (a) shows that a reduction in national saving lowers the supply of loans. The equilibrium interest rate rises. Panel (b) shows that the higher interest rate lowers net foreign investment. Panel (c) shows that the reduced level of net foreign investment means a reduced supply of dollars in the market for foreign currency exchange. The reduced supply of dollars causes the real exchange rate to appreciate and net exports to fall.

(c) The Market for Foreign Exchange

reduces both domestic investment I and net foreign investment NFI. The fall in net foreign investment reduces the supply of dollars to be exchanged into foreign currency. The exchange rate appreciates, and net exports fall.

Note that the impact of fiscal policy in this model combines its impact in the closed economy and its impact in the small open economy. As in the closed economy, a fiscal expansion in a large open economy raises the interest rate and crowds out investment. As in the small open economy, a fiscal expansion causes a trade deficit and an appreciation in the exchange rate.

One way to see how the three types of economy are related is to consider the identity

$$S = I + NX.$$

In all three cases, expansionary fiscal policy reduces national saving S. In the closed economy, the fall in S coincides with an equal fall in I, and NX stays constant at zero. In the small open economy, the fall in S coincides with an equal fall in NX, and I remains constant at the level fixed by the world interest rate. The large open economy is the intermediate case: both I and NX fall, each by less than the fall in S.

Shifts in Investment Demand   Suppose that the investment demand schedule shifts outward, perhaps because the U.S. Congress passes an investment tax credit. Figure 7-22 shows the effect. The demand for loans rises, raising the equilibrium interest rate. The higher interest rate reduces net foreign investment: Americans make fewer loans abroad, and foreigners make more loans in the United States. The fall in net foreign investment reduces the supply of dollars in the market for foreign exchange. The exchange rate appreciates, and net exports fall.

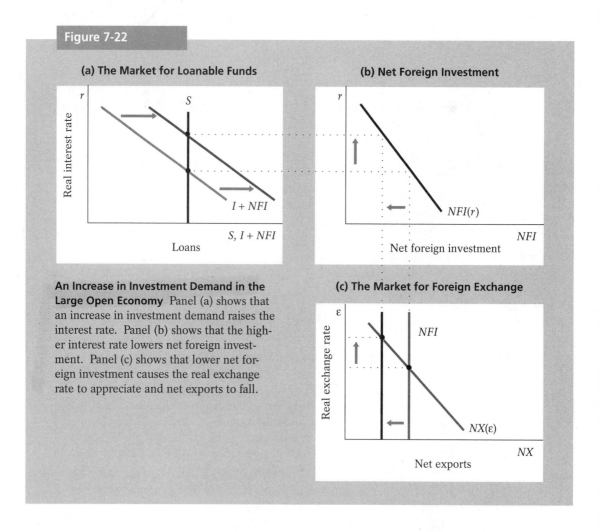

Figure 7-22

(a) The Market for Loanable Funds

(b) Net Foreign Investment

An Increase in Investment Demand in the Large Open Economy   Panel (a) shows that an increase in investment demand raises the interest rate. Panel (b) shows that the higher interest rate lowers net foreign investment. Panel (c) shows that lower net foreign investment causes the real exchange rate to appreciate and net exports to fall.

(c) The Market for Foreign Exchange

Trade Policies   Figure 7-23 shows the effect of a trade restriction, such as an import quota. The reduced demand for imports shifts the net exports schedule outward. Since nothing has changed in the market for loanable funds, the interest rate remains the same, which in turn implies that net foreign investment

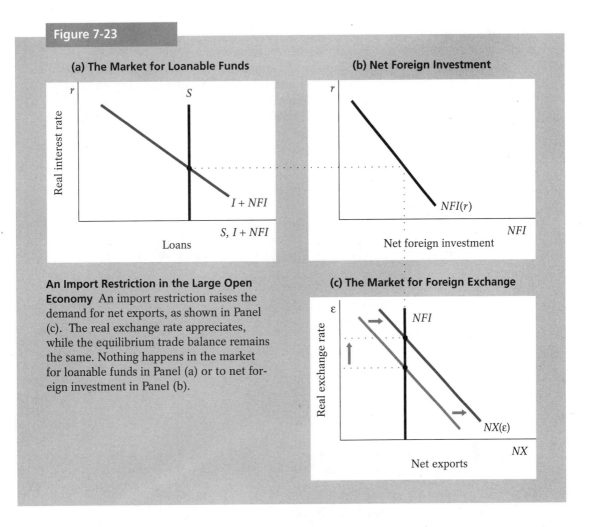

Figure 7-23

(a) The Market for Loanable Funds

(b) Net Foreign Investment

An Import Restriction in the Large Open Economy An import restriction raises the demand for net exports, as shown in Panel (c). The real exchange rate appreciates, while the equilibrium trade balance remains the same. Nothing happens in the market for loanable funds in Panel (a) or to net foreign investment in Panel (b).

(c) The Market for Foreign Exchange

remains the same. The shift in the net exports schedule causes the exchange rate to appreciate. The rise in the exchange rate makes U.S. goods expensive relative to foreign goods, which depresses exports and stimulates imports. In the end, the trade restriction does not affect the trade balance.

Shifts in Net Foreign Investment There are various reasons that the *NFI* schedule might shift. One reason is fiscal policy abroad. For example, suppose that Germany pursues a fiscal policy that raises German saving. This policy reduces the German interest rate. The lower German interest rate discourages American investors from lending in Germany and encourages German investors to lend in the United States. For any given U.S. interest rate, U.S. net foreign investment falls.

Another reason that the *NFI* schedule might shift is political instability abroad. Suppose that a war or revolution breaks out in another country. Investors around the world will try to withdraw their assets from that country and seek a "safe haven" in a stable country such as the United States. The result is a reduction in U.S. net foreign investment.

Figure 7-24 shows the impact of a shift in the *NFI* schedule. The reduced demand for loans lowers the equilibrium interest rate. The lower interest rate tends to raise net foreign investment, but this only partly mitigates the shift in the *NFI* schedule. The reduced level of net foreign investment reduces the supply of dollars in the market for foreign exchange. The exchange rate appreciates, and net exports fall.

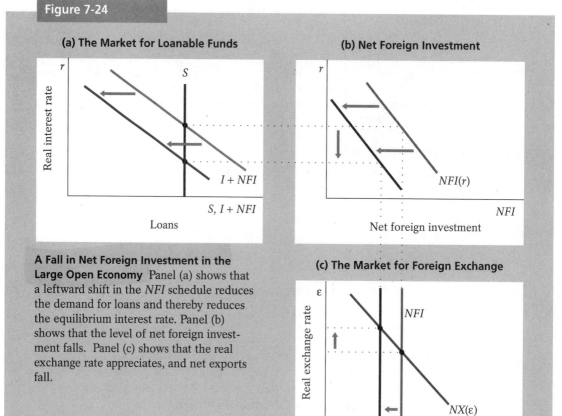

Figure 7-24

(a) The Market for Loanable Funds

(b) Net Foreign Investment

(c) The Market for Foreign Exchange

A Fall in Net Foreign Investment in the Large Open Economy Panel (a) shows that a leftward shift in the *NFI* schedule reduces the demand for loans and thereby reduces the equilibrium interest rate. Panel (b) shows that the level of net foreign investment falls. Panel (c) shows that the real exchange rate appreciates, and net exports fall.

Conclusion

How different are large and small open economies? Certainly, policies affect the interest rate in a large open economy, unlike in a small open economy. But, in other ways, the two models yield similar conclusions. In both large and small open economies, policies that raise saving or reduce investment lead to trade surpluses, whereas policies that lower saving or raise investment lead to trade deficits. In both economies, protectionist trade policies cause the exchange rate to appreciate, and they do not influence the trade balance. Because the results are so similar, for most questions one can use the simpler model of the small open economy, even if the economy being examined is not really small.

PROBLEMS AND APPLICATIONS

1. If a war broke out abroad, it would affect the U.S. economy in many ways. Use the model of the large open economy to examine each of the following effects of such a war. What happens in the United States to saving, investment, the trade balance, the interest rate, and the exchange rate? (To keep things simple, consider each effect separately.)

a. The U.S. government, fearing it may need to enter the war, increases its purchases of military equipment.

b. Other countries raise their demand for high-tech weapons, a major export of the United States.

c. The war makes U.S. firms uncertain about the future, and the firms delay some investment projects.

d. The war makes U.S. consumers uncertain about the future, and the consumers save more in response.

e. Americans become apprehensive about traveling abroad, so more of them spend their vacations in the United States.

f. Foreign investors seek a safe haven for their portfolios in the United States.

PART THREE

The Economy in the Short Run

In Part Two we developed theories to explain how the economy behaves in the long run. Those theories were based on the classical dichotomy—the premise that real variables such as production and employment are independent of nominal variables such as the money supply. Although the classical dichotomy holds approximately in the long run, most economists believe that it does not hold at all in the short run. Here, in Part Three, we see how economists explain short-run economic fluctuations.

Chapter 8 discusses the key differences between the long run and the short run, and it introduces the model of aggregate supply and aggregate demand. With this model we can show how shocks to the economy lead to fluctuations in output and employment. We can also show how monetary policy can cause or limit those fluctuations.

The next three chapters develop more fully the model of aggregate supply and aggregate demand. Chapters 9 and 10 present a theory of aggregate demand, called the *IS-LM* model, which shows how monetary and fiscal policy affect the aggregate demand for goods and services. Chapter 11 discusses theories of aggregate supply and their implications.

In Chapter 12 we enter the debate over how policymakers should respond to short-run fluctuations. Should monetary and fiscal policy take an active or passive role? Should policy be conducted by rule or by discretion?

Chapter 13 brings international issues into our analysis. It presents a theory of short-run fluctuations in an open economy, called the Mundell-Fleming model.

The final chapter in this part, Chapter 14, presents the theory of real business cycles. This alternative theory of short-run fluctuations, which a small but influential group of economists advocates, holds that the classical dichotomy describes the short run as well as the long run. It contrasts sharply with the short-run theory developed in Chapters 8 through 13, which most economists advocate.

Introduction to Economic Fluctuations

*The modern world regards business cycles much as the ancient
Egyptians regarded the overflowing of the Nile. The phenomenon
recurs at intervals, it is of great importance to everyone, and natural
causes of it are not in sight.*

John Bates Clark, 1898

Economic fluctuations present a recurring problem for economists and policy-makers. As you can see in Figure 8-1, real GDP does not grow smoothly. Recessions—periods of falling incomes and rising unemployment—are frequent. In the first two years of this decade, real GDP fell almost 2 percent, and the unemployment rate rose from 7.5 percent in 1989 to 11.3 percent in 1992. Recessions are also associated with shorter workweeks: more workers have part-time jobs, and fewer workers work overtime.

Economists call these fluctuations in output and employment the *business cycle*. Although this term suggests that fluctuations in the economy are regular and predictable, neither is the case, as Figure 8-1 makes clear.

In Part Two of this book, we developed models to identify the determinants of national income, unemployment, inflation, and other economic variables. Yet we did not examine why these variables fluctuate so much from year to year. Here in Part Three we develop a model to explain these short-run fluctuations.

Just as Egypt has attempted to stem the flooding of the Nile Valley with the Aswan Dam, modern society tries to control the business cycle with appropriate economic policies. The model we develop over the next several chapters shows how monetary and fiscal policies influence the business cycle. We will see that these policies can either stabilize or magnify economic fluctuations.

8•1 How the Short Run and Long Run Differ

To build a model of short-run fluctuations, we must first decide how that model will differ from the long-run classical model we developed in Chapters 3 through 7. Almost all economists agree that the classical model gives an accurate description of the economy in the long run, and most believe that the key difference between the short run and the long run is the behaviour of prices. *In*

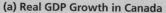

(a) Real GDP Growth in Canada

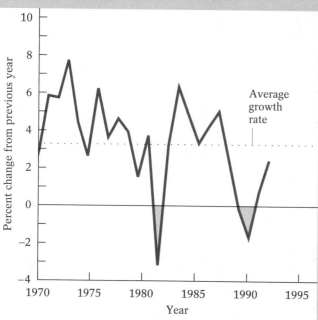

Real GDP Growth in Canada and the United States In Canada the growth rate in real GDP averages around 3.2 percent per year, as indicated by the dotted line in Panel (a). But there is a wide variation around this average. Recessions are periods during which real GDP falls—that is, during which real GDP growth is negative. U.S. GDP is shown in Panel (b). Clearly business cycles in the two economies are closely connected. But the state of the U.S. economy is not the only important thing for Canada. For example, the recession in the early 1990s started earlier and lasted longer in Canada.

Source: Reproduced and adapted by authority of the Minister of Industry, 1994, "Statistics Canada," *Canadian Economic Observer, Catalogue 11-210,* Series D20463, (Historical Statistical Supplement, 1991/92): 7 and (Statistical Supplement, March 1994): 4.

(b) Real GDP Growth in the United States

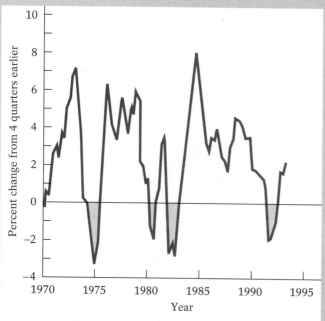

the long run, prices are flexible and can respond to changes in supply or demand. In the short run, many prices are "stuck" at some predetermined level. Because prices behave differently in the short run than in the long run, economic policies have different effects over different time horizons.

To see how the short run and the long run differ, consider the effects of a change in monetary policy. Suppose that the Bank of Canada suddenly reduced the money supply by 5 percent. According to the classical model, the money supply affects nominal variables—variables measured in terms of money—but not real variables. As we discussed in Chapter 6, this principle is known as the *classical dichotomy*. In the long run, a 5 percent reduction in the money supply lowers all prices (including nominal wages) by 5 percent while leaving real wages, employment, and output unaltered.

In the short run, however, many prices do not respond to changes in monetary policy. A reduction in the money supply does not immediately cause all firms to cut the wages they pay, all stores to change the price tags on their goods, all mail-order firms to issue new catalogs, and all restaurants to print new menus. Instead, there is little immediate change in many prices; that is, many prices are sticky. This short-run price stickiness implies that the short-run impact of a change in the money supply is not the same as the long-run impact.

A model of economic fluctuations must take into account this short-run price stickiness. We will see that since prices do not adjust instantly to changes in the money supply, the classical dichotomy breaks down—monetary policy does affect output and employment. The failure of prices to adjust to changes in the money supply implies that, in the short run, output and employment must do some of the adjusting instead.

As a general principle, the amount of output produced can deviate from the level implied by the classical model if prices are sticky. In the classical model, the amount of output depends on the economy's ability to *supply* goods and services, which, in turn, depends on the supplies of capital and labour and on the available technology. Here we will see that flexible prices are a crucial feature of the classical model: the model assumes that prices adjust to make the quantity of output demanded equal the quantity supplied. By contrast, when prices are sticky, output also depends on the *demand* for goods and services. Demand in turn is influenced by monetary policy, fiscal policy, and a variety of other factors. Thus, price stickiness provides a rationale for the usefulness of monetary and fiscal policy in stabilizing the economy in the short run.

In the remainder of this chapter we introduce a model that can explain short-run economic fluctuations. The model of supply and demand, which we used to discuss the market for bread in Chapter 1, offers some of the most fundamental insights in economics. This model shows how the supply and demand for any good jointly determine the good's price and the quantity sold, and how changes in exogenous variables affect the price and quantity. Here we present the "economy-size" version of this model—*the model of aggregate supply and aggregate demand*. This macroeconomic model allows us to study how the aggregate price level and the quantity of aggregate output are determined. It also provides a way to contrast how the economy behaves in the long run and how it behaves in the short run.

Although the model of aggregate supply and aggregate demand resembles the model of supply and demand for a single good, the analogy is not exact. The model of supply and demand for a single good considers only one good within a large economy. By contrast, the model of aggregate supply and aggregate demand is a sophisticated model that considers all goods at once and that incorporates the interactions among markets and both input markets and financial markets.

The Puzzle of Sticky Magazine Prices

How sticky are prices? The answer to this question depends on what price we consider. Some commodities, such as wheat, soybeans, and pork bellies, are traded on organized exchanges, and their prices change every minute. No one would call these prices sticky. Yet the prices of most goods and services change much less frequently. One survey found that 37.7 percent of firms change their prices once a year, and another 17.4 percent change their prices less than once a year.[1]

The reasons for price stickiness are not always apparent. Consider, for example, the market for magazines. A study has documented that magazines change their newsstand prices very infrequently. The typical magazine allows inflation to erode its real price by about 25 percent before it raises its nominal price. When inflation is 4 percent per year, the typical magazine changes its price about every 6 years.[2]

Why do magazines leave their prices unchanged for so long? Economists do not have a definitive answer. The question is puzzling because it would seem that, for magazines, the cost of a price change is small: to change prices, a mail-order firm must issue a new catalog and a restaurant must print a new menu, but a magazine publisher can simply print a new price on the cover of the next issue. Perhaps the cost to the publisher of charging the wrong price is also not very great. Or maybe customers would find it inconvenient if the price of their favorite magazine changed every month.

Thus, it is often not easy to explain sticky prices at the microeconomic level. The cause of price stickiness is, therefore, an active area of research. In Chapter 11 we discuss some recent theories about why prices are sticky.

Although not yet fully explained, price stickiness is widely believed to be crucial for understanding economic fluctuations. In this chapter we begin to develop the link between sticky prices and economic fluctuations.

8·2 Aggregate Demand

Aggregate demand (*AD*) is the relationship between the quantity of output demanded and the aggregate price level. In other words, the aggregate de-

---

[1] Alan S. Blinder, "Why Are Prices Sticky? Preliminary Results from an Interview Study," *American Economic Review Papers and Proceedings* 81 (May 1991): 89–100.

[2] Stephen G. Cecchetti, "The Frequency of Price Adjustment: A Study of the Newsstand Prices of Magazines," *Journal of Econometrics* 31 (1986): 255–274.

mand curve tells us the quantity of goods and services people will buy for any given level of prices. We examine the theory of aggregate demand thoroughly in Chapters 9 and 10. By way of introduction, however, in this chapter we use the quantity theory of money to provide a very simple, although incomplete, derivation of the aggregate demand curve.

The Quantity Equation as Aggregate Demand

Recall from Chapter 6 that the quantity theory says that

$$MV = PY,$$

where M is the money supply, V is the velocity of money (which for now we assume is constant), P is the price level, and Y is the amount of output. This equation states that the money supply determines the nominal value of output, which, in turn, is the product of the price level and the amount of output.

You might recall that the quantity equation can be rewritten in terms of the supply and demand for real money balances:

$$M/P = (M/P)^d = kY,$$

where $k = 1/V$. In this form, the quantity equation states that the supply of real money balances M/P equals the demand $(M/P)^d$ and that the demand is proportional to the amount of output Y.

For any fixed money supply, the quantity equation yields a negative relationship between the price level P and output Y. Figure 8-2 graphs the combinations of P and Y that satisfy the quantity equation holding the money supply constant. This is called the aggregate demand curve.

Figure 8-2

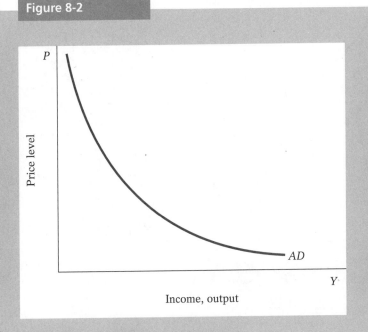

The Aggregate Demand Curve The aggregate demand curve AD expresses the relationship between the price level P and the quantity of goods and services demanded Y. It is drawn for a given value of the money supply M. The aggregate demand curve slopes downward: the higher the price level P, the lower the level of real balances M/P, and therefore the lower the quantity of goods and services demanded Y.

Why the Aggregate Demand Curve Slopes Downward

The aggregate demand curve slopes downward. For any fixed money supply, the quantity equation fixes the nominal value of output PY. Therefore, if the price level P goes up, output Y must go down.

One way to understand the negative relationship between P and Y is to consider the link between money and transactions. Because we have assumed that the velocity of money is fixed, the money supply determines the dollar value of all transactions in the economy. If the price level rises, so that each transaction requires more dollars, the quantity of transactions and thus the quantity of goods and services purchased must fall.

Equivalently, we could look at the supply and demand for real money balances. If output is higher, people engage in more transactions and need higher real balances M/P. For a fixed money supply M, higher real balances imply a lower price level. Conversely, if the price level is lower, real money balances are higher; the higher level of real balances allows a greater volume of transactions and thus a higher level of output.

Figure 8-3

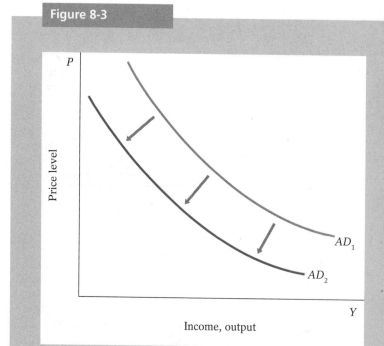

Inward Shifts in the Aggregate Demand Curve A change in the money supply shifts the aggregate demand curve. For any given price level P, a reduction in the money supply M implies that real balances M/P are lower and thus that output Y is lower. Therefore, a reduction in the money supply shifts the aggregate demand curve inward.

Shifts in the Aggregate Demand Curve

The aggregate demand curve is drawn for a fixed value of the money supply. In other words, it tells us the possible combinations of P and Y for a given value of M. If the money supply changes, then the possible combinations of P and Y change—that is, the aggregate demand curve shifts. Let's examine some situations in which a shift may occur.

First, consider what happens if the Bank of Canada reduces the money supply. The quantity equation, $MV = PY$, tells us that the reduction in the money supply leads to a proportionate reduction in the nominal value of output, PY. For any given price level, the amount of output is lower, and for any given amount of output, the price level is lower. As in Figure 8-3, the aggregate demand curve relating P and Y shifts inward.

Next, consider what happens if the Bank of Canada increases the money supply. The quantity equation tells us that there is an increase in PY. For any given price level, the amount of output is higher, and for any given amount of output, the price level is higher. As shown in Figure 8-4, the aggregate demand curve shifts outward.

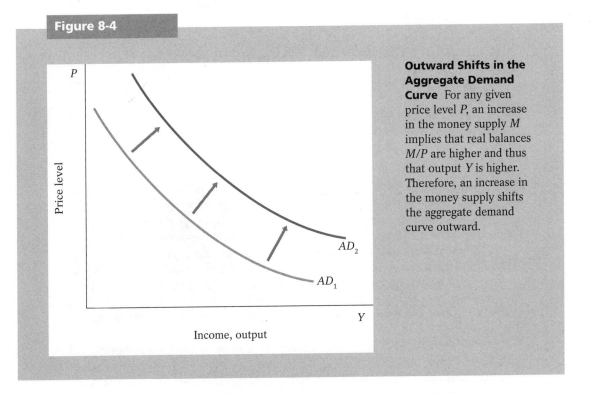

Figure 8-4

Outward Shifts in the Aggregate Demand Curve For any given price level P, an increase in the money supply M implies that real balances M/P are higher and thus that output Y is higher. Therefore, an increase in the money supply shifts the aggregate demand curve outward.

Fluctuations in the money supply are not the only source of fluctuations in aggregate demand. Even if the money supply is held constant, the aggregate demand curve shifts because of changes in the velocity of money. When we study the aggregate demand curve more fully in Chapters 9 and 10, we consider many possible reasons that it might shift.

8·3 Aggregate Supply

By itself, the aggregate demand curve does not tell us the price level or the amount of output; it merely gives a relationship between these two variables. To accompany the aggregate demand curve, we need another relationship between P and Y that crosses the aggregate demand curve—an aggregate supply curve. The aggregate demand curve and the aggregate supply curve together pin down the price level and the amount of output.

Aggregate supply (*AS*) is the relationship between the quantity of goods and services supplied and the price level. Because prices are flexible in the long run and sticky in the short run, this relationship depends on the time horizon under consideration. We need to discuss two different aggregate supply curves: the long-run aggregate supply curve (*LRAS*) and the short-run aggregate supply curve (*SRAS*). We also need to discuss the transition from the short run to the long run.

The Long Run: The Vertical Aggregate Supply Curve

Since the classical model describes how the economy behaves in the long run, we derive the long-run aggregate supply curve from the classical model. Recall from Chapter 3 that the amount of output produced depends on the fixed amounts of capital and labour and on the available technology. To show this, we write

$$Y = F(\bar{K}, \bar{L})$$
$$= \bar{Y}.$$

According to the classical model, output does not depend on the price level. To show that output is the same for all price levels, we draw a vertical aggregate supply curve, as in Figure 8-5. The intersection of the aggregate demand curve with this vertical aggregate supply curve determines the price level.

If the aggregate supply curve is vertical, then changes in aggregate demand affect prices but not output. For example, if the money supply falls, the aggregate demand curve shifts downward, as in Figure 8-6. The economy moves from the old intersection of aggregate supply and aggregate demand, point A, to the new intersection, point B. The shift in aggregate demand affects only prices.

The vertical curve satisfies the classical dichotomy, since it implies that the level of output is independent of the money supply. This long-run level of output, $\bar{Y}$, is called the *natural* level of output. It is the level of output that the economy produces when unemployment is at its natural rate. (We discussed the determinants of the natural unemployment rate in Chapter 5.) Short-run macroeconomic analysis focuses on cyclical unemployment—that is, deviations

Figure 8-5

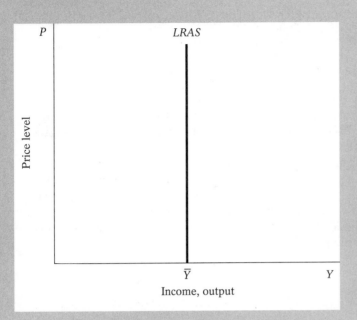

The Long-Run Aggregate Supply Curve In the long run, the level of output is determined by the amounts of capital and labour and by the available technology. Thus, it does not depend on the price level. The long-run aggregate supply curve, *LRAS*, is vertical.

Figure 8-6

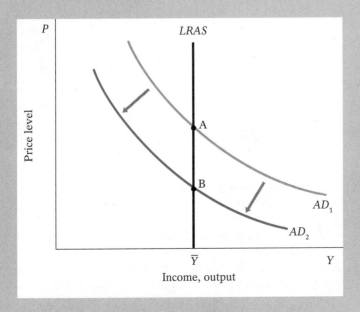

Shifts in Aggregate Demand in the Long Run A reduction in the money supply shifts the aggregate demand curve downward. The equilibrium for the economy moves from point A to point B. Since the aggregate supply curve is vertical in the long run, the reduction in aggregate demand affects the price level but not the level of output.

of actual unemployment from its full-equilibrium value. With just cyclical unemployment in mind, some economists use the term "full" employment to describe the natural rate. Thus, the natural level of output is also referred to as the *full-employment* level of output.

The Short Run: The Horizontal Aggregate Supply Curve

The classical model and the vertical aggregate supply curve apply only in the long run. In the short run, some prices are sticky and, therefore, do not adjust to changes in demand. This price stickiness implies that the short-run aggregate supply curve is not vertical.

As an extreme example, suppose that all firms have issued price catalogues and that it is costly for them to issue new ones. Thus, all prices are stuck at predetermined levels. At these prices, firms are willing to sell as much as their customers are willing to buy, and they hire just enough labour to produce the amount demanded. Since the price level is fixed, we represent this situation in Figure 8-7 with a horizontal aggregate supply curve.

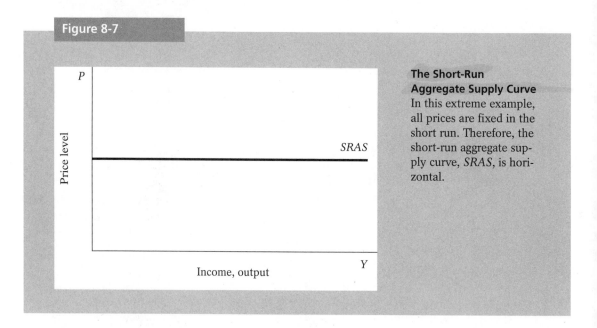

Figure 8-7

The Short-Run Aggregate Supply Curve
In this extreme example, all prices are fixed in the short run. Therefore, the short-run aggregate supply curve, *SRAS*, is horizontal.

The short-run equilibrium of the economy is the intersection of the aggregate demand curve and this horizontal short-run aggregate supply curve. In this case, changes in aggregate demand do affect the level of output. For example, if the Bank of Canada suddenly reduces the money supply, the aggregate demand curve shifts inward, as in Figure 8-8. The economy moves from the old intersection of aggregate demand and aggregate supply, point A, to the new intersection, point B. Since the price level is fixed, the shift in aggregate demand causes output to fall.

A fall in aggregate demand reduces output in the short run because prices do not adjust instantly. After the sudden fall in aggregate demand, firms are stuck with prices that are too high. With demand low and prices high, firms sell less of their product, which causes them to reduce employment and production.

Figure 8-8

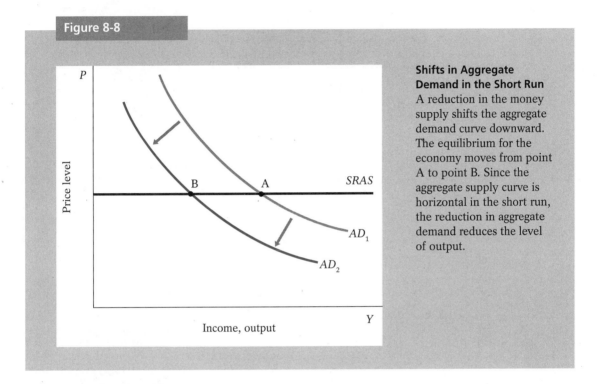

Shifts in Aggregate Demand in the Short Run A reduction in the money supply shifts the aggregate demand curve downward. The equilibrium for the economy moves from point A to point B. Since the aggregate supply curve is horizontal in the short run, the reduction in aggregate demand reduces the level of output.

From the Short Run to the Long Run

We can summarize our analysis so far as follows: *Over short periods of time, prices are sticky, the aggregate supply curve is flat, and changes in aggregate demand affect the output of the economy. Over long periods of time, prices are flexible, the aggregate supply curve is vertical, and changes in aggregate demand affect only the price level.* Thus, changes in aggregate demand have different effects over different time horizons.

Let's trace the effects over time of a fall in aggregate demand. Suppose that the economy begins in long-run equilibrium, as shown in Figure 8-9. In this figure, there are three curves: the aggregate demand curve, the long-run aggregate supply curve, and the short-run aggregate supply curve. The long-run equilibrium is the point at which aggregate demand crosses the long-run aggregate supply curve. Prices have adjusted to reach this equilibrium. Therefore, when the economy is in its long-run equilibrium, the short-run aggregate supply curve must cross this point as well.

Figure 8-9

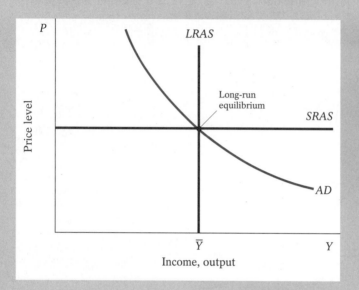

Long-Run Equilibrium In the long run, the economy finds itself at the intersection of the long-run aggregate supply curve and the aggregate demand curve. Since prices have adjusted to this level, the short-run aggregate supply curve crosses this point as well.

Figure 8-10

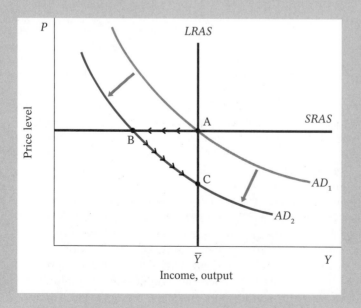

A Reduction in Aggregate Demand The economy begins in long-run equilibrium, point A. A reduction in aggregate demand, perhaps caused by a decrease in the money supply, moves the economy from point A to point B, where output is below its natural level. As prices fall, the economy gradually recovers from the recession, moving from point B to point C. To avoid clutter, the lower positions that are appropriate for *SRAS* as prices fall are not shown.

FYI

The Short Run, the Long Run, and the Very Long Run

This book discusses numerous models of the economy, each with its own set of simplifying assumptions. One way to categorize the models is by the time horizon over which they apply. The models fall into three categories:

- **The Short Run** This chapter and the following ones present the short-run theory of the economy. This theory assumes that prices are sticky and that, because of this price stickiness, capital and labour are sometimes not fully employed. Price stickiness is widely viewed as being important for explaining the economic fluctuations we observe from month to month or from year to year.

- **The Long Run** Chapter 3 presented the basic long-run theory of the economy, called the classical model. Chapter 6 presented the classical theory of money, and Chapter 7 presented the classical theory of the open economy. These chapters assumed that prices are flexible and, therefore, that capital and labour are fully employed. These chapters also took as fixed the quantities of capital and labour, as well as the technology for turning capital and labour into output. These assumptions apply best over a time horizon of several years. Over this period, prices can adjust to equilibrium levels, yet capital, labour, and technology are relatively constant.

- **The Very Long Run** Chapter 4 presented the basic theory of economic growth, called the Solow model. This model analyzes the time horizon over which the capital stock, the labour force, and the available technology can change. This model is designed to explain how the economy works over a period of several decades.

When analyzing economic policies, it is important to keep in mind that they influence the economy over all time horizons. We must, therefore, draw on the insights of all these models.

Now suppose that the Bank of Canada reduces the money supply and the demand curve shifts downward, as in Figure 8-10. In the short run, prices are sticky, so the economy moves from point A to point B. Output and employment fall below their natural levels, which means the economy is in a recession. Over time, in response to the low demand, wages and prices fall. The gradual reduction in the price level moves the economy downward along the aggregate demand curve to point C, which is the new long-run equilibrium. In the new long-run equilibrium (point C), output and employment are back to their natural levels, but prices are lower than in the old long-run equilibrium (point A).

8·2   **The U.S. Civil War**

The aftermath of the Civil War in the United States provides a vivid example of how contractionary monetary policy affects the economy. Before the war, the United States was on a gold standard. Paper dollars were readily convertible into gold. Under this policy, the quantity of gold determined the money supply and the price level.

In 1862, after the Civil War broke out, the Treasury announced that it would no longer exchange gold for dollars. In essence, this act replaced the gold standard with a system of fiat money. Over the next few years, the government printed large quantities of paper currency—called *greenbacks* for their colour—and used the seigniorage to finance wartime expenditure. Because of this increase in the money supply, the price level approximately doubled during the war.

When the war was over, much political debate centered on the question of whether to return to the gold standard. The Greenback Party was formed with the primary goal of maintaining the system of fiat money. Eventually, however, the Greenback Party lost the debate. Policymakers decided to retire the greenbacks over time in order to reinstate the gold standard at the rate of exchange between dollars and gold that had prevailed before the war. Their goal was to return the value of the dollar to its former level.

Returning to the gold standard in this way required reversing the wartime rise in prices, which meant a fall in aggregate demand. (To be more precise, the growth in aggregate demand needed to fall short of the growth in the natural rate of output.) As the price level fell, the U.S. economy experienced a recession from 1873 to 1879, the longest on record. By 1879, the price level was back to its level before the war, and the gold standard was reinstated.

8·4 Stabilization Policy

Fluctuations in the economy as a whole come from changes in aggregate supply or aggregate demand. Economists call exogenous changes in these curves **shocks** to the economy. Shocks can disrupt economic well-being by pushing output and employment away from their natural rates. The model of aggregate supply and aggregate demand shows how shocks cause economic fluctuations.

The model is also useful for evaluating how macroeconomic policy can respond to shocks in order to dampen fluctuations. **Stabilization policy** is public policy aimed at keeping output and employment at their natural rates. Because the money supply has a powerful impact on aggregate demand, monetary policy is an important component of stabilization policy.

Shocks to Aggregate Demand

Consider an example of a shock to aggregate demand: the invention of automatic teller machines. These machines make cash easier to obtain and, therefore, reduce the demand for money. For example, suppose that before the introduction of teller machines, everyone goes to the bank once a week, withdraws $100, and then spends the money gradually over the week; in this case, average money holdings equal $50. After the introduction of teller machines, everyone goes to the bank twice a week and withdraws $50; now, average money holdings equal $25. In this example, money demand falls by half.

This reduction in money demand is equivalent to an increase in the velocity of money. To see this, remember that

$$M/P = kY,$$

where $k = 1/V$. A decrease in real money balances for any given amount of output implies a decrease in k and an increase in V. Because the introduction of automatic teller machines allows people to hold fewer dollars in their wallets, the dollars circulate more quickly. That is, because people obtain money more often, there is less time between when a dollar is received and when it is spent. Hence, velocity increases.

If the money supply is held constant, the increase in velocity causes nominal spending to rise and the aggregate demand curve to shift outward, as in Figure 8-11. In the short run, the increase in demand raises the output of the economy—it causes an economic boom. At the old prices, firms now sell more output. Therefore, they hire more workers, ask their existing workers to work longer hours, and make greater use of their factories and equipment.

Over time, the high level of aggregate demand pulls up wages and prices. As the price level rises, the quantity of output demanded declines, and the

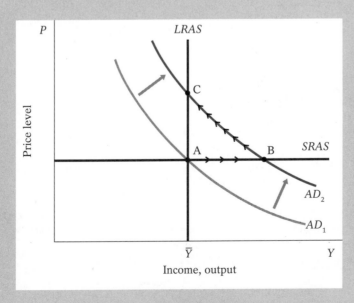

An Increase in Aggregate Demand The economy begins in long-run equilibrium, point A. An increase in aggregate demand, due to an increase in the velocity of money, moves the economy from point A to point B, where output is above its natural level. As prices rise, output gradually returns to its natural rate, and the economy moves from point B to point C. *SRAS* rises as prices rise but to avoid clutter, these shifts are not shown.

economy gradually approaches the natural rate of production. But during the transition to the higher price level, the economy's output is higher than the natural rate.

What can the Bank of Canada do to dampen this boom, keep output closer to the natural rate, and limit price increases? The Bank of Canada might reduce the money supply to offset the increase in velocity. Offsetting the change in velocity would stabilize aggregate demand. Thus, the Bank of Canada can reduce or even eliminate the impact of demand shocks on output and employment if it can skillfully control the money supply. Whether the Bank of Canada in fact has the necessary skill is a more difficult question, which we take up in Chapter 12.

CASE STUDY

8·3 **Velocity and the Recession of the 1990s**

Is the velocity of money steady, or is it highly volatile? The answer to this question influences how the Bank of Canada should conduct monetary policy. On the one hand, if velocity is steady, then it is easy to stabilize aggregate demand:

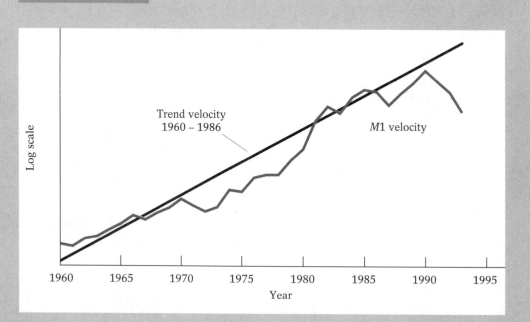

Figure 8-12

The Velocity of Money For reasons that are still not fully understood, the velocity of money (nominal GDP divided by *M*1) stopped rising after about 1985. This fall contributed to a reduction in aggregate demand, leading to the recession of the early 1990s, one of the deepest in recent history.

Source: Review (Ottawa: Bank of Canada).

the Bank of Canada needs only to keep the money supply constant or allow it to grow at a steady rate. On the other hand, if velocity is highly volatile, then stabilizing aggregate demand requires adjusting the money supply frequently to offset the changes in velocity.

The deep recession that Canada experienced in the early 1990s may be partly attributable to an unexpected decline in the growth of velocity. Figure 8-12 graphs velocity (measured here as nominal GDP divided by $M1$) since 1960. The figure shows that velocity rose steadily in the 1960–1985 period, but then essentially stopped rising after 1985. The experience of the early 1990s shows that the Bank of Canada cannot rely on the velocity of money to remain predictable.

The Bank of Canada could have offset the fall in velocity growth by raising the money supply. Containing inflation was the Bank of Canada's primary concern in the early 1990s, however, so it slowed the rate of money growth instead, further depressing aggregate demand. The combination of these two forces—falling velocity and anti-inflationary monetary policy—led to a deep recession.

How should we evaluate the Bank of Canada's actions? The Bank attained its goal of lower inflation more quickly than it expected (since it did not fully appreciate the leveling off of velocity until later). But the cost was a substantial fall in output and employment. The early 1990s recession highlights the conflicting goals of macroeconomics: maintaining full employment and keeping inflation under control. Stabilization policy often involves a tradeoff between these two objectives.

Shocks to Aggregate Supply

Shocks to aggregate supply, as well as shocks to aggregate demand, can cause economic fluctuations. A supply shock is a shock to the economy that alters the cost of producing goods and services and, as a result, the prices that firms charge. Because supply shocks have a direct impact on the price level, they are sometimes called price shocks. Examples are:

- A drought that destroys crops—the reduction in food supply pushes up food prices.

- A new environmental protection law requiring firms to reduce their emissions of pollutants—firms pass on the added costs to customers in the form of higher prices.

- An increase in union aggressiveness—this pushes up wages and the prices of the goods produced by union workers.

- The organization of an international oil cartel—by curtailing competition, the major oil producers can raise the world price of oil.

All these events are adverse supply shocks: they push up costs and prices. A favourable supply shock, such as the breakup of an international oil cartel, reduces costs and prices.

Figure 8-13 shows how an adverse supply shock affects the economy. The short-run aggregate supply curve shifts upward. (Some supply shocks may also lower the natural level of output, and thus shift the long-run aggregate supply curve to the left, but we ignore that effect here.) If aggregate demand is held constant, the economy moves from point A to point B: the price level rises and the amount of output falls below the natural rate. An experience like this is called **stagflation**, because it combines stagnation (falling output) with inflation (rising prices).

Figure 8-13

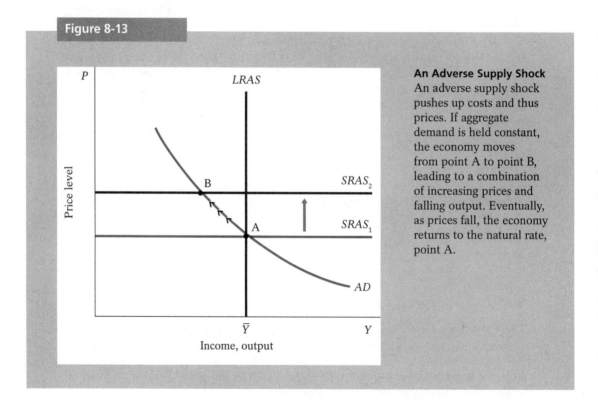

An Adverse Supply Shock An adverse supply shock pushes up costs and thus prices. If aggregate demand is held constant, the economy moves from point A to point B, leading to a combination of increasing prices and falling output. Eventually, as prices fall, the economy returns to the natural rate, point A.

Faced with an adverse supply shock, a policymaker controlling aggregate demand, such as the Bank of Canada, has a difficult choice between two options. The first option, implicit in Figure 8-13, is to hold aggregate demand constant. In this case, output and employment are lower than the natural rate. Eventually, prices will fall (the short-run aggregate supply curve shifts back down) to restore full employment at the old price level (point A). But the cost of this process is a painful recession.

The second option, illustrated in Figure 8-14, is to expand aggregate demand to bring the economy toward the natural rate more quickly. If the increase in aggregate demand coincides with the shock to aggregate supply, the economy goes immediately from point A to point C. In this case, the Bank of Canada is said to *accommodate* the supply shock. The drawback of this option,

Figure 8-14

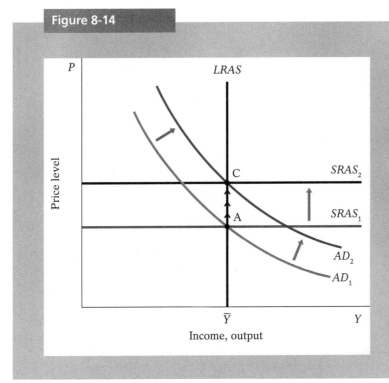

Accommodating an Adverse Supply Shock In response to an adverse supply shock, the Bank of Canada can increase aggregate demand to prevent a reduction in output. The economy moves from point A to point C. The cost of this policy is a permanently higher level of prices.

of course, is that the price level is permanently higher. There is no way to adjust aggregate demand both to maintain full employment and to keep the price level stable.

CASE STUDY

8·4 How OPEC Helped Cause Stagflation in the 1970s

The most disruptive supply shocks in recent history are due to OPEC, the Organization of Petroleum Exporting Countries. In the early 1970s, OPEC's coordinated reduction in the supply of oil nearly doubled the world price. This increase in oil prices caused stagflation in most industrial countries. For example, in the United States, inflation rose from 6.2 percent to 11 percent between 1973 and 1974, while the unemployment rate almost doubled, from 4.9 percent in 1973 to 8.5 percent in 1975.

The unemployment effects of the OPEC oil-price increase were less dramatic in Canada for two reasons. First, using expansionary aggregate demand policies, the federal government cushioned the recession that would have followed from the large drop in export sales to the United States. Second, the government imposed a price control that precluded domestic oil prices from increasing as much as world prices. This price limit irritated many in western Canada whose incomes were tied to the oil industry. In any event, the federal government's policy kept Canada's aggregate supply curve from shifting upward as much as it otherwise would have. Canada's inflation rate only went up by 3.3 percentage points in 1974 (compared to 4.8 percentage points in the United States), and Canada's unemployment rate increased by only 1.5 percentage points in the 1973–1975 period (compared to 3.6 percentage points in the United States).

A few years later, when the world economy had nearly recovered from the first OPEC recession, almost the same thing happened again. OPEC raised oil prices, causing further stagflation. The average increase in world oil prices in the 1979–1981 period was almost 40 percent. U.S. inflation rose from 7.7 percent in 1978 to 10.3 percent by 1981, while unemployment rose from 6.1 percent to 7.5 percent over the same period. In Canada, the federal government did not attempt the same insulation of the Canadian economy from this world event, so responses were more dramatic than in the mid-1970s. Inflation rose from 8.9 percent in 1978 to 12.5 percent in 1981, while unemployment rose from 8.3 percent to 11 percent. When less protected from an adverse supply-side shock, Canada suffered a bigger bout of stagflation.[3]

8·5 Conclusion

This chapter has introduced a framework to study economic fluctuations, the model of aggregate supply and aggregate demand. It is built on the assumption that prices are sticky in the short run and flexible in the long run. The model shows how shocks to the economy cause output to deviate temporarily from the level implied by the classical model.

The model also highlights the role of monetary policy. Poor monetary policy can be a source of shocks to the economy. A well-run monetary policy can respond to shocks and help stabilize the economy.

In the chapters that follow, we refine our understanding of this model and our analysis of stabilization policy. Chapters 9 and 10 go beyond the quantity equation to refine our theory of aggregate demand. This refinement shows that aggregate demand depends on fiscal policy as well as monetary policy. Chapter 11 examines aggregate supply in more detail and discusses why wages and prices are sticky. Chapter 12 examines the debate over the virtues and limits of stabilization policy.

Summary

1. The crucial difference between the long run and the short run is that prices are flexible in the long run but sticky in the short run. The model of aggregate supply and aggregate demand provides a framework to analyze economic fluctuations and to see how the impact of policies varies over different time horizons.

---

[3] Some economists have suggested that changes in oil prices played a major role in economic fluctuations even before the 1970s. See James D. Hamilton, "Oil and the Macroeconomy Since World War II," *Journal of Political Economy* 91 (April 1983): 228–248.

2. The aggregate demand curve slopes downward. It tells us that the lower the price level, the greater the aggregate demand for goods and services.

3. In the long run, the aggregate supply curve is vertical: output is determined by the amounts of capital and labour and by the available technology. Therefore, shifts in aggregate demand affect the price level but not output or employment.

4. In the short run, the aggregate supply curve is horizontal, since wages and prices are predetermined. Therefore, shifts in aggregate demand affect output and employment.

5. Shocks to aggregate demand and aggregate supply cause economic fluctuations. Since the Bank of Canada can shift the aggregate demand curve, it can attempt to offset these shocks to maintain output and employment at their natural rates.

KEY CONCEPTS

Aggregate demand

Aggregate supply

Shocks

Stabilization policy

Stagflation

QUESTIONS FOR REVIEW

1. Give an example of a price that is sticky in the short run and flexible in the long run.

2. Why does the aggregate demand curve slope downward?

3. Explain the impact of an increase in the money supply in the short run and in the long run.

4. Why is it easier for the Bank of Canada to deal with demand shocks than with supply shocks?

PROBLEMS AND APPLICATIONS

1. Suppose that a change in government regulations allows banks to start paying interest on chequing accounts. (Before the change, chequing accounts paid no interest.) Recall that the money stock is the sum of currency and demand deposits, including chequing accounts, so this regulatory change makes holding money more attractive.

    a. How does this change affect the demand for money?

    b. What happens to the velocity of money?

    c. If the Bank of Canada keeps the money supply the same, what will happen to output and prices in the short run and long run?

    d. Should the Bank of Canada keep the money supply the same in response to this regulatory change? Why or why not?

2. The Bank of Canada reduces the money supply by 5 percent.

   a. What happens to the aggregate demand curve?

   b. What happens to the level of output and the price level in the short run and in the long run?

   c. According to Okun's law, what happens to unemployment in the short run and in the long run? (*Hint:* Okun's law is the relationship between output and unemployment discussed in Chapter 2.)

   d. What happens to the real interest rate in the short run and in the long run? (*Hint:* Use the model of the real interest rate in Chapter 3 to see what happens when output changes.)

3. Let's examine how the goals of the Bank of Canada influence its response to shocks. Suppose central bank A cares only about keeping the price level stable, and central bank B cares only about keeping output and employment at their natural rates. Explain how each central bank would respond to

   a. an exogenous decrease in the velocity of money.

   b. an exogenous increase in the price of oil.

Aggregate Demand I

I shall argue that the postulates of the classical theory are applicable to a special case only and not to the general case. . . . Moreover, the characteristics of the special case assumed by the classical theory happen not to be those of the economic society in which we actually live, with the result that its teaching is misleading and disastrous if we attempt to apply it to the facts of experience.

John Maynard Keynes, *The General Theory*

The most disruptive economic fluctuation in Canadian history was the Great Depression. In the 1930s Canada experienced massive unemployment and greatly reduced incomes. In the Depression's worst year, 1933, one fifth of the Canadian labour force was unemployed, and real GDP was 28 percent below its 1929 level.

This devastating episode caused many economists to question the validity of classical economic theory—the theory we examined in Chapters 3 through 7. Classical theory seemed incapable of explaining the Depression. It states that national income depends on factor supplies and the available technology, neither of which changed substantially from 1929 to 1933. After the onset of the Depression, many economists believed that a new model was needed to explain such a large and sudden economic downturn and to suggest government policies that might reduce the economic hardship so many people faced.

In 1936 the British economist John Maynard Keynes revolutionized economics with his book, *The General Theory of Employment, Interest, and Money*. Keynes proposed a new way to analyze the economy, which he presented as an alternative to classical theory. His vision of how the economy works quickly became a center of controversy. Yet, as economists debated *The General Theory*, a new understanding of economic fluctuations gradually developed.

Keynes proposed that low aggregate demand is responsible for the low income and high unemployment that characterize economic downturns. He criticized classical theory for assuming that aggregate supply alone—capital, labour, and technology—determines national income. Economists today reconcile these two views with the model of aggregate demand and aggregate supply introduced in Chapter 8. In the long run, prices are flexible, and aggregate supply determines income. But in the short run, prices are sticky, so changes in aggregate demand influence income.

In this chapter and the next one, we continue our study of economic fluctuations by looking more closely at aggregate demand. Our goal is to identify the variables that shift the aggregate demand curve, causing fluctuations in national income. We also examine more fully the tools policymakers can use to influence aggregate demand. In Chapter 8 we derived the aggregate demand curve from the quantity theory of money, and we showed that monetary policy can shift the aggregate demand curve. In this chapter we see that the government can influence aggregate demand with both monetary and fiscal policy.

The model of aggregate demand developed in this chapter, called the **IS-LM model**, is the leading interpretation of Keynes's theory. This model takes the price level as exogenous and then shows what determines national income. There are two ways to view the *IS-LM* model. One can view it as showing what causes income to change in the short run when the price level is fixed. Or one can view the *IS-LM* model as showing what causes the aggregate demand curve to shift. These two views are equivalent because, as Figure 9-1 illustrates, changes in income for a fixed price level are the same as shifts in the aggregate demand curve. That is, in the short run when the price level is fixed, shifts in the aggregate demand curve determine changes in income.

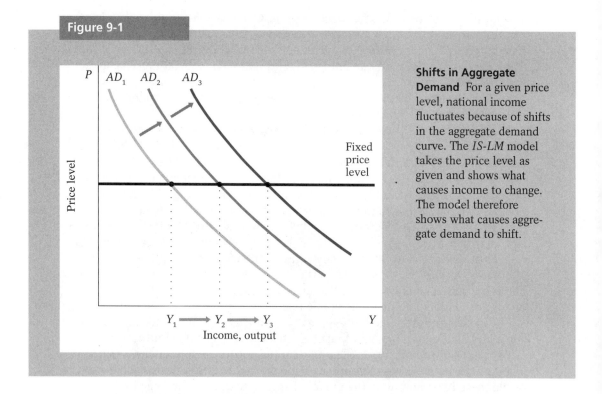

Figure 9-1

Shifts in Aggregate Demand For a given price level, national income fluctuates because of shifts in the aggregate demand curve. The *IS-LM* model takes the price level as given and shows what causes income to change. The model therefore shows what causes aggregate demand to shift.

The two parts of the *IS-LM* model are, not surprisingly, the **IS curve** and the **LM curve**. *IS* stands for "investment" and "saving." The *IS* curve represents the market for goods and services we discussed in Chapter 3. *LM* stands for "liquidity" and "money." The *LM* curve represents the supply and demand for money we discussed in Chapter 6. Because the interest rate influences both investment and money demand, it is the variable that links the two halves of the *IS-LM* model. The model shows how interactions between these markets determine aggregate demand.[1]

9•1 The Goods Market and the *IS* Curve

The *IS* curve plots the relationship between the interest rate and the level of income that arises in the market for goods and services. To understand this relationship, we begin with a simple theory of the demand for goods and services, called the **Keynesian cross**.

The Keynesian Cross

The Keynesian cross is the simplest interpretation of Keynes's theory of national income and is a building block for the more complex and realistic *IS-LM* model. Many of the elements of the Keynesian cross should be familiar from our discussion of the market for goods and services in Chapter 3.

Planned Expenditure To derive the Keynesian cross, we begin by looking at the determinants of planned expenditure. Planned expenditure is the amount households, firms, and the government plan to spend on goods and services.

The difference between actual and planned expenditure is unplanned inventory investment. When firms sell less of their product than they planned, their stock of inventories automatically rises. Conversely, when firms sell more than planned, their stock of inventories falls. Because these unplanned changes in inventory are counted as spending by firms, actual expenditure can be either above or below planned expenditure.

Assuming that the economy is closed, so that net exports are zero, we write planned expenditure E as the sum of consumption C, planned investment I, and government purchases G:

$$E = C + I + G.$$

To this equation, we add the consumption function

$$C = C(Y - T).$$

The consumption function states that consumption depends on disposable income $(Y - T)$. Disposable income is total income Y minus taxes T. In addition, we assume that planned investment is fixed

$$I = \overline{I},$$

---

[1] The *IS-LM* model was introduced in a classic article by the Nobel-prize-winning economist John R. Hicks, "Mr. Keynes and the Classics: A Suggested Interpretation," *Econometrica* 5 (1937): 147–159.

and that fiscal policy—the levels of government purchases and taxes—is fixed:

$$G = \bar{G}$$
$$T = \bar{T}.$$

Combining these equations, we obtain

$$E = C(Y - \bar{T}) + \bar{I} + \bar{G}.$$

This equation states that planned expenditure is a function of income Y, the exogenous level of planned investment $\bar{I}$, and the exogenous fiscal policy variables $\bar{G}$ and $\bar{T}$.

Figure 9-2 graphs planned expenditure as a function of the level of income. This line slopes upward because higher income leads to higher consumption and thus higher planned expenditure. The slope of this line is the marginal propensity to consume, the *MPC:* it shows how much planned expenditure increases when income rises by one dollar.

Figure 9-2

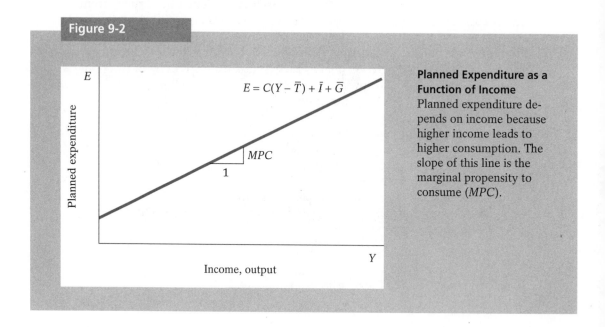

$$E = C(Y - \bar{T}) + \bar{I} + \bar{G}$$

MPC

1

E

Planned expenditure

Income, output

Y

Planned Expenditure as a Function of Income Planned expenditure depends on income because higher income leads to higher consumption. The slope of this line is the marginal propensity to consume (*MPC*).

The Economy in Equilibrium We now assume that the economy is in equilibrium when actual expenditure equals planned expenditure. Recall that Y equals not only total income but also actual expenditure on goods and services. We write the equilibrium condition as

Actual Expenditure = Planned Expenditure
$$Y = E.$$

The 45-degree line in Figure 9-3 plots the points where this condition holds. With the addition of the planned-expenditure function, this diagram becomes the Keynesian cross. The equilibrium of this economy is at point A, where the planned-expenditure function crosses the 45-degree line.

Figure 9-3

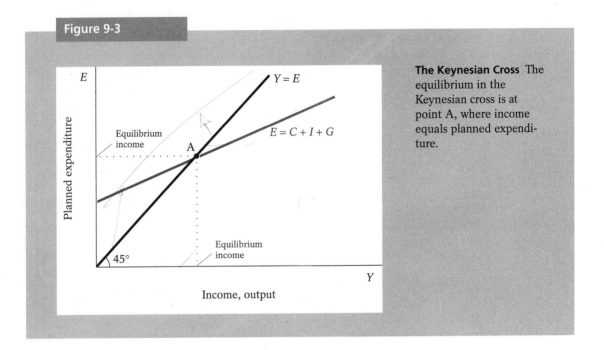

The Keynesian Cross The equilibrium in the Keynesian cross is at point A, where income equals planned expenditure.

How does the economy get to the equilibrium? For many firms, inventories play an important role in the adjustment process. Unplanned changes in inventories induce firms to change production levels, which in turn changes income and expenditure.

For example, suppose GDP is at a level greater than the equilibrium level, such as the level Y_1 in Figure 9-4. In this case, planned expenditure is E_1, which is less than Y_1. Because planned expenditure is less than production, firms are selling less than they produce. Firms add the unsold goods to their stock of inventories. This unplanned rise in inventories induces firms to lay off workers and reduce production, which reduces GDP. This process of unintended inventory accumulation and falling income continues until income falls to the equilibrium level. At the equilibrium, income equals planned expenditure.

Similarly, suppose GDP is at a level lower than the equilibrium level, such as the level Y_2 in Figure 9-4. In this case, planned expenditure is E_2, which is more than Y_2. Because planned expenditure exceeds production, firms are selling more than they are producing. As firms see their stock of inventories fall, they hire more workers and increase production. This process continues until income equals planned expenditure.

Figure 9-4

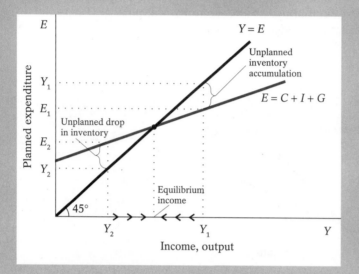

The Adjustment to Equilibrium in the Keynesian Cross If firms are producing at level Y_1, then planned expenditure E_1 falls short of production, so that firms accumulate inventories. This inventory accumulation induces firms to reduce production. Similarly, if firms are producing at level Y_2, then planned expenditure E_2 exceeds production, so that firms run down their inventories. This fall in inventories induces firms to raise production.

In summary, the Keynesian cross shows how income Y is determined for given levels of planned investment I and fiscal policy G and T. We can use this model to show how income changes when one of these exogenous variables changes.

Fiscal Policy and the Multiplier: Government Purchases Consider how changes in government purchases affect the economy. Because government purchases are one component of expenditure, higher government purchases imply, for any given level of income, higher planned expenditure. If government purchases rise by ΔG, then the planned-expenditure schedule shifts upward by ΔG, as in Figure 9-5. The equilibrium of the economy moves from point A to point B.

This graph shows that an increase in government purchases leads to an even greater increase in income. That is, ΔY is larger than ΔG. The ratio $\Delta Y/\Delta G$ is called the **government-purchases multiplier**; it tells us how much income rises in response to a one-dollar increase in government purchases. An implication of the Keynesian cross is that the government-purchases multiplier is larger than one.

Why does fiscal policy have a multiplied effect on income? The reason is that, according to the consumption function, higher income causes higher consumption. Because an increase in government purchases raises income, it also raises consumption, which further raises income, which further raises consumption, and so on. Therefore, in this model, an increase in government purchases causes a greater increase in income.

Figure 9-5

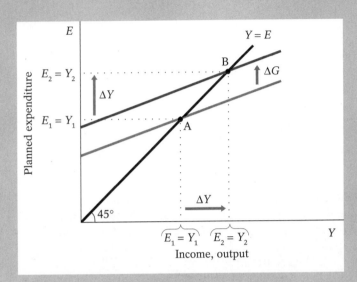

An Increase in Government Purchases in the Keynesian Cross   An increase in government purchases of ΔG raises planned expenditure by that amount for any given level of income. The equilibrium moves from point A to point B, and income rises from Y_1 to Y_2. Note that the increase in income (ΔY) exceeds the increase in government purchases (ΔG = the vertical distance between the two planned expenditure lines). Thus, fiscal policy has a multiplied effect on income.

How big is the multiplier? To answer this question, we trace through each step of the change in income. The process begins when expenditure rises by ΔG, which implies that income rises by ΔG as well. This increase in income in turn raises consumption by $MPC \times \Delta G$, where MPC is the marginal propensity to consume. This increase in consumption raises expenditure and income once again. This second increase in income of $MPC \times \Delta G$ again raises consumption, this time by $MPC \times (MPC \times \Delta G)$, which again raises expenditure and income, and so on. This feedback from consumption to income to consumption continues indefinitely. The total effect on income is:

Initial Change in Government Purchases = ΔG
First Change in Consumption $= MPC \times \Delta G$
Second Change in Consumption $= MPC^2 \times \Delta G$
Third Change in Consumption $= MPC^3 \times \Delta G$

$$\cdot \qquad\qquad\qquad\qquad \cdot$$
$$\cdot \qquad\qquad\qquad\qquad \cdot$$
$$\cdot \qquad\qquad\qquad\qquad \cdot$$

$$\Delta Y = (1 + MPC + MPC^2 + MPC^3 + \ldots)\Delta G.$$

The government-purchases multiplier is

$$\Delta Y/\Delta G = 1 + MPC + MPC^2 + MPC^3 + \ldots.$$

This expression for the multiplier is an example of an *infinite geometric series*. A result from algebra allows us to write the multiplier as[2]

$$\Delta Y / \Delta G = 1/(1 - MPC).$$

For example, if the marginal propensity to consume is 0.6, the multiplier is

$$\Delta Y / \Delta G = 1 + 0.6 + 0.6^2 + 0.6^3 + \ldots$$
$$= 1/(1 - 0.6)$$
$$= 2.5.$$

In this case, a \$1.00 increase in government purchases raises equilibrium income by \$2.50.[3]

Fiscal Policy and the Multiplier: Taxes   Consider now how changes in taxes affect equilibrium income. A decrease in taxes of ΔT immediately raises disposable income $Y - T$ by ΔT and, therefore, consumption by $MPC \times \Delta T$. For any given level of income Y, planned expenditure is now higher. As in Figure 9-6, the planned-expenditure schedule shifts upward by $MPC \times \Delta T$. The equilibrium of the economy moves from point A to point B.

Just as the increase in government purchases has a multiplied effect on income, so does a decrease in taxes. As before, the initial change in expenditure, $-(MPC)\Delta T$, is multiplied by $1/(1 - MPC)$. The overall effect on income of the change in taxes is

$$\Delta Y / \Delta T = -MPC/(1 - MPC).$$

This expression is the **tax multiplier**: the amount income changes in response

---

[2] *Mathematical note*: We prove this algebraic result as follows. Let

$$z = 1 + x + x^2 + \ldots.$$

Multiply both sides of this equation by x:

$$xz = x + x^2 + x^3 + \ldots.$$

Subtract the second equation from the first:

$$z - xz = 1.$$

Rearrange this last equation to obtain

$$z(1 - x) = 1,$$

which implies

$$z = 1/(1 - x).$$

This completes the proof.

[3] *Mathematical note*: The government-purchases multiplier is most easily derived using a little calculus. Begin with the equation

$$Y = C(Y - T) + I + G.$$

Differentiate to obtain

$$dY = C'dY + dG,$$

and then rearrange to find

$$dY/dG = 1/(1 - C').$$

This is the same as the equation in the text.

Figure 9-6

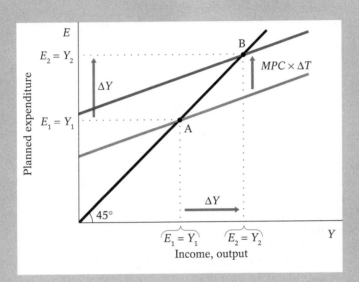

A Decrease in Taxes in the Keynesian Cross A decrease in taxes of ΔT raises planned expenditure by $MPC \times \Delta T$ for any given level of income. The equilibrium moves from point A to point B, and income rises from Y_1 to Y_2. Again, fiscal policy has a multiplied effect on income.

to a one-dollar change in taxes. For example, if the marginal propensity to consume is 0.6, then the tax multiplier is

$$\Delta Y / \Delta T = -0.6 / (1 - 0.6) = -1.5.$$

In this example, a \$1.00 cut in taxes raises equilibrium income by \$1.50.[4] Note that in our model, "taxes" stand for net taxes paid by individuals—that is, taxes less transfer payments received, like unemployment insurance benefits. Canadian fiscal policies often take the form of changes in these transfer payments. Thus, we analyze a cut in unemployment insurance benefits as an increase in T.

CASE STUDY

9•1

Modest Expectations Concerning Job Creation

Canada's Liberal government was elected in 1993 on a platform of "jobs, jobs, jobs." Many students, when hearing the term "multiplier," expect that it could be fairly straightforward for governments to fulfill job-creation promises of this sort. But economists now believe that the multiplier terminology may create

---

4   *Mathematical note:* As before, the multiplier is most easily derived using a little calculus. Begin with the equation

$$Y = C(Y - T) + I + G.$$

Differentiate to obtain

$$dY = C'(dY - dT),$$

and then rearrange to find

$$dY/dT = -C'/(1 - C').$$

This is the same as the equation in the text.

unrealistic expectations. This trend in thinking will become clearer as our understanding of aggregate demand progresses through this book. For example, we will be considering developments in financial markets—the effects of fiscal policy on interest rates and the exchange rate. We will learn that the size of our fiscal policy multipliers is much reduced by these considerations.

What is a plausible value for the government spending multiplier—given that, at this point, we must limit our attention to the simple formula $1/(1 - MPC)$? To answer this question, we must think of taxes, imports, and saving—the main things that keep a new dollar of income earned from being spent on domestically produced goods. The first consideration is the tax system; taxes increase by about $0.25 for each $1 increase in GDP. The second consideration is that the transfer payments people receive from the government decrease as their income increases, and in aggregate this variation means that transfer payments fall by about $0.15 for each $1 increase in GDP. Since "taxes" in our model stand for *net* payments by individuals to government—taxes less transfer receipts—we must take the overall "tax rate" to be 0.25 plus 0.15, or 0.40. Thus the proporion of income not taxed is 0.60. Finally, Canadians tend to import about one quarter of all goods consumed. With a propensity to spend about 75 percent of each extra dollar of disposable income, we have an overall marginal propensity to consume domestically produced goods (out of each dollar of pretax income, GDP) equal to:

Proportion of Income Not Taxed	$\times$	Proportion of Spending Not Spent on Imports	$\times$	Propensity to Spend	$=$	MPC
(0.60)		(0.75)		(0.75)	$=$	0.34

With the *MPC* estimated at 0.34, the spending multiplier, $1/(1 - MPC)$, is 1.5.

The 1994 federal budget involved an average change in government spending of $5 billion per year. Thus, we can take $\Delta G = \$5$ billion as representing the magnitude of a typical fiscal policy. The multiplier formula then predicts that ΔY is $7.5 billion. Since Canada's economy's GDP was just over $700 billion in early 1994, this typical fiscal policy involves changing output by about 1 percent.

How much can this initiative be expected to change unemployment? The answer to this question can be had by relying on Okun's law, which was explained in Chapter 2. Okun's law states that unemployment usually falls by about one half the percentage rise in GDP. Thus, the effect of this typical fiscal policy is estimated to be a change in the unemployment rate of only one half of 1 percentage point. With an unemployment rate over 10 percent, not many would summarize this change as "jobs, jobs, jobs." We must also keep in mind that the simple formula, $1/(1 - MPC)$, overestimates the effects of policy.

It is also important to realize that a small multiplier is sometimes exactly what the government desires. For example, when cutting expendentures to reduce the budget deficit (as was the government's aim in 1994), the government does not want to destroy many jobs. A small fiscal multiplier is just what is needed in that case.

The Interest Rate, Investment, and the *IS* Curve

The Keynesian cross is only a stepping stone on our road to developing the *IS-LM* model. The Keynesian cross is useful because it shows what determines the economy's income for any given level of planned investment. Yet it makes the unrealistic assumption that the level of planned investment is fixed. As we discussed in Chapter 3, we can expect planned investment to depend negatively on the interest rate.

To add this relationship between the interest rate and investment to our model, we write the level of planned investment as

$$I = I(r).$$

This investment function is graphed in Figure 9-7(a). Because the interest rate is the cost of borrowing to finance investment projects, an increase in the interest rate reduces planned investment.

Figure 9-7

Deriving the *IS* Curve Panel (a) shows the investment function: an increase in the interest rate from r_1 to r_2 reduces planned investment from $I(r_1)$ to $I(r_2)$. Panel (b) shows the Keynesian cross: a decrease in planned investment from $I(r_1)$ to $I(r_2)$ reduces income from Y_1 to Y_2. Panel (c) shows the *IS* curve summarizing this relationship between the interest rate and income: the higher the interest rate, the lower the level of income.

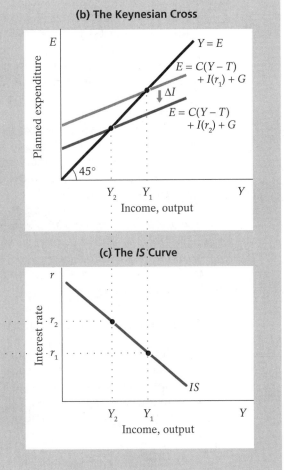

(b) The Keynesian Cross

(a) The Investment Function

(c) The *IS* Curve

We can use the investment function and the Keynesian-cross diagram to determine how income changes when the interest rate changes. Because investment is inversely related to the interest rate, an increase in the interest rate from r_1 to r_2 reduces the quantity of investment from $I(r_1)$ to $I(r_2)$. The reduction in planned investment, in turn, shifts the expenditure function downward, as in Figure 9-7(b). The shift in the expenditure function leads to a lower level of income. Hence, an increase in the interest rate lowers income.

The IS curve summarizes the relationship between the interest rate and the level of income that results from the investment function and the Keynesian cross. The higher the interest rate, the lower the level of planned investment, and thus the lower the level of income. For this reason, the IS curve slopes downward, as in Figure 9-7(c).

How Fiscal Policy Shifts the *IS* Curve

The IS curve shows us the level of income for any given interest rate. As we learned from the Keynesian cross, the level of income also depends on fiscal policy. The IS curve is drawn for a given fiscal policy; that is, the IS curve holds G and T fixed. When fiscal policy changes, the IS curve shifts.

Figure 9-8 uses the Keynesian cross to examine how an increase in government purchases from G_1 to G_2 shifts the IS curve. This figure is drawn for a given interest rate $\bar{r}$ and thus for a given level of planned investment. The Keynesian cross shows that this change in fiscal policy raises planned expenditure and thereby increases equilibrium income from Y_1 to Y_2. A similar analysis holds for any given interest rate. Therefore, an increase in government purchases shifts the entire IS curve outward.

We can use the Keynesian cross to see how other changes in fiscal policy shift the IS curve. Because a decrease in taxes also expands expenditure and income, it too shifts the IS curve outward. A decrease in government purchases or an increase in taxes reduces income; therefore, such a change in fiscal policy shifts the IS curve inward.

In summary, the IS curve shows the relationship between the interest rate and the level of income that arises from the market for goods and services. The IS curve is drawn for a given fiscal policy. Changes in fiscal policy that raise the demand for goods and services shift the IS curve to the right. Changes in fiscal policy that reduce the demand for goods and services shift the IS curve to the left.

A Loanable-Funds Interpretation of the *IS* Curve

When we first studied the market for goods and services in Chapter 3, we noted an equivalence between the supply and demand for goods and services and the supply and demand for loanable funds. This equivalence provides another way to interpret the IS curve.

Recall that the national income accounts identity can be written as

$$Y - C - G = I$$
$$S = I.$$

Figure 9-8

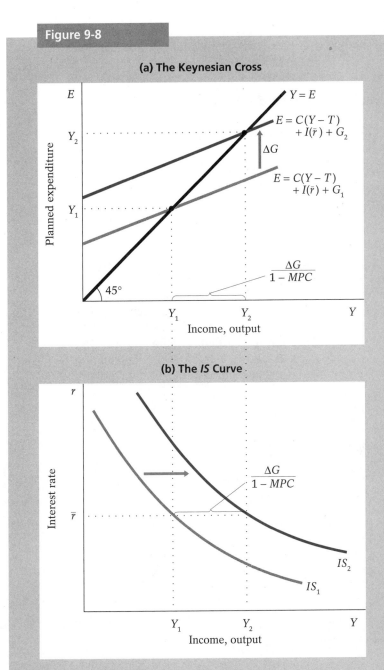

(a) The Keynesian Cross

An Increase in Government Purchases Shifts the *IS* Curve Outward Panel (a) shows that an increase in government purchases raises planned expenditure. For any given interest rate, the upward shift in planned expenditure of ΔG leads to an increase in income of $\Delta G/(1 - MPC)$. Therefore, in Panel (b), the *IS* curve shifts to the right by this amount.

(b) The *IS* Curve

The left-hand side of this equation is national saving S, the sum of private saving $Y - T - C$ and public saving $T - G$, and the right-hand side is investment I. National saving represents the supply of loanable funds, and investment represents the demand for these funds.

To see how the market for loanable funds produces the *IS* curve, substitute the consumption function for *C* and the investment function for *I*:

$$Y - C(Y - T) - G = I(r).$$

The left-hand side of this equation states that the supply of loanable funds depends on income and fiscal policy. The right-hand side states that the demand for loanable funds depends on the interest rate. The interest rate adjusts to equilibrate the supply and demand for loans.

As Figure 9-9 illustrates, we can interpret the *IS* curve as showing the interest rate that equilibrates the market for loanable funds for any given level of income. When income rises from Y_1 to Y_2, national saving, which equals $Y - C - G$, increases. (Consumption rises by less than income, because the marginal propensity to consume is less than one.) The increased supply of loanable funds drives down the interest rate from r_1 to r_2. The *IS* curve summarizes this relationship: higher income implies higher saving, which in turn implies a lower equilibrium interest rate. For this reason, the *IS* curve slopes downward.

This alternative interpretation of the *IS* curve also explains why a change in fiscal policy shifts the *IS* curve. An increase in government purchases or a decrease in taxes reduces national saving for any given level of income. The reduced supply of loanable funds raises the interest rate that equilibrates the market. Because the interest rate is now higher for any given level of income, the *IS* curve shifts upward in response to the expansionary change in fiscal policy.

Figure 9-9

(a) The Market for Loanable Funds

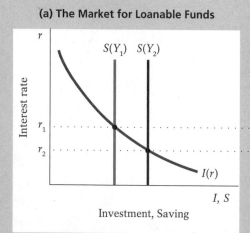

(b) The *IS* Curve

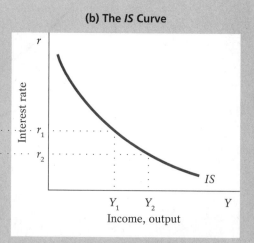

A Loanable-Funds Interpretation of the *IS* Curve Panel (a) shows that an increase in income from Y_1 to Y_2 raises saving and thus lowers the interest rate that equilibrates the supply and demand for loanable funds. The *IS* curve in Panel (b) expresses this negative relationship between income and the interest rate.

Finally, note that, by itself, the *IS* curve does not determine either income *Y* or the interest rate *r*. Instead, the *IS* curve is a relationship between *Y* and *r* arising in the market for goods and services or, equivalently, the market for loanable funds. To determine the equilibrium of the economy, we need another relationship between these two variables, to which we now turn.

9•2 The Money Market and the *LM* Curve

The *LM* curve is the relationship between the interest rate and the level of income that arises in the market for money balances. To understand this relationship, we begin by looking at a simple theory of the interest rate, called the **theory of liquidity preference.**

The Theory of Liquidity Preference

The theory of liquidity preference is the simplest interpretation of Keynes's theory of the interest rate. Just as the Keynesian cross provides a building block for the *IS* curve, the theory of liquidity preference provides a building block for the *LM* curve. The theory explains how the supply and demand for real money balances, which we studied in Chapter 6, determine the interest rate.

We begin with the supply of real money balances. If *M* stands for the supply of money and *P* stands for the price level, then *M/P* is the supply of real money balances. The theory of liquidity preference assumes there is a fixed supply of real balances. That is,

$$(M/P)^s = \bar{M}/\bar{P}.$$

The money supply *M* is an exogenous policy variable chosen by the central bank, such as the Bank of Canada. The price level *P* is also an exogenous variable in this model. (We take the price level as given because the *IS-LM* model—our ultimate goal in this chapter—considers the short run when the price level is fixed.) These assumptions imply that the supply of real balances is fixed and, in particular, does not depend on the interest rate. When we plot the supply of real money balances against the interest rate in Figure 9-10, we obtain a vertical supply curve.

Next, consider the demand for real money balances. People hold money because it is a "liquid" asset—that is, because it is easily used to make transactions. The theory of liquidity preference postulates that the quantity of real money balances demanded depends on the interest rate. The interest rate is the opportunity cost of holding money: it is what you forgo by holding money, which does not bear interest, instead of interest-bearing bank deposits or bonds. When the interest rate rises, people want to hold less of their wealth in the form of money.

We write the demand for real money balances as

$$(M/P)^d = L(r),$$

where the function *L*( ) denotes the demand for the liquid asset—money. This

Figure 9-10

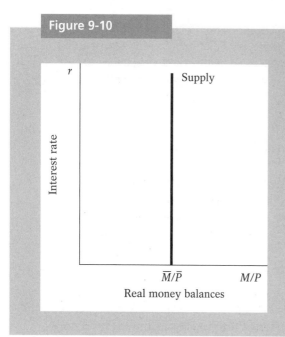

The Supply of Real Money Balances The supply curve for real balances is vertical because the supply does not depend on the interest rate.

equation states that the quantity of real balances demanded is a function of the interest rate. Figure 9-11 shows the relationship between the interest rate and the quantity of real balances demanded. This demand curve slopes downward because higher interest rates reduce the quantity of real balances demanded.[5]

To obtain a theory of the interest rate, we combine the supply and demand for real money balances in Figure 9-12. According to the theory of liquidity preference, the interest rate adjusts to equilibrate the money market. At the equilibrium interest rate, the quantity of real balances demanded equals the quantity supplied.

The adjustment of the interest rate to this equilibrium of money supply and money demand occurs because people try to adjust their portfolios of assets if the interest rate is not at the equilibrium level. If the interest rate is too high, the quantity of real balances supplied exceeds the quantity demanded. Individuals holding the excess supply of money try to convert some of their non-interest-bearing money into interest-bearing bank deposits or bonds. Banks and bond issuers, who prefer to pay lower interest rates, respond to this excess supply of money by lowering the interest rates they offer. Conversely, if the interest rate is too low, so that the quantity of money demanded exceeds the quantity sup-

---

[5]   Note that r is being used to denote the interest rate here, as it was in our discussion of the *IS* curve. More accurately, it is the nominal interest rate that determines money demand and the real interest rate that determines firms' investment in new plant and equipment. Household investment in residential housing can depend on the nominal interest rate, since bank rules concerning maximum mortgage limits are fixed in nominal terms. To keep things simple, we are ignoring expected inflation, which creates the difference between the real and nominal interest rates. The role of expected inflation in the *IS-LM* model is explored in Chapter 10.

Figure 9-11

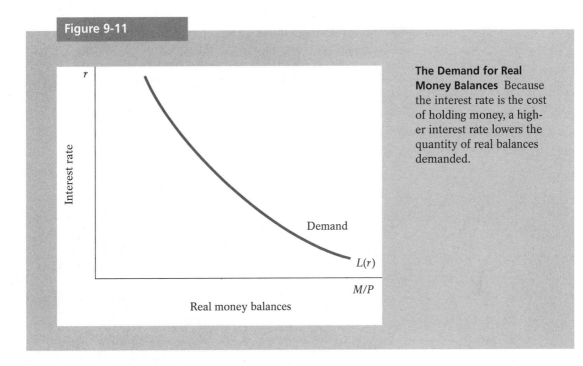

The Demand for Real Money Balances Because the interest rate is the cost of holding money, a higher interest rate lowers the quantity of real balances demanded.

plied, individuals try to obtain money by selling bonds or making bank withdrawals, which drives the interest rate up. At the equilibrium interest rate people are content with their portfolios of monetary and nonmonetary assets.

Figure 9-12

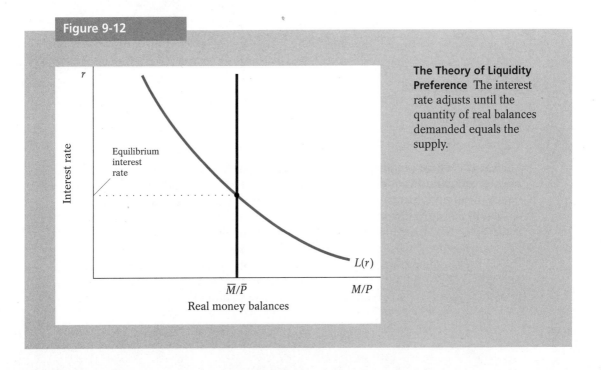

The Theory of Liquidity Preference The interest rate adjusts until the quantity of real balances demanded equals the supply.

The theory of liquidity preference implies that decreases in the money supply raise the interest rate and that increases in the money supply lower the interest rate. To see why, suppose that the Bank of Canada reduces the money supply. A reduction in M reduces M/P, since P is fixed in the model. The supply of real balances shifts to the left, as in Figure 9-13. The equilibrium interest rate rises from r_1 to r_2. The higher interest rate induces people to hold a smaller quantity of their wealth in the form of real money balances.

Figure 9-13

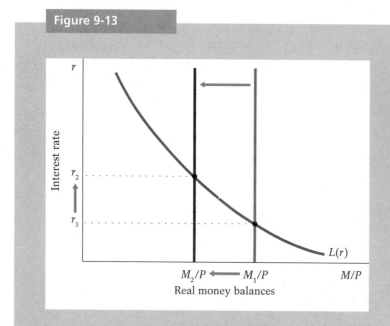

A Reduction in the Money Supply in the Theory of Liquidity Preference A reduction in the money supply from M_1 to M_2 reduces the supply of real balances, since the price level is fixed. The equilibrium interest rate therefore rises from r_1 to r_2.

CASE STUDY

9•2   **Tight Money and Rising Interest Rates**

The early 1980s saw a large and speedy reduction in North American inflation rates. During the 1980–1982 period, Canada's CPI increased at an average annual rate of 11.2 percent; during the next three years, that rate of increase slowed to just 4.7 percent. This 6.5 percentage point reduction in inflation was achieved by a dramatic tightening of monetary policy.

During the 1970s, the quantity of real money balances ($M1$ divided by the CPI) had been growing at an average rate of 2.8 percent per year. Then, during the 1980–1982 period, Canadian real money growth was pushed down to an average of −7.8 percent per year. After that, monetary policy was eased significantly; average growth in real balances was 1.7 percent per year in the 1983–1985 period.

How does such a monetary tightening influence interest rates? The answer depends on the time horizon. Our analysis of the Fisher effect in Chapter 6 suggests that the change in monetary policy would lower inflation, which, in turn, would lead to lower nominal interest rates. Yet the theory of liquidity preference predicts that, in the short run when prices are sluggish, anti-inflationary monetary policy involves a leftward shift of the *LM* curve and higher nominal interest rates.

Both conclusions are consistent with experience. Nominal interest rates did fall in the 1980s as inflation fell. For example, the three-month treasury bill rate fell from an average of 14.7 percent in the 1980–1982 period to an average of 10 percent in the 1983–1985 period. But it is instructive to consider the year-to-year sequence. The interest rate rose from 12.7 percent in 1980 to 17.8 percent in 1981, and it did not fall below 12.7 percent until 1983.

Income, Money Demand, and the *LM* Curve

We now use the theory of liquidity preference to derive the *LM* curve. We see that the equilibrium interest rate—the interest rate that equilibrates money supply and money demand—depends on the level of income. The *LM* curve expresses this relationship between the level of income and the interest rate.

So far we have assumed that only the interest rate influences the quantity of real balances demanded. More realistically, the level of income Y also affects money demand. When income is high, expenditure is high, so people engage in more transactions that require the use of money. Thus, greater income implies greater money demand. We now write the money demand function as

$$(M/P)^d = L(r, Y).$$

The quantity of real money balances demanded is negatively related to the interest rate and positively related to income.

Using the theory of liquidity preference, we can see what happens to the interest rate when the level of income changes. For example, consider what happens when income increases from Y_1 to Y_2. As Figure 9-14(a) illustrates, this increase in income shifts the money demand curve outward. To equilibrate the market for real money balances, the interest rate must rise from r_1 to r_2. Therefore, higher income leads to a higher interest rate.

The *LM* curve plots this relationship between the level of income and the interest rate. The higher the level of income, the higher the demand for real money balances, and the higher the equilibrium interest rate. For this reason, the *LM* curve slopes upward, as in Figure 9-14(b).

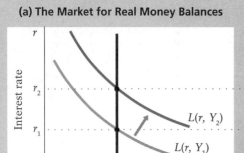

(a) The Market for Real Money Balances

(b) The LM Curve

Deriving the LM Curve Panel (a) shows the market for real balances: an increase in income from Y_1 to Y_2 raises the demand for money and thus raises the interest rate from r_1 to r_2. Panel (b) shows the LM curve summarizing this relationship between the interest rate and income: the higher the level of income, the higher the interest rate.

How Monetary Policy Shifts the LM Curve

The LM curve tells us the interest rate that equilibrates the money market for any given level of income. The theory of liquidity preference shows that the equilibrium interest rate depends on the supply of real balances. The LM curve is drawn for a given supply of real money balances. If real balances change— for example, if the Bank of Canada alters the money supply—the LM curve shifts.

We can use the theory of liquidity preference to understand how monetary policy shifts the LM curve. Suppose that the Bank of Canada decreases the money supply from M_1 to M_2, which causes the supply of real balances to fall from M_1/P to M_2/P. Figure 9-15 shows what happens. Holding constant the amount of income and thus the demand curve for real balances, a reduction in the supply of real balances raises the interest rate that equilibrates the money market. A similar analysis holds for all levels of income, other than Y. Hence, a decrease in real balances shifts the entire LM curve upward.

In summary, the LM curve shows the relationship between the interest rate and the level of income that arises in the market for real money balances. The LM curve is drawn for a given supply of real money balances. Decreases in the supply of real money balances shift the LM curve upward. Increases in the supply of real money balances shift the LM curve downward.

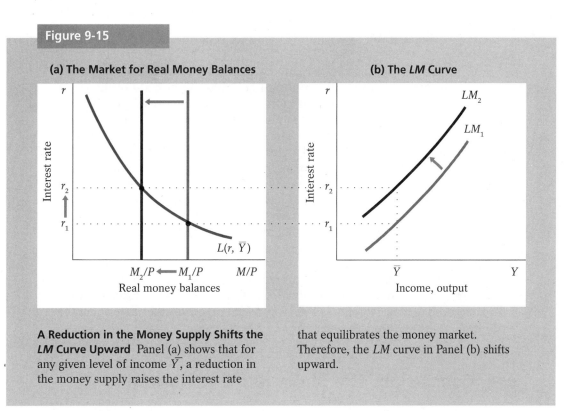

Figure 9-15

(a) The Market for Real Money Balances

(b) The *LM* Curve

A Reduction in the Money Supply Shifts the *LM* Curve Upward Panel (a) shows that for any given level of income $\overline{Y}$, a reduction in the money supply raises the interest rate that equilibrates the money market. Therefore, the *LM* curve in Panel (b) shifts upward.

A Quantity-Equation Interpretation of the *LM* Curve

When we first discussed aggregate demand and the short-run determination of income in Chapter 8, we derived the aggregate demand curve from the quantity theory of money. We wrote the quantity equation,

$$MV = PY,$$

and assumed that velocity V is constant. This assumption implies that, for any given price level, the supply of money alone determines the level of income. Because this level of income does not depend on the interest rate, the quantity theory is equivalent to a vertical *LM* curve.

We can derive the more realistic upward-sloping *LM* curve from the quantity equation by relaxing the assumption that velocity is constant. The assumption of constant velocity is equivalent to the assumption that the demand for real money balances depends only on the level of income. In reality, the demand for real money balances also depends on the interest rate: a higher interest rate raises the cost of holding money and reduces money demand. As people respond to a higher interest rate by reducing the amount of money they hold, each dollar in the economy circulates from person to person more quickly— that is, the velocity of money increases. We can write this as

$$MV(r) = PY.$$

The velocity function $V(r)$ indicates that velocity is positively related to the interest rate.

This form of the quantity equation yields an *LM* curve that slopes upward. Because an increase in the interest rate raises the velocity of money, it raises the level of income for any given money supply and price level. The *LM* curve expresses this positive relationship between the interest rate and income.

This equation also shows why changes in the money supply shift the *LM* curve. For any given interest rate and price level, an increase in the money supply raises the level of income. Thus, increases in the money supply shift the *LM* curve to the right, and decreases in the money supply shift the *LM* curve to the left.

Keep in mind that the quantity equation merely provides another way to express the theory behind the *LM* curve. This interpretation of the *LM* curve is substantively the same as that provided by the theory of liquidity preference. In both cases, the *LM* curve represents a positive relationship between income and the interest rate that arises from the money market.[6]

Finally, remember that the *LM* curve by itself does not determine either income Y or the interest rate r. Like the *IS* curve, it is only a relationship between these two endogenous variables. The *IS* and *LM* curves together determine the equilibrium in the economy.

9•3 Conclusion: The Short-Run Equilibrium

We now have all the components of the *IS-LM* model. The two equations of this model are

$$Y = C(Y - T) + I(r) + G \qquad IS$$
$$M/P = L(r, Y). \qquad LM$$

The model takes fiscal policy, G and T, monetary policy M, and the price level P as exogenous. Given these exogenous variables, the *IS* curve provides the combinations of r and Y that satisfy the equation representing the goods market, and the *LM* curve provides the combinations of r and Y that satisfy the equation representing the money market. These two curves are shown together in Figure 9-16.

The equilibrium of the economy is the point at which the *IS* curve and the *LM* curve cross. This point gives the interest rate r and the level of income Y that satisfy both the goods-market equilibrium condition and the money-market equilibrium condition. In other words, at this intersection, actual expenditure equals planned expenditure, and the demand for real money balances equals the supply.

Economists use the *IS-LM* model to analyze the short-run effects of policy changes and other events on national income. We apply it to that purpose in the next chapter, where we also see how the *IS-LM* model explains the position and slope of the aggregate demand curve.

---

[6] Mathematical Note: The liquidity preference relationship is $M/P = L(r, Y)$. A special case of this is $M/P = YH(r)$. Since velocity is PY/M, this special case can be written as $V(r) = 1/H(r)$. Thus, to say that velocity is positively related to interest rates is just another way of saying that money demand is negatively related to interest rates.

Figure 9-16

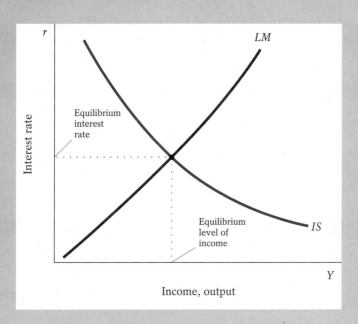

Equilibrium in the IS-LM Model The intersection of *IS* and *LM* represents simultaneous equilibrium in the market for goods and services and in the market for real money balances.

Summary

1. The Keynesian cross is a simple model of income determination. It takes fiscal policy and planned investment as exogenous and then shows that there is one level of national income at which actual expenditure equals planned expenditure. It shows that changes in fiscal policy have a multiplied impact on income.

2. Once we allow planned investment to depend on the interest rate, the Keynesian cross yields a relationship between the interest rate and national income. A higher interest rate lowers planned investment, which in turn lowers national income. The *IS* curve summarizes this negative relationship between the interest rate and income.

3. The theory of liquidity preference is a simple model of the determination of the interest rate. It takes the money supply and the price level as exogenous and assumes that the interest rate adjusts to equilibrate the supply and demand for real money balances. The theory implies that increases in the money supply lower the interest rate.

4. Once we allow the demand for real balances to depend on national income, the theory of liquidity preference yields a relationship between income and the interest rate. A higher level of income raises the demand for real balances, which in turn raises the interest rate. The *LM* curve summarizes this positive relationship between income and the interest rate.

5. The *IS-LM* model combines the elements of the Keynesian cross and the elements of the theory of liquidity preference. The intersection of the *IS* curve and the *LM* curve shows the interest rate and income that satisfy both equilibrium in the goods market and equilibrium in the money market.

KEY CONCEPTS

IS-LM model

IS curve

LM curve

Keynesian cross

Government-purchases multiplier

Tax multiplier

Theory of liquidity preference

QUESTIONS FOR REVIEW

1. Use the Keynesian cross to explain why fiscal policy has a multiplied effect on national income.

2. Use the theory of liquidity preference to explain why an increase in the money supply lowers the interest rate. What does this explanation assume about the price level?

3. Why does the *IS* curve slope downward?

4. Why does the *LM* curve slope upward?

PROBLEMS AND APPLICATIONS

1. Use the Keynesian cross to examine the impact of:

   a. an increase in government purchases.

   b. an increase in taxes.

   c. an equal increase in government purchases and taxes.

2. In the Keynesian cross, assume that the consumption function is given by

$$C = 200 + 0.75(Y - T).$$

Planned investment is 100; government purchases and taxes are both 100.

   a. Graph planned expenditure as a function of income.

   b. What is the equilibrium level of income?

   c. If government purchases increase to 125, what is the new equilibrium income?

   d. What level of government purchases is needed to achieve an income of 1,600?

3. Although our development of the Keynesian cross in this chapter assumes that taxes are a fixed amount, in many countries taxes depend on income. Let's represent the tax system by writing tax revenue as

$$T = \bar{T} + tY,$$

where $\bar{T}$ and t are parameters of the tax code. The parameter t is the marginal tax rate: if income rises by $1.00, taxes rise by $t \times \$1.00$.

   a. How does this tax system change the way consumption responds to changes in GDP?

   b. How does this tax system alter the response of the economy to a change in government purchases?

c. In the *IS-LM* model, how does this tax system alter the slope of the *IS* curve?

4. Consider the impact of an increase in thriftiness in the Keynesian cross. Suppose the consumption function is

$$C = \bar{C} + c(Y - T),$$

where $\bar{C}$ is a parameter called *autonomous consumption* and c is the marginal propensity to consume.

a. What happens to equilibrium income when the society becomes more thrifty, as represented by a decline in $\bar{C}$?

b. What happens to equilibrium saving?

c. Why do you suppose this result is called the *paradox of thrift*?

d. Does this paradox arise in the classical model of Chapter 3? Why or why not?

5. Suppose that the money demand function is

$$(M/P)^d = 1000 - 100r,$$

where r is the interest rate in percent. The money supply M is 1,000 and the price level P is 2.

a. Graph the supply and demand for real money balances.

b. What is the equilibrium interest rate?

c. Assuming the price level is fixed, what happens to the equilibrium interest rate if the supply of money is raised from 1,000 to 1,200?

d. If the central bank wishes to raise the interest rate to 7 percent, what money supply should it set?

Aggregate Demand II

Science is a parasite: the greater the patient population the better the advance in physiology and pathology; and out of pathology arises therapy. The year 1932 was the trough of the great depression, and from its rotten soil was belatedly begot a new subject that today we call macroeconomics.

Paul Samuelson

In Chapter 9 we assembled the pieces of the *IS-LM* model. We saw that the *IS* curve represents the equilibrium in the market for goods and services, that the *LM* curve represents the equilibrium in the market for real money balances, and that the *IS* and *LM* curves together determine national income in the short run when the price level is fixed. Now we turn our attention to applying the model. This chapter uses the *IS-LM* model to analyze three issues.

First, we examine the potential causes of fluctuations in national income. To be more precise, we use the *IS-LM* model to see how changes in the exogenous variables influence the endogenous variables. Because monetary and fiscal policy are among the exogenous variables, the *IS-LM* model shows how these policies influence the economy in the short run. The model also shows how various shocks to the money and goods markets influence the economy.

Second, we discuss how the *IS-LM* model fits into the model of aggregate supply and aggregate demand we developed in Chapter 8. In particular, we examine how the *IS-LM* model provides a theory of the aggregate demand curve. Here we relax the assumption that the price level is fixed, and we show that the *IS-LM* model implies a negative relationship between the price level and national income.

Third, we study the Great Depression, the episode that motivated Keynes to emphasize aggregate demand as a key determinant of national income. As the quotation at the beginning of this chapter indicates, the Great Depression is the event that gave birth to short-run macroeconomic theory. We can use the *IS-LM* model to discuss the various explanations of this traumatic economic downturn.

10•1 Explaining Fluctuations With the IS-LM Model

The intersection of the *IS* curve and the *LM* curve determines the level of national income. National income fluctuates when one of these curves shifts, changing the short-run equilibrium of the economy. In this section we examine how changes in policy and exogenous shocks to the economy can cause these curves to shift.

Changes in Fiscal Policy

We first examine the impact of changes in fiscal policy on the economy. Recall that changes in fiscal policy shift the *IS* curve. The *IS-LM* model shows how these shifts in the *IS* curve affect income and the interest rate.

Consider the effect of an increase in government purchases of ΔG. The government-purchases multiplier in the Keynesian cross tells us that, at any given interest rate, this change in fiscal policy raises the level of income by $\Delta G/(1 - MPC)$. Therefore, as Figure 10-1 illustrates, the *IS* curve shifts outward by this amount. The equilibrium of the economy moves from point A to point B. The increase in government purchases raises both income and the interest rate.

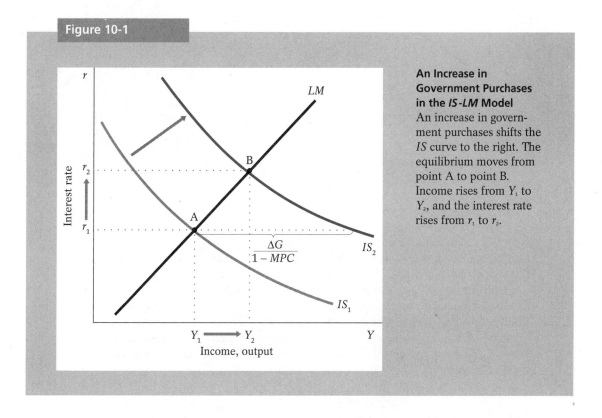

Figure 10-1

An Increase in Government Purchases in the *IS-LM* Model An increase in government purchases shifts the *IS* curve to the right. The equilibrium moves from point A to point B. Income rises from Y_1 to Y_2, and the interest rate rises from r_1 to r_2.

Similarly, consider the effect of a decrease in taxes of ΔT. The tax multiplier in the Keynesian cross tells us that, at any given interest rate, this change in policy raises the level of income by $\Delta T \times MPC/(1 - MPC)$. Therefore, as Figure

10-2 illustrates, the *IS* curve shifts outward by this amount. The equilibrium of the economy moves from point A to point B. The tax cut raises both income and the interest rate.

Figure 10-2

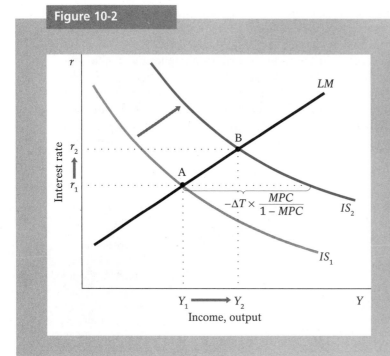

A Decrease in Taxes in the *IS-LM* Model A decrease in taxes shifts the *IS* curve to the right. The equilibrium moves from point A to point B. Income rises from Y_1 to Y_2, and the interest rate rises from r_1 to r_2.

Note that the increase in income in response to either form of fiscal expansion is smaller in the *IS-LM* model than in the Keynesian cross. You can see this in Figures 10-1 and 10-2. The horizontal shift in the *IS* curve equals the rise in equilibrium income in the Keynesian cross. This amount is larger than the increase in equilibrium income here in the *IS-LM* model. The difference arises because the Keynesian cross assumes that investment is fixed, whereas the *IS-LM* model takes into account that investment falls when the interest rate rises. In the *IS-LM* model, a fiscal expansion raises the interest rate and crowds out some investment. Thus, fiscal policy is less powerful in this more realistic model of the economy.

Changes in Monetary Policy

We now examine the impact of a change in monetary policy. Recall that a change in monetary policy shifts the *LM* curve. The *IS-LM* model shows how a shift in the *LM* curve affects income and the interest rate.

Consider the impact of an increase in the money supply. An increase in M leads to an increase in M/P, since P is fixed. The theory of liquidity preference shows that, for any given level of income, an increase in real money balances leads to a lower interest rate. Therefore, the LM curve shifts downward, as in Figure 10-3. The equilibrium moves from point A to point B. The increase in the money supply lowers the interest rate and raises the level of income.

Thus, the IS-LM model shows that monetary policy influences income by changing the interest rate. This conclusion sheds light on our analysis of monetary policy in Chapter 8. In that chapter we showed that in the short run, when prices are sticky, an expansion in the money supply raises income. But we did not discuss how a monetary expansion induces greater spending on goods and services—a process that is called the **monetary transmission mechanism**. The IS-LM model shows that an increase in the money supply lowers the interest rate, which stimulates investment and thereby expands the overall demand for goods and services.

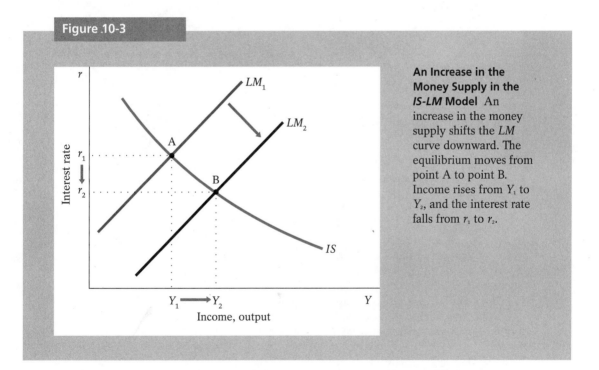

Figure 10-3

An Increase in the Money Supply in the *IS-LM* Model An increase in the money supply shifts the LM curve downward. The equilibrium moves from point A to point B. Income rises from Y_1 to Y_2, and the interest rate falls from r_1 to r_2.

The Interaction Between Monetary and Fiscal Policy

When analyzing any change in monetary or fiscal policy, it is important to keep in mind that these policies may not be independent of each other. A change in one may influence the other. This interdependence may alter the impact of a policy change.

For example, consider the plan proposed by the federal government in 1994 to reduce the budget deficit by cutting government spending. What effect should this policy have on the economy? According to the *IS-LM* model, the answer depends on how the Bank of Canada responds to the spending cut.

Figure 10-4 shows three of the many possible outcomes. In Figure 10-4(a), the Bank of Canada holds the money supply constant. The spending cut shifts the *IS* curve inward, which reduces income and the interest rate. In Figure

Figure 10-4

(a) The Bank of Canada Holds Money Supply Constant

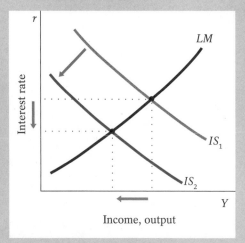

(b) The Bank of Canada Holds Interest Rate Constant

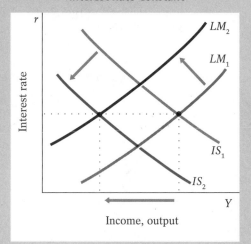

(c) The Bank of Canada Holds Income Constant

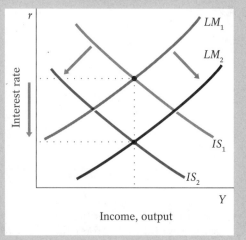

The Response of the Economy to a Cut in Government Spending How the economy responds to a cut in government spending depends on how monetary policy responds. In Panel (a) the Bank of Canada holds the money supply constant. In Panel (b) the Bank of Canada holds the interest rate constant by reducing the money supply. In Panel (c) the Bank of Canada holds the level of income constant by raising the money supply.

10-4(b), the Bank of Canada wants to hold the interest rate constant. In this case, when the spending cut shifts the *IS* curve inward, the Bank of Canada must decrease the money supply to keep the interest rate at its original level. This shifts the *LM* curve upward. The interest rate does not fall, but income falls by a larger amount than if the Bank of Canada had held the money supply constant.

In Figure 10-4(c), the Bank of Canada wants to prevent the spending cut from lowering income. It must, therefore, raise the money supply. In this case, the spending cut does not cause a recession, but it does cause a large fall in the interest rate. Although the level of income is unchanged, the combination of a spending cut and a monetary expansion changes the allocation of the economy's resources. The spending cut shrinks the government sector while the lower interest rate stimulates investment.

From this example we can see that the impact of the change in fiscal policy depends on the policy the Bank of Canada pursues—that is, on whether it holds the money supply, the interest rate, or the level of income constant. More generally, whenever analyzing a change in one policy, one must make an assumption about its effects on the other policy. What assumption is most appropriate depends on the case at hand and the many political considerations that lie behind economic policymaking.

Perhaps the most significant interaction between monetary and fiscal policy occurs in the case of a small open economy. In that case, the fundamental choice for monetary policy is whether to fix the exchange rate or to allow a floating exchange rate. As we shall see in Chapter 13, this choice dramatically affects the power of fiscal policy. With a floating exchange rate (and this has been Canada's policy for years), the effect of fiscal policy on real GDP is very much blunted. This is good news for those who do not want spending cuts to raise unemployment very much, but this is bad news for those who want to use expansionary fiscal policy to create jobs. We will explore these issues more fully in Chapter 13, after we have completed our development of the closed-economy model of aggregate demand.

CASE STUDY

10•1 Policy Analysis With Macroeconometric Models

The *IS-LM* model shows how monetary and fiscal policy influence the equilibrium level of income. The predictions of the model, however, are qualitative, not quantitative. The *IS-LM* model shows that increases in government purchases raise GDP and that increases in taxes lower GDP. But when economists analyze specific policy proposals, they need to know not just the direction of the effect but the size as well. For example, if the federal government cuts spending by $5 billion and if monetary policy is not altered, how much will GDP fall? To answer this question economists need to go beyond the graphical representation of the *IS-LM* model.

Macroeconometric models of the economy provide one way to evaluate policy proposals. A **macroeconometric model** is a model that describes the economy quantitatively, rather than just qualitatively. Many of these models are essentially more complicated and more realistic versions of our *IS-LM* model. The economists who build macroeconometric models use historical data to estimate parameters such as the marginal propensity to consume, the sensitivity of investment to the interest rate, and the sensitivity of money demand to the interest rate. Once a model is built, economists can simulate the effects of alternative policies with the help of a computer.

It is interesting to note that estimates of Canada's one-year government spending multiplier have changed substantially over the years. In the situation in which the Bank of Canada keeps the money supply constant, $\Delta Y/\Delta G$ was estimated to be 1.42 fifteen years ago.[1] This estimate meant that an increase in government spending of $1 billion was expected to raise overall GDP by $1.42 billion after one year. By 1986, multiplier estimates had fallen to 0.77.[2] Finally, by the early 1990s, those using macroeconometric models were reporting government spending multipliers in the 0.50–0.67 range.[3] This wide variation in estimates for $\Delta Y/\Delta G$, all involving the same behaviour on the part of the Bank of Canada, implies a great deal of imprecision in the planning of fiscal policy. Why do the estimates of the power of fiscal policy keep shrinking as more research proceeds? Economists believe there are two reasons for this trend.

The first concerns the role of expectations on the part of households and firms. To see the importance of expectations, compare a temporary increase in government spending to a permanent one. The *IS* curve shifts out to the right in both cases, so interest rates rise, and this causes some cutback in the investment component of aggregate demand. But the size of this investment response depends on how permanent firms expect the rise in interest rates to be. If the increase in government spending is temporary, the rise in interest rates should be temporary as well, so firms' investment spending is not curtailed to a very great extent. But if the increase in government spending is expected to be permanent, the rise in interest rates matters much more in firms' long-range planning decisions, and there is a much bigger cutback in investment spending. Thus, the government spending multiplier is smaller when the change in spending is expected to last a long time.

You might think that, since changes in investment spending lag behind interest rate changes, this expectations issue cannot matter much for determining the multiplier value for a time horizon of just one year. But such a view amounts to assuming that individuals cannot see the interest changes coming. Anyone who understands the *IS-LM* model knows that permanently higher government spending raises interest rates. They also know that the value of existing financial assets (stocks and bonds) will fall when newly issued bonds promising higher yields are issued. No one wants to hold an asset with a low

[1] John Helliwell, T. Maxwell, and H.E.L. Waslander, "Comparing the Dynamics of Canadian Macro Models," *Canadian Journal of Economics* 12 (May 1979): 133–138.

[2] John Bossons, "Issues in the Analysis of Government Deficits," in John Sargent, ed., *Fiscal and Monetary Policy*, Research Studies of the Royal Commission on the Economic Union and Development Prospects for Canada 21 (Toronto: University of Toronto Press, 1986): 85–112

[3] John Helliwell, "What's Left for Macroeconomic and Growth Policies?," *Bell Canada Papers on Economic and Public Policy* 2 (1994): 5–48.

yield when better yields are expected. Thus, in an attempt to avoid a capital loss on existing financial assets, owners sell them the moment they expect a capital loss. That moment occurs as soon as they see a reason for interest rate increases—that is, *just* after the government spending increase has been *announced* (even before it is implemented). But if everyone tries to sell financial assets at the same time, the price of those assets drops quickly. As a result, the effective yield that a new purchaser can earn on them—the going rate of interest—rises immediately. The moral of the story is that when individuals react to well-informed expectations, their reactions have the effect of bringing the long-run implications of fiscal policy forward in time.

Over the last 15 years, economists have made major strides in their ability to model and simulate how individuals form expectations. Because of this development, the estimated econometric models have done a much better job of including the short-run implications of future government policies. This is a fundamental reason why the estimates of $\Delta Y/\Delta G$ have shrunk so much over time as research methods have improved.

The second explanation for the decrease in $\Delta Y/\Delta G$ estimates follows from increased globalization. With financial markets becoming evermore integrated throughout the world, there has developed an ever-expanding pool of "hot money." These funds move into or out of a country like Canada the moment that the interest rate rises above or below interest rate levels in other countries. This flow of funds dominates the trading in the foreign exchange markets, and so it results in large changes in exchange rates. We must wait until Chapter 13 to learn how these exchange-rate changes reduce the power of fiscal policy. But it is worth noting now that globalization has increased the size and speed of these exchange-rate effects, and so it is not surprising that estimated fiscal policy multipliers have shrunk over time.

Shocks in the *IS-LM* Model

Because the *IS-LM* model shows how national income is determined in the short run, we can use the model to examine how various economic disturbances affect income. So far we have seen how changes in fiscal policy shift the *IS* curve and how changes in monetary policy shift the *LM* curve. Similarly, we can group other disturbances into two categories: shocks to the *IS* curve and shocks to the *LM* curve.

Shocks to the *IS* curve are exogenous changes in the demand for goods and services. Some economists, including Keynes, have emphasized that changes in demand can arise from investors' *animal spirits*—exogenous and perhaps self-fulfilling waves of optimism and pessimism. For example, suppose that firms become pessimistic about the future of the economy and that this pessimism causes them to build fewer new factories. This reduction in the demand for investment goods causes a contractionary shift in the investment function: at every interest rate, firms want to invest less. The fall in investment shifts the *IS* curve inward, which reduces income and employment. This fall in equilibrium income in part validates the firms' initial pessimism.

Shocks to the *IS* curve may also arise from changes in the demand for consumer goods. Suppose that consumer confidence rises, as people become less worried about losing their jobs. This changed attitude induces consumers to save less for the future and consume more today. We can interpret this change as an upward shift in the consumption function. This shift in the consumption function causes the *IS* curve to shift outward, raising income, and, in part, validating the households' initial optimism.

Shocks to the *LM* curve arise from exogenous changes in the demand for money. Suppose that the demand for money increases substantially, as it does when people become worried about the security of holding wealth in less liquid forms. An increase in money demand implies that, for any given level of income and money supply, the interest rate necessary to equilibrate the money market is higher. Hence, an increase in money demand shifts the *LM* curve upward, which tends to raise the interest rate and depress income.

Calvin and Hobbes   by Bill Watterson

Calvin and Hobbes copyright 1992 Watterson Dist. by Universal Press Syndicate

In summary, several kinds of events can cause economic fluctuations by shifting the *IS* curve or the *LM* curve. Remember, however, that such fluctuations are not inevitable. Monetary and fiscal policy can try to offset exogenous shocks. If changes in policy are well timed, shocks to the *IS* or *LM* curves may not lead to large fluctuations in income or employment.

CASE STUDY

10•2   **The Recession of the Early 1990s**

As the Liberal government took office in 1993, Canada was recovering from a recession. Real GDP had fallen by about 1.25 percent over the 1990–1992 period, and unemployment had risen from 7.5 percent in 1989 to 11.3 percent in 1992. High unemployment became a major concern, and it was a central issue in the 1993 federal election.

What caused this recession? It appears that there is no single culprit, but there is a group of likely suspects.

First, there was a recession in the United States. The U.S. central bank, the Federal Reserve, engineered a substantial tightening of monetary policy (so the *LM* curve in the United States shifted to the left), and there was a drop in consumer confidence (so the *IS* curve in the United States shifted left, too). The drop in confidence was partly due to a wave of bankruptcies among savings and loan companies in the United States and partly due to the invasion of Kuwait by Iraq in the summer of 1990. Apparently, households thought it best to reduce spending. Since Canadians export about one quarter of Canada's GDP and 80 percent of that goes to the United States, the recession there meant a major loss in export sales. Thus, Canada's *IS* curve shifted to the left as well, putting downward pressure on Canadian real GDP. There was low consumer confidence in Canada, too, partly because of the uncertainty concerning the national referendum on constitutional change.

Canada also had a tight monetary policy in the early 1990s. Indeed, the Bank of Canada was more committed to eliminating inflation than was the U.S. central bank, so Canada's *LM* curve shifted dramatically to the left—so much so that the leftward *LM* shift dominated the leftward *IS* shift in terms of interest rate effects. Canadian interest rates rose, both in absolute terms and in relative terms to U.S. interest rates. This development had the direct effect of reducing investment spending by firms, and the indirect effect of raising the value of the Canadian dollar by 15 percent in two years, since "hot money" flowed into Canada to take advantage of the high interest rates. The more expensive Canadian dollar made it very difficult for Canadian exporters, and so accentuated the loss of jobs in the export sector.

Many commentators assumed that the recession of the early 1990s was a result of the Free Trade Agreement with the United States (signed in January 1989). But this agreement involved cutting tariffs gradually over 10 years, from levels that were already low. Also, while Canadians lost some jobs as a result of cutting Canadian tariffs, employment opportunities were gained through the simultaneous reduction of U.S. tariffs. Thus, the role of the free trade deal has been exaggerated; the other reasons for the leftward shifts in the *IS* and *LM* curves were the major causes of the recession.

Many commentators argue that the severity of the recession could have been avoided if monetary policy had not been so tight. Since the Bank of Canada surpassed its goal of reducing inflation to 2 percent and it achieved this goal sooner than was intended, it appears that monetary policy was tighter than necessary. But this assessment has the benefit of hindsight. Most economic data are available only after a lag, and the economy responds to monetary policy with a lag.

The 1990 recession shows some of the difficulties in short-run stabilization policy. There are many sources of shocks to the economy, and the magnitudes of the shocks are not easily observed. Policymakers can recognize and offset the shocks only after a substantial lag. As we discuss more fully in Chapter 12, these lags limit the ability of policymakers to stabilize the economy.

10·2 *IS-LM* as a Theory of Aggregate Demand

We have been using the *IS-LM* model to explain national income in the short run when the price level is fixed. To see how the *IS-LM* model fits into the model of aggregate supply and aggregate demand developed in Chapter 8, we now examine what happens in the *IS-LM* model as the price level changes. As was promised when we began our study of this model, the *IS-LM* model provides a theory to explain the position and slope of the aggregate demand curve.

From the *IS-LM* Model to the Aggregate Demand Curve

Recall from Chapter 8 that the aggregate demand curve is a relationship between the price level and the level of national income. In Chapter 8 this relationship was derived from the quantity theory of money. For a given money supply, a higher price level implies a lower level of income. Increases in the money supply shift the aggregate demand curve outward, and decreases in the money supply shift the aggregate demand curve inward.

We now use the *IS-LM* model, rather than the quantity theory, to derive the aggregate demand curve. First, we use the *IS-LM* model to show that national income falls as the price level rises; the downward-sloping aggregate demand curve expresses this relationship. Second, we examine what causes the aggregate demand curve to shift.

Why does the aggregate demand curve slope downward? To answer this question, we examine what happens in the *IS-LM* model when the price level changes. Figure 10-5 illustrates the impact of a changing price level. For any given money supply M, a higher price level P causes a lower supply of real money balances M/P. A lower supply of real money balances shifts the *LM* curve upward, which raises the interest rate and lowers the equilibrium level of income, as in Figure 10-5(a). Here we see that when the price level rises from P_1 to P_2, national income falls from Y_1 to Y_2. The curve in Figure 10-5(b) is the summary of the entire *IS-LM* system. It plots the negative relationship between national income and the price level that arises from the *IS-LM* model.

What causes the aggregate demand curve to shift? Because the aggregate demand curve summarizes the results of the *IS-LM* model, shocks that shift the *IS* curve or the *LM* curve cause the aggregate demand curve to shift. Expansionary monetary or fiscal policy raises income in the *IS-LM* model and thus shifts the aggregate demand curve outward, as in Figure 10-6. Similarly, contractionary monetary or fiscal policy lowers income in the *IS-LM* model and thus shifts the aggregate demand curve inward.

We can summarize these results as follows. A change in income in the IS-LM model resulting from a change in the price level represents a movement along the aggregate demand curve. A change in income in the IS-LM model for a fixed price level represents a shift in the position of the aggregate demand curve.

Figure 10-5

(a) The *IS-LM* Model

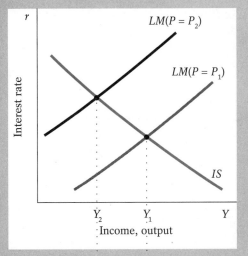

(b) The Aggregate Demand Curve

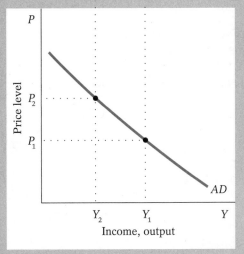

Deriving the Aggregate Demand Curve With the *IS-LM* Model Panel (a) shows the *IS-LM* model: an increase in the price level from P_1 to P_2 lowers real money balances and thus shifts the *LM* curve upward. The shift in the *LM* curve lowers income from Y_1 to Y_2. Panel (b) shows the aggregate demand curve summarizing this relationship between the price level and income: the higher the price level, the lower the level of income.

Figure 10-6

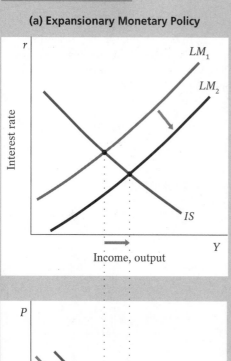

(a) Expansionary Monetary Policy

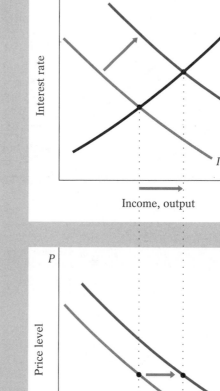

(b) Expansionary Fiscal Policy

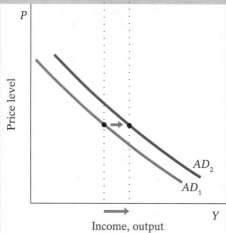

How Monetary and Fiscal Policy Shift the Aggregate Demand Curve Panel (a) shows a monetary expansion. For any given price level, an increase in the money supply raises real money balances, shifts the *LM* curve downward, and raises income. Hence, an increase in the money supply shifts the aggregate demand curve outward.

Panel (b) shows a fiscal expansion, such as an increase in government purchases or a decrease in taxes. The fiscal expansion shifts the *IS* curve outward and, for any given price level, raises income. Hence, a fiscal expansion shifts the aggregate demand curve outward.

The *IS-LM* Model in the Short Run and Long Run

The *IS-LM* model is designed to explain the economy in the short run when the price level is fixed. Yet, now that we have seen how a change in the price level influences the equilibrium, we can use the *IS-LM* model also to describe the economy in the long run when the price level adjusts to ensure that the economy produces at its natural rate. By using the *IS-LM* model to describe the long run, we can show clearly how the Keynesian model of national income differs from the classical model of Chapter 3.

Figure 10-7(a) shows the three curves that are necessary for understanding the short-run and long-run equilibria: the *IS* curve, the *LM* curve, and the vertical line representing the natural rate of output $\bar{Y}$. The *LM* curve is, as always, drawn for a fixed price level, P_1. The short-run equilibrium of the economy is point K, where the *IS* curve crosses the *LM* curve.

Figure 10-7(b) shows the same situation in the diagram of aggregate supply and aggregate demand. At the price level P_1, the quantity of output de-

Figure 10-7

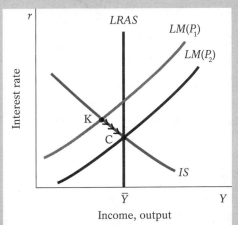

(a) The *IS-LM* Model

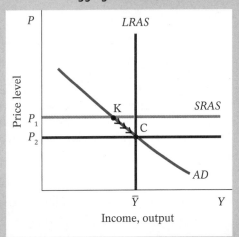

(b) The Model of Aggregate Supply and Aggregate Demand

The Short-Run and Long-Run Equilibria We can compare the short-run and long-run equilibria using either the *IS-LM* diagram in Panel (a) or the aggregate supply–aggregate demand diagram in Panel (b). In the short run, the price level is stuck at P_1. The short-run equilibrium of the economy is therefore point K. In the long run, the price level adjusts so that the economy is at the natural rate. The long-run equilibrium is therefore point C.

manded is below the natural rate. In other words, at the existing price level, there is insufficient demand for goods and services to keep the economy at its natural rate.

In these two diagrams we can examine the short-run equilibrium at which the economy finds itself and the long-run equilibrium toward which the economy evolves. Point K describes the short-run equilibrium, because it assumes that the price level is stuck at P_1. Eventually, the low demand for goods and services causes prices to fall, which moves the economy back toward its natural rate. When the price level reaches P_2, the economy is at point C, which is the long-run equilibrium. The diagram of aggregate supply and aggregate demand shows that, at point C, the quantity of goods and services demanded equals the natural rate of output. This long-run equilibrium is achieved in the *IS-LM* diagram by a shift in the *LM* curve: the fall in the price level raises real money balances and therefore shifts the *LM* curve to the right automatically.

We can now see the key difference between Keynesian and classical approaches to the determination of national income. The Keynesian assumption (represented by point K) is that the price level is stuck. Depending on monetary policy, fiscal policy, and the other determinants of aggregate demand, output may deviate from the natural rate. The classical assumption (represented by point C) is that the price level is flexible. The price level adjusts to ensure that national income is always at the natural rate.

To make the same point somewhat differently, we can think of the economy as being described by three equations. The first two are the *IS* and *LM* equations:

$$Y = C(Y - T) + I(r) + G \qquad IS$$
$$M/P = L(r, Y). \qquad LM$$

The *IS* equation describes the goods market, and the *LM* equation describes the money market. These two equations contain three variables of interest: Y, P, and r. The Keynesian approach is to complete the model with the assumption of fixed prices, so the third equation is

$$P = P_1.$$

This assumption implies that r and Y must adjust to satisfy the *IS* and *LM* equations. The classical approach is to complete the model with the assumption that output reaches the natural rate, so the third equation is

$$Y = \bar{Y}.$$

This assumption implies that r and P must adjust to satisfy the *IS* and *LM* equations.

Which assumption is most appropriate? The answer depends on the time horizon. The classical assumption best describes the long run. Hence, our long-run analysis of national income in Chapter 3 and prices in Chapter 6 assumes that output equals the natural rate. The Keynesian assumption best describes the short run. Therefore, our analysis of economic fluctuations relies on the assumption of a fixed price level.

10•3   The Great Depression

Now that we have developed the model of aggregate demand, let's use it to address the question that originally motivated Keynes: what caused the Great Depression in the United States? For Canada, there is not such a puzzle. Since Canada exports such a large fraction of Canadian GDP to the United States, a depression in that country means a very big decrease in aggregate demand in Canada. Canada had no bank failures, so there is every reason to suspect that the loss in export sales was the dominant event. But what caused the Great Depression in the United States? Even today, more than half a century after the event, economists continue to debate the cause of this major economic downturn in the world's most powerful economy. The Great Depression provides an extended case study to show how economists use the *IS-LM* model to analyze economic fluctuations.[4]

The Spending Hypothesis: Shocks to the *IS* Curve

Since the decline in U.S. income in the early 1930s coincided with falling interest rates, some economists have suggested that the cause of the decline was a contractionary shift in the *IS* curve. This view is sometimes called the *spending hypothesis,* because it places primary blame for the Depression on an exogenous fall in spending on goods and services. Economists have attempted to explain this decline in spending in several ways.

Some argue that a downward shift in the consumption function caused the contractionary shift in the *IS* curve. The stock market crash of 1929 may have been partly responsible for this decline in consumption. By reducing wealth and increasing uncertainty, the crash may have induced consumers to save more of their income.

Others explain the decline in spending by pointing to the large drop in investment in housing. Some economists believe that the residential investment boom of the 1920s was excessive, and that once this "overbuilding" became apparent, the demand for residential investment declined drastically. Another possible explanation for the fall in residential investment is the reduction in immigration in the 1930s: a more slowly growing population demands less new housing.

Once the Depression began, several events occurred that could have reduced spending further. First, the widespread bank failures in the United States (some 9,000 banks failed in the 1930–1933 period) may have reduced investment. Banks play the crucial role of getting the funds available for investment to those investors who can best use them. The closing of many banks in the early 1930s may have prevented some investors from getting the funds they

---

[4] For a flavour of the debate, see Milton Friedman and Anna J. Schwartz, *A Monetary History of the United States, 1867–1960* (Princeton, N.J.: Princeton University Press, 1963); Peter Temin, *Did Monetary Forces Cause the Great Depression?* (New York: W. W. Norton, 1976); and the essays in Karl Brunner, ed., *The Great Depression Revisited* (Boston: Martinus Nijhoff Publishing, 1981).

needed and thus may have led to a further contractionary shift in the invest-ment function.[5]

In addition, U.S. fiscal policy of the 1930s caused a contractionary shift in the *IS* curve. Politicians at that time were more concerned with balancing the budget than with using fiscal policy to stimulate the economy. The Revenue Act of 1932 increased various taxes, especially those falling on lower- and middle-income consumers.[6] The Democratic platform of that year expressed concern about the budget deficit and advocated an "immediate and drastic reduction of governmental expenditures." In the midst of historically high unemployment, policymakers searched for ways to raise taxes and reduce government spending.

There are, therefore, several ways to explain a contractionary shift in the *IS* curve. Keep in mind that these different views are not inconsistent with one another. There may be no single explanation for the decline in spending. It is possible that all of these changes coincided, and together they led to a major reduction in spending.

The Money Hypothesis: A Shock to the *LM* Curve

The U.S. money supply fell 25 percent from 1929 to 1933, during which time the unemployment rate rose from 3.2 percent to 25.2 percent. This fact provides the motivation and support for what is called the *money hypothesis*, which places primary blame for the Depression on the Federal Reserve for allowing the money supply to fall by such a large amount.[7] The best known advocates of this interpretation are Milton Friedman and Anna Schwartz, who defend it in their treatise on U.S. monetary history. Friedman and Schwartz argue that con-tractions in the money supply have caused most economic downturns and that the Great Depression is a particularly vivid example.

Using the *IS-LM* model, we might interpret the money hypothesis as ex-plaining the Depression by a contractionary shift in the *LM* curve. Seen in this way, however, the money hypothesis runs into two problems.

The first problem is the behaviour of *real* money balances. Monetary policy leads to a contractionary shift in the *LM* curve only if real money balances fall. Yet from 1929 to 1931, real money balances rose slightly, since the fall in the money supply was accompanied by an even greater fall in the price level. Al-though the monetary contraction may be responsible for the rise in unemploy-ment from 1931 to 1933, when real money balances did fall, it probably should not be blamed for the initial downturn from 1929 to 1931.

The second problem for the money hypothesis is the behaviour of interest rates. If a contractionary shift in the *LM* curve triggered the Depression, we

---

[5] Ben Bernanke, "Non-Monetary Effects of the Financial Crisis in the Propagation of the Great De-pression," *American Economic Review* 73 (June 1983): 257–276.

[6] E. Cary Brown, "Fiscal Policy in the 'Thirties: A Reappraisal," *American Economic Review* 46 (December 1956): 857–879.

[7] We discuss the reason for this large decrease in the money supply in Chapter 18 (Case Study 18·1), where we examine the money supply process in more detail.

should have observed higher interest rates. Yet nominal interest rates fell continuously from 1929 to 1933.

These two reasons appear sufficient to reject the view that the Depression was instigated by a contractionary shift in the *LM* curve. But was the fall in the money stock irrelevant? Next, we turn to another mechanism through which monetary policy might have been responsible for the severity of the Depression—the deflation of the 1930s.

The Money Hypothesis Again: The Effects of Falling Prices

From 1929 to 1933 the U.S. price level fell 25 percent. Many economists blame this deflation for the severity of the Great Depression. They argue that the deflation may have turned what in 1931 was a typical economic downturn into an unprecedented period of high unemployment and depressed income. If correct, this argument gives new life to the money hypothesis. Since the falling money supply was, plausibly, responsible for the falling price level, it could be responsible for the severity of the Depression. To evaluate this argument, we must discuss how changes in the price level affect income in the *IS-LM* model.

The Stabilizing Effects of Deflation   In the *IS-LM* model we have developed so far, falling prices raise income. For any given supply of money M, a lower price level implies higher real money balances M/P. An increase in real money balances causes an expansionary shift in the *LM* curve, which leads to higher income.

Another channel through which falling prices expand income is called the **Pigou effect**. Arthur Pigou, a prominent classical economist in the 1930s, pointed out that real money balances are part of households' wealth. As prices fall and real money balances rise, consumers should feel wealthier and spend more. This increase in consumer spending should cause an expansionary shift in the *IS* curve, also leading to higher income.

These two reasons led some economists in the 1930s to believe that falling prices would help the economy restore itself to full employment. Yet other economists were less confident in the economy's ability to correct itself. They pointed to other effects of falling prices, to which we now turn.

The Destabilizing Effects of Deflation   Economists have proposed two theories to explain how falling prices could depress income rather than raise it. The first, called **debt-deflation**, concerns the effects of unexpected falls in the price level. The second concerns the effects of expected deflation.

The debt-deflation theory begins with an observation that should be familiar from Chapter 6: unanticipated changes in the price level redistribute wealth between debtors and creditors. If a debtor owes a creditor $1,000, then the real amount of this debt is $1,000/P$, where P is the price level. A fall in the price level raises the real amount of this debt—the amount of purchasing power the debtor must repay the creditor. Therefore, an unexpected deflation enriches creditors and impoverishes debtors.

The debt-deflation theory then posits that this redistribution of wealth affects spending on goods and services. In response to the redistribution from debtors to creditors, debtors spend less and creditors spend more. If these two groups have equal spending propensities, there is no aggregate impact. But it seems reasonable to assume that debtors have higher propensities to spend than creditors—perhaps that is why the debtors are in debt in the first place. In this case, debtors reduce their spending by more than creditors raise theirs. The net effect is a reduction in spending, a contractionary shift in the *IS* curve, and lower national income.

To understand how *expected* changes in prices can affect income, we need to add a new variable to the *IS-LM* model. Our discussion of the model so far has not distinguished between the nominal and real interest rates. Yet we know from previous chapters that investment depends on the real interest rate and that money demand depends on the nominal interest rate. If i is the nominal interest rate and π^e is expected inflation, then the *ex ante* real interest rate $r = i - \pi^e$. We can now write the *IS-LM* model as

$$Y = C(Y - T) + I(i - \pi^e) + G \qquad IS$$
$$M/P = L(i, Y). \qquad LM$$

Expected inflation enters as a variable in the *IS* curve. Thus, changes in expected inflation shift the *IS* curve.

Let's use this extended *IS-LM* model to examine how changes in expected inflation influence the level of income. We begin by assuming that

Figure 10-8

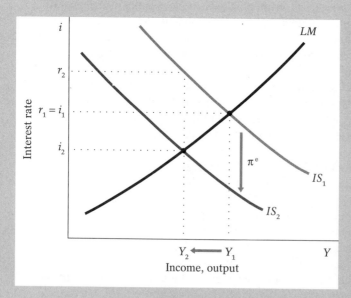

Expected Deflation in the *IS-LM* Model An expected deflation raises the real interest rate for any given nominal interest rate, which reduces desired investment. This reduction in investment shifts the *IS* curve downward (measuring vertically, by an amount equal to the expected deflation). The level of income falls from Y_1 to Y_2. The nominal interest rate falls from i_1 to i_2, and the real interest rate rises from r_1 to r_2.

everyone expects the price level to remain the same. In this case, there is no expected inflation ($\pi^e = 0$), and these two equations produce the familiar *IS-LM* model. Now suppose that everyone suddenly expects that the price level will fall in the future, so that π^e becomes negative. Figure 10-8 shows what happens. At any given nominal interest rate, the real interest rate is higher by the amount that π^e has dropped. Thus, the *IS* curve shifts down by this amount, as investment spending is reduced. An expected deflation thus leads to a reduction in national income from Y_1 to Y_2. The nominal interest rate falls from i_1 to i_2, and since this is less than the drop in π^e, the real interest rate rises from r_1 to r_2.

Note that there is a common thread in these two stories of destabilizing deflation. In both, falling prices depress national income by causing a contractionary shift in the *IS* curve. Since a deflation of the size observed from 1929 to 1933 is unlikely except in the presence of a major contraction in the money supply, these two explanations give some of the responsibility for the Depression—especially its severity—to the Federal Reserve in the United States. In other words, if falling prices are destabilizing, then a contraction in the money supply can lead to a fall in income, even without a decrease in real money balances or a rise in nominal interest rates.

Could the Depression Happen Again?

Economists study the Depression both because of its intrinsic interest as a major economic event and to provide guidance to policymakers so that it will not happen again. To state with confidence whether this event could recur one would need to know why it happened. Since there is not yet agreement on the causes of the Great Depression, it is impossible to rule out with certainty another depression of this magnitude.

Yet most economists believe that the mistakes that led to the Great Depression are unlikely to be repeated. Central banks seem unlikely to allow the money supply to fall by one fourth. Many economists believe that the deflation of the early 1930s was responsible for the depth and length of the Depression. And it seems likely that such a prolonged deflation was possible only in the presence of a falling money supply.

The fiscal-policy mistakes of the Depression are also unlikely to be repeated. Fiscal policy in the 1930s not only failed to help but actually further depressed aggregate demand. Few economists today would advocate such a rigid adherence to a balanced budget in the face of massive unemployment.

In addition, there are many institutions today that would help to prevent the events of the 1930s from recurring. The system of deposit insurance (now available in both Canada and the United States, and discussed in Chapter 18) makes widespread bank failures less likely. The income tax causes an automatic reduction in taxes when income falls, which stabilizes the economy. Finally, economists know more today than they did in the 1930s. Our knowledge of how the economy works, limited as it still is, should help policymakers formulate better policies to combat such widespread unemployment.

10•4 Conclusion

The purpose of this chapter and the previous one has been to deepen our understanding of aggregate demand. We now have the tools to analyze monetary and fiscal policy in the long run and in the short run. In the long run, prices are flexible, and we use the classical analysis of Part Two of this book. In the short run, prices are sticky, and we use the *IS-LM* model to examine how changes in policy influence the economy.

Although the model presented in this chapter provides the basic framework for analyzing aggregate demand, it is not the whole story. In later chapters, we examine in more detail the elements of this model and thereby refine our understanding of aggregate demand. In Chapter 15, for example, we study theories of consumption. Since the consumption function is a crucial element of the *IS-LM* model, a change in our analysis of consumption may modify our view of the impact of monetary and fiscal policy on the economy. The simple *IS-LM* model presented in Chapters 9 and 10 provides the benchmark for this further analysis.

Summary

1. The *IS-LM* model provides a general theory of aggregate demand. The exogenous variables in the model are fiscal policy, monetary policy, and the price level. The model explains two endogenous variables: the interest rate and the level of national income.

2. The *IS* curve represents the negative relationship between the interest rate and the level of income that arises from equilibrium in the market for goods and services. The *LM* curve represents a positive relationship between the interest rate and the level of income that arises from equilibrium in the market for real money balances. Equilibrium in the *IS-LM* model—the intersection of the *IS* and *LM* curves—represents simultaneous equilibrium in the market for goods and services and in the market for real money balances.

3. Expansionary fiscal policy—an increase in government purchases or a decrease in taxes—shifts the *IS* curve outward. This shift in the *IS* curve increases the interest rate and income. The increase in income represents an outward shift in the aggregate demand curve. Similarly, contractionary fiscal policy shifts the *IS* curve inward, lowers the interest rate and income, and shifts the aggregate demand curve inward.

4. Expansionary monetary policy shifts the *LM* curve downward. This shift in the *LM* curve lowers the interest rate and raises income. The increase in income represents an outward shift of the aggregate demand curve. Similarly, contractionary monetary policy shifts the *LM* curve upward, raises the interest rate and lowers income, and shifts the aggregate demand curve inward.

KEY CONCEPTS

Monetary transmission mechanism

Macroeconometric model

Pigou effect

Debt-deflation theory

QUESTIONS FOR REVIEW

1. Explain why the aggregate demand curve slopes downward.

2. What is the impact of an increase in taxes on the interest rate, income, consumption, and investment?

3. What is the impact of a decrease in the money supply on the interest rate, income, consumption, and investment?

4. Describe the possible effects of falling prices on equilibrium income.

PROBLEMS AND APPLICATIONS

1. According to the *IS-LM* model, what happens to the interest rate, income, consumption, and investment when

   a. the central bank increases the money supply?

   b. the government increases government purchases?

   c. the government increases taxes?

   d. the government increases government purchases and taxes by equal amounts?

2. Consider the economy of Hicksonia.

   a. The consumption function is given by

   $$C = 200 + 0.75(Y - T).$$

   The investment function is

   $$I = 200 - 25r.$$

   Government purchases and taxes are both 100. For this economy, graph the IS curve for r ranging from 0 to 8.

   b. The money demand function in Hicksonia is

   $$(M/P)^d = Y - 100r.$$

   The money supply M is 1,000 and the price level P is 2. For this economy, graph the LM curve for r ranging from 0 to 8.

   c. Find the equilibrium interest rate r and level of income Y.

   d. Suppose that government purchases are raised from 100 to 150. How much does the IS curve shift? What are the new equilibrium interest rate and level of income?

   e. Suppose instead that the money supply is raised from 1,000 to 1,200. How much does the LM curve shift? What are the new equilibrium interest rate and level of income?

   f. With the initial values for monetary and fiscal policy, suppose that the price level rises from 2 to 4. What happens? What are the new equilibrium interest rate and level of income?

g. Derive and graph an equation for the aggregate demand curve. What happens to this aggregate demand curve if fiscal or monetary policy changes, as in parts (d) and (e)?

3. Explain why each of the following statements is true. Discuss the impact of monetary and fiscal policy in each of these special cases.

a. If investment does not depend on the interest rate, the *IS* curve is vertical.

b. If money demand does not depend on the interest rate, the *LM* curve is vertical.

c. If money demand does not depend on income, the *LM* curve is horizontal.

d. If money demand is extremely sensitive to the interest rate, the *LM* curve is horizontal.

4. Suppose that the government wants to raise investment but keep output constant. In the *IS-LM* model, what mix of monetary and fiscal policy will achieve this goal? In the 1980s, the Canadian government ran budget deficits while the Bank of Canada pursued tight monetary policy. What effect should this policy mix have?

5. Use the *IS-LM* diagram to describe the short-run and long-run impact on national income, the price level, and the interest rate of

a. an increase in the money supply.

b. an increase in government purchases.

c. an increase in taxes.

6. The central bank is considering two alternative monetary policies:

• Holding the money supply constant

• Adjusting the money supply to hold the interest rate constant

In the *IS-LM* model, which policy will better stabilize output if

a. all shocks to the economy arise from exogenous changes in the demand for goods and services?

b. all shocks to the economy arise from exogenous changes in the demand for money?

7. Suppose that the demand for real money balances depends on consumption rather than on total expenditure. That is, the money demand function is

$$M/P = L(r, C).$$

Using the *IS-LM* model, discuss whether this change in the money demand function alters

a. the analysis of changes in government purchases.

b. the analysis of changes in taxes.

[*Hint:* Substitute the consumption function, $C = C(Y - T)$, into the money demand function.]

The Simple Algebra of the *IS-LM* Model and the Aggregate Demand Curve

The chapter analyzes the *IS-LM* model graphically. With the use of some simple algebra, however, we can gain more insight into how monetary and fiscal policy influence aggregate demand.

The *IS* Curve

One way to think about the *IS* curve is that it describes the combinations of income Y and the interest rate r that satisfy an equation we first saw in Chapter 3:

$$Y = C(Y - T) + I(r) + G.$$

This equation combines the national income accounts identity, the consumption function, and the investment function. It states that the quantity of goods produced Y must equal the quantity of goods demanded, $C + I + G$.

We can learn more about the *IS* curve by considering the special case in which the consumption function and investment function are linear. We begin with the national income accounts identity

$$Y = C + I + G.$$

Now suppose that the consumption function is

$$C = a + b(Y - T),$$

where a and b are numbers greater than zero, and the investment function is

$$I = c - dr,$$

where c and d also are numbers greater than zero. The parameter b is the marginal propensity to consume, so we expect b to be between zero and one. The parameter d determines how much investment responds to the interest rate; because investment rises when the interest rate falls, there is a minus sign in front of d.

From these three equations, we can derive an algebraic expression for the *IS* curve and see what influences the *IS* curve's position and slope. If we substitute the consumption and investment functions into the national income accounts identity, we obtain

$$Y = [a + b(Y - T)] + (c - dr) + G.$$

Note that Y shows up on both sides of this equation. We can simplify this equation by bringing all the Y terms to the left-hand side and rearranging the terms on the right-hand side:

$$Y - bY = (a + c) + (G - bT) - dr.$$

We solve for Y to get

$$Y = \frac{a + c}{1 - b} + \frac{1}{1 - b}G + \frac{-b}{1 - b}T + \frac{-d}{1 - b}r.$$

This equation expresses the *IS* curve algebraically. It tells us the level of income Y for any given interest rate r and fiscal policy G and T. Holding fiscal policy fixed, the equation gives us a relationship between the interest rate and the level of income: the higher the interest rate, the lower the level of income. The *IS* curve graphs this equation for different values of Y and r given fixed values of G and T.

Using this last equation, we can verify our previous conclusions about the *IS* curve. First, because the coefficient of the interest rate is negative, the *IS* curve slopes downward: higher interest rates reduce income. Second, because the coefficient of government purchases is positive, an increase in government purchases shifts the *IS* curve outward. Third, because the coefficient of taxes is negative, an increase in taxes shifts the *IS* curve inward.

The coefficient of the interest rate, $-d/(1 - b)$, tells us what determines whether the *IS* curve is steep or flat. If investment is highly sensitive to the interest rate, then d is large, and income is highly sensitive to the interest rate as well. In this case, small changes in the interest rate lead to large changes in income: the *IS* curve is relatively flat. Conversely, if investment is not very sensitive to the interest rate, then d is small, and income is also not very sensitive to the interest rate. In this case, large changes in interest rates lead to small changes in income: the *IS* curve is relatively steep.

Similarly, the slope of the *IS* curve depends on the marginal propensity to consume, b. The larger the marginal propensity to consume, the larger the change in income resulting from a given change in the interest rate. The reason is that a large marginal propensity to consume leads to a large multiplier for changes in investment. The larger the multiplier, the larger the impact of a change in investment on income, and the flatter the *IS* curve.

The marginal propensity to consume b also determines how much changes in fiscal policy shift the *IS* curve. The coefficient of G, $1/(1 - b)$, is the government-purchases multiplier in the Keynesian cross. Similarly, the coefficient of T, $-b/(1 - b)$, is the tax multiplier in the Keynesian cross. The larger the marginal propensity to consume, the greater the multiplier, and thus the greater the shift in the *IS* curve that arises from a change in fiscal policy.

The *LM* Curve

The *LM* curve describes the combinations of income Y and the interest rate r that satisfy the money-market equilibrium condition

$$M/P = L(r, Y).$$

This equation simply equates money supply and money demand.

We can learn more about the *LM* curve by considering the case in which the money demand function is linear—that is,

$$L(r, Y) = eY - fr,$$

where e and f are numbers greater than zero. The value of e determines how much the demand for money rises when income rises. The value of f determines how much the demand for money falls when the interest rate rises. There is a minus sign in front of the interest rate term because money demand is inversely related to the interest rate.

The equilibrium in the money market is now described by

$$M/P = eY - fr.$$

To see what this equation implies, rearrange the terms so that r is on the left-hand side. We obtain

$$r = (e/f)Y - (1/f)M/P.$$

This equation gives us the interest rate that equilibrates the money market for any values of income and real money balances. The *LM* curve graphs this equation for different values of Y and r given a fixed value of M/P.

From this last equation, we can verify some of our conclusions about the *LM* curve. First, because the coefficient of income is positive, the *LM* curve slopes upward: higher income requires a higher interest rate to equilibrate the money market. Second, because the coefficient of real money balances is negative, decreases in real balances shift the *LM* curve upward, and increases in real balances shift the *LM* curve downward.

From the coefficient of income, e/f, we can see what determines whether the *LM* curve is steep or flat. If money demand is not very sensitive to the level of income, then e is small. In this case, only a small change in the interest rate is necessary to offset the small increase in money demand caused by a change in income: the *LM* curve is relatively flat. Similarly, if the quantity of money demanded is not very sensitive to the interest rate, then f is small. In this case, a shift in money demand due to a change in income leads to a large change in the equilibrium interest rate: the *LM* curve is relatively steep.

The Aggregate Demand Curve

To find the aggregate demand equation, we must find the level of income that satisfies both the *IS* equation and the *LM* equation. To do this, substitute the *LM* equation for the interest rate *r* into the *IS* equation to obtain

$$Y = \frac{a+c}{1-b} + \frac{1}{1-b}G + \frac{-b}{1-b}T + \frac{-d}{1-b}[(e/f)Y - (1/f)M/P].$$

With some algebraic manipulation, we can solve for *Y*. The final equation for *Y* is

$$Y = \frac{z(a+c)}{1-b} + \frac{z}{1-b}G + \frac{-zb}{1-b}T + \frac{d}{(1-b)[f+de/(1-b)]}M/P,$$

where $z = f/[f + de/(1-b)]$ is a composite of some of the parameters and is between zero and one.

This last equation expresses the aggregate demand curve algebraically. It says that income depends on fiscal policy *G* and *T*, monetary policy *M*, and the price level *P*. The aggregate demand curve graphs this equation for different values of *Y* and *P* given fixed values of *G*, *T*, and *M*.

We can verify several features of the aggregate demand curve from this equation. First, the aggregate demand curve slopes downward, since an increase in *P* lowers *M/P* and thus lowers *Y*. Second, increases in the money supply raise income and shift the aggregate demand curve outward. Third, increases in government purchases or decreases in taxes also raise income and shift the aggregate demand curve outward. Note that, because *z* is less than one, the multipliers for fiscal policy are smaller in the *IS-LM* model than in the Keynesian cross. Hence, the parameter *z* reflects the crowding out of investment discussed earlier.

Finally, this equation shows the relationship between the aggregate demand curve derived in this chapter from the *IS-LM* model and the aggregate demand curve derived in Chapter 8 from the quantity theory of money. The quantity theory assumes that the interest rate does not influence the quantity of real money balances demanded. Put differently, the quantity theory assumes that the parameter *f* equals zero. If *f* equals zero, then the composite parameter *z* also equals zero, so that fiscal policy does not influence aggregate demand. Thus, the aggregate demand curve derived in Chapter 8 is a special case of the aggregate demand curve derived here.

CASE STUDY

10•3

The Effectiveness of Monetary and Fiscal Policy

Economists have long debated whether monetary or fiscal policy exerts a more powerful influence on aggregate demand. According to the *IS-LM* model, the answer to this question depends on the parameters of the *IS* and *LM* curves. Therefore, economists have spent much energy arguing about the size of these parameters. The most hotly contested parameters are those that describe the influence of the interest rate on economic decisions.

Those economists who believe that fiscal policy is more potent than monetary policy argue that the responsiveness of investment to the interest rate—measured by the parameter d—is small. If you look at the algebraic equation for aggregate demand, you will see that a small value of d implies a small effect of the money supply on income. The reason is that when d is small, the IS curve is nearly vertical, so that shifts in the LM curve do not cause much of a change in income. In addition, a small value of d implies a large value of z, which in turn implies that fiscal policy has a large effect on income. The reason for this large effect is that when investment is not very responsive to the interest rate, there is little crowding out.

Those economists who believe that monetary policy is more potent than fiscal policy argue that the responsiveness of money demand to the interest rate—measured by the parameter f—is small. When f is small, z is small, so that fiscal policy has a small effect on income; in this case, the LM curve is nearly vertical. In addition, when f is small, changes in the money supply have a large effect on income.

Most economists today do not endorse either of these extreme views. The evidence indicates that the interest rate affects both investment and money demand. This finding implies that both monetary and fiscal policy are important determinants of aggregate demand.

Aggregate Supply

There is always a temporary tradeoff between inflation and unemployment; there is no permanent tradeoff. The temporary tradeoff comes not from inflation per se, but from unanticipated inflation, which generally means, from a rising rate of inflation.

Milton Friedman

We now turn our attention to aggregate supply. In Chapters 9 and 10, we used the *IS-LM* model to show how changes in monetary and fiscal policy and exogenous shocks to the money and goods markets shift the aggregate demand curve. To see how shifts in aggregate demand affect the quantity of output and the level of prices, we must add aggregate supply to the analysis. In particular, we must understand what determines the position and slope of the aggregate supply curve. That is our goal in this chapter.

When we introduced the aggregate supply curve in Chapter 8, we established that aggregate supply behaves very differently in the short run than in the long run. In the long run, prices are flexible, and the aggregate supply curve is vertical. A vertical aggregate supply curve implies that shifts in the aggregate demand curve affect the price level but not aggregate output. By contrast, in the short run, prices are sticky, and the aggregate supply curve is not vertical. In this case, shifts in aggregate demand do cause fluctuations in aggregate output. In Chapter 8 we took a simplified view of price stickiness by drawing the short-run aggregate supply curve as a horizontal line, representing the extreme situation in which all prices are fixed.

To refine our understanding of aggregate supply, we begin by looking more closely at explanations for the slope of the short-run aggregate supply curve. Because economists disagree about how best to explain aggregate supply, we examine four prominent models. Although different in some important details, these models share a common theme about what makes the short-run and long-run aggregate supply curves differ and a common conclusion that the short-run aggregate supply curve is upward-sloping.

After examining the models, we see that the short-run aggregate supply curve implies a tradeoff between two measures of economic performance: inflation and unemployment. This tradeoff states that to reduce the rate of inflation policymakers must temporarily raise unemployment, and to reduce unemployment they must accept higher inflation. As the quotation at the beginning of the chapter suggests, the tradeoff between inflation and unemployment holds only in the short run.

Aggregate supply is an active area of research. The last section of this chapter examines some recent developments in the theory of aggregate supply. It is not yet clear which of these developments will prove most useful, but they show how macroeconomists are attempting to gain new insights into aggregate supply.

11•1 Four Models of Aggregate Supply

Here we present four prominent models of aggregate supply, roughly in the order of their development. In all the models, the short-run aggregate supply curve is not vertical because of some market imperfection. As a result, shifts in the aggregate demand curve cause the level of output to deviate temporarily from the natural rate.

All four models imply an aggregate supply equation of the form

$$Y = \bar{Y} + \alpha(P - P^e) \qquad \alpha > 0,$$

where Y is output, $\bar{Y}$ is the natural rate of output, P is the price level, and P^e is the expected price level. This equation states that output deviates from its natural rate when the price level deviates from the expected price level. The parameter α indicates how much output responds to unexpected changes in the price level; $1/\alpha$ is the slope of the aggregate supply curve.

Each of the four models tells a different story about what lies behind this equation. In other words, each highlights a particular reason that unexpected price movements are associated with fluctuations in output.

The Sticky-Wage Model

To explain why the short-run aggregate supply curve is not vertical, many economists stress the sluggish behaviour of nominal wages. In many industries, especially those that are unionized, nominal wages are set by long-term contracts, so they cannot adjust quickly when economic conditions change. Even in industries not covered by formal contracts, implicit agreements between workers and firms may limit wage changes. Wages may also depend on social norms and notions of fairness that evolve slowly. For these reasons, many economists believe that nominal wages are sluggish, or "sticky," in the short run.

The **sticky-wage model** shows what a sticky nominal wage implies for aggregate supply. To preview the model, consider what happens to the amount of output produced when the price level rises.

1. When the nominal wage is stuck, a rise in the price level lowers the real wage, making labour cheaper.

2. The lower real wage induces firms to hire more labour.

3. The additional labour hired produces more output.

This positive relationship between the price level and the amount of output means that the aggregate supply curve slopes upward during the time when the nominal wage cannot adjust.

To develop this story of aggregate supply more formally, assume that workers and firms bargain over and agree on the nominal wage before they know what the price level will be when their agreement takes effect. The bargaining parties—the workers and the firms—have in mind a target real wage. The target may be the real wage that equilibrates labour supply and demand. More likely, it also depends on the various factors that keep the real wage above the equilibrium level—union power, efficiency-wage considerations, and so on—which we discussed in Chapter 5.

The two parties set the nominal wage W based on the target real wage ω and on their expectation of the price level P^e. The nominal wage they set is

$$
\begin{array}{ccccc}
W & = & \omega & \times & P^e \\
\text{Nominal} & = & \text{Target} & \times & \text{Expected} \\
\text{Wage} & & \text{Real Wage} & & \text{Price Level.}
\end{array}
$$

After the nominal wage has been set and before labour has been hired, firms learn the actual price level P. The real wage turns out to be

$$
\begin{array}{ccccc}
W/P & = & \omega & \times & (P^e/P) \\
\text{Real} & = & \text{Target} & \times & \dfrac{\text{Expected Price Level}}{\text{Actual Price Level}} .\\
\text{Wage} & & \text{Real Wage} & &
\end{array}
$$

This equation shows that the real wage deviates from its target if the actual price level differs from the expected price level. When the actual price level is greater than expected, the real wage is less than its target; when the actual price level is less than expected, the real wage is greater than its target.

The final assumption of the model is that the quantity of labour demanded determines employment. In other words, the bargain between the workers and the firms does not determine the level of employment in advance; instead, the workers agree to provide as much labour as the firms wish to buy at the predetermined wage. We describe the firms' hiring decisions by the labour demand function,

$$
L = L^d(W/P),
$$

which states that the lower the real wage, the more labour is hired. The labour demand curve is shown in Panel (a) of Figure 11-1. Output is determined by the production function

$$
Y = F(L),
$$

which states that the more labour is hired, the more output is produced. This is shown in Panel (b) of Figure 11-1.

Panel (c) of Figure 11-1 shows the resulting aggregate supply curve. Unex-

Figure 11-1

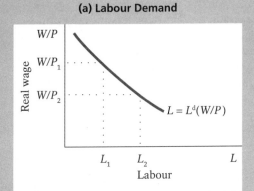

(a) Labour Demand

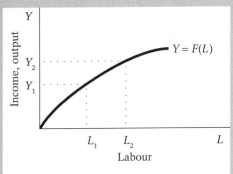

(b) Production Function

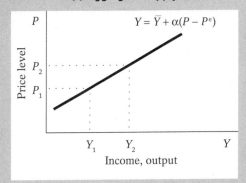

(c) Aggregate Supply

The Sticky-Wage Model Panel (a) shows the labour demand curve. Since the nominal wage W is stuck, an increase in the price level from P_1 to P_2 reduces the real wage from W/P_1 to W/P_2. The lower real wage raises the quantity of labour demanded from L_1 to L_2. Panel (b) shows the production function. An increase in the quantity of labour from L_1 to L_2 raises output from Y_1 to Y_2. Panel (c) shows the aggregate supply curve summarizing this relationship between the price level and output. An increase in the price level from P_1 to P_2 raises output from Y_1 to Y_2.

pected price changes move the real wage away from the target real wage. The change in the real wage in turn influences the amounts of labour hired and output produced. The aggregate supply curve can be written as

$$Y = \bar{Y} + \alpha(P - P^e).$$

Output deviates from its natural level when the price level deviates from the expected price level.[1]

---

[1] For more on the sticky-wage model, see Jo Anna Gray, "Wage Indexation: A Macroeconomic Approach," *Journal of Monetary Economics* 2 (April 1976): 221–235; and Stanley Fischer, "Long-term Contracts, Rational Expectations, and the Optimal Money Supply Rule," *Journal of Political Economy* 85 (February 1977): 191–205.

The Worker-Misperception Model

The next model of the short-run aggregate supply curve also focuses on the labour market. Yet, unlike the sticky-wage model, the **worker-misperception model** assumes that wages are free to equilibrate supply and demand. Its key assumption is that workers temporarily confuse real and nominal wages.

The two components of the worker-misperception model are labour supply and labour demand. As before, the quantity of labour demanded depends on the real wage:

$$L^d = L^d(W/P).$$

The labour supply curve is new:

$$L^s = L^s(W/P^e).$$

This equation states that the quantity of labour supplied depends on the real wage that workers expect. Workers know their nominal wage W, but they do not know the overall price level P. When deciding how much to work, they consider the expected real wage, which equals the nominal wage W divided by their expectation of the price level P^e. We can write the expected real wage as

$$\frac{W}{P^e} = \frac{W}{P} \times \frac{P}{P^e}.$$

The expected real wage is the product of the actual real wage W/P and workers' misperception of the level of prices, as measured by P/P^e. To see what determines labour supply, we can substitute this expression for W/P^e and write

$$L^s = L^s(W/P \times P/P^e).$$

The quantity of labour supplied depends on the real wage and on workers' misperceptions.

To see the implications of this model for aggregate supply, consider the equilibrium in the labour market, shown in Figure 11-2. As is usual, the labour demand curve slopes downward, the labour supply curve slopes upward, and the wage adjusts to equilibrate supply and demand. Note that the position of the labour supply curve and thus the equilibrium in the labour market depend on worker misperception P/P^e.

When the price level P rises, there are two possible reactions. If workers had anticipated the change, then P^e rises proportionately with P. In this case, neither labour supply nor labour demand changes. The real wage and the level of employment remain the same. The nominal wage rises by the same amount as prices.

By contrast, suppose that the price level rises without workers being aware of it. In this case, P^e remains the same. Then, at every real wage, workers are

Figure 11-2

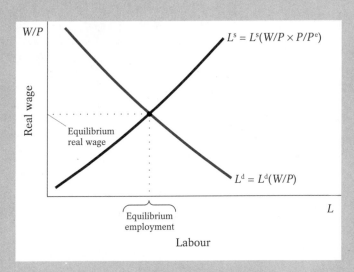

The Worker Misperception Model: Equilibrium in the Labour Market In the worker-misperception model, the labour market clears, so the intersection of the labour supply and labour demand curves determines the quantity of labour hired. Remember that the position of the labour supply curve depends on workers' misperceptions of the price level.

willing to supply more labour because they believe that their real wage is higher than it actually is. The increase in P/P^e shifts the labour supply curve outward, as in Figure 11-3. The outward shift in labour supply lowers the real wage and raises the level of employment. In essence, the increase in the nominal wage caused by the rise in the price level leads workers to think that their real wage is higher, which induces them to supply more labour. In actuality, the nominal wage rises by less than the price level. Firms are assumed to be better informed than workers and to recognize the fall in the real wage, so they hire more labour and produce more output.

To sum up, the worker-misperception model says that deviations of prices from expected prices induce workers to alter their supply of labour. The model implies an aggregate supply curve of the same form as the sticky-wage model:

$$Y = \bar{Y} + \alpha(P - P^e).$$

Output deviates from the natural rate when the price level deviates from the expected price level.[2]

---

[2] The worker-misperception model as presented here comes from the classic article by Milton Friedman, "The Role of Monetary Policy," *American Economic Review* 68 (March 1968): 1–17.

Figure 11-3

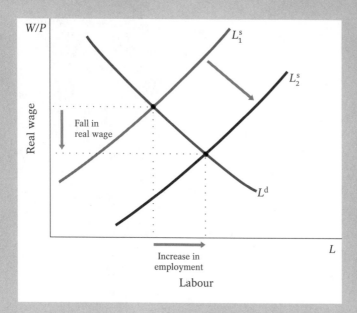

The Worker-Misperception Model: An Unexpected Increase in the Price Level If the price level rises unexpectedly, workers are willing to supply more labour at any given real wage, since they believe the real wage is higher than it actually is. The equilibrium level of employment therefore rises.

The Cyclical Behaviour of the Real Wage

In any model with an unchanging labour demand curve, such as the two models we just discussed, employment rises when the real wage falls. In the sticky-wage and worker-misperception models, an unexpected rise in the price level lowers the real wage and thereby raises the quantity of labour hired and the amount of output produced. The real wage should be *countercyclical*: it should fluctuate in the opposite direction from employment and output. Keynes himself wrote in *The General Theory* that "an increase in employment can only occur to the accompaniment of a decline in the rate of real wages."

The earliest attacks on *The General Theory* came from economists challenging Keynes's prediction. Figure 11-4 is a scatterplot of the percentage change in average weekly earnings (measured in real terms) and the percentage change in real GDP using annual data for Canada. If Keynes's prediction were correct, this figure would show a negative relationship. Yet it shows only a weak correlation between the real wage and output. If the real wage is cyclical at all, it is slightly *procyclical*: the real wage tends to rise when output rises. Thus, abnormally high labour costs cannot explain the low employment and output observed in recessions.

How should we interpret this evidence? Most economists conclude that the sticky-wage and worker-misperception models cannot, by themselves, fully explain aggregate supply. They advocate models in which the labour demand

Figure 11-4

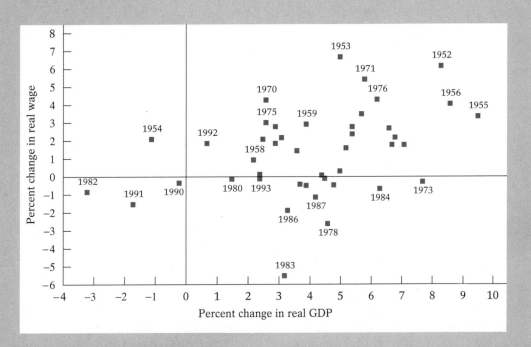

The Cyclical Behaviour of the Real Wage
This figure is a scatterplot of the percent change in real GDP and the percent change in average weekly wages (measured in real terms). It shows that as output fluctuates, the real wage typically moves in the same direction. That is, the real wage is somewhat procyclical. This observation is inconsistent with the sticky-wage and worker-misperception models.

Source: Reproduced and adapted by authority of the Minister of Industry, 1994, "Statistics Canada," *Canadian Economic Observer, Catalogue 11-210,* Series D20463, D59668, P484000.

curve shifts over the business cycle. These shifts may arise because firms have sticky prices and cannot sell all they want at those prices; we discuss this possibility in the next section. Alternatively, the labour demand curve may shift because of shocks to technology, which alter labour productivity, or changes in raw materials prices. The theory we discuss in Chapter 14, called the theory of real business cycles, gives a prominent role to technology shocks as a source of economic fluctuations.[3]

---

[3] For some of the recent work on this topic, see Patrick T. Geary and John Kennan, "The Employment-Real Wage Relationship: An International Study," *Journal of Political Economy* 90 (August 1982): 854–871; Mark J. Bils, "Real Wages over the Business Cycle: Evidence from Panel Data," *Journal of Political Economy* 93 (1985): 666–689; and Scott Sumner and Stephen Silver, "Real Wages, Employment, and the Phillips Curve," *Journal of Political Economy* 97 (June 1989): 706–720.

The Imperfect-Information Model

The third model of aggregate supply, the **imperfect-information model**, also assumes that markets clear and that the short-run and long-run aggregate supply curves differ because of short-run misperceptions about prices. But unlike the worker-misperception model, it does not assume that firms are better informed than their workers. In its simplest form, the model does not distinguish between workers and firms at all.

The imperfect-information model assumes that each supplier in the economy produces a single good and consumes many goods. Because the number of goods is so large, suppliers cannot observe all prices at all times. They monitor closely the prices of what they produce but less closely the prices of all the goods that they consume. Because of imperfect information, they sometimes confuse changes in the overall level of prices with changes in relative prices. This confusion influences decisions about how much to supply, and it leads to a short-run relationship between the price level and output.

Consider the decision facing a single supplier—say, a wheat farmer. Because the farmer earns income from selling wheat and uses this income to buy goods and services, the amount of wheat she chooses to produce depends on the price of wheat relative to the prices of other goods and services in the economy. If the relative price of wheat is high, the farmer is motivated to work hard and produce more wheat, because the reward is great. If the relative price of wheat is low, she would prefer to enjoy more leisure and produce less wheat.

Unfortunately, when the farmer makes her production decision, she does not know the relative price of wheat. Being a wheat producer, she monitors the wheat market closely and always knows the nominal price of wheat. But she does not know the prices of all the other goods in the economy. She must, therefore, estimate the relative price of wheat using the nominal price of wheat and her expectation of the overall price level.

Consider how the farmer responds if all prices in the economy, including the price of wheat, increase. One possibility is that she expected this change in prices. When she observes an increase in the price of wheat, her estimate of its relative price is unchanged. She does not work any harder.

The other possibility is that the farmer did not expect the price level to increase (or to increase by this much). When she observes the increase in the price of wheat, she is not sure whether other prices have risen (in which case wheat's relative price is unchanged) or whether only the price of wheat has risen (in which case its relative price is higher). The rational inference is that some of each has happened. In other words, the farmer infers from the increase in the nominal price of wheat that its relative price has risen somewhat. She works harder and produces more.

Our wheat farmer is not unique. When the price level rises unexpectedly, all suppliers in the economy observe increases in the prices of the goods they produce. They all infer, rationally but mistakenly, that the relative prices of the goods they produce have risen. They work harder and produce more.

To sum up, the imperfect-information model says that when prices exceed expected prices, suppliers raise their output. The model implies an aggregate supply curve that is now familiar:

$$Y = \bar{Y} + \alpha(P - P^e).$$

Output deviates from the natural rate when the price level deviates from the expected price level.[4]

The Sticky-Price Model

Our fourth and final model of aggregate supply, the **sticky-price model**, emphasizes that firms do not instantly adjust the prices they charge in response to changes in demand. Sometimes prices are set by long-term contracts between firms and customers. Even without formal agreements, firms may hold prices steady in order not to annoy their regular customers with frequent price changes. Some prices are sticky because of the way markets are structured: once a firm has printed and distributed its catalogue or price list, it is costly to alter prices.

To see what sticky prices imply for aggregate supply, we must first consider the pricing decisions of individual firms. We can then add together the decisions of many firms to obtain the aggregate supply curve.

Consider the decision facing a single firm that has some monopoly control over the price it charges. The firm's desired price p depends on two macroeconomic variables:

- **The Overall Level of Prices P**   A higher price level implies that the firm's costs are higher. Hence, the higher the overall price level, the more the firm would like to charge for its product.

- **The Level of Aggregate Income Y**   A higher level of income raises the demand for the firm's product. Because marginal cost increases at higher levels of production, the greater the demand, the higher the firm's desired price.

We write the firm's desired price as

$$p = P + a(Y - \bar{Y}),$$

where a is a parameter greater than zero. This equation says that the desired price p depends on the overall level of prices P and on the level of aggregate output relative to the natural rate $Y - \bar{Y}$.[5]

Now assume that there are two types of firms. Some have flexible prices: they always set their prices according to this equation. Others have sticky

---

[4] To read more on the imperfect-information model, see Robert E. Lucas, Jr., "Understanding Business Cycles," *Stabilization of the Domestic and International Economy*, vol. 5 of Carnegie-Rochester Conference on Public Policy (Amsterdam: North-Holland Publishing Company, 1977); reprinted in Robert E. Lucas, Jr., *Studies in Business Cycle Theory* (Cambridge, Mass.: MIT Press, 1981).

[5] *Mathematical note*: The firm cares most about its relative price, which is the ratio of its nominal price to the overall price level. If we interpret p and P as the logarithm of the firm's price and the price level, then this equation states that the desired relative price depends on the deviation of output from the natural rate.

prices: they announce their prices in advance based on what they expect economic conditions to be. These firms set prices according to

$$p = P^e + a(Y^e - \bar{Y}^e),$$

where, as before, a superscript "e" represents the expected value of a variable.
For simplicity, assume that these firms expect output to be at its natural rate, so
that the last term, $a(Y^e - \bar{Y}^e)$, is zero. Then these firms set the price

$$p = P^e.$$

That is, they set their prices based on what they expect other firms to charge.

We can use the pricing rules of the two groups of firms to derive the aggregate supply equation. To do this, we find the overall price level in the economy, which is the weighted average of the prices set by the two groups. If s is
the fraction of firms with sticky prices and $1 - s$ the fraction with flexible
prices, then the overall price level is

$$P = sP^e + (1 - s)[P + a(Y - \bar{Y})].$$

The first term is the price of the sticky-price firms weighted by their fraction of
the economy, and the second term is the price of the flexible-price firms
weighted by their fraction. Now subtract $(1 - s)P$ from both sides of this equation to obtain

$$sP = sP^e + (1 - s)[a(Y - \bar{Y})].$$

Divide both sides by s to solve for the overall price level:

$$P = P^e + [(1 - s)a/s](Y - \bar{Y}).$$

The two terms in this equation are explained as follows:

- When firms expect a high price level, they expect high costs. Those firms
  that fix prices in advance set their prices high. These high prices cause the
  other firms to set high prices also. Hence, a high expected price level
  leads to a high actual price level.

- When output is high, the demand for goods is high. Those firms with flexible prices set their prices high, which leads to a high price level. The effect of output on the price level depends on the proportion of firms with
  flexible prices.

Hence, the overall price level depends on the expected price level and on the
level of output.

Algebraic rearrangement puts this aggregate pricing equation into a more
familiar form:

$$Y = \bar{Y} + \alpha(P - P^e),$$

where $\alpha = s/[(1 - s)a]$. Like the other models, the sticky-price model says that
the deviation of output from the natural rate is associated with the deviation of
the price level from the expected price level.

Although the sticky-price model emphasizes the goods market, consider briefly what is happening in the labour market. If a firm's price is stuck in the short run, then a reduction in aggregate demand reduces the amount that the firm is able to sell. The firm responds to the drop in sales by reducing its production and its demand for labour. Unlike in the sticky-wage and worker-misperception models, the firm does not move along a fixed labour demand curve. Instead, fluctuations in output are associated with shifts in the labour demand curve. Because of these shifts in labour demand, employment, production, and the real wage can all move in the same direction. Thus, the real wage can be procyclical.[6]

CASE STUDY

11·2 **International Differences in the Aggregate Supply Curve**

Although all countries experience economic fluctuations, these fluctuations are not exactly the same everywhere. International differences are intriguing puzzles in themselves, and they often provide a way to test alternative economic theories. Examining international differences has been especially fruitful in research on aggregate supply.

When economist Robert Lucas proposed the imperfect-information model, he noted that the slope of the aggregate supply curve should depend on the variability of aggregate demand. In countries where aggregate demand fluctuates widely, the aggregate price level fluctuates widely as well. Because most movements in prices in these countries do not represent movements in relative prices, suppliers should have learned not to respond much to unexpected changes in the price level. Therefore, the aggregate supply curve should be relatively steep (that is, α will be small). Conversely, in countries where aggregate demand is relatively stable, suppliers should have learned that most price changes are relative price changes. Accordingly, in these countries, suppliers should be more responsive to unexpected price changes, making the aggregate supply curve relatively flat (that is, α will be large).

Lucas tested this prediction by examining international data on output and prices. He found that changes in aggregate demand have the biggest effect on output in those countries where aggregate demand and prices are most stable. Lucas concluded that the evidence supports the imperfect-information model.[7]

The sticky-price model also makes predictions about the slope of the short-run aggregate supply curve. In particular, it predicts that the average rate of inflation should influence the slope of the short-run aggregate supply curve. When the average rate of inflation is high, it is very costly for firms to keep

---

[6] For a more advanced development of the sticky-price model, see Julio Rotemberg, "Monopolistic Price Adjustment and Aggregate Output," *Review of Economic Studies* 49 (1982): 517–531; or Laurence Ball, N. Gregory Mankiw, and David Romer, "The New Keynesian Economics and the Output-Inflation Tradeoff," *Brookings Papers on Economic Activity* (1988:1): 1–65.

[7] Robert E. Lucas, Jr., "Some International Evidence on Output-Inflation Tradeoffs," *American Economic Review* 63 (June 1973): 326–334; reprinted in Robert E. Lucas, Jr., *Studies in Business Cycle Theory* (Cambridge, Mass.: MIT Press, 1981).

prices fixed for long intervals. Thus, firms adjust prices more frequently. More frequent price adjustment in turn allows the overall price level to respond more quickly to shocks to aggregate demand. Hence, a high rate of inflation should make the short-run aggregate supply curve steeper.

International data support this prediction of the sticky-price model. In countries with low average inflation, the short-run aggregate supply curve is relatively flat: fluctuations in aggregate demand have large effects on output and are slowly reflected in prices. High-inflation countries have steep short-run aggregate supply curves. In other words, high inflation appears to erode the frictions that cause prices to be sticky.[8]

Note that the sticky-price model can also explain Lucas's finding that countries with variable aggregate demand have steep aggregate supply curves. If the price level is highly variable, few firms will commit to prices in advance (s will be small). Hence, the aggregate supply curve will be steep (α will be small).

Summary and Implications

Figure 11-5 lists the four models of aggregate supply and the market imperfection that each uses to explain why the short-run aggregate supply curve is not vertical. The figure divides the models according to two characteristics. The first is whether the model assumes that markets clear—that is, whether wages

Figure 11-5

| | Market With Imperfection | |
	Labour	Goods
Markets Clear? — Yes	**Worker-Misperception Model:** Workers confuse nominal wage changes with real wage changes.	**Imperfect-Information Model:** Suppliers confuse changes in the price level with changes in relative prices.
Markets Clear? — No	**Sticky-Wage Model:** Nominal wages adjust slowly.	**Sticky-Price Model:** The prices of goods and services adjust slowly.

Comparison of Models of Aggregate Supply The four models of aggregate supply differ by two characteristics: whether they assume that markets clear and whether the key market imperfection lies in the goods market or in the labour market.

[8] Laurence Ball, N. Gregory Mankiw, and David Romer, "The New Keynesian Economics and the Output-Inflation Tradeoff," *Brookings Papers on Economic Activity* (1988:1): 1–65.

and prices are free to equilibrate supply and demand. The second is whether the model emphasizes the labour or the goods market as the location of the market imperfection.

Keep in mind that these models of aggregate supply are not necessarily incompatible with one another. We need not accept one model and reject the others. The world may contain all four of these market imperfections, and all may contribute to the behaviour of short-run aggregate supply.

Although the four models of aggregate supply differ in their assumptions and emphases, their implications for the economy are similar. All can be summarized in the equation

$$Y = \bar{Y} + \alpha(P - P^e).$$

This equation, illustrated in Figure 11-6, relates deviations of output from the natural rate to deviations of the price level from the expected price level. *If the price level is higher than the expected price level, output exceeds its natural rate. If the price level is lower than the expected price level, output falls short of its natural rate.*

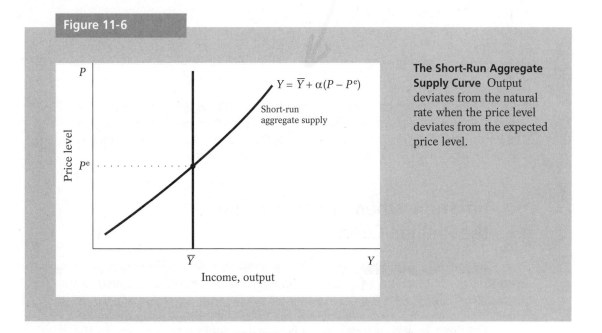

Figure 11-6

The Short-Run Aggregate Supply Curve Output deviates from the natural rate when the price level deviates from the expected price level.

$Y = \bar{Y} + \alpha(P - P^e)$

Short-run aggregate supply

Figure 11-7 uses this aggregate supply equation to show how the economy responds to an unexpected increase in aggregate demand. In the short run, the equilibrium moves from point A to point B. The increase in aggregate demand raises the price level above the expected price level and output above the

Figure 11-7

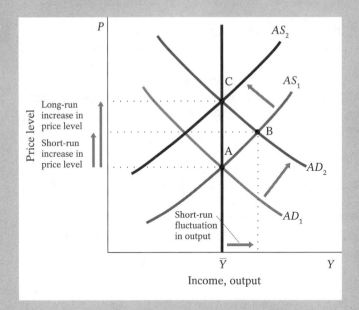

A Shift in Aggregate Demand When aggregate demand increases unexpectedly, the price level rises above the expected price level and output rises above the natural rate, moving the economy along the short-run aggregate supply curve from point A to point B. In the long run, the expected price level rises, the short-run aggregate supply curve shifts upward, and output returns to the natural rate at point C. In this way, shifts in the aggregate demand curve lead to short-run fluctuations in output.

natural rate. In the long run, the expected price level rises, so that the short-run aggregate supply curve shifts upward. As the expected price level rises, the equilibrium of the economy moves from point B to point C. The economy returns to the natural level of output, but with an even higher price level.

11·2 Inflation, Unemployment, and the Phillips Curve

Two goals of economic policymakers are low inflation and low unemployment. Here we examine a relationship between inflation and unemployment called the **Phillips curve**. The Phillips curve shows the short-run tradeoff between inflation and unemployment implied by the short-run aggregate supply curve.

The Phillips curve is merely another way to express aggregate supply. The short-run aggregate supply curve shows a positive relationship between the price level and output. Since inflation is the rate of change in the price level, and since unemployment fluctuates inversely with output, the aggregate supply curve implies a negative relationship between inflation and unemployment. The Phillips curve expresses this negative relationship.

The Phillips curve posits that the inflation rate—the percentage change in the price level—depends on three forces:

1. Expected inflation
2. The deviation of unemployment from the natural rate, called *cyclical unemployment*
3. Supply shocks

These three forces are expressed in the following equation:

$$\pi = \pi^e - \beta(u - u^n) + \varepsilon$$

$$\text{Inflation} = \begin{matrix} \text{Expected} \\ \text{Inflation} \end{matrix} - \left(\beta \times \begin{matrix} \text{Cyclical} \\ \text{Unemployment} \end{matrix}\right) + \begin{matrix} \text{Supply} \\ \text{Shock} \end{matrix}$$

where β is a parameter greater than zero. Notice that there is a minus sign before the cyclical unemployment term: high unemployment tends to reduce inflation.

From Aggregate Supply to the Phillips Curve

To see that the Phillips curve and the aggregate supply curve express essentially the same relationship, write the aggregate supply equation as

$$P = P^e + (1/\alpha)(Y - \bar{Y}).$$

With one subtraction, one substitution, and one addition, we can derive the Phillips curve.

First, subtract last year's price level P_{-1} from both sides of the equation to obtain

$$(P - P_{-1}) = (P^e - P_{-1}) + (1/\alpha)(Y - \bar{Y}).$$

The term on the left-hand side, $P - P_{-1}$, is the difference between the current price level and last year's price level, which is inflation π.[9] The term on the right-hand side, $P^e - P_{-1}$, is the difference between the expected price level and last year's price level, which is expected inflation π^e. Therefore, we can replace $P - P_{-1}$ with π and $P^e - P_{-1}$ with π^e:

$$\pi = \pi^e + (1/\alpha)(Y - \bar{Y}).$$

Next, recall from Chapter 2 that Okun's law gives a relationship between output and unemployment. One version of Okun's law states that the deviation of output from its natural rate is inversely related to the deviation of unemploy-

---

[9] *Mathematical note*: This statement is not precise, because inflation is really the *percentage* change in the price level. To make the statement more precise, interpret P as the logarithm of the price level. By the properties of logarithms, the change in P is roughly the inflation rate. The reason is that $dP = d(\log \text{price level}) = d(\text{price level})/\text{price level}$.

FYI

The History of the Modern Phillips Curve

The Phillips curve is named after British economist A.W. Phillips. In 1958 Phillips observed a negative relationship between the unemployment rate and the rate of wage inflation.[10] The Phillips curve that economists use today differs from the relationship Phillips examined in three ways.

First, the modern Phillips curve substitutes price inflation for wage inflation. This difference is not crucial, because price inflation and wage inflation are closely related. In periods when wages are rising quickly, prices are rising quickly as well.

Second, the modern Phillips curve includes expected inflation. This addition is due to the work of Milton Friedman and Edmund Phelps. In developing the worker-misperception model in the 1960s, these two economists emphasized the importance of expectations for aggregate supply.

Third, the modern Phillips curve includes supply shocks. Credit for this addition goes to OPEC, the Organization of Petroleum Exporting Countries. In the 1970s OPEC caused large increases in the world price of oil, which made economists more aware of the importance of shocks to aggregate supply.

ment from its natural rate; that is, when output is higher than the natural rate of output, unemployment is lower than the natural rate of unemployment.[11] Using this relationship, we can substitute $-\beta(u - u^n)$ for $(1/\alpha)(Y - \bar{Y})$. The equation becomes

$$\pi = \pi^e - \beta(u - u^n).$$

Finally, add a supply shock ε to represent exogenous influences on prices, such as a change in oil prices, a change in the minimum wage, or the imposition of government controls on prices:

$$\pi = \pi^e - \beta(u - u^n) + \varepsilon.$$

Thus, we obtain the Phillips curve from the aggregate supply equation.

Now step back from this algebra. Notice that the Phillips curve retains the key feature of the short-run aggregate supply curve: a link between real and nominal variables that causes the classical dichotomy to fail. More precisely, the Phillips curve demonstrates the connection between real economic activity and unexpected changes in the price level. *The Phillips curve is merely a convenient way to express and analyze aggregate supply.*

---

[10] A. W. Phillips, "The Relationship between Unemployment and the Rate of Change of Money Wages in the United Kingdom, 1861–1957," *Economica* 25 (November 1958): 283–299.

[11] *Mathematical note*: this version of Okun's law can be written as $(u - u^n) = -(1/\alpha\beta)$ $(Y - \bar{Y})$. Abstracting from changes in the natural rates, this relationship implies $\Delta u = -(1/\alpha\beta)$ ΔY, which is Okun's law in change form—the version that is graphed in Chapter 2.

Expectations and Inflation Inertia

To make the Phillips curve useful for analyzing the choices facing policymakers, we need to say what determines expected inflation. A simple and an often plausible assumption, referred to as **adaptive expectations**, is that people form their expectations of inflation based on recently observed inflation. For example, suppose that people expect prices will rise this year at the same rate they did last year. Then

$$\pi^e = \pi_{-1}.$$

In this case, we can write the Phillips curve as

$$\pi = \pi_{-1} - \beta(u - u^n) + \varepsilon,$$

which states that inflation depends on past inflation, cyclical unemployment, and a supply shock.

The first term in this form of the Phillips curve, π_{-1}, implies that inflation is inertial. If unemployment is at its natural rate and if there are no supply shocks, prices will continue to rise at the prevailing rate of inflation. This inertia arises because past inflation influences expectations of future inflation and because these expectations influence the wages and prices that people set. Robert Solow captured the concept of inflation inertia well when, during the high inflation of the 1970s, he wrote, "Why is our money ever less valuable? Perhaps it is simply that we have inflation because we expect inflation, and we expect inflation because we've had it."

In the model of aggregate supply and aggregate demand, inflation inertia is interpreted as persistent upward shifts in both the aggregate supply curve and the aggregate demand curve. Consider first aggregate supply. If prices have been rising quickly, people will expect them to continue to rise quickly. Because the position of the short-run aggregate supply curve depends on the expected price level, the short-run aggregate supply curve will shift upward over time. It will continue to shift upward until some event, such as a recession or a supply shock, changes inflation and thereby changes expectations of inflation.

The aggregate demand curve must also be shifting upward in order to confirm the expectations of inflation. Most often, the continued rise in aggregate demand is due to persistent growth in the money supply. If the Bank of Canada suddenly halted money growth, aggregate demand would stabilize, and the upward shift in aggregate supply would cause a recession. The high unemployment in the recession would reduce both actual and then expected inflation, causing inflation inertia to subside.

The Two Causes of Rising and Falling Inflation

The second and third terms in the Phillips curve show the two forces that can change the rate of inflation.

The second term, $\beta(u - u^n)$, shows that cyclical unemployment—the deviation of unemployment from its natural rate—exerts upward or downward pressure on inflation. Low unemployment pulls the inflation rate up. This is called **demand-pull inflation** because high aggregate demand is responsible for this type of inflation. High unemployment pulls the inflation rate down. The parameter β measures how responsive inflation is to cyclical unemployment.

The third term, ε, shows that inflation also rises and falls because of supply shocks. An adverse supply shock, such as the rise in world oil prices in the 1970s, implies a positive value of ε and causes inflation to rise. This is called **cost-push inflation** because adverse supply shocks are typically events that push up the costs of production. A beneficial supply shock, such as the oil glut that led to a fall in oil prices in the 1980s, implies a negative value of ε and causes inflation to fall. An increase in sales taxes represents another adverse supply shock, while a decrease in the sales tax rate constitutes a beneficial supply shock.

The Short-Run Tradeoff Between Inflation and Unemployment

Consider the options the Phillips curve gives to a policymaker who can influence aggregate demand with monetary or fiscal policy. At any moment, expected inflation and supply shocks are beyond the policymaker's immediate control. Yet, by changing aggregate demand, the policymaker can alter output, unemployment, and inflation. The policymaker can expand aggregate demand to lower unemployment and raise inflation. Or the policymaker can depress aggregate demand to raise unemployment and lower inflation.

Figure 11-8 shows the short-run tradeoff between inflation and unemployment implied by the Phillips-curve equation. The policymaker can manipulate aggregate demand to choose a combination of inflation and unemployment on this curve, called the *short-run Phillips curve*.

Notice that the short-run Phillips curve depends on expected inflation. If expected inflation rises, the curve shifts upward, and the policymaker's tradeoff becomes less favourable: inflation is higher for any level of unemployment. Figure 11-9 shows how the tradeoff depends on expected inflation.

Because people adjust their expectations of inflation over time, this tradeoff between inflation and unemployment holds only in the short run. The policymaker cannot keep inflation above expected inflation forever. Eventually, expectations adapt to whatever inflation rate the policymaker chooses. In the long run, the classical dichotomy holds, unemployment returns to its natural rate, and there is no tradeoff between inflation and unemployment.

To follow this process explicitly, assume that the economy is initially at point A in Figure 11-9—a point at which actual and expected inflation coincide. Then, assume that expansionary monetary or fiscal policy is used to move the economy from point A to point B. The short-run tradeoff is operating; there are lower unemployment and higher inflation. But the economy cannot stay at point B since it involves actual inflation being greater than peoples' expectations of inflation. As individuals revise their expectations upward, there is a tendency for the point showing the economy's outcome to move up in Figure 11-9. Often, in this situation, the government begins to contract aggregate de-

Figure 11-8

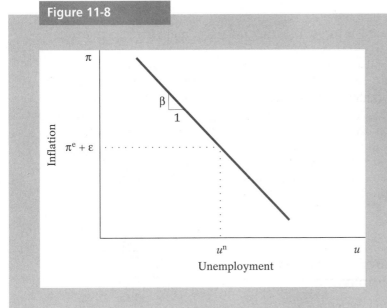

The Short-Run Tradeoff Between Inflation and Unemployment In the short run, there is a negative relationship between inflation and unemployment. At any point in time, a policymaker who controls aggregate demand can choose a combination of inflation and unemployment on this short-run Phillips curve.

mand—now that it realizes that the inflationary consequences of its previous policy are larger than first assumed. This reaction creates a tendency for the point showing the economy's outcome to move back to the right in Figure 11-9. The net effect of these two tendencies—the upward revision in inflationary

Figure 11-9

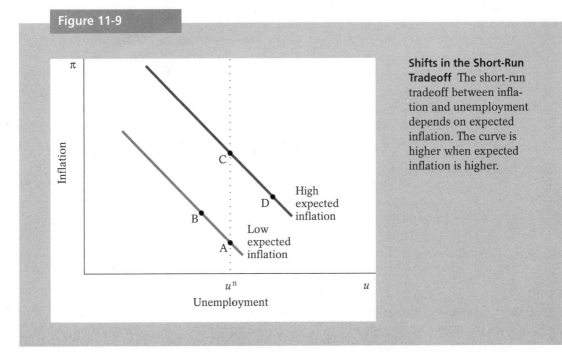

Shifts in the Short-Run Tradeoff The short-run tradeoff between inflation and unemployment depends on expected inflation. The curve is higher when expected inflation is higher.

expectations and the backing off of aggregate demand policy—is an upward-sloping move from point B to point C. At this stage, there is not a tradeoff; both unemployment and inflation are rising.

Point C is sustainable in the long run. Unemployment has returned to the natural rate and actual and expected inflation are consistent (they are both high). When the government wants to fight inflation, contractionary monetary and fiscal policy move the outcome from point C to point D. Again we see a short-run tradeoff—inflation falling but unemployment rising. But because actual inflation is less than expected inflation at point D, expectations are revised down. The economy spends a long time at point D if people are slow to adjust expectations, and there will be a significant sacrifice involved in fighting inflation—a prolonged period of high unemployment.

CASE STUDY

11·3 Inflation and Unemployment in Canada

Figure 11-10 depicts the history of inflation and unemployment in Canada since 1956. We see that the pre-1970 observations (all dots without a date label) are well summarized by the negatively sloped Phillips curve. During this period, there were few large supply shocks, and the government never allowed aggregate demand to expand so much that a sustained inflation developed. As a result, inflationary expectations played little role.

Then, in the 1970s, things changed. The large supply shock of the OPEC oil price increases and the government's shift to more expansionary monetary and fiscal policy caused inflation to shoot up with little reduction in unemployment. The time path for the early 1970s is shown by the upward-pointing arrows in Figure 11-10. In the later 1970s, aggregate demand policy was tightened somewhat, and wage and price controls were imposed for the 1975–1978 period. As a result, the economy slid down its short-run Phillips curve; but with inflationary expectations much higher by then, that short-run Phillips curve was further out from the origin than the earlier one.

The second OPEC shock occurred in 1979. Again, given that demand policy was used to try to insulate unemployment from this event, inflation shot up (see the second set of arrows pointing up in Figure 11-10). By 1981, concern about high inflation peaked, and the Bank of Canada embarked on an enthusiastic disinflation. The contractionary monetary policy pushed the economy down its short-run Phillips curve once again (see the arrows that are farthest to the right in Figure 11-10). But, after two bouts of high inflation, inflationary expectations had ratcheted up to very high levels. As a result the short-run Phillips curve was even farther out from the origin.

Both actual and expected inflation came down during the 1981–1985 period. Perhaps because the inflation problem had become less severe, there was a partial reverse of policy in the 1986–1990 period, so unemployment fell and inflation started rising again. The arrows for this period in Figure 11-10 indicate that Canada's short-run Phillips curve had returned some of the way back toward the origin by then (and this is consistent with the fact that lower inflationary expectations had become widespread by then).

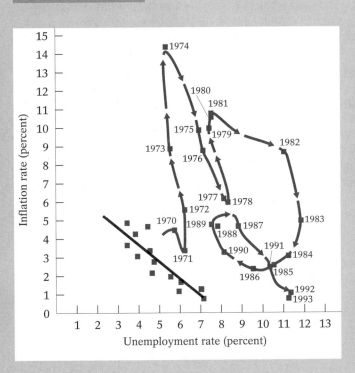

Inflation and Unemployment in Canada Since 1956 This figure uses annual data on the unemployment rate and the inflation rate (percent change in the GDP deflator) to illustrate macroeconomic developments over the last four decades.

Source: Reproduced and adapted by authority of the Minister of Industry, 1994, Statistics Canada. For details, see source lines of Figures 1-2 and 1-3.

Finally, beginning in 1990, the second contractionary monetary policy was initiated. Again, inflation dropped quite dramatically, while unemployment was pushed higher again. By 1994, the battle against inflation had been won, but unemployment remained discouragingly high.

Since there were no obvious adverse supply shocks in the early 1990s and since inflationary expectations were eliminated, it remains a puzzle as to why the unemployment rate remains high. Despite this puzzle, the modern Phillips curve (augmented by supply shocks and inflationary expectations) is a very useful vehicle for interpreting Canada's unemployment and inflation experience of the last 40 years.

Disinflation and the Sacrifice Ratio

Imagine an economy in which unemployment is at its natural rate and inflation is running at 6 percent. What would happen to unemployment and output if the central bank pursued a policy to reduce inflation from 6 to 2 percent?

The Phillips curve shows that, in the absence of a beneficial supply shock, lowering inflation requires a period of high unemployment and reduced output. But by how much and for how long would unemployment need to rise above the natural rate? Before deciding whether to reduce inflation, policy-makers must know how much output would be lost during the transition to lower inflation. This cost can then be compared with the benefits of lower inflation.

Much research has used the available data to examine the Phillips curve quantitatively. The results of these studies are often summarized in a number called the **sacrifice ratio**, the percentage of a year's real GDP that must be forgone to reduce inflation by 1 percentage point. Estimates of the sacrifice ratio vary substantially—between 2 percent and 5 percent. These estimates mean that, for every percentage point that inflation is to fall, something between 2 percent and 5 percent of one year's GDP must be sacrificed.[12]

We can also express the sacrifice ratio in terms of unemployment. Okun's law says that a change of 1 percentage point in the unemployment rate translates into a change of 2 percentage points in GDP. Therefore, reducing inflation by 1 percentage point requires between 1 percentage point and 2.5 percentage points of cyclical unemployment.

We can use the midrange values for the sacrifice ratio to estimate by how much and for how long unemployment must rise to reduce inflation. Since reducing inflation by 1 percentage point requires a sacrifice of 3.5 percent of a year's GDP, reducing inflation by 4 percentage points requires a sacrifice of 14 percent of a year's GDP. Equivalently, this reduction in inflation requires a sacrifice of 7 percentage points of cyclical unemployment.

This disinflation could take various forms, each totaling the same sacrifice of 14 percent of a year's GDP. For example, a rapid disinflation would lower output by 7 percent for two years: this is sometimes called the *cold turkey* solution to inflation. A gradual disinflation would depress output by 2 percent for seven years.

Rational Expectations and Painless Disinflation

Because the expectation of inflation influences the short-run tradeoff between inflation and unemployment, a crucial question is how people form expectations. So far, we have been assuming that expected inflation depends on recently observed inflation. Although this assumption of adaptive expectations is plausible, it is probably too simple to be applicable in all circumstances.

An approach called **rational expectations** assumes that people optimally use all the available information, including information about current policies, to forecast the future. Because monetary and fiscal policies influence inflation, expected inflation should also depend on the monetary and fiscal policies in effect. According to the theory of rational expectations, a change in monetary or fiscal policy will change expectations, and an evaluation of any policy change

---

[12] Barry Cozier and G. Wilkinson, *Some Evidence on Hysteresis and the Costs of Disinflation in Canada*, Technical Report No. 55 (Ottawa: Bank of Canada, 1991); William M. Scarth, "Fighting Inflation: Are the Costs of Getting to Zero Too High?," in Robert C. York, ed., *Taking Aim: The Debate on Zero Inflation*, Study No. 10 (Toronto: C.D. Howe Institute, 1990): 81–103.

must incorporate this effect on expectations. This approach implies that inflation is less inertial than it first appears.

Here is how Thomas Sargent, a prominent advocate of rational expectations, describes its implications for the Phillips curve:

> An alternative "rational expectations" view denies that there is any inherent momentum to the present process of inflation. This view maintains that firms and workers have now come to expect high rates of inflation in the future and that they strike inflationary bargains in light of these expectations. However, it is held that people expect high rates of inflation in the future precisely because the government's current and prospective monetary and fiscal policies warrant those expectations. . . . Thus inflation only seems to have a momentum of its own; it is actually the long-term government policy of persistently running large deficits and creating money at high rates which imparts the momentum to the inflation rate. An implication of this view is that inflation can be stopped much more quickly than advocates of the "momentum" view have indicated and that their estimates of the length of time and the costs of stopping inflation in terms of forgone output are erroneous. . . . [Stopping inflation] would require a change in the policy regime: there must be an abrupt change in the continuing government policy, or strategy, for setting deficits now and in the future that is sufficiently binding as to be widely believed. . . . How costly such a move would be in terms of forgone output and how long it would be in taking effect would depend partly on how resolute and evident the government's commitment was.[13]

Thus, advocates of rational expectations argue that the short-run Phillips curve does not accurately represent the options available. They believe that if policymakers are credibly committed to reducing inflation, rational people will understand the commitment and quickly lower their expectations of inflation. According to the theory of rational expectations, traditional estimates of the sacrifice ratio are not useful for evaluating the impact of alternative policies. Under a credible policy, the costs of reducing inflation may be much lower than estimates of the sacrifice ratio suggest.

In the most extreme case, one can imagine reducing the rate of inflation without causing any recession at all. A painless disinflation has two requirements. First, the plan to reduce inflation must be announced before the workers and firms who set wages and prices have formed their expectations. Second, the workers and firms must believe the announcement; otherwise, they will not reduce their expectations of inflation. If both requirements are met, the announcement will immediately shift the short-run tradeoff between inflation and unemployment downward, permitting a lower rate of inflation without higher unemployment.

Although the rational-expectations approach remains controversial, almost all economists agree that expectations of inflation influence the short-run

13 Thomas J. Sargent, "The Ends of Four Big Inflations," in Robert E. Hall, ed., *Inflation: Causes and Effects* (Chicago: University of Chicago Press, 1982).

tradeoff between inflation and unemployment. The credibility of a policy to reduce inflation is therefore one determinant of how costly the policy will be.
Unfortunately, it is often difficult to predict whether the public will view the
announcement of a new policy as credible. The central role of expectations
makes forecasting the results of alternative policies far more difficult.

CASE STUDY

11·4   The Sacrifice Ratio in Practice

The Phillips curve with adaptive expectations implies that reducing inflation requires a period of high unemployment and low output. By contrast, the rational-
expectations approach suggests that reducing inflation can be much less costly.
What happens during actual disinflations?

Consider the Canadian disinflation in the early 1980s. This decade began
with inflation over 10 percent. Yet because of the tight monetary policies pursued by the Bank of Canada, the rate of inflation fell substantially in the first
few years of the decade. This episode provides a natural experiment with
which to estimate how much output is lost in the process of disinflation.

The first question is, how much did inflation fall? As measured by the
GDP inflator, inflation reached a peak of 10.8 percent in 1981 and then hit a
low of 2.5 percent by the end of 1985. Thus, we can estimate that the Bank of
Canada engineered a reduction in inflation of 8.3 points over four years.

The second question is, how much output was lost during this period?
Table 11-1 shows the unemployment rate from 1982 to 1985. Assuming that
the natural rate of unemployment was 8.5 percent (see Figure 5-1 in Chapter
5), we can compute the amount of cyclical unemployment in each year. In total
over this period, there were 11.5 point-years of cyclical unemployment.
Okun's law says that 1 percentage point of unemployment implies 2 percentage
points of GDP. Therefore, 22 percentage points of annual GDP were lost during the disinflation.

Now we can compute the sacrifice ratio for this episode. We know that 22
percentage points of GDP were lost, and that inflation fell by 8.3 percentage
points. Hence, 22/8.3, or 2.7, percentage points of GDP were lost for each
percentage-point reduction in inflation. The estimate of the sacrifice ratio from
the disinflation of the 1980s is 2.7.

This estimate of the sacrifice ratio is at the low end of the estimates made
before this episode. Why is it that inflation was reduced at a smaller cost than
many economists had predicted? One explanation is that the contractionary
monetary policy of the early 1980s was far more dramatic than the earlier less-
concerted attempts to reduce inflation. Perhaps the Bank of Canada's tough
stand was credible enough to influence expectations of inflation directly. Yet
the change in expectations was not large enough to make the disinflation
painless: in 1983 unemployment reached its highest level since the Great
Depression.

Table 11-1	Unemployment During the Disinflation of the 1980s		
Year	Unemployment Rate	Natural Rate	Cyclical Unemployment
1982	11.0%	8.5%	2.5%
1983	11.8	8.5	3.3
1984	11.2	8.5	3.7
1985	10.5	8.5	2.0
		Total	11.5%

Another interpretation of our estimate of the sacrifice ratio is that it is a miscalculation. In the three years previous to the disinflation policy, the unemployment rate was 7.5 percent, and this value was what most Canadian economists (including those working at the Bank of Canada) had been estimating the natural unemployment rate to be back then. If we change the third column of Table 11-1 to a series of 7.5 percent entries, instead of a column of 8.5 percent entries, the total point-years of cyclical unemployment over this period rises from 11.5 percent to 15.5 percent. The estimated sacrifice ratio jumps to 3.7 percent, not 2.7 percent. Furthermore, since unemployment did not return to 7.5 percent until 1989, it can be argued that the cyclical unemployment in the 1986–1988 period should also be attributed to the disinflation policy. During the 1986–1988 years there was an additional 3.6 point-years of cyclical unemployment, and counting this additional excess capacity boosts the overall sacrifice ratio to 4.6. Thus, disinflation is seen as much more costly if a lower estimate of the natural unemployment rate is used in the calculations.

Which estimate of the natural rate is more credible? A glance back at Figure 5-1 in Chapter 5 suggests that the natural rate *did* rise form 7.5 percent to 8.5 percent over this period. But the important issue is *why*. If this rise is due to such things as increased generosity of the unemployment insurance system, as some believe, then our first estimate of the sacrifice ratio using the 8.5 percent natural rate is the better one. But if the natural unemployment rate rose *only because* the actual unemployment rate did, then our second estimate of the sacrifice ratio is more accurate.

The possibility that the natural rate could depend on the actual rate is discussed more fully later in this chapter. It remains a controversial topic of current research. At this point, economists must simply admit that their estimates of the sacrifice ratio are not pinned down with a great degree of accuracy.

Although the Canadian disinflation of the 1980s is only one historical episode, this kind of analysis can be applied to other disinflations. A recent study documented the results of 65 disinflations in 19 countries. In almost all these episodes, the reduction in inflation came at the cost of temporarily lower out-

put. Yet the size of the output loss varied from episode to episode. Rapid disinflations usually had smaller sacrifice ratios than slower ones. That is, in contrast
to what the Phillips curve with adaptive expectations suggests, a cold-turkey
approach appears less costly than a gradual one. Moreover, countries with
more flexible wage-setting institutions, such as shorter labour contracts, had
smaller sacrifice ratios. These findings indicate that reducing inflation always
has some cost, but that policies and institutions can affect its magnitude.[14]

11•3 Recent Developments: New Keynesian Economics

Economists do not agree on the best way to explain short-run economic
fluctuations. There are two major schools of thought: new classical economics
and new Keynesian economics.

New classical economists advocate models in which wages and prices adjust quickly to clear markets. The market-clearing models examined in the
chapter—the worker-misperception and imperfect-information models—were
popular among new classical economists in the 1970s. More recently, many new
classical economists have turned their attention to *real-business-cycle theory*,
which applies the tenets of the classical model—price flexibility and monetary
neutrality—to explain economic fluctuations. We discuss this theory in Chapter 14.

New Keynesian economists believe that market-clearing models cannot
explain short-run economic fluctuations, and so they advocate models with
sticky wages and prices. In *The General Theory*, Keynes urged economists to
abandon the classical presumption that wages and prices adjust quickly to equilibrate markets. He emphasized that aggregate demand is a primary determinant of national income in the short run. New Keynesian economists accept
these basic conclusions.

In their research, new Keynesian economists try to develop more fully the
Keynesian approach to economic fluctuations. Much new Keynesian research is
aimed at refining the theory of aggregate supply by explaining how wages and
prices behave in the short run. This work tries to identify more precisely the
market imperfections that make wages and prices sticky and that cause the
economy to return only slowly to the natural rate. Other new Keynesian research calls into question an underlying premise of our model of economic
fluctuations. In this section we discuss some of these recent developments.

Small Menu Costs and Aggregate-Demand Externalities

One reason that prices do not adjust immediately in the short run is that there are
costs involved in adjusting prices. To change its prices, a firm may need to send

---

[14] Laurence Ball, "What Determines the Sacrifice Ratio?" in N.G. Mankiw, ed., *Monetary Policy*
(Chicago: University of Chicago Press, 1994), forthcoming.

out a new catalogue to customers, distribute new price lists to its sales staff, or, in the case of a restaurant, print new menus. These costs of price adjustment, called **menu costs**, lead firms to adjust prices intermittently rather than continuously.

Economists disagree about whether menu costs explain the short-run stickiness of prices. Skeptics point out that menu costs are usually very small. How can small menu costs help to explain recessions, which are very costly for society? Proponents reply that small does not mean inconsequential: even though menu costs are small for the individual firm, they can have large effects on the economy as a whole.

According to proponents of the menu-cost hypothesis, to understand why prices adjust slowly, we must acknowledge that there are externalities to price adjustment: a price reduction by one firm benefits other firms in the economy. When a firm lowers the price it charges, it slightly lowers the average price level and thereby raises real money balances. The increase in real money balances expands aggregate income (by shifting the *LM* curve outward). The economic expansion in turn raises the demand for the products of all firms. This macroeconomic impact of one firm's price adjustment on the demand for all other firms' products is called an **aggregate-demand externality**. For any one firm, the externality effect is small; but for all firms taken together, it is large.

In the presence of this aggregate-demand externality, small menu costs can make prices sticky, and this stickiness can have a large cost to society. Suppose that a firm originally sets its price too high and later must decide whether to cut its price. Because of the aggregate-demand externality, the benefit to society of the price cut would exceed the benefit to the firm. Because the firm ignores this externality when making its decision, it sometimes fails to pay the menu cost and cut its price even though the price cut is socially desirable. *Hence, sticky prices may be optimal for those setting prices, even though they are undesirable for the economy as a whole.*[15]

The Staggering of Wages and Prices

Not everyone in the economy sets new wages and prices at the same time. Instead, the adjustment of wages and prices throughout the economy is staggered. *Staggering makes the overall level of wages and prices adjust slowly, even when individual wages and prices change frequently.*

Consider the following example. Suppose first that price setting is synchronized: every firm adjusts its price on the first day of every month. If the money supply and aggregate demand rise on May 10, output will be higher from May 10 to June 1 because prices are fixed during this interval. But on

---

[15] For more on this topic, see N. Gregory Mankiw, "Small Menu Costs and Large Business Cycles: A Macroeconomic Model of Monopoly," *Quarterly Journal of Economics* 100 (May 1985): 529–537; George A. Akerlof and Janet L. Yellen, "A Near Rational Model of the Business Cycle, with Wage and Price Inertia," *Quarterly Journal of Economics* 100 (Supplement 1985): 823–838; and Olivier Jean Blanchard and Nobuhiro Kiyotaki, "Monopolistic Competition and the Effects of Aggregate Demand," *American Economic Review* 77 (September 1987): 647–666. These three articles are reprinted in N. Gregory Mankiw and David Romer, eds., *New Keynesian Economics* (Cambridge, Mass.: MIT Press, 1991).

June 1 all firms will raise their prices in response to the higher demand, ending the boom.

Now suppose that price setting is staggered: half the firms set prices on the first of each month and half on the fifteenth. If the money supply rises on May 10, then half the firms can raise their prices on May 15. But these firms will probably not raise their prices very much. Because half the firms will not be changing their prices on the fifteenth, a price increase by any firm will raise that firm's *relative* price, which will cause it to lose customers. (In contrast, if all firms are synchronized, all firms can raise prices together, leaving relative prices unaffected.) If the May 15 price-setters make little adjustment in their prices, then the other firms will make little adjustment when their turn comes on June 1, because they also want to avoid relative price changes that put their sales in jeopardy. And so on. The price level rises slowly as the result of small price increases on the first and the fifteenth of each month. Hence, staggering makes the price level sluggish, because no firm wishes to be the first to post a substantial price increase.

Staggering also affects wage determination. Consider, for example, how a fall in the money supply works its way through the economy. A smaller money supply implies reduced aggregate demand, which in turn requires a proportionate fall in nominal wages to maintain full employment. Each worker might be willing to take a cut in his nominal wage if all other wages were to fall proportionately. The worker could then reasonably expect a reduction in the overall level of goods prices. But each worker is reluctant to be the first to take a pay cut, knowing that this means, at least temporarily, a fall in his relative wage. Since the setting of wages is staggered, the reluctance of each worker to reduce his wage first makes the overall level of wages slow to respond to changes in aggregate demand. In other words, the staggered setting of individual wages makes the overall level of wages sticky.[16]

Recessions as Coordination Failure

Some new Keynesian economists suggest that recessions result from a failure of coordination. In recessions, output is low, workers are unemployed, and factories sit idle. It is possible to imagine allocations of resources in which everyone is better off—for example, the high output and employment of the 1920s is clearly preferable to the low output and employment of the 1930s. If society fails to reach an outcome that is feasible and that everyone prefers, then the members of society have failed to coordinate in some way.

Coordination problems can arise in the setting of wages and prices because those who set them must anticipate the actions of other wage and price setters. Union leaders negotiating wages are concerned about the concessions

---

[16] For more on the effects of staggering, see John Taylor, "Staggered Price Setting in a Macro Model," *American Economic Review* 69 (May 1979): 108–113; and Olivier J. Blanchard, "Price Asynchronization and Price Level Inertia," in R. Dornbusch and Mario Henrique Simonsen, eds., *Inflation, Debt, and Indexation* (Cambridge, Mass.: MIT Press, 1983), 3–24. Both are reprinted in N. Gregory Mankiw and David Romer, eds., *New Keynesian Economics* (Cambridge, Mass.: MIT Press, 1991).

other unions will win. Firms setting prices are mindful of the prices other firms will charge.

To see how a recession could arise as a failure of coordination, consider the following parable. The economy is made up of two firms. After a fall in the money supply, each firm must decide whether to cut its price. Each firm wants to maximize its profit, but its profit depends not only on its pricing decision, but also on the decision made by the other firm.

The choices facing each firm are listed in Figure 11-11, which shows how the profits of the two firms depend on their actions. If neither firm cuts its price, real money balances are low, a recession ensues, and each firm makes a profit of only $15. If both firms cut their prices, real money balances are high, a recession is avoided, and each firm makes a profit of $30. Although both firms prefer to avoid a recession, neither can do so by its own actions. If one firm cuts its price while the other does not, a mild recession follows. The firm making the price cut makes only $10, while the other firm makes $20.

Figure 11-11

| | | Firm 2 | |
		Cut Price	Keep High Price
Firm 1	Cut Price	Firm 1 makes $30 Firm 2 makes $30	Firm 1 makes $10 Firm 2 makes $20
	Keep High Price	Firm 1 makes $20 Firm 2 makes $10	Firm 1 makes $15 Firm 2 makes $15

Price Setting and Coordination Failure
This figure shows a hypothetical "game" between two firms, each of which is deciding whether to cut prices after a fall in the money supply. Each firm must choose a strategy without knowing the strategy the other firm will choose. What outcome would you expect?

The essence of this parable is that each firm's decision influences the set of outcomes available to the other firm. When one firm cuts its price, it improves the position of the other firm, because part of the recession is avoided, and the other firm suffers a smaller loss in sales. This positive impact of one firm's price cut on the other firm's profit opportunities might arise from an aggregate-demand externality.

What outcome should we expect in this economy? On the one hand, if each firm expects the other to cut its price, both will cut prices, resulting in the preferred outcome in which each makes $30. On the other hand, if each firm expects the other to maintain its price, both will maintain their prices, resulting in the inferior solution in which each makes $15. Either of these outcomes is possible: economists say that there are *multiple equilibria*.

The inferior outcome, in which each firm makes $15, is an example of a **coordination failure**. If the two firms could coordinate, they would both cut their price and reach the preferred outcome. In the real world, unlike in our parable, coordination is often difficult because the number of firms setting prices is large. *The moral of the story is that prices can be sticky simply because people expect them to be sticky, even though stickiness is in no one's interest.*[17]

Hysteresis and the Challenge to the Natural-Rate Hypothesis

Our discussion of economic fluctuations in Chapters 8 through 11 has been based on an assumption called the **natural-rate hypothesis**, summarized in the following statement.

> *Fluctuations in aggregate demand affect output and employment only in the short run. In the long run, the economy returns to the levels of output, employment, and unemployment described by the classical model.*

The natural-rate hypothesis allows macroeconomists to study separately short-run and long-run developments in the economy.

Recently, some new Keynesian economists have challenged the natural-rate hypothesis by suggesting that aggregate demand may affect output and employment even in the long run. They have pointed out a number of mechanisms through which recessions might leave permanent scars on the economy by altering the natural rate of unemployment. **Hysteresis** is the term used to describe the long-lasting influence of history on the natural rate.

A recession can have permanent effects if it changes the people who become unemployed. For instance, workers might lose valuable job skills when unemployed, lowering their ability to find a job even after the recession ends. Alternatively, a long period of unemployment may change an individual's attitude toward work and reduce the desire to find employment. In either case, the recession permanently inhibits the process of job search and raises the amount of frictional unemployment.

Another way in which a recession can permanently affect the economy is by changing the process that determines wages. Those who become unemployed may lose their influence on the wage-setting process. Unemployed workers may lose their status as union members, for example. More generally, some of the *insiders* in the wage-setting process become *outsiders*. If the smaller group of insiders cares more about high real wages and less about high employment, then the recession may permanently push real wages farther above the equilibrium level and raise the amount of wait unemployment.

Hysteresis remains a controversial topic. It is still not clear whether this phenomenon is significant, or why it might be more pronounced in some countries than in others. Yet the topic is important, because hysteresis implies that

---

[17] For more on coordination failure, see Russell Cooper and Andrew John, "Coordinating Coordination Failures in Keynesian Models," *Quarterly Journal of Economics* 103 (1988): 441–463; reprinted in N. Gregory Mankiw and David Romer, eds., *New Keynesian Economics* (Cambridge, Mass.: MIT Press, 1991); and Laurence Ball and David Romer, "Sticky Prices as Coordination Failure," *American Economic Review*, 81 (June 1991): 539–552.

recessions are much more costly than the natural-rate hypothesis would suggest. Put another way, hysteresis raises the sacrifice ratio.

CASE STUDY

11·5 Unemployment in the United Kingdom in the 1980s

Doubts about the natural-rate hypothesis and interest in hysteresis arose largely in response to the experience in the 1980s of several European countries, especially the United Kingdom. In the 1970s U.K. unemployment averaged 3.4 percent, whereas in the 1980s it averaged 9.4 percent. This rise in unemployment presented a problem for policymakers and a puzzle for economists.

The rise in unemployment was caused in large part by the policies designed by the Thatcher government to reduce inflation. When the Conservative party won control and Margaret Thatcher became prime minister in 1979, inflation was running almost 18 percent per year. Contractionary monetary and fiscal policies caused the rate of unemployment to rise from 4.3 percent in 1979 to 11.1 percent in 1984. As the Phillips curve predicts, the rise in unemployment lowered inflation to less than 5 percent in 1984.

The puzzle is that unemployment remained high even after inflation had stabilized. Since this high unemployment did not lower inflation further, it appeared that the natural rate of unemployment had risen. Theories of hysteresis provide reasons for why the recession might have raised the natural rate of unemployment.[18]

11·4 Conclusion

In this chapter we discussed four models of aggregate supply and the implied tradeoff between inflation and unemployment. We saw that the four models are similar in their implications for the aggregate economy. We also saw that the Phillips curve, according to which inflation depends on expected inflation, cyclical unemployment, and supply shocks, provides a convenient way to express and analyze aggregate supply.

The last section of this chapter presented some recent developments in the theory of aggregate supply. Keep in mind that not all economists endorse all the ideas discussed here. Some of these developments, such as the theories of hysteresis, challenge traditional views about aggregate supply. If you find it difficult to fit all the pieces together, you are not alone. The study of aggregate supply remains one of the most unsettled—and therefore one of the most exciting—research areas in macroeconomics.

---

[18] For a review of some of these theories, see Olivier J. Blanchard and Lawrence H. Summers, "Beyond the Natural Rate Hypothesis," *American Economic Review* 78 (May 1988): 182–187. For some evidence that hysteresis may apply to Canada, see Pierre Fortin, "Innis Lecture: The Phillips Curve, Macroeconomic Policy, and the Welfare of Canadians," *Canadian Journal of Economics* 24 (November 1991): 774–803.

Summary

1. The four theories of aggregate supply—the sticky-wage, worker-misperception, imperfect-information, and sticky-price models—attribute deviations of output and employment from the natural rate to various market imperfections. All the theories imply that output rises above the natural rate when the price level exceeds the expected price level, and that output falls below the natural rate when the price level is less than the expected price level.

2. Economists often express aggregate supply in a relationship called the Phillips curve. The Phillips curve says that inflation depends on expected inflation, the deviation of unemployment from its natural rate, and supply shocks. It implies that policymakers who control aggregate demand face a short-run tradeoff between inflation and unemployment.

3. If expected inflation depends on recently observed inflation, then inflation has inertia, which implies that reducing inflation requires either a beneficial supply shock or a period of high unemployment and reduced output. If people have rational expectations, however, then a credible announcement of a change in policy might be able to influence expectations directly and, therefore, reduce inflation without causing a recession.

4. Recent developments in the theory of aggregate supply have tried to explain why wages and prices are sticky in the short run. They have also challenged the natural-rate hypothesis by suggesting ways in which recessions can leave permanent scars on the economy.

KEY CONCEPTS

Sticky-wage model

Worker-misperception model

Imperfect-information model

Sticky-price model

Phillips curve

Adaptive expectations

Demand-pull inflation

Cost-push inflation

Sacrifice ratio

Rational expectations

New classical economics

New Keynesian economics

Menu costs

Aggregate-demand externality

Coordination failure

Natural-rate hypothesis

Hysteresis

QUESTIONS FOR REVIEW

1. Explain the four theories of aggregate supply. On what market imperfection does each theory rely? What do the theories have in common?

2. How is the Phillips curve related to aggregate supply?

3. Why might inflation be inertial?

4. Explain the differences between demand-pull inflation and cost-push inflation.

5. Under what circumstances might it be possible to reduce inflation without causing a recession?

6. Explain two ways in which a recession might raise the natural rate of unemployment.

PROBLEMS AND APPLICATIONS

1. Consider the following changes in the sticky-wage model.

   a. Suppose that labour contracts specify that the nominal wage be fully indexed for inflation. That is, the nominal wage is to be adjusted to fully compensate for changes in the consumer price index. How does full indexation alter the aggregate supply curve implied by the model?

   b. Suppose now that indexation is only partial. That is, for every increase in the CPI, the nominal wage rises, but by a smaller percentage. How does partial indexation alter the aggregate supply curve implied by the model?

2. In the sticky-price model, describe the aggregate supply curve in the following special cases. How do these cases compare to the short-run aggregate supply curve we discussed in Chapter 8?

   a. No firms have flexible prices ($s = 1$).

   b. The desired price does not depend on aggregate output ($a = 0$).

3. Suppose that an economy has the Phillips curve

$$\pi = \pi_{-1} - 0.5(u - 0.06).$$

   a. What is the natural rate of unemployment?

   b. Graph the short-run and long-run relationship between inflation and unemployment.

   c. How much cyclical unemployment is necessary to reduce inflation by 5 percentage points? Using Okun's law, compute the sacrifice ratio.

   d. Inflation is running at 10 percent. The central bank wants to reduce it to 5 percent. Give two scenarios that will achieve that goal.

4. According to the rational-expectations approach, if everyone believes that policymakers are committed to reducing inflation, the cost of reducing inflation—the sacrifice ratio—will be lower than if the public is skeptical about the policymakers' intentions. Why might this be true? How might credibility be achieved?

5. Assume that people have rational expectations and that the economy is described by the sticky-wage or sticky-price model. Explain why each of the following propositions is true:

   a. Only unanticipated changes in the money supply affect real GDP. Changes in the money supply that were anticipated when wages and prices were set do not have any real effects.

   b. If the Bank of Canada chooses the money supply at the same time that people are setting wages and prices, so that everyone has the same information about the state of the economy, then monetary policy cannot be used systematically to stabilize output. Hence, a policy of keeping the money supply constant will have the same real effects as a policy of adjusting the money supply in response to the state of the economy. (This is called the *policy irrelevance proposition.*)

c. If the Bank of Canada sets the money supply substantially after people have set wages and prices, so the Bank of Canada has collected more information about the state of the economy, then monetary policy can be used systematically to stabilize output.

6. Suppose that an economy has the Phillips curve

$$\pi = \pi_{-1} - 0.5(u - u^n)$$

and that the natural rate of unemployment is given by an average of the past two years' unemployment:

$$u^n = 0.5(u_{-1} + u_{-2}).$$

a. Why might the natural rate of unemployment depend on recent unemployment (as is assumed in the preceding equation)?

b. Suppose that the Bank of Canada follows a policy to reduce permanently the inflation rate by 1 percentage point. What effect will that policy have on the unemployment rate over time?

c. What is the sacrifice ratio in this economy? Explain.

d. What do these equations imply about the short-run and long-run tradeoff between inflation and unemployment?

The Macroeconomic Policy Debate

The Federal Reserve's job is to take away the punch bowl just as the party gets going.

William McChesney Martin

What we need is not a skilled monetary driver of the economic vehicle continuously turning the steering wheel to adjust to the unexpected irregularities of the route, but some means of keeping the monetary passenger who is in the back seat as ballast from occasionally leaning over and giving the steering wheel a jerk that threatens to send the car off the road.

Milton Friedman

Economists argue most vehemently during discussions of economic policy. The two quotations above—the first from a former chairman of the Federal Reserve (the U.S. central bank), the second from a prominent critic of central banks—exemplify the diversity of opinion over how macroeconomic policy should be conducted.

Some economists, such as William McChesney Martin, view the economy as inherently unstable. They argue that the economy experiences frequent shocks to aggregate demand and aggregate supply. Unless policymakers use monetary and fiscal policy to stabilize the economy, these shocks will lead to unnecessary and inefficient fluctuations in output, unemployment, and inflation. According to the popular saying, macroeconomic policy should "lean against the wind," stimulating the economy when it is depressed and slowing the economy when it is overheated.

Other economists, such as Milton Friedman, view the economy as naturally stable. They blame bad economic policies for the large and inefficient fluctuations we have sometimes experienced. They argue that economic policy should not try to "fine tune" the economy. Instead, economic policymakers should recognize their limitations and be satisfied if they do no harm.

This debate has continued for many years with numerous protagonists advancing varied arguments for their positions. The fundamental issue is how policymakers should use the theory of economic fluctuations developed in the last four chapters. In this chapter we ask two questions that have arisen in this

343

debate. First, should monetary and fiscal policy take an active role in trying to stabilize the economy, or should policy remain passive? Second, should policy-makers be free to use their discretion in responding to changing economic conditions, or should they be committed to following a fixed policy rule?

12•1 Should Policy Be Active or Passive?

Policymakers in the federal government view economic stabilization as one of their primary responsibilities. The analysis of macroeconomic policy is a regular duty of the Department of Finance and the Bank of Canada. When the government is considering a major change in either fiscal policy or monetary policy, foremost in the discussion are whether the change will influence inflation and unemployment and whether aggregate demand needs to be stimulated or depressed.

Although the government has long conducted monetary and fiscal policy, the view that it should try to stabilize the economy is more recent. The federal *White Paper* of 1945 was the key document in which the government held itself accountable for macroeconomic performance. The *White Paper* states that the "the government will be prepared, in periods when unemployment threatens, to incur deficits and increases in the national debt resulting from its employment and income policy." This policy commitment was written when the memory of the Great Depression was still fresh. The lawmakers who wrote it believed, as many economists do, that in the absence of an active government role in the economy, events like the Great Depression could occur regularly.

To many economists the case for active government policy is clear and simple. Recessions are periods of high unemployment, low incomes, and reduced economic well-being. The model of aggregate demand and aggregate supply shows how shocks to the economy cause recessions. It also shows how monetary and fiscal policy can prevent recessions by responding to these shocks. These economists consider it wasteful not to use these policy instruments to stabilize the economy.

Other economists are critical of the government's attempts to stabilize the economy. These critics argue that the government should take a "hands off" approach to macroeconomic policy. At first, this view might seem surprising. If our model shows how to prevent or reduce the severity of recessions, why do these critics want the government to refrain from using monetary and fiscal policy for economic stabilization? To find out, let's consider some of their arguments.

Lags in the Implementation and Effects of Policies

Economic stabilization would be easy if the effects of policy were immediate. Making policy would be like driving a car: policymakers would simply adjust their instruments to keep the economy on the desired path. Driving comes naturally to most people because a car changes direction almost immediately after the steering wheel is turned.

Yet economic policymakers face a problem more similar to that of a pilot of a large ship. Steering a ship is difficult because a ship changes course long after the pilot adjusts the rudder. And once the ship starts to turn, it continues long after the rudder is returned to normal. A novice is likely to oversteer and, after noticing his mistake, overreact by steering too much in the opposite direction. The result could be unstable, as the novice responds to previous mistakes by making larger and larger corrections.

Like a ship's pilot, economic policymakers face the problem of long lags. Indeed, the problem for policymakers is even more difficult, because the lengths of the lags are hard to predict. These long and variable lags greatly complicate the conduct of monetary and fiscal policy.

Economists distinguish between two lags in the conduct of stabilization policy: the inside lag and the outside lag. The **inside lag** is the time between a shock to the economy and the policy action that responds to that shock. This lag arises because it takes time for policymakers first to recognize that a shock has occurred and then to put appropriate policies into effect. The **outside lag** is the time between a policy action and its influence on the economy. This lag arises because policies do not immediately influence spending, income, and employment.

Fiscal policy can have a long inside lag, since changes in spending or taxes must be voted through both the House of Commons and the Senate. The process of parliamentary committee hearings can be slow and cumbersome. An additional problem concerning fiscal policy is that provincial governments sometimes want to push the economy in the opposite direction from what is intended by the federal government. (This coordination problem is discussed more fully in Chapter 13.) While monetary policy has a short inside lag, it can have a long outside lag. Monetary policy works through interest rates, which in turn influence investment. But many firms make investment plans far in advance. Therefore, a change in monetary policy is thought not to affect economic activity until about six months after it is made.[1]

The long and variable lags associated with monetary and fiscal policy certainly make stabilizing the economy more difficult. Advocates of passive policy argue that, because of these lags, successful stabilization policy is almost impossible. Indeed, attempts to stabilize the economy are all too often destabilizing. Suppose that the economy's condition changes between the time when a policy action begins and the time when the policy affects the economy. In this case, active policy may end up stimulating the economy when it is overheated or depressing the economy when it is cooling off. Advocates of active policy admit that such lags do require policymakers to be cautious. But, they argue, these lags do not necessarily imply that policy should be completely passive, especially in the face of a severe and protracted economic downturn.

Some policies, called **automatic stabilizers**, are designed to reduce the lags associated with stabilization policy. Automatic stabilizers are policies that stimulate or depress the economy when necessary without any deliberate policy change. For example, the system of income taxes automatically reduces taxes when the economy goes into a recession, without any change in the tax

---

[1] As we shall see in Chapter 13, monetary policy also works through the exchange rate.

laws, because individuals and corporations pay less tax when their incomes fall. Similarly, the unemployment-insurance system and the welfare programs automatically raise transfer payments when the economy moves into a recession, because more people apply for benefits. One can view these automatic stabilizers as fiscal policy without any inside lag.

CASE STUDY

12•1   Profit-Sharing as an Automatic Stabilizer

Economists often propose policies to improve the automatic-stabilizing powers of the economy. The economist Martin Weitzman has made one of the most intriguing suggestions: profit sharing. Today, most labour contracts specify a fixed wage. For example, General Motors might pay assembly-line workers $20 an hour. Weitzman recommends that the workers' total pay should depend on their firm's profits. A profit-sharing contract for General Motors might pay workers $10 for each hour of work, but in addition the workers would divide among themselves a share of the firm's profit.

Weitzman argues that profit sharing would act as an automatic stabilizer. Under the current wage system, a fall in demand for a firm's product causes the firm to lay off workers: it is no longer profitable to employ them at the old wage. The firm will rehire these workers only if the wage falls or if demand recovers. Under a profit-sharing system, Weitzman argues, firms would be more likely to maintain employment after a fall in demand. Under our hypothetical profit-sharing contract for General Motors, for example, each additional hour of work would cost the firm only $10; the rest of the compensation for additional workers would come from the workers' share of profits. Because the marginal cost of labour would be so much lower under profit sharing, a fall in demand would not normally cause a firm to lay off workers.

To provide evidence for the advantages of profit sharing, Weitzman points to Japan. Most Japanese workers receive a large fraction of their compensation in the form of year-end bonuses. Weitzman argues that, because of these bonuses, Japanese workers "think of themselves more as permanently employed partners than as hired hands." And, as Weitzman's theory predicts, employment in Japan is much more stable than in countries without any form of profit sharing.

The New York Times dubbed Weitzman's proposal "the best idea since Keynes." Advocates of his theory want the government to provide tax incentives to encourage firms to adopt profit-sharing plans. Others, however, have expressed skepticism. They wonder why, if profit sharing is such a good idea, firms and workers don't sign such contracts without prodding from the government. Whether profit sharing would help stabilize the economy, as Weitzman suggests, remains an open question.[2]

---

[2] Martin L. Weitzman, *The Share Economy* (Cambridge, Mass.: Harvard University Press, 1984).

The Difficult Job of Economic Forecasting

Because policy influences the economy after a substantial lag, successful stabilization policy requires the ability to predict accurately future economic conditions. If we cannot predict whether the economy will be in a boom or a recession in six months or a year, we cannot evaluate whether monetary and fiscal policy should now be trying to expand or contract aggregate demand. Unfortunately, economic developments are often unpredictable, at least given our current understanding of the economy.

One way forecasters try to look ahead is with the **index of leading indicators**. This index, called the composite index, is composed of 10 data series—such as stock prices, the number of housing starts, the U.S. leading indicator, the value of orders for new plants and equipment, and the money supply—that often fluctuate in advance of the economy. A large fall in the leading indicators signals that a recession is likely.

Another way forecasters look ahead is with models of the economy. Both government agencies and private forecasting firms maintain large-scale computer models. These models are made up of many

"It's true, Caesar. Rome is declining, but I expect it to pick up in the next quarter."

equations, each representing a part of the economy. After making assumptions about the path of the exogenous variables, such as monetary policy, fiscal policy, and foreign variables such as oil prices and tariffs, these models yield predictions about unemployment, inflation, and other endogenous variables. One must always keep in mind, however, that the validity of these predictions is only as good as the model and the assumptions about the exogenous variables.

CASE STUDY

Two Episodes in Economic Forecasting

Economic forecasting is a crucial input to private and public decisionmaking. Business executives rely on forecasts when deciding how much to produce and how much to invest. Government policymakers also rely on them when developing economic policies.

How accurate is economic forecasting? We can answer this question by looking at how well forecasters have done in the past.

The most severe economic downturn in modern history, the Great Depression of the 1930s, caught economic forecasters by surprise. Even after the stock market crash of 1929, they remained confident that the economy would not suffer a substantial setback. In late 1931, when all western economies were clearly in bad shape, the eminent economist Irving Fisher predicted that it would recover quickly. Subsequent events showed that these forecasts were much too optimistic.[3]

Forecasting success is still an elusive goal, as the recession of the early 1990s illustrates. On average, during the first three years of the decade, Canada's real GDP fell by 0.4 percentage points each year. Throughout this period, the federal government surveyed private forecasters to ensure that their own projections of GDP growth agreed with the existing consensus. One of the reasons the government's budget deficit increased so much during the 1990–1992 period is that Finance Department officials (and other forecasters) overestimated GDP growth by over 3 percentage points per year! (With lower levels of income being earned, the existing set of tax rates did not generate the amount of revenue that the government expected.)

This low level of forecasting accuracy is discouraging for those who favour an active stabilization policy. Furthermore, there is significant disparity among the various forecasters' estimates. For example, in the Federal Budget of 1994 (delivered in February of that year), it was noted that the private forecasts for real GDP growth in that year ranged from 2.9 percent to 4.3 percent. More important, Statistics Canada (one of the most respected statistical agencies in the world) finds that it must revise its estimates of real GDP *several* times—even *after* the period in question has become a matter of history. Journalist Bruce

Figure 12-1

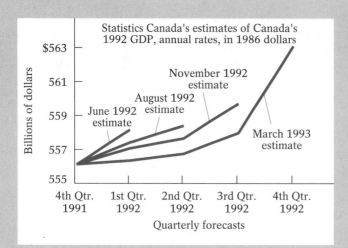

Statistics Canada's estimates of Canada's 1992 GDP, annual rates, in 1986 dollars

Recording the Recession of the Early 1990s
Forecasting is particularly difficult if the figure being forecasted is constantly being revised. This graph shows how often Statistics Canada data for real GDP are revised during the year following the issue of their preliminary estimates.

Source: Bruce Little, "Revised Recovery not so Robust," *The Globe and Mail*, March 13, 1993, p. B21.

[3] Kathryn M. Dominguez, Ray C. Fair, and Matthew D. Shapiro, "Forecasting the Depression: Harvard versus Yale," *American Economic Review* 78 (September 1988): 595–612. This article shows how badly economic forecasters did during the Great Depression, and it argues that one could not have done any better with the modern forecasting techniques available today.

Little used the graph shown in Figure 12-1 to indicate how much data revision goes on. For example, in just the nine months between June 1992 and March 1993, the estimate for GDP growth during the first quarter of 1992 was revised downward *four* times, with the final estimate's being a growth rate that is only *one-sixth* of the initial measurement. And this is just getting recorded history straight—this is not forecasting at all. Although economic forecasts are an essential input to private and public decisionmaking, they are very uncertain.

Ignorance, Expectations, and the Lucas Critique

The prominent macroeconomist Robert Lucas once wrote, "As an advice-giving profession we are in way over our heads." Even many of those who frequently advise policymakers would agree with this assessment. Economics is a young science, and there is still much that we do not know. This ignorance suggests that economists should be cautious when advising policymakers. Economists cannot be completely confident when they make assessments about the effects of alternative policies.

Although there are many topics about which economists' knowledge is limited, Lucas has emphasized the question of how people form expectations of the future. Expectations play a crucial role in the economy because they influence the behaviour of consumers, investors, and other economic actors. People's expectations depend on many things, including the economic policies being pursued by the government. Thus, estimating the effect of a policy change requires knowing how people's expectations will respond to the policy change. Lucas has argued that traditional methods of policy evaluation do not adequately take into account this impact of policy on expectations. This criticism of traditional policy evaluation is known as the **Lucas critique**.[4]

We saw one example of the Lucas critique in Chapter 11 when we discussed the role of rational expectations in the cost of reducing inflation. Traditional estimates of the sacrifice ratio—the percentage points of GDP that must be forgone to reduce inflation by 1 percentage point—rely on the assumption of adaptive expectations. That is, they assume that expected inflation depends on past inflation. Advocates of the rational-expectations approach claim that reducing inflation can be much less costly because expectations will respond directly to a credible change in policy. In other words, they claim that traditional estimates of the sacrifice ratio are unreliable because they are subject to the Lucas critique.

We will encounter another example of the Lucas critique in our study of the consumption function in Chapter 15. We will learn that economists have sometimes made very inaccurate predictions concerning how consumers respond to changes in personal-income tax rates. This is because analysts have ignored the effect of the government's policies on consumers' expectations. In Chapter

---

[4] Robert E. Lucas, Jr., "Econometric Policy Evaluation: A Critique," *Carnegie Rochester Conference on Public Policy* 1 (Amsterdam: North-Holland Publishing Company, 1976), 19–46; reprinted in Robert E. Lucas, Jr., *Studies in Business Cycle Theory* (Cambridge, Mass.: MIT Press, 1981).

15, we see how economists have learned to respect the Lucas critique by modifying their theory of consumer behaviour.

The Historical Record

In judging whether government policy should play an active or passive role in the economy, we must give some weight to the historical record. If the economy has experienced many large shocks to aggregate supply and aggregate demand, and if policy has successfully insulated the economy from these shocks, then the case for active policy would be clear. Conversely, if the economy has experienced few large shocks, and if the fluctuations we have observed can be traced to inept economic policy, then the case for passive policy would be clear. In other words, our view of stabilization policy should be influenced by whether policy has historically been stabilizing or destabilizing. For this reason, the debate over macroeconomic policy frequently turns into a debate over macroeconomic history.

Yet history does not settle the debate over stabilization policy. Disagreements over history arise because it is not easy to identify the sources of economic fluctuations. The historical record often permits more than one interpretation.

The Great Depression is a case in point. Economists' views on macroeconomic policy are often related to their views on the cause of the Depression. Some economists believe that a large contractionary shock to private spending caused the Depression. They assert that policymakers should have responded by stimulating aggregate demand. Other economists believe that the large fall in the money supply in the United States caused the Depression. They assert that the Depression would have been avoided if the U.S. central bank, the Fed, had been pursuing a passive monetary policy of increasing the money supply at a steady rate. Hence, depending on one's beliefs about its cause, the Great Depression can be viewed as an example either of why active monetary and fiscal policy is necessary, or of why it is dangerous.

CASE STUDY

12•3 Is the Stabilization of the Economy a Figment of the Data?

Keynes wrote *The General Theory* in the 1930s, and in the wake of the Keynesian revolution, governments around the world began to view economic stabilization as a primary responsibility. Some economists believe that the development of Keynesian theory has had a profound influence on the behaviour of the economy. Comparing data from before World War I and after World War II, they find that real GDP and unemployment have become much more stable. (Notice how the wiggles in the real GDP per-capita graph (Figure 1-1 in Chapter 1) are less pronounced after World War II.) This, some Keynesians claim, is the best argument for active stabilization policy: it has worked.

In a series of provocative and influential papers, Christina Romer has challenged this assessment of the historical record. She argues that the measured reduction in volatility reflects not an improvement in economic policy and performance but rather an improvement in the economic data. The older data are much less accurate than the newer data. Romer claims that the higher volatility of unemployment and real GDP that has been reported for the United States for the period before World War I is largely a figment of the data.

Romer uses various techniques to make her case. One is to try to construct more accurate data for the earlier period. This task is difficult because data sources are not readily available. A second way is to try to construct *less* accurate data for the recent period—that is, data that are comparable to the older data and thus suffer from the same imperfections. After constructing new "bad" data, Romer finds that the recent period appears much more volatile—indeed, almost as volatile as the early period—suggesting that the volatility of the early period may be largely an artifact of data construction.

Romer's work is an important part of the continuing debate over whether macroeconomic policy has improved the performance of the economy. Although her work remains controversial, most economists now believe that the economy is only slightly more stable than it was in the past.[5]

12•2 Should Policy Be Conducted by Rule or by Discretion?

A second topic of debate among economists is whether economic policy should be conducted by rule or by discretion. Policy is conducted by rule if policymakers announce in advance how policy will respond to various situations and commit themselves to following through on this announcement. Policy is conducted by discretion if policymakers are free to size up the situation case by case and choose whatever policy seems appropriate at the time.

The debate over rules versus discretion is distinct from the debate over passive versus active policy. Policy can be conducted by a rule and yet be either passive or active. For example, a passive policy rule might specify steady growth in the money supply of 3 percent per year. An active policy rule might specify that

$$\text{Money Growth} = 3\% + (\text{Unemployment Rate} - 8.5\%).$$

Under this rule, the money supply grows at 3 percent if the unemployment rate is 8.5 percent, but for every percentage point the unemployment rate exceeds 8.5 percent, money growth increases by an extra percentage point. This rule tries to stabilize the economy by raising money growth when the economy is in a recession (when unemployment exceeds the natural rate).

We begin this section by discussing the reasons that policy might be improved by a commitment to a fixed policy rule. We then examine several possible policy rules.

[5] Christina D. Romer, "Spurious Volatility in Historical Unemployment Data," *Journal of Political Economy* 94 (February 1986): 1–37; Christina D. Romer, "Is the Stabilization of the Postwar Economy a Figment of the Data?" *American Economic Review* 76 (June 1986): 314–334.

Distrust of Policymakers and the Political Process

Some economists believe that economic policy is too important to be left to the discretion of policymakers. Although this view is more political than economic, evaluating it is central to how we judge the role of economic policy. If politicians are incompetent or opportunistic, then we may not want to give them the discretion to use the powerful tools of monetary and fiscal policy.

Incompetence in economic policy arises for several reasons. Some economists view the political process as erratic, perhaps because it reflects the shifting power of special interest groups. In addition, macroeconomics is complicated, and politicians often do not have sufficient knowledge of it to make informed judgments. This ignorance allows charlatans to propose incorrect but superficially appealing solutions to complex problems. The political process often cannot weed out the advice of charlatans from that of competent economists.

Opportunism in economic policy arises when the objectives of policymakers conflict with the well-being of the public. Some economists fear that politicians use macroeconomic policy to further their own electoral ends. If citizens vote on the basis of economic conditions prevailing at the time of the election, then politicians have an incentive to pursue policies that will make the economy look good during election years. A new government might cause a recession soon after coming into office in order to lower inflation and then stimulate the economy as the next election approaches to lower unemployment; this would ensure that both inflation and unemployment are low on election day. Manipulation of the economy for electoral gain, called the political business cycle, has been the subject of extensive research by economists and political scientists.[6]

Politicians have not fully abided by the principles set out in the 1945 *White Paper* on income and employment. We noted earlier that this statement of government intent involved the government's increasing the national debt during recessions, by having spending exceed taxes when the economy might benefit from stimulation. Most politicians like this message—it excuses budget deficits. Indeed, it is based on the proposition that running a deficit *is* the responsible policy in some instances. But many politicians seem to have ignored a later section of the *White Paper*, in which it is clearly stated that "in periods of buoyant employment and income, budget plans will call for surpluses." If this part of the *White Paper*'s advice had been heeded, then Canadians would have witnessed budget surpluses as often as budget deficits. The result would have been no long-run increase in the national debt.

Distrust of the political process leads some economists to advocate placing economic policy outside the realm of politics. Some have proposed constitutional amendments, such as a balanced-budget amendment, that would tie the hands of legislators and insulate the economy from both incompetence and opportunism.

---

[6] William Nordhaus, "The Political Business Cycle," *Review of Economic Studies* 42 (1975): 169–190; Edward Tufte, *Political Control of the Economy* (Princeton, N. J.: Princeton University Press, 1978).

The Time Inconsistency of Discretionary Policy

If we assume that we can trust our policymakers, discretion at first glance appears superior to a fixed policy rule. Discretionary policy is, by its nature, flexible. As long as policymakers are intelligent and benevolent, there might appear to be little reason to deny them flexibility in responding to changing conditions.

Yet a case for rules over discretion arises from the problem of **time inconsistency** of policy. In some situations policymakers may want to announce in advance the policy they will follow in order to influence the expectations of private decisionmakers. But later, after the private decisionmakers have acted on the basis of their expectations, these policymakers may be tempted to renege on their announcement. Understanding that policymakers may be inconsistent over time, private decisionmakers are led to distrust policy announcements. In this situation, to make their announcements credible, policymakers may want to make a commitment to a fixed policy rule.

Time inconsistency is illustrated most simply in an example involving not economics but politics—specifically, public policy about negotiating with terrorists over the release of hostages. The announced policy of most nations is that they will not negotiate over hostages. Such an announcement is intended to deter terrorists: if there is nothing to be gained from kidnapping hostages, rational terrorists won't kidnap any. In other words, the purpose of the announcement is to influence the expectations of terrorists and thereby their behaviour.

But, in fact, unless the policymakers are credibly committed to the policy, the announcement has little effect. Terrorists know that once hostages are taken, the temptation to make some concession to obtain their release can be overwhelming. The only way to deter rational terrorists is somehow to take away the discretion of policymakers and commit them to a rule of never negotiating. If policymakers were truly unable to make concessions, the incentive for terrorists to take hostages would be largely eliminated.

The same problem arises less dramatically in the conduct of monetary policy. Consider the dilemma of a central bank that cares about both inflation and unemployment. According to the Phillips curve, the tradeoff between inflation and unemployment depends on expected inflation. The Bank of Canada would prefer everyone to expect low inflation so that it will face a favourable tradeoff. To reduce expected inflation, the Bank of Canada often announces that low inflation is the paramount goal of monetary policy.

But an announcement of a policy of low inflation is by itself not credible. Once expectations are formed, the Bank of Canada has an incentive to renege on its announcement in order to reduce unemployment. Private economic actors understand the incentive to renege and therefore do not believe the announcement in the first place. Just as a government leader facing a hostage crisis is sorely tempted to negotiate their release, a central bank with discretion is sorely tempted to inflate in order to reduce unemployment. And just as terrorists discount announced policies of never negotiating, private economic actors discount announced policies of low inflation.

The surprising implication of this analysis is that policymakers can sometimes better achieve their goals by having their discretion taken away from them. In the case of rational terrorists, there will be fewer hostages taken and fewer hostages killed if policymakers are committed to following the seemingly harsh rule of refusing to negotiate for hostages' freedom. In the case of monetary policy, there will be lower inflation without higher unemployment if the Bank of Canada is committed to a policy of zero inflation.

The time inconsistency of policy arises in many other contexts. Here are some examples:

- To encourage investment, the government announces that it will not tax income from capital. But after the capital is in place, the government is tempted to renege on its promise because the taxation of existing capital does not distort economic incentives. (Individuals will not destroy existing capital just to avoid taxes.)

- To encourage research, the government announces that it will give a temporary monopoly to companies that discover new drugs. But after a drug has been discovered, the government is tempted to revoke the patent or to regulate the price in order to make the drug more affordable.

- To encourage good behaviour, a parent announces that he or she will punish a child whenever the child breaks a rule. But after the child has misbehaved, the parent is tempted to forgive this transgression, because punishment is unpleasant for the parent as well as the child.

- To encourage you to work hard, your professor announces that this course will end with an exam. But after you have studied and learned all the material, the professor is tempted to cancel the exam so that he or she won't have to grade it.

In each of these cases, rational agents understand the incentive for the policymaker to renege, and this expectation affects their behaviour. And in each case, the solution is to take away the policymaker's discretion with a commitment to a fixed policy rule.[7]

CASE STUDY

12•4 Alexander Hamilton versus Time Inconsistency

Time inconsistency has long been a problem associated with discretionary policy. In fact, it was one of the first problems that confronted Alexander Hamilton when President George Washington appointed him the first U.S. Secretary of the Treasury in 1789.

---

[7] The appendix to this chapter examines more analytically the time-inconsistency problem in monetary policy. For more on time inconsistency, see Finn E. Kydland and Edward C. Prescott, "Rules Rather Than Discretion: The Inconsistency of Optimal Plans," *Journal of Political Economy* 85 (June 1977): 473–492; and Robert J. Barro and David Gordon, "A Positive Theory of Monetary Policy in a Natural Rate Model," *Journal of Political Economy* 91 (August 1983): 589–610.

Hamilton faced the question of how to deal with the debts that the new nation had accumulated as it fought for its independence from Britain. When the revolutionary government incurred the debts, it promised to honour them when the war was over. But after the war, many Americans advocated defaulting on the debt because repaying the creditors would require taxation, which is always costly and unpopular.

Hamilton opposed the time inconsistent policy of repudiating the debt. He knew that the nation would likely need to borrow again sometime in the future. In his *First Report on the Public Credit*, which he presented to the U.S. Congress in 1790, he wrote

> If the maintenance of public credit, then, be truly so important, the next inquiry which suggests itself is: By what means is it to be effected? The ready answer to which question is, by good faith; by a punctual performance of contracts. States, like individuals, who observe their engagements are respected and trusted, while the reverse is the fate of those who pursue an opposite conduct.

Thus, Hamilton proposed that the nation make a commitment to the policy rule of honouring its debts.

The policy rule that Hamilton originally proposed has continued for over two centuries. Today, unlike in Hamilton's time, when most governments debate spending priorities, people do not propose defaulting on the public debt. However, there have been exceptions. For example, the provinces of Alberta and Saskatchewan defaulted on their debts in the 1930s, and several developing countries were forgiven part of their international debts in the 1980s. Nevertheless, these exceptions represent extreme situations in which alternative actions were extraordinarily difficult. In the case of public debt, almost everyone now agrees that the government should be committed to a fixed policy rule.

Rules for Monetary Policy

Even if we are convinced that policy rules are superior to discretion, the debate over macroeconomic policy is not over. If the Bank of Canada were to commit to a rule for monetary policy, what rule should it choose? Let's discuss briefly three policy rules that various economists advocate.

Some economists, called **monetarists**, advocate that the Bank of Canada keep the money supply growing at a steady rate. The quotation at the beginning of this chapter from Milton Friedman—the most famous monetarist—exemplifies this view of monetary policy. Monetarists believe that fluctuations in the money supply are responsible for most large fluctuations in the economy. They argue that slow and steady growth in the money supply would yield stable output, employment, and prices.

Although a monetarist policy rule might have prevented many of the economic fluctuations we have experienced historically, most economists believe that it is not the best possible policy rule. Steady growth in the money supply stabilizes aggregate demand only if the velocity of money is stable. But the

356 The Economy in the Short Run

variations in velocity in the 1980s, which we discussed in Chapter 8, show that velocity is sometimes unpredictable. Most economists believe that a policy rule needs to allow the money supply to adjust to various shocks to the economy.

A second policy rule that economists widely advocate is a nominal GDP target. Under this rule, the Bank of Canada announces a planned path for nominal GDP. If nominal GDP rises above the target, the Bank of Canada reduces money growth to dampen aggregate demand. If it falls below the target, the Bank of Canada raises money growth to stimulate aggregate demand. Since a nominal GDP target allows monetary policy to adjust to changes in the velocity of money, most economists believe it would lead to greater stability in output and prices than a monetarist policy rule.

A third policy rule that is often advocated is a target for the price level. Under this rule, the Bank of Canada announces a planned path for the price level and adjusts the money supply when the actual price level deviates from the target. Proponents of this rule usually believe that price stability should be the primary goal of monetary policy.

Notice that all these rules are expressed in terms of some nominal variable—the money supply, nominal GDP, or the price level. One can also imagine policy rules expressed in terms of real variables. For example, the Bank of Canada might try to target the unemployment rate at 5 percent. The problem with such a rule is that no one knows exactly what the natural rate of unemployment is. If the Bank of Canada chose a target for the unemployment rate below the natural rate, the result would be accelerating inflation (as was explained in Chapter 11). Conversely, if the Bank of Canada chose a target for the unemployment rate above the natural rate, the result would be accelerating deflation. For this reason, economists rarely advocate rules for monetary policy expressed solely in terms of real variables, even though real variables such as unemployment and real GDP are among the best measures of economic performance.

Rules for Fiscal Policy

Although most discussion of policy rules centers on monetary policy, economists and politicians also frequently propose rules for fiscal policy. The rule that has received the most attention is the balanced-budget rule. Under a balanced-budget rule, the government would not be allowed to spend more than it receives in tax revenue. In the United States, many state governments operate under such a fiscal policy rule, since state constitutions often require a balanced budget. A recurring topic of political debate in the United States is whether the constitution should require a balanced budget for the federal government. The Canadian debate focuses on whether both federal and provincial governments should adopt such a rule. In the early 1990s, both Alberta and New Brunswick took steps in this direction.

Most economists oppose a strict rule requiring the government to balance its budget. Three considerations lead them to believe that a budget deficit or surplus is sometimes appropriate.

First, a budget deficit or surplus can help stabilize the economy. In essence, a balanced-budget rule would revoke the automatic stabilizing powers of the system of taxes and transfers. When the economy goes into a recession, taxes automatically fall, and transfers automatically rise. While these automatic responses help stabilize the economy, they push the budget into deficit. A strict balanced-budget rule would require that the government raise taxes or reduce spending in a recession, which would further depress aggregate demand.

Second, a budget deficit or surplus can be used to minimize the distortion of incentives caused by the tax system. High tax rates impose a cost on society by discouraging economic activity. The higher the tax rates, the greater the social cost of taxes. The total social cost of taxes is minimized by keeping tax rates relatively stable, rather than making them high in some years and low in others. Economists call this policy *tax smoothing*. To keep tax rates smooth, a deficit is necessary in years of unusually low income (recessions) and unusually high expenditure (wars).

Third, a budget deficit can be used to shift a tax burden from current to future generations. For example, some economists argue that if the current generation fights a war to maintain freedom, future generations benefit. To make the future beneficiaries pay some of the costs, the current generation can finance the war with a budget deficit. The government can retire the debt issued during the war by levying taxes on the next generation.

These considerations lead most economists to reject a strict balanced-budget rule. At the very least, a rule for fiscal policy needs to take account of the recurring episodes, such as recessions and wars, during which a budget deficit is a reasonable policy response. Nevertheless, if the government runs a deficit much more frequently than it runs a surplus, the national debt grows. Chapter 16 is devoted to examining this problem.

CASE STUDY

12•5 The Bank of Canada's Low-Inflation Target: Implications for Fiscal Policy

In an effort to acquire credibility as an inflation-fighter, the Bank of Canada has repeatedly emphasized since 1987 that its *sole* target is zero inflation. In 1994, in an attempt to show its support for a slightly more flexible form of this commitment, the federal government published its (and the Bank's) inflation target for the next 5 years—that the annual rise in the CPI stay within the 1–3 percent range.

The Bank of Canada continues to argue that reducing unemployment is *not* part of what it sees as its mandate. Many Canadians are critical of the Bank's taking this narrow view; they want the Bank of Canada to care about unemployment, too. Some of those criticizing the Bank of Canada ignore the fact that the Bank officials are not strict monetarists, and that, by pursuing an inflation rate close to zero, the Bank of Canada *will automatically help to stabilize employment*. We are now in a position to appreciate this important implication of the Bank of Canada's monetary rule.

Consider a decrease in aggregate demand, as shown in panel (a) of Figure 12-2. If the Bank of Canada holds the money supply constant, the economy moves from point A to point B in the short run, and a recession occurs. But

Figure 12-2

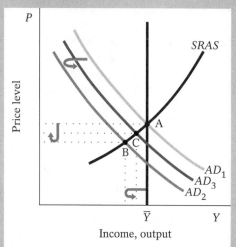

(a) A Shift in Aggregate Demand

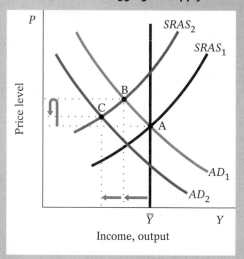

(b) A Shift in Aggregate Supply

A decrease in aggregate demand (from AD_1 to AD_2) is automatically resisted by the Bank of Canada if it adopts a zero-inflation target; the money supply must be increased (moving aggregate demand from AD_2 to

AD_3) to resist the change in prices. The employment effects of a decrease in aggregate supply (from $SRAS_1$ to $SRAS_2$) are accentuated by the Bank of Canada's attempt to limit price changes.

some deflation in prices occurs as well, and this evokes an automatic reaction from the Bank of Canada if it has adopted a zero-inflation target instead of a constant money supply rule. To implement a zero-inflation target, the Bank of Canada must increase the money supply whenever there is a downward pressure on the price level (as shown in panel (a) of Figure 12-2). Even if the Bank does not fully accomplish its goal, the result is that the aggregate demand curve shifts somewhat back to the right. The economy ends up at point C, and the magnitude of the recession is reduced. Thus, as far as aggregate demand disturbances are concerned, inflation targeting involves the very built-in stabilization feature that many Bank of Canada critics want the economy to have. So the Bank of Canada *does* care about unemployment, even if indirectly.

One way of interpreting this analysis is to say that inflation targeting makes fiscal policy multipliers smaller than they would otherwise be. Inflation targeting reduces the importance of both the undesired shifts in the aggregate demand curve *and* the shifts that are deliberately planned by fiscal policy. So a high degree of built-in stability involves good news and bad. The good news is that unforeseen events have a limited effect on unemployment; the bad news is that demand policies that are intended to lower unemployment by shifting aggregate demand to the right have limited effects as well.

In Chapter 10, we noted that the numerical estimates of fiscal policy multipliers from macroeconometric models have been falling in recent years. We can now appreciate another reason why this trend in estimated multiplier values is not something we should find surprising. The Bank of Canada has switched from money-growth targeting to inflation targeting.

What about aggregate supply shocks? The effects of a leftward shift in the aggregate supply curve is shown in panel (b) of Figure 12-2. If the Bank of Canada holds the money supply constant in the face of this event, the economy moves from point A to point B. Again, a recession occurs, but in this case, it is accompanied by inflation, not deflation. If the Bank of Canada adopts a zero-inflation target, it must decrease the money supply in an attempt to reduce the upward pressure on prices. With this response accounted for, the economy moves to point C instead of point B, and the magnitude of the recession is made larger by monetary policy. Thus, inflation targeting is *de*stabilizing in the face of supply-side shocks.

Since the Bank of Canada's critics are concerned about limiting the losses in Canadian output and employment, our analysis suggests that they must be expecting supply shocks to be more prominent than demand shocks. However, it is likely that leftward shifts in the aggregate demand curve will be the dominant influence in the next several years. With deficit reduction being the primary focus of fiscal policy, spending cuts and tax increases will be pushing the aggregate demand curve to the left in a rather big way. If these initiatives are the dominant macroeconomic events, it will be fortunate for Canada that the Bank of Canada has adopted an inflation target. By adopting this target, the Bank of Canada has forced itself to limit the short-run costs involved in deficit reduction.

12•3 Conclusion: Making Policy in an Uncertain World

In this chapter we have examined whether policy should take an active or passive role in responding to economic fluctuations and whether policy should be conducted by rule or by discretion. There are many arguments on both sides of these questions. Perhaps the only clear conclusion is that there is no simple and compelling case for any particular view of macroeconomic policy. In the end, you must weigh the various arguments, both economic and political, and decide for yourself what kind of role the government should play in trying to stabilize the economy.

For better or worse, economists play a key role in the formulation of economic policy. Because the economy is complex, this role is often difficult. Yet it is also inevitable. Economists cannot sit back and wait until our knowledge of the economy has been perfected before giving advice. In the meantime, someone must advise economic policymakers. That job, difficult as it sometimes is, falls to economists.

The role of economists in the policymaking process goes beyond giving advice to policymakers. Even economists cloistered in academia influence policy indirectly through their research and writing. In the conclusion of *The General Theory*, John Maynard Keynes wrote that

> . . . the ideas of economists and political philosophers, both when they are right and when they are wrong, are more powerful than is commonly understood. Indeed, the world is ruled by little else. Practical men, who believe themselves to be quite exempt from intellectual influences, are usually the slaves of some defunct economist. Madmen in authority, who hear voices in the air, are distilling their frenzy from some academic scribbler of a few years back.

This is as true today as it was when Keynes wrote it in 1935—except now that academic scribbler is often Keynes himself.

Summary

1. Advocates of active policy view the economy as subject to frequent shocks that will lead to inefficient fluctuations in output and employment unless monetary or fiscal policy responds. Many believe that economic policy has been successful in stabilizing the economy.

2. Advocates of passive policy argue that because monetary and fiscal policies work with long and variable lags, attempts to stabilize the economy are likely to end up being destabilizing. In addition, they believe that our present understanding of the economy is too limited to be useful in formulating successful stabilization policy and that inept policy is a frequent source of economic fluctuations.

3. Advocates of discretionary policy argue that discretion gives more flexibility to policymakers in responding to various unforeseen situations.

4. Advocates of policy rules argue that the political process cannot be trusted. They believe that politicians make frequent mistakes in conducting economic policy and sometimes use economic policy for their own political ends. In addition, advocates of policy rules argue that a commitment to a fixed policy rule is necessary to solve the problem of time inconsistency.

KEY CONCEPTS

Inside lag

Outside lag

Automatic stabilizers

Index of leading indicators

Lucas critique

Time inconsistency

Monetarists

QUESTIONS FOR REVIEW

1. What are the inside lag and the outside lag? Which has the longer inside lag—monetary or fiscal policy? Which has the longer outside lag? Why?

2. Why would more accurate economic forecasting make it easier for policymakers to stabilize the economy? Describe two ways economists try to forecast developments in the economy.

3. Describe the Lucas critique.

4. Why is macroeconomic history important for macroeconomic policy?

5. What is meant by the "time inconsistency" of economic policy? Why might policymakers be tempted to renege on an announcement they made earlier? In this situation, what is the advantage of a policy rule?

6. List three policy rules that the Bank of Canada might follow. Which of these would you advocate? Why?

7. Give three reasons why requiring a balanced budget might be too restrictive a rule for fiscal policy.

PROBLEMS AND APPLICATIONS

1. Suppose that the tradeoff between unemployment and inflation is determined by the Phillips curve:

$$u = u^n - \alpha(\pi - \pi^e),$$

where u denotes the unemployment rate, u^n the natural rate, π the rate of inflation, and π^e the expected rate of inflation. In addition, suppose that the country involves two parties, the Left and the Right. Suppose that the Left party always follows a policy of high money growth, and the Right party always follows a policy of low money growth. What "political business cycle" pattern of inflation and unemployment would you predict if

   a. every five years one of the parties took control based on a random flip of a coin?

   b. the two parties took turns?

2. When cities pass laws limiting the rent landlords can charge on apartments, the laws usually apply to existing buildings and exempt buildings not yet built. Advocates of rent control argue that this exemption ensures that rent control does not discourage the construction of new housing. Evaluate this argument in light of the time-inconsistency problem.

3. The *cyclically adjusted budget deficit* is the budget deficit corrected for the effects of the business cycle. In other words, it is the budget deficit that the government would be running if unemployment were at the natural rate. (It is also called the *full-employment budget deficit.*) Some economists have proposed the rule that the cyclically adjusted budget deficit always be balanced. Compare this proposal to a strict balanced-budget rule. Which is preferable? What problems do you see with the rule requiring a balanced cyclically adjusted budget?

Time Inconsistency and the Tradeoff Between Inflation and Unemployment

In this appendix, we examine more analytically the time-inconsistency argument for rules rather than discretion. This material is relegated to an appendix because we will need to use some calculus.

Suppose that the Phillips curve describes the relationship between inflation and unemployment. Letting u denote the unemployment rate, u^n the natural rate of unemployment, π the rate of inflation, and π^e the expected rate of inflation, unemployment is determined by

$$u = u^n - \alpha(\pi - \pi^e).$$

Unemployment is low when inflation exceeds expected inflation and high when inflation falls below expected inflation.

For simplicity, suppose also that the Bank of Canada chooses the rate of inflation. Of course, more realistically, the Bank of Canada controls inflation only imperfectly through its control of the money supply. But for the purposes of illustration, it is useful to assume that the Bank of Canada can control inflation perfectly.

The Bank of Canada likes low unemployment and low inflation. Suppose that the cost of unemployment and inflation, as perceived by the Bank of Canada, can be represented as

$$L(u, \pi) = u + \gamma\pi^2,$$

where the parameter γ represents how much the Bank of Canada dislikes inflation relative to unemployment. $L(u, \pi)$ is called the *loss function*; according to this relationship the Bank dislikes unemployment and *both* positive and negative values of inflation. The Bank of Canada's objective is to make the loss as small as possible.

Having specified how the economy works and the Bank of Canada's objective, let's compare monetary policy made under a fixed rule and under discretion.

First, consider policy under a fixed rule. A rule commits the Bank of Canada to a particular level of inflation. As long as private agents understand that the Bank of Canada is committed to this rule, the expected level of inflation will be the level the Bank of Canada is committed to produce. Since expected inflation equals actual inflation ($\pi^e = \pi$), unemployment will be at its natural rate ($u = u^n$).

What is the optimal rule? Since unemployment is at its natural rate regardless of the level of inflation legislated by the rule, there is no benefit to having any inflation at all. Therefore, the optimal fixed rule requires that the Bank of Canada produce zero inflation.

Second, consider discretionary monetary policy. Under discretion, the economy works as follows:

1. Private agents form their expectations of inflation π^e.

2. The Bank of Canada chooses the actual level of inflation π.

3. Based on expected and actual inflation, unemployment is determined.

Under this arrangement, the Bank of Canada minimizes its loss $L(u, \pi)$ subject to the constraint that the Phillips curve imposes. When making its decision about the rate of inflation, the Bank of Canada takes expected inflation as already determined.

To find what outcome we would obtain under discretionary policy, we must examine what level of inflation the Bank of Canada would choose. By substituting the Phillips curve into the Bank of Canada's loss function we obtain

$$L(u, \pi) = u^n - \alpha(\pi - \pi^e) + \gamma\pi^2.$$

Notice that the Bank of Canada's loss is negatively related to unexpected inflation (the second term) and positively related to actual inflation (the third term). To find the level of inflation that minimizes this loss, differentiate with respect to π to obtain

$$dL/d\pi = -\alpha + 2\gamma\pi.$$

The loss is minimized when this derivative equals zero. This implies that

$$\pi = \alpha/(2\gamma).$$

Whatever level of inflation private agents expected, this is the "optimal" level of inflation for the Bank of Canada to choose. Of course, rational private agents understand the objective of the Bank of Canada and the constraint that the Phillips curve imposes. They therefore expect that the Bank of Canada will choose this level of inflation. Expected inflation equals actual inflation [$\pi^e = \pi = \alpha/(2\gamma)$], and unemployment equals its natural rate ($u = u^n$).

Now compare the outcome under optimal discretion to the outcome under the optimal rule. In both cases, unemployment is at its natural rate. Yet discretionary policy produces more inflation than does policy under the rule. Thus, optimal discretion is worse than the optimal rule, even though the Bank of Canada under discretion was attempting to minimize its loss $L(u, \pi)$.

At first it may seem bizarre that the Bank of Canada can achieve a better outcome by being committed to a fixed rule. Why can't the Bank of Canada with discretion mimic its behaviour when committed to a zero-inflation rule? The answer is that the Bank of Canada is playing a game against private decisionmakers who have rational expectations. Without being committed to a fixed rule of zero inflation, the Bank of Canada is not able to get private agents to expect zero inflation.

Suppose, for example, that the Bank of Canada simply announces that it will follow a zero-inflation policy. Such an announcement by itself cannot be credible. Once expectations of inflation are formed, the Bank of Canada has the incentive to renege on its announcement in order to decrease unemployment. Private agents understand the incentive to renege and therefore do not believe the announcement in the first place.

This theory of monetary policy has an important corollary. Under one circumstance, the Bank of Canada with discretion achieves the same outcome as the Bank of Canada committed to a fixed rule of zero inflation. If the Bank of Canada dislikes inflation much more than it dislikes unemployment (so that γ is very large), inflation under discretion is near zero, since the Bank of Canada has little incentive to inflate. This finding provides some guidance to those who have the job of appointing central bankers. An alternative to imposing a fixed rule is to appoint an individual with a fervent distaste for inflation. Perhaps this is why even liberal politicians who are more concerned about unemployment than inflation often appoint conservative central bankers who are more concerned about inflation.

MORE PROBLEMS AND APPLICATIONS

1. In the 1970s in Canada, the inflation rate and the natural rate of unemployment both rose. Let's use this model of time inconsistency to examine this phenomenon. Assume that policy is discretionary.

a. In the model as developed so far, what happens to the inflation rate when the natural rate of unemployment rises?

b. Let's now change the model slightly by supposing that the Bank of Canada's loss function is quadratic in both inflation and unemployment. That is,

$$L(u, \pi) = u^2 + \gamma\pi^2.$$

Follow steps similar to those in the text to solve for the inflation rate under discretionary policy.

c. Now what happens to the inflation rate when the natural rate of unemployment rises?

d. In 1987, Prime Minister Brian Mulroney's government appointed the conservative central banker John Crow to head the Bank of Canada. According to this model, what should have happened to inflation and unemployment?

The Open Economy in the Short Run

We now extend our analysis of economic fluctuations to include international trade and finance. As we first discussed in Chapter 7, the world's major economies are open. Open economies export some of the goods and services they produce, and they import some of the goods and services they consume. Open economies also borrow and lend in world financial markets.

In this chapter we discuss how open economies behave in the short run. Our primary goal is to understand how monetary and fiscal policies influence aggregate demand in an open economy. The model we develop in this chapter, called the **Mundell-Fleming model**, is an open-economy version of the *IS-LM* system. Both models assume that the price level is fixed and then show what causes fluctuations in aggregate demand. Both also stress the interaction between the goods market and the money market. The key difference is that the *IS-LM* model assumes a closed economy, whereas the Mundell-Fleming model assumes a small open economy. The Mundell-Fleming model introduces the international considerations we discussed in Chapter 7 into the short-run model of national income we developed in Chapters 9 and 10.

One of the lessons of the Mundell-Fleming model is that the behaviour of an economy depends on the exchange-rate system it has adopted. We begin by assuming a floating exchange rate. That is, we assume that the central bank allows the exchange rate to adjust to changing economic conditions. We then examine how the economy operates under a fixed exchange rate, and we discuss the debate over whether exchange rates should be floating or fixed.

13•1 The Mundell-Fleming Model

In this section we build the Mundell-Fleming model.[1] In the following sections we use the model to evaluate the impact of various policies under floating and fixed exchange rates.

---

[1] The Mundell-Fleming model was developed in the early 1960s. Mundell's contributions are collected in Robert A. Mundell, *International Economics* (New York: Macmillan, 1968). For Fleming's contribution, see J. Marcus Fleming, "Domestic Financial Policies Under Fixed and Under Floating Exchange Rates," *IMF Staff Papers* 9 (November 1962): 369–379.

Components of the Model

The Mundell-Fleming model is made up of components that should be familiar to you from previous chapters. We begin by simply stating the three equations that make up the model. They are

$$Y = C(Y - T) + I(r) + G + NX(e) \qquad IS$$
$$M/P = L(r, Y) \qquad LM$$
$$r = r^*.$$

Before putting these equations together to make a short-run model of a small open economy, let's review each of them in turn.

The first equation describes the goods market. It states that aggregate supply Y is equal to aggregate demand—the sum of consumption C, investment I, government purchases G, and net exports NX. Consumption depends positively on disposable income $Y - T$. Investment depends negatively on the interest rate r. Net exports depend negatively on the exchange rate e. Canadian imports depend positively on the level of disposable income, so net exports depend negatively on this variable. For simplicity, we ignore this effect. It is left for the reader (see Problems and Applications item 4 at the end of this chapter) to check that the basic conclusions of this chapter are unaffected by this simplification.

Recall that we define the exchange rate e as the amount of foreign currency per unit of domestic currency—for example, e might be $0.75 (U.S.) per Canadian dollar. For the purposes of the Mundell-Fleming model, we do not need to distinguish between the real and nominal exchange rates. In Chapter 7 we related net exports to the real exchange rate ε, which equals eP/P^*, where P is the domestic price level and P^* is the foreign price level. Because the Mundell-Fleming model assumes that prices are fixed, changes in the real exchange rate are proportional to changes in the nominal exchange rate. That is, when the nominal exchange rate rises, foreign goods become less expensive compared to domestic goods, which depresses exports and stimulates imports.

The second equation describes the money market. It states that the supply of real money balances, M/P, equals the demand, $L(r, Y)$. The demand for real balances depends negatively on the interest rate and positively on overall output. As long as we have a floating exchange rate, the money supply M is an exogenous variable controlled by the central bank. Like the IS-LM model, the Mundell-Fleming model takes the price level P as an exogenous variable, so there is no difference between nominal and real interest rates.

The third equation states that the world interest rate r^* determines the interest rate in this economy. This equation holds because we are examining a small open economy. That is, the economy is sufficiently small relative to the world economy that it can borrow or lend as much as it wants in world financial markets without affecting the world interest rate.

It should be recalled from our discussion in Chapter 7 (in particular from Figure 7-2) that there are deviations of the Canadian interest rate from the world interest rate. One form of departure is a risk premium that depends on such factors as international concern about political instability in Canada (for example, Quebec separation). Political considerations of this sort are ignored in this chapter. Nevertheless, we consider increases in world interest rates which, from the model's point of view, are the same thing as an increase in the Canadian risk premium. The second reason for departures from the $r = r^*$ condition is that it takes some time for international lenders to react to yield differentials (and in doing so, to eliminate them). Thus, we view $r = r^*$ as representing full equilibrium, and we can consider temporary deviations from this full equilibrium while discussing the time sequence involved in the Mundell-Fleming model.

These three equations fully describe the Mundell-Fleming model. Our job is to examine the implications of these equations for short-run fluctuations in a small open economy. If you do not understand the equations, you should review Chapters 7 and 9 before continuing.

The Model on a *Y–r* Graph

One way to depict the Mundell-Fleming model is to use a graph in which income Y is on the horizontal axis and the interest rate r is on the vertical axis. This presentation is comparable to our analysis of the closed economy in the *IS-LM* model. As Figure 13-1 shows, the *IS* curve slopes downward, and the *LM* curve slopes upward. New in this graph is the horizontal line representing the world interest rate.

Two features of this graph deserve special attention. First, because the exchange rate influences the demand for goods, the *IS* curve is drawn for a given value of the exchange rate (say, $0.75 (U.S.) per Canadian dollar). An increase in the exchange rate (say, to $0.90 (U.S.) per Canadian dollar) makes Canadian goods more expensive relative to foreign goods, which reduces net exports. Hence, an increase in the exchange rate shifts the *IS* curve to the left. To remind us that the position of the *IS* curve depends on the exchange rate, the *IS* curve is labeled *IS(e)*.

Figure 13-1

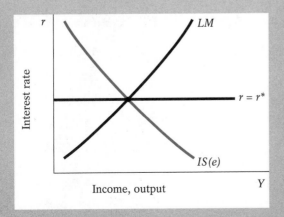

The Mundell-Fleming Model on a *Y – r* Graph This presentation of the Mundell-Fleming model is similar to that of the closed-economy *IS–LM* model. In the small open economy, however, the position of the *IS* curve depends on the exchange rate. The exchange rate adjusts to ensure that the *IS* curve crosses the point where the *LM* curve intersects the horizontal line that represents the world interest rate r^*.

Second, the three curves in Figure 13-1 all intersect at the same point. This might seem an unlikely coincidence. But, in fact, the exchange rate adjusts to ensure that all three curves pass through the same point.

To see why all three curves must intersect at a single point, let's imagine a hypothetical situation in which they did not, as in Figure 13-2(a). Here, the domestic interest rate—the point where the *IS* and *LM* curves intersect—would be higher than the world interest rate. Since Canada would be offering a higher rate of return than is available in world financial markets, investors from around the world would want to buy Canadian financial assets. But first these foreign investors must convert their funds into dollars. In the process, they

Figure 13-2

(a) The Exchange Rate Is Too Low

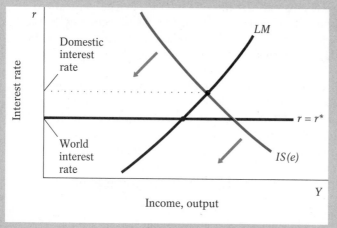

(b) The Exchange Rate Is Too High

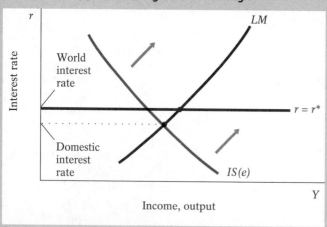

The Mundell-Fleming Model With the Exchange Rate at the Wrong Level. This figure shows why the *IS* curve must intersect at the point at which the *LM* curve and the $r = r^*$ line cross. In Panel (a), because the three curves do not cross at the same point, the domestic interest rate would exceed the world interest rate. Foreign investors would try to invest their funds in Canada. In the process, they would bid up the Canadian dollar and shift the *IS* curve downward. In Panel (b), the domestic interest rate would be less than the world interest rate. Investors would try to invest their funds abroad. In the process, they would sell Canadian dollars, depressing its value. This shifts the *IS* curve upward.

would bid up the value of the Canadian dollar. This rise in the exchange rate would shift the IS curve downward until the domestic interest rate equaled the world interest rate.

Alternatively, imagine that the IS and LM curves intersect at a point where the domestic interest rate is below the world interest rate, as in Figure 13-2(b). Since Canada would be offering a lower rate of return, investors would want to invest in world financial markets. But, to be able to buy foreign financial assets, they must convert their Canadian dollars into foreign currency. In the process of doing so, they would depress the value of the Canadian dollar. The fall in the exchange rate would stimulate Canadian export sales and so shift the IS curve upward until the domestic interest rate equaled the world interest rate.

To sum up, the equilibrium in this graph is found where the LM curve crosses the line representing the world interest rate. The exchange rate then adjusts and shifts the IS curve so that the IS curve crosses this point as well.

The Model on a Y–e Graph

The second way to depict the model is to use a graph in which income is on the horizontal axis and the exchange rate is on the vertical axis, as in Figure 13-3. This graph is drawn holding the interest rate constant at the world interest rate. The two equations in this figure are

$$Y = C(Y - T) + I(r^*) + G + NX(e) \qquad IS^*$$
$$M/P = L(r^*, Y). \qquad LM^*$$

Figure 13-3

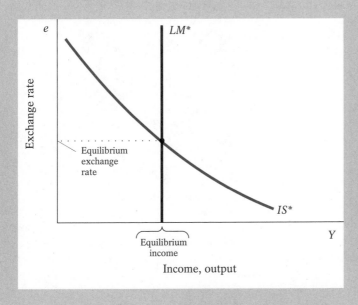

The Mundell-Fleming Model This graph of the Mundell-Fleming model plots the goods-market equilibrium condition IS^* and the money-market equilibrium condition LM^* holding the interest rate constant at the world interest rate. It shows the equilibrium level of income and the equilibrium exchange rate.

We label these curves IS^* and LM^* to remind us that we are holding the interest rate constant at the world interest rate r^*. The equilibrium of the economy is found where the IS^* curve and the LM^* curve intersect. This intersection determines the exchange rate and the level of income.

The LM^* curve is vertical because the exchange rate does not enter into the LM^* equation. Given the world interest rate, the LM^* equation determines aggregate income, regardless of the exchange rate. Figure 13-4 shows how the LM^* curve arises from the world interest rate and the LM curve, which relates the interest rate and income.

Figure 13-4

(a) The *LM* Curve

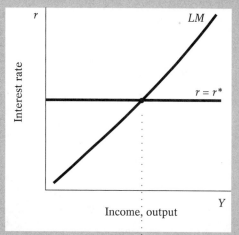

(b) The *LM** Curve

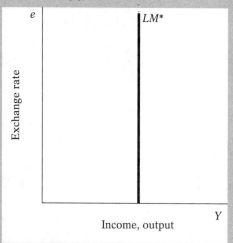

The *LM** Curve Panel (a) shows the standard *LM* curve together with a horizontal line representing the world interest rate r^*. These determine the level of income, regardless of the exchange rate. Therefore, as Panel (b) shows, the *LM** curve is vertical. The higher the level of world interest rates (i.e., the higher the r^* line), the farther to the right the *LM** summary line is.

Figure 13-5

(a) The Net Exports Schedule

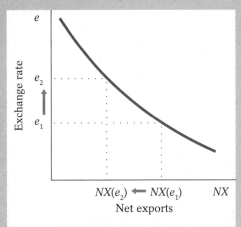

(b) The Keynesian Cross

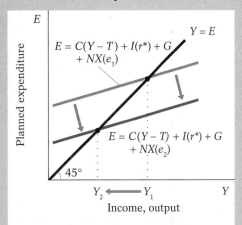

(c) The *IS** Curve

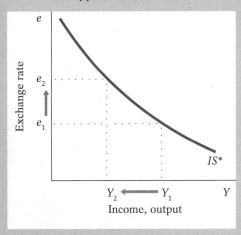

The *IS Curve** The *IS** curve is derived from the net-exports schedule and the Keynesian cross. Panel (a) shows the net-exports schedule: an increase in the exchange rate from e_1 to e_2 lowers net exports from $NX(e_1)$ to $NX(e_2)$. Panel (b) shows the Keynesian cross: a decrease in net exports from $NX(e_1)$ to $NX(e_2)$ reduces income from Y_1 to Y_2. Panel (c) shows the *IS** curve summarizing this relationship between the exchange rate and income: the higher the exchange rate, the lower the level of income.

The *IS** curve slopes downward because a higher exchange rate lowers net exports and thus lowers aggregate income. To show how this works, Figure 13-5 combines the net-exports schedule and the Keynesian cross diagram to derive the *IS** curve. An increase in the Canadian dollar from e_1 to e_2 lowers net exports from $NX(e_1)$ to $NX(e_2)$. The reduction in net exports reduces planned expenditure and thus lowers income. Just as the standard *IS* curve combines the investment schedule and the Keynesian cross, the *IS** curve combines the net-exports schedule and the Keynesian cross.

We can now use this diagram for the Mundell-Fleming model to show how aggregate income Y and the Canadian dollar e respond to changes in policy.

13•2   The Small Open Economy Under Floating Exchange Rates

Before analyzing the impact of policies in an open economy, we must specify the international monetary system in which the country has chosen to operate. We start with the system relevant for most major economies today: **floating exchange rates**. Under floating exchange rates, the exchange rate is allowed to fluctuate freely in response to changing economic conditions.

Fiscal Policy

Suppose that the government stimulates domestic spending by increasing government purchases or by cutting taxes. This expansionary fiscal policy shifts the IS^* curve outward, as in Figure 13-6. The exchange rate rises, and the level of income remains the same.

This conclusion about fiscal policy stands in stark contrast to the conclusion implied by the closed-economy IS-LM model. In a closed economy, a fiscal expansion raises income. In a small open economy with a floating exchange rate, a fiscal expansion leaves income at the same level. The reason for the difference is that, in an open economy, the reduction in national saving due to a fiscal expansion causes net foreign investment to fall and the exchange rate to appreciate.

Figure 13-6

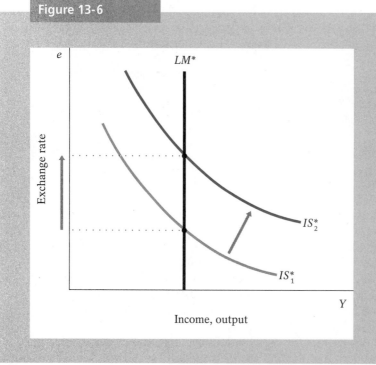

A Fiscal Expansion Under Floating Exchange Rates An increase in government purchases or a decrease in taxes shifts the IS^* curve to the right. This raises the exchange rate but has no effect on income.

The appreciation of the exchange rate reduces net exports, which offsets the expansion in the domestic demand for goods and services.

To better understand the difference between the closed and open economies, consider the equation describing equilibrium in the money market:

$$M/P = L(r, Y).$$

The supply of real money balances M/P is fixed, and the demand must always equal this fixed supply. In a closed economy, a fiscal expansion causes the interest rate to rise, which allows equilibrium income to rise. By contrast, in a small open economy, r is fixed at r^*, so there is only one level of income that can satisfy this equation. Hence, in a small open economy, the appreciation of the exchange rate and the fall in net exports must be exactly large enough to offset fully the expansionary impact of fiscal policy.

Monetary Policy

Suppose now that the Bank of Canada increases the money supply. Because the price level is assumed to be fixed, the increase in the money supply means an increase in real balances. The increase in real balances shifts the LM^* curve to the right, as in Figure 13-7. Hence, an increase in the money supply raises income and lowers the exchange rate.

Figure 13-7

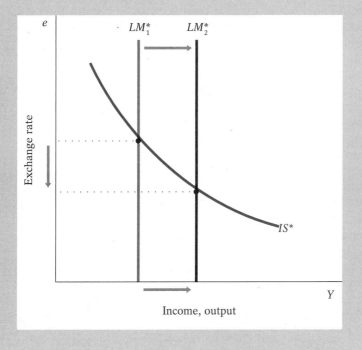

A Monetary Expansion Under Floating Exchange Rates An increase in the money supply shifts the LM^* curve to the right, lowering the exchange rate and raising income.

Although monetary policy influences income in an open economy, as it does in a closed economy, the monetary transmission mechanism is different. Recall that in a closed economy an increase in the money supply lowers the interest rate, which stimulates investment. In a small open economy, the interest rate is fixed by the world interest rate. As soon as an increase in the money supply puts downward pressure on the domestic interest rate, capital flows out of the economy, as investors seek a higher return elsewhere. This capital flow prevents the interest rate from falling, and it causes the domestic currency to depreciate. The fall in the exchange rate makes domestic goods inexpensive relative to foreign goods, which stimulates net exports. Hence, in a small open economy, monetary policy influences income by altering the exchange rate rather than the interest rate.

CASE STUDY

13·1

Tight Monetary Policy Combined With Loose Fiscal Policy

During the late 1980s, Canada experienced a combination of tight monetary policy and loose fiscal policy. The governor of the Bank of Canada, John Crow, was committed to bringing inflation down to zero, and his success earned him quite a reputation among the world central bankers. But both the federal and provincial governments were following an expansionary fiscal policy; their expenditures were far in excess of their tax revenues. Government deficits were increasing at record rates.

The Mundell-Fleming model predicts that both policies would raise the value of the Canadian dollar, and, indeed, Canadian currency did rise. In 1985 one Canadian dollar could be purchased for $0.71 (U.S.), and by 1991 its price had risen to $0.89 (U.S.). This rise in the Canadian dollar made imported goods less expensive, and it made Canadian industries that compete against these foreign sellers less competitive. It is no wonder that this period witnessed a dramatic increase in "cross-border shopping."

Many analysts have noted that it was unfortunate that Canada's monetary-fiscal policy mix during this period was so counterproductive for Canadian firms' gaining a foothold in the U.S. markets following the signing of the Free Trade Agreement in January 1989. At the very time Canadian producers were becoming more competitive in the United States, because of the removal of U.S. tariffs on Canadian exports, these firms were becoming less competitive because of the dramatic rise in the value of the Canadian dollar.

Canada witnessed a similar mix of tight money and loose fiscal policy some 30 years before this most recent situation. John Diefenbaker, Canada's prime minister at the time, was trying to reduce unemployment during the worst postwar recession up to that point by raising government spending and cutting taxes. But James Coyne, the governor of the Bank of Canada, was focused exclusively on keeping the inflation rate close to zero. Thus, Coyne refused to print any new currency to help finance the government's deficit. The result was just what our model predicts. Funds flowed into Canada, and the value of the Canadian dollar increased dramatically. This put a further profit squeeze on Canadian exporting firms, so that as rapidly as the government was creating jobs in the government sector, the rising Canadian dollar was destroying jobs in the exporting and import-competing sectors.

The dispute between the government and the Bank of Canada governor became so bitter during the Coyne affair that the Bank of Canada Act was changed following this incident. Now the governor must resign immediately if he or she is issued a written directive from the minister of finance that directs monetary policy to be other than what the governor thinks is appropriate. Many analysts speculated that a directive might be issued in late 1993, when the Liberal government of Jean Chrétien came to power. The Liberals had campaigned on a platform of expansionary fiscal policy to create jobs, and they had been critical of John Crow's tight monetary policy. But as it turned out, a directive was not necessary, because Crow's seven-year appointment ended in February 1994. The Liberals simply waited out John Crow's tenure and then appointed Gordon Thiesson, Crow's senior deputy governor. This appointment seems to imply that the Liberals intend to control spending, and that they will continue to pursue the government's support of the Bank of Canada's low-inflation policy.

Trade Policy

Suppose that the government reduces the demand for imported goods by imposing an import quota or a tariff. What happens to aggregate income and the exchange rate?

Since net exports equal exports minus imports, a reduction in imports means an increase in net exports. That is, the net-exports schedule shifts outward, as in Figure 13-8. This shift in the net-exports schedule moves the IS^* curve to the right. Hence, the trade restriction raises the exchange rate and has no effect on income.

A stated goal of policies to restrict trade is often to alter the trade balance NX. Yet, as we first saw in Chapter 7, such policies do not necessarily have that effect. The same conclusion holds in the Mundell-Fleming model under floating exchange rates. Recall that

$$NX(e) = Y - C(Y - T) - I(r) - G.$$

Because a trade restriction does not affect income, consumption, investment, or government purchases, it does not affect the trade balance. Although the shift in the net-exports schedule tends to raise NX, the increase in the exchange rate reduces NX by the same amount.

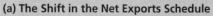

Figure 13-8

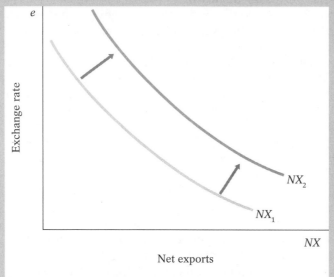

(a) The Shift in the Net Exports Schedule

e (Exchange rate)

NX_2

NX_1

NX

Net exports

A Trade Restriction Under Floating Exchange Rates A tariff or an import quota shifts the net-exports schedule outward. This causes the IS^* curve to shift outward, raising the exchange rate and leaving income unchanged.

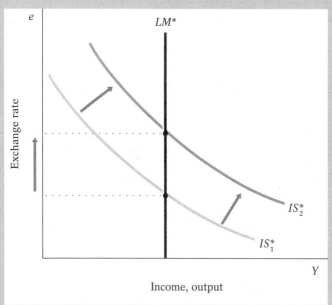

(b) The Change in the Economy's Equilibrium

e (Exchange rate)

LM^*

IS_2^*

IS_1^*

Y

Income, output

Figure 13-9

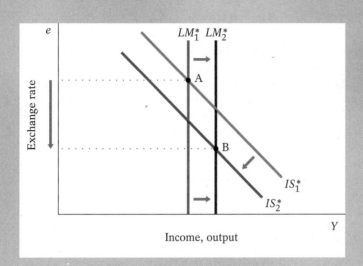

An Increase in World Interest Rates Under Floating Exchange Rates Higher interest rates depress investment spending (which shifts IS* inward) and decrease the demand for money (which shifts LM* outward). The fall in exchange rate raises net exports more than the rise in interest rates lowers investment, so national output increases.

World Interest Rate Changes

Consider an increase in the general level of world interest rates. In the Mundell-Fleming model, this means that Canadian interest rates must rise (as the law of one price operates in the world bond markets). But will this cause a rise or fall in the level of aggregate demand in Canada? Clearly, the higher borrowing cost will depress the investment spending component of aggregate demand, but can the exchange-rate change insulate aggregate demand from this depressing effect of higher interest rates? We now use the model to answer this question.

From Figure 13-4 we know that higher world interest rates cause LM* to shift to the right. Also, since higher interest rates depress firms' investment spending on new plant and equipment, IS* shifts back to the left. These shifts are shown in Figure 13-9, where equilibrium moves from point A to point B. With funds initially leaving the country in pursuit of the high yields available in other parts of the world, the domestic currency depreciates, as shown in Figure 13-9. The model shows that this depreciation in the Canadian dollar must be of such a magnitude that aggregate demand rises. Net exports are stimulated more than investment expenditure is reduced.[2] Thus, one advantage of allowing a floating exchange rate is that we do not have to suffer a recession just because there are increases in either world tariffs or world interest rates.

---

[2] This strong prediction follows from the fact that the exchange rate plays no role in the LM* equation in the Mundell-Fleming model. Some analysts prefer to assume that the price level that is relevant for money demand is an index involving the price of domestically produced goods (which we are taking as fixed in this chapter) and the Canadian dollar price of imports. Imports become less expensive whenever the Canadian dollar appreciates. Thus, a higher value for e lowers the price index P, and so raises the real money supply. The result is that the LM* line has a positive slope, and in this case an increase in world interest rates can cause a recession. This extension of the basic Mundell-Fleming model is considered in Problems and Applications item 6 at the end of this chapter.

13•3 The Small Open Economy Under Fixed Exchange Rates

We now turn to the second type of exchange-rate system: **fixed exchange rates**. In the 1950s and 1960s, most of the world's major economies operated within the Bretton Woods system—an international monetary system under which most governments agreed to fix exchange rates. The world abandoned this system in the early 1970s, and exchange rates were allowed to float freely. Recently, many European countries have reinstated a system of fixed exchange rates among themselves, and some economists have advocated a return to a worldwide system of fixed exchange rates. In this section we discuss how such a system works, and we examine the impact of economic policies on an economy with a fixed exchange rate.

How a Fixed-Exchange-Rate System Works

Under a system of fixed exchange rates, a central bank stands ready to buy or sell the domestic currency for foreign currencies at a predetermined price. Suppose, for example, that the Bank of Canada announced that it was going to fix the exchange rate at $0.75 (U.S.) per dollar. It would then stand ready to give $1 (Canadian) in exchange for $0.75 (U.S.) or to give $0.75 (U.S.) in exchange for $1 (Canadian). To carry out this policy, the Bank of Canada would need a reserve of Canadian dollars (which it can print) and a reserve of U.S. dollars (which it must have accumulated in past transactions).

Fixing the exchange rate dedicates monetary policy to the single goal of keeping the exchange rate at the announced level. In other words, the essence of a fixed-exchange-rate system is the commitment of the central bank to allow the money supply to adjust to whatever level will ensure that the equilibrium exchange rate equals the announced exchange rate. Moreover, as long as the central bank stands ready to buy or sell foreign currency at the fixed exchange rate, the money supply adjusts automatically to the necessary level.

To see how fixing the exchange rate determines the money supply, consider the following example. Suppose that the Bank of Canada announces that it will fix the exchange rate at $0.75 (U.S.) per dollar. But, in the current equilibrium with the current money supply, the exchange rate is $0.85 (U.S.) per dollar, $0.10 (U.S.) above the announced rate. This situation is illustrated in Figure 13-10(a). Notice that there is a profit opportunity: an arbitrageur could buy $85 (U.S.) in the marketplace for $100 (Canadian), and then sell the U.S. dollars to the Bank of Canada for $113 ($85/$0.75), making $13 in profit. When the Bank of Canada buys these U.S. dollars from the arbitrageur, the Canadian dollars it pays automatically increase the money supply. The rise in the money shifts the LM^* curve outward, lowering the equilibrium exchange rate. In this way, the money supply continues to rise until the equilibrium exchange rate falls to the announced level.

Figure 13-10

(a) The Equilibrium Exchange Rate Is Greater Than the Fixed Exchange Rate

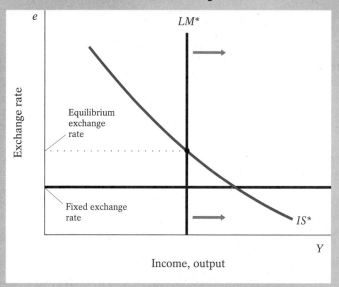

(b) The Equilibrium Exchange Rate Is Less Than the Fixed Exchange Rate

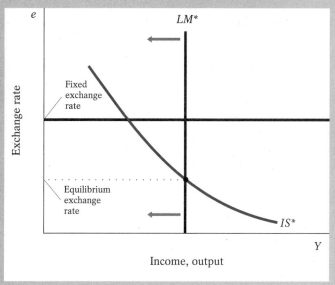

How a Fixed Exchange Rate Governs the Money Supply In Panel (a), the equilibrium exchange rate exceeds the fixed level. Arbitrageurs will buy foreign currency in foreign-exchange markets and sell it to the Bank of Canada for a profit. This process automatically increases the money supply, shifting the LM* curve and lowering the exchange rate. In Panel (b), the equilibrium exchange rate is below the fixed level. Arbitrageurs will buy dollars in foreign-exchange markets and use them to buy foreign exchange from the Bank of Canada. This process automatically reduces the money supply, shifting the LM* curve and raising the exchange rate.

Conversely, suppose that when the Bank of Canada announces that it will fix the exchange rate at $0.85 (U.S.) per dollar, the equilibrium is $1 (U.S.) per $1 (Canadian). Figure 13-10(b) shows this situation. In this case, an arbitrageur could make a profit by buying $85 (U.S.) from the Bank of Canada for $100 (Canadian) and then selling the U.S. dollars in the marketplace for $118 Canadian ($100/$0.85). When the Bank of Canada sells these U.S. dollars, the Canadian dollars it receives are no longer circulating among private transactors, so this policy automatically reduces the money supply. The fall in the money supply shifts the LM^* curve inward, raising the equilibrium exchange rate. The money supply continues to fall until the equilibrium exchange rate rises to the announced level.

CASE STUDY

13·2 The International Gold Standard

During the late nineteenth and early twentieth centuries, most of the world's major economies operated under a gold standard. Each country maintained a reserve of gold and agreed to exchange one unit of its currency for a specified amount of gold. Through the gold standard, the world economies maintained a system of fixed exchange rates.

To see how an international gold standard fixes exchange rates, suppose that the U.S. Treasury stands ready to buy or sell an ounce of gold for $100, and the Bank of England stands ready to buy or sell an ounce of gold for 100 pounds. Together, these policies fix the rate of exchange between dollars and pounds: 1 dollar must trade for 1 pound. Otherwise, the law of one price would be violated, and it would be profitable to buy gold in one country and sell it in the other.

Suppose, for example, that the exchange rate were 2 pounds per dollar. In this case, an arbitrageur could buy 200 pounds for $100, use the pounds to buy 2 ounces of gold from the Bank of England, bring the gold to the United States, and sell it for $200 to the Treasury—making a $100 profit. Moreover, by bringing the gold to the United States from England, the arbitrageur would increase the money supply in the United States and decrease the money supply in England.

Thus, during the era of the gold standard, the international transport of gold by arbitrageurs was an automatic mechanism adjusting money supplies and stabilizing exchange rates. This system did not completely fix exchange rates, because shipping gold across the Atlantic was costly. Yet the international gold standard did keep the exchange rate within a range dictated by transportation costs. It thereby prevented large and persistent movements in exchange rates.[3]

---

[3] For more on how the gold standard worked, see the essays in Barry Eichengreen, ed., *The Gold Standard in Theory and History* (New York: Methuen, 1985).

These examples make clear that fixing the exchange rate requires a commitment on the part of the Bank of Canada to either buy or sell whatever amount of foreign exchange is demanded by private participants in foreign currency markets. Fixing a Canadian dollar price below the free market equilibrium can be done indefinitely, because all the Bank of Canada needs is an unlimited supply of Canadian dollars (which it can print). Nevertheless, this policy is limited by the willingness of Canadians to tolerate the inflation that eventually accompanies rapid growth in the domestic money supply.

Fixing the Canadian dollar at a price below the free market equilibrium, on the other hand, cannot be done indefinitely. This follows from the basic fact that the Bank of Canada cannot print foreign exchange. Private traders know this, and they can easily determine how rapidly the Bank of Canada's reserves of foreign exchange are running out. Canada's balance of payments data record precisely this—the amount by which the country's foreign exchange reserves have been depleted each period. Armed with this information, private traders can readily guess when the Bank of Canada will have to give up fixing the exchange rate at such a high value. It is in this situation that we hear about a "speculative run against the currency" in the media. Once private traders see that a country's currency is about to fall in value, they sell off that currency to avoid the almost certain capital loss. This very action hastens the exchange rate change and verifies the speculators' expectations.

It is important to understand that a fixed-exchange-rate system fixes the nominal exchange rate. Whether it also fixes the real exchange rate depends on the time horizon under consideration. If prices are flexible, as they are in the long run, then the real exchange rate can change even while the nominal exchange rate is fixed. Therefore, in the long run described in Chapter 7, a policy to fix the nominal exchange rate would not influence any real variable, including the real exchange rate. A fixed nominal exchange rate would influence only the money supply and the price level. Yet in the short run described by the Mundell-Fleming model, prices are fixed, so a fixed nominal exchange rate implies a fixed real exchange rate as well.

Fiscal Policy

Let's now examine how economic policies affect a small open economy with a fixed exchange rate. Suppose that the government stimulates domestic spending by increasing government purchases or by cutting taxes. This policy shifts the IS^* curve outward, as in Figure 13-11, putting upward pressure on the exchange rate. But since the money supply adjusts to keep the exchange rate unchanged, the money supply must rise, shifting the LM^* curve outward. In contrast to the situation under floating exchange rates, a fiscal expansion under fixed exchange rates raises aggregate income. The rise in income occurs because a fiscal expansion under a fixed-exchange-rate system causes an automatic monetary expansion.

Figure 13-11

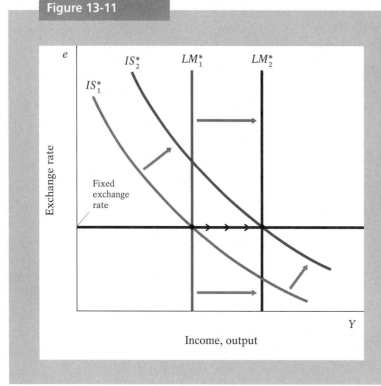

A Fiscal Expansion Under Fixed Exchange Rates A fiscal expansion shifts the IS^* curve to the right. To maintain the fixed exchange rate, the Bank of Canada must increase the money supply and shift the LM^* curve to the right as well. Hence, in contrast to the case of floating exchange rates, under fixed exchange rates a fiscal expansion raises income.

Monetary Policy

What happens if the Bank of Canada tries to increase the money supply—for example, by buying bonds from the public? The initial impact of this policy is to shift the LM^* curve outward, lowering the exchange rate, as in Figure 13-12. But, since the Bank of Canada is committed to buying and selling foreign currency at a fixed exchange rate, arbitrageurs quickly sell dollars to the Bank of Canada, causing the money supply and the LM^* curve to return to their initial positions. Hence, monetary policy as usually conducted is ineffectual under a fixed exchange rate. By agreeing to fix the exchange rate, the Bank of Canada gives up its control over the money supply.

A country with a fixed exchange rate can, however, conduct a type of monetary policy: it can decide to change the level at which the exchange rate is fixed. A reduction in the value of the currency is called a **devaluation**, and an increase in its value is called a **revaluation**. In the Mundell-Fleming model, a devaluation shifts the fixed-exchange-rate line down and the LM^* curve outward; it acts like an increase in the money supply under a floating exchange rate. A devaluation thus expands net exports and raises aggregate income. Conversely, a revaluation shifts the fixed-exchange-rate line up and the LM^* curve inward, thereby reducing net exports and lowering aggregate income.

Figure 13-12

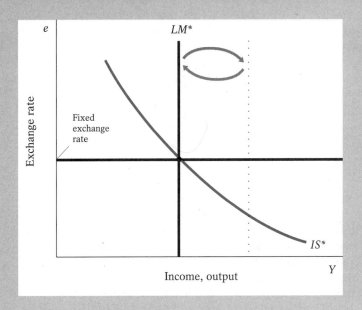

A Monetary Expansion Under Fixed Exchange Rates If the Bank of Canada tries to increase the money supply—for example, by buying bonds from the public—it will put downward pressure on the exchange rate. To maintain the fixed exchange rate, the money supply and *LM** curve must return to their initial positions. Hence, under fixed exchange rates, normal monetary policy is ineffectual.

CASE STUDY

13·3   Devaluation and the Recovery From the Great Depression

The Great Depression of the 1930s was a global event. Although events in the United States may have precipitated the downturn for many other western countries like Canada, all of the world's major economies experienced huge declines in production and employment. Yet not all governments responded to this calamity in the same way.

One key difference among governments was how committed they were to the fixed exchange rate set by the international gold standard. Some countries, such as France, Germany, Italy, and the Netherlands, maintained the old rate of exchange between gold and currency. Other countries, such as Denmark, Finland, Norway, Sweden, and the United Kingdom, reduced the amount of gold they would pay for each unit of currency by about 50 percent. By reducing the gold content of their currencies, these governments devalued their currencies relative to those of other countries.

The subsequent experience of these two groups of countries conforms to the prediction of the Mundell-Fleming model. Those countries that pursued a policy of devaluation recovered quickly from the Depression. The lower value of the currency raised the money supply, stimulated exports, and expanded production. By contrast, those countries that maintained the old exchange rate suffered longer with a depressed level of economic activity.[4]

[4] Barry Eichengreen and Jeffrey Sachs, "Exchange Rates and Economic Recovery in the 1930s," *Journal of Economic History* 45 (December 1985): 925–946.

Because of this successful experience with devaluation, several analysts have called for a shift to fixed exchange rates, with a noticeable devaluation initially, for Canada in the 1990s. The idea is to get the stimulation that this policy can provide in order to help counteract any negative effect on aggregate demand that may follow the contractionary fiscal policies involved in deficit reduction. Those who disagree with this suggestion fear that wages and prices are far more prone to increase in the face of devaluation today than they were during the Great Depression of the 1930s.

Trade Policy

Suppose that the government reduces imports by imposing an import quota or a tariff. This policy shifts the net-exports schedule outward and thus shifts the IS^* curve outward, as in Figure 13-13. The shift in the IS^* curve tends to raise the exchange rate. To keep the exchange rate at the fixed level, the money supply must rise, shifting the LM^* curve outward.

The result of a trade restriction under a fixed exchange rate is very different from that under a floating exchange rate. Under a fixed exchange rate, a trade restriction raises aggregate income. Moreover, the trade restriction also raises net exports NX. Because the exchange rate is fixed, an outward shift in

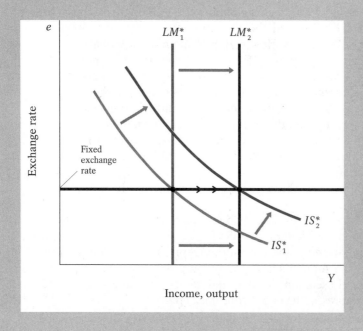

Figure 13-13

A Trade Restriction Under Fixed Exchange Rates A tariff or an import quota imposed by the domestic government shifts the IS^* curve outward. This induces an increase in the money supply to maintain the fixed exchange rate. Hence, aggregate income increases.

the net-exports schedule implies an increase in net exports. To see this result another way, recall that

$$NX = S - I.$$

The expansion in income leads to an increase in saving, which implies an increase in net exports.

This analysis can be used to consider tariffs levied by foreigners as well. In that case, our net exports are reduced so the shifts in IS^* and LM^* are to the left, instead of to the right, as they were in Figure 13-13. In contrast to the floating exchange rate case, then, Canada must suffer a recession following the imposition of foreign trade restrictions, if the exchange rate is fixed.

World Interest Rate Changes

The analysis of foreign interest rate increases under fixed exchange rates is similar to that for trade restrictions imposed by other countries. Higher interest rates lower investment spending by firms, so IS^* shifts to the left for this reason, rather than because of a reduction in net exports. However, whatever causes the aggregate demand curve to shift is insignificant. IS^* and LM^* still shift to the left to keep the exchange rate fixed. (Again, just picture Figure 13-13 running in reverse.) Thus, Canada must suffer a recession following an increase in world interest rates, if the exchange rate is fixed.

This same analysis applies to small open economies in Europe that have maintained fixed exchange rates with one another. In the early 1990s, German reunification meant a big increase in government spending to improve conditions in the former East Germany. Given the commitment to low inflation on the part of the German central bank, this spending led to higher German interest rates. Our model shows that the only way that the other European countries could avoid a recession as a result the changes happening in Germany was to shift away from fixed exchange rates. This is exactly what happened in 1992.

Summary of the Mundell-Fleming Model

The most important lesson of the Mundell-Fleming model is that the effect of almost any domestic policy or world event on a small open economy depends on whether the exchange rate is floating or fixed. Table 13-1 summarizes our analysis of the effects of monetary, fiscal, and trade policies, and world interest rate changes on income and the exchange rate. It also shows the effect of these policies on the trade balance. What is most striking is that all of the results are different under floating and fixed exchange rates.

To be more specific, the Mundell-Fleming model shows that the power of monetary and fiscal policy to influence aggregate income depends on the exchange-rate regime. Under floating exchange rates, only monetary policy can affect income. The usual expansionary impact of fiscal policy is offset by a rise in the value of the currency. Under fixed exchange rates, only fiscal policy can affect income. The normal potency of monetary policy is lost because the money supply is dedicated to maintaining the exchange rate at the announced level.

Table 13-1

The Mundell-Fleming Model: Summary of Policy Effects and the Impact of Events in the Rest of the World

	Exchange-Rate Regime					
	Floating			Fixed		
	Impact on:					
Policy/World Event	Y	e	NX	Y	e	NX
Fiscal Expansion	0	↑	↓	↑	0	0
Monetary Expansion	↑	↓	↑	0	0	0
Import Restriction	0	↑	0	↑	0	↑
Export Restriction	0	↓	0	↓	0	↓
Higher Interest Rates	↑	↓	↑	↓	0	0

Note: This table shows the direction of impact of various economic policies on income Y, the exchange rate e, and the trade balance NX. A "↑" indicates that the variable increases; a "↓" indicates that it decreases; a "0" indicates no effect. Remember that the exchange rate is defined as the amount of foreign currency per unit of domestic currency (for example, $0.75 (U.S.)/Canadian dollar).

CASE STUDY

13·4 Regional Tensions Within Canada

The Mundell-Fleming model can be used to help explain why regional tensions increased in Canada during the late 1980s. At that time, the Ontario government was running an expansionary fiscal policy. We now know that the overall impact of such a policy (throughout the country) has no effect on aggregate demand. Instead it creates a higher Canadian dollar, which forces net exports to be reduced by the same amount as government spending is increased. But consider the distribution of these two effects within the country.

The increase in the government spending component of aggregate demand is concentrated entirely within Ontario whereas the crowding out of preexisting net export demand is felt in all provinces. The result is that demand in Ontario is increased, while that in the rest of the country is decreased. The two effects add up to zero as far as overall demand in the entire country is concerned. Thus, fiscal policy *does* work under floating exchange rates after all, but only from one province's point of view. Ontario can reduce its unemployment problem, but *only* by worsening the same problem for the other regions!

13·4 Should Exchange Rates Be Floating or Fixed?

Having analyzed how an economy works under floating and fixed exchange rates, we turn to the question of which exchange-rate regime is preferable. The international monetary system is often a topic of heated debate among international economists and policymakers. Historically, most economists have favoured a system of floating exchange rates. Yet, in recent years, some have advocated a return to fixed exchange rates.

The primary argument for a floating exchange rate is that it allows monetary policy to be used for other purposes. Under fixed rates, monetary policy is committed to the single goal of maintaining the exchange rate at its announced level. Yet the exchange rate is only one macroeconomic variable among many that monetary policy can influence and about which policymakers are concerned. A system of floating exchange rates leaves monetary policymakers free to pursue other goals, such as stabilizing employment or prices.

Advocates of fixed exchange rates argue that exchange-rate uncertainty makes international trade more difficult. After the world abandoned the Bretton Woods system of fixed exchange rates in the early 1970s, both real and nominal exchange rates became more volatile than anyone had expected. Some economists attribute this volatility to irrational and destabilizing speculation by international investors. Business executives often claim that this volatility is harmful because it increases the uncertainty associated with international business transactions. Yet, despite this exchange-rate volatility, the amount of world trade has continued to rise under floating exchange rates.

Furthermore, foreign exchange crises have often occurred under fixed-exchange-rate regimes. As noted earlier, when a central bank fixes a value for the domestic currency that is above the equilibrium level, it must buy its own currency to maintain its price. In order to buy its own currency, it must sell foreign exchange. Because private traders can observe both the central bank's balance sheet (to see the current size of the country's foreign exchange reserves) and the balance of payments (to see the amount by which the foreign exchange stock is falling), they have all the information needed to speculate against the currency. This speculation forces a foreign exchange crisis.

Advocates of fixed exchange rates sometimes argue that a commitment to a fixed exchange rate is one way to discipline the monetary authority and prevent excessive growth in the money supply. Yet there are many other policy rules to which the central bank could be committed. A policy of fixing the exchange rate should be compared to the policy rules we discussed in Chapter 11, such as targeting nominal GDP or the price level. Fixing the exchange rate has the advantage of being simpler to implement than some other policy rules, since the money supply adjusts automatically, but this policy can lead to greater instability in income and employment.

In Canada's case, fixing the exchange rate means having the same monetary policy as the United States. It is easiest to see this by considering the definition of the real exchange rate, eP/P^*. Trade flows cannot remain in long-run equilibrium unless the real exchange rate is constant. Since a fixed exchange rate means that e is constant, a constant real exchange rate requires that the percentage changes in P and P^* be the same—that is, that we have the same inflation rate as that of our major trading partner. For many years, Canadians did not want as rapid an inflation rate as that occurring in the United States, so there was widespread support for a floating exchange rate. However, since the late 1980s, the Bank of Canada has become more ambitious about fighting inflation, and some Canadians (who were against this policy) now favour a fixed-exchange-rate policy (to force Canadian monetary policy to become somewhat more expansionary, as it has been in the United States).

In the end, the choice between floating and fixed rates is not as stark as it may seem at first. During periods of fixed exchange rates, countries can change the value of their currency if maintaining the exchange rate conflicts too severely with other goals. During periods of floating exchange rates, countries often use formal or informal targets for the exchange rate when deciding whether to expand or contract the money supply. We rarely observe exchange rates that are completely fixed or completely floating. Instead, under both systems, stability of the exchange rate is usually one among many of the central bank's objectives.

CASE STUDY

13·5 **The European Monetary System**

Since 1979, most European countries have participated in the *European Monetary System* (*EMS*). The goal of the EMS is to limit fluctuations in the exchange rates among the member countries. Relative to currencies not included in the EMS, such as the U.S. dollar, these European currencies fluctuate together. An organization of countries like the EMS is called an **exchange-rate union**.

The EMS does not completely fix exchange rates. The central banks of the member countries allow their exchange rates to fluctuate within bands around specific targets. The exchange rate can float as long as it remains inside the band. But when the exchange rate approaches its upper or lower limit, the intention is that the central bank must intervene in the market for foreign exchange. That is, the central bank must adjust the money supply to keep the exchange rate within its band. Thus, members of the EMS lose some of their ability to conduct independent monetary policy.

When maintaining the targets appears to be causing other economic problems, the targets can be changed. Such a change is called a *realignment*. One of the goals of the EMS is to make realignments less necessary by coordinating monetary and fiscal policies among member countries. Eventually, if such coordination is successful, the EMS may be the first step toward *monetary union*—a single currency for all of Europe. As noted above, however, such events as the reunification of Germany force the monetary and fiscal policies of the member countries to diverge. This divergence has stalled the move toward European monetary union.

13·5 The Mundell-Fleming Model With a Changing Price Level

So far we have been using the Mundell-Fleming model to study the small open economy in the short run when the price level is fixed. To see how this model relates to models we have considered previously, let's consider what happens when the price level changes.

Figure 13-14

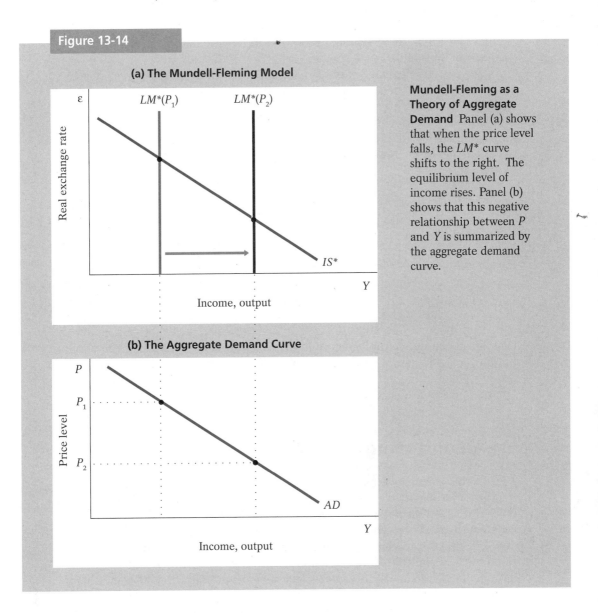

(a) The Mundell-Fleming Model

Real exchange rate (ε) / Income, output (Y)

$LM^*(P_1)$ $LM^*(P_2)$ IS^*

(b) The Aggregate Demand Curve

Price level (P) / Income, output (Y)

P_1 P_2 AD

Mundell-Fleming as a Theory of Aggregate Demand Panel (a) shows that when the price level falls, the LM^* curve shifts to the right. The equilibrium level of income rises. Panel (b) shows that this negative relationship between P and Y is summarized by the aggregate demand curve.

To examine price adjustment in an open economy, we must distinguish between the nominal exchange rate e and the real exchange rate ε, which equals eP/P^*. We can write the Mundell-Fleming model as

$$Y = C(Y - T) + I(r^*) + G + NX(\varepsilon) \qquad IS^*$$
$$M/P = L(r^*, Y). \qquad LM^*$$

These equations should be familiar. The first equation describes the IS^* curve, and the second equation describes the LM^* curve. Note that net exports depend on the real exchange rate.

Figure 13-14 shows what happens when the price level falls. Because a lower price level implies a higher level of real money balances, the LM^* curve shifts to the right, as in Figure 13-14(a). The real exchange rate depreciates, and the equilibrium level of income rises.

The aggregate demand curve summarizes this negative relationship between the price level and the level of income, as shown in Figure 13-14(b). Thus, the aggregate demand curve implied by the Mundell-Fleming model is similar to that implied by the *IS-LM* model. Policies that raise income in the Mundell-Fleming model shift the aggregate demand curve to the right; policies that lower income in the Mundell-Fleming model shift the aggregate demand curve to the left.

We can use this diagram to show how the short-run model in this chapter is related to the long-run model in Chapter 7. Figure 13-15 shows the short-run and long-run equilibria. Point K describes the short-run equilibrium, because it assumes a fixed price level. At this equilibrium, the demand for goods and services is too low to keep the economy producing at its natural rate. Over time, low demand causes the price level to fall. The fall in the price level raises real money balances, which shifts the LM^* curve outward. The real exchange rate depreciates, which stimulates net exports. Eventually, the economy reaches point C, which is the long-run equilibrium.

Both point K and point C are of interest. Point K, the short-run equilibrium, has been our central concern in this chapter. Point C, the long-run equilibrium, was our central concern in Chapter 7. The speed of transition between the short-run and long-run equilibria depends on how quickly the price level adjusts to restore the economy to the natural rate.

13·6   A Concluding Reminder

In this chapter we have examined how a small open economy works in the short run when prices are sticky. We have seen how monetary and fiscal policy influence income and the exchange rate, and how the behaviour of the economy depends on whether the exchange rate is floating or fixed. We have also seen that this model is very relevant for Canada. But, in closing, it is worth repeating a lesson from Chapter 7. Many countries, such as the United States, have neither closed economies nor small open economies: they lie somewhere in between.

A large open economy like the United States combines the behaviour of a closed economy and the behaviour of a small open economy. When analyzing policies in a large open economy, we need to consider both the closed-economy logic of Chapter 10 and the open-economy logic developed in this chapter. The appendix to this chapter presents a model for the intermediate case of a large open economy. The results of that model are, as one would guess, a mixture of the two polar cases we have already examined.

Figure 13-15

(a) The Mundell-Fleming Model

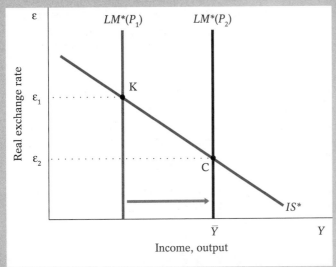

The Short-Run and Long-Run Equilibria in a Small Open Economy Point K shows the equilibrium under the Keynesian assumption that the price level is fixed at P_1. Point C shows the equilibrium under the classical assumption that the price level adjusts to maintain income at its natural rate $\bar{Y}$.

(b) The Model of Aggregate Supply and Aggregate Demand

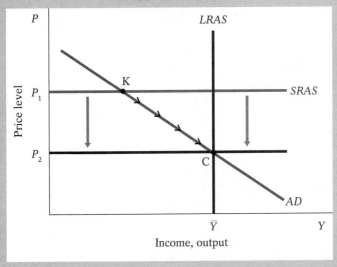

To see how we can draw on the logic of both the closed and small open economies and apply these insights to the United States, consider how a monetary contraction affects the economy in the short run. In a closed economy, a monetary contraction raises the interest rate, lowers investment, and thus lowers aggregate income. In a small open economy with a floating exchange rate, a monetary contraction raises the exchange rate, lowers net exports, and thus lowers aggregate income. The interest rate is unaffected, however, because it is determined by world financial markets.

The U.S. economy contains elements of both cases. Because the United States is large enough to affect the world interest rate and because capital is not perfectly mobile across countries, a monetary contraction does raise the interest rate and depress investment. At the same time, a monetary contraction also raises the value of the U.S. dollar, thereby depressing net exports. Hence, although the Mundell-Fleming model does not precisely describe an economy like that of the United States, it does predict correctly what happens to international variables such as the exchange rate, and it shows how international interactions alter the effects of monetary and fiscal policies.

Summary

1. The Mundell-Fleming model is the *IS-LM* model for a small open economy. It takes the price level as given and then shows what causes fluctuations in income and the exchange rate.

2. The Mundell-Fleming model shows that fiscal policy does not influence aggregate income under floating exchange rates. A fiscal expansion causes the currency to appreciate, which reduces net exports and offsets the usual expansionary impact on aggregate income. Fiscal policy does influence aggregate income under fixed exchange rates.

3. The Mundell-Fleming model shows that monetary policy does not influence aggregate income under fixed exchange rates. Any attempt to expand the money supply is futile, because the money supply must adjust to ensure that the exchange rate stays at its announced level. Monetary policy does influence aggregate income under floating exchange rates.

4. There are advantages to both floating and fixed exchange rates. Floating exchange rates leave monetary policymakers free to pursue objectives other than exchange-rate stability, and they provide insulation from foreign shocks. Fixed exchange rates reduce some of the uncertainty in international business transactions, and they remove the negative spillover effects to other regions of the country that result from provincial-level fiscal policies that are undertaken with a flexible exchange rate.

KEY CONCEPTS

Mundell-Fleming model

Floating exchange rates

Fixed exchange rates

Devaluation

Revaluation

Exchange-rate union

QUESTIONS FOR REVIEW

1. In the Mundell-Fleming model with floating exchange rates, explain what happens to aggregate income, the exchange rate, and the trade balance when taxes are raised. What would happen if exchange rates were fixed rather than floating?

2. In the Mundell-Fleming model with floating exchange rates, explain what happens to aggregate income, the exchange rate, and the trade balance when the money supply is reduced. What would happen if exchange rates were fixed rather than floating?

3. In the Mundell-Fleming model with floating exchange rates, explain what happens to aggregate income, the exchange rate, and the trade balance when foreign countries impose import quotas. What would happen if exchange rates were fixed rather than floating?

4. What are the advantages of floating exchange rates and fixed exchange rates?

PROBLEMS AND APPLICATIONS

1. Use the Mundell-Fleming model to predict what would happen to aggregate income, the exchange rate, and the trade balance under both floating and fixed exchange rates in response to each of the following shocks:

a. A fall in consumer confidence about the future induces consumers to spend less and save more.

b. The introduction of a stylish line of Toyotas makes some consumers prefer foreign cars over domestic cars.

c. The introduction of automatic teller machines reduces the demand for money.

2. The Mundell-Fleming model takes the world interest rate r^* as an exogenous variable. Consider what happens when this variable changes.

a. What might cause the world interest rate to rise?

b. In the Mundell-Fleming model with a floating exchange rate, what happens to aggregate income, the exchange rate, and the trade balance when the world interest rate rises?

c. In the Mundell-Fleming model with a fixed exchange rate, what happens to aggregate income, the exchange rate, and the trade balance when the world interest rate rises?

3. Business executives and policymakers are often concerned about the "competitiveness" of Canadian industry (the abil-

ity of Canadian industries to sell their goods profitably in world markets).

a. How would a change in the exchange rate affect competitiveness?

b. Suppose you wanted to make domestic industries more competitive but did not want to alter aggregate income. According to the Mundell-Fleming model, what combination of monetary and fiscal policies should you pursue?

4. Suppose that higher income implies higher imports and thus lower net exports. That is, the net exports function is

$$NX = NX(e, Y).$$

Examine the effects in a small open economy of a fiscal expansion on income and the trade balance under

a. a floating exchange rate.

b. a fixed exchange rate.

How does your answer compare to those given in Table 13-1?

5. Suppose that money demand depends on consumption rather than on income, so that the equation for the money market becomes

$$M/P = L[r, C(Y - T)].$$

Analyze the impact of a tax cut in a small open economy on the exchange rate and income under both floating and fixed exchange rates.

6. Suppose that the price level relevant for money demand includes the price of imported goods and that the price of imported goods depends on the exchange rate. That is, the money market is described by

$$M/P = L(r, Y),$$

where

$$P = \lambda P_d + (1 - \lambda)P_f/e.$$

The parameter λ is the share of domestic goods in the price index P. Assume the price of domestic goods P_d and the price of foreign goods measured in foreign currency P_f are fixed.

a. Explain why in this model the LM^* curve is upward sloping rather than vertical.

b. What is the impact of expansionary fiscal policy under floating exchange rates in this model? Explain. Contrast with the standard Mundell-Fleming model.

c. The effect of the exchange rate on the price level is sometimes called an "endogenous supply shock." Why might it be called this?

7. Use the Mundell-Fleming model to answer the following questions about the province of Alberta (a small open economy).

a. If Alberta suffers from a recession, should the provincial government use monetary or fiscal policy to stimulate employment? Explain. (*Note*: For this question, assume that the provinicial government can print dollar bills.)

b. If Alberta prohibited the import of machines from Ontario, what would happen to output, the exchange rate, and the trade balance? Consider both the short-run and the long-run impacts.

A Short-Run Model of the Large Open Economy

When analyzing policies in an economy such as the United States, we need to combine the closed-economy logic of the *IS-LM* model and the small-open-economy logic of the Mundell-Fleming model. In this appendix we present a model for the intermediate case of a large open economy.

As we discussed in the appendix to Chapter 7, a large open economy differs from a small open economy because its interest rate is not fixed by world financial markets. In a large open economy, we must consider the relationship between the interest rate and net foreign investment. Net foreign investment is the amount that domestic investors lend abroad minus the amount that foreign investors lend here. As the domestic interest rate falls, domestic investors find foreign lending more attractive, and foreign investors find lending here less attractive. Thus, net foreign investment is negatively related to the interest rate. Here we add this relationship to our short-run model of national income.

The three equations of the model are

$$Y = C(Y - T) + I(r) + G + NX(e)$$
$$M/P = L(r, Y)$$
$$NX(e) = NFI(r).$$

The first two equations are the same as those used in the Mundell-Fleming model of this chapter. The third equation, taken from the appendix to Chapter 7, states that the trade balance *NX* equals net foreign investment *NFI* and that net foreign investment depends on the domestic interest rate.

To see what this model implies, substitute the third equation into the first, so the model becomes

$$Y = C(Y - T) + I(r) + G + NFI(r) \qquad IS$$
$$M/P = L(r, Y). \qquad\qquad\qquad\qquad LM$$

These two equations are much like the two equations of the closed-economy *IS-LM* model. The only difference is that expenditure now depends on the interest rate for two reasons. As before, a higher interest rate implies lower investment. But now, a higher interest rate also implies lower net foreign investment and thus lower net exports.

To analyze this model, we can use the three graphs in Figure 13-16. Panel (a) shows the *IS-LM* diagram. As in the closed-economy model in Chapters 9 and 10, the interest rate r is on the vertical axis, and income Y is on the horizontal axis. The *IS* and *LM* curves together determine the equilibrium level of income and the equilibrium interest rate.

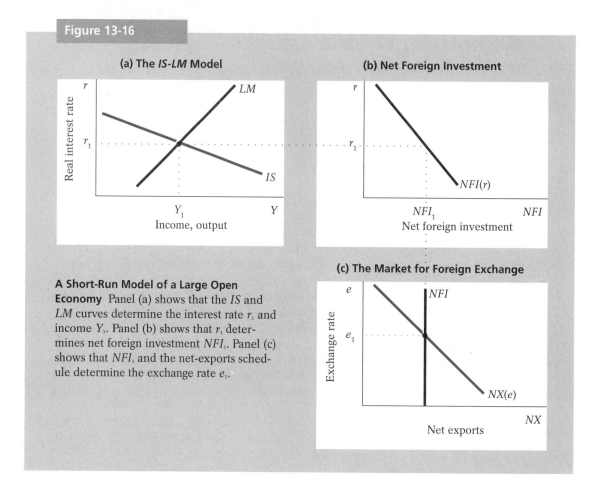

Figure 13-16

(a) The *IS-LM* Model

(b) Net Foreign Investment

(c) The Market for Foreign Exchange

A Short-Run Model of a Large Open Economy Panel (a) shows that the *IS* and *LM* curves determine the interest rate r_1 and income Y_1. Panel (b) shows that r_1 determines net foreign investment NFI_1. Panel (c) shows that NFI_1 and the net-exports schedule determine the exchange rate e_1.

The new net-foreign-investment term in the *IS* equation, $NFI(r)$, makes this *IS* curve flatter than it would be in a closed economy. The more responsive that net foreign investment is to the interest rate, the flatter the *IS* curve is. You might recall from the Chapter 7 appendix that the small open economy represents the extreme case in which net foreign investment is infinitely elastic at the world interest rate. In this extreme case, the *IS* curve is completely flat. Hence, a small open economy would be depicted in this figure with a horizontal *IS* curve.[5]

Panels (b) and (c) show how the equilibrium from the *IS-LM* model determines net foreign investment, the trade balance, and the exchange rate. In Panel (b) we see that the interest rate determines net foreign investment. This curve slopes downward because a higher interest rate discourages domestic in-

---

[5] A word of warning: Do not confuse the *IS* curve used here in Figure 13-16(a) with the *IS* curve used in Figure 13-1. In Figure 13-1, the *IS* curve is graphed holding the exchange rate and net exports *constant*. By contrast in Figure 13-16(a), the *IS* curve is graphed using the condition *NX* (*e*) = *NFI* (*r*), which implies that net exports and the exchange rate vary as the interest rate changes. Since this *IS* curve is not drawn for a given exchange rate, changes in the exchange rate do not shift it.

vestors from lending abroad and encourages foreign investors to lend here. In Panel (c) we see that the exchange rate adjusts to ensure that net exports of goods and services equal net foreign investment.

Now let's use this model to examine the impact of various policies. We assume that the economy has a floating exchange rate, since this assumption is correct for most large open economies such as the United States.

Fiscal Policy

Figure 13-17 examines the impact of a fiscal expansion. An increase in government purchases or a cut in taxes shifts the *IS* curve outward. As Panel (a) illustrates, this shift in the *IS* curve leads to an increase in the level of income and an increase in the interest rate. These two effects are similar to those in a closed economy.

Figure 13-17

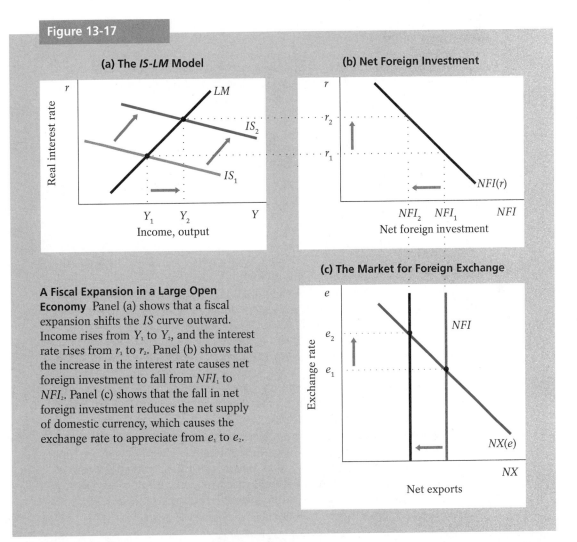

(a) The *IS-LM* Model

(b) Net Foreign Investment

(c) The Market for Foreign Exchange

A Fiscal Expansion in a Large Open Economy Panel (a) shows that a fiscal expansion shifts the *IS* curve outward. Income rises from Y_1 to Y_2, and the interest rate rises from r_1 to r_2. Panel (b) shows that the increase in the interest rate causes net foreign investment to fall from NFI_1 to NFI_2. Panel (c) shows that the fall in net foreign investment reduces the net supply of domestic currency, which causes the exchange rate to appreciate from e_1 to e_2.

Yet, in the large open economy, the higher interest rate reduces net foreign investment, as in Panel (b). The fall in net foreign investment reduces the supply of dollars in the market for foreign exchange. The exchange rate appreciates, as in Panel (c). Because domestic goods become more expensive relative to foreign goods, net exports fall.

Figure 13-17 shows that a fiscal expansion does raise income in the large open economy, unlike in a small open economy under a floating exchange rate. The impact on income, however, is smaller than in a closed economy. In a closed economy, the expansionary impact of fiscal policy is mitigated by the crowding out of investment: as the interest rate rises, investment falls, reducing the fiscal-policy multipliers. In a large open economy, there is yet another mitigating factor: as the interest rate rises, net foreign investment falls, the exchange rate appreciates, and net exports fall. Together these effects are not large enough to make fiscal policy powerless, as it is in a small open economy, but they do reduce fiscal policy's impact.

Monetary Policy

Figure 13-18 examines the impact of a monetary expansion. An increase in the money supply shifts the *LM* curve outward, as in Panel (a). The level of income rises, and the interest rate falls. Once again, these effects are similar to those in a closed economy.

Yet, as Panel (b) shows, the lower interest rate leads to higher net foreign investment. The increase in *NFI* raises the supply of domestic currency in the market for foreign exchange. The exchange rate depreciates, as in Panel (c). As domestic goods become cheaper relative to foreign goods, net exports rise.

A Rule of Thumb

This model of the large open economy describes well the U.S. economy today. Yet it is somewhat more complicated and cumbersome than the model of the closed economy we studied in Chapters 9 and 10 and the model of the small open economy we developed in this chapter. Fortunately, there is a useful rule of thumb to help you determine how policies influence a large open economy without remembering all the details of the model: *The large open economy is an average of the closed economy and the small open economy. To find how any policy will affect any variable, find the answer in the two extreme cases and take an average.*

For example, how does a monetary contraction affect the interest rate and investment in the short run? In a closed economy, the interest rate rises and investment falls. In a small open economy, neither the interest rate nor investment changes. The effect in the large open economy is an average of these two cases: a monetary contraction raises the interest rate and reduces investment, but only somewhat. The fall in net foreign investment mitigates the rise in the interest rate and the fall in investment that would occur in a closed economy. But unlike in a small open economy, the international flow of capital is not so strong as to negate fully these effects.

Figure 13-18

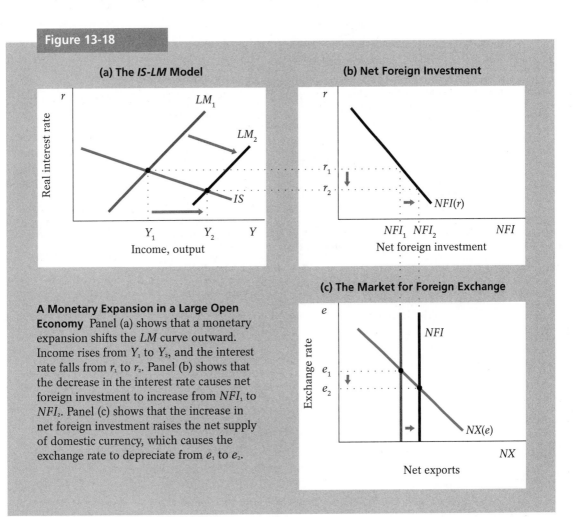

(a) The *IS-LM* Model

r — Real interest rate

LM_1

LM_2

IS

Y_1 Y_2 *Y*

Income, output

(b) Net Foreign Investment

r

r_1

r_2

$NFI(r)$

NFI_1 NFI_2 *NFI*

Net foreign investment

A Monetary Expansion in a Large Open Economy Panel (a) shows that a monetary expansion shifts the *LM* curve outward. Income rises from Y_1 to Y_2, and the interest rate falls from r_1 to r_2. Panel (b) shows that the decrease in the interest rate causes net foreign investment to increase from NFI_1 to NFI_2. Panel (c) shows that the increase in net foreign investment raises the net supply of domestic currency, which causes the exchange rate to depreciate from e_1 to e_2.

(c) The Market for Foreign Exchange

e — Exchange rate

NFI

e_1

e_2

$NX(e)$

NX

Net exports

This rule of thumb makes the simple models all the more valuable. For example, the Mundell-Fleming model not only describes the policy options for a small open economy like Canada; it also provides part of what is needed to understand the policy options of large economies like the United States.

MORE PROBLEMS AND APPLICATIONS

1. Imagine that you run the central bank in a large open economy. Your goal is to stabilize income. Under your policy, what happens to the money supply, the interest rate, the exchange rate, and the trade balance in response to each of the following shocks?

a. The president raises taxes to reduce the budget deficit.

b. The president restricts the import of Japanese cars.

2. Over the past several decades, investors around the world have become

more willing to take advantage of opportunities in other countries. Because of this increasing sophistication, economies are more open today than in the past. Consider how this development affects the ability of monetary policy to influence the economy.

a. If investors become more willing to substitute foreign and domestic assets, what happens to the slope of the *NFI* function?

b. If the *NFI* function changes in this way, what happens to the slope of the *IS* curve?

c. How does this change in the *IS* curve affect the central bank's ability to control the interest rate?

d. How does this change in the *IS* curve affect the central bank's ability to control national income?

3. Suppose that a large open economy has a fixed exchange rate.

a. Describe what happens in response to a fiscal contraction, such as a tax increase. Compare your answer to the case of a small open economy.

b. Describe what happens if the central bank expands the money supply by buying bonds from the public. Compare your answer to the case of a small open economy.

CHAPTER 14

The Theory of Real Business Cycles

What is the best way to explain short-run fluctuations in output and employment? How should policymakers who control monetary and fiscal policy respond to these fluctuations? These are the central questions of short-run macroeconomics. Unfortunately, there is no consensus on the answers.

Most economists endorse the approach taken in the preceding chapters. They believe that the classical model cannot account for economic fluctuations and that, to explain the economy in the short run, we need a model in which prices are sticky.

Others question this judgment. A small but influential group, called the **new classical economists**, believes that we can explain short-run economic fluctuations while maintaining the assumptions of the classical model. They believe that it is best to assume that prices are fully flexible, even in the short run. Almost all microeconomic analysis is based on the premise that prices adjust to clear markets. New classical economists argue that macroeconomic analysis should be grounded on the same assumption.

The leading new classical explanation of economic fluctuations is called the theory of **real business cycles**. According to this theory, the assumptions that we have used to study the long run apply to the short run as well. Most important, real-business-cycle theory holds that the economy obeys the classical dichotomy: nominal variables, such as the money supply and the price level, are assumed not to influence real variables, such as output and employment. To explain fluctuations in real variables, real-business-cycle theory emphasizes real changes in the economy, such as changes in fiscal policy and production technologies. The "real" in real-business-cycle theory refers to the theory's exclusion of nominal variables in explaining economic fluctuations.

In this chapter we examine the theory of real business cycles. Although a complete development of the theory would take many chapters, in this single chapter we can build a simplified model that exhibits the key elements of the approach. We can then discuss the pros and cons of this new classical view of economic fluctuations.

14•1 A Review of the Economy Under Flexible Prices

Although real-business-cycle theory is a new theory of fluctuations, many of the economic relationships we saw in previous chapters appear in it, sometimes with different names attached to them. To build a real-business-cycle model, we begin with the *IS-LM* model, recalling how it works under the assumption that prices are flexible. We then modify it to develop a "real" model of short-run fluctuations.

Recall that the *IS-LM* model describes the economy using the following equations for the goods market and the money market:

$$Y = C(Y - T) + I(r) + G \qquad IS$$
$$M/P = L(r, Y). \qquad LM$$

The first equation states that output Y is the sum of consumption C, investment I, and government purchases G. Consumption depends on disposable income $Y - T$, and investment depends on the real interest rate r. The second equation states that the supply of real money balances M/P equals the demand, which is a function of the interest rate and the level of output. For simplicity, we are assuming that expected inflation equals zero, so that the nominal interest rate—which determines money demand—equals the real interest rate. These equations should be familiar from Chapters 9 and 10.

To analyze short-run fluctuations with the *IS-LM* model, we usually assume that the price level is fixed. If prices are flexible, however, then the price level adjusts so that output is at its natural rate:

$$Y = \bar{Y} = F(\bar{K}, \bar{L}).$$

These three equations determine three endogenous variables: the level of output Y, the real interest rate r, and the price level P.

Figure 14-1 shows the equilibrium of the economy under flexible prices. Output is at its natural rate $\bar{Y}$. The intersection of the *IS* curve and the vertical

Figure 14-1

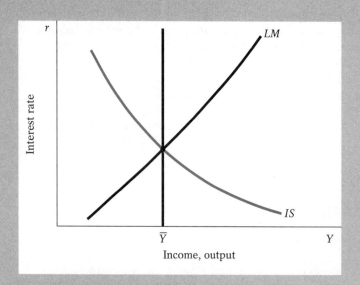

The *IS-LM* Model With Flexible Prices Under flexible prices, the level of output Y is determined by the supply of the factors of production and the production function. The interest rate is determined by the intersection of the *IS* curve and the vertical line at $\bar{Y}$, the natural rate of output. The price level adjusts so that the *LM* curve crosses the intersection of the other two curves.

line representing the natural rate determines the interest rate. The price level adjusts to ensure that the *LM* curve crosses this point as well.

Note that the *LM* curve is not very important here. Because prices are flexible, the price level adjusts to equilibrate the money market. This adjustment of prices implies that the *LM* curve always crosses the intersection of the other two curves. For the purpose of understanding real variables, such as output and the real interest rate, we can ignore the money market.

We can study the economy under flexible prices using the two relationships shown in Figure 14-2. First, the *IS* curve tells us how the demand for goods and services depends on the interest rate. For the remainder of this chapter, we call the *IS* curve the **real aggregate demand curve**. Second, the vertical line at the natural rate of output shows the supply of goods and services. We call this the **real aggregate supply curve**. The real interest rate adjusts to equilibrate the supply and demand for goods and services.

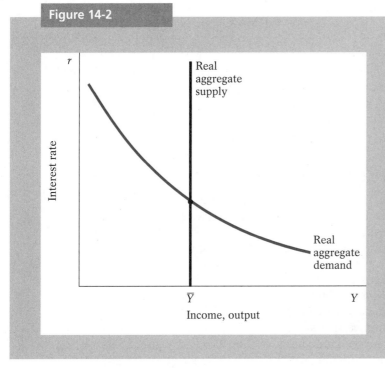

Figure 14-2

The Two Key Relationships Under Flexible Prices Under flexible prices, the two key relationships are real aggregate demand and real aggregate supply. Real aggregate demand shows the demand for goods and services as a function of the interest rate: it is another name for the *IS* curve. Real aggregate supply shows the supply of goods and services, which is determined by the supplies of capital and labour and by the available technology.

So far we have not said anything new. We have merely expressed in a new way the model of national income that we first saw in Chapter 3. In this model, factor supplies and the production technology determine the supply of goods and services, and the real interest rate adjusts to ensure that the demand for goods and services equals the supply.

In interpreting Figure 14-2, do not confuse the real aggregate demand curve and the real aggregate supply curve with the aggregate demand curve and aggregate supply curve we analyzed earlier. In previous chapters, the price level was on the vertical axis, whereas here the interest rate is. In real-business-cycle theory, the price level is not important, because it is a nominal variable and does not affect real variables. We are now developing a completely different theory of economic fluctuations.

14·2   A Real-Business-Cycle Model

In this section we turn our model of the economy under flexible prices into a model of fluctuations. The new feature of the model is the behaviour of labour supply. In the classical model discussed so far, the supply of labour is fixed, and this fixed supply determines the level of employment. Yet employment fluctuates substantially over the business cycle. If we want to maintain the classical assumption that the labour market clears, as new classical economists do, then we must examine what causes fluctuations in the quantity of labour supplied.

After discussing the determinants of labour supply, we modify our classical model of aggregate income to include changes in labour supply. The supply of goods and services depends in part on the supply of labour. The greater the number of hours people are willing to work, the more output the economy can produce. We examine how, according to real-business-cycle theory, various events influence labour supply and aggregate income.

Intertemporal Substitution and Labour Supply

Real-business-cycle theory emphasizes that the quantity of labour supplied at any point in time depends on the incentives that workers face. When workers are well rewarded, they are willing to work more hours; when the rewards are less, they are willing to work fewer hours. Sometimes, if the reward for working is sufficiently small, workers choose to forgo working altogether—at least temporarily. This willingness to reallocate hours of work over time is called the **intertemporal substitution of labour.**

To see how intertemporal substitution affects labour supply, consider the following example. A university student finishing her second year has two summer vacations left before graduating with her honours degree. She wishes to work for one of these summers (so she can buy a car after she graduates) and to relax at the beach during the other summer. How should she choose which summer to work?

Let W_1 be her real wage in the first summer, and W_2 the real wage she expects in the second summer. Choosing which summer to work involves comparing these two wages. Yet, because the student can earn interest on money earned earlier, a dollar earned in the first summer is more valuable than a dollar earned in the second summer. Let r be the real interest rate. If the student works in the first summer and saves her earnings, she will have $(1 + r)W_1$ a year later. If she works in the second summer, she will have W_2. The intertemporal relative wage—that is, the earnings from working the first summer relative to the earnings from working the second summer—is

$$\text{Intertemporal Relative Wage} = \frac{(1 + r)W_1}{W_2}.$$

Working the first summer is more attractive if the interest rate is high or if the wage is high relative to the wage expected to prevail in the future.

According to real-business-cycle theory, all workers perform this cost–benefit analysis to decide when to work and when to enjoy leisure. If the wage is temporarily high or if the interest rate is high, it is a good time to work. If the wage is temporarily low or if the interest rate is low, it is a good time to enjoy leisure.

Real-business-cycle theory uses the intertemporal substitution of labour to explain why employment and output fluctuate. Shocks to the economy that cause the interest rate to rise or the wage to be temporarily high cause people to want to work more. The increase in work effort raises employment and production.[1]

Real Aggregate Supply and Real Aggregate Demand

Real-business-cycle theory incorporates intertemporal substitution of labour into the classical model of the economy. The key insight from our analysis of labour supply is that the interest rate influences the attractiveness of working today. The higher the interest rate, the greater the amount of labour supplied, and the greater the amount of output produced.

Figure 14-3 shows the real-business-cycle model of the economy. Because of intertemporal substitution, the real aggregate supply curve is now upward-sloping rather than vertical. That is, a higher interest rate increases labour supply, which in turn increases the quantity of output supplied. Here, as before, the real interest rate adjusts to equilibrate the supply and demand for goods.

We can now use this model of the economy to explain fluctuations in output. Any shock to the economy that shifts real aggregate demand or real aggregate supply changes equilibrium output. Intertemporal substitution of labour leads to a corresponding change in the level of employment as well.

To explain shifts in real aggregate demand and real aggregate supply, real-business-cycle theorists have emphasized changes in fiscal policy and changes in technology. We now examine these sources of short-run fluctuations.

[1] The classic article emphasizing the role of intertemporal substitution in the labour market is Robert E. Lucas, Jr., and Leonard A. Rapping, "Real Wages, Employment, and Inflation," *Journal of Political Economy* 77 (September/October 1969): 721–754.

Figure 14-3

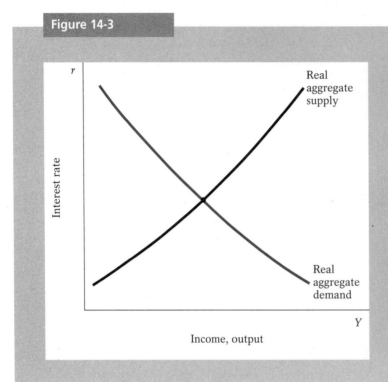

Real Aggregate Demand and Real Aggregate Supply Because of intertemporal substitution of labour, the real aggregate supply curve slopes upward: a higher interest rate makes working more attractive, which raises labour supply and thus output. The real interest rate adjusts to equilibrate real aggregate supply and real aggregate demand.

Fiscal Policy

Suppose that government purchases increase. Figure 14-4 shows how, according to real-business-cycle theory, this change affects the economy. For any given interest rate, the quantity of goods and services demanded is now higher. The increase in government purchases shifts the real aggregate demand curve outward. Output and the interest rate both rise.

Note that there are similarities between this explanation of the effects of fiscal policy and the one we saw when we studied the *IS-LM* model in Chapter 10. An increase in government purchases shifts the real aggregate demand curve outward for the same reason that it shifts the *IS* curve outward in the *IS-LM* model: for any given interest rate, expenditure on goods and services is higher. In both cases, the result is higher output and a higher interest rate. Thus, the two models make similar predictions.

Yet there are important differences between the two explanations. In the *IS-LM* model, prices are sticky, and aggregate demand determines output and employment; labour supply and intertemporal substitution play no role in explaining how fiscal policy influences output. In the real-business-cycle model, prices are flexible, and workers intertemporally substitute labour. The expansion of output results from an increase in labour supply: people respond to the higher interest rate by choosing to defer leisure and to work longer hours.[2]

---

[2] To read more about the real-business-cycle interpretation of how changes in government purchases affect the economy, see Robert J. Barro, "Output Effects of Government Purchases," *Journal of Political Economy* 89 (December 1981): 1086–1121.

Figure 14-4

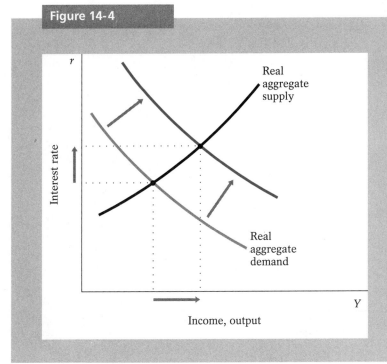

An Increase in Government Purchases in the Real-Business-Cycle Model An increase in government purchases shifts the real aggregate demand curve outward. The result is higher output and a higher real interest rate.

Technology

Many real-business-cycle theorists emphasize the role of shocks to technology. To see how technology shocks cause fluctuations, suppose that someone improves the available technology, such as by inventing a new faster computer. According to real-business-cycle theory, this change affects the economy in two ways.

First, the improved technology increases the supply of goods and services. In other words, because the production function is now improved, more output is produced for any given interest rate. The real aggregate supply curve shifts outward.

Second, the availability of the new technology raises the demand for goods. For example, if the new technology is a faster computer, firms wishing to buy these computers will raise their demand for investment goods. The real aggregate demand curve shifts outward as well.

Figure 14-5 shows these two effects. In Panel (a), the effect of the technology shock on demand is larger than the effect on supply, so output and the interest rate both rise. In Panel (b), the effect on demand is smaller than the effect on supply, so output rises and the interest rate falls. (Which case prevails depends on whether the shock is believed to be permanent or transitory. See Problem 1 at the end of the chapter.) The important lesson is that technology shocks change output and the interest rate. And, as we have seen, because of intertemporal substitution of labour, shocks that change the interest rate influence employment as well.

Figure 14-5

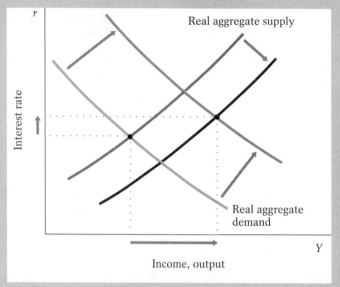

(a) Real Aggregate Demand Shifts More Than Real Aggregate Supply

An Improvement in Technology in the Real-Business-Cycle Model A beneficial shock to the technology raises both real aggregate supply and real aggregate demand. In Panel (a), demand shifts more than supply. In Panel (b), demand shifts less than supply.

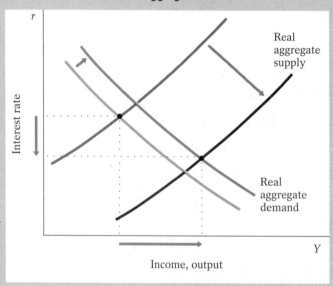

(b) Real Aggregate Supply Shifts More Than Real Aggregate Demand

14•3 The Debate Over Real-Business-Cycle Theory

Economists disagree about the empirical importance of real-business-cycle theory. At the heart of the debate are four basic issues:

- The importance of technology shocks
- The interpretation of unemployment
- The neutrality of money
- The flexibility of wages and prices

We now examine each of these.

The Importance of Technology Shocks

Real-business-cycle theory assumes that the economy experiences fluctuations in its ability to turn inputs (capital and labour) into output (goods and services) and that these fluctuations in technology cause fluctuations in output and employment. When the available production technology improves, the economy produces more output. Because of intertemporal substitution of labour, the improved technology also leads to greater employment. Real-business-cycle theorists often explain recessions as periods of technological regress. According to these models, output and employment fall during recessions because the available production technology deteriorates, which reduces output and the incentive to work.

Critics of real-business-cycle theory are skeptical that the economy experiences large shocks to technology. It is a more common presumption that technological progress occurs gradually. Critics argue that technological regress is especially implausible: the accumulation of technological knowledge may slow down, but it is hard to imagine that it would go in reverse.

Advocates respond by taking a broad view of shocks to technology. They argue that there are many events that, although not literally technological, affect the economy much as technology shocks do. For example, bad weather, the passage of strict environmental regulations, or increases in raw material prices have effects similar to adverse changes in technology: they all reduce our ability to turn capital and labour into goods and services. Whether such events are sufficiently common to explain the frequency and magnitude of business cycles is an open question.

CASE STUDY

14•1 **The Solow Residual and the Business Cycle**

To demonstrate the role of technology shocks in generating business cycles, the new classical economist Edward Prescott looked at data on the U.S. economy's inputs (capital and labour) and its output (GDP). For every year, he computed the **Solow residual**—the percentage change in output minus the percentage change in inputs, where the different inputs are weighted by their factor shares. The Solow residual measures the change in the economy's output of goods and services that cannot be explained by changes in the amounts of capital and labour. Prescott interprets it as a measure of the rate of technological progress.[3]

Figure 14-6 shows the Solow residual and the growth in output for the United States (1948–1992), and it allows us to evaluate Prescott's reasoning. Notice that the Solow residual fluctuates substantially. It tells us, for example, that technology worsened in 1982 and improved in 1984. In addition, the Solow

Figure 14-6

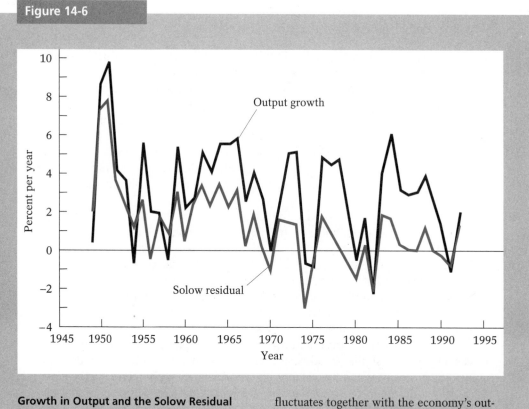

Growth in Output and the Solow Residual
The Solow residual, which some economists interpret as a measure of technology shocks, fluctuates together with the economy's output of goods and services.

Source: U.S. Department of Commerce and authors' calculations.

---

[3] The appendix to Chapter 4 shows that the Solow residual is

$$\frac{\Delta A}{A} = \frac{\Delta Y}{Y} - \alpha \, \frac{\Delta K}{K} - (1 - \alpha) \, \frac{\Delta L}{L}$$

where A is total factor productivity, Y is output, K is capital, L is labour, and α is capital's share of income.

residual moves closely with output: in years when output falls, technology worsens. According to Prescott, these large fluctuations in the Solow residual show that technology shocks are an important source of economic fluctuations.

Prescott's interpretation of this figure is controversial, however. Many economists believe that the Solow residual does not accurately represent changes in technology over short periods of time. The standard explanation of the cyclical behaviour of the Solow residual is that it reflects two problems of measurement.

First, during recessions, firms may continue to employ workers they do not need to save the large fixed costs that are associated with hiring and firing labour and so that they will have these workers on hand when the economy recovers—a phenomenon called **labour hoarding**. If firms do hoard labour, then labour input is overestimated in recessions, because the hoarded workers are probably not working as hard as usual. Labour hoarding makes the Solow residual more cyclical than the available production technology.

Second, when demand is low, firms may produce things that are not easily measured. In recessions, workers may clean the factory, organize the inventory, and do other useful tasks that standard measures of output fail to include. If so, then output is underestimated in recessions, which also makes the measured Solow residual more cyclical than technology.

Thus, economists can interpret the cyclical behaviour of the Solow residual in different ways. Real-business-cycle theorists point to the low productivity in recessions as evidence for adverse technology shocks. Other economists believe that measured productivity is low in recessions because workers are not working as hard as usual and because more of their output is not measured. Unfortunately, there is no clear evidence on the importance of labour hoarding and the cyclical mismeasurement of output. Therefore, different interpretations of Figure 14-6 persist. This disagreement is one part of the debate between advocates and critics of real-business-cycle theory.[4]

The Interpretation of Unemployment

Real-business-cycle theory assumes that fluctuations in employment reflect changes in the amount people want to work. In other words, it assumes that the economy is always on the labour supply curve: everyone who wants a job at the prevailing wage can find one. To explain fluctuations in employment, advocates of this theory argue that changes in wages and interest rates cause intertemporal substitution of labour.

Critics of this theory believe that fluctuations in employment do not reflect changes in the amount people want to work. They believe that desired employment is not very sensitive to the real wage and the real interest rate. They point out that the unemployment rate fluctuates substantially over the

---

[4] For the two sides of this debate, see Edward C. Prescott, "Theory Ahead of Business Cycle Measurement," and Lawrence H. Summers, "Some Skeptical Observations on Real Business Cycle Theory." Both are in *Quarterly Review*, Federal Reserve Bank of Minneapolis (Fall 1986).

business cycle. The high unemployment in recessions suggests that the labour market does not clear: if people were voluntarily choosing not to work in recessions, they would not call themselves unemployed. These critics conclude that wages do not adjust to equilibrate labour supply and labour demand, as real-business-cycle models assume.

In reply, advocates of real-business-cycle theory argue that unemployment statistics are difficult to interpret. The mere fact that the unemployment rate is high does not imply that intertemporal substitution of labour is unimportant. Individuals who voluntarily choose not to work may call themselves unemployed to collect unemployment-insurance benefits. Or they may call themselves unemployed because, if they were offered the wage they receive in most years, they would be willing to work.

Economists engage in similar disputes concerning the "unemployment" of capital equipment. Data on their capacity utilization show that firms fully use their capital during boom periods, but leave a significant amount of equipment unused (30 percent of the existing capital) during recessions. Obviously, we cannot argue that these inanimate objects engage in a set of intertemporal substitution calculations. Why would the owners of this capital want the machines to remain idle? Advocates of real-business-cycle theory answer this question by building more complicated models in which firms are subject to costs whenever they adjust the level of either labour or capital. Critics of this approach tend to be dissatisfied with this response, however, because this equilibrium theory presumes that no one is frustrated. Critics think that at least some out-of-work individuals are involuntarily unemployed and that at least some unused equipment is unplanned.

CASE STUDY

14·2 Looking for Intertemporal Substitution

Since intertemporal substitution of labour is a central element of real-business-cycle theory, much research has been aimed at examining whether it is an important determinant of labour supply. This research looks at data on wages and hours to see whether people alter the amount they work in response to small changes in the real wage. If leisure were highly intertemporally substitutable, then individuals expecting increases in the real wage should work little today and much in the future. Those expecting decreases in their real wage should work hard today and enjoy leisure in the future.

Studies of labour supply find that expected changes in the real wage lead to only small changes in hours worked. Individuals appear not to respond to expected real-wage changes by substantially reallocating leisure over time. This evidence suggests that intertemporal substitution is not important, contrary to the claims of real-business-cycle theorists.

This evidence does not convince everyone, however. One reason is that the data are often far from perfect. For example, to study labour supply, we need data on wages; yet when a person is not working, we do not observe the wage he could have earned if he had taken a job. Thus, although these studies of labour supply find little evidence for intertemporal substitution, they do not end the debate over real-business-cycle theory.[5]

The Neutrality of Money

Real-business-cycle theory assumes that money is neutral. That is, monetary policy is assumed not to affect real variables such as output and employment. The neutrality of money not only gives real-business-cycle theory its name, but it is also the most radical feature of the theory.

Critics argue that the evidence does not support the assumption of monetary neutrality. They point out that reductions in money growth and inflation are almost always associated with periods of high unemployment. Monetary policy appears to have a strong influence on the real economy.

Advocates of real-business-cycle theory argue that their critics confuse the direction of causation between money and output. These advocates claim that the money supply is endogenous: fluctuations in output might cause fluctuations in the money supply. For example, when output rises because of a beneficial technology shock, the quantity of money demanded rises. The Bank of Canada may respond by raising the money supply to accommodate the greater demand. This endogenous response of money to economic activity may give the illusion of monetary non-neutrality.[6]

CASE STUDY

14·3   Testing for Monetary Neutrality

The direction of causation between fluctuations in the money supply and fluctuations in output is hard to establish. The only way to be sure would be to conduct a controlled experiment. Imagine that the central bank set the money supply according to some random process. Every January, the governor of the Bank of Canada would flip a coin. Heads would mean an expansionary monetary policy

---

5   Joseph G. Altonji, "Intertemporal Substitution in Labour Supply: Evidence from Micro Data," *Journal of Political Economy* 94 (June 1986, Part 2): S176–S215; Laurence Ball, "Intertemporal Substitution and Constraints on Labour Supply: Evidence from Panel Data," *Economic Inquiry* 28 (October 1990): 706–724.

6   Robert G. King and Charles I. Plosser, "Money, Credit, and Prices in a Real Business Cycle," *American Economic Review* 74 (June 1984): 363–380.

for the coming year; tails a contractionary one. After a number of years we would know with confidence the effects of monetary policy. If output and employment usually rose after the coin came up heads, and usually fell after it came up tails, then we would conclude that monetary policy has real effects. Yet if the flip of the coin were unrelated to subsequent economic performance, then we would conclude that real-business-cycle theorists are right about the neutrality of money.

Unfortunately for scientific progress, but fortunately for the economy, economists are not allowed to conduct such experiments. Instead, we must glean what we can from the data that history gives us.

In an important and controversial study, Christina Romer and David Romer proposed one way to study the historical record. The Romers read through the minutes of all the meetings of the main policymaking committee of the U.S. central bank, the Federal Reserve (the Fed). From these minutes, they identified dates when the Fed appears to have shifted its policy toward reducing the rate of inflation. These dates, they argue, are the equivalent of the Fed's coin coming up tails. After each of these dates, the economy experienced a decline in output and employment. The Romers interpret this evidence as establishing the non-neutrality of money.[7]

The Flexibility of Wages and Prices

Real-business-cycle theory assumes that wages and prices adjust quickly to clear markets. Advocates of this theory believe that the stickiness of wages and prices is not important for understanding economic fluctuations. They also believe that the assumption of flexible prices is superior methodologically to the assumption of sticky prices, because it ties macroeconomic theory more closely to microeconomic theory. Most of microeconomic analysis is based on the assumption that prices adjust to equilibrate supply and demand. Advocates of real-business-cycle theory believe that macroeconomists should base the analysis of economic fluctuations on the same assumption.

Critics point out that many wages and prices are, in fact, not flexible. They believe that this inflexibility explains both the existence of unemployment and the non-neutrality of money. To explain why prices are sticky, they rely on the various new Keynesian theories that we discussed in Chapter 11.

---

[7] Christina Romer and David Romer, "Does Monetary Policy Matter? A New Test in the Spirit of Friedman and Schwartz," *NBER Macroeconomics Annual* (1989).

What Is New Classical Economics?

Real-business-cycle theory is called "new classical" because it uses the assumptions of the classical model—especially flexible prices and monetary neutrality—to study short-run economic fluctuations. Yet real-business-cycle theory is not the only part of macroeconomics that bears the label "new classical." Most economists use the term broadly to describe the many challenges to the Keynesian orthodoxy that prevailed in the 1960s.

According to this broad definition, one can apply the label "new classical" to some of the ideas we discussed in earlier chapters, including rational expectations (Chapter 11), the Lucas critique (Chapter 12), and the problem of time inconsistency (Chapter 12). And, as we shall see, the Ricardian view of government debt (Chapter 16) can be called "new classical." Some economists apply the label "new classical" to any model in which prices are fully flexible in the short run. By this definition, the worker-misperception and imperfect-information models of aggregate supply (Chapter 11) are new classical, even though they violate the classical dichotomy.

Although real-business-cycle theory is widely called "new classical," in some ways the term is a misnomer, for the classical economists themselves never suggested that money was neutral in the short run. For example, David Hume, in his 1752 essay "Of Money," stressed that money was neutral only in the long run:

> In my opinion, it is only in the interval or intermediate situation, between the acquisition of money and the rise in prices, that the increasing quantity of gold or silver is favourable to industry. . . . The farmer or gardener, finding that their commodities are taken off, apply themselves with alacrity to the raising of more. . . . It is easy to trace the money in its progress through the whole commonwealth; where we shall find that it must first quicken the diligence of every individual, before it increases the price of labour.

In claiming that money is neutral in the short run, real-business-cycle theorists take the assumptions of classical economics more seriously than did the classical economists themselves.[8]

---

[8] For a textbook that emphasizes the new classical approach, see Robert J. Barro and Robert F. Lucas, *Macroeconomics*, 1st ed. (Canadian) (Burr Ridge, IL: Richard D. Irwin, 1994). The real-business-cycle model presented in this chapter is a simplified version of the one presented by Barro and Lucas.

14•4   Conclusion

Real-business-cycle theory reminds us that we do not understand economic fluctuations as well as we would like. Fundamental questions about the economy remain open to dispute. Is the stickiness of wages and prices a key to understanding economic fluctuations? Does monetary policy have real effects?

The way an economist answers these questions influences the way he or she views the role of economic policy. Those economists who believe that wages and prices are sticky often believe that monetary and fiscal policy should be used to try to stabilize the economy. Price stickiness is a type of market imperfection. This imperfection leaves open the possibility that government policies can raise economic well-being.

By contrast, real-business-cycle theorists believe that government's ability to stabilize the economy is limited and that, even if the government could do so, it should not try. They view the business cycle as the natural and efficient response of the economy to changing technological possibilities. Most real-business-cycle models do not include any type of market imperfection. In these models, the invisible hand of the marketplace guides the economy to an optimal allocation of resources.

These two views of economic fluctuations are a source of frequent and heated debate among economists. Much is at stake, both in economic science and in economic policy. It is this kind of debate that makes macroeconomics an exciting and attractive field of study.[9]

Summary

1. The theory of real business cycles is an alternative explanation of economic fluctuations. It applies the assumptions of the classical model, including the flexibility of wages and prices, to the short run.

2. Real-business-cycle models rely on the intertemporal substitution of labour. If the wage is temporarily high, or if the interest rate is high, working today is more attractive than working in the future. Individuals respond to these incentives by changing the amount of labour they supply.

3. Real-business-cycle models show how changes in fiscal policy or shocks to technology induce intertemporal substitution of labour and influence output and the real interest rate.

---

[9]   To read more about real-business-cycle theory, see N. Gregory Mankiw, "Real Business Cycles: A New Keynesian Perspective," *Journal of Economic Perspectives* 3 (Summer 1989): 79–90; Bennett T. McCallum, "Real Business Cycle Models," in R. Barro, ed., *Modern Business Cycle Theory* (Cambridge, Mass.: Harvard University Press, 1989), 16–50; and Charles I. Plosser, "Understanding Real Business Cycles," *Journal of Economic Perspectives* 3 (Summer 1989): 51–77.

4. Advocates and critics of real-business-cycle theory disagree about whether technology shocks cause most economic fluctuations, whether high unemployment implies that the labour market does not clear, whether monetary policy affects real variables, and whether the short-run stickiness of wages and prices is important for understanding economic fluctuations.

KEY CONCEPTS

New classical economics

Real-business-cycle theory

Real aggregate demand curve

Real aggregate supply curve

Intertemporal substitution of labour

Solow residual

Labour hoarding

QUESTIONS FOR REVIEW

1. How does real-business-cycle theory explain fluctuations in employment?

2. According to real-business-cycle theory, how does an increase in government purchases affect the economy?

3. What are the four central disagreements in the debate over real-business-cycle theory?

PROBLEMS AND APPLICATIONS

1. According to real-business-cycle theory, permanent and transitory shocks should have very different effects on the economy. Let's therefore compare the effects of a transitory technology shock (such as good weather) and a permanent technology shock (such as the invention of a new production process).

a. Which shock would have the larger impact on the demand for investment goods? Which shock would cause the larger shift in real aggregate demand?

b. Which shock would raise the current real wage above the expected future real wage? Which shock would cause the larger shift in real aggregate supply?

c. Compare the effects of the two shocks on output and the real interest rate.

2. Suppose that prices are fully flexible and that the output of the economy fluctuates because of shocks to technology, as real-business-cycle theory claims.

a. If the Bank of Canada holds the money supply constant, what will happen to the price level as output fluctuates?

b. If the Bank of Canada adjusts the money supply to stabilize the price level, what will happen to the money supply as output fluctuates?

c. Many economists have observed that fluctuations in the money supply are positively correlated with fluctuations in output. Is this evidence against real-business-cycle theory?

PART FOUR

More on the Microeconomics Behind Macroeconomics

To understand the economy as a whole, we must understand the households and firms that make up the economy. In the next four chapters we look more closely at the behaviour of households and firms. These chapters present microeconomic models that help refine our macroeconomic analysis.

Chapter 15 looks at how consumers behave and provides a more thorough explanation of the consumption function. As we see in Chapter 16, different views about consumer behaviour can lead to different views about how government debt affects the economy.

Chapter 17 examines the determinants of the three types of investment—business fixed investment, residential investment, and inventory investment. It discusses why investment depends on the interest rate, what might cause the investment function to shift, and why investment fluctuates so much over the business cycle.

Chapter 18 studies the supply and demand for money. It discusses the role of the banking system in determining the money supply, as well as the various theories of the money demand function. The discussion offers new insights into the instruments and problems of monetary policy.

These chapters offer a taste of modern research. Much recent progress in macroeconomics has come from applying microeconomic models. Most often, these models refine, rather than overturn, traditional macroeconomic theory. They are important to learn, for they can enhance our understanding of the economy and economic policies.

CHAPTER 15

Consumption

Consumption is the sole end and purpose of all production.

Adam Smith

How do households decide how much of their income to consume today and how much to save for the future? This is a microeconomic question because it addresses the behaviour of individual decisionmakers. Yet its answer is important for macroeconomics as well. As we have seen in previous chapters, households' consumption decisions affect the way the economy as a whole behaves both in the long run and in the short run.

The consumption decision is crucial for long-run analysis because of its role in economic growth. The Solow growth model of Chapter 4 shows that the saving rate is a key determinant of the steady-state capital stock and thus of the level of economic well-being. The saving rate measures how much of its income the present generation is putting aside for its own future and for future generations.

The consumption decision is crucial for short-run analysis because of its role in aggregate demand. Since consumption is six tenths of GDP, fluctuations in consumption are a key element of booms and recessions. The *IS-LM* model of Chapters 9 and 10 shows that changes in consumer confidence can be a source of shocks to the economy, and that the marginal propensity to consume is a key determinant of the fiscal-policy multipliers.

In previous chapters we explained consumption with a function that relates consumption to disposable income: $C = C(Y - T)$. This approximation allowed us to develop simple models for long-run and short-run analysis. But it is too simple to provide a complete explanation of consumer behaviour. In this chapter we examine the consumption function in greater detail and develop a more thorough explanation of what determines aggregate consumption.

Since macroeconomics began as a field of study, many economists have written about the theory of consumer behaviour and suggested alternative ways of interpreting the data on consumption and income. This chapter presents the views of four prominent economists, roughly in historical order. By examining the theories of consumer behaviour developed by John Maynard Keynes, Irving Fisher, Franco Modigliani, and Milton Friedman, this chapter provides an overview of the diverse approaches to explaining consumption.

15•1 John Maynard Keynes and the Consumption Function

We begin our study of consumption with John Maynard Keynes's *General Theory*, which was published in 1936. Keynes made the consumption function central to his theory of economic fluctuations, and it has played a key role in macroeconomic analysis ever since. Let's consider what Keynes thought about the consumption function, and then see what puzzles arose when his ideas were confronted with the data.

Keynes's Conjectures

Today, economists who study consumption rely on sophisticated techniques of data analysis. With the help of computers, they analyze aggregate data on the behaviour of the overall economy from the national income accounts, and detailed data on the behaviour of individual households from surveys. Because Keynes wrote in the 1930s, however, he had neither the advantage of these data nor the computers necessary to analyze such large data sets. Instead of relying on statistical analysis, Keynes made conjectures about the consumption function based on introspection and casual observation.

First and most important, Keynes conjectured that the **marginal propensity to consume**—the amount consumed out of an additional dollar of income—is between zero and one. He wrote that the "fundamental psychological law, upon which we are entitled to depend with great confidence, . . . is that men are disposed, as a rule and on the average, to increase their consumption as their income increases, but not by as much as the increase in their income." The marginal propensity to consume was crucial to Keynes's policy recommendations for how to deal with widespread unemployment. The power of fiscal policy to influence the economy—as expressed by the fiscal policy multipliers—arises from the feedback between income and consumption.

Second, Keynes posited that the ratio of consumption to income, called the **average propensity to consume**, falls as income rises. He believed that saving was a luxury, so he expected the rich to save a higher proportion of their income than the poor. Although not essential for Keynes's own analysis, the postulate of a falling average propensity to consume became a central part of early Keynesian economics.

Third, Keynes thought that income is the primary determinant of consumption and that the interest rate does not have an important role. This conjecture stood in stark contrast to the beliefs of the classical economists who preceded him. The classical economists held that a higher interest rate encourages saving and discourages consumption. Keynes admitted that the interest rate could influence consumption as a matter of theory. Yet he wrote that "the main conclusion suggested by experience, I think, is that the short-period influence of the rate of interest on individual spending out of a given income is secondary and relatively unimportant."

On the basis of these three conjectures, the Keynesian consumption function is often written as

$$C = \bar{C} + cY \qquad \bar{C} > 0, 0 < c < 1,$$

where C is consumption, Y is disposable income, $\bar{C}$ is a constant sometimes called *autonomous consumption*, and c is the marginal propensity to consume. This consumption function, shown in Figure 15-1, is graphed as a straight line.

Figure 15-1

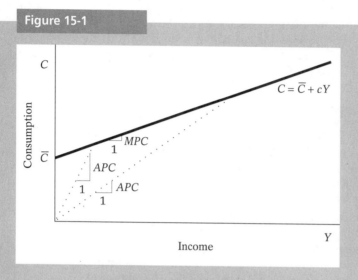

The Keynesian Consumption Function This figure graphs a consumption function with the three properties that Keynes conjectured. First, the marginal propensity to consume c is between zero and one. Second, the average propensity to consume falls as income rises. Third, consumption is determined by current income.

Note: The marginal propensity to consume is the slope of the consumption function. The average propensity to consume, C/Y, equals the slope of a line drawn from the origin to a point on the consumption function.

Notice that this consumption function exhibits the three properties that Keynes posited. It satisfies Keynes's first property because the marginal propensity to consume c is between zero and one, so that higher income leads to higher consumption and also to higher saving. This consumption function satisfies Keynes's second property because the average propensity to consume (APC) is

$$APC = C/Y = \bar{C}/Y + c.$$

As Y rises, $\bar{C}/Y$ falls, and so the average propensity to consume C/Y falls. And finally, this consumption function satisfies Keynes's third property because the interest rate is not included in this equation as a determinant of consumption.

The Early Empirical Successes

Soon after Keynes proposed the consumption function, economists began collecting and examining data to test his conjectures. The earliest studies indicated that the Keynesian consumption function is a good approximation of how consumers behave.

In some of these studies, researchers surveyed households and collected data on consumption and income. From these cross-section studies, they found that households with higher income consumed more, which implies that the marginal propensity to consume is greater than zero. They also found that households with higher income saved more, which implies that the marginal propensity to consume is less than one. These data supported Keynes's prediction that the marginal propensity to consume is between zero and one. In addition, these researchers found that higher-income households saved a larger fraction of their income, which verified Keynes's conjecture that the average propensity to consume falls as income rises.

In other studies, researchers examined aggregate data on consumption and income for the period between the two world wars. These data also supported the Keynesian consumption function. In years when income was unusually low, such as during the depths of the Great Depression, both consumption and saving were low, indicating that the marginal propensity to consume is between zero and one. In addition, during those years of low income, the ratio of consumption to income was high, confirming Keynes's second conjecture. Finally, because the correlation between income and consumption was so strong, no other variable appeared to be important for explaining consumption. Thus, the data also confirmed Keynes's third conjecture that income is the primary determinant of how much people choose to consume.

Secular Stagnation, Simon Kuznets, and the Consumption Puzzle

Although the Keynesian consumption function met with early successes, two anomalies soon arose. Both concern Keynes's conjecture that the average propensity to consume falls as income rises.

The first anomaly came from a prediction some economists made during World War II. On the basis of the Keynesian consumption function, these economists reasoned that as incomes in the economy grew over time, households would consume a smaller and smaller fraction of their incomes. They feared that there might not be enough profitable investment projects to absorb all this saving. If so, the low consumption would lead to an inadequate demand for goods and services, resulting in a depression once the wartime demand from the government ceased. In other words, on the basis of the Keynesian consumption function, these economists predicted that the economy would experience what they called *secular stagnation*—a long depression of indefinite duration—unless fiscal policy was used to expand aggregate demand.

Fortunately for the economy, but unfortunately for the Keynesian consumption function, the end of World War II did not throw western economies into another depression. Although incomes were much higher after the war than before, these higher incomes did not lead to large increases in the rate of saving. Keynes's conjecture that the average propensity to consume would fall as income rose appeared not to hold.

The second anomaly came from new data on consumption and income for the United States, dating back to 1869. These data were constructed in the 1940s by the economist Simon Kuznets, who later received the Nobel Prize for this work. Kuznets discovered that the ratio of consumption to income was remarkably stable from decade to decade, despite large increases in income over the period he studied. Again, Keynes's conjecture that the average propensity to consume would fall as income rose appeared not to hold.

The failure of the secular-stagnation hypothesis and the findings of Kuznets both indicated that the average propensity to consume is fairly constant over long periods of time. This fact presented a puzzle that motivated much of the subsequent work on consumption. Economists wanted to know why some studies confirmed Keynes's conjectures and others refuted them. That is, why did Keynes's conjectures hold up well in the cross-section studies of household data and in the studies of short time-series, but fail when long time-series were examined?

Figure 15-2 illustrates this puzzle. The evidence suggested that there were two consumption functions. For the household data or for the short time-series, the Keynesian consumption function appeared to work well. Yet for the long time-series, the consumption function appeared to have a constant average propensity to consume. In Figure 15-2, these two relationships between consumption and income are called the short-run and long-run consumption functions. Economists needed to explain how these two consumption functions could be consistent with each other.

In the 1950s, Franco Modigliani and Milton Friedman each proposed explanations of these seemingly contradictory findings. Both economists later won Nobel Prizes, in part because of their work on consumption. But before we see how Modigliani and Friedman tried to solve the consumption puzzle, we must discuss Irving Fisher's contribution to consumption theory. Both Modigliani's life-cycle hypothesis and Friedman's permanent-income hypothesis rely on the theory of consumer behaviour proposed much earlier by Irving Fisher.

Figure 15-2

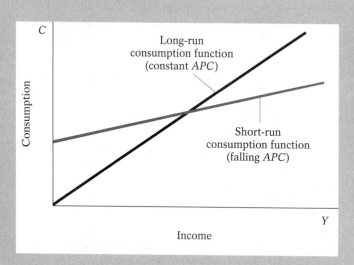

The Consumption Puzzle Studies of household data and short time-series found a relationship between consumption and income similar to the one Keynes conjectured. In the figure, this relationship is called the short-run consumption function. But studies of long time-series found that the average propensity to consume did not vary systematically with income. This relationship is called the long-run consumption function. Notice that the short-run consumption function has a falling average propensity to consume, whereas the long-run consumption function has a constant average propensity to consume.

15•2 Irving Fisher and Intertemporal Choice

When people decide how much to consume and how much to save, they must consider both the present and the future. The more consumption they enjoy today, the less they will be able to enjoy tomorrow. In making this tradeoff, households must look ahead to the income they expect to receive in the future and to the consumption of goods and services they hope to be able to afford.

The economist Irving Fisher developed the model with which economists analyze how rational, forward-looking consumers make intertemporal choices—that is, choices involving different periods of time. Fisher's model shows the constraints consumers face and how they choose consumption and saving.

The Intertemporal Budget Constraint

Almost everyone would prefer to increase the quantity or quality of the goods and services they consume—to wear nicer clothes, eat at better restaurants, or see more movies. The reason people consume less than they desire is that their consumption is constrained by their income. In other words, consumers face a limit on how much they can spend, called a *budget constraint*. When they are deciding how much to consume today versus how much to save for the future, they face an **intertemporal budget constraint**. To understand how people choose their level of consumption, we must examine this constraint.

To keep things simple, we examine the decision facing a consumer who lives for two periods. Period one represents the consumer's youth, and period two represents the consumer's old age. The consumer earns income Y_1 and consumes C_1 in period one, and earns income Y_2 and consumes C_2 in period two. (All variables are real—that is, adjusted for inflation.) Because the consumer has the opportunity to borrow and save, consumption in any single period can be either greater or less than income in that period.

Consider how the consumer's income in the two periods constrains consumption in the two periods. In the first period, saving equals income minus consumption. That is,

$$S = Y_1 - C_1,$$

where S is saving. In the second period, consumption equals the accumulated saving, including the interest earned on that saving, plus second-period income. That is,

$$C_2 = (1 + r)S + Y_2,$$

where r is the real interest rate. For example, if the interest rate is 5 percent, then for every dollar of saving in period one, the consumer enjoys an extra $1.05 of consumption in period two. Because there is no third period, the consumer does not save in the second period.

Note that these two equations still apply if the consumer is borrowing rather than saving in the first period. The variable S represents both saving and borrowing. If first-period consumption is less than first-period income, the consumer is saving, and S is greater than zero. If first-period consumption exceeds first-period income, the consumer is borrowing, and S is less than zero. For simplicity, we assume that the interest rate for borrowing is the same as the interest rate for saving.

To derive the consumer's budget constraint, combine the two equations above. Substitute the first equation for S into the second equation to obtain

$$C_2 = (1 + r)(Y_1 - C_1) + Y_2.$$

To make the equation easier to interpret, we must rearrange terms. To place all the consumption terms together, bring $(1 + r)C_1$ from the right-hand side to the left-hand side of the equation to obtain

$$(1 + r)C_1 + C_2 = (1 + r)Y_1 + Y_2.$$

Now divide both sides by $(1 + r)$ to obtain

$$C_1 + \frac{C_2}{1 + r} = Y_1 + \frac{Y_2}{1 + r}.$$

This equation relates consumption in the two periods to income in the two periods. It is the standard way of expressing the consumer's intertemporal budget constraint.

The consumer's budget constraint is easily interpreted. If the interest rate is zero, the budget constraint says that total consumption in the two periods equals total income in the two periods. In the usual case in which the interest rate is greater than zero, future consumption and future income are discounted by a factor $1 + r$. This **discounting** arises from the interest earned on savings. In essence, because the consumer earns interest on current income that is saved, future income is worth less than current income. Similarly, because future consumption is paid for out of savings that have earned interest, future consumption costs less than current consumption. The factor $1/(1 + r)$ is the price of second-period consumption measured in terms of first-period consumption: it is the amount of first-period consumption that the consumer must forgo to obtain one unit of second-period consumption.

Figure 15-3 graphs the consumer's budget constraint. Three points are marked on this figure. At point A, first-period consumption is Y_1 and second-period consumption is Y_2, so there is neither saving nor borrowing between the two periods. At point B, the consumer consumes nothing in the first period and saves all income, so second-period consumption is $(1 + r)Y_1 + Y_2$. At point C, the consumer plans to consume nothing in the second period and borrows as much as possible against second-period income, so first-period consumption is $Y_1 + Y_2/(1 + r)$. Of course, these are only three of the many combinations of first- and second-period consumption that the consumer can choose: all the points on the line from B to C are possible.

The shaded area below the budget constraint shows other combinations of first-period and second-period consumption available to the consumer. The consumer can choose points below the budget constraint because he can discard some of his income. The important points are those on the budget constraint, however. As long as more consumption is preferred to less, the consumer will always choose a point on—rather than below—this budget line. The slope of the budget line can be determined by dividing the vertical distance between points A and B, $(1 + r)Y_1$, by the horizontal distance between points A and B, Y_1. Thus, the slope is $1 + r$ in absolute value.

Figure 15-3

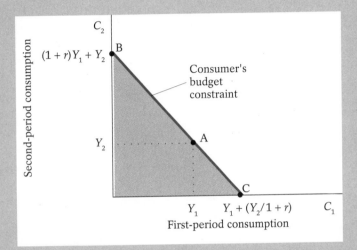

The Consumer's Budget Constraint This figure shows the combinations of first-period and second-period consumption that the consumer can choose. If he chooses points between A and B, he consumes less than his income in the first period and saves the rest for the second period. If he chooses points between A and C, he consumes more than his income in the first period and borrows to make up the difference.

Consumer Preferences

The consumer's preferences regarding consumption in the two periods can be represented by **indifference curves**. An indifference curve shows the combinations of first-period and second-period consumption that make the consumer equally happy.

Figure 15-4 shows two possible indifference curves. The consumer is indifferent among combinations W, X, and Y, because they are all on the same curve. Not surprisingly, if the consumer's first-period consumption is reduced, say from point W to point X, second-period consumption must increase to keep him equally happy. If first-period consumption is reduced again, from point X to point Y, the amount of extra second-period consumption he requires for compensation is greater.

The slope at any point on the indifference curve shows how much second-period consumption the consumer requires in order to be compensated for a one-unit reduction in first-period consumption. We call this slope the **marginal rate of substitution** between first-period consumption and second-period consumption. It tells us the rate at which the consumer is willing to substitute second-period consumption for first-period consumption.

We can see from Figure 15-4 that the marginal rate of substitution depends on the levels of consumption in the two periods. When first-period con-

Figure 15-4

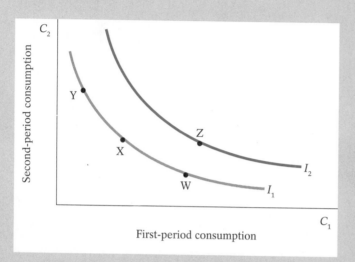

The Consumer's Preferences The consumer's preferences over first-period and second-period consumption are represented by indifference curves. An indifference curve gives the combinations of consumption in the two periods that make the consumer equally happy. Higher indifference curves are preferred to lower ones. This figure shows two of many indifference curves. The consumer is equally happy at points W, X, and Y, but prefers point Z to points W, X, or Y.

sumption is high and second-period consumption is low, such as at point W, the marginal rate of substitution is low: the consumer requires only a little extra second-period consumption to give up a unit of first-period consumption. When first-period consumption is low and second-period consumption is high, such as at point Y, the marginal rate of substitution is high: the consumer requires much additional second-period consumption to give up a unit of first-period consumption.

The consumer is equally happy at all points on a given indifference curve, but prefers some indifference curves to others. Because he prefers more consumption to less, higher indifference curves are preferred to lower ones. In Figure 15-4, the points on curve I_2 are preferred to the points on curve I_1.

The set of indifference curves gives a complete ranking of the consumer's preferences. They tell us that point Z is preferred to point W, but that may be obvious because point Z has more consumption in both periods. Yet compare point Z and point Y: point Z has more consumption in period one and less in period two. Which is preferred, Z or Y? Since Z is on a higher indifference curve than Y, point Z is preferred to point Y. Hence, we can use the set of indifference curves to rank any combinations of first-period and second-period consumption.

Optimization

Having discussed the consumer's budget constraint and preferences, we can consider the decision about how much to consume. The consumer would like to end up with the best possible combination of consumption in the two periods—that is, on the highest possible indifference curve. But the budget constraint requires that the consumer also end up on or below the budget line, because the budget line measures the total resources available to him.

Figure 15-5 shows that many indifference curves cross the budget line. The highest indifference curve that the consumer can obtain without violating the budget constraint is the indifference curve that just barely touches the budget line, which is curve I_3 in the figure. The point at which the curve and line touch—point O for optimum—is the best combination of consumption in the two periods available to the consumer.

Notice that, at the optimum, the slope of the indifference curve equals the slope of the budget line. We say that the indifference curve is *tangent* to the budget line. The slope of the indifference curve is the marginal rate of substitution (*MRS*), and the slope of the budget line is one plus the real interest rate. We conclude that, at point O,

$$MRS = 1 + r.$$

The consumer chooses consumption in the two periods so that the marginal rate of substitution equals one plus the real interest rate.

Figure 15-5

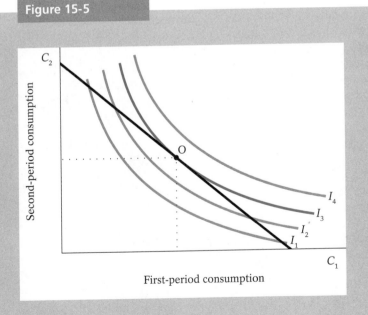

The Consumer's Optimum The consumer achieves his highest level of satisfaction by choosing the point on the budget constraint that is on the highest indifference curve. At the optimum, the indifference curve is tangent to the budget constraint.

How Changes in Income Affect Consumption

Now that we have seen how the consumer makes the consumption decision, let's examine how consumption responds to an increase in income. An increase in either Y_1 or Y_2 shifts the budget constraint outward, as in Figure 15-6. The higher budget constraint allows the consumer to choose a better combination of first- and second-period consumption—that is, the consumer can now reach a higher indifference curve.

Notice that, in Figure 15-6, the consumer chooses more consumption in both periods. Although not implied by the logic of the model alone, this situation is the most usual. If a consumer wants more of a good when his or her income rises, economists call it a **normal good**. The indifference curves in Figure 15-6 are drawn under the assumption that consumption in period one and consumption in period two are both normal goods.

The key implication of Figure 15-6 is that regardless of whether the increase in income occurs in the first period or the second period, the consumer spreads it over consumption in both periods. Because the consumer can borrow and lend between periods, the timing of the income is irrelevant to how much is consumed today (except, of course, that future income is discounted by the interest rate). The lesson of this analysis is that consumption depends on the present value of current and future income—that is, on

$$\text{Present Value of Income} = Y_1 + \frac{Y_2}{1 + r}.$$

Figure 15-6

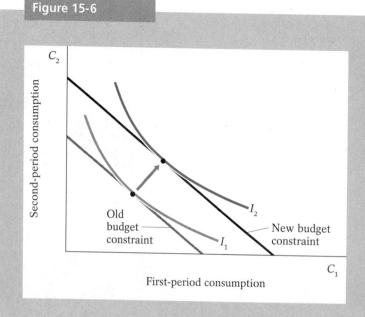

Second-period consumption

Old budget constraint

New budget constraint

I_1

I_2

C_1

First-period consumption

An Increase in Income An increase in either first-period income or second-period income shifts the budget constraint outward. If consumption in period one and consumption in period two are both normal goods, this increase in income raises consumption in both periods.

In contrast to Keynes's consumption function, Fisher's model says that consumption does not depend primarily on current income. Instead, consumption depends on the resources the consumer expects over his or her lifetime.

How Changes in the Real Interest Rate Affect Consumption

Let's now use Fisher's model to consider how a change in the real interest rate alters the consumer's choices. There are two cases to consider: the case in which the consumer is initially saving and the case in which he is initially borrowing. Here we discuss the saving case, and Problem 1 at the end of the chapter asks you to analyze the borrowing case.

Figure 15-7 shows that an increase in the real interest rate rotates the consumer's budget line around the point (Y_1, Y_2). This change alters the amount of consumption he chooses in both periods. You can see that, for the indifference curves drawn in this figure, first-period consumption falls and second-period consumption rises.

Economists decompose the impact of an increase in the real interest rate on consumption into two effects: an **income effect** and a **substitution effect**.

Figure 15-7

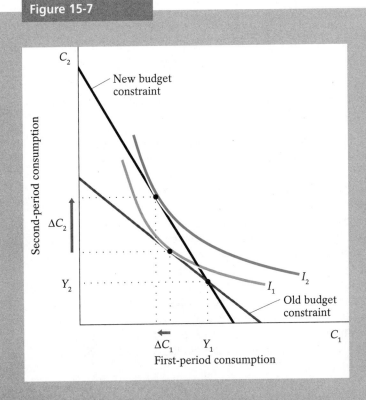

An Increase in the Interest Rate An increase in the interest rate tilts the budget constraint around the point (Y_1, Y_2). In this figure, the higher interest rate reduces first-period consumption and raises second-period consumption.

Textbooks in microeconomics discuss these effects in detail. We summarize them briefly here.

The income effect is the change in consumption that results from the movement to a higher indifference curve. Because the consumer is a saver rather than a borrower, the increase in the interest rate makes him better off. If consumption in period one and consumption in period two are both normal goods, the consumer will want to spread this improvement in his welfare over both periods. This income effect tends to make the consumer choose more consumption in both periods.

The substitution effect is the change in consumption that results from the change in the relative price of consumption in the two periods. In particular, consumption in period two becomes less expensive relative to consumption in period one when the interest rate rises. That is, because the real interest rate earned on saving is higher, the consumer must now give up less first-period consumption to obtain an extra unit of second-period consumption. This substitution effect tends to make the consumer choose more consumption in period two and less consumption in period one.

The consumer's choice depends on both the income effect and the substitution effect. Both effects act to increase the amount of second-period consumption; hence, we can confidently conclude that an increase in the real interest rate raises second-period consumption. But the two effects have opposite impacts on first-period consumption. Hence, the increase in the interest rate could either lower or raise first-period consumption.

CASE STUDY

Consumption and the Real Interest Rate

Irving Fisher's model shows that, depending on the consumer's preferences, changes in the real interest rate could either raise or lower current consumption. In other words, economic theory alone cannot predict how the interest rate influences consumption. Therefore, economists have devoted much energy to examining empirically how the interest rate affects consumption and saving.

Figure 15-8 presents a scatterplot of the personal saving rate and the real interest rate for Canada. This figure shows that there is no apparent relationship between the two variables. The evidence suggests that saving does not depend on the interest rate. In other words, it appears that the income and substitution effects of higher interest rates approximately cancel each other.

Yet this sort of evidence is not completely persuasive. The task of estimating the sensitivity of saving to the interest rate is complicated by the identification problem discussed in Chapter 3. Nonetheless, more sophisticated examinations of the data usually find that the real interest rate has little effect on consump-

Figure 15-8

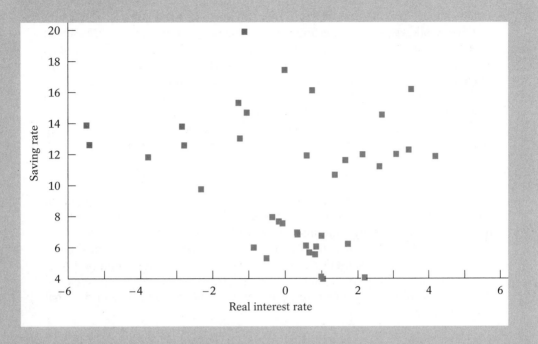

A Scatterplot of Saving and the Interest Rate This figure uses annual data from 1956 to 1993 to examine whether there is any relationship between the personal saving rate and the real interest rate. No relationship is evident.

Note: The personal saving rate is personal disposable income minus consumer spending as a fraction of personal disposable income. The real interest rate is the after-tax interest rate on three-month treasury bills minus that year's inflation rate; this was calculated assuming a tax rate of 30 percent.

Source: Reproduced and adapted by authority of the Minister of Industry, 1994, "Statistics Canada," *Canadian Economic Observer*, Series B14007, D20103, D20111, P484000 (Historical Statistical Supplement 1991/92): 10-11, 27, 51, 92 and (Statistical Summary, March 1994): 5, 22-23, 52.

tion and saving. Keynes's conjecture that consumption depends primarily on income and not on the interest rate has held up well in the face of much empirical testing.[1]

---

[1] For some of the recent research on the relationship between consumption and the real interest rate, see Robert E. Hall, "Intertemporal Substitution and Consumption," *Journal of Political Economy* 96 (April 1988): 339–357; and John Y. Campbell and N. Gregory Mankiw, "Consumption, Income, and Interest Rates: Reinterpreting the Time-Series Evidence," *NBER Macroeconomics Annual* (1989): 185–216.

Constraints on Borrowing

Fisher's model assumes that the consumer can borrow as well as save. The ability to borrow allows current consumption to exceed current income. In essence, when the consumer borrows, he consumes some of his future income today. Yet for many people such borrowing is impossible. For example, an unemployed individual wishing to go skiing at Whistler or to relax in Florida would probably be unable to finance these vacations with a bank loan. Let's examine how Fisher's analysis changes if the consumer cannot borrow.

The inability to borrow prevents current consumption from exceeding current income. A constraint on borrowing can therefore be expressed as

$$C_1 \le Y_1.$$

This inequality states that consumption in period one is less than or equal to income in period one. This additional constraint on the consumer is called a **borrowing constraint** or, sometimes, a *liquidity constraint*.

Figure 15-9 shows how this borrowing constraint restricts the consumer's set of choices. The consumer's choice must satisfy both the intertemporal budget constraint and the borrowing constraint. The shaded area represents the combinations of first-period consumption and second-period consumption that satisfy both constraints.

Figure 15-9

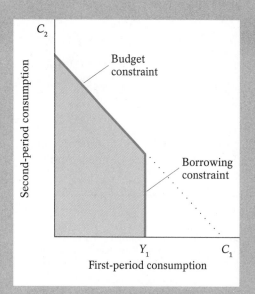

A Borrowing Constraint If the consumer cannot borrow, he faces the additional constraint that first-period consumption cannot exceed first-period income. The shaded area represents the combination of first-period and second-period consumption the consumer can choose.

Figure 15-10 shows how this borrowing constraint affects the consumption decision. There are two possibilities. In Panel (a), the consumer wishes to consume less in period one than he earns. The borrowing constraint is not binding in this case and, therefore, does not affect consumption. In Panel (b), the consumer would like to consume more than he earns in period one. In this case, the consumer consumes all his first-period income, and the borrowing constraint prevents him from consuming more.

"What I'd like, basically, is a temporary line of credit just to tide me over the rest of my life."

Figure 15-10

(a) The Borrowing Constraint Is Not Binding

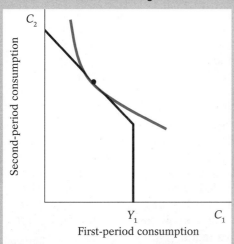

(b) The Borrowing Constraint Is Binding

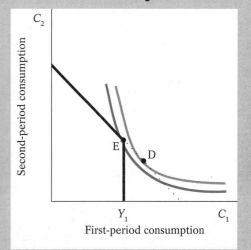

The Consumer's Optimum With a Borrowing Constraint When the consumer faces a borrowing constraint, there are two possible situations. In Panel (a), the consumer chooses first-period consumption to be less than first-period income, so the borrowing constraint is not binding and does not affect consumption.

In Panel (b), the borrowing constraint is binding. The consumer would like to borrow and choose point D. But because borrowing is not allowed, the best available choice is point E. When the borrowing constraint is binding, first-period consumption equals first-period income.

The analysis of borrowing constraints leads us to conclude that there are two consumption functions. For some consumers, the borrowing constraint is not binding, and consumption depends on the present value of lifetime income, $Y_1 + [Y_2/(1 + r)]$. For other consumers, the borrowing constraint binds, and the consumption function is $C_1 = Y_1$. Hence, *for those consumers who would like to borrow but cannot, consumption depends only on current income.*

CASE STUDY

15·2   The High Japanese Saving Rate

Japan has one of the world's highest saving rates, and many economists believe that this is a key to its economic success. The Solow growth model in Chapter 4 shows that, in the long run, the saving rate is a primary determinant of a country's level of income. Because saving is so important for long-run economic performance, economists spend much time studying international differences in saving.

Why do the Japanese consume a much smaller fraction of their income than do North Americans? One reason is that it is harder for households to borrow in Japan. As Fisher's model shows, a household facing a binding borrowing constraint consumes less than it would without the borrowing constraint. Hence, societies in which borrowing constraints are common will tend to have higher rates of saving.

One reason that households often wish to borrow is to buy a home. In Canada, a person can usually buy a home with a down payment of 10 percent. A home buyer in Japan can borrow much less: down payments of 40 percent are common. Moreover, housing prices are very high in Japan, primarily because land prices are high. A Japanese family must save a great deal in order to eventually afford its own home.

Although constraints on borrowing are part of the explanation of high Japanese saving, there are many other differences between Japan and Canada that contribute to the difference in the saving rates. For example, cultural differences may lead to differences in consumer preferences regarding present and future consumption. One prominent Japanese economist writes, "The Japanese are simply *different*. They are more risk averse and more patient. If this is true, the long-run implication is that Japan will absorb all the wealth in the world. I refuse to comment on this explanation."[2]

Many economists believe that a low saving rate is one of Canada's biggest economic problems. As we discussed in Chapter 4, increasing national saving is often a stated goal of economic policy. Keep in mind, however, that policies designed to raise saving have their costs. Home buyers in Canada would not be happy if they faced the borrowing constraints that are so common in Japan.

---

[2] Fumio Hayashi, "Why Is Japan's Saving Rate So Apparently High?" *NBER Macroeconomics Annual* (1986): 147–210.

15•3 Franco Modigliani and the Life-Cycle Hypothesis

In a series of papers written in the 1950s, Franco Modigliani and his collaborators Albert Ando and Richard Brumberg used Fisher's model of consumer behaviour to study the consumption function. One of their goals was to solve the consumption puzzle—that is, to explain the apparently conflicting pieces of evidence that came to light when Keynes's consumption function was brought to the data. According to Fisher's model, consumption depends on a person's lifetime income. Modigliani emphasized that income varies systematically over people's lives and that saving allows consumers to move income from those times in life when income is high to those times when it is low—an interpretation of consumer behaviour that formed the basis for his **life-cycle hypothesis.**[3]

The Hypothesis

One important reason that income varies over a person's life is retirement. Most people plan to stop working at about age 65, and they expect their incomes to fall when they retire. Yet they do not want a large drop in their standard of living, as measured by their consumption. To maintain consumption after retirement, people must save during their working years. Let's see what this motive for saving implies for the consumption function.

Consider a consumer who expects to live another T years, has wealth of W, and expects to earn income Y until she retires R years from now. What level of consumption will the consumer choose if she wishes to maintain a smooth level of consumption over her life?

The consumer's lifetime resources are composed of initial wealth W and lifetime earnings of $R \times Y$. (For simplicity, we are assuming an interest rate of zero; if the interest rate were greater than zero, we would need to take account of interest earned on savings as well.) The consumer can divide up her lifetime resources among her T remaining years of life. We assume that she wishes to achieve the smoothest possible path of consumption over her lifetime. Therefore, she divides this total of $W + RY$ equally among the T years and each year consumes

$$C = (W + RY)/T.$$

We can write this person's consumption function as

$$C = (1/T)W + (R/T)Y.$$

---

[3] For references to the large body of work on the life-cycle hypothesis, a good place to start is the lecture Modigliani gave when he won the Nobel Prize. Franco Modigliani, "Life Cycle, Individual Thrift, and the Wealth of Nations," *American Economic Review* 76 (June 1986): 297–313.

For example, if the consumer expects to live for 50 more years and work for 30 of them, then $T = 50$ and $R = 30$, so her consumption function is

$$C = 0.02W + 0.6Y.$$

This equation says that consumption depends on both income and wealth. An extra \$1 of income per year raises consumption by \$0.60 per year, and an extra \$1 of wealth raises consumption by \$0.02 per year.

 If every individual in the economy plans consumption like this, then the aggregate consumption function is much the same as the individual one. In particular, aggregate consumption depends on both wealth and income. That is, the economy's consumption function is

$$C = \alpha W + \beta Y,$$

where the parameter α is the marginal propensity to consume out of wealth, and the parameter β is the marginal propensity to consume out of income.

Implications

Figure 15-11 graphs the relationship between consumption and income predicted by the life-cycle model. For any given level of wealth, the model yields a conventional consumption function, such as in Figure 15-1. Notice, however, that the intercept of the consumption function, αW, is not a fixed value but depends on the level of wealth.

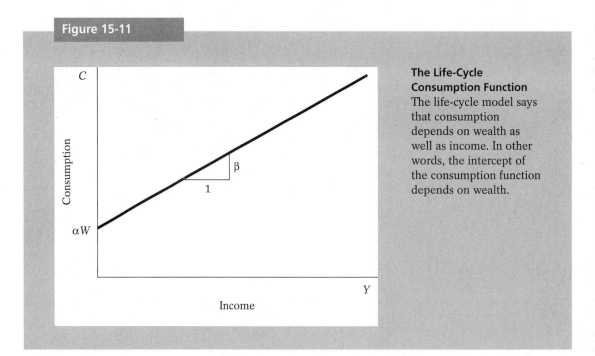

Figure 15-11

The Life-Cycle Consumption Function The life-cycle model says that consumption depends on wealth as well as income. In other words, the intercept of the consumption function depends on wealth.

This life-cycle model of consumer behaviour can solve the consumption puzzle. The life-cycle consumption function implies that the average propensity to consume is

$$C/Y = \alpha(W/Y) + \beta.$$

Because wealth does not vary proportionately with income from person to person or from year to year, we should find that high income implies a low average propensity to consume when looking at data across individuals or over short periods of time. But, over long periods of time, wealth and income grow together, which implies a constant ratio W/Y and thus a constant average propensity to consume.

To make the same point somewhat differently, consider how the consumption function changes over time. As Figure 15-11 shows, for any given level of wealth, the life-cycle consumption function looks like the one Keynes suggested. But this function holds only in the short run when wealth is constant. In the long run, as wealth increases, the consumption function shifts upward, as in Figure 15-12. This upward shift prevents the average propensity to consume from falling as income increases. In this way, Modigliani reconciled the apparently conflicting studies of the consumption function.

Figure 15-12

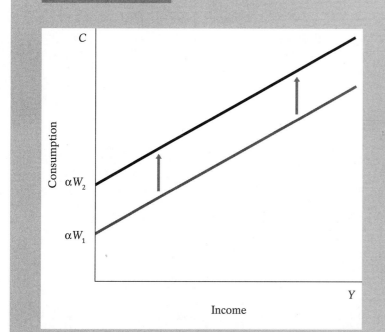

How Changes in Wealth Shift the Consumption Function If consumption depends on wealth, then an increase in wealth shifts the consumption function upward.

The life-cycle model makes many other predictions as well. Most important, it implies that saving varies over a person's life in a predictable way. If a person begins adulthood with no wealth, she will accumulate wealth during her working years and then run down her wealth during her retirement years. Figure 15-13 illustrates the consumer's income, consumption, and wealth over her adult life. A key implication is that the young who are working save, while the old who are retired dissave.

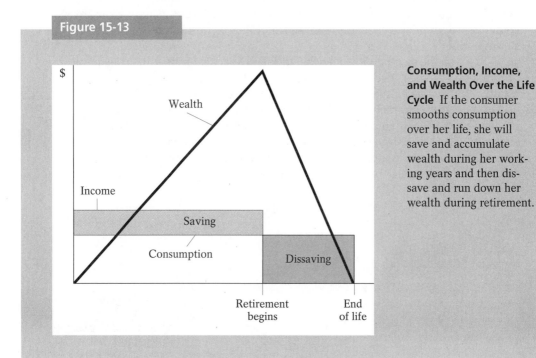

Figure 15-13

Consumption, Income, and Wealth Over the Life Cycle If the consumer smooths consumption over her life, she will save and accumulate wealth during her working years and then dissave and run down her wealth during retirement.

CASE STUDY

15·3   The Consumption and Saving of the Elderly

Many economists have studied the consumption and saving of the elderly. Their findings present a problem for the life-cycle model. It appears that the elderly do not dissave as much as the model predicts. In other words, the elderly do not run down their wealth as quickly as one would expect if they were trying to smooth their consumption over their remaining years of life.

There are two chief explanations for why the elderly do not dissave to the extent that the model predicts. Each suggests a direction for further research on consumption.

The first explanation is that the elderly are concerned about unpredictable expenses. Additional saving that arises from uncertainty is called **precautionary saving**. One reason for precautionary saving by the elderly is the possibility of living longer than expected and thus having to provide for a longer than average span of retirement. Another reason is the possibility of illness and large medical bills. The elderly may respond to this uncertainty by saving more in order to be better prepared for these contingencies.

The precautionary-saving explanation is not completely persuasive, because the elderly can largely insure against these risks. To protect against life-span uncertainty, they can buy *annuities* from insurance companies. For a fixed fee, annuities offer a stream of income that lasts as long as the recipient lives. Uncertainty about medical expenses should be largely eliminated by medicare and by private health insurance plans.

The second explanation for the failure of the elderly to dissave is that they may want to leave bequests to their children. Economists have proposed various theories of the parent–child relationship and the bequest motive. In Chapter 16 we discuss some of these theories and their implications for consumption.

Overall, research on the elderly suggests that the simplest life-cycle model cannot fully explain consumer behaviour. There is no doubt that providing for retirement is an important motive for saving, but other motives, such as precautionary saving and bequests, appear important as well.[4]

15•4 Milton Friedman and the Permanent-Income Hypothesis

In a book published in 1957, Milton Friedman proposed the **permanent-income hypothesis** to explain consumer behaviour. Friedman's permanent-income hypothesis complements Modigliani's life-cycle hypothesis: both use Irving Fisher's theory of the consumer to argue that consumption should not depend on current income alone. But unlike the life-cycle hypothesis, which emphasizes that income follows a regular pattern over a person's lifetime, the permanent-income hypothesis emphasizes that people experience random and temporary changes in their incomes from year to year.[5]

The Hypothesis

Friedman suggested that we view current income Y as the sum of two components, **permanent income** Y^P and **transitory income** Y^T. That is,

$$Y = Y^P + Y^T.$$

---

[4] To read more about the consumption and saving of the elderly, see Albert Ando and Arthur Kennickell, "How Much (or Little) Life Cycle Saving Is There in Micro Data?" in Rudiger Dornbusch, Stanley Fischer, and John Bossons, eds., *Macroeconomics and Finance: Essays in Honor of Franco Modigliani* (Cambridge, Mass.: MIT Press, 1986); and Michael Hurd, "Research on the Elderly: Economic Status, Retirement, and Consumption and Saving," *Journal of Economic Literature* 28 (June 1990): 565–589.

[5] Milton Friedman, *A Theory of the Consumption Function* (Princeton, N.J.: Princeton University Press, 1957).

Permanent income is the part of income that people expect to persist into the future. Transitory income is the part of income that people do not expect to persist. Put differently, permanent income is average income, and transitory income is the random deviation from that average.

To see how we might separate income into these two parts, consider these examples:

- Maria, who has a law degree, earned more this year than John, who is a high-school drop-out. Maria's higher income resulted from higher permanent income, because her education will continue to provide her a higher salary.

- Sue, a strawberry grower in the Niagara peninsula in Ontario, earned less than usual this year because dry weather reduced her crop. Bill, a strawberry grower in British Columbia, earned more than usual because the scarcity of strawberries in Ontario drove up selling prices. Bill's higher income resulted from higher transitory income, because he is no more likely to have good weather next year than Sue.

These examples show that different forms of income have different degrees of persistence. A good education provides a permanently higher income, whereas good weather provides only transitorily higher income. Although one can imagine intermediate cases, it is useful to keep things simple by supposing that there are only two kinds of income: permanent and transitory.

Friedman reasoned that consumption should depend primarily on permanent income, because consumers use saving and borrowing to smooth consumption in response to transitory changes in income. For example, if a person received a permanent raise of $10,000, his consumption would rise by about as much. Yet if a person won $10,000 in a lottery, he would not consume it all in one year. Instead, he would spread the extra consumption over the rest of his life. Assuming an interest rate of zero and a remaining lifespan of 50 years, consumption would rise by only $200 per year in response to the $10,000 prize. Thus, consumers spend their permanent income, but they save rather than spend most of their transitory income.

Friedman concluded that we should view the consumption function as approximately

$$C = \alpha Y^P,$$

where α is a constant. The permanent-income hypothesis, as expressed by this equation, states that consumption is proportional to permanent income.

Implications

The permanent-income hypothesis solves the consumption puzzle by suggesting that the standard Keynesian consumption function uses the wrong variable. According to the permanent-income hypothesis, consumption depends on permanent income; yet many studies of the consumption function try to relate consumption to current income. Friedman argued that this *errors-in-variables problem* explains the seemingly contradictory findings.

Let's see what Friedman's hypothesis implies for the average propensity to consume. Divide both sides of his consumption function by Y to obtain

$$APC = C/Y = \alpha Y^P/Y.$$

According to the permanent-income hypothesis, the average propensity to consume depends on the ratio of permanent income to current income. When current income temporarily rises above permanent income, the average propensity to consume temporarily falls; when current income temporarily falls below permanent income, the average propensity to consume temporarily rises.

Now consider the studies of household data. Friedman reasoned that these data reflect a combination of permanent and transitory income. Households with high permanent income would have proportionately higher consumption. If all variation in current income came from the permanent component, one would not observe differences in the average propensity to consume across households. But some of the variation in income comes from the transitory component, and households with high transitory income would not have higher consumption. Therefore, researchers would find that high-income households had, on average, lower average propensities to consume.

Similarly, consider the studies of time-series data. Friedman reasoned that year-to-year fluctuations in income are dominated by transitory income. Therefore, years of high income should be years of low average propensities to consume. But over long periods of time—say, from decade to decade—the variation in income comes from the permanent component. Hence, in long time-series, one should observe a constant average propensity to consume.

CASE STUDY

15·4   Income Taxes versus Sales Taxes as an Instrument for Stabilization Policy

The permanent-income hypothesis can help us to interpret how the economy responds to changes in fiscal policy. According to the *IS-LM* model of Chapters 9 and 10, income-tax cuts stimulate consumption and raise aggregate demand, and income-tax increases depress consumption and reduce aggregate demand. The permanent-income hypothesis, however, states that consumption responds only to changes in permanent income. Therefore, transitory changes in income taxes will have only a negligible effect on consumption and aggregate demand. If a change in personal income taxes is to have a large effect on aggregate demand, it must be permanent.

Several income-tax changes in the United States illustrate the relevance of this reasoning. The first example occurred in 1964 when personal income-tax rates were cut by about 18 percent. At the time, the public was told that the growth in U.S. GDP since World War II had been sufficient to permit the government's revenue needs to be met with lower tax rates. Thus, the tax cut was viewed as permanent, and consumer spending rose markedly. Then, in 1968, the U.S. government wanted to dampen private spending temporarily (while government spending was very high because of the war in Vietnam). The U.S.

government introduced a temporary personal income-tax "surcharge" of about 10 percent. Consumption, however, was reduced by only a small amount, just as the permanent-income theory predicts.

The U.S. government tried another temporary tax change in 1975. Because of the recession that followed the Oil Petroleum Exporting Countries (OPEC) crisis, the U.S. government returned to taxpayers some of the taxes already paid in 1974 and reduced income-tax rates for the balance of 1975. Once again, the public realized that this tax break was temporary, and so it had little effect on households' expectations about their long-run average income. Not surprisingly, households saved a large part of their tax rebates instead of spending them.

Finally, President Ronald Reagan introduced a series of tax cuts in the 1981–1984 period, reducing personal income-tax rates by about 23 percent. Households knew that Reagan had campaigned on a promise of smaller government, so the tax cuts were interpreted as likely to be permanent. As a result, these tax cuts did stimulate consumption spending significantly.

How have Canadian authorities responded to these U.S. policy experiments? In the 1978 federal budget, the Canadian government tried to stimulate spending with a sales-tax cut instead of an income-tax cut. A sales tax does not affect consumption only by raising or lowering households' estimates of their permanent income. Instead, a temporary sales-tax cut lowers the price of buying goods now, compared to the price in the future. Indeed, the *more* temporary a sales-tax change is, the more effective it is in changing the timing of people's spending.[6] Thus, sales taxes represent a much more reliable instrument for accomplishing stabilization policy. After all, the whole point of stabilization is to introduce a series of temporary stimuli to aggregate demand.

Unfortunately, until the GST was introduced in 1991, the federal government did not have a retail sales tax with which to implement stabilization policy. The 1978 budget tried to overcome this problem by having the federal government transfer some of its share of the personal income-tax revenue to the provinces in exchange for the provinces agreeing to lower sales-tax rates for a specified time period. Even though an agreement was reached "behind closed doors," the Quebec government refused to cooperate after the federal budget was made public. Quebec officials claimed that they must resist Ottawa's meddling in provincial affairs. Unfortunately, the political wrangling that ensued left the federal government uninterested in pursuing agreements of this sort again.

By 1991 the federal government had the GST, which gave the government a more predictable and powerful lever to use in attempts to adjust consumer expenditures for stabilization policy purposes. But, as this book goes to press, the government is considering replacing the GST with an increase in personal income taxes. The government feels that this switch might enhance political support, and this appeal may be stronger than any technical argument, based on the permanent-income hypothesis, that a sales tax is a better instrument for short-run stabilization policy.

---

[6]   Solid evidence is provided in Peter Gusson, "The Role of Provincial Governments in Economic Stabilization: The Case of Ontario's Auto Sales Tax Rebate" (Ottawa: Conference Board of Canada, 1978).

The fact that personal income-tax changes have significant effects on consumer spending only when those changes are expected to be permanent, is a dramatic illustration of the importance of the Lucas critique (that we discussed in Chapter 12). As explained there, the prominent economist Robert Lucas has emphasized that predictions of policy impact are quite inaccurate if economists do not focus on how policy affects expectations. The permanent-income hypothesis is a convenient way of organizing our analysis so that the Lucas critique is respected.

The permanent-income hypothesis has received support from numerous episodes other than government fiscal policies. For example, the dramatic stock market crash of 1987 was widely viewed as transitory, and (as the theory predicts) that event had little effect on consumer spending.

Rational Expectations and Consumption

The permanent-income hypothesis is founded on Fisher's model of intertemporal choice. It builds on the idea that forward-looking consumers base their consumption decisions not only on their current income but also on the income they expect to receive in the future. Thus, the permanent-income hypothesis highlights that consumption depends on people's expectations.

Recent research on consumption has combined this view of the consumer with the assumption of rational expectations. The rational-expectations assumption states that people use all available information to make optimal forecasts about the future. You might recall from Chapter 11 that this assumption has potentially profound implications for the costs of stopping inflation. It can also have profound implications for consumption.

The economist Robert Hall was the first to derive the implications of rational expectations for consumption. He showed that if the permanent-income hypothesis is correct, and if consumers have rational expectations, then changes in consumption over time should be unpredictable. When changes in a variable are unpredictable, the variable is said to follow a *random walk*. According to Hall, the combination of the permanent-income hypothesis and rational expectations implies that consumption follows a random walk.

Hall reasoned as follows. According to the permanent-income hypothesis, consumers face fluctuating income and try their best to smooth their consumption over time. At any moment, consumers choose consumption based on their current expectations of their lifetime incomes. Over time, they change their consumption because they receive news, which causes them to revise their expectations. For example, a person getting an unexpected promotion increases consumption, whereas a person getting an unexpected demotion decreases consumption. In other words, changes in consumption reflect "surprises" about lifetime income. If consumers are optimally using all available information, then these surprises should be unpredictable. Therefore, changes in their consumption should be unpredictable as well.

The evidence shows that the random-walk theory does not describe the world exactly. That is, changes in aggregate consumption are somewhat predictable.

Yet because the degree of predictability is small, some economists view the random-walk theory—and therefore the rational-expectations assumption—as a good approximation to reality.[7]

The rational-expectations approach to consumption has implications not only for forecasting but also for the analysis of economic policies. *If consumers obey the permanent-income hypothesis and have rational expectations, then only unexpected policy changes influence consumption. These policy changes take effect when they change expectations.* For example, suppose that today the federal government passes a tax increase to be effective next year. In this case, consumers receive the news about their lifetime incomes when the government passes the law (or even earlier if the law's passage was predictable). The arrival of this news causes consumers to revise their expectations and reduce their consumption. The following year, when the tax hike goes into effect, consumption is unchanged because no new news has arrived.

Hence, if the consumers have rational expectations, policymakers influence the economy not only through their actions but also through the public's expectation of their actions. Expectations, however, cannot be observed directly. Therefore, it is often hard to know how and when changes in fiscal policy alter aggregate demand.

CASE STUDY

15·5 **Do Consumers Anticipate Future Income?**

The essence of Fisher's model of the consumer—and of almost all subsequent work on consumption—is that consumption today depends not just on income today but also on income in the future. The more consumers expect to earn in the future, the more they consume today.

The model suggests that saving rates should help forecast future income growth. If consumers are saving a low fraction of current income, then they must be optimistic about future income. Conversely, if consumers are saving a high fraction of current income, then they must be pessimistic about future income. If this theory is correct, we should be able to examine data on the saving rate and find that periods of low saving are typically followed by periods of high income growth.[8]

Studies of time-series data on consumption and income provide support for this prediction. The saving rate does tend to rise when recessions are approaching, and booms are often preceded by low saving rates. Consumers do look ahead to their future income when making their consumption decisions.

The evidence is not completely consistent with the theory, however. In particular, saving moves less than predicted. In other words, it appears that future

---

[7]   Robert E. Hall, "Stochastic Implications of the Life Cycle-Permanent Income Hypothesis: Theory and Evidence," *Journal of Political Economy* 86 (April 1978): 971–987.

[8]   *Mathematical note*: To see how this works, consider our two-period example. Suppose that the interest rate is zero and that the consumer divides his total resources between the two periods, so that $C_1 = (Y_1 + Y_2)/2$. Then with simple algebraic rearrangement, you can show that $g = -2s$, where $g = (Y_2 - Y_1)/Y_1$ is the growth rate of income between the two periods and $s = (Y_1 - C_1)/Y_1$ is the first-period saving rate. Hence, saving and subsequent growth are negatively related.

income has a weaker influence on consumption, and current income has a stronger influence, than the permanent-income hypothesis predicts. One possible reason for this behaviour is that some consumers may not have rational expectations: they may base their expectations of future income excessively on current income. Another possible reason is that some consumers are borrowing-constrained and therefore base their consumption on current income alone.[9]

15•5 Conclusion

In the work of Keynes, Fisher, Modigliani, and Friedman, we have seen a progression of views on consumer behaviour. As a simplification, Keynes proposed that consumption depends largely on current income. Since then, economists have emphasized that consumers understand that they face an intertemporal decision. Consumers look ahead to their future resources and needs, implying a more complex consumption function than the one that Keynes proposed. Keynes suggested a consumption function of the form

$$\text{Consumption} = f(\text{Current Income}).$$

Recent work suggests instead that

$$\text{Consumption} = f(\text{Current Income, Wealth,}$$
$$\text{Expected Future Income, Interest Rates}).$$

In other words, current income is only one determinant of aggregate consumption.

Economists continue to debate the relative importance of these determinants of consumption. There remains disagreement, for example, on the effect of interest rates and the prevalence of borrowing constraints. One reason economists sometimes disagree about the effects of economic policy is that they are assuming different consumption functions. In the next chapter, we examine the debates about the impact of government debt, which are largely about alternative views of consumer behaviour.

Summary

1. Keynes conjectured that the marginal propensity to consume is between zero and one, that the average propensity to consume falls as income rises, and that current income is the primary determinant of consumption. Studies of household data and short time-series confirmed Keynes's conjectures. Yet studies of long time-series found no tendency for the average propensity to consume to fall as income rises over time.

---

[9]   John Y. Campbell, "Does Saving Anticipate Declining Labor Income?" *Econometrica* 55 (November 1982): 1249–1273; John Y. Campbell and N. Gregory Mankiw, "Consumption, Income, and Interest Rates: Reinterpreting the Time-Series Evidence," *NBER Macroeconomics Annual* (1989): 185–216.

2. Recent work on consumption builds on Irving Fisher's model of the consumer. In this model, the consumer faces an intertemporal budget constraint and chooses consumption for the present and the future to achieve the highest level of lifetime satisfaction. As long as the consumer can save and borrow, consumption depends on the consumer's lifetime resources.

3. Modigliani's life-cycle hypothesis emphasizes that income varies somewhat predictably over a person's life and that consumers use saving and borrowing to smooth their consumption over their lifetimes. The hypothesis implies that consumption depends on both income and wealth.

4. Friedman's permanent-income hypothesis emphasizes that individuals experience both permanent and transitory fluctuations in their income. Because consumers can save and borrow, and because they want to smooth their consumption, consumption does not respond much to transitory income. Consumption depends primarily on permanent income.

KEY CONCEPTS

Marginal propensity to consume

Average propensity to consume

Intertemporal budget constraint

Discounting

Indifference curves

Marginal rate of substitution

Normal good

Income effect

Substitution effect

Borrowing constraint

Life-cycle hypothesis

Precautionary saving

Permanent-income hypothesis

Permanent income

Transitory income

QUESTIONS FOR REVIEW

1. What were Keynes's three conjectures about the consumption function?

2. Describe the evidence that was consistent with Keynes's conjectures and the evidence that was inconsistent with them.

3. How do the life-cycle and permanent-income hypotheses resolve the seemingly contradictory pieces of evidence regarding consumption behaviour?

4. Use Fisher's model of consumption to analyze an increase in second-period income. Compare the case in which the consumer faces a binding borrowing constraint and the case in which he does not.

5. Explain why changes in consumption are unpredictable if consumers obey the permanent-income hypothesis and have rational expectations.

PROBLEMS AND APPLICATIONS

1. The chapter uses the Fisher model to discuss a change in the interest rate for a consumer who saves some of his first-period income. Suppose, instead, that the consumer is a borrower. How does that alter the analysis? Discuss the income and substitution effects on consumption in both periods.

2. The chapter analyzes Fisher's model for the case in which the consumer can save or borrow at an interest rate of r and for the case in which the consumer can save at this rate but cannot borrow at all. Consider now the intermediate case in which the consumer can save at rate r_s and borrow at rate r_b, where $r_s < r_b$.

   a. What is the consumer's budget constraint in the case in which he consumes less than his income in period one?

   b. What is the consumer's budget constraint in the case in which he consumes more than his income in period one?

   c. Graph the two budget constraints and shade the area that represents the combination of first-period and second-period consumption the consumer can choose.

   d. Now add to your graph the consumer's indifference curves. Show three possible outcomes: one in which the consumer saves, one in which he borrows, and one in which he neither saves nor borrows.

   e. What determines first-period consumption in each of the three cases?

3. Explain whether borrowing constraints increase or decrease the potency of fiscal policy to influence aggregate demand in each of the following two cases:

   a. a temporary tax cut

   b. an announced future tax cut

4. In the discussion of the life-cycle hypothesis in the text, income is assumed to be constant during the period before retirement. For most people, however, income grows over their lifetimes. How does this growth in income influence the lifetime pattern of consumption and wealth accumulation shown in Figure 15-13 under the following conditions?

   a. Consumers can borrow, so that their wealth can be negative.

   b. Consumers face borrowing constraints, which prevents their wealth from falling below zero.

Do you consider case (a) or case (b) to be more realistic? Why?

5. Demographers predict that the fraction of the population that is elderly will increase over the next 35 years. What does the life-cycle model predict for the influence of this demographic change on the national saving rate?

6. One study found that the elderly who do not have children dissave at about the same rate as the elderly who do have children. What might this finding imply about the reason the elderly do not dissave as much as the life-cycle model predicts?

CHAPTER 16

The Debates Over Government Debt

All decent people live beyond their incomes nowadays and those
who aren't respectable live beyond other people's. A few gifted indi-
viduals manage to do both.

Saki

When a government spends more than it collects in taxes, it borrows from the private sector to finance the budget deficit. The accumulation of past borrowing is the government debt. All national governments have some debt, although the amount varies substantially from country to country. Table 16-1 shows the amount of government debt (all levels) for 18 major countries.

Focusing on just the Canadian federal government, national debt is the sum total of all the annual budget deficits incurred since confederation in 1867. That debt reached the $500 billion mark in 1994. Most of this debt accumulated in recent years—only 5 percent can be attributed to the country's first 100 years of existence! The federal debt shot up during the Great Depression of the 1930s and ballooned during World War II, as Figure 16-1 shows. These developments have not been interpreted as government mismanagement, however, because people have reasoned that the government had no choice but to get involved in

Table 16-1

How Indebted Are the World's Governments?

Country	Government Debt as a Percentage of GDP	Country	Government Debt as a Percentage of GDP
Belgium	141 %	United States	66
Italy	116	France	61
Ireland	93	Spain	59
Greece	91	Austria	56
Canada	87	United Kingdom	52
Netherlands	81	Finland	50
Sweden	76	Germany	50
Denmark	68	Norway	50
Japan	66	Australia	39

Source: OECD Economic Outlook. Figures are based on estimates of the gross public debt and GDP for 1994.

Figure 16-1

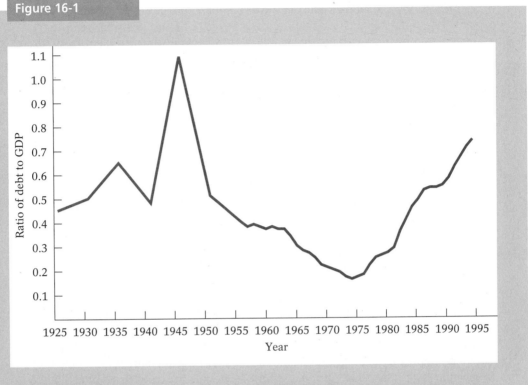

Ratio of National Debt This graph shows the federal government debt as a proportion of GDP. The debt rose dramatically during the Great Depression and World War II and then was brought back down. The rise in the debt ratio since the early 1970s has caused concern, because it has occurred with neither a massive depression nor a war.

Source: Department of Finance.

these crises. Most people think that because future generations have benefited from the freedom that the war ensured, it is only fair that they shoulder some of the burden. Issuing debt during the war, therefore, was the government's way of spreading some of the costs to future generations.

Following the war, the federal government's debt/GDP ratio was 110 percent. By 1970, it was less than 20 percent. The debt ratio was brought under control in three main ways. First, the government ran budget surpluses for a number of years in the 1945–1970 period, and in each of those years the debt was decreased by the amount of the surplus. Second, Canada enjoyed a long period of rapid economic growth. With real GDP growing briskly, the ratio of the outstanding debt to GDP shrank at a rapid rate. Finally, during the Korean War period in the early 1950s, and during the 1965–1980 period, Canada's inflation rate reduced the real value of the debt by a significant amount. Unexpected inflation is simply a gradual (some would say "civilized") way for a country to default on some of its debt.

By 1994, the federal debt ratio had climbed back up to 75 percent. There were two main reasons for this dramatic reversal of the postwar trend. First, Canada's average growth rate for real GDP has been lower since the mid-1970s, when most western countries began suffering from a slowdown in productivity growth. Second, the government has simply overspent. The federal government has not run a surplus since the early 1970s. Even with the debt as big as it has become, the size of recent annual deficits guarantees that the total will continue to increase substantially. For example, the federal deficit of $40 billion in the 1994–1995 fiscal year increased the debt by another 8 percent in just that one year.

Broadly speaking, there are three reasons why we should be concerned about this increase in debt. First, Canadians are getting more indebted to foreigners. As a proportion of GDP, Canada's net foreign debt (including all forms, not just government debt) was almost 50 percent in 1994. This put Canada in *first* place among G7 countries in foreign debt standings. (The second- and third-place finishers were Italy at 12 percent and the United States at 10 percent.) Just to pay the interest on that debt, Canadians had to give up 4.5 percent of GDP in 1994. On average, it is unrealistic to expect Canada's economy to grow at that rate, so the prospects for an improvement in the Canadian standard of living are bleak. Second, many regard the debt as worrisome because it may lead to further tax increases in order to pay for the interest. The tax/GDP ratio in Canada increased from 31.5 percent in 1980 to 37.5 percent in 1993, and despite higher taxes, federal debt service costs rose from 20 percent of tax revenue to 32 percent of revenue over this same period. Some individuals are concerned that higher taxes have already reduced labour supply, investment, and economic efficiency. Finally, the existence of the debt raises issues of equity. Some regard it as immoral that one generation "spends beyond its means," thereby lowering the standard of living for future generations through such mechanisms as reduced government programs, (for example, unemployment insurance and support for education and health).

Thus, our current high debt levels have sparked a renewed interest among economists and policymakers in the economic effects of government debt. Some view these large budget deficits as the worst mistake of economic policy since the Great Depression. Perhaps surprisingly, others think that the deficits matter very little.

This chapter presents the various views of government debt. Section 16·1 describes the traditional view of government debt, according to which government borrowing reduces national saving and crowds out capital accumulation. This view is held by most economists and has been implicit in the discussion of fiscal policy throughout this textbook.

Section 16·2 discusses an alternative view, called Ricardian equivalence, which is held by a small but influential minority of economists. According to the Ricardian view, government debt does not influence saving and capital accumulation. We will see that this debate over government debt arises from disagreements over the theory of consumption. In evaluating whether the traditional or the Ricardian view of government debt is correct, the key question is how fiscal policy affects consumer spending. To analyze the effects of government budget deficits on the economy, we must take a stand on whether consumers are short-sighted or forward-looking, on whether they face borrowing constraints or not, and on other aspects of consumer behaviour.

Section 16·3 turns to another set of issues in the debate over government debt. We will see that the budget deficit is not as easy to measure as it might seem. Some economists have argued that traditional measures of the budget deficit are misleading. We discuss the federal government's deficit reduction targets and estimate the benefits of deficit reduction in Section 16·3 and in the Appendix to this chapter.

16·1 The Traditional View of Government Debt

You are an economist working for the Department of Finance in Ottawa. You receive this letter from a member of Parliament (MP):

> Dear Finance Canada Economist:
>
> Parliament is about to consider the government's proposal to cut all taxes by 20 percent. Before deciding whether to endorse the policy, I would like your analysis. I see little hope of reducing government spending, so the tax cut would mean an increase in the budget deficit. How would the tax cut and budget deficit affect the economy and the economic well-being of the country?
>
> Sincerely,
>
> Member of Parliament

Before responding to the MP, you open up your favourite economics text-book—this one, of course—to see what the models predict for such a change in fiscal policy.

To analyze the long-run effects of this policy change, you turn to the models in Chapters 3 and 4. The model in Chapter 3 shows that a tax cut stimulates consumer spending and reduces national saving. The reduction in saving raises the interest rate, which crowds out investment. The Solow growth model in Chapter 4 shows that lower investment eventually leads to a lower steady-state capital stock and a lower level of output. Because the economy starts with less capital than in the Golden Rule steady state, the reduction in steady-state capital implies lower consumption and reduced economic well-being.

To analyze the short-run effects of the policy change, you turn to the *IS-LM* model in Chapters 9 and 10. This model shows that a tax cut stimulates consumer spending, which implies an expansionary shift in the *IS* curve. If there is no change in monetary policy, the shift in the *IS* curve leads to an expansionary shift in the aggregate demand curve. In the short run, when prices are sticky, the expansion in aggregate demand leads to higher output and lower unemployment. Over time, as prices adjust, the economy returns to the natural rate of output, and the higher aggregate demand results in a higher price level.

To see how international trade affects your analysis, you turn to the open-economy models in Chapters 7 and 13. The model in Chapter 7 shows that reduced national saving causes a trade deficit. Although the inflow of capital from abroad lessens the effect of the fiscal policy change on capital accumulation, it implies that Canada becomes indebted to foreign countries. The fiscal policy change also causes the Canadian dollar to appreciate, which makes foreign goods cheaper in Canada and domestic goods more expensive abroad. The Mundell-Fleming model in Chapter 13 shows that this appreciation of the Canadian dollar and fall in net exports reduce the short-run expansionary impact of the fiscal change on output and employment.

With all these models in mind, you draft a response:

Dear MP:

A tax cut financed by government borrowing would have many effects on the economy. The immediate impact of the tax cut would be to stimulate consumer spending. Higher consumer spending affects the economy in both the short run and the long run.

In the short run, higher consumer spending would raise the demand for goods and services and thus raise output and employment. Interest rates would also rise, however, as investors competed for a smaller flow of saving. Higher interest rates would discourage investment and would encourage capital to flow in from abroad. The dollar would rise in value against foreign currencies, which would make Canadian firms less competitive in world markets.

In the long run, the smaller national saving caused by the tax cut would mean a smaller capital stock and a greater foreign debt. Therefore, the output of the nation would be smaller, and a greater share of that output would be owed to foreigners.

The overall effect of the tax cut on economic well-being is hard to judge. Current generations would benefit from higher consumption and higher employment, although inflation would likely be higher as well. Future generations would bear much of the burden of today's budget deficits: they would be born into a nation with a smaller capital stock and a larger foreign debt.

Your faithful servant,

Finance Canada Economist

The MP replies:

Dear Finance Canada Economist:

Thank you for your letter. It made sense to me. But yesterday my committee heard testimony from a prominent economist who called herself a "Ricardian" and who reached quite a different conclusion. She said that a tax cut by itself would not stimulate consumer spending. She concluded that the budget deficit would therefore not have all the effects you listed. What's going on here?

Sincerely,

MP

After studying the next section, you write back to the MP, explaining in detail the debate over Ricardian equivalence.

16•2 The Ricardian View of Government Debt

Modern theories of consumer behaviour emphasize that, because consumers are forward-looking, consumption does not depend on current income alone. The forward-looking consumer is at the heart of Franco Modigliani's life-cycle hypothesis and Milton Friedman's permanent-income hypothesis. The Ricardian view of government debt applies the logic of the forward-looking consumer to analyze the impact of fiscal policy.

The Basic Logic of Ricardian Equivalence

Consider the response of a forward-looking consumer to the tax cut that Parliament is debating. The consumer might reason as follows:

> The government is cutting taxes without any plans to reduce government spending. Does this policy alter my set of opportunities? Am I richer because of this tax cut? Should I consume more?
>
> Maybe not. The government is financing the tax cut by running a budget deficit. At some point in the future, the government will have to raise taxes to pay off the debt and accumulated interest. So the policy really represents a tax cut today coupled with a tax hike in the future. The tax cut merely gives me transitory income that eventually will be taken back. I am not any better off, so I will leave my consumption unchanged.

The forward-looking consumer understands that government borrowing today means higher taxes in the future. A tax cut financed by government debt does not reduce the tax burden; it merely reschedules it. It does not raise the consumer's permanent income and, therefore, does not increase consumption.

One can view this argument another way. Suppose that the government borrows $1,000 from the typical citizen to give that citizen a $1,000 tax cut. In essence, this policy is the same as giving the citizen a $1,000 government bond as a gift. One side of the bond says, "The government owes you, the bondholder, $1,000 plus interest." The other side says, "You, the taxpayer, owe the government $1,000 plus interest." Overall, the gift of a bond from the government to the typical citizen does not make the citizen richer or poorer, because the value of the bond is offset by the value of the future tax liability.

The general principle is that government debt is equivalent to future taxes, and if consumers are sufficiently forward-looking, future taxes are equivalent to current taxes. Hence, financing the government by debt is equivalent to financing it by taxes. This view, called **Ricardian equivalence**, is named after the famous nineteenth-century economist David Ricardo, because he first noted the theoretical argument.[1]

---

[1] Ironically, Ricardo was not a Ricardian. He was skeptical about the theory that now bears his name.

The implication of Ricardian equivalence is that a debt-financed tax cut leaves consumption unaffected. Households save the extra disposable income to pay the future tax liability that the tax cut implies. This increase in private saving just offsets the decrease in public saving. National saving—the sum of private and public saving—remains the same. The tax cut therefore has none of the effects that the traditional analysis predicts.

The logic of Ricardian equivalence does not imply that all changes in fiscal policy are irrelevant. Changes in fiscal policy do influence consumer spending if they influence present or future government purchases. For example, suppose that the government cuts taxes today because it plans to reduce government purchases in the future. If the consumer understands that this tax cut does not imply an increase in future taxes, he feels richer and raises his consumption. But note that it is the reduction in government purchases, rather than the reduction in taxes, that stimulates consumption: the announcement of a future reduction in government purchases would raise consumption today even if current taxes were unchanged, because it would imply lower taxes at some time in the future.

The Government Budget Constraint

To better understand the link between government debt and future taxes, it is useful to imagine that the economy lasts for only two periods. Period one represents the present, and period two the future. In period one, the government collects taxes T_1 and makes purchases G_1; in period two, it collects taxes T_2 and makes purchases G_2. Because the government can run a budget deficit or a budget surplus, taxes and purchases in any single period need not be closely related.

We want to see how the government's tax receipts in the two periods are related to its purchases in the two periods. In the first period, the budget deficit equals government purchases minus taxes. That is,

$$D = G_1 - T_1,$$

where D is the deficit. The government finances this deficit by selling an equal amount of government bonds. In the second period, the government must collect enough taxes to repay the debt, including the accumulated interest, and to pay for its second-period purchases. Thus,

$$T_2 = (1 + r)D + G_2,$$

where r is the interest rate.

To derive the equation linking taxes and purchases, combine the two equations above. Substitute the first equation for D into the second equation to obtain

$$T_2 = (1 + r)(G_1 - T_1) + G_2.$$

This equation relates purchases in the two periods to taxes in the two periods.

To make the equation easier to interpret, we rearrange terms. After a little algebra, we obtain

$$T_1 + \frac{T_2}{1 + r} = G_1 + \frac{G_2}{1 + r}.$$

This equation is the **government budget constraint**. It states that the present value of government purchases must equal the present value of taxes.

The government budget constraint shows how changes in fiscal policy today are linked to changes in fiscal policy in the future. If the government cuts first-period taxes without altering first-period purchases, then it enters the second period owing a debt to the holders of government bonds. This debt forces the government to choose between reducing purchases and raising taxes.

Figure 16-2 uses the Fisher diagram from Chapter 15 to show how a tax cut in period one affects the consumer under the assumption that the government does not alter its purchases in either period. In period one, the government cuts taxes by ΔT and finances this tax cut by borrowing. In period two, the government must raise taxes by $(1 + r)\Delta T$ to repay its debt and accumulated

Figure 16-2

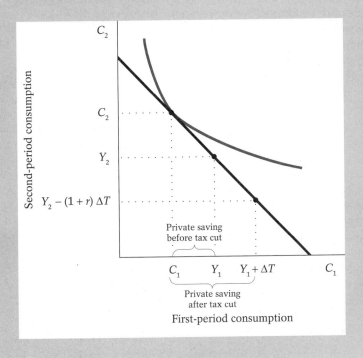

A Debt-Financed Tax Cut in the Fisher Diagram A debt-financed tax cut of ΔT raises first-period income. Yet if government purchases are unchanged, then the government budget constraint requires that second period taxes be raised by $(1 + r)\Delta T$. Because the present value of income is unchanged, the budget constraint is unchanged, and the consumer chooses the same consumption as before the tax cut. Hence, Ricardian equivalence holds.

interest. Thus, the change in fiscal policy raises the consumer's income by ΔT in period one and reduces it by $(1 + r)\Delta T$ in period two. The consumer's set of opportunities is unchanged, however, because the present value of the consumer's lifetime income is the same as before the change in fiscal policy. Therefore, the consumer chooses the same level of consumption as he would have without the tax cut, which implies that private saving rises by the amount of the tax cut. Hence, by combining the government budget constraint and Fisher's model of intertemporal choice, we obtain the Ricardian result that a debt-financed tax cut does not affect consumption.

Consumers and Future Taxes

The essence of the Ricardian view is that when people choose their consumption, they rationally look ahead to the future taxes implied by government debt. But how forward-looking are consumers? Defenders of the traditional view of government debt believe that future taxes do not have as large an influence on current consumption as the Ricardian view assumes. Here are some of their arguments.[2]

Myopia   Economists who support the Ricardian view of fiscal policy assume that people are rational when making important decisions such as choosing how much of their income to consume and how much to save. Rational consumers look ahead to the future taxes implied by current government borrowing. Thus, the Ricardian view presumes that people have substantial knowledge and foresight.

One possible argument for the traditional view of tax cuts is that people are short-sighted, perhaps because they do not fully comprehend the implications of government budget deficits. It is possible that some people follow simple and not fully rational rules of thumb when choosing how much to save. Suppose, for example, that a person acts on the assumption that future taxes will be the same as current taxes. This person will fail to take account of future changes in taxes implied by current government policies. A debt-financed tax cut will lead this person to believe that his permanent income has increased, even if it hasn't. The tax cut will therefore lead to higher consumption and lower national saving.

Borrowing Constraints   The Ricardian view of government debt is based on the permanent-income hypothesis. This view assumes that consumption does not depend on current income alone, but on permanent income, which includes both current and expected future income. According to the Ricardian view, a debt-financed tax cut increases current income, but it leaves permanent income and consumption unchanged.

Advocates of the traditional view of government debt argue that we should not rely totally on the permanent-income hypothesis, because some consumers face borrowing constraints. As we discussed in Chapter 15, a person fac-

---

[2] For a thorough survey of the debate over Ricardian equivalence, see Douglas Bernheim, "Ricardian Equivalence: An Evaluation of Theory and Evidence," *NBER Macroeconomics Annual* (1987), 263–303.

ing a binding borrowing constraint can consume only his current income. For this person, current income rather than permanent income determines consumption; a debt-financed tax cut raises current income and thus consumption, even though future income is lower. In essence, when the government cuts current taxes and raises future taxes, it is giving taxpayers a loan. For individuals who wanted to obtain a loan but were unable to, the tax cut raises consumption.

Figure 16-3 uses the Fisher diagram to illustrate how a debt-financed tax cut raises consumption for a consumer facing a borrowing constraint. As we saw previously, this change in fiscal policy raises first-period income by ΔT and lowers second-period income by $(1 + r)\Delta T$. But the result is now different. Although the present value of income is the same, the consumer's set of opportunities is larger: the tax cut has loosened the borrowing constraint that prevents first-period consumption from exceeding first-period income. The consumer can now choose point B rather than point A.

Figure 16-3

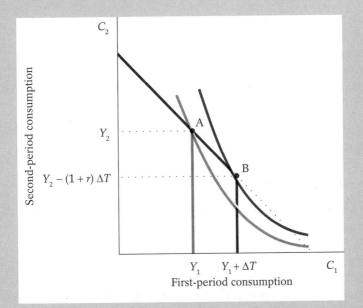

How a Debt-Financed Tax Cut Relaxes a Borrowing Constraint The consumer here faces two constraints. The budget constraint says that the present value of consumption must not exceed the present value of income. The borrowing constraint says that first-period consumption must not exceed first-period income. A debt-financed tax cut of ΔT raises first-period income by ΔT and reduces second-period income by $(1 + r)\Delta T$. Because the present value of income is unchanged, the budget constraint is unchanged. Yet because first-period income is higher, the borrowing constraint allows a higher level of first-period consumption. The consumer now chooses point B rather than point A. Hence, Ricardian equivalence fails to hold.

You can see that the debate over government debt naturally evolves into a debate over consumer behaviour. If many consumers would like to borrow to consume but cannot, then a debt-financed tax cut will stimulate consumption, as the traditional view assumes. Yet if borrowing constraints are unimportant for most consumers and if the permanent-income hypothesis is valid, then consumers are more likely to take into account the future taxes implied by government debt.

CASE STUDY

16•1 A Test of Ricardian Equivalence

In 1994, changes in Canada's personal income tax system forced many individuals to increase the amount of taxes they paid on a quarterly installment basis (rather than paying taxes just once each year in April on income that does not involve automatic tax deductions by one's employer). Is this change likely to affect consumer spending? Some evidence is available from a similar change that was introduced in the United States just two years earlier.

The American policy was an attempt to deal with a lingering recession by lowering the amount of income taxes that were being withheld from workers' pay cheques. The policy did not lower the amount of taxes that workers owed; it merely delayed payment. The higher take-home pay that workers received during 1992 was to be offset by higher tax payments, or smaller tax refunds, when income taxes were due in April 1993.

What effect would you predict for this policy? According to the logic of Ricardian equivalence, consumers should realize that their lifetime resources were unchanged and, therefore, save the extra take-home pay to meet the upcoming tax liability. Yet George Bush, the U.S. president at the time, claimed his policy would provide "money people can use to help pay for clothing, college, or to get a new car." That is, he believed that consumers would spend the extra income, thereby stimulating aggregate demand and helping the economy to recover from the recession. Bush seemed to be assuming that consumers were short-sighted or faced binding borrowing constraints.

Gauging the actual effects of this policy is difficult with aggregate data, because many other things were happening at the same time. Yet some evidence comes from a survey two economists conducted shortly after the policy was announced. The survey asked people what they would do with the extra income. Fifty-seven percent of the respondents said they would save it, use it to repay debts, or adjust their withholding in order to reverse the effect of Bush's executive order. Forty-three percent said they would spend the extra income. Thus, for this policy change, a majority of the population was planning to act Ricardian. Nonetheless, Bush was partly right: many people planned to spend the extra income, even though they understood that the following year's tax bill would be higher.[3]

[3] Matthew D. Shapiro and Joel Slemrod, "Consumer Response to the Timing of Income: Evidence from a Change in Tax Withholding," NBER Working Paper No. 4344 (1993).

These U.S. results suggest that the Canadian policy (which is essentially the reverse of the American initiative in 1992) would lower the government's budget deficit temporarily and dampen aggregate demand temporarily (thereby weakening Canada's recovery slightly). It is the first of these two effects that appeals to the government.

Future Generations Besides myopia and borrowing constraints, a third argument for the traditional view of government debt is that consumers expect the implied future taxes to fall not on them but on future generations. Suppose, for example, that the government cuts taxes today, issues 30-year bonds to finance the budget deficit, and then raises taxes in 30 years to repay the loan. In this case, the government debt represents a transfer of wealth from the next generation of taxpayers (which faces the tax hike) to the current generation of taxpayers (which gets the tax cut). This transfer raises the lifetime resources of the current generation, so it raises their consumption. In essence, a debt-financed tax cut stimulates consumption because it gives the current generation the opportunity to consume at the expense of the next generation.

Economist Robert Barro has provided a clever rejoinder to this argument to support the Ricardian view. Barro argues that because future generations are the children and grandchildren of the current generation, we should not view them as independent economic actors. Instead, he argues, the appropriate assumption is that current generations care about future generations. This altruism between generations is evidenced by the gifts that many people give their children, often in the form of bequests at the time of their death. The existence of bequests suggests that many people are not eager to take advantage of the opportunity to consume at their children's expense.

According to Barro's analysis, the relevant decisionmaking unit is not the individual who lives only a finite number of years, but the family, which continues indefinitely. In other words, an individual decides how much to consume based not only on his own income but also on the income of future members of his family. A debt-financed tax cut may raise the income an individual receives in his lifetime, but it does not raise his family's permanent income. Instead of consuming the extra income from the tax cut, the individual saves it and leaves it as a bequest to his children who will bear the future tax liability.

Drawing by Dave Carpenter. From *The Wall Street Journal*. Permission, Cartoon Features Syndicate.

"What's this I hear about you adults mortgaging my future?"

Again, we see that the debate over government debt is really a debate over consumer behaviour. The Ricardian view assumes that consumers have a long time horizon. Barro's analysis of the family implies that the consumer's time horizon, like the government's, is effectively infinite. Yet it is possible that consumers do not look ahead to the tax liabilities of future generations, perhaps because they do not care enough about their children to leave them a bequest. In this case, a debt-financed tax cut can alter consumption by redistributing wealth among generations.[4]

CASE STUDY

16•2   Why Do Parents Leave Bequests?

The debate over Ricardian equivalence is partly a debate over how different generations are linked to one another. Robert Barro's defense of the Ricardian view is based on the assumption that parents leave their children bequests because they care about them. But is altruism really the reason that parents leave bequests?

One group of economists has suggested that parents use bequests to control their children. Parents often want their children to do certain things for them, such as phoning home regularly and visiting on holidays. Perhaps parents use the implicit threat of disinheritance to induce their children to be more attentive.

To test this "strategic bequest motive," these economists examined data on how often children visit their parents. They found that the more wealthy the parent, the more often the children visit. Even more striking was another result: only wealth that can be left as a bequest induces more frequent visits. Wealth that cannot be bequeathed, such as pension wealth which reverts back to the pension company in the event of an early death, does not encourage children to visit. These findings suggest that there may be more to the relationships among generations than mere altruism.[5]

Making a Choice

Having considered the traditional and Ricardian views of government debt, you should ask yourself two sets of questions.

First, which view do you agree with? If the government cuts taxes today, runs a budget deficit, and raises taxes in the future, how will the policy affect the economy? Will it stimulate consumption, as the traditional view holds? Or will consumers understand that their permanent income is unchanged and, therefore, offset the budget deficit with higher private saving?

---

[4] Robert J. Barro, "Are Government Bonds Net Wealth?" *Journal of Political Economy* 81 (1974): 1095–1117.

[5] B. Douglas Bernheim, Andrei Shleifer, and Lawrence H. Summers, "The Strategic Bequest Motive," *Journal of Political Economy* 93 (1985): 1045–1076.

Second, why do you hold the view that you do? If you agree with the traditional view of government debt, what is the reason? Do consumers fail to understand that higher government borrowing today means higher taxes tomorrow? Or do they ignore future taxes, either because they are borrowing-constrained or because future taxes fall on future generations with which they do not feel an economic link? If you hold the Ricardian view, do you believe that consumers have the foresight to see that government borrowing today implies future taxes to be levied on them or their descendants? Do you believe that consumers will save the extra income to offset that future tax liability?

One might have hoped that we could turn to the evidence to decide between these two views of government debt. Yet when economists examine historical episodes of large budget deficits, the evidence is inconclusive. History can be interpreted in different ways.

Consider, for example, the experience of the 1980s. The large budget deficits run by most western countries seem to offer a natural experiment to test the two views of government debt. At first glance, this episode appears decisively to support the traditional view. The large budget deficits coincided with low national saving, high real interest rates, and large trade deficits. Indeed, advocates of the traditional view of government debt often claim that the experience of the 1980s confirms their position.

Yet those who hold the Ricardian view of government debt interpret these events differently. Perhaps saving was low in the 1980s because people were optimistic about future economic growth—an optimism that was also reflected in a booming stock market. Or perhaps saving was low because people expected that budget deficits would eventually lead not to higher taxes but to lower government spending instead. Because it is hard to rule out any of these interpretations, both views of government debt survive.

16•3   Is the Budget Deficit Correctly Measured?

Although the debate between the traditional and Ricardian views of government debt is central to the disagreements among economists over fiscal policy, it is not the only source of controversy. Even economists who hold the traditional view that government borrowing has important effects on the economy argue among themselves about how best to evaluate fiscal policy.

Many of the arguments concern the question of how the budget deficit should be measured. Some economists believe that the deficit as currently measured is not a good indicator of the stance of fiscal policy. They believe that the budget deficit does not accurately gauge either the impact of fiscal policy on today's economy or the burden being placed on future generations of taxpayers. In this section we discuss four problems with the usual measure of the budget deficit.

The general principle is that *the government budget deficit should accurately reflect the change in the government's overall indebtedness*. This principle seems simple enough. But its application is not as straightforward as one might expect.

Measurement Problem No. 1: Inflation

The least controversial of the measurement issues is the correction for inflation. Almost all economists agree that the government's indebtedness should be measured in real terms, not in nominal terms. The measured deficit should equal the change in the government's real debt, not the change in its nominal debt.

The budget deficit as commonly measured, however, does not correct for inflation. To see how large an error this induces, consider the following example. Suppose that the real government debt is not changing; in other words, in real terms, the budget is balanced. In this case, the nominal debt must be rising at the rate of inflation. That is,

$$\Delta B/B = \pi,$$

where π is the inflation rate and B is the stock of government bonds. This implies

$$\Delta B = \pi B.$$

The government would look at the change in the nominal debt ΔB and would report a budget deficit of πB. Hence, most economists believe that the reported budget deficit is overstated by the amount πB.

One can make the same argument another way. The deficit is government expenditure minus government revenue. Part of expenditure is the interest paid on the government bonds. Expenditure should include only the real interest paid on the debt rB, not the nominal interest paid iB. Because the difference between the nominal interest rate i and the real interest rate r is the inflation rate π, the budget deficit is overstated by πB.

This correction for inflation can be large, especially when inflation is high, and it can often change one's evaluation of fiscal policy. For example, in 1981, the federal government reported a budget deficit of over \$7 billion. But inflation was over 12 percent, and after correction for inflation, the deficit turned into a small surplus.

Measurement Problem No. 2: The Business Cycle

Many economists believe that government spending and tax rates should be set so that the budget *would* be balanced *if* real GDP was at the natural rate. If this were accomplished, we would observe deficits during recessions (when unemployment is high and the government is making more transfer payments and collecting fewer tax dollars), and we would observe surpluses during booms (when employment and tax revenue are high and unemployment insurance and welfare payments are low). To assess fiscal policy, then, we need to know what the deficit would be if we were not undergoing a business cycle.

To solve this problem, the Department of Finance calculates what it calls the **cyclically adjusted budget deficit**—what the excess of spending over revenue would be if Canadian GDP were at its natural-rate value. We can now clarify how these data are used. In 1994, the actual federal deficit was about \$40 billion, while the cyclically adjusted deficit was estimated to be approximately $25 billion. According to these calculations, about $15 billion of the $40 billion total resulted from the fact that unemployment was so high in 1994. According to this approach, any attempt to push the deficit below $15 billion is regarded as inappropriate, since that part of the deficit was simply due to the state of the economy. It would vanish automatically when the economy returned to the natural rate. Efforts to eliminate it any earlier just prolong and deepen the recession. It is true that the national debt increases while we wait for this automatic elimination of that fraction of the deficit to take place. However, since there should be budget surpluses in the boom years, there should be no tendency for debt to grow over the longer run.

As the 1994 example makes clear, however, an appeal to cyclical corrections can hardly excuse recent fiscal policy. There was still no justification for the remaining cyclically adjusted deficit of $25 billion in 1994.

Measurement Problem No. 3: Capital Assets

Many economists believe that an accurate assessment of the government's budget deficit requires accounting for the government's assets as well as its liabilities. In particular, when measuring the government's overall indebtedness, we should subtract government assets from government debt. Therefore, the budget deficit should be measured as the change in debt minus the change in assets.

Certainly, individuals and firms treat assets and liabilities symmetrically. When a person borrows to buy a house, we do not say that he is running a budget deficit. Instead, we offset the increase in assets (the house) against the increase in debt (the mortgage) and record no change in net wealth. Perhaps we should treat the government's finances the same way.

A budget procedure that accounts for assets as well as liabilities is called **capital budgeting**, because it takes into account changes in capital. For example, suppose that the government sells one of its office buildings or some of its land and uses the proceeds to reduce the government debt. Under current budget procedures, the reported deficit would be lower. Under capital budgeting, the revenue received from the sale would not lower the deficit because the reduction in debt would be offset by a reduction in assets. Similarly, under capital budgeting, government borrowing to finance the purchase of a capital good would not raise the deficit.

The major difficulty with capital budgeting is that it is hard to decide which government expenditures should count as capital expenditures. For example, should the highway system be counted as an asset of the government? If so, what is its value? Should spending on education and health be treated as expenditure on human capital? These difficult questions must be answered if the government is to adopt a capital budget.

Economists and policymakers disagree about whether governments should use capital budgeting. Opponents of capital budgeting argue that, although the system is superior in principle to the current system, it is too difficult to implement in practice. Proponents of capital budgeting argue that even an imperfect treatment of capital assets would be better than ignoring them altogether.

Measurement Problem No. 4: Uncounted Liabilities

Some economists argue that the measured budget deficit is misleading because it excludes some important government liabilities. For example, consider the Canada and Quebec Pension Plans. People pay some of their income into the system when young and expect to receive benefits when old. Perhaps accumulated future pension benefits should be included in the government's liabilities.

One might argue that pension liabilities are different from government debt because the government can change the laws determining pension benefits. Yet, in principle, the government could always choose not to repay all of its debt: the government honours its debt only because it chooses to do so. Promises to pay the holders of government debt may not be fundamentally different from promises to pay the future recipients of the public pension system. As of 1994, the unfunded debt of the Canada Pension Plan was about $500 billion—an amount that is just as big as the entire federal debt that is usually reported.

A particularly difficult form of government liability to measure is its *contingent liability*—the liability that is due only if a specified event occurs. For example, the government guarantees many forms of private credit, such as student loans, mortgages for low- and moderate-income families, and deposits in banks and trust companies. If the borrower repays the loan, the government pays nothing; if the borrower defaults, the government makes the repayment. When the government provides this guarantee, it undertakes a liability contingent on the borrower's default. Yet this contingent liability is not reflected in the budget deficit, in part because it is not clear what dollar value to attach to it.

Whither the Budget Deficit?

Economists differ in the importance they place on these measurement problems. Some believe that the problems are so severe that the measured budget deficit is almost meaningless. Most take these measurement problems seriously but still view the measured budget deficit as a useful indicator of fiscal policy.

The undisputed lesson is that, to evaluate fully the course of fiscal policy, economists and policymakers must look at more than just the measured budget deficit. And, in fact, they do. No economic statistic is perfect. Whenever one sees a number reported in the media, it is important to know what it is measuring and what it is leaving out. This is especially true for the government budget deficit.

CASE STUDY

16•3   **The Federal Government Deficit Reduction Targets**

The primary deficit is the excess of all the government's program spending over its tax revenue. Program spending is all government expenditure except interest payments. The overall deficit is the primary deficit plus the government's interest payment obligations on its outstanding debt. To reduce the outstanding debt, the government must run an overall surplus, and this, in turn, requires a primary surplus that exceeds the existing interest payment obligations. As a first step, then, the government must eliminate its primary deficit. While this first step is not sufficient to reduce Canada's national debt, is it at least enough to eliminate the explosive growth we have observed in debt? A quick look at Canadian history suggests not.

Brian Mulroney's Conservative government maintained a small primary surplus (on average) over its nine years (1984–1993) in office. This compares with a sizable primary deficit (an average of $6.6 billion each year) for the Liberals during the 1976–1984 period. Despite this effort by the Conservatives, the deficit problem worsened during their term of office. To see why, it is helpful to check the basic arithmetic of deficits and debt.

Letting D and B stand for the government's deficit and the stock of outstanding bonds, respectively, we can summarize the key relationships as follows. The deficit is the excess of government spending over tax revenue (the primary deficit, $G - T$) plus interest payments on the outstanding bonds, rB:

$$D = G - T + rB.$$

The national debt increases by the size of the current deficit:

$$\Delta B = D.$$

Using lowercase letters to stand for the ratio of each item to GDP (i.e., $g = G/Y$, $t = T/Y$, $d = D/Y$, and $b = B/Y$), then the deficit ratio is

$$d = g - t + rb,$$

and the increase in the debt ratio is

$$\Delta b = d - nb,$$

where n stands for the long-run average growth rate in output (which takes place because of productivity increases and population growth). This last relationship may require further explanation. Since $b = B/Y$, b rises whenever its numerator grows more than its denominator does. B grows when we have a deficit, and Y grows at rate n. $(n = \Delta Y/Y)$.[6]

If the government sets the primary deficit at some target value, it is setting $(g - t)$ as an exogenous constant. The implications for the debt ratio can then be seen by eliminating d from our two key relationships:

$$\Delta b = (g - t) + (r - n)b.$$

Consider the Conservatives' policy of setting $(g - t)$ at zero. This relationship says that the debt ratio must *forever* rise—Δb is forever positive—if r exceeds n. That is, debt rises without bound if the interest rate the government pays on government bonds (the growth rate for the numerator of the debt ratio) ex-

---

[6] *Mathematical note:*
Applying the quotient rule for differentiation to $b = B/Y$, we have

$$\Delta b = \frac{\Delta B}{Y} - \frac{B}{Y}\frac{\Delta Y}{Y} = \frac{D}{Y} - bn = d - nb.$$

ceeds the economy's underlying average growth rate (the growth rate for the denominator of the debt ratio). Since r has exceeded n for many years now, it is not surprising that Canada's debt ratio has *inexorably risen*, despite the effort by the federal Conservative government to keep $(g - t)$ at zero.

The economy's average growth rate did exceed interest rates during the 1950s and 1960s in Canada, when such factors as the postwar reconstruction of industry, the shift of population to the cities, and the development of Canada's natural resources made growth particularly high. Given this temporary excess of n over r and the fact that the federal government often ran budget surpluses, it is not surprising that the debt ratio fell during these years (as shown in Figure 16-1). But considering long-run average values, we must realize that r exceeds n, so it is impossible to grow out of the debt problem by keeping the primary deficit at zero.[7]

When the Liberals took over in 1993, they switched to targeting the overall deficit instead of targeting just the primary deficit. Is this policy likely to have greater success in controlling the debt ratio?

The Liberal policy involves switching the exogenous and endogenous variables. Under the previous regime, $g - t$ was exogenous and d was endogenous. The Liberals' plan makes d exogenous, and to accomplish this, they must allow g or t to become endogenous. Since the plan is to accomplish most of the deficit reduction through expenditure cuts and not to allow tax increases, we take g as the endogenous variable in the following illustration.

Using a subscript of -1 to stand for previous period's values, the debt-ratio growth equation can be rewritten as

$$b = (1 - n)\, b_{-1} + d$$

This debt-ratio growth equation says that the value of this period's debt ratio is equal to the value of last period's debt ratio plus the adjustments that indicate how both the numerator and the denominator of the debt ratio have grown over the period. The numerator has grown by the size of the deficit, and the denominator has grown by the economy's rate of growth. The debt-ratio growth equation involves both these adjustments in ratio terms.

If d is an exogenous constant, the debt-ratio growth equation states that b *cannot* keep growing forever. Except for the constant d, this year's debt ratio is just a *fraction*, $(1 - n)$, of last period's value. So the Liberal plan can work. It involves the government's "making room" in its budget by cutting programs by whatever is necessary to meet both the interest payment obligations *and* the overall deficit target. The required time path for the spending rate is given by

$$g = d = t + rb.$$

---

[7] When evaluating whether Canada was above or below the Golden Rule level of saving (described in Chapter 4), we noted that the net marginal product of capital, $MPK - \delta$, exceeded the growth rate, here denoted simply by n, by a wide margin. In Chapter 17, we will see that $MPK = r + \delta$ in full equilibrium. In terms of long-run averages, then, we conclude that r exceeds n.

A simulation of the Liberal plan is given in Table 16-2. The Liberals took power in the 1993–1994 fiscal year. At that time, they announced that the deficit ratio would be reduced from 6.3 percent of GDP to 3 percent in three years, as indicated in column 2 of Table 16-2.

Table 16-2

A Simulation of Deficit Reduction

Fiscal Year	(Deficit/GDP) = d	(Spending/GDP) = g	(Debt/GDP) = b
1993–1994	6.3%	17.4%	75%
1994–1995	5.4	16.3	76
1995–1996	4.2	15.0	77
1996–1997	3.0	13.7	76

Source: Authors' calculations

As their plan started, the relevant values were $d = 0.063$, $g = 0.174$, $t = 0.165$, $b = 0.72$, $r = 0.075$, and $n = 0.05$. (Since we are measuring the interest rate in nominal terms, comparability requires that we measure the economy's growth rate in nominal terms as well. Forecasters expect real growth of 3.5 percent and inflation of 1.5 percent as an average for the remaining years in the 1990s, so we take 5 percent as a plausible value for the nominal growth rate. Some of these values are listed in the first line of the table. For this simulation, we take the tax rate, the interest rate, and the growth rate as constant and use our two equations to determine the expected time paths for b and g (and we report the results in Table 16-2).[8]

Table 16-2 suggests that the ratio of government spending to GDP must be cut by about 1.25 percentage points in each of three years. The government's projections, which were given in the 1994 Budget, were very close to those presented in Table 16-2. But, as far as implementing these required spending cuts is concerned, the Budget documents only spelled out the details for about one half of the cutbacks. Without the full details being presented, many individuals became skeptical regarding the government's commitment to reducing the deficit.

The longer the government delays in clarifying how it will actually reach its deficit reduction target, the less credible that target becomes. As credibility fades, the interest rate premium that foreigners demand when buying Canadian debt rises.

---

[8] For example, for the second line in Table 16-2, $b = (1 - n)b_{-1} + d = (0.95)(0.75) + 0.054 = 0.77$, while $g = d + t - rb = 0.054 + 0.165 - (0.075)(0.75) = 0.163$.

16•4 Conclusion

Fiscal policy and government debt have been central in Canadian political debate over the past decade. When Paul Martin became minister of finance in 1993, he made reducing the budget deficit a high priority of the Liberal government. Some members of the Liberal party worried that they might lose popular support since deficit reduction is perceived as a Conservative priority. This chapter has discussed the parallel debate among economists. Economists disagree about how fiscal policy affects the economy and how fiscal policy is best measured. To be sure, these are among the most important and controversial questions facing policymakers today. We can be confident that, as long as the Canadian government runs large budget deficits, these debates will continue.

Summary

1. According to the traditional view of government debt, a debt-financed tax cut stimulates consumer spending and lowers national saving. This increase in consumer spending raises aggregate demand and income in the short run but leads to a lower capital stock and lower income in the long run.

2. According to the Ricardian view of government debt, a debt-financed tax cut does not stimulate consumer spending because it does not raise permanent income—it merely reschedules taxes from the present to the future.

3. The debate between the traditional and Ricardian views of government debt is ultimately a debate over how consumers behave. Are consumers rational or short-sighted? Do they face binding borrowing constraints? Are they economically linked to future generations through altruistic bequests? Economists' views of government debt hinge on their answers to these questions.

4. Standard measures of the budget deficit are imperfect measures of fiscal policy for several reasons. In particular, these measures do not correct for the effects of inflation or the business cycle, do not offset changes in liabilities with changes in assets, and omit some liabilities altogether.

KEY CONCEPTS

Ricardian equivalence

Government budget constraint

Cyclically adjusted budget deficit

Capital budgeting

QUESTIONS FOR REVIEW

1. According to the traditional view, how does a debt-financed tax cut affect public saving, private saving, and national saving?

2. According to the Ricardian view, how does a debt-financed tax cut affect public saving, private saving, and national saving?

3. Do you believe the traditional or the Ricardian view of government debt? Why?

4. Describe three problems affecting measurement of the government budget deficit.

PROBLEMS AND APPLICATIONS

1. Draft a letter to the member of Parliament described in Section 16·1 explaining and evaluating the Ricardian view of government debt.

2. Chapter 15 discusses various theories of the consumption function: Keynes's three conjectures, the life-cycle hypothesis, and the permanent-income hypothesis. What do these different views about consumption imply for the debate between the traditional and Ricardian views of government debt?

3. The Canadian Pension system levies a tax on workers and pays benefits to the elderly. Suppose that the federal government increases both the tax and the benefits. For simplicity, assume that the federal government announces that the increases will last for one year only.

   a. How would this change affect the economy?

   b. Does your answer depend on whether generations are altruistically linked?

Estimating the Benefits
of Deficit Reduction

Canadian governments have been fighting major deficit-reduction battles in recent years—a period during which the unemployment rate has exceeded 10 percent. For example, the first budget of the federal Liberals in 1994 involved a commitment to reduce the federal deficit (measured as a ratio of GDP) from 6.3 percent to 3 percent within three years. By focusing so heavily on deficits, governments seem to have rejected the Ricardian equivalence view. Given this position, governments expect expenditure cuts and tax hikes to decrease aggregate demand. Thus, deficit reduction exacerbates the unemployment problem in the short run. Why are governments willing to incur this cost? It must be because they think that the long-run benefits of deficit reduction are worth incurring these costs.

Part of the answer to this puzzle lies in the fact that aggregate-demand multipliers are small. As noted in Chapters 10, 12, and 13, especially with a floating exchange rate, fiscal policy has only limited effects on output and therefore on unemployment. Another part of the answer lies in the governments' fear that foreign lenders may cease to buy Canadian bonds. International bond-rating agencies have downgraded Canadian federal and provincial government bonds several times in recent years, and the spectre of New Zealand's experience in the 1980s looms ever larger in the minds of many officials. Canada's debt ratio has already surpassed that of New Zealand's in the 1980s, which left New Zealand completely shunned by foreign lenders.[9]

But a large part of the explanation of the federal government's drive toward deficit reduction follows from a desire to increase the standard of living for future generations. Current generations have been "living beyond their means," and many people feel that this is unfair. By how much will future living standards be increased by deficit reduction today? We can provide an answer to this question by recalling a key relationship from our analysis of a small open economy in Chapter 7. We learned there that a country's net exports equals the excess of the country's output over total spending. That is,

$$\left(\begin{array}{c}\text{Net} \\ \text{Exports}\end{array}\right) = NX = Y - C - I - G.$$

Now let us note how each of the terms in this equation are determined.

---

[9] In general, the provinces have been more effective at controlling their debts, and some analysts attribute this more prudent behaviour (compared to the federal government) to the fact that more credit downgrades have occurred at the provincial level. See Ronald Kneebone, "Deficits and Debt in Canada: Some Lessons from Recent History," *Canadian Public Policy* 20 (1994).

First, long-run equlibrium implies that the level of a country's international indebtedness be a constant proportion of its GDP. If we define B^f as the quantity
of bonds sold to foreigners, then the foreign debt-GDP ratio is B^f/Y. This ratio
is constant if $\Delta B^f/B^f = \Delta Y/Y$. Denoting the output growth rate by n, this constant ratio requirement is satisfied when:

$$\Delta B^f = nB^f.$$

The country's debt increases each period by ΔB^f, and this debt must rise whenever the trade surplus, NX, earns less foreign exchange than is necessary to
cover the existing interest obligations to foreigners, rB^f. That is,

$$\Delta B^f = rB^f - NX.$$

Combining this definition of debt growth with the long-run equilibrium requirement that the debt-GDP ratio be constant yields:

$$NX = (r - n)B^f.$$

This expression for net exports can be substituted into the left side of the original GDP identity on the previous page. Now we present expressions for the
terms on the right side of that identity.
    We take consumption to be proportional to disposable income:

$$C = c(Y + rB - T - rB^f),$$

where B is the outstanding stock of government bonds. Disposable income is
pre-tax factor earnings plus interest payment receipts from the domestic government debt minus taxes and interest payment obligations to foreigners.
    The government budget deficit, D, is:

$$D = G + rB - T.$$

Using this equation to replace the transfer payments less taxes term, $rB - T$, in
the consumption function, we have

$$C = c(Y + D - G - rB^f).$$

Finally, investment is a function of the interest rate:

$$\text{Investment} = I(r).$$

All these relationships can be combined to yield:

$$(r - n)B^f = Y - c(Y + D - G - rB^f) - I(r) - G$$

or

$$B^f = \left(\frac{1}{r(1 - c) - n}\right)\left(Y - c(Y + D - G) - I(r) - G\right).$$

This expression for foreign debt obligations can be used to estimate the effects
of deficit reduction on domestic living standards. For simplicity, and to ensure

that our calculation underestimates the full benefits of deficit reduction, we assume that lower debt does not decrease the risk premium demanded by foreign lenders.[10] With no change in the interest rate premium, the interest rate is exogenous for a small open economy. This fact means that investment spending is not affected by deficit reduction. Also, since the marginal product of capital equals the interest rate in long-run equilibrium, the quantity of capital and overall real GDP must be independent of deficit reduction as well.

But even though GDP for a small open economy is unaffected by deficit reduction in the long run, GNP *is* affected. GNP equals GDP minus interest payments to foreigners, so we can estimate the benefits of deficit reduction by calculating how much a lower deficit reduces our debt to foreigners.

As just noted, GNP represents the level of domestic income, $Y - rB^f$. We substitute the expression for B^f into this definition. Since the government's policy is phrased in terms of reducing the deficit-GDP ratio, we divide the resulting equation through by Y and use lowercase letters to denote ratios to GDP: $d = D/Y$, $g = G/Y$, $v = I/Y$, and $a = GNP/Y$. The result is:

$$a = 1 - \left(\frac{r}{r(1-c) - n}\right)\left(1 - c(1 + d - g) - v - g\right).$$

We assume that deficit reduction is accomplished through variations in taxes and transfer payments, so that, as a proportion of the economy, the size of government is constant ($\Delta g = 0$). Given this assumption, and the fact that the interest rate is exogenous for a small open economy (so that $\Delta v = 0$), this equation implies the following relationship when written in change form:

$$\Delta a = \left(\frac{rc}{r(1-c) - n}\right)\Delta d.$$

As 1994 began, the deficit-GDP ratio for the federal government was 6.3 percent. Reducing that deficit to 3 percent (the government's policy) means $\Delta d = -.033$. Since the propensity to consume, c, is approximately 0.9, and since representative values for the interest rate and the growth rate are .075 and .05 respectively, this last equation implies $\Delta a = .052$, so that the living standards of future generations would be 5.2 percent higher if we reduce the federal deficit as the government has planned.[11] At 1994 values, this increase in living standards amounts to an extra $4,600 of income for a four-person family *every* year.

Thus, it is not so surprising afterall that governments are willing to incur some increase in umemployment in the short run to secure this substantial benefit for future generations.

[10]   For an estimate of the benefits of lower interest rates, see Case Study 17-1.

[11]   Estimates of this same order of magnitude emerge when a more sophisticated comsumption function, only very slight departures from pure Ricardian equivalence, and technological change are involved in the calculations. See W.M. Scarth, "Deficit Reduction: Costs and Benefits," *Commentary No. 61* (Toronto: C.D., Howe Institute, 1994).

Investment

Investment is the most volatile component of GDP. When expenditure on goods and services falls during a recession, much of the decline is usually due to a drop in investment spending. In the severe recession of 1982, for example, real GDP fell just over $14 billion whereas investment spending fell $11 billion, accounting for more than three-quarters fall in spending.

Economists study investment to better understand fluctuations in the economy's output of goods and services. In previous chapters our models of GDP used a simple investment function relating investment to the real interest rate: $I = I(r)$. That function states that an increase in the real interest rate reduces investment. In this chapter we look more closely at the theory behind this investment function.

There are three types of investment spending. **Business fixed investment** includes the machinery, equipment, and structures that businesses buy to use in production. **Residential investment** includes the new housing that people buy to live in and that landlords buy to rent out. **Inventory investment** includes those goods that businesses put aside in storage, including materials and supplies, work in process, and finished goods. Figure 17-1 plots total investment and its three components in Canada during the past two decades. You can see that all types of investment fall substantially during recessions, which are shown as shaded areas in the figure.

In this chapter we build models of each type of investment to explain these fluctuations. As we develop the models, it is useful to keep in mind the following three questions:

- Why is investment negatively related to the interest rate?

- What causes the investment function to shift?

- Why does investment rise during booms and fall during recessions?

At the end of the chapter, we return to these questions and summarize the answers that the models offer.

17•1 Business Fixed Investment

The standard model of business fixed investment is called the **neoclassical model of investment**. The neoclassical model examines the benefits and costs to firms of owning capital goods. The model shows how the level of investment—the addition to the stock of capital—is related to the marginal product of capital, the interest rate, and the tax rules affecting firms.

Figure 17-1

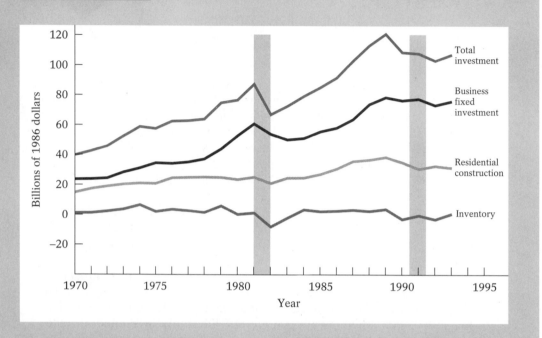

The Three Components of Investment This
figure shows total investment, business fixed
investment, residential construction, and
inventory investment from 1970 to 1993.

Notice that all types of investment fall substantially during recessions, which are indicated here by the shaded areas.

Source: Reproduced and adapted by authority of the Minister of Industry, 1994, "Statistics Canada," *Canadian
Economic Observer*, Series D20468, D20469, D20473 (Historical Statistical Supplement 1991/92): 6-7 and (Statistical
Summary, March 1994): 4.

To develop the model, imagine that there are two kinds of firms in the
economy. *Production firms* produce goods and services using capital that they
rent. *Rental firms* make all the investments in the economy; they buy capital and
rent it out to the production firms. Of course, most firms in the actual economy
perform both functions: they produce goods and services and they invest in
capital for future production. For our analysis, however, it is instructive to separate these two activities by imagining that they take place in different firms.

The Rental Price of Capital

Let's first consider the typical production firm. As we discussed in Chapter 3,
this firm decides how much capital to rent by comparing the cost and benefit of
each unit of capital. The firm rents capital at a rental rate R and sells its output
at a price P; the real cost of a unit of capital to the production firm is R/P. The
real benefit of a unit of capital is the marginal product of capital MPK—the

extra output produced with one more unit of capital. The marginal product of capital declines as the amount of capital rises: the more capital the firm has, the less an additional unit of capital will add to its production. Chapter 3 concluded that, to maximize profit, the firm rents capital until the marginal product of capital falls to equal the real rental price.

Figure 17-2 shows the equilibrium in the rental market for capital. For the reason just discussed, the marginal product of capital determines the demand curve. The demand curve slopes downward because the marginal product of capital is low when the level of capital is high. At any point in time, the amount of capital in the economy is fixed, so the supply curve is vertical. The real rental price of capital adjusts to equilibrate supply and demand.

Figure 17-2

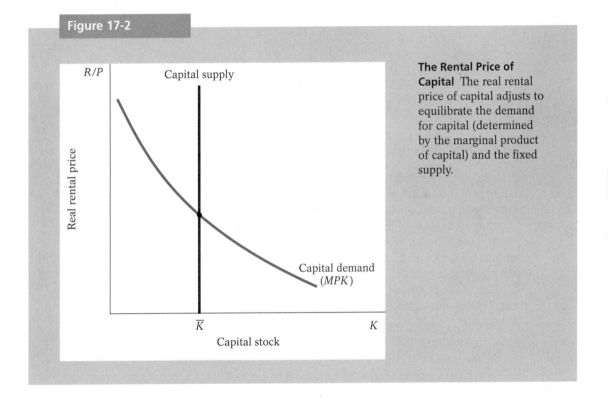

The Rental Price of Capital The real rental price of capital adjusts to equilibrate the demand for capital (determined by the marginal product of capital) and the fixed supply.

To see what variables influence the equilibrium rental price, it is instructive to consider a particular production function. As the appendix to Chapter 3 discusses, many economists consider the Cobb-Douglas production function a good approximation of how the actual economy turns capital and labour into goods and services. The Cobb-Douglas production function is

$$Y = AK^{\alpha}L^{1-\alpha},$$

where Y is output, K capital, L labour, A a parameter measuring the level of technology, and α a parameter between zero and one that measures capital's share of output. The marginal product of capital for the Cobb-Douglas production function is

$$MPK = \alpha A(L/K)^{1-\alpha}.$$

Because the real rental price equals the marginal product of capital in equilibrium, we can write

$$R/P = \alpha A(L/K)^{1-\alpha}.$$

This expression identifies the variables that determine the real rental price. It shows the following:

- The lower the stock of capital, the higher the real rental price of capital.
- The greater the amount of labour employed, the higher the real rental price of capital.
- The better the technology, the higher the real rental price of capital.

Events that reduce the capital stock (an earthquake), or raise employment (an expansion in aggregate demand), or improve the technology (a scientific discovery) raise the equilibrium real rental price of capital.

The Cost of Capital

Next consider the rental firms. These firms, like car-rental companies, merely buy capital goods and rent them out. Since our goal is to explain the investments made by the rental firms, we begin by considering the benefit and cost of owning capital.

The benefit of owning capital is the revenue from renting it to the production firms. The rental firm receives the real rental price of capital, R/P, for each unit of capital it owns and rents out.

The cost of owning capital is more complex. For each period of time that it rents out a unit of capital, the rental firm bears three costs:

1. When a rental firm buys a unit of capital and rents it out, it loses the interest it could have earned by depositing the purchase price of the capital in the bank. Or, equivalently, if the firm borrows to buy the capital, it must pay interest on the loan. If P_K is the purchase price of a unit of capital, and i is the nominal interest rate, then iP_K is the interest cost.

2. While the rental firm is renting out the capital, the price of capital can change. If the price of capital falls, the firm loses, because the firm's asset has fallen in value. If the price of capital rises, the firm gains, because the firm's asset has risen in value. The cost of this loss or gain is $-\Delta P_K$.

3. While the capital is rented out, it suffers wear and tear, called **depreciation**. If δ is the rate of depreciation—the fraction of value lost per period due to wear and tear—then the dollar cost of depreciation is δP_K.

The total cost of renting out a unit of capital for one period is therefore

$$\text{Cost of Capital} = iP_K - \Delta P_K + \delta P_K$$
$$= P_K(i - \Delta P_K/P_K + \delta).$$

The cost of capital depends on the price of capital, the interest rate, the rate at which capital prices are changing, and the depreciation rate.

For example, consider the cost of capital to a car-rental company. The company buys cars at $10,000 each and rents them out to other businesses. The company faces an interest rate i of 10 percent per year, so the interest cost iP_K is $1,000 per year for each car the company owns. Car prices are rising at 6 percent per year, so, excluding wear and tear, the firm gets a capital gain ΔP_K of $600 per year. Cars depreciate at 20 percent per year, so the loss due to wear and tear δP_K is $2,000 per year. Therefore, the company's cost of capital is

$$\text{Cost of Capital} = \$1,000 - \$600 + \$2,000$$
$$= \$2,400.$$

The cost to the car-rental company of keeping a car in its capital stock is $2,400 per year.

To make the expression for the cost of capital simpler and easier to interpret, we assume that the price of capital goods rises with the prices of other goods. In this case, $\Delta P_K/P_K$ equals the overall rate of inflation π. Because $i - \pi$ equals the real interest rate r, we can write the cost of capital as

$$\text{Cost of Capital} = P_K(r + \delta).$$

This equation states that the cost of capital depends on the price of capital, the real interest rate, and the depreciation rate.

Finally, we want to express the cost of capital relative to other goods in the economy. The **real cost of capital**—the cost of buying and renting out a unit of capital measured in units of the economy's output—is

$$\text{Real Cost of Capital} = (P_K/P)(r + \delta).$$

This equation states that the real cost of capital depends on the relative price of a capital good P_K/P, the real interest rate r, and the depreciation rate δ.

The Determinants of Investment

Now consider a rental firm's decision about whether to increase or decrease its capital stock. For each unit of capital, the firm earns real revenue R/P and bears the real cost $(P_K/P)(r + \delta)$. The real profit per unit of capital is

$$\text{Profit Rate} = \text{Revenue} - \text{Cost}$$
$$= R/P - (P_K/P)(r + \delta).$$

Since the real rental price in equilibrium equals the marginal product of capital, we can write the profit rate as

$$\text{Profit Rate} = MPK - (P_K/P)(r + \delta).$$

The rental firm makes a profit if the marginal product of capital is greater than the cost of capital. It incurs a loss if the marginal product is less than the cost of capital.

We can now see the economic incentives that lie behind the rental firm's investment decision. The firm's decision regarding its capital stock—that is, whether to add to it or to let it depreciate—depends on whether owning and renting out capital is profitable. The change in the capital stock, called **net investment**, depends on the difference between the marginal product of capital and the cost of capital. *If the marginal product of capital exceeds the cost of capital, firms find it profitable to add to their capital stock. If the marginal product of capital falls short of the cost of capital, they let their capital stock shrink.*

We can also now see that the separation of economic activity between production and rental firms—although useful to clarify our thinking—is not necessary for our conclusion regarding how firms choose investment. For a firm that both uses and owns capital, the benefit of an extra unit of capital is the marginal product of capital, and the cost is the cost of capital. Like a firm that owns and rents out capital, this firm adds to its capital stock if the marginal product exceeds the cost of capital. Thus, we can write

$$\Delta K = I_n [MPK - (P_K/P)(r + \delta)],$$

where $I_n(\ )$ is the function showing how much net investment responds to the incentive to invest.

We can now derive the investment function. Total spending on business fixed investment is the sum of net investment and the replacement of depreciated capital. The investment function is

$$I = I_n [MPK - (P_K/P)(r + \delta)] + \delta K.$$

Business fixed investment depends on the marginal product of capital, the cost of capital, and the amount of depreciation.

This model shows why investment depends on the interest rate. An increase in the real interest rate raises the cost of capital. It therefore reduces the amount of profit from owning capital and reduces the incentive to accumulate more capital. Similarly, a decrease in the real interest rate reduces the cost of capital and stimulates investment. For this reason, the investment schedule relating investment to the interest rate slopes downward, as in Figure 17-3.

The model also shows what causes the investment schedule to shift. Any event that raises the marginal product of capital increases the profitability of investment and causes the investment schedule to shift outward, as in Figure 17-4. For example, a technological innovation that increases the production function parameter A raises the marginal product of capital and, for any given interest rate, raises the amount of capital goods that rental firms wish to buy.

Figure 17-3

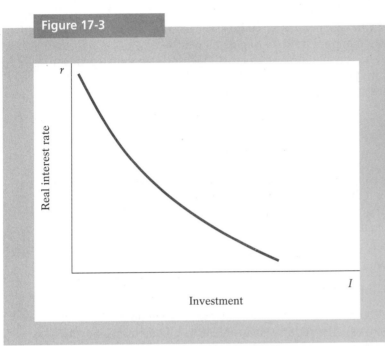

The Investment Function Business fixed investment increases when the interest rate falls, because a lower interest rate reduces the cost of capital and therefore makes owning capital more profitable.

Figure 17-4

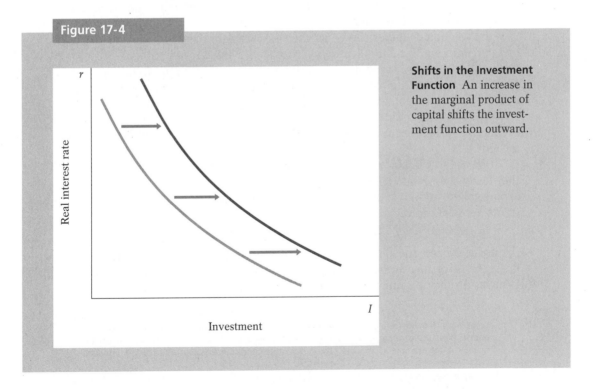

Shifts in the Investment Function An increase in the marginal product of capital shifts the investment function outward.

Finally, consider what happens as this adjustment of the capital stock continues over time. If the marginal product begins above the cost of capital, the
capital stock will rise and the marginal product will fall. If the marginal product
of capital begins below the cost of capital, the capital stock will fall and the
marginal product will rise. Eventually, as the capital stock adjusts, the marginal
product of capital approaches the cost of capital. When the capital stock
reaches a steady-state level, we can write

$$MPK = (P_K/P)(r + \delta).$$

Thus, in the long run, the marginal product of capital equals the real cost of
capital. The speed of adjustment toward the steady state depends on how
quickly firms adjust their capital stock, which, in turn, depends on how costly
it is to build, deliver, and install new capital.[1]

CASE STUDY

17•1 The Burden of Higher Interest Rates

The spread between Canadian and U.S. interest rates has widened in recent
years (as Figure 7-2 shows). The federal government has blamed this development on the fact that foreign lenders have demanded a higher risk premium to
compensate for the uncertainty associated with the possibility of Quebec separation. While acknowledging this factor, many analysts argue that the increased
spread also is caused by Canada's rising debt-GDP ratio.

International studies show that the risk premium rises by about one third
of 1 percentage point if the debt ratio climbs by 25 percentage points.[2] Because
Canada's federal government debt-GDP ratio has risen from 0.5 to 0.75 in just
five years, it is reasonable to expect that Canadian interest rates are roughly
one third of a percentage point higher than they would otherwise be, as a result of this overspending. Journalists frequently refer to this debt-related risk
premium as a significant burden for Canadians. How can this conclusion be de-
fended?

We are in a position to answer this question, because we now understand
the steady-state relationship firms use to adjust their holdings of capital. Firms
arrange their affairs so that the marginal product of capital equals the real
(rental) cost of capital:

$$MPK = r + \delta.$$

(Units have been chosen so that the purchase price of capital, P_K, equals the
purchase price of other goods, P.) In Chapter 3, we learned that the Cobb-
Douglas production function is a good approximation of production processes

---

[1] Economists often measure capital goods in units such that the price of one unit of capital equals the
price of one unit of other goods and services ($P_K = P$). This was the approach taken implicitly in
Chapter 4, for example. In this case, the steady-state condition says that the marginal product of
capital net of depreciation, $MPK - \delta$, equals the real interest rate r.

[2] See W. Robson and W. Scarth, *Deficit Reduction: What Pain? And What Gain?* (Toronto: C.D. Howe
Institute, 1994).

in Canada, and that for this production function, the marginal product of capital is given by

$$MPK = \alpha Y/K = \alpha y/k,$$

where α is capital's share of output. Substituting this expression for MPK into the steady-state capital-demand relationship yields

$$\alpha y = (r + \delta)k.$$

Rewriting this equilibrium condition in change form (holding α and δ constant) results in

$$\alpha \Delta y = (r + \delta)\Delta k + k\Delta r.$$

Since we also know that $\Delta y = MPK\Delta k = (r + \delta)\Delta k$, we can use this relationship to eliminate Δk by substitution. The result, after dividing by y, is

$$\Delta y/y = \frac{(-k/y)}{(1 - \alpha)} \Delta r.$$

Representative numbers ($k/y = 3$), $\alpha = 0.33$, $\Delta r = 0.0033$ imply that

$$\Delta y/y = -1.5 \text{ percent.}$$

Given the 1994 value for GDP, this loss amounts to $11 billion *every* year. This finding means that we can expect Canadians to give up about $11 billion worth of goods and services *every* year, if steps are not taken to get interest rates down by one third of a percentage point on a lasting basis. This *annual* loss represents *a lot* of valuable items, such as hospitals and day-care facilities. It appears that standard macroeconomic analysis supports journalists who refer to even "small" increases in interest rates as a major "burden."

Taxes and Investment

The tax laws influence firms' incentives to accumulate capital in many ways. Sometimes policymakers change the tax laws in order to shift the investment function and influence aggregate demand. Here we consider three of the most important provisions of corporate taxation: the corporate income tax rate itself, depreciation allowances, and the investment tax credit.

The effect of a **corporate profit tax** on investment depends on how the law defines "profit" for the purpose of taxation. Suppose, first, that the law defined profit as we did above—the rental price of capital minus the cost of capital. In this case, even though firms would be sharing a fraction of their profits with the government, it would still be rational for them to invest if the rental price of capital exceeded the cost of capital, and to disinvest if the rental price fell short of the cost of capital. A tax on profit, measured in this way, would not alter investment incentives.

Yet, because of the tax law's definition of profit, the corporate income tax can affect investment decisions. There are many differences between the law's definition of profit and ours. One major difference is the treatment of depreciation. Our definition of profit deducts the *current* value of depreciation as a cost. That is, it bases depreciation on how much it would cost today to replace worn out capital. By contrast, under the corporate tax laws, firms deduct depreciation using *historical* cost. That is, the **depreciation allowance** is based on the price of the capital when it was originally purchased. In periods of inflation, replacement cost is greater than historical cost, so the corporate tax tends to understate the cost of depreciation and overstate profit. As a result, the tax law sees a profit and levies a tax even when economic profit is zero, which makes owning capital less attractive. For this and other reasons, many economists believe that the corporate profit tax can discourage investment.

The **investment tax credit** is a tax provision that encourages the accumulation of capital. The investment tax credit reduces a firm's taxes by a certain amount for each dollar spent on capital goods. Because a firm recoups part of its expenditure on new capital in lower taxes, the credit reduces the effective purchase price of a unit of capital P_K. Thus, the investment tax credit reduces the cost of capital and raises investment.

Tax incentives for investment are one tool policymakers can use to control aggregate demand. For example, an increase in the investment tax credit reduces the cost of capital, shifts the investment function outward, and raises aggregate demand. Similarly, a reduction in the tax credit reduces aggregate demand by making investment more costly.

From the mid-1950s to the mid-1970s, the government of Sweden attempted to control aggregate demand by encouraging or discouraging investment. A system called the *investment fund* subsidized investment, much like an investment tax credit, during periods of recession. When government officials decided that economic growth had slowed, they authorized a temporary investment subsidy. When the officials concluded that the economy had recovered sufficiently, they revoked the subsidy. Eventually, however, Sweden abandoned the use of temporary investment subsidies to control the business cycle, and the subsidy became a permanent feature of Swedish tax policy.

Should investment subsidies be used to combat economic fluctuations? Some economists believe that, for the two decades it was in effect, the Swedish policy reduced the magnitude of the business cycle. Others believe that such a policy can have unintended and perverse effects: for example, if the economy begins to slow down, firms may anticipate a future subsidy and delay investment, making the slowdown worse. Thus, the implications of this policy are complex, which makes its effect on economic performance hard to evaluate.[3]

---

[3] John B. Taylor, "The Swedish Investment Funds System as a Stabilization Rule," *Brookings Papers on Economic Activity* (1982:1): 57–106.

CASE STUDY

17•2 Canada's Experience With Corporate Tax Concessions

Capital goods typically wear out at a slower rate than that assumed by the tax laws. Firms would like governments to think that all capital goods completely wear out during the purchase year, so that they can claim the entire cost of the machine as a *current* expense. By reducing *reported* profits that first year, tax obligations are less. Of course in later years, because firms have already claimed the full expense for the machine, *reported* profits (and therefore tax obligations) are then larger. But a tax saving today is worth more than one in the future, and firms are happy to accept an interest-free loan from governments whenever they can.

The corporate tax laws define how rapidly machinery wears out for tax purposes. For example, in the manufacturing and processing sector, depreciation allowances have allowed one half the machinery expense to be claimed in each of the first two years following its purchase. As far as generating a tax deduction, the present value of each dollar spent on investment is

$$v = 0.5 + 0.5/(1 + r),$$

where r is the rate of interest. With an interest rate of 8 percent, this formula implies that v is 0.963.

The Canadian legislation is almost as generous as the tax law can be. The maximum possible value for v is 1, and this occurs if firms are allowed to claim the entire cost of the machinery in the first year. A less generous depreciation allowance makes v lower. For example, if, for tax purposes, machinery is deemed to wear out over five years, the formula for v is

$$v = 0.2 + \frac{0.2}{1 + r} + \frac{0.2}{(1 + r)^2} + \frac{0.2}{(1 + r)^3} + \frac{0.2}{(1 + r)^4},$$

and, for the assumed 8 percent interest rate, v is 0.86. The federal government has opted for generous depreciation allowances in an attempt to stimulate investment expenditures.

Another initiative of the government is to reduce the corporate income tax rate itself. But this policy has often proven to be a very inefficient way to stimulate investment spending. We can understand why by noting that a lower tax rate brings both a benefit *and* a cost to firms. If it were not for the allowed deductions for depreciation, a 10-percent cut in the corporate tax rate would lower tax obligations by 10 percent. But a lower tax rate means that smaller deductions can be claimed. The loss in deductions equals v times 10 percent.

With v *almost* unity in Canada, it makes *almost* no sense to cut the corporate tax rate. The benefit and the cost to firms change by almost the same amount, so the incentive for firms to invest is hardly increased at all—despite a

major revenue loss for the government. Thus introducing accelerated depreciation allowances (raising v) can stimulate investment spending, but once this has
been done, the rationale for cutting the tax rate itself is reduced.

This discussion pertains to Canadian-owned firms. The case against using
corporate tax concessions as a means of stimulating investment spending is
even stronger in the case of foreign-owned firms. Firms that are subsidiaries of
multinationals based in other countries get to deduct all taxes paid in Canada
when calculating corporate taxes in their home countries. In this case, no corporate tax concession in Canada can lower the rental cost of capital. These tax
concessions simply transfer revenue to foreign governments, and so they have
no effect on investment.

The Stock Market and Tobin's q

Many economists see a link between fluctuations in investment and fluctuations in the stock market. The term *stock* refers to the shares in the ownership
of corporations, and the **stock market** is the market in which these shares are
traded. Stock prices tend to be high when firms have many opportunities for
profitable investment, since these profit opportunities mean higher future income for the shareholders. Thus, stock prices reflect the incentives to invest.

The Nobel-Prize–winning economist James Tobin proposed that firms
base their investment decisions on the following ratio, which is now called
Tobin's q:

$$q = \frac{\text{Market Value of Installed Capital}}{\text{Replacement Cost of Installed Capital}}.$$

The numerator of Tobin's q is the value of the economy's capital as determined
by the stock market. The denominator is the price of the capital if it were purchased today.

Tobin reasoned that net investment should depend on whether q is
greater or less than one. If q is greater than one, then the stock market values
installed capital at more than its replacement cost. In this case, managers can
raise the market value of their firms' stock by buying more capital. Conversely,
if q is less than one, the stock market values capital at less than its replacement
cost. In this case, managers will not replace capital as it wears out.

Although at first the q theory of investment may appear quite different from
the neoclassical model developed above, in fact the two theories are closely related. The connection comes from the observation that Tobin's q depends on
current and future expected profits from installed capital. If the marginal product
of capital exceeds the cost of capital, then installed capital is earning profits.
These profits make the rental firms desirable to own, which raises the market
value of these firms' stock, implying a high value of q. Similarly, if the marginal

product of capital falls short of the cost of capital, then installed capital is incurring losses, implying a low market value and a low value of q.[4]

The advantage of Tobin's q as a measure of the incentive to invest is that it reflects the expected future profitability of capital as well as the current profitability. For example, suppose that the federal government introduces a reduction in the corporate profit tax beginning next year. This expected fall in the corporate tax implies greater profits for the owners of capital. These higher expected profits raise the value of stock today, raise Tobin's q, and therefore encourage investment today. Thus, Tobin's q theory of investment emphasizes that investment decisions depend not only on current economic policies, but also on policies expected to prevail in the future.

Tobin's q theory provides a simple way of interpreting the role of the stock market in the economy. Suppose, for example, that you observe a fall in stock prices. Because the replacement cost of capital is fairly stable, a fall in the stock market usually implies a fall in Tobin's q. A fall in q reflects investors' pessimism about the current or future profitability of capital. According to q theory, the fall in q will lead to a fall in investment, which could lower aggregate demand. In essence, q theory gives a reason to expect fluctuations in the stock market to be closely tied to fluctuations in output and employment.[5]

CASE STUDY

17.3 The Stock Market as an Economic Indicator

"The stock market has predicted nine out of the past five recessions." So goes the famous quip about the stock market's reliability as an economic indicator. The stock market is in fact quite volatile, and it can give false signals about the future of the economy.

Yet the link between the stock market and the economy should not be ignored. Figure 17-5 shows that changes in the stock market often reflect

---

[4] Formally, the q theory and the neoclassical model can be related as follows. The owners of capital receive the MPK for each unit of capital every year forever. Assuming, for simplicity, that capital's marginal product is expected to stay constant in the future, the present value of that stream of receipts in nominal terms is $P(MPK) / (r + \delta)$ for each unit of capital. The discount rate involves the rate at which interest is forgone by tying up funds in the ownership of capital, r, and the rate at which capital is wearing out, δ. Buyers and sellers in the stock market should recognize that this present value is what an owner of the stock receives. Thus, this present value, when multiplied by the total quantity of capital, is the market value of the existing capital stock. q is the ratio of this market value to the purchase cost of capital $P_K K$. Thus, q is

$$\frac{MPK}{(P_K/P)(r + \delta)},$$

and $q > 1$ implies that investment is profitable.

[5] To read more about the relationship between the neoclassical model of investment and q theory, see Fumio Hayashi, "Tobin's Marginal q and Average q: A Neoclassical Approach," *Econometrica* 50 (January 1982): 213–224; Lawrence H. Summers, "Taxation and Corporate Investment: A q-theory Approach," *Brookings Papers on Economic Activity* (1981:1): 67–140.

Figure 17-5

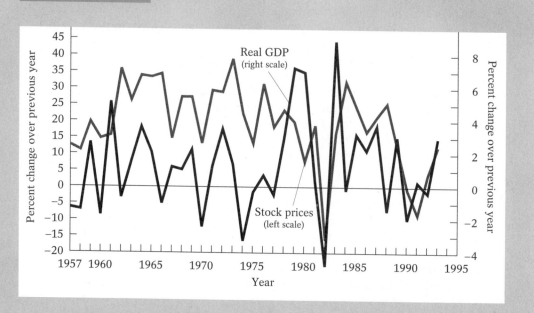

The Stock Market and the Economy This figure shows the association between the stock market and real economic activity. Using quarterly data from 1957 to 1993, it presents the percentage change from one year earlier in the Toronto Stock Exchange index and real GDP. The Toronto Stock Exchange index traces the prices of major industrial companies.

Source: Reproduced and adapted by authority of the Minister of Industry, 1994, "Statistics Canada," *Canadian Economic Observer*, Series B4237, D20463 (Historical Statistical Supplement 1991/92): 7, 96 and (Statistical Summary, March 1994): 4, 53.

changes in real GDP. This fact is not lost on policymakers, such as those at the Bank of Canada. Indeed, because the stock market often anticipates changes in real GDP, and because data on the stock market are available more quickly than data on GDP, the stock market is a closely watched indicator of economic activity.

Financing Constraints

When a firm wants to invest in new capital, such as building a new factory, it often raises the necessary funds in financial markets. This financing may take several forms—obtaining loans from banks, selling bonds to the public, or selling shares in future profits on the stock market. The neoclassical model assumes that if a firm is willing to pay the cost of capital, the financial markets will make the funds available.

Yet sometimes firms face **financing constraints**—limits on the amount they can raise in financial markets. Financing constraints can prevent firms from undertaking profitable investments. When a firm is unable to raise funds in financial markets, the amount it can spend on new capital goods is limited to the amount it is currently earning. Financing constraints influence the investment behaviour of firms just as borrowing constraints influence the consumption behaviour of households. Borrowing constraints cause households to determine their consumption on the basis of current rather than permanent income; financing constraints cause firms to determine their investment on the basis of their current cash flow rather than expected profitability.

To see the impact of financing constraints, consider the effect of a short recession on investment spending. A recession reduces employment, the rental price of capital, and profits. If firms expect the recession to be short-lived, however, they will want to continue investing, knowing that their investments will be profitable in the future. That is, a short recession will have only a small effect on Tobin's q. For firms that can raise funds in financial markets, the recession should have only a small effect on investment.

Quite the opposite is true for firms that face financing constraints. The fall in current profits restricts the amount that these firms can spend on new capital goods and may prevent them from making profitable investments. Financing constraints make investment more sensitive to current economic conditions.

17•2 Residential Investment

In this section we consider the determinants of residential investment. We begin by presenting a simple model of the housing market. Residential investment includes the purchase of new housing both by people who plan to live in it themselves and by landlords who plan to rent it to others. To keep things simple, however, it is useful to imagine that all housing is owner-occupied.

The Stock Equilibrium and the Flow Supply

There are two parts to the model. First, the market for the existing stock of houses determines the equilibrium housing price. Second, the housing price determines the flow of residential investment.

Figure 17-6(a) shows how the relative price of housing P_H/P is determined by the supply and demand for the existing stock of houses. At any point in time, the supply of houses is fixed. We represent this stock with a vertical supply curve. The demand curve for houses slopes downward, because high prices cause people to live in smaller houses, to share residences, or sometimes even to become homeless. The price of housing adjusts to equilibrate supply and demand.

Figure 17-6(b) shows how the relative price of housing determines the supply of new houses. Construction firms buy materials and hire labour to build houses, and then sell the houses at the market price. Their costs depend on the overall price level P, and their revenue depends on the price of houses P_H. The higher the relative price of housing, the greater the incentive to build houses, and the more houses are built. The flow of new houses—residential investment—therefore depends on the equilibrium price set in the market for existing houses.

This model of residential investment is closely related to the q theory of business fixed investment. According to q theory, business fixed investment depends on the market price of installed capital relative to its replacement cost; this relative price, in turn, depends on the expected profits from owning installed capital. According to this model of the housing market, residential investment depends on the relative price of housing. The relative price of housing, in turn, depends on the demand for housing, which depends on the imputed rent that individuals expect to receive from their housing. Hence, the relative price of housing plays much the same role for residential investment as Tobin's q does for business fixed investment.

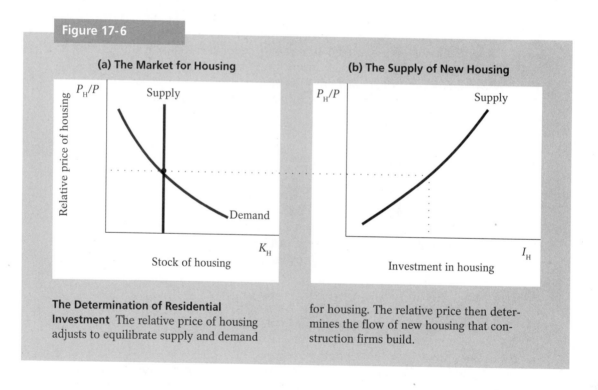

Figure 17-6

(a) The Market for Housing

(b) The Supply of New Housing

The Determination of Residential Investment The relative price of housing adjusts to equilibrate supply and demand for housing. The relative price then determines the flow of new housing that construction firms build.

Changes in Housing Demand

When the demand for housing shifts, the equilibrium housing price changes, which in turn affects residential investment. The demand curve for housing can shift for various reasons. An economic boom raises national income and therefore the demand for housing. A large increase in the population, perhaps due to immigration, also raises the demand for housing. Figure 17-7(a) shows that an expansionary shift in demand raises the equilibrium price. Figure 17-7(b) shows that the increase in the housing price increases residential investment.

One of the most important determinants of housing demand is the real interest rate. Many people take out loans—mortgages—to buy their homes; the interest rate is the cost of the loan. Even the few people who do not have to borrow to purchase a home will respond to the interest rate, because the interest rate is the opportunity cost of holding their wealth in housing rather than putting it in a bank. A reduction in the interest rate therefore raises housing demand, housing prices, and residential investment.

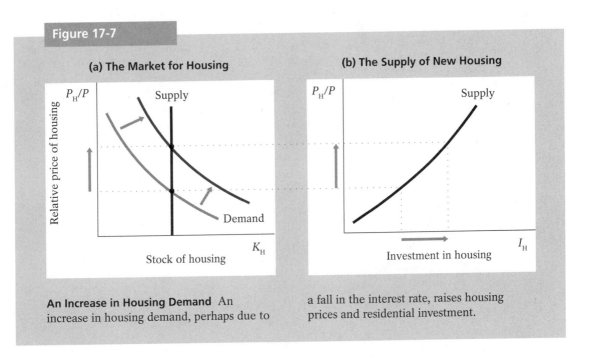

Figure 17-7

(a) The Market for Housing

(b) The Supply of New Housing

An Increase in Housing Demand An increase in housing demand, perhaps due to a fall in the interest rate, raises housing prices and residential investment.

The Tax Treatment of Housing

Just as the tax laws affect the accumulation of business fixed investment, they affect the accumulation of residential investment. In this case, however, their effects are nearly the opposite. Rather than discouraging investment, as the corporate income tax does for businesses, the personal income tax encourages households to invest in housing.

One can view a homeowner as a landlord with himself as a tenant. But he is a landlord with a special tax treatment. The Canadian income-tax system does not require him to pay tax on the imputed rent (the rent he "pays" himself). Nor does he have to pay any capital gains tax when the value of his home increases. Many economists have criticized the tax treatment of homeownership. They believe that, because of this subsidy, Canada invests too much in housing compared to other forms of capital.

What Price House Can You Afford?

When someone takes out a mortgage to buy a house, the bank often places a ceiling on the size of the loan. That ceiling depends on the person's income and the market interest rate. A typical bank or trust company requirement is that the monthly mortgage payment—including both interest and repayment of principal—not exceed 30 percent of the borrower's monthly income.

Table 17-1 shows how the interest rate affects monthly payments on a $100,000 25-year mortgage, and how the interest rate affects the minimum annual income that is required before banks and trust companies will grant a mortgage.

As you can see, small changes in the interest rate can have a large influence on who can buy a home. For example, an increase in the interest rate from 8 percent to 10 percent raises the monthly payment on a typical mortgage by 17 percent. It also cuts out of the mortgage market all families in the $30,520–$35,760 income range. An increase in the interest rate therefore reduces housing demand, which in turn depresses housing prices and residential investment.

Table 17-1

How High Interest Rates Reduce Mortgage Eligibility and Housing Demand for a 25-year $100,000 Mortgage

Interest Rate	Monthly Payment	Annual Income Required
5%	$ 582	$23,280
6	640	25,600
7	700	28,000
8	763	30,520
9	828	33,120
10	894	35,760
11	963	38,520
12	1,032	41,280

17•3 Inventory Investment

Inventory investment is one of the smallest components of spending, averaging about 1 percent of GDP. Yet its remarkable volatility makes it important. In recessions, inventory investment becomes negative because firms stop replenishing their inventory as goods are sold. In a typical recession, more than half the fall in spending comes from a decline in inventory investment.

Reasons for Holding Inventories

Inventories serve many purposes. Before presenting a model to explain fluctuations in inventory investment, let's discuss some of the motives firms have for holding inventories.

One use of inventories is to smooth the level of production over time. Consider a firm that experiences temporary booms and busts in sales. Rather than adjusting production to match the fluctuations in sales, it may be cheaper to produce goods at a steady rate. When sales are low, the firm produces more than it sells and puts the extra goods into inventory. When sales are high, the firm produces less than it sells and takes goods out of inventory. This motive for holding inventories is called **production smoothing**.

A second reason for holding inventories is that they may allow a firm to operate more efficiently. Retail stores, for example, can sell merchandise more effectively if they have goods on hand to show to customers. Manufacturing firms keep inventories of spare parts in order to reduce the time that the assembly line is shut down when a machine breaks. In some ways, we can view **inventories as a factor of production**: the larger the stock of inventories a firm holds, the more output it can produce.

A third reason for holding inventories is to avoid running out of goods when sales are unexpectedly high. Firms often have to make production decisions before knowing how much customers will demand. For example, a publisher must decide on how many copies of a new book to print before knowing whether the book will be popular. If demand exceeds production and there are no inventories, the good will be out of stock for a period, and the firm will lose sales and profit. Inventories can prevent this from happening. This motive for holding inventories is called **stock-out avoidance**.

A fourth explanation of inventories is dictated by the production process. Many goods require a number of steps in production and, therefore, take time to produce. When a product is only partly completed, its components are counted as part of a firm's inventory. These inventories are called **work in process**.

CASE STUDY

◆ **17•4** **Seasonal Fluctuations and Production Smoothing**

Economists have spent much time studying data on production, sales, and inventories to test alternative theories of inventory holding. Much of this research examines whether the production-smoothing theory accurately describes the behaviour of firms. Contrary to what many economists expected, most of the evidence suggests that firms do not use inventories to smooth production over time.

The clearest evidence against production smoothing comes from industries with seasonal fluctuations in demand. In many industries, sales fluctuate regularly over the course of a year. For example, the toy industry sells more of its output in December than in January. One might expect that firms would build up inventories in times of low sales and draw them down in times of high sales.

Yet, in most industries, firms do not use inventories to smooth production over the year. Instead, the seasonal pattern in production closely matches the seasonal pattern in sales. The evidence from seasonal fluctuations suggests that, in most industries, firms see little benefit to smoothing production.[6]

The Accelerator Model of Inventories

Because there are many motives for holding inventories, there are many models of inventory investment. One simple model that explains the data reasonably well, without endorsing a particular motive, is the **accelerator model**. This model was developed about half a century ago, and it is sometimes applied to all types of investment. Here we apply it to the type for which it works best—inventory investment.

The accelerator model of inventories assumes that firms hold a stock of inventories that is proportional to the firms' level of output. There are various reasons for this assumption. When output is high, manufacturing firms need more materials and supplies on hand, and they have more goods in the process of being completed. When the economy is booming, retail firms want to have more merchandise on the shelves to show customers. This assumption implies that if N is the stock of inventories and Y is output, then

$$N = \beta Y,$$

where β is a parameter reflecting how much inventory firms wish to hold as a proportion of output.

Inventory investment I is the change in the stock of inventories ΔN. Therefore,

$$I = \Delta N = \beta \Delta Y.$$

The accelerator model predicts that inventory investment will be proportional to the change in output. When output rises, firms want to hold more inventories, so they invest in them. When output falls, firms want to hold fewer inventories, so they allow their inventories to run down.

---

[6] Jeffrey A. Miron and Stephen P. Zeldes, "Seasonality, Cost Shocks, and the Production Smoothing Model of Inventories," *Econometrica* 56 (July 1988): 877–908.

We can now see how the model earned its name. Because the variable Y is the rate at which firms are producing goods, ΔY is the "acceleration" of production. The model says that inventory investment depends on whether the economy is speeding up or slowing down.

The accelerator mechanism is one of the reasons that business cycles develop momentum and are therefore so difficult to control. We can appreciate this fact by considering the following scenario and applying the accelerator to all components of investment. Suppose that the economy is at its natural rate and that a loss in export sales then reduces GDP and causes a recession. The fact that output has fallen (ΔY is negative) means that investment falls. This makes the recession more severe. Then, when the economy is recovering (ΔY is positive), investment rises. This fact forces the economy to overshoot the natural rate (since ΔY is positive at that point, and that keeps investment high). As time proceeds, the (positive) changes in output get smaller, and this pushes investment lower. The fall-off in investment is what causes the next recession. Thus, it is quite likely that a *onetime* shock like a drop in export sales can set in motion a whole series of overshoots—an *ongoing* business cycle—because of the accelerator mechanism.

Inventories and the Real Interest Rate

Like other components of investment, inventory investment depends on the real interest rate. When a firm holds a good in inventory and sells it tomorrow, rather than selling it today, it gives up the interest it could have earned between today and tomorrow. Thus, the real interest rate measures the opportunity cost of holding inventories.

When the real interest rate rises, holding inventories becomes more costly, so rational firms try to reduce their stock. Therefore, an increase in the real interest rate depresses inventory investment. For example, in the 1980s many firms adopted "just-in-time" production plans, which were designed to reduce the amount of inventory by producing goods just before sale. The high real interest rates that prevailed during most of that decade are one possible explanation for this change in business strategy.

17•4 Conclusion

The purpose of this chapter has been to examine the determinants of investment in more detail. Looking back on the various models of investment, three themes arise.

First, we have seen that all types of investment spending are inversely related to the real interest rate. A higher interest rate raises the cost of capital to firms that invest in plant and equipment, raises the cost of borrowing to homebuyers, and raises the cost of holding inventories. Thus, the models of investment developed here justify the investment function we have used throughout this book.

Second, we have seen what can cause the investment function to shift. An improvement in the available technology raises the marginal product of capital and raises business fixed investment. An increase in the population raises the demand for housing and raises residential investment. Finally, various economic policies, such as changes in the investment tax credit and the corporate profit tax, alter the incentives to invest and thus shift the investment function.

Third, we have learned why investment is so volatile over the business cycle: investment spending depends on the output of the economy as well as on the interest rate. In the neoclassical model of business fixed investment, higher employment raises the marginal product of capital and the incentive to invest. Higher income also raises the demand for houses, which raises housing prices and residential investment. Higher output raises the stock of inventories firms wish to hold, stimulating inventory investment. Our models predict that an economic boom should stimulate investment, and a recession should depress it. This is exactly what we observe.

Summary

1. The marginal product of capital determines the real rental price of capital. The real interest rate, the depreciation rate, and the relative price of capital goods determine the cost of capital. According to the neoclassical model, firms invest if the rental price is greater than the cost of capital, and disinvest if the rental price is less than the cost of capital.

2. Various parts of the corporate profit tax system influence the incentive to invest. The tax itself discourages investment, while generous depreciation allowances and investment tax credits encourage it.

3. An alternative way of expressing the neoclassical model is to state that investment depends on Tobin's q, the ratio of the market value of installed capital to its replacement cost. This ratio reflects the current and expected future profitability of capital.

4. In contrast to the assumption of the neoclassical model, firms cannot always raise funds to finance investment. Financing constraints make investment sensitive to firms' current cash flow.

5. Residential investment depends on the relative price of housing. Housing prices in turn depend on the demand for housing and the fixed supply. An increase in housing demand, perhaps due to a reduction in the interest rate, raises housing prices and residential investment.

6. Firms have various motives for holding inventories of goods: smoothing production, using them as a factor of production, avoiding stock-outs, and storing work in process. One model of inventory investment that works well without endorsing a particular motive is the accelerator model, according to which the stock of inventories is proportional to GDP. It implies that inventory investment depends on the change in GDP.

KEY CONCEPTS

Business fixed investment

Residential investment

Inventory investment

Neoclassical model of investment

Depreciation

Real cost of capital

Net investment

Corporate profit tax

Depreciation allowance

Investment tax credit

Stock market

Tobin's q

Financing constraints

Production smoothing

Inventories as a factor of production

Stock-out avoidance

Work in process

Accelerator model

QUESTIONS FOR REVIEW

1. In the neoclassical model of business fixed investment, under what conditions will firms find it profitable to add to their capital stock?

2. What is Tobin's q, and what does it have to do with investment?

3. Explain why an increase in the interest rate reduces the amount of residential investment.

4. List four reasons firms might hold inventories.

PROBLEMS AND APPLICATIONS

1. Use the neoclassical model of investment to explain the impact of each of the following on the rental price of capital, the cost of capital, and investment:

a. Anti-inflationary monetary policy raises the real interest rate.

b. An earthquake destroys part of the capital stock.

c. Immigration of foreign workers increases the size of the labour force.

2. Suppose that the government levies a tax on oil companies equal to a proportion of the value of the company's oil reserves. (The government assures the firms that the tax is for one time only.) According to the neoclassical model, what effect will the tax have on business fixed investment by these firms? What if these firms face financing constraints?

3. The *IS-LM* model developed in Chapters 9 and 10 assumes that investment depends only on the interest rate. Yet our theories of investment suggest that investment might also depend on national income: higher income might induce firms to invest more.

a. Explain why investment might depend on national income.

b. Suppose that investment is determined by

$$I = \overline{I} + aY,$$

where a is a constant between zero and one. With investment set this way, what are the fiscal-policy multipliers in the Keynesian cross model? Explain.

c. Suppose that investment depends on both income and the interest rate. That is, the investment function is

$$I = \bar{I} + aY - br,$$

where a is a constant between zero and one, and b is a constant greater than zero. Use the *IS-LM* model to consider the short-run impact of an increase in government purchases on national income Y, the interest rate r, consumption C, and investment I. How might this investment function alter the conclusions implied by the basic *IS-LM* model?

4. When the stock market crashes, as it did in October 1929 and October 1987, how should the Bank of Canada respond? Why?

5. It is an election year, and the economy is in a recession. The opposition candidate campaigns on a platform of passing an investment tax credit, which would be effective next year, after she takes office. What impact does this campaign promise have on economic conditions during the current year?

6. In the 1950s, Canada experienced a large increase in the number of births. This baby-boom generation reached adulthood and started forming their own households in the 1970s.

a. Use the model of residential investment to predict the impact of this event on housing prices and residential investment.

b. For the years 1970 and 1980, compute the real price of housing, measured as the residential investment deflator divided by the GDP deflator. What do you find? Is this finding consistent with the model? (*Hint*: A good source of data is the Canadian Economic Observer, which is published monthly by Statistics Canada.) Another good source of data is the Department of Finance's June Quarterly Economic Review. These publications are available in the Government Documents section of your university library.

7. Canadian tax laws encourage investment in housing and discourage investment in business capital. What are the long-run effects of this policy? (*Hint*: Think about the labour market.)

Money Supply and Money Demand

The supply and demand for money are key to many issues in macroeconomics. Chapter 6 discussed how economists use the term "money," and it showed how monetary policy affects prices and interest rates in the long run when prices are flexible. Chapters 9 and 10 showed that the money market is a central element of the *IS-LM* model, which describes the economy in the short run when prices are sticky.

This chapter examines money supply and money demand more closely. In Section 18·1 we see that the banking system plays a key role in determining the money supply, and we discuss various policy instruments that the Bank of Canada can use to alter the money supply. In Section 18·2 we consider the motives behind money demand, and we analyze the household's decision about how much money to hold. In Section 18·3 we discuss how recent changes in the financial system have blurred the distinction between money and other assets and how this development complicates the conduct of monetary policy.

18·1 Money Supply

Chapter 6 introduced the concept of "money supply" in a highly simplified manner. In that chapter we defined the quantity of money as the number of dollars held by the public, and we assumed that the Bank of Canada controls the supply of money by increasing or decreasing the number of dollars in circulation through open-market operations. Although this explanation is acceptable as a first approximation, it is not complete. This is because it omits the role of the banking system in determining the money supply. We now present a more complete explanation.

In this section we see that the money supply is determined not only by Bank of Canada policy, but also by the behaviour of households which hold money and of banks in which money is held. We begin by recalling that the money supply includes both currency in the hands of the public and the deposits at banks that households can use on demand for transactions. That is, letting M denote the money supply, C currency, and D deposits, we can write

$$\text{Money Supply} = \text{Currency} + \text{Deposits}$$
$$M = C + D.$$

To understand the money supply, we must understand the interaction between currency and deposits and how Bank of Canada policy influences these two components of the money supply.

100-Percent-Reserve Banking

We begin by imagining a world without banks. In such a world, all money takes the form of currency, and the quantity of money is simply the amount of currency that the public holds. For this discussion, suppose that there is $1,000 of currency in the economy.

Now introduce banks. At first, suppose that banks accept deposits but do not make loans. The only purpose of the banks is to provide a safe place for depositors to keep their money.

The deposits that banks have received but have not lent out are called **reserves**. Some reserves are held in the vaults of local banks throughout the country, but most are held at a central bank, such as the Bank of Canada. In our hypothetical economy, all deposits are held as reserves: banks simply accept deposits, place the money in reserve, and leave the money there until the depositor makes a withdrawal or writes a cheque against the balance. This system is called **100-percent-reserve banking**.

Suppose that households deposit the economy's entire $1,000 in Firstbank. Figure 18-1 shows Firstbank's **balance sheet**—its accounting statement of assets and liabilities. The bank's assets are the $1,000 it holds as reserves; the bank's liabilities are the $1,000 it owes to depositors. Unlike banks in our economy, this bank is not making loans, so it will not earn profit from its assets. The bank presumably charges depositors a small fee to cover its costs.

Figure 18-1	

Firstbank's Balance Sheet

Assets		Liabilities	
Reserves	$1,000	Deposits	$1,000

A Balance Sheet Under 100-Percent-Reserve Banking A bank's balance sheet shows its assets and liabilities. Under 100-percent-reserve banking, banks hold all deposits as reserves.

What is the money supply in this economy? Before the creation of Firstbank, the money supply was the $1,000 of currency. After the creation of Firstbank, the money supply is the $1,000 of deposits. A dollar deposited in a bank reduces currency by one dollar and raises deposits by one dollar, so the money supply remains the same. *If banks hold 100 percent of deposits in reserve, the banking system does not affect the supply of money.*

Fractional-Reserve Banking

Now imagine that banks start to use some of their deposits to make loans—for example, to families who are buying houses or to firms that are investing in new plants and equipment. The advantage to banks is that interest can be charged on the loans. The banks must keep some reserves on hand so that reserves are available whenever depositors want to make withdrawals. But as long as the amount of new deposits approximately equals the amount of withdrawals, a bank need not keep many of its deposits in reserve. Thus, bankers have an incentive to make loans. When they do so, we have **fractional-reserve banking**, a system under which banks keep only a fraction of their deposits in reserve.

Figure 18-2(a) shows the balance sheet of Firstbank after it makes a loan. This balance sheet assumes that the bank's *reserve–deposit ratio*—the fraction of deposits kept in reserve—is 20 percent. Firstbank keeps $200 of the $1,000 in deposits in reserve and lends out the remaining $800.

Notice that Firstbank increases the supply of money by $800 when it makes this loan. Before the loan is made, the money supply is $1,000, equaling the deposits in Firstbank. After the loan is made, the money supply is $1,800: the depositor still has a deposit of $1,000, but now the borrower holds $800 in currency. *Thus, in a system of fractional-reserve banking, banks create money.*

The creation of money does not stop with Firstbank. If the borrower deposits the $800 in another bank (or if the borrower uses the $800 to pay someone who then deposits it), the process of money creation continues. Figure 18-2(b) shows the balance sheet of Secondbank. Secondbank receives the $800 in deposits, keeps 20 percent, or $160, in reserve, and then loans out $640. Thus, Secondbank creates $640 of money. If this $640 is eventually deposited in Thirdbank, this bank keeps 20 percent, or $128, in reserve and loans out $512, and so on. With each deposit and loan, more money is created.

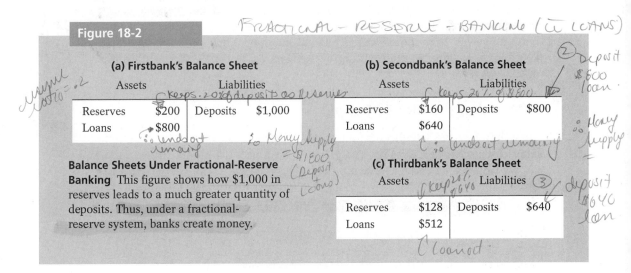

Figure 18-2

(a) Firstbank's Balance Sheet

Assets		Liabilities	
Reserves	$200	Deposits	$1,000
Loans	$800		

(b) Secondbank's Balance Sheet

Assets		Liabilities	
Reserves	$160	Deposits	$800
Loans	$640		

(c) Thirdbank's Balance Sheet

Assets		Liabilities	
Reserves	$128	Deposits	$640
Loans	$512		

Balance Sheets Under Fractional-Reserve Banking This figure shows how $1,000 in reserves leads to a much greater quantity of deposits. Thus, under a fractional-reserve system, banks create money.

Although this process of money creation can continue forever, it does not create an infinite amount of money. Letting rr denote the reserve–deposit ratio, the amount of money that the original $1,000 creates is:

Original Deposit　　　　= $1,000
Firstbank Lending　　　= $(1 - rr) \times \$1,000$
Secondbank Lending = $(1 - rr)^2 \times \$1,000$
Thirdbank Lending　　= $(1 - rr)^3 \times \$1,000$

Total Money Supply = $[1 + (1 - rr) + (1 - rr)^2 + (1 - rr)^3 + \ldots] \times \$1,000$
　　　　　　　　　= $(1/rr) \times \$1,000$

Each $1 of reserves generates $$(1/rr)$ of money. In our example, $rr = 0.2$, so the original $1,000 generates $5,000 of money.[1]

The banking system's ability to create money is the primary difference between banks and other financial institutions. As we first discussed in Chapter 3, financial markets have the important function of transferring the economy's resources from those households that wish to save some of their income for the future to those households and firms that wish to borrow to buy investment goods to be used in future production. This process is called **financial intermediation**. Many institutions in the economy act as financial intermediaries: the most prominent examples are the stock market, the bond market, mortgage loan companies, credit unions, trust companies, and the banking system. For simplicity, we focus on just the chartered banks in this chapter.

Note that although the system of fractional-reserve banking creates money, it does not create wealth. When a bank loans out some of its reserves, it gives borrowers the ability to make transactions and therefore increases the supply of money. The borrowers are also undertaking a debt obligation to the bank, however, so the loan does not make them wealthier. In other words, the creation of money by the banking system increases the economy's liquidity, not its wealth.

A Model of the Money Supply

Now that we have seen how banks create money, let's examine in more detail what determines the money supply. Here we present a model of the money supply under fractional-reserve banking. The model has three exogenous variables:

- The **monetary base** B is the total number of dollars held by the public as

---

[1] *Mathematical note*: The last step in the derivation of the total money supply uses the algebraic result for the sum of an infinite geometric series (which we used previously in computing the multiplier in Chapter 9). This result states that if x is a number between -1 and 1, then

$$1 + x + x^2 + x^3 + \ldots = 1/(1 - x).$$

In this application, $x = (1 - rr)$.

currency C and by the banks as reserves R. It can be controlled by the Bank of Canada.

- The **reserve–deposit ratio** rr is the fraction of deposits that banks hold in reserve. It is determined by the business policies of banks and, for many years, by the laws regulating banks. By mid-1994 the phasing out of reserve requirement laws was complete, and Canadian banks were no longer subject to any minimum reserve requirement.

- The **currency–deposit ratio** cr expresses the preferences of the public about how much money to hold in the form of currency C and how much to hold in the form of deposits D.

Our model shows how the money supply depends on the monetary base, the reserve–deposit ratio, and the currency–deposit ratio. It allows us to examine how Bank of Canada policy and the choices of banks and households influence the money supply.

We begin with the definitions of the money supply and the monetary base:

$$M = C + D,$$
$$B = C + R.$$

The first equation states that the money supply is the sum of currency and deposits. The second equation states that the monetary base is the sum of currency and bank reserves. Now divide the first equation by the second to obtain:

$$\frac{M}{B} = \frac{C + D}{C + R}.$$

Then divide both the top and bottom of the expression on the right by D.

$$\frac{M}{B} = \frac{C/D + 1}{C/D + R/D}.$$

Note that C/D is the currency–deposit ratio cr, and that R/D is the reserve–deposit ratio rr. Making these substitutions, and bringing the B from the left to the right side of the equation, we obtain

$$M = \frac{cr + 1}{cr + rr} \times B.$$

This equation shows how the money supply depends on the three exogenous variables.

We can now see that the money supply is proportional to the monetary base. The factor of proportionality, $(cr + 1)/(cr + rr)$, is denoted m and is called the **money multiplier**. We can write

$$M = m \times B.$$

Each dollar of the monetary base produces m dollars of money. Because the monetary base has a multiplied effect on the money supply, the monetary base is sometimes called **high-powered money**.

Here's a numerical example which approximately describes the Canadian economy in 1994. Suppose that the monetary base B is \$25 billion, the reserve–deposit ratio rr is 0.12, and the currency–deposit ratio cr is 0.64. In this case, the money multiplier for $M1$ is

$$m = \frac{0.64 + 1}{0.64 + 0.12} = 2.16,$$

and the money supply, $M1$, is

$$2.16 \times 25 = 54.$$

Each dollar of the monetary base generates 2.16 dollars of money, so the total money supply, using $M1$ as the measure, is \$54 billion.

We can now see how changes in the three exogenous variables—B, rr, and cr—cause the money supply to change:

1. The money supply is proportional to the monetary base. Thus, an increase in the monetary base increases the money supply by the same percentage.

2. The lower the reserve–deposit ratio, the more loans banks make, and the more money banks create from every dollar of reserves. Thus, a decrease in the reserve–deposit ratio raises the money multiplier and the money supply.

3. The lower the currency–deposit ratio, the fewer dollars of the monetary base the public holds as currency, the more base dollars banks hold as reserves, and the more money banks can create. Thus, a decrease in the currency–deposit ratio raises the money multiplier and the money supply.

With this model in mind, we can discuss the ways in which the Bank of Canada influences the money supply.

The Two Instruments of Monetary Policy

In previous chapters we made the simplifying assumption that the Bank of Canada controls the money supply directly. In fact, the Bank of Canada controls the money supply indirectly by altering the monetary base. To do this, the Bank of Canada has at its disposal two instruments of monetary policy: open-market operations and deposit-switching.

Open-market operations are the purchases and sales of federal government bonds by the Bank of Canada. When the Bank of Canada buys bonds from the public, the dollars it pays for the bonds increase the monetary base and thereby increase the money supply. When the Bank of Canada sells bonds to the public, the dollars it receives reduce the monetary base and thus decrease the money supply.

Open-market operations are also carried out in the foreign exchange market. To fix the exchange rate, and even just to limit what exchange-rate changes are occurring, the Bank of Canada enters the foreign exchange market. To keep the Canadian dollar high when the market pressure is pushing it down, the

Bank buys lots of Canadian dollars. This is done by selling some of Canada's foreign exchange reserves, which are held by the Bank of Canada. Since the Canadian dollars bought by the Bank are no longer in private use, the monetary base is reduced. Similarly, to keep the Canadian dollar from rising in value, the Bank sells lots of Canadian dollars. The Bank does this by using the currency to purchase foreign exchange (thus building up the country's foreign exchange reserves). The new currency that is used to pay for the foreign exchange forms part of the domestic monetary base. As a result, buying foreign exchange causes a multiple expansion in the money supply, just like an open-market purchase of bonds does.

Understanding the mechanics behind these open-market operations is fundamental to having an informed opinion about the plausibility of a small country like Canada having a monetary policy that is independent from that of the United States. If a completely floating exchange-rate policy is chosen, the Bank of Canada is under no obligation to make any trades in the foreign exchange market. Thus, open-market operations can be confined to the domestic bond market, and they can be initiated only when domestic monetary policy objectives call for action. If a fixed-exchange-rate policy is chosen, however, the Bank of Canada gets to decide neither the timing nor the magnitude of its open-market operations. These decisions are made by the private participants in the foreign exchange market, and the Bank's role is a residual one—just issuing or withdrawing whatever quantity of domestic monetary base necessary to keep the exchange rate constant.

The moral of the story is this: We *cannot* fix *both* the quantity and the price of our currency. A fixed-exchange-rate is inconsistent with independent monetary policy. A floating exchange rate is what permits independent monetary policy.

Deposit-switching is the other method used by the Bank of Canada to alter the monetary base. The government of Canada holds large bank deposits because it receives tax payments on a daily basis. These deposits are held both at the Bank of Canada and at the various chartered banks. In terms of the security of its funds, the government does not care where these deposits are held. But from the perspective of monetary policy, the government *does* have a preference. To understand why, consider a switch of government deposits from the Bank of Canada to any one of the chartered banks. (This operation or its reverse is performed daily by the Bank of Canada, on behalf of the government.) The deposit switch increases chartered bank reserves and deposits on a one-for-one basis. With a fractional reserve system, we know that the chartered bank will use a good part of this increase in reserves to extend new loans. Thus, the deposit switch toward chartered banks sets in motion a multiple expansion of the money supply. Similarly, a switch of government deposits away from chartered banks depletes their reserves—inducing a contraction of loans and so a decrease in the money supply.

The **Bank rate** is the interest rate that the Bank of Canada uses to determine how much it charges if it ever has to lend reserves to chartered banks. Because an increase in the Bank rate can be interpreted as an increase in chartered bank costs, it is taken as a signal that banks will be cutting back loans and that the

↑ Bank rate = ↑ chartered Bank Costs ∴ ↓ loans ∴ M ↓ (shrinking)
↓ Bank rate = ↑ loans ∴ ↑ M (expanding)

money supply is shrinking. Similarly, a decrease in the Bank rate is a signal that banks can afford to expand loans and that the monetary policy is expansionary.

Although the broad outline of this interpretation is perfectly correct, it is misleading in its detail. Because Canada has only a few major banks, with branch offices all over the country, they rarely have to borrow reserves from the Bank of Canada. If one branch runs a bit short to meet its customers' needs, reserves are just passed on from another branch, or from the "head office." Given this fact, an increase in the Bank rate has no effect on chartered bank costs. If reserves are rarely borrowed, who cares what the borrowing rate is?

Note? ↔

Individuals and firms write a great many cheques every day to finance their purchases. When these cheques are cleared at the end of the day, they represent instructions for banks to transfer funds to each other (for honouring each other's cheques). Banks make these transfers on a net basis by writing cheques to each other against their own deposit accounts at the Bank of Canada. The total of these accounts is known as the quantity of settlement balances. Banks are not allowed to end the day with a negative balance in their settlement account. The Bank of Canada uses deposit-switching to alter the overall quantity of settlement balances, and so affect the ability of charter banks to make loans.

Bank of Can uses deposit switching to change qty. of settlement Balances.

It is convenient to pay attention to the weekly changes in the Bank rate because it represents a summary indicator of what the Bank of Canada has been doing. By following the Bank rate, individuals can be aware of the stance of monetary policy without having to know the details of the fundamental instruments of policy—open-market operations and deposit-switching. Here's why. Every Tuesday, there is an auction sale of short-term government bonds called treasury bills. The more people pay for those bonds, the lower the effective yield received on them. After the auction, the government calculates the resulting yield and sets the Bank rate at one quarter of 1 percentage point above the treasury bill yield. Thus, the Bank rate is set to be consistent with the market-determined interest rates. It does not determine those market rates. Market rates are determined by the demand and supply of money, and the supply of money is, in turn, affected by the Bank of Canada's open-market and deposit-switching operations. Most journalists report changes in the Bank rate as if it is the trend-setting rate. In fact, it is the follower, not the leader. Nevertheless, we can still follow its ups and downs and have a good summary indicator of whether monetary policy is getting tighter or easier.

∴ Follow changes in Bank rate to tell you what Bank of Can is doing. Be aware of monetary policy.

Bank rate is consistent w/ market-determined interest rates.

Although the two instruments—open-market operations and deposit-switching, and the summary indicator of these operations—the Bank rate—give the Bank of Canada substantial power to influence the money supply, the Bank cannot control the money supply perfectly. Chartered bank discretion in conducting business can cause the money supply to change. For example, banks may decide to hold more reserves than usual, and households may choose to hold more cash. Such increases in *rr* and *cr* reduce the money supply, even though the Bank of Canada might have thought the initial size of the money supply was the appropriate level for maintaining aggregate demand in the economy.

↑ in rr ↓ M
↑ in cr ↓ M

There is a frustrating irony in this sort of development. When banks and their customers get nervous about the future and rearrange their assets to have a higher proportion of cash, they raise the chances that there will actually be a recession. One of the reasons that the Bank of Canada constantly monitors financial market developments is to try to counteract events like this. The Bank tries to use open-market and deposit-switching operations in such a way that the monetary base moves in the opposite direction to the change in the money multiplier (that are caused by the changes in household and banking preferences and practices).

There is a second method of dealing with crises of confidence in financial institutions: the government can insure individuals' deposits in banks and trust companies, a system called **deposit insurance**. Canada has the Canada Deposit Insurance Corporation (CDIC), which insures all deposits up to a maximum of $60,000 per customer. The idea is quite simple. If a bank or trust company extends too many risky loans and goes bankrupt as a result, customers do not lose their deposits. The general taxpayer, through the CDIC, will pay the customer up to $60,000 to protect them from the company's failure. Armed with this insurance, depositors do not have to move more into cash when they get nervous, and, as a result, the Bank of Canada has an easier job trying to keep the money supply on course.

CASE STUDY

18•1   Bank Failures and Deposit Insurance

As noted earlier, given Canada's branch banking system, banks almost never go bankrupt. Some smaller trust companies, however, have failed. Indeed, there were several such failures in the late 1980s and early 1990s, and since the CDIC went beyond the $60,000 limit and covered *all* deposits, the CDIC has run up quite a bill for taxpayers to cover. This development has sparked some controversy concerning possible reforms to the deposit insurance system. Before evaluating this controversy, however, it is instructive to consider the situation in the United States. U.S. banking is regulated at the state level, which means that there is very little branch banking. Many banks operate in only one state, and some are limited to an even more local region. This unit banking system is far more prone to bank failures. Indeed, whereas Canada had no bank failures during the Great Depression of the 1930s, there were a great many in the United States. And these failures help explain the severity of the Great Depression.

Between August 1929 and March 1933, the U.S. money supply fell 28 percent. As we discussed in Chapter 10, some economists believe that this large decline in the U.S. money supply was the primary cause of the Great Depression. But we did not discuss why the money supply fell so dramatically.

The three variables that determine the money supply—the monetary base, the reserve–deposit ratio, and the currency–deposit ratio—are shown in Table 18-1 for 1929 and 1933. You can see that the fall in the money supply cannot be attributed to a fall in the monetary base: in fact, the monetary base rose 18

Table 18-1		
The U.S. Money Supply and Its Determinants: 1929 and 1933		
	August 1929	March 1933
Money Supply	26.5	19.0
Currency	3.9	5.5
Demand deposits	22.6	13.5
Monetary Base	7.1	8.4
Currency	3.9	5.5
Reserves	3.2	2.9
Money Multiplier	3.7	2.3
Reserve–deposit ratio	0.14	0.21
Currency–deposit ratio	0.17	0.41

Source: Adapted from Milton Friedman and Anna Schwartz, *A Monetary History of the United States, 1867–1960* (Princeton, N.J.: Princeton University Press, 1963), Appendix A.

percent over this period. Instead, the money supply fell because the money multiplier fell 38 percent. The money multiplier fell because the currency–deposit and reserve–deposit ratios both rose substantially.

Most economists attribute the fall in the money multiplier to the large number of bank failures in the early 1930s. From 1930 to 1933, more than 9,000 banks suspended operations, often defaulting on their depositors. The bank failures caused the money supply to fall by altering the behaviour of both depositors and bankers.

Bank failures raised the currency–deposit ratio by reducing public confidence in the banking system. People feared that bank failures would continue, and they began to view currency as a more desirable form of money than deposits. When they withdrew their deposits, they drained the banks of reserves. The process of money creation reversed itself, as banks responded to lower reserves by reducing their outstanding balance of loans.

In addition, the bank failures raised the reserve–deposit ratio by making bankers more cautious. Having just observed many bank runs, bankers became apprehensive about operating with a small amount of reserves. They therefore increased their holdings of reserves to well above the legal minimum. Just as households responded to the banking crisis by holding more currency relative to deposits, bankers responded by holding more reserves relative to loans. Together these changes caused a large fall in the money multiplier.

Although it is easy to explain why the money supply fell, it is more difficult to decide whether to blame the U.S. central bank, the Federal Reserve. One might argue that the monetary base did not fall, so the Fed should not be blamed. Critics of Fed policy during this period make two arguments. First, they claim that the Fed should have taken a more vigorous role in preventing bank failures by acting as a *lender of last resort* when banks needed cash during bank runs; this would have helped maintain confidence in the banking system and prevented the large fall in the money multiplier. Second, they point out that the Fed could have responded to the fall in the money multiplier by increasing the monetary base even more than it did. Either of these actions would likely have prevented such a large fall in the money supply, which, in turn, might have reduced the severity of the Great Depression.

Like Canada, the United States now has deposit insurance, so a sudden fall in the money multiplier is much less likely today. But also like Canada, U.S. taxpayers are frustrated with how the deposit insurance system requires the general taxpayer to subsidize depositors that do not exercise care concerning where they deposit their funds. This is a classic problem that is involved with any form of insurance. In this case, insurance lowers the cost to depositors of failures, but it also raises the probability that those very failures will occur. This is because the insurance eliminates the need for depositors to assess and monitor the riskiness of financial institutions. Current discussions in Canada have raised suggestions like following the "co-insurance" system of Great Britain. The essential feature of this reform is that there is a deductible, so that individuals lose 2 percent or 3 percent of their deposits when the institution fails. With this feature, depositors remain well-protected, but they still have some incentive to avoid institutions that are obviously shaky.

18•2 Money Demand

We now turn to the other side of the money market and examine what determines money demand. In previous chapters, we used simple money demand functions. We started with the quantity theory, which assumes that the demand for real balances is proportional to income. That is, the quantity theory assumes

$$(M/P)^d = kY,$$

where k is a constant. We then considered a more general and realistic money demand function that assumes the demand for real balances depends on both the interest rate and income:

$$(M/P)^d = L(i, Y).$$

We used this money demand function when we discussed how to stop a hyperinflation in Chapter 6 and when we developed the *IS-LM* model in Chapters 9 and 10.

The purpose of studying money demand in more detail is to gain insight about the money demand function. Just as studies of the consumption function rely on microeconomic models of the consumption decision, studies of the money-demand function rely on microeconomic models of the money-demand decision. In this section we first discuss in broad terms the different ways to model money demand. We then develop one prominent model.

Recall that money serves three functions: it is a unit of account, a store of value, and a medium of exchange. The first function—money as a unit of account—does not by itself generate any demand for money, because one can quote prices in dollars without holding any. By contrast, money can serve its other two functions only if people hold it. Theories of money demand emphasize the role of money either as a store of value or as a medium of exchange.

Portfolio Theories of Money Demand

Theories of money demand that emphasize the role of money as a store of value are called **portfolio theories**. These theories stress that people hold money as part of their portfolio of assets. The key insight is that money offers a different combination of risk and return than other assets. In particular, money offers a safe (nominal) return, whereas the prices of stocks and bonds may rise or fall. Thus, some economists have suggested that households choose to hold money as part of their optimal portfolio.[2]

Portfolio theories predict that the demand for money should depend on the risk and return offered by money and by the various assets households can hold instead of money. In addition, money demand should depend on total wealth, because wealth measures the size of the portfolio to be allocated among money and the alternative assets. For example, we might write the money demand function as

$$(M/P)^d = L(r_s, \sigma_s, r_b, \sigma_b, \pi^e, W),$$

where r_s is the expected real return on stock, σ_s is the expected risk incurred by holding stock (typically measured by the past volatility in r_s), r_b is the expected real return on bonds, σ_b is the expected risk incurred by holding bonds (measured by the past volatility in the bond rate), π^e is the expected inflation rate, and W is real wealth. An increase in r_s or r_b reduces money demand, because other assets become more attractive. An increase in the riskiness of either stocks or bonds increases money demand, because these other assets become less attractive. An increase in π^e also reduces money demand, because money becomes less attractive. (Recall that $-\pi^e$ is the expected real return to holding money.) An increase in W raises money demand, because higher wealth implies a larger portfolio.

From the standpoint of portfolio theories, we can view our money demand function, $L(i, Y)$, as a useful simplification. First, it uses real income Y as a proxy for real wealth W. If we think of wealth very broadly defined to include human capital, income is the yield on wealth. Second, the only return variable it includes is the nominal interest rate, which is the sum of the real return on bonds and expected inflation (that is, $i = r_b + \pi^e$). According to portfolio theories, however, the money demand function should include the expected returns and risks associated with other assets as well.

[2] James Tobin, "Liquidity Preference as Behavior Toward Risk," *Review of Economic Studies* 25 (February 1958): 65–86.

Are portfolio theories useful for studying money demand? The answer depends on which measure of money we are considering. The most narrow measures of money, such as $M1$, include only currency and chequing accounts. These forms of money earn zero or very low rates of interest. There are other assets—such as savings accounts, treasury bills, and guaranteed investment certificates—that earn higher rates of interest and have the same risk characteristics as currency and chequing accounts. Economists say that money ($M1$) is a **dominated asset**: as a store of value, it exists alongside other assets that are always better. Thus, it is not optimal for people to hold money as part of their portfolio, implying that portfolio theories cannot explain the demand for these dominated forms of money.

Portfolio theories are more plausible as theories of money demand if we adopt a broad measure of money. The broad measures include many of those assets that dominate currency and chequing accounts. $M2$, for example, includes savings and other notice accounts. When we examine why people hold assets in the form of $M2$, rather than bonds or stock, the portfolio considerations of risk and return may be paramount. Hence, although the portfolio approach to money demand may not be plausible when applied to $M1$, it may be a good theory to explain the demand for $M2$ or $M3$.

CASE STUDY

18•2 Currency and the Underground Economy

How much currency are you holding right now in your wallet? How many $100 bills?

In Canada today, the amount of currency per person is about $960, and about half of that is in large-denomination notes. Most people find this fact surprising because they hold much smaller amounts and in smaller denominations.

Some of this currency is used by people in the underground economy— that is, by those engaged in illegal activity such as the drug trade and by those trying to hide income in order to evade taxes. People whose wealth was earned illegally may have fewer options for investing their portfolio, because by holding wealth in banks, bonds, or stock, they assume a greater risk of detection. For criminals, currency may not be a dominated asset: it may be the best store of value available.

Some economists point to the large amount of currency in the underground economy as one reason that some inflation may be desirable. Recall that inflation is a tax on the holders of money, because inflation erodes the real value of money. A drug dealer holding $20,000 in cash pays an inflation tax of $2000 per year when the inflation rate is 10 percent. The inflation tax may be the only tax those in the underground economy cannot evade. Government estimates of the underground economy put it at 4.5 percent of GDP in 1994.

Transactions Theories of Money Demand

Theories of money demand that emphasize the role of money as a medium of exchange are called **transactions theories**. These theories acknowledge that money is a dominated asset and emphasize that money, unlike other assets, is held to make purchases. These theories best explain why people hold narrow measures of money, such as currency and chequing accounts, as opposed to holding assets that dominate them, such as savings accounts or treasury bills.

Transactions theories of money demand take many forms, depending on how one models the process of obtaining money and making transactions. All these theories assume that money has the cost of earning a low rate of return and the benefit of making transactions more convenient. People decide how much money to hold by trading off these costs and benefits.

To see how transactions theories explain the money demand function, let's develop one prominent model of this type. The **Baumol-Tobin model** was developed in the 1950s by economists William Baumol and James Tobin, and it remains a leading theory of money demand.[3]

The Baumol-Tobin Model of Cash Management

The Baumol-Tobin model analyzes the costs and benefits of holding money. The benefit of holding money is convenience: people hold money to avoid making a trip to the bank every time they wish to buy something. The cost of this convenience is the forgone interest they would have received had they left the money deposited in a savings account that paid interest.

To see how people trade off these benefits and costs, consider a person who plans to spend Y dollars gradually over the course of a year. (For simplicity, assume that the price level is constant, so real spending is constant over the year.) How much money should she hold in the process of spending this amount? That is, what is the optimal size of average cash balances?

Consider the possibilities. She could withdraw the Y dollars at the beginning of the year and gradually spend the money. Figure 18-3(a) shows her money holdings over the course of the year under this plan. Her money holdings begin the year at Y and end the year at zero, averaging $Y/2$ over the year.

A second possible plan is to make two trips to the bank. In this case, she withdraws $Y/2$ dollars at the beginning of the year, gradually spends this amount over the first half of the year, and then makes another trip to withdraw $Y/2$ for the second half of the year. Figure 18-3(b) shows that money holdings over the year vary between $Y/2$ and zero, averaging $Y/4$. This plan has the advantage that less money is held on average, so less interest is forgone, but it has the disadvantage of requiring two trips to the bank rather than one.

More generally, suppose the individual makes N trips to the bank over the course of the year. On each trip, she withdraws Y/N dollars; she then spends

---

[3] William Baumol, "The Transactions Demand for Cash: An Inventory Theoretic Approach," *Quarterly Journal of Economics* 66 (November 1952): 545–556; James Tobin, "The Interest Elasticity of the Transactions Demand for Cash," *Review of Economics and Statistics* (August 1956): 241–247.

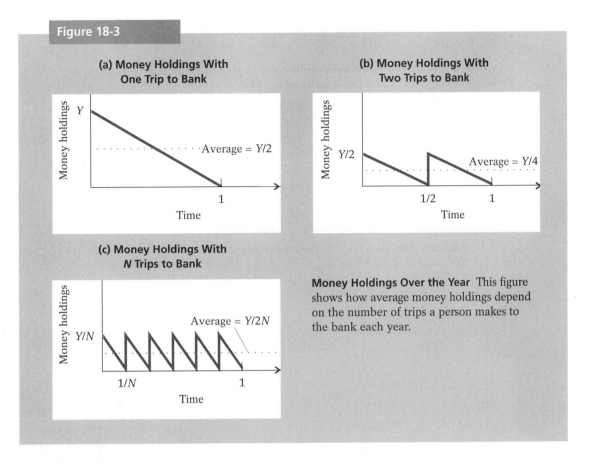

Figure 18-3

(a) Money Holdings With One Trip to Bank

Money holdings

Y

Average = $Y/2$

1

Time

(b) Money Holdings With Two Trips to Bank

Money holdings

$Y/2$

Average = $Y/4$

1/2   1

Time

(c) Money Holdings With N Trips to Bank

Money holdings

Y/N

Average = $Y/2N$

1/N   1

Time

Money Holdings Over the Year This figure shows how average money holdings depend on the number of trips a person makes to the bank each year.

the money gradually over the following $1/N$th of the year. Figure 18-3(c) shows that money holdings vary between Y/N and zero, averaging $Y/(2N)$.

The question is, what is the optimal choice of N? The greater N is, the less money is held on average and the less interest is forgone. But as N increases, so does the inconvenience of making frequent trips to the bank.

Suppose that the cost of going to the bank is some fixed amount F. F represents the value of the time spent traveling to and from the bank and waiting in line to make the withdrawal. For example, if a trip to the bank takes 15 minutes and a person's wage is $12 per hour, then F is $3. Also, let i denote the interest rate; because money does not bear interest, i measures the opportunity cost of holding money.

Now we can analyze the optimal choice of N, which determines money demand. For any N, the average amount of money held is $Y/(2N)$, so the forgone interest is $iY/(2N)$. Because F is the cost per trip to the bank, the total cost of making trips to the bank is FN. The total cost the individual bears is the sum of the forgone interest and the cost of trips to the bank:

$$\text{Total Cost} = \text{Forgone Interest} + \text{Cost of Trips}$$
$$= iY/(2N) + FN.$$

The larger the number of trips N, the smaller the forgone interest, and the larger the cost of going to the bank.

Figure 18-4 shows how total cost depends on N. There is one value of N that minimizes total cost. The optimal value of N, denoted N^*, is[4]

$$N^* = \sqrt{\frac{iY}{2F}}.$$

Average money holding is

$$\text{Average Money Holding} = Y/(2N^*)$$

$$= \sqrt{\frac{YF}{2i}}.$$

This expression shows that the individual holds more money if the fixed cost of going to the bank F is higher, if expenditure Y is higher, or if the interest rate i is lower.

Figure 18-4

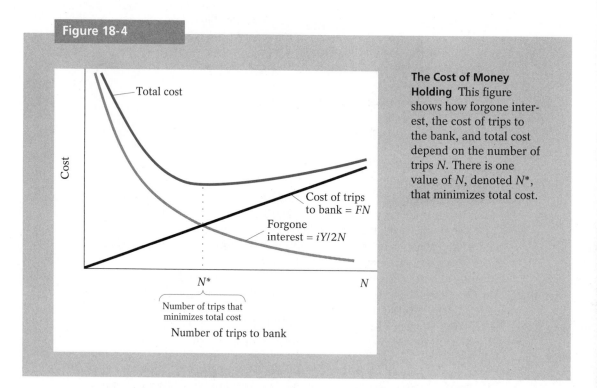

The Cost of Money Holding This figure shows how forgone interest, the cost of trips to the bank, and total cost depend on the number of trips N. There is one value of N, denoted N^*, that minimizes total cost.

---

[4] *Mathematical note:* Deriving this expression for the optimal choice of N requires simple calculus. Differentiate total cost C with respect to N to obtain

$$dC/dN = -iYN^{-2}/2 + F.$$

At the optimum, $dC/dN = 0$, which yields the formula for N^*.

So far, we have been interpreting the Baumol-Tobin model as a model of the demand for currency. That is, we have used it to explain the amount of money held outside of banks. Yet one can interpret the model more broadly. Imagine a person who holds a portfolio of monetary assets (currency and chequing accounts) and non-monetary assets (stocks and bonds). Monetary assets are used for transactions but offer a low rate of return. Let i be the difference in the return between monetary and non-monetary assets, and let F be the cost of transferring non-monetary assets into monetary assets, such as a brokerage fee. The decision about how often to pay the brokerage fee is analogous to the decision about how often to make a trip to the bank. Therefore, the Baumol-Tobin model describes this person's demand for monetary assets. By showing that money demand depends positively on expenditure Y and negatively on the interest rate i, the model provides a microeconomic justification for the money demand function, $L(i, Y)$, that we have used throughout this book.

CASE STUDY

18•3   Empirical Studies of Money Demand

Many economists have studied the data on money, income, and interest rates to learn more about the money demand function. One purpose of these studies is to estimate how money demand responds to changes in income and the interest rate. The sensitivity of money demand to these two variables determines the slope of the *LM* curve; it thus influences how monetary and fiscal policy affect the economy.

Another purpose of the empirical studies is to test the theories of money demand. The Baumol-Tobin model, for example, makes precise predictions for how income and interest rates influence money demand. The model's square-root formula implies that the income elasticity of money demand is one-half: a 10 percent increase in income should lead to a 5 percent increase in the demand for real balances. It also says that the interest elasticity of money demand is one-half: a 10 percent increase in the interest rate (say, from 10 percent to 11 percent) should lead to a 5 percent decrease in the demand for real balances.

Most empirical studies of money demand do not confirm these predictions. They find that the income elasticity of money demand is larger than one-half and that the interest elasticity is smaller than one-half. Thus, although the Baumol-Tobin model may capture part of the story behind the money demand function, it is not completely correct.

One possible explanation for the failure of the Baumol-Tobin model is that some people may have less discretion over their money holdings than the model assumes. For example, the model assumes that peoples' pay goes straight into their bank accounts—sent directly from their employers. Suppose instead that some people must go to the bank once a week to deposit their pay cheques. While at the bank, these individuals would take advantage of their visit to withdraw the currency needed for the coming week. For these individuals, the number of trips to the bank N does not respond to changes in expenditure or the interest rate. Because N is fixed, average money holdings ($Y/2N$) are proportional to expenditure and insensitive to the interest rate.

Now imagine that the world is populated with two sorts of people. Some obey the Baumol-Tobin model, so they have income and interest elasticities of one-half. The others have a fixed N, so they have an income elasticity of one and an interest elasticity of zero. In this case, the overall money demand function is a weighted average of the two groups. The income elasticity will be between one-half and one, and the interest elasticity will be between one-half and zero, as the empirical studies find.[5]

18•3   Financial Innovation and the Rise of Near Money

Traditional macroeconomic analysis groups assets into two categories: those used as a medium of exchange as well as a store of value (currency, chequing accounts) and those used only as a store of value (stocks, bonds, savings accounts). The first category of assets is called "money." In this chapter we discussed its supply and demand.

Although the distinction between monetary and non-monetary assets remains a useful theoretical tool, in recent years it has become more difficult to use in practice. In part because of deregulation of banks and other financial institutions, and in part because of improved computer technology, the past decade has seen rapid financial innovation. Monetary assets such as chequing accounts once paid no interest; today they earn market interest rates and are comparable to non-monetary assets as stores of value. Non-monetary assets such as stocks and bonds were once inconvenient to buy and sell; today mutual funds allow depositors to hold stocks and bonds and to make withdrawals simply by writing cheques from their accounts. Treasury bills are as easy to buy and sell as it is to make deposits into, and withdrawals out of, a "T bill" savings account at a neighbourhood trust company. These non-monetary assets that have acquired some of the liquidity of money are called **near money**.

The existence of near money complicates monetary policy by making the demand for money unstable. Since money and near money are close substitutes, households can easily switch their assets from one form to the other. Such changes can occur for minor reasons and do not necessarily reflect changes in spending. Thus, the velocity of money becomes less predictable, and the quantity of money can give faulty signals about aggregate demand.

One response to this problem is to use a broad definition of money that includes near money. Yet, since there is a continuum of assets in the world with

---

[5] To learn more about the empirical studies of money demand, see Stephen M. Goldfeld, "The Demand for Money Revisited," *Brookings Papers on Economic Activity* (1973:1): 577–638; and David Laidler, *The Demand for Money: Theories and Evidence*, 3rd ed. (New York: Harper and Row, 1985).

varying characteristics, it is not clear how to choose a subset to label "money." Moreover, if we adopt a broad definition of money, the Bank of Canada's ability to control this quantity may be limited.

The potential instability in money demand caused by near money has been an important practical problem for the Bank of Canada. In recent years, different measures of the money supply have given rather conflicting signals. For example, in 1990, M2 grew by almost 11 percent while M1 shrank by 1 percent. Then, in 1993, M2 growth had fallen to 3.2 percent while M1 growth had shot up to 10.4 percent. It is partly because of these problems that the Bank of Canada shifted away from attempting to target any particular monetary aggregate in the early 1980s. Since then, the Bank has been adjusting the monetary base by whatever it takes to target the inflation rate directly.

18•4 Conclusion

Money is at the heart of much macroeconomic analysis. Models of money supply and money demand can help shed light on the long-run determinants of the price level and the short-run causes of economic fluctuations. The rise of near money in recent years has shown that there is still much to be learned. Building reliable microeconomic models of money and near money remains a central challenge for macroeconomists.

Summary

1. The system of fractional-reserve banking creates money, because each dollar of reserves generates many dollars of deposits.

2. The supply of money depends on the monetary base, the reserve–deposit ratio, and the currency–deposit ratio. An increase in the monetary base leads to a proportionate increase in the money supply. A decrease in the reserve–deposit ratio or in the currency–deposit ratio increases the money multiplier and thus the money supply.

3. The Bank of Canada changes the money supply using two policy instruments. It can increase the monetary base by making an open-market purchase of bonds or foreign exchange, or by switching government deposits out of the Bank of Canada and into the chartered banks. Both of these operations cause a reduction of interest rates, and so they can be monitored by observing a drop in the Bank rate, which is set every Tuesday.

4. Portfolio theories of money demand stress that money is a store of value. They predict that the demand for money depends on the risk and return on money and alternative assets.

5. Transactions theories of money demand, such as the Baumol-Tobin model, stress that money is a medium of exchange. They predict that the demand for money depends positively on expenditure and negatively on the interest rate.

6. Financial innovation has led to the creation of assets with many of the attributes of money. These near monies make the demand for money less stable, which complicates the conduct of monetary policy.

KEY CONCEPTS

Reserves

100-percent-reserve banking

Balance sheet

Fractional-reserve banking

Financial intermediation

Monetary base

Reserve–deposit ratio

Currency–deposit ratio

Money multiplier

High-powered money

Open-market operations

Deposit-switching

Bank rate

Deposit insurance

Portfolio theories

Dominated asset

Transactions theories

Baumol-Tobin model

Near money

QUESTIONS FOR REVIEW

1. Explain how banks create money.

2. What are the two ways in which the Bank of Canada can influence the money supply?

3. Why might a banking crisis lead to a fall in the money supply?

4. Explain the difference between portfolio and transactions theories of money demand.

5. According to the Baumol-Tobin model, what determines how often people go to the bank? What does this decision have to do with money demand?

6. In what way does the existence of near money complicate the conduct of monetary policy?

PROBLEMS AND APPLICATIONS

1. The U.S. money supply fell during the years 1929 to 1933 because both the currency–deposit ratio and the reserve–deposit ratio increased. Use the model of the money supply and the data in Table 18-1 to answer the following hypothetical questions about this episode.

   a. What would have happened to the money supply if the currency–deposit ratio had risen but the reserve–deposit ratio had remained the same?

   b. What would have happened to the money supply if the reserve–deposit ratio had risen but the currency–deposit ratio had remained the same?

   c. Which of the two changes was more responsible for the fall in the money supply?

2. Let's see what the Baumol-Tobin model says about how often you should go to the bank to withdraw cash.

a. How much do you buy per year using currency (as opposed to cheques or credit cards)? This is your value of Y.

b. How long does it take you to go to the bank? What is your hourly wage? Use these two figures to compute your value of F.

c. What interest rate do you earn on the money you leave in your bank account? This is your value of i. (Be sure to write i in decimal form—that is, 6 percent should be expressed 0.06.)

d. According to the Baumol-Tobin model, how many times should you go to the bank each year, and how much should you withdraw each time?

e. In practice, how often do you go to the bank, and how much do you withdraw?

f. Compare the predictions of the Baumol-Tobin model to your behaviour. Does the model describe how you actually behave? If not, why not? How would you change the model to make it a better description of your behaviour?

3. In Chapter 6, we defined the velocity of money as the ratio of nominal expenditure to the quantity of money. Let's now use the Baumol-Tobin model to examine what determines velocity.

a. Recalling that average money holdings equal $Y/(2N)$, write velocity as a function of the number of trips to the bank N. Explain your result.

b. Use the formula for the optimal number of trips to express velocity as a function of expenditure Y, the interest rate i, and the cost of a trip to the bank F.

c. What happens to velocity when the interest rate rises? Explain.

d. What happens to velocity when the price level rises? Explain.

e. As the economy grows, what should happen to the velocity of money? (*Hint:* Think about how economic growth will influence Y and F.)

f. Suppose now that the number of trips to the bank is fixed rather than discretionary. What does this assumption imply about velocity?

What We Know,
What We Don't

*If all economists were laid end to end, they would not reach
a conclusion.*

George Bernard Shaw

*The theory of economics does not furnish a body of settled conclu-
sions immediately applicable to policy. It is a method rather than a
doctrine, an apparatus of the mind, which helps its possessor to
draw correct conclusions.*

John Maynard Keynes

The first chapter of this book states that the purpose of macroeconomics is to
understand economic events and to improve economic policy. Now that we
have developed and used many of the most important models in the macroeconomist's toolbox, we can assess whether macroeconomists have achieved
these goals.

Any fair assessment of macroeconomics today must admit that the science is incomplete. There are some principles that almost all macroeconomists
accept and on which we can rely when trying to analyze events or formulate
policies. Yet there are also many questions about the economy that remain
open to debate. In this last chapter we briefly review the central lessons of
macroeconomics, and we discuss the most pressing unresolved questions.

The Four Most Important
Lessons of Macroeconomics

We begin with four lessons that have recurred throughout this book and
that most economists today would endorse. Each lesson tells us how policy can
influence a key economic variable—output, inflation, or unemployment—
either in the long run or in the short run.

Lesson No. 1: In the long run, a country's capacity to produce goods and services determines the standard of living of its citizens.

Of all the measures of economic performance introduced in Chapter 2 and used throughout this book, the one that best measures economic well-being is GDP. Real GDP measures the economy's total output of goods and services and, therefore, a country's ability to satisfy the needs and desires of its citizens. Perhaps the most important question in macroeconomics is what determines the level and the growth of GDP.

The models in Chapters 3 and 4 identify the long-run determinants of GDP. In the long run, GDP depends on the factors of production—capital and labour—and on the technology for turning capital and labour into output. GDP grows when the factors of production increase or when the available technology improves.

This lesson has an obvious but important corollary: public policy can raise GDP in the long run only by improving the productive capability of the economy. There are many ways in which policymakers can attempt to do this. Policies that raise national saving—either through higher public saving (reduced deficits) or higher private saving—eventually lead to a larger capital stock (and in the small open economy case, a lower level of foreign indebtedness). Policies that raise the efficiency of labour—such as those that improve education or increase technological progress—lead to a more productive use of capital and labour. All these policies raise the economy's output of goods and services and, thereby, the standard of living. It is less clear, however, which is the best way to raise the economy's productive capability.

Lesson No. 2: In the short run, aggregate demand influences the amount of goods and services that a country produces.

Although the economy's ability to *supply* goods and services is the sole determinant of GDP in the long run, in the short run GDP depends also on the aggregate *demand* for goods and services. Aggregate demand is of key importance because prices are sticky in the short run. The *IS-LM* model developed in Chapters 9, 10, and 13 shows what causes changes in aggregate demand and, therefore, short-run fluctuations in GDP.

Because aggregate demand influences output in the short run, all the variables that affect aggregate demand can influence economic fluctuations. Monetary policy, fiscal policy, and shocks to the money and goods markets are often responsible for year-to-year changes in output and employment. Since aggregate demand is crucial to short-run fluctuations, policymakers monitor the economy closely. Before making any change in monetary or fiscal policy, they want to know whether the economy is booming or heading into a recession.

Lesson No. 3: In the long run, the rate of money growth determines the rate of inflation, but it does not affect the rate of unemployment.

In addition to GDP, inflation and unemployment are among the most closely watched measures of economic performance. Chapter 2 discussed how these two variables are measured, and subsequent chapters developed models to explain how they are determined.

The long-run analysis of Chapter 6 stresses that growth in the money supply is the ultimate determinant of inflation. That is, in the long run, a currency loses real value over time if and only if the central bank prints more and more of it. This lesson can explain the decade-to-decade variation in the inflation rate that we have observed in Canada, as well as the far more dramatic hyperinflations that various countries have experienced from time to time.

We have also seen many of the long-run effects of high money growth and high inflation. In Chapter 6 we saw that, according to the Fisher effect, high inflation raises the nominal interest rate (so that the real interest rate would remain unaffected if it were not for the fact that the Canadian personal income tax system is not indexed). In Chapter 7 we saw that high inflation leads to a depreciation of the currency in the market for foreign exchange.

The long-run determinants of unemployment are very different. The classical dichotomy—the irrelevance of nominal variables in the determination of real variables—implies that growth in the money supply does not affect unemployment in the long run. As we saw in Chapter 5, the natural rate of unemployment is determined by the rates of job separation and job finding, which in turn are determined by the process of job search and by the rigidity of the real wage.

These conclusions imply that persistent inflation and persistent unemployment are unrelated problems. To combat inflation in the long run, policymakers must reduce the growth in the money supply. To combat unemployment, they must alter the structure of labour markets. In the long run, there is no tradeoff between inflation and unemployment.

Lesson No. 4: In the short run, policymakers who control monetary and fiscal policy face a tradeoff between inflation and unemployment.

Although inflation and unemployment are not related in the long run, in the short run there is a tradeoff between these two variables, which is illustrated by the short-run Phillips curve. As we discussed in Chapter 11, policymakers can use monetary and fiscal policies to expand aggregate demand, which lowers unemployment and raises inflation. Or they can use these policies to contract aggregate demand, which raises unemployment and lowers inflation.

Policymakers face a fixed tradeoff between inflation and unemployment only in the short run. Over time, the short-run Phillips curve shifts for two reasons. First, supply shocks, such as changes in the price of oil, change the short-run tradeoff; an adverse supply shock offers policymakers the difficult choice between higher inflation or higher unemployment. Second, when people change their expectations of inflation, the short-run tradeoff between inflation and unemployment changes. The adjustment of expectations ensures that the tradeoff exists only in the short run. That is, only in the short run does unemployment deviate from its natural rate, and only in the short run does monetary policy have real effects. In the long run, the classical model of Chapters 3 through 7 describes the world.

The Four Most Important Unresolved Questions of Macroeconomics

So far, we have been discussing some of the broad lessons about which most economists would agree. We now turn to four questions about which there is continuing debate. Some of the disagreements concern the validity of alternative economic theories; others concern the ways in which economic theory should be applied to economic policy.

Question No. 1: How should policymakers try to raise the economy's natural rate of output?

The economy's natural rate of output depends on the amount of capital, the amount of labour, and the level of technology. Any policy designed to raise output in the long run must aim to increase the amount of capital, improve the use of labour, or enhance the available technology. There is, however, no simple and costless way to achieve these goals.

The Solow growth model of Chapter 4 shows that increasing the amount of capital requires raising the economy's rate of saving and investment. Therefore, many economists advocate policies to raise national saving. Yet the Solow model also shows that raising the capital stock requires a period of reduced consumption for current generations. Some argue that policymakers should not encourage current generations to make this sacrifice, because technological progress will ensure that future generations are better off than current generations. Moreover, even those who advocate increased saving and investment disagree about how to encourage additional saving and whether the investment should be in privately owned plants and equipment or in public infrastructure, such as roads and schools.

To improve the economy's use of its labour force, most policymakers would like to lower the natural rate of unemployment. Yet, as we discussed in Chapter 5, this is not an easy task. Reducing unemployment-insurance benefits would decrease the amount of frictional unemployment, and reducing the minimum wage would decrease the amount of wait unemployment. Yet these policies do not command a consensus among economists, because they would also hurt some of those members of society most in need.

Raising the rate of technological progress is, according to some economists, the most important objective for public policy. The Solow growth model shows that persistent growth in living standards ultimately requires continuing technological progress. This conclusion suggests that the worldwide slowdown in productivity growth that began in the early 1970s may have been the worst economic development of the past half century. Economists have not been successful at explaining this slowdown, and policymakers have not been successful at finding ways to reverse it.

Question No. 2: Should policymakers try to stabilize the economy?

The model of aggregate supply and aggregate demand developed in Chapters 8 through 11 and in Chapter 13 shows how various shocks to the economy cause economic fluctuations and how monetary and fiscal policy can influence these fluctuations. Some economists believe that policymakers should use this analysis in an attempt to stabilize the economy. They believe that monetary and fiscal policy should try to offset shocks in order to keep output and employment close to their natural rates.

Yet, as we discussed in Chapter 12, others are skeptical about our ability to stabilize the economy. These economists emphasize the long and variable lags inherent in economic policymaking, the poor record of economic forecasting, and our still-limited understanding of the economy. They conclude that the best policy is a passive one. In addition, many economists believe that policymakers are all too often opportunistic or follow time-inconsistent policies. They conclude that policymakers should not have discretion over monetary and fiscal policy but should be committed to following a fixed policy rule.

A related question is whether the benefits of economic stabilization—assuming stabilization could be achieved—would be large or small. Without any change in the natural rate of unemployment, stabilization policy can only reduce the magnitude of fluctuations around the natural rate. Thus, successful stabilization policy would eliminate booms as well as recessions. Some economists have suggested that the average gain from stabilization would be small.

Finally, not all economists endorse the standard model of economic fluctuations, which assumes sticky prices and monetary non-neutrality in the short run. According to real-business-cycle theory, which we discussed in Chapter 14, economic fluctuations are the optimal response of the economy to changing technology. Advocates of this approach believe that policymakers should not stabilize the economy, even if it were possible.

Question No. 3: How costly is inflation, and how costly is reducing inflation?

Whenever prices are rising, policymakers confront the question of whether to pursue policies to reduce the rate of inflation. To make this decision, they must compare the cost of allowing inflation to continue to the cost of reducing it. Yet economists cannot offer accurate estimates of either of these two costs.

The cost of inflation is a topic on which economists and laymen frequently disagree. When inflation exceeded 10 percent per year in the late 1970s, opinion polls showed that the public viewed inflation as a major economic problem. Yet, as we discussed in Chapter 6, when economists try to identify the social costs of inflation, they can point only to shoe-leather costs, menu costs, the costs of a nonindexed tax system, and so on. These costs become large when countries experience hyperinflation, but some economists regard them as modest at the moderate rates of inflation experienced in most major economies. Some economists believe that the public confuses inflation with other economic problems that coincide with inflation. For example, growth in productivity and real wages slowed in the 1970s; some laymen might have viewed inflation as the cause of the slowdown in real wages. Yet it is also possible that economists are mistaken: perhaps inflation is in fact very costly, and we have yet to figure out why.

The cost of reducing inflation is a topic on which economists often disagree among themselves. As we discussed in Chapter 11, the standard view— as described by the short-run Phillips curve—is that reducing inflation requires a period of low output and high unemployment. According to this view, the cost of reducing inflation is measured by the sacrifice ratio, which gives the number of percentage points of one year's GDP that must be forgone to reduce inflation by one percentage point.

Some economists think that the cost of reducing inflation can be much smaller than standard estimates of the sacrifice ratio indicate. According to the rational-expectations approach discussed in Chapter 11, if a disinflationary policy is announced in advance and is credible, people will adjust their expectations quickly, so the disinflation need not cause a recession. According to the real-business-cycle models discussed in Chapter 14, prices are fully flexible, and money is neutral, so disinflationary monetary policy will not affect the economy's output of goods and services.

Other economists believe that the cost of reducing inflation is much larger than standard estimates of the sacrifice ratio indicate. The theories of hysteresis discussed in Chapter 11 suggest that a recession caused by disinflationary policy could raise the natural rate of unemployment. If so, then the cost of reducing inflation is not merely a temporary recession but a persistently higher level of unemployment.

Because the costs of inflation and disinflation remain open to debate, economists frequently offer conflicting advice to policymakers. Perhaps with further research, we can reach a consensus on the benefits of low inflation and the best way to achieve that goal.

Question No. 4: How big a problem are government budget deficits?

In recent years, large budget deficits have been a primary topic of debate among policymakers. In 1994, the Canadian federal government promised to cut its deficit in half within three years, during a period when unemployment already exceeded 10 percent. As we discussed in Chapter 16, the budget deficit is a topic about which economists often disagree.

Most of the models in this book—and most economists—take the traditional view of government debt. According to this view, a budget deficit leads to lower national saving, lower investment, and a trade deficit. In the long run, it leads to a smaller steady-state capital stock and a larger foreign debt. Those who hold the traditional view conclude that budget deficits place a burden on future generations.

Yet not all economists agree with this assessment. Advocates of the Ricardian view of government debt are skeptical. They stress that a budget deficit represents merely a substitution of future taxes for current taxes. As long as consumers are forward-looking, as the theories of consumption presented in Chapter 15 assume, they will save today to meet their or their children's future tax liability. These economists believe that budget deficits have only a minor effect on the economy.

Still other economists believe that the budget deficit is an imperfect measure of fiscal policy. They agree that the government's choices regarding taxes and spending have important effects on different generations. Yet, according to these economists, the budget deficit does not accurately capture these generational impacts.

Conclusion

Economists and policymakers must deal with ambiguity. The current state of macroeconomics offers many insights, but it also leaves many questions open. The challenge for economists is to find answers to these questions and to expand our knowledge. The challenge for policymakers is to use the knowledge we now have to improve economic performance. Both challenges are formidable, but neither is insuperable.

Glossary

Accelerator model: The model according to which investment depends on the change in output.

Accommodating policy: A policy that yields to the effect of a shock and thereby prevents the shock from being disruptive; for example, a policy that raises aggregate demand in response to an adverse supply shock, sustaining the effect of the shock on prices and keeping output at the natural rate.

Accounting profit: The amount of revenue remaining for the owners of a firm after all the factors of production except capital have been compensated. (Cf. economic profit, profit.)

Acyclical: Moving in no consistent direction over the business cycle. (Cf. countercyclical, procyclical.)

Adaptive expectations: An approach that assumes that people form their expection of a variable based on recently observed values of the variable. (Cf. rational expectations.)

Adverse selection: An unfavourable sorting of individuals by their own choices; for example, in efficiency-wage theory, when a wage cut induces good workers to quit and bad workers to remain with the firm.

Aggregate: Total for the whole economy.

Aggregate demand curve: The negative relationship between the price level and the aggregate quantity of output demanded that arises from the interaction between the goods market and the money market.

Aggregate demand externality: The macroeconomic impact of one firm's price adjustment on the demand for all other firms' products.

Aggregate supply curve: The relationship between the price level and the aggregate quantity of output firms produce.

Animal spirits: Exogenous and perhaps self-fulfilling waves of optimism and pessimism about the state of the economy, which, according to some economists, influence the level of investment.

Appreciation: A rise in the value of a currency relative to other currencies in the market for foreign exchange. (Cf. depreciation.)

Arbitrage: The act of buying an item in one market and selling it at a higher price in another market in order to profit from the price differential in the two markets.

Automatic stabilizer: A policy that reduces the amplitude of economic fluctuations without regular and deliberate changes in economic policy; for example, an income tax system that automatically reduces taxes when income falls.

Average propensity to consume (APC): The ratio of consumption to income (C/Y).

Balance sheet: An accounting statement that shows assets and liabilities.

Balanced budget: A budget in which receipts equal expenditures.

Bank of Canada: The central bank of Canada.

Bank rate: The interest rate that the Bank of Canada charges if it makes loans to chartered banks.

Baumol-Tobin model: A model of money demand positing that people choose optimal money holdings by comparing the opportunity cost of the forgone interest from holding money and the benefit of making less frequent trips to the bank.

Bond: A document representing an interest-bearing debt of the issuer, usually a corporation or the government.

Borrowing constraint: A restriction on the amount a person can borrow from financial institutions, limiting that person's ability to spend his or her future income today; also called a liquidity constraint.

Budget constraint: The limit that income places on expenditure. (Cf. intertemporal budget constraint.)

Budget deficit: A shortfall of receipts from expenditure.

Budget surplus: An excess of receipts over expenditure.

Business cycle: Economy-wide fluctuations in output, incomes, and employment.

Business fixed investment: Equipment and structures that businesses buy for use in future production.

Capital: 1. The stock of equipment and structures used in production. 2. The funds to finance the accumulation of equipment and structures.

Capital budgeting: An accounting procedure that measures both assets and liabilities.

Central bank: The institution responsible for the conduct of monetary policy, such as the Bank of Canada in Canada.

Classical dichotomy: The theoretical separation of real and nominal variables in the classical model, which implies that nominal variables do not influence real variables. (Cf. neutrality of money.)

Classical model: A model of the economy derived from the ideas of the classical, or pre-Keynesian, economists; a model based on the assumptions that wages and prices adjust to clear markets and that monetary policy does not influence real variables. (Cf. Keynesian model.)

Closed economy: An economy that does not engage in international trade. (Cf. open economy.)

Cobb-Douglas production function: A production function of the form $F(K, L) = AK^\alpha L^{1-\alpha}$, where K is capital, L is labour, and A and α are parameters.

Commodity money: Money that is intrinsically useful and would be valued even if it did not serve as money. (Cf. fiat money, money.)

Competition: A situation in which there are many individuals or firms so that the actions of any one of them do not influence market prices.

Constant returns to scale: A property of a production function whereby a proportionate increase in all factors of production leads to an increase in output of the same proportion.

Consumer price index (CPI): A measure of the overall level of prices that shows the cost of a fixed basket of consumer goods relative to the cost of the same basket in a base year.

Consumption: Goods and services purchased by consumers.

Consumption function: A relationship showing the determinants of consumption; for example, a relationship between consumption and disposable income, $C = C(Y - T)$.

Contractionary policy: Policy that reduces aggregate demand, real income, and employment. (Cf. expansionary policy.)

Coordination failure: A situation in which decisionmakers reach an outcome that is inferior for all of them because of their inability to jointly choose strategies that would result in a preferred outcome.

Corporate profit tax: The tax levied on the accounting profit of corporations.

Cost of capital: The amount forgone by holding a unit of capital for one period, including interest, depreciation, and the gain or loss from the change in the price of capital.

Cost-push inflation: Inflation resulting from shocks to aggregate supply. (Cf. demand-pull inflation.)

Countercyclical: Moving in the opposite direction from output, incomes, and employment over the business cycle; rising during recessions and falling during recoveries. (Cf. acyclical, procyclical.)

CPI: *See* consumer price index.

Crowding out: The reduction in investment that results when expansionary fiscal policy raises the interest rate.

Currency: The sum of outstanding paper money and coins.

Cyclical unemployment: The employment associated with short-run economic fluctuations; the deviation of the unemployment rate from the natural rate.

Cyclically adjusted budget deficit: The value that the government budget deficit would be if real GDP equalled its average value over the business cycle.

Debt-deflation: A theory according to which an unexpected fall in the price level redistributes real wealth from debtors to creditors and, therefore, reduces total spending in the economy.

Deflation: A decrease in the overall level of prices. (Cf. disinflation, inflation.)

Deflator: *See* GDP deflator.

Demand deposits: Assets that are held in banks and can be used on demand to make transactions, such as chequing accounts.

Demand-pull inflation: Inflation resulting from shocks to aggregate demand. (Cf. cost-push inflation.)

Deposit insurance: Insurance provided by the Canada Deposit Insurance Corporation (CDIC) to individuals or firms that deposited funds in a bank or trust company that has gone bankrupt.

Deposit-switching: The switching of federal government deposits between the Bank of Canada and the chartered banks for the purpose of changing the money supply.

Depreciation: 1. The reduction in the capital stock that occurs over time because of aging and use. 2. A fall in the value of a currency relative to other currencies in the market for foreign exchange. (Cf. appreciation.)

Depreciation allowances: Deductions permitted in the calculation of corporate taxes to allow for the wearing out of capital equipment.

Depression: A very severe recession.

Devaluation: An action by the central bank to decrease the value of a currency under a system of fixed exchange rates. (Cf. revaluation).

Diminishing marginal product: A characteristic of a production function whereby the marginal product of a factor falls as the amount of the factor increases while all other factors are held constant.

Discounting: The reduction in value of future expenditure and receipts, compared to current expenditure and receipts, resulting from the presence of a positive interest rate.

Discouraged workers: Individuals who have left the labour force because they believe that there is little hope of finding a job.

Disinflation: A reduction in the rate at which prices are rising. (Cf. deflation, inflation.)

Disposable income: Income remaining after the payment of taxes and the receipt of transfer payments.

Dominated asset: An asset that offers an inferior return compared to another asset in all possible realizations of future uncertainty.

Double coincidence of wants: A situation in which two individuals each have precisely the good that the other wants.

Economic profit: The amount of revenue remaining for the owners of a firm after all the factors of production have been compensated. (Cf. accounting profit, profit.)

Efficiency of labour: A variable in the Solow growth model that measures the health, education, skills, and knowledge of the labour force.

Efficiency units of labour: A measure of the labour force that incorporates both the number of workers and the efficiency of each worker.

Efficiency-wage theories: Theories of real-wage rigidity and unemployment according to which firms raise labour productivity and profits by keeping real wages above the equilibrium level.

Elasticity: The percent change in a variable caused by a 1 percent change in another variable.

Endogenous variable: A variable that is explained by a particular model; a variable whose value is determined by the model's solution. (Cf. exogenous variable.)

Equilibrium: A state of balance between opposing forces, such as the balance of supply and demand in a market.

Euler's theorem: The mathematical result economists use to show that economic profit must be zero if the production function has constant returns to scale and if factors are paid their marginal products.

Ex ante **real interest rate:** The real interest rate anticipated when a loan is made; the nominal interest rate minus expected inflation. (Cf. *ex post* real interest rate.)

Ex post **real interest rate:** The real interest rate actually realized; the nominal interest rate minus actual inflation. (Cf. *ex ante* real interest rate.)

Exchange rate: The rate at which a country makes exchanges in world markets. (Cf. nominal exchange rate, real exchange rate.)

Exchange-rate union: A group of countries that agree to limit exchange-rate fluctuations among their currencies.

Exogenous variable: A variable that a particular model takes as given; a variable whose value is independent of the model's solution. (Cf. endogenous variable.)

Expansionary policy: Policy that raises aggregate demand, real income, and employment. (Cf. contractionary policy.)

Exports: Goods and services sold to other countries.

Factor of production: An input used to produce goods and services; for example, capital or labour.

Factor price: The amount paid for one unit of a factor of production.

Factor share: The proportion of total income being paid to a factor of production.

Federal Reserve (the Fed): The central bank of the United States.

Fiat money: Money that is not intrinsically useful and is valued only because it is used as money. (Cf. commodity money, money.)

Financial intermediation: The process by which resources are allocated from those individuals who wish to save some of their income for future consumption to those individuals and firms who wish to borrow to buy investment goods for future production.

Financing constraint: A limit on the quantity of funds a firm can raise—such as through borrowing—in order to buy capital.

Fiscal policy: The government's choice regarding levels of spending and taxation.

Fisher effect: The one-for-one influence of expected inflation on the nominal interest rate.

Fisher equation: The equation stating that the nominal interest rate is the sum of the real interest rate and expected inflation ($i = r + \pi^e$).

Fixed exchange rate: An exchange rate that is set by the central bank's willingness to buy and sell the domestic currency for foreign currencies at a predetermined price. (Cf. floating exchange rate.)

Flexible prices: Prices that adjust quickly to equilibrate supply and demand. (Cf. sticky prices.)

Floating exchange rate: An exchange rate that the central bank allows to change in response to changing economic conditions and economic policies. (Cf. fixed exchange rate.)

Flow: A variable measured as a quantity per unit of time. (Cf. stock.)

Fractional-reserve banking: A system in which banks keep only some of their deposits on reserve. (Cf. 100-percent-reserve banking.)

Frictional unemployment: The unemployment that results because it takes time for workers to search for the jobs that best suit their skills and tastes. (Cf. wait unemployment.)

GDP: *See* gross domestic product.

GDP deflator: The ratio of nominal GDP to real GDP; a measure of the overall level of prices that shows the cost of the currently produced basket of goods relative to the cost of that basket in a base year.

General equilibrium: The simultaneous equilibrium of all the markets in the economy.

GNP: *See* gross national product.

Gold standard: A monetary system in which gold serves as money or in which all money is convertible into gold.

Golden rule: The saving rate in the Solow growth model that leads to the steady state in which consumption per worker (or consumption per efficiency unit of labour) is maximized.

Government purchases: Goods and services bought by the government. (Cf. transfer payments.)

Government-purchases multiplier: The change in aggregate income resulting from a one-dollar change in government purchases.

Gross domestic product (GDP): The total income earned domestically, including the income earned by foreign-owned factors of production; the total expenditure on domestically produced final goods and services.

Gross national product (GNP): The total income of all residents of a nation, including the income from factors of production used abroad, but excluding both the income of foreign-owned factors of production operating within the country and interest payments on the foreign debt.

High-powered money: The sum of currency and bank reserves; also called the monetary base.

Hyperinflation: Extremely high inflation.

Hysteresis: The long-lasting influence of history, such as on the natural rate of unemployment.

Identification problem: The difficulty of isolating a particular relationship in data when two or more variables are related in more than one way.

Imperfect-information model: The model of aggregate supply emphasizing that individuals do not always know the overall price level because they cannot observe the prices of all goods and services in the economy.

Import quota: A legal limit on the amount of a good that can be imported.

Imports: Goods and services bought from other countries.

Imputed value: An estimate of the value of a good or service that is not sold in the marketplace and therefore does not have a market price.

Income effect: The change in consumption of a good resulting from a movement to a higher or lower indifference curve, holding the relative price constant. (Cf. substitution effect.)

Index of leading indicators: *See* leading indicators.

Indifference curves: A graphical representation of preferences that shows different combinations of goods producing the same level of satisfaction.

Inflation: An increase in the overall level of prices. (Cf. deflation, disinflation.)

Inflation tax: The revenue raised by the government through the creation of money; seigniorage.

Inside lag: The time between a shock hitting the economy and the policy action taken to respond to the shock. (Cf. outside lag.)

Insiders: Workers who are already employed and therefore have an influence on wage bargaining. (Cf. outsiders.)

Interest rate: The market price at which resources are transferred between the present and the future; the return to saving and the cost of borrowing.

Intermediation: *See* financial intermediation.

Intertemporal budget constraint: The budget constraint applying to expenditure and income

in more than one period of time. (Cf. budget constraint.)

Intertemporal substitution of labour: The willingness of people to trade off working in one period for working in future periods.

Inventory investment: The change in the quantity of goods that firms hold in storage, including materials and supplies, work in process, and finished goods.

Investment: Goods purchased by individuals and firms to add to their stock of capital.

Investment tax credit: A provision of the corporate income tax that reduces a firm's tax when it buys new capital goods.

IS **curve**: The negative relationship between the interest rate and the level of income that arises in the market for goods and services. (Cf. *IS-LM* model, *LM* curve.)

IS-LM **model**: A model of aggregate demand that shows what determines aggregate income for a given price level by analyzing the interaction between the goods market and the money market. (Cf. *IS* curve, *LM* curve.)

Keynesian cross: A simple model of income determination, based on the ideas in Keynes's *General Theory*, which shows how changes in spending can have a multiplied effect on aggregate income.

Keynesian model: A model derived from the ideas of Keynes's *General Theory*; a model based on the assumptions that wages and prices do not adjust to clear markets and that aggregate demand determines the economy's output and employment. (Cf. classical model.)

Labour-augmenting technological progress: Advances in productive capability that raise the efficiency of labour.

Labour force: Those in the population who have a job or are looking for a job.

Labour-force participation rate: The percent of the adult population in the labour force.

Labour hoarding: The phenomenon of firms employing workers whom they do not need when the demand for their products is low, so that they will still have these workers when demand recovers.

Large open economy: An open economy that can influence its domestic interest rate; an economy that, by virtue of its size, can have a substantial impact on world markets and, in particular, on the world interest rate. (Cf. small open economy.)

Laspeyres price index: A measure of the level of prices based on a fixed basket of goods. (Cf. Paasche price index.)

Leading indicators: Economic variables that fluctuate in advance of the economy's output and thus signal the direction of economic fluctuations.

Life-cycle hypothesis: The theory of consumption that emphasizes the role of saving and borrowing as transferring resources from those times in life when income is high to those times in life when income is low, such as from working years to retirement.

Liquid: Readily convertible into the medium of exchange; easily used to make transactions.

Liquidity constraint: A restriction on the amount a person can borrow from a financial institution, which limits the person's ability to spend his future income today; also called a borrowing constraint.

Liquidity-preference theory: A simple model of the interest rate, based on the ideas in Keynes's *General Theory*, which says that the interest rate adjusts to equilibrate the supply and demand for real money balances.

***LM* curve**: The positive relationship between the interest rate and the level of income (while holding the price level fixed) that arises in the market for real money balances. (Cf. *IS-LM* model, *IS* curve.)

Loanable funds: The flow of resources available to finance capital accumulation.

Lucas critique: The argument that traditional policy analysis does not adequately take into account the impact of policy changes on people's expectations.

***M*1, *M*2, *M*2⁺, *M*3**: Various measures of the stock of money, where larger numbers signify a broader definition of money.

Macroeconometric model: A model that uses data and statistical techniques to describe the economy quantitatively, rather than just qualitatively.

Macroeconomics: The study of the economy as a whole. (Cf. microeconomics.)

Marginal product of capital (*MPK*): The amount of extra output produced when the capital input is increased by one unit.

Marginal product of labour (*MPL*): The amount of extra output produced when the labour input is increased by one unit.

Marginal propensity to consume (*MPC*): The increase in consumption resulting from a one-dollar increase in disposable income.

Marginal rate of substitution (*MRS*): The rate at which a consumer is willing to give up some of one good in exchange for more of another; the slope of the indifference curve.

Market-clearing model: A model that assumes that prices freely adjust to equilibrate supply and demand.

Medium of exchange: The item widely accepted in transactions for goods and services; one of the functions of money. (Cf. store of value, unit of account.)

Menu cost: The cost of changing a price.

Microeconomics: The study of individual markets and decisionmakers. (Cf. macroeconomics.)

Model: A simplified representation of reality, often using diagrams or equations, that shows how variables interact.

Monetarism: The doctrine according to which changes in the money supply are the primary cause of economic fluctuations, implying that a stable money supply would lead to a stable economy.

Monetary base: The sum of currency and bank reserves; also called high-powered money.

Monetary neutrality: *See* neutrality of money.

Monetary policy: The central bank's choice regarding the supply of money.

Monetary transmission mechanism: The process by which changes in the money supply influence the amount that households and firms wish to spend on goods and services.

Money: The stock of assets used for transactions. (Cf. commodity money, fiat money.)

Money demand function: A function showing the determinants of the demand for real money balances; for example, $(M/P)^\mathrm{d} = L(i, Y)$.

Money multiplier: The increase in the money supply resulting from a one-dollar increase in the monetary base.

Moral hazard: The possibility of dishonest behaviour in situations in which behaviour is imperfectly monitored; for example, in efficiency-wage theory, the possibility that low-wage workers may shirk their responsibilities and risk getting caught and fired.

Multiplier: *See* government-purchases multiplier, money multiplier, or tax multiplier.

Mundell-Fleming model: The *IS-LM* model for a small open economy.

Mundell-Tobin effect: The fall in the real interest rate that results when an increase in expected inflation raises the nominal interest rate, lowers real money balances and real wealth, and thereby reduces consumption and raises saving.

National income accounting: The accounting system that measures GDP and many other related statistics.

National income accounts identity: The equation showing that GDP is the sum of consumption, investment, government purchases, and net exports.

National saving: A nation's income minus consumption and government purchases; the sum of private and public saving.

Natural rate of unemployment: The steady-state rate of unemployment; the rate of unemployment toward which the economy gravitates in the long run.

Natural-rate hypothesis: The premise that fluctuations in aggregate demand influence output, employment, and unemployment only in the short run, and that in the long run these variables return to the levels implied by the classical model.

Near money: Assets that are almost as useful as money for engaging in transactions and, therefore, are close substitutes for money.

Neoclassical model of investment: The theory according to which investment depends on the deviation of the marginal product of capital from the cost of capital.

Net exports: Exports minus imports.

Net foreign investment: The net flow of funds being invested abroad; domestic saving minus domestic investment.

Net investment: The amount of investment after the replacement of depreciated capital; the change in the capital stock.

Neutrality of money: The property that a change in the money supply does not influence real variables. (Cf. classical dichotomy.)

New classical economics: The school of thought according to which economic fluctuations can be explained while maintaining the assumptions of the classical model. (Cf. new Keynesian economics.)

New Keynesian economics: The school of thought according to which economic fluctuations can be explained only by admitting a role for some microeconomic imperfection, such as sticky wages or prices. (Cf. new classical economics.)

Nominal: Measured in current dollars; not adjusted for inflation. (Cf. real.)

Nominal exchange rate: The rate at which one country's currency trades for another country's currency. (Cf. exchange rate, real exchange rate.)

Nominal interest rate: The return to saving and the cost of borrowing without adjustment for inflation. (Cf. real interest rate.)

Normal good: A good that a consumer demands in greater quantity when his or her income rises.

Okun's law: The negative relationship between unemployment and real GDP, according to which a decrease of 2 percentage points in the growth of real GDP is associated with approximately 1 additional percentage point in the unemployment rate.

100-percent-reserve banking: A system in which banks keep all deposits on reserve. (Cf. fractional-reserve banking.)

Open economy: An economy in which people can freely engage in international trade in goods and capital. (Cf. closed economy.)

Open-market operations: The purchase or sale of government bonds by the central bank for the purpose of increasing or decreasing the money supply.

Outside lag: The time between a policy action and its influence on the economy. (Cf. inside lag.)

Outsiders: Workers who are not employed and therefore have no influence on wage bargaining. (Cf. insiders.)

Paasche price index: A measure of the level of prices based on a changing basket of goods. (Cf. Laspeyres price index.)

Permanent income: Income that people expect to persist into the future; normal income. (Cf. transitory income.)

Permanent-income hypothesis: The theory of consumption according to which people choose consumption based on their permanent income, and use saving and borrowing to smooth consumption in response to transitory variations in income.

Phillips curve: A negative relationship between inflation and unemployment; in its modern form, a relationship among inflation, cyclical unemployment, expected inflation, and supply shocks, derived from the short-run aggregate supply curve.

Pigou effect: The increase in consumer spending that results when a fall in the price level raises real money balances and, thereby, consumers' wealth.

Portfolio theories of money demand: Theories that explain how much money people choose to hold and that stress the role of money as a store of value. (Cf. transactions theories of money demand.)

Precautionary saving: The extra saving that results from uncertainty regarding, for example, longevity or future income.

Present value: The amount today that is equivalent to an amount to be received in the future, taking into account the interest that could be earned over the interval of time.

Private saving: Disposable income minus consumption.

Procyclical: Moving in the same direction as output, incomes, and employment over the business cycle; falling during recessions and rising during recoveries. (Cf. acyclical, counter-cyclical.)

Production function: The mathematical relationship showing how the quantities of the factors of production determine the quantity of goods and services produced; for example, $Y = F(K, L)$.

Production smoothing: The motive for holding inventories according to which a firm can reduce its costs by keeping the amount of output it produces steady and allowing its stock of inventories to respond to fluctuating sales.

Profit: The income of firm owners; firm revenue minus firm costs. (Cf. accounting profit, economic profit.)

Public saving: Government receipts minus government spending; the budget surplus.

Purchasing-power parity: The doctrine according to which goods must sell for the same price in every country, implying that the nominal exchange rate reflects differences in price levels.

q-theory of investment: The theory according to which expenditure on capital goods depends on the ratio of the market value of installed capital to its replacement cost.

Quantity equation: The identity stating that the product of the money supply and the velocity of money equals nominal expenditure ($MV = PY$); coupled with the assumption of stable velocity, an explanation of nominal expenditure called the quantity theory of money.

Quantity theory of money: The doctrine emphasizing that changes in the quantity of money lead to changes in nominal expenditure.

Quota: *See* import quota.

Random walk: The path of a variable whose changes over time are unpredictable.

Rational expectations: An approach that assumes that people optimally use all available information—including information about current and prospective policies—to forecast the future. (Cf. adaptive expectations.)

Real: Measured in constant dollars; adjusted for inflation. (Cf. nominal.)

Real aggregate demand curve: In real-business-cycle theory, the negative relationship arising from the goods market between the real interest rate and the aggregate quantity of output demanded.

Real aggregate supply curve: In real-business-cycle theory, the positive relationship arising from intertemporal substitution in the labour market between the real interest rate and the aggregate quantity of output supplied.

Real-business-cycle theory: The theory according to which economic fluctuations can be explained by real changes in the economy (such as changes in technology) and without any role for nominal variables (such as the money supply).

Real exchange rate: The rate at which one country's goods trade for another country's goods. (Cf. exchange rate, nominal exchange rate.)

Real interest rate: The return to saving and the cost of borrowing after adjustment for inflation. (Cf. nominal interest rate.)

Real money balances: The quantity of money expressed in terms of the quantity of goods and services it can buy; the quantity of money divided by the price level (M/P).

Recession: A sustained period of falling real income.

Rental price of capital: The amount paid to rent one unit of capital.

Reserves: The money that banks have received from depositors but have not used to make loans.

Residential investment: New housing bought by people to live in and by landlords to rent out.

Revaluation: An action undertaken by the central bank to raise the value of a currency under a system of fixed exchange rates. (Cf. devaluation.)

Ricardian equivalence: The theory according to which forward-looking consumers fully anticipate the future taxes implied by government debt, so that government borrowing today coupled with a tax increase in the future to repay the debt has the same effect on the economy as a tax increase today.

Sacrifice ratio: The number of percentage points of a year's real GDP that must be forgone to reduce inflation by 1 percentage point.

Saving: See national saving, private saving, and public saving.

Seasonal adjustment: The removal of the regular fluctuations in an economic variable that occur as a function of the time of year.

Sectoral shift: A change in the composition of demand among industries or regions.

Seigniorage: The revenue raised by the government through the creation of money; the inflation tax.

Shock: An exogenous change in an economic relationship, such as the aggregate demand or aggregate supply curve.

Shoeleather cost: The cost of inflation from reducing real money balances, such as the inconvenience of needing to make more frequent trips to the bank.

Small open economy: An open economy that takes its interest rate as given by world financial markets; an economy that, by virtue of its size, has a negligible impact on world markets and, in particular, on the world interest rate. (Cf. large open economy.)

Solow growth model: A model showing how

saving, population growth, and technological progress determine the level of and growth in the standard of living.

Solow residual: The growth in total factor productivity, measured as the percentage change in output minus the percentage change in inputs, where the inputs are weighted by their factor shares. (Cf. total factor productivity.)

Stabilization policy: Public policy aimed at keeping output and employment at their natural-rate levels.

Stagflation: A situation of falling output and rising prices; combination of stagnation and inflation.

Steady state: A condition in which key variables are not changing.

Sticky prices: Prices that adjust sluggishly and, therefore, do not always equilibrate supply and demand. (Cf. flexible prices.)

Sticky-price model: The model of aggregate supply emphasizing the slow adjustment of the prices of goods and services.

Sticky-wage model: The model of aggregate supply emphasizing the slow adjustment of nominal wages.

Stock: 1. A variable measured as a quantity at a point in time. (Cf. flow.) 2. Shares of ownership in a corporation.

Stock market: A market in which shares of ownership in corporations are bought and sold.

Stock-out avoidance: The motive for holding inventories according to which firms keep extra goods on hand to prevent running out if sales are unexpectedly high.

Store of value: A way of transferring purchasing power from the present to the future; one of the functions of money. (Cf. medium of exchange, unit of account.)

Substitution effect: The change in consumption of a good resulting from a movement along an indifference curve because of a change in the relative price. (Cf. income effect.)

Tariff: A tax on imported goods.

Tax multiplier: The change in aggregate income resulting from a one-dollar change in taxes.

Time inconsistency: The tendency of policymakers to announce policies in advance in order to influence the expectations of private decisionmakers, and then to follow different policies after those expectations have been formed and acted upon.

Tobin's q: The ratio of the market value of installed capital to its replacement cost.

Total factor productivity: A measure of the level of technology; the amount of output per unit of input, where different inputs are combined on the basis of their factor shares. (Cf. Solow residual.)

Trade balance: The receipts from exports minus the payments for imports.

Transactions theories of money demand: Theories that explain how much money people choose to hold and that stress the role of money as a medium of exchange. (Cf. portfolio theories of money demand.)

Transfer payments: Payments from the government to individuals that are not in exchange for goods and services, such as welfare receipts and unemployment insurance benefits. (Cf. government purchases.)

Transitory income: Income that people do not expect to persist into the future; current income minus normal income. (Cf. permanent income.)

Underground economy: Economic transactions that are hidden in order to evade taxes or conceal illegal activity.

Unemployment insurance: A government program under which unemployed workers can collect benefits for a certain period of time after losing their jobs.

Unemployment rate: The percentage of those in the labour force who do not have jobs.

Unit of account: The measure in which prices and other accounting records are recorded; one of the functions of money. (Cf. medium of exchange, store of value.)

Value-added: The value of a firm's output minus the value of the intermediate goods the firm purchased.

Velocity of money: The ratio of nominal expenditure to the money supply; the rate at which money changes hands.

Wage: The amount paid for one unit of labour.

Wage rigidity: The failure of wages to adjust to equilibrate labour supply and labour demand.

Wait unemployment: The unemployment resulting from wage rigidity and job rationing. (Cf. frictional unemployment.)

Work in process: Goods in inventory that are in the process of being completed.

Worker-misperception model: The model of aggregate supply emphasizing that workers sometimes perceive incorrectly the overall level of prices.

World interest rate: The interest rate prevailing in world financial markets.

Index

Federal Government Deficit-GDP Ratio

(Public Accounts Basis)

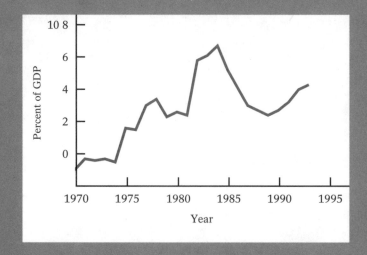

Money Growth

(*M*1)

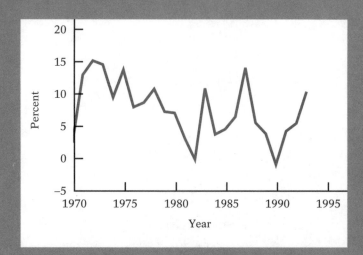